Khakhanate

Khakhanate

THOMAS LANKENAU

RED ANVIL PRESS

OAKLAND

RED ANVIL PRESS
1393 Old Homestead Drive, Second floor
Oakland, Oregon 97462—9506.
E-MAIL: editor@elderberrypress.com
TEL/FAX: 541.459.6043
http://elderberrypress.com

All Red Anvil books are available from your favorite bookstore, amazon.
com, or from our 24 hour order line: 1.800.431.1579

Library of Congress Control Number: 2007928395

Publisher's Catalog—in—Publication Data
Khakhanate/Thomas Lankenau
ISBN-13: 978-1-932762-81-5
ISBN-10: 1-932762817

1. Native American—fiction.
2. Mongol—fiction.
3. Mongol Migration—fiction.
4. Native American Tribes—fiction.
5. Mongol Warrior—fiction.
I. Title

This book was written, printed and bound in the United States of
America.

For
Deena

BOOK ONE

THE RAVEN

1

Cuauhnahuac
71st Year of the Khanate
(Cuernavaca, Mexico, 1440)

Cuauhnahuac is a beautiful place. The climate is temperate, none of the searing heat of the central desert, the bitter cold of far north, the humidity of the coastal areas or the damp fetid smells of the city. The air is fresh, lightly tinged with the delicate but changing scent of many flowers and warm during the day and cool and silken at night. The view is of green hillsides dotted with colors and mottled with light and shadows during the day and shining ethereally in the muted light of the moon or barely visible in the dim light of the endless stars on moonless nights. Yes, I picked the perfect place to end my days. And yet, in all this perfection, I am, for the first time in my life truly alone. Of course, I've been by myself many times, but I was always on a mission or a journey to or from somewhere and consumed by that purpose. Now, while I am not exactly by myself, for there are servants and family about, I am alone. I have nothing to do and nowhere to go. I suppose this is the inevitable fate of anyone who lives long enough, achieves an exalted position, and has the grace to step down before he becomes senile, but that is small comfort. There is the occasional visitor, but I have outlived almost all of my contemporaries, and the few remaining are too decrepit to travel all the way down here. My grandson drops by when he comes here to get away from the capital much like I used to do, and he's gracious enough to ask my advice as though he really needed it. Very rarely I see my other children and grandchildren, and they always bring their children with them. Last spring, my youngest son, John, came back from the north with a new wife and to everyone's surprise because of her age, she delivered a healthy baby boy in the winter. He then told me that he had decided to name the child Karl after me. I warned him about the consequences, but he insisted it was time for another Karl. So I started thinking about the past and the many events that brought me to this place at this time. I reread all the books in my library in their many strange languages, including the now-fragile book in this ancient language. Finally it came to me—I can have one more mission in my life! I can set down my story for my family in this ancient tongue so no strangers can read it. It will enable me to relive my life, and I needn't worry about anyone taking offense, to my family's detriment. And who knows, perhaps one of my descendants will be moved to carry the tale forward, for I know there is still much adventure ahead in this wonderful new world. Maybe the tale will interest this newborn Karl when he is old enough, and maybe he will outdo me, but I doubt it.

Since there is no written family history for me to build on, I'll have to start at the beginning. Most of you have noticed we do look a bit different from our fellow Mongols, although that difference is diminishing with intermarriage. Our ancestry is, strictly speaking, not Mongol. There never really was a tribe called the Mongols, but the Tungus tribes that coalesced into the core of what became the Mongols could be given first priority to the title. As time went on, many different tribes were taken into the Mongols even though they were not related. Some, like the Tatars, only provided women and children, but others came in fully and freely or were recruited to fill out the ranks. The Hanjen resisted joining since they always felt superior to Mongol "barbarians," and in the end drove us out of what they called the Middle Kingdom. Our "tribe" was never in a position to choose to join or not join the Mongols, so our allegiance requires a bit more explanation.

According to my grandfather, our ancestors were, perhaps fortunately, obscure and forgettable until the first Karl wandered out of the primeval forest and into a no-longer-remembered village in an area called Schwabia far to the west. His apparent source led to his surname, Waldmann, Man of the Forest in the dialect of that place. This Karl was, not surprisingly, a woodcutter, and since he had considerable skill at carving, he was welcomed to the village.

The family continued in modest obscurity until the next Karl, some few generations later, who was bored with wood but fascinated with iron and bucking the family traditions, moved to a city named Regensburg to learn the blacksmith trade. Being a perfectionist, he spent a long time working for many masters throughout what was called the Holy Roman Empire, the obscure if pretentiously titled principality that governed his "tribe." When he was admitted to the Guild as a master blacksmith, he had become a legendary sword maker, and settled in Innsbruck, a city in the same empire which was incongruously ruled by a bishop, a type of leader of the Christian religion prevalent in the far west. His descendants remained there continuing in the trade uneventfully until the next Karl came to maturity. This Karl, my great-great-grandfather, did continue the family skill of sword making, but being the second son left Innsbruck, and began to ply his trade eastward. He happened to be at the court of King Bela of Hungary, when a certain minor Christian cleric named John came to the court on his way back from performing an embassy from the pope, the leader or high priest of the Christian religion, to the Great Khan in Karakorum, Kuyuk, the second successor of the immortal Chingis. Karl managed to talk to this cleric and his companions and was fascinated by their tale. His curiosity got the best of him, and he decided to pack up his wife and two young children and go visit this Karakorum and offer his not inconsiderable talents to the Khan.

The story of his journey is a long, sometimes amusing, and some-times sad saga, but it is of no significance to this history. Suffice it to say, after some three very eventful years, he arrived at Karakorum just in time for his wife to be delivered of a son, my great-grandfather, whom he named John for the cleric who was responsible for the trip. Whether Karl regretted his journey, my grandfather couldn't say, but his acceptance at the court of the Khan was immediate, and he was soon hard at work at his first love, sword making. My great-grandfather John moved to Khanbalikh when the Great Khan Kubilai moved the capital there.

My great-grandfather, his brother, one of his sons, and both of his brother's sons met an untimely end during the ill-fated second invasion of Yapon uls (a group of large islands east of the old Khanate). Of course, the first invasion was also ill-fated, but the losses incurred were considerably less. My grandfather George decided to ply his trade more humbly to avoid the dubious honor of being invited on any more such fiascoes. He moved to the outskirts of Khanbalikh, and although he continued to make swords, he also made many other things as well, catering to the tastes of the Khan's subjects rather than the court. My father, Henry, also followed in my grandfather's footsteps and continued the general ironsmith business, and married Christina, the daughter of a Nestorian Christian priest, Peter. In the next ten years he had three sons and three daughters. Only two of the former and one of the latter survived infancy. These were the eldest son, Henry; the second daughter, Mathilde; and the youngest son, John. Curiously, the family always used the old tribal names rather than more Mongol names. Even more curiously, we still generally do.

Father happened to befriend an officer in the Khan's army who greatly admired his skills and frequently called between campaigns. He had confided to my father his pessimism about the future of the Khanate since much of it was in revolt and most of the army's energy had been wasted in the fratricidal power struggles since the death of Kubilai. This officer, Kaidu, rose through the ranks and finally came to be commander of a tumen. When Dorji, the Chancellor of the Right (yes, there was also a Chancellor of the Left, and between them they ran the Khanate for the Khan) was forced from power, he invited Kaidu to join him in the north and take command of the tumen then guarding the northern border of the Khanate along the Karamuren River between the ancient home of the Khitans and the frozen lands of the reindeer-herding Tungus tribes. Since a tumen was like a self-contained mobile city with skilled artisans as well as soldiers and their families, Kaidu invited my father to join him and, of course, bring along his family. Because my father shared Kaidu's pessimism about the future and feared for his family's safety should the revolts reach Khanbalikh, he agreed to join him as soon as his wife had been delivered of their latest child.

Late in the winter, the child, a boy, made his appearance, and over the grave misgivings of my grandfather, my father decided it was time for another Karl in the family to commemorate the definite change the family was about to experience. My grandfather elected to remain in Khanbalikh rather than finishing his years as a nomad. It seems my mother too had misgivings of undertaking a very new and strange lifestyle but trusted my father's judgment and went along. So it was that soon after birth, I was whisked away from the great capital to the very different northern landscape and the Ordu of Kaidu.

2

KARAMUREN RIVER,
20-8TH YEARS OF TOGHON TEMUR
(AMUR RIVER, N. MANCHURIA, 1350-8)

How can I describe a place so strange and so foreign to all your experiences? My earliest memories are of the clear, blue sky spreading overhead like the vaulted roof of a great yurt, the wide, cold, blue and white Karamuren River, dotted with islands and sandbars in the spring and early summer, a vast lake after the monsoon rains of late summer and frozen over during the long cold, dry winters. I remember visiting the small fishing villages of the native tribes, the Nanai on the tributaries of the Karamuren and the strange Nivkh in the delta. I remember studying the fantastic carvings of masks and animals in the stone of the riverbank on the lower river. I remember the dark green forested mountains and the interspersed grasslands where we camped and moved about with our herds always in the same pattern: winter in the lee of the coastal mountains sheltered from the bitter northwest wind, spring moving slowly upriver along the Karamuren until we reached the Sungari in early summer, up the Sungari a short way then east across the Ussuri to the highlands for the monsoon season, then to the designated hunting ground for the annual fall hunt, and back to the coastal mountains for winter.

I learned to ride the steppe horse almost before I learned to walk. Many an hour was spent with the other children charging across the plain, the wind rushing around us as we were choked by dust or covered with mud according to the season. I also learned to use the bow and like a good Mongol became quite proficient with it. When I was five years old, a pestilence swept the camp and many died including my mother, my one sister and my middle brother, John. My older brother, Henry, and I also caught the disease but were spared. I have little memory of the time, but my brother told

me we were cured by the shaman, Givevneu, whom Kaidu brought
in after our own shaman proved to be ineffective.

Givevneu was from a tribe of people far to the north called the
An'kalym. He fascinated me as a child, and I often followed him
around, and he would kindly tell me stories. He told me I was very
close to the sky god, Tengri, because my eyes reflected the sky. This
was because I had dark blue eyes like my mother while my brother
and father had gray-blue eyes. Givevneu had come to our camp
apparently by accident. It seems he was resisting his "call" to be a
shaman and had left his home and wandered along the forests near
the coast of the great ocean. He stayed to himself and struggled with
the spirits for some years until he finally gave in and then spent more
years communing with the spirits. The spirits taught him during
meditation and in dreams. Over time he learned how to heal the
sick by finding and then overcoming the ke'let or evil spirit that
caused the sickness. He told me the ke'let who had attacked our
camp was one of the harder ones to defeat. He had used his "ship"
(as he called his drum) to find the ke'let, and he forced the spirit
to leave the encampment after a mighty struggle. This victory had
been in the nick of time to save my brother and me, but too late to
save the others. I never quite understood what he was talking about,
and what I learned from the Hanjen treatises on disease was quite
different, but it was clear to me then as it still is that Givevneu was
a wonderful man who could indeed heal the sick. We were very
fortunate that he was nearby in our time of need, and some of the
local people sent him to us more out of fear that the pestilence would
spread to them than desire to help us. He told me that he had agreed
to stay with us because of the dream that had guided him south in
the first place. In it he saw a walrus leave the rest of his herd and
swim south until it reached the mouth of a great river. It then swam
up the river until it found a herd of horses. It got out of the river
and found that many were sick and dying, so it helped them and
was invited to join. He said he finally understood the dream when
he saw all our horses and knew that the spirits wanted him to stay.
Unlike many shamans he never tried to frighten anyone or impress
anyone with his powers. He was loved and respected by all and was

always honored by Kaidu while he lived. As it turned out, he had a profound affect on our future.

My mother's death greatly affected my father. Even though I was quite young, I remember how happy he had been before she died. He would always hum or whistle little tunes as he worked, and his cheerful mien was so infectious, people loved to hang around and talk and laugh with him while he worked. After Mother's death when I fully recovered from my illness, I found him a changed man. He seldom smiled, he sat for hours staring into space, his job seemed to be a burden to him, he drank too much kumis, and he barely noticed my brother and me. My brother, Henry, was also greatly affected by Mother's death. He had always been happy and carefree much like my father. He had a lot of friends and always had time for his younger brothers. It was he who taught me how to ride and use the bow. He became very quiet and serious spending all his time working at his forge. A year after Mother died, Kaidu insisted that my father take another wife. Her name was Yesui, and she was related to Kaidu, making it impossible for my father to refuse. She was a small wiry woman, much stronger than she looked. She also had been widowed by the pestilence, but she had never had any children. She was a remarkable woman. She took us all in hand and tried to turn us back into a family again. No stranger to hard work, she made sure we all ate well and were well clothed. She got my father back to the forge and was even able to make him laugh on occasion with her raunchy Mongol humor. She encouraged my older brother's blacksmithing interest and got him and my father working together again. She got me out from under Givevneu's feet and turned me over to her brother, Katan, to work on my hunting skills.

Yesui had been born and raised near Khanbalikh, but her family had always clung to the old Mongol ways, and she had readily adjusted back to the life of a nomad. Taking us over required more adjustment, but she was game up to a point. The long influence of the Hanjen and the surfeit of water in the Middle Kingdom had weaned away the Mongols from their almost manic fear of wasting water. In the old days, a Mongol only bathed or washed his clothes to the degree this could be accomplished by crossing a river or stream or being out in a rainstorm. According to my grandfather, George, our ancestors thought bathing was unhealthy but did wash clothes. It was only his father who got us on a regular cleanliness regime, and then only because his wife insisted. Yesui thought we overdid the cleanliness, but adjusted. She was also puzzled by our possession of and interest in books, as she could neither read nor write and couldn't be bothered learning either skill. She did insist on bringing in her ongons or domestic gods (little idols made of felt) and rearranged our yurt so that my father's bed was on the north side opposite the door, her bed was on the east side, and my brother and I slept on the west side. The little felt gods were over her and my father's beds as well as between and above the "bed gods." Also she put two protective figures on either side of the entrance to the yurt, to watch over the herd. We did have a few goats as well as about twenty horses. We had to patiently wait before eating while she smeared some fat on the idols' mouths and poured a little broth out the front door to feed the spirits. But in spite of all the nonsense, she was cheerful, respectful, honest, kind, fun, and full of energy, and I still think of her very fondly.

I should explain that my mother was a strict Christian and, I was told, had tried to encourage our adherence to that particular sect, but my father and my grandfather, George, considered all religions to be an obstacle to one's relationship to the one God. It seems this attitude dates back to an old tradition before the family came east. All good craftsmen strove for perfection in their work and were greatly offended that the religious "craftsmen" or priests betrayed, in general, no such striving. Disgust over the apparent hypocrisy led to a gradual disinterest in the religion, but they always believed in God and felt it was important to pray to him and dedicate their work to him. In any case, Yesui never presumed to tell us what to believe, but simply stated her beliefs as if they were facts, and my father instructed us to respect her and her beliefs but not accept them unless we personally agreed with them. My brother never did, but I might have if I had stayed with the Ordu.

Yesui's brother, Katan, took my training very seriously. He was also short but rather broad shouldered and very strong, although no longer young. His children were grown, and being a born teacher, he welcomed the chance to get a new pupil. Once he was satisfied with my use of the bow, he introduced me to the sword and the knife, getting my brother to make me a small sword. He drilled me endlessly. Once he was satisfied with my progress, he taught me how to hunt. We would be gone for days at a time during all four seasons. His favorite hunting grounds were the river valleys and the low densely forested hills east of the Ussuri River. This was a beautiful area. It was almost tropical, with lianas climbing among the oak, hornbeam, maple, elm, willow, and lime trees. Shrubs like ginseng, honeysuckle, mock orange, peonies, and wild pepper covered the ground, making movement—and tracking—very difficult and dangerous. Colorful butterflies and beautiful birds often distracted me until Katan had me identify the various birds by their songs or just their flight. Not just the common buntings, flycatchers, cuckoos, and thrushes, but also the white eyes, minivets, drongos, plovers, and mergansers. Then there were the hunting birds, the eagles, hawks, falcons, osprey, owls, and especially the tiny screeching sparrow hawk. Here we hunted leopard, boar, bear, tiger, and on occasion marten, forest cat, and the small sika deer. While we were often successful, we would also have to settle for a rabbit or grouse on bad days. I still preferred the open plain where you could see what you were hunting and chase it down on horseback. Of course, such areas were limited along the Karamuren, and Katan taught me skills, which, fortunately, stayed with me for life.

When I was seven years old, I was allowed to participate in the annual fall hunt. In full battle regalia, the whole Ordu went out and surrounded a large tract of land and then began moving in on the great circle they had formed, driving all game before them. It was a matter of pride to let no animal, large or small, escape the ring. I and the other youngsters on their first hunt were with Kaidu advancing slowly on horseback, with more experienced hunters nearby to make sure we did not disgrace the Ordu. Over the next two days as the circle became smaller, we could see all sorts of different animals, deer, reindeer, bears, wild dogs, wolves, antelope, wolverines, boars, mink, sable, hedgehogs, even rabbits, pheasants, ptarmigan, grouse, and other small game. At night the surrounding fires kept the trap intact, and we could see the glowing eyes balefully staring at us from a safe distance and hear their roars, hisses, and snorts. No prey evaded the trap. Finally in the early afternoon of the third day, the circle was perceived by Kaidu to be small enough, and he signaled a halt. Then, as was the custom, he moved forward alone and entered the wooded hills before us armed only with a bow and a sword. We sat on our horses and quietly waited while the game could be heard crashing around in the wood. After a short time, Kaidu emerged from the wood riding calmly and pulling behind his horse a tiger and a boar. Over the rump of his horse lay a huge silver wolf. Each animal had only a single arrow in it. On reaching us, he instructed some of the men to retrieve the bear and three deer they would find in a small clearing just into the wood. When these were brought out, he gave the signal for the other leaders to move into the wood. After a short pause, Kaidu greased the middle finger of the bow hand of each of us first-time hunters according to the custom and then sent us in with the rest of the hunters while he took a good vantage point from which to watch the hunt and his women set to work on his game.

We youngsters tried to stay together as we entered the woods but were soon separated by the irregularity of the terrain, for it was broken by ravines and there were rocky outcrops interspersed with thickly wooded hillsides. Soon I found myself with only one companion as we moved deeper into the wood. The shouts of the hunters and the screams and grunts and thrashings of the hunted could be heard on all sides. I saw some small game, rabbits, mink, an otter, and a wild dog scurry to evade us, but in my childish arrogance I disdained them, for I wanted a noble prize for my first hunt. My companion rushed after a wild dog he thought was a wolf, and I went on alone urging my horse into the din. Finally, I saw a young stag hiding motionless behind a screen of birch. Taking careful aim I dropped him with one shot right to the heart. Swelling with pride I walked my horse over to my prize and jumped off and tied a rope around its neck so that my horse could drag it out. I remounted, secured the other end of the rope, and started slowly moving back to the starting point. Then out of all the noise around me I distinctly heard a nearby menacing growl. I fit an arrow to my bow as I carefully looked around peering into the bushes from where the sound had come. I started moving forward again keeping my bow ready, but my horse snorted and shied away from the path in which I was directing it, so I halted again and tried to see what was in the low brush ahead. Suddenly a figure hurled itself out of the brush toward me and only the instinct born of constant practice enabled me to fire off an arrow before it was on me, but the arrow hit its mark, and my frightened horse lashed out with its hooves to finish off what proved to be a young tiger. Badly shaken, I fit another arrow into the bow lest the limp figure should spring back to life. Just then Katan came out of the woods and stared in amazement at my prizes. Without a word, he jumped down and tied the tiger to the stag for me, then remounted and went back into the woods muttering something about the student trying to show up the teacher. I could tell he was pleased.

Uneventfully, although slowly because of the underbrush, I dragged my prizes back to the encampment and encountered some of the other returning hunters on the way. Some of the men were dragging much more formidable prey than I was, but I could see that they were impressed with my success. The others my own age had much less to show for their first hunt, and by the time I cleared the wood, I was feeling rather puffed up with pride. My brother rushed up to greet me only to look in awe at my catch. His stag was bigger, but he had only bagged a fox not a tiger and besides he was nine years older than me and had only gotten a wild dog and two rabbits on his first hunt. Word got around and Kaidu himself came over to see my kill. He praised me and gave me a cup of kumis. My very proud stepmother took over the game while I basked in the glow of all the praise as well as the glow of the kumis. As more of the men came in, more toasts were drunk to my first hunt, and soon my head was swimming. I don't recall much about the feast that followed the hunt, except I do remember retching uncontrollably at one point. Eventually my brother found me and hauled me home dropping me off at the entrance to our yurt and throwing a skin over me because of my condition. The next day I spent trying to keep my head from exploding, while receiving no sympathy from any of my family. I suppose that ended any enthusiasm I might have had for kumis, and I have never had the stomach for the stuff since.

In the spring of the following year my stepmother managed to make my father aware that his second son was becoming quite the Mongol, except for my curious interest in reading the family books. He decided my future needed to be considered and called me in for a talk. He first asked if I had any interest in the family skill, sword making, and was not at all surprised to hear I had none. He then asked if I wanted to be a soldier like my stepuncle, Katan, and again I said no. "What then?" he asked.

I wish I could get back into my head at the time and understand my reply to him, but I have no recall of what I was thinking when I answered simply, "Learning things." I did indeed enjoy reading the family books and liked the strange language in which one of them was written and the beautiful illuminations or pictures made out of the first letter on each page. I liked the feel of the pages, so unlike the Hanjen paper I would later get to know. It was a strange book I couldn't really understand until I was much older. Father couldn't really understand it either and had no idea how or which ancestor acquired it. He speculated that someone probably gave it to one of our ancestors in lieu of payment. It was called, De Politica and was written by an Aristotelis. We all used it to learn the written language—as we called it. I also liked the Mongol books in the Uighur script I had laboriously learned. But I really liked knowing how things were made and why they were made that way. In general I was quite a nuisance to anyone who would make the mistake of letting me ask them a question. After some thought, my father decided that it would be best if I returned to Khanbalikh to live with my grandfather, and perhaps with more options available, I could learn a skill that would make me of use to the Ordu. My stepmother was upset to lose me, but didn't feel she had a right to interfere, so she got my things ready for the trip.

I had never been away from the camp before for more than a few days while on a hunt and was a little apprehensive about living with strangers (for I had no memory of my grandfather). Still the idea of returning to my birthplace and seeing many of the wonderful sights my brother had told me about excited me, and I looked forward to the adventure. In early summer I set off with some men Kaidu was sending to the capital after first promising my stepmother and Katan to keep up the skills he had patiently imparted.

At the time of my departure our camp was near where the Karamuren River is joined by the Sungari and turns northeast to empty finally into the Great Sea some fifteen hundred li away. At this point, the few "tribal Mongols" among the Ordu, especially Kaidu, would be seen staring westward along the river toward Mongolia. For it was along the Onon River which flows into the Karamuren, way upstream from this point, that the tribes which became the first Mongols arose. My own origins being far too distant to even contemplate, I could never get into the idea. In any case, Kaidu and his few fellows were so engaged when I left that morning. I remember the sight of them as we moved steadily southwestward up the muddy Sungari River, which drained the Manchurian plain into the Karamuren. It occurred to me looking at the water flow by that soon it would pass the Ordu and everything I had known so far, and I began to understand the behavior of the old Mongols. Little time was allowed for dreaming however, since we moved very steadily in order to reach the first yam by nightfall, and no one was going to be held up by a boy—I had to keep up or make it on my own. The others were especially anxious to make good time because the monsoon season was approaching and the rivers would become impassable and the ground marshy if we tarried.

The yam system established long ago by Chingis was still in fairly good condition in the north, but by now had fallen into great disrepair to the south and west of the capital. I was, of course, blissfully unaware of the fact that the great Khanate of the Mongols was slowly being torn apart. At this time, the Great Khan, Toghon Temur, held sway over only a fraction of the Khanate of Kubilai. But here in the rugged and sparsely populated north, there was no rebellion seething under the surface of the scattered nomad herders and farmers we encountered on our way. The yams were about ninety li apart, and so we moved just that distance each day. Nights were spent in the yurts of the yams. These were not very fancy and were often rather dirty and foul smelling, but after a day in the saddle and the fresh air, I, at least, was too tired to press the issue and simply ate what was put before me and promptly lay down on whatever sort of rug was provided and quickly fell asleep. In the morning we ate millet gruel, were given dried milk or meat to eat on our way, received fresh horses, and continued on to the next yam.

Our path followed the Sungari until it turned southeastward, where we crossed it, and moved due south for a while to avoid a desert, finally turned southwestward again following for a time a tributary of the Liao River, although we never saw the Liao itself. On we moved threading our way along the low mountains that separated Manchuria from the Han Plain. Finally, almost a month after our departure, we came to the Great Wall. In spite of my companions' disdain for the ineffective barrier, I was awestruck and wanted to explore it carefully. They refused, but suggested that my grandfather could take me to it since part of the wall came very near Khanbalikh. For the next four days the Wall slipped tantalizingly into and out of our view. Then we saw it no more but began to see the sprawling suburbs of Khanbalikh and beyond them, the outer earthen walls of the city itself. While I gaped in wonder at the increasing concentration of people as we moved through the suburbs and the corresponding increase in traffic on the road, the people we encountered showed no particular interest in us. Soon we had to wind our way through merchant caravans of camels and asses laden with trade goods, venders' carts, wagons drawn by horses or yaks, and many, many individual men and women carrying burdens on their backs. Through all our journey, we had skirted by the larger cities, and I had only seen towns and villages which, while the larger ones were like nothing I had ever seen along the Karamuren, had hardly prepared me for the teeming cacophony of noise, the riot of color, and the barrage of odors that assaulted my senses as we approached the steadily looming city walls. Finally we entered the gates and found ourselves on a broad, paved street stretching out before us. Shortly, we turned aside and soon stopped before a house from the back of which could be heard the unmistakable sound of a smithy. My companions told me that this was my grandfather's house and bidding me farewell, went on to complete their mission.

3

KHANBALIKH

28TH TO 37TH YEARS OF TOGHON TEMUR

(BEIJING, CHINA 1358-67)

I stared after my traveling companions for a while as they disappeared among the throng along the road. Then with some misgivings, I dismounted and approached what appeared to be a horse shed next to the main house. I entered the shed, tethered the horse next to the two horses already there, and taking my pack, slowly walked up to the house. Not sure what to do, I opened the door and peered in. Seeing no one, I entered the house and looked all around the large airy room with glass windows, colorful wall coverings, and rugs. The walls and floor were made of polished wood, as were the benches I could see about the room. There were also doors that led to other rooms. This was nothing like a yurt! Curious though I was, I stopped staring about and moved toward the hammering sounds I knew so well from my father's forge. The sound led me through the house and out another door into an enclosed backyard with trees, bushes and flowers, and in the center, a forge. At the forge lost in his work so much that he did not detect my approach was a white-haired replica of my father. Before I left the Ordu, my father assured me that I would have no trouble recognizing his father—he was right. I put my gear down and squatted down to watch just as I sometimes watched my father, and the sounds transported me home for a while, until my grandfather finally noticed me.

"Who might you be, child?" He peered at me as if he was trying to recognize me, "And how did you get in here?"

"I'm Karl," I stammered, "and I came through the door there." I pointed back to the door from which I had entered the garden.

"Karl?" My grandfather seemed puzzled. "What Karl? Should I know you?"

It was foolish of me to think the poor man would recognize a grandson he had only seen as a babe some eight years before, and, of course, no one warned him I was coming, since our family's business hardly rated a dispatch rider. In fact, I carried with me my father's announcement of my advent in a hastily scribbled note, which I thoughtfully produced from my pack at this strategic moment. The light was fading so my grandfather took the note near the forge to read. Finishing the note, he again studied me as if to see if there was any family resemblance to give credence to the note. Finally, he burst out laughing, a laud, raucous, infectious laughter, which I finally joined in, puzzled but relieved.

"So, you are Karl," he chuckled. "I finally see it. You look just like your mother, although you smell like a Mongol from the old days—after a long campaign. Come, we'll clean you up and then decide what to do with you."

So it was that I came to live in Khanbalikh with my grandfather George. He was not a bit surprised at my not wanting to be a blacksmith, (after all I was named Karl, wasn't I?) and was glad I didn't want to simply be a soldier. He decided, and I agreed, that since I wanted to learn, he would see that I was taught. He also had some books that I could read, but more importantly, my maternal grandfather, Peter, a Nestorian priest, who was immersed in things of the Hanjen, could teach me to speak, read, and write in that language and perhaps also in his native Farsi. With these two languages along with Mongol under my belt, I could learn all there was to learn in Khanbalikh.

Grandfather Peter, a pale, short, and thin man with a long white beard, a large nose, and bright blue almost feverish eyes, bawled like a woman in mourning when he first saw me, because I reminded him of his daughter, my mother. Soon, he decided the resemblance was purely superficial, and he was scandalized by my "crude Mongol manners" which were all because my father had dragged his poor gentle baby girl off into the wilds to live as a barbarian. He also held my father responsible for her untimely death. When he wasn't carrying on so, he did try to teach me Hanjen and Farsi over the next few years as my grandfather George had requested. Fortunately, I was allowed to live with Grandfather George and go to Grandfather Peter only for lessons. I was much more comfortable with the former as he was more easygoing—more of a Mongol than the latter. I was also subjected to both sides of a debate on the merits of Grandfather Peter's religion. Grandfather George warned me not to clutter my brain with Grandfather Peter's "religious puffery," but to learn only the languages, so I could learn useful things. Grandfather Peter was incensed at my imperviousness to his religion and was certain that I would end up in an unpleasant place called hell, where I would no doubt find my grandfather George. Since I had grown quite fond of the latter, I wasn't too concerned by the prospect. Grandfather Peter also tried to introduce me to Hanjen "culture." He would first read to me, then help me read his Hanjen books (implausible accounts of old heroes overcoming devils, dragons, and other insurmountable obstacles), and he would haul me to what proved to be completely incomprehensible formal entertainments, which he greatly enjoyed. These latter consisted of skits and rather tedious songs—long and in one key. I hated these and didn't really like his poetry and tales either, but I very much enjoyed the less literary works. These were compendiums of history, medicine, science, warfare, geography, and technology. I devoured all such that he had and was allowed to read some owned by his friends since I always treated the books with proper reverence. He never could understand my interests, but was pleased that I had impressed his friends with my questions. He would also take me far out of our way all over the sprawling city of Tatu (as he and most of the Hanjen insisted on calling Khanbalikh) to show me some painting or piece of crockery he greatly admired. The former tended to be landscapes and somewhat nice, but no match for the real thing—not nearly enough color. The latter were quite attractive, bright blues, yellows, reds, and greens with imaginative decorations like dragons, flowers and animals on them, but the porcelain was thin and fragile, not very practical for the Ordu. He did not cry when Grandfather George decided it was time I had a new teacher.

My next teacher was Ibrahim, a chemist and a Muslim, fortunately in that order. A tall, thin, quiet man with a sallow complexion, a large hooked nose, small hazel eyes topped by bushy black eyebrows and a long, rather unkempt black beard. He always wore a turban, even indoors, and he was rather stoop shouldered. He taught me what he knew about the elements of the earth, where they could be found and isolated and how they could be used. He also tried to teach me his religion, but he wasn't as pushy about it as Grandfather Peter had been and didn't appear to be offended by my intransigence. Again, I still lived with Grandfather George and each day we went over whatever I had learned. He always encouraged me to question until I fully understood and was very supportive. After two years with Ibrahim, I knew where and how to find all metal-bearing ores and how to smelt the metal free from the slag. I could make the various strengths of gunpowder and poison and smoke bombs, knew how and when to use acids and various salts, and could recognize many gases by their smell. I could detect many poisons and salts by simple tests and could distill petroleum and alcohol. He only showed me the last skill, because, like him, I didn't drink alcohol. One could make a very potent drink called strong beer by distilling ordinary beer. I can imagine what could be done with kumis!

My next teacher was Kuang Tung, a Hanjen engineer. He was a short, rather portly Han, with intense dark eyes, a thin wispy beard, and a broad mouth usually smiling with enthusiasm. He explained to me the various ingenious inventions the Hanjen had developed over the centuries to make their lives more comfortable or their wars more successful. Some of the former were clever but impractical in the Ordu, but the mechanics were interesting, and I paid close attention. The war machinery was quite intriguing, especially if one was to engage in siege warfare, either offensively or defensively, which seemed to be the main application. It was the development of a very strong brass that was 70 percent copper, which enabled such creations as the "flying fire machine." This weapon had a clever double acting piston bellows enabling it to deliver a continuous directed flow of fire. The fire came by holding a lighted fuse in front of the nozzle while pumping out the lighter petroleum distillates. He also showed me the designs for various sizes of cannon made of cast iron. Grandfather made one of the handheld-sized ones for me, and it actually worked for many years. I also learned the intricacies of fireworks both as show and as weapons. Kuang Tung belonged to an odd Tibetan religion, Buddhism. As warlike as the Tibetans were I was curious about their beliefs, but they proved to be rather passive and too reflective. Perhaps that was why their incursions into the Middle Kingdom were always beaten back. In any case, he was a most patient teacher, tirelessly explaining the inner workings of his machinery until I could actually get a feel for how they were developed—a skill that would serve me well later on.

At last I came to my final teacher, the formidable Tsu Chi'a. He was of moderate height for a Han, and rather thin, but ramrod straight, rather than the typical stooped posture of the Hanjen. His small dark eyes were heavily lidded and perversely expressionless. His thin, clean-shaved face was almost cadaverous with its pale, parchmentlike skin. He proposed to teach me history, geography, cartography, navigation, tactics, philosophy, and most important, manners. He was a remarkable teacher. He could actually answer all my questions and demanded and received my complete attention at all times. This was simple for I was fascinated by everything except the manners. These were tedious and, to put it mildly, excessive. Still, if I didn't put on his manners for him, he wouldn't go on to the interesting things. It was blackmail, but a small price to pay for all he taught me. I wish I could say that the manners were a help to me as years went by, but I can't. No other people I have encountered were that silly about interpersonal encounters. As Grandfather George said, the Hanjen have a flair for complicating the mundane. Everything else he taught me, however, proved to be very useful. Most importantly, he taught me how all these subjects were synergistic, and if applied that way the potential was unlimited. For example, if I decided to be a general, from history I would know what had been tried before and how successfully, from geography I would know how to shape the lessons of the past to the problem at hand, from cartography I could be secure in my knowledge of the terrain in detail, from navigation I could explore the unknown and find my way back home safely by studying the stars, or should they be obscured by means of the lodestone (a marvelous discovery that always pointed north), from tactics I would understand how others used the strengths and limitations of their forces to best advantage, and from philosophy I would be able to think clearly and logically to bring all my knowledge to bear on the problem at hand. I was with this last teacher the longest and was a young man of seventeen years when he dismissed me. I suspect that under his cold, impassive front he was as fond of me as I was of him.

By now I have managed to give the impression that I spent my youth in hard study with never a thought to frivolity or diversion. But the truth is, that while I did apply myself to my studies, my grandfather George was not too old to remember what it was like to be young. And, I suspect having me around made him feel younger. We dedicated one day a week to what he called my bookless education. We explored the city, both the new part where we lived and the old part across the river. We always steered clear of the palace, however, not wishing to be noticed, or by any accident be drawn into the constant intrigue there. It was like a city within the city, large and imposing, but Grandfather George had an exaggerated fear of getting too close. Whenever the current Khan, Toghon Temur, or his chancellors deigned to wander forth, we would always stay far out of their path. I still think it was unlikely we would have been of any interest to the Khan or his court, but Grandfather was right in keeping me away from the very empty court life, and, in truth, it really didn't interest me at all.

We also explored beyond the city, taking day trips on horseback, for my grandfather also loved to ride. As my traveling companions had suggested, I got him to take me to the Great Wall. In fact it was one of his favorite sites, and we spent hours studying it and speculating on what it must have taken to build it. While most Mongols saw it as a monument to Hanjen folly, to me it was rather a monument to ingenuity, determination, and engineering skill. It always comes to mind when I think of the Hanjen, and I think it is a good symbol for them, strong, enduring but not impermeable or as forbidding as they first appear. It was during our excursions outside the city that I would practice with the bow both on foot and from horseback as well as hunting and tracking. It was also during one of these outings that I met my first and only love, Paula.

Paula was the niece of a Polish (from Poland, a large kingdom east of the Holy Roman Empire) merchant who had found himself trapped in Karakorum during the disintegration of the Empire of Kubilai. Unable to return home, he moved to Khanbalikh and continued his trade. His brother, Paula's father, had been with him but died when she was still a child. She was just my age and breathtakingly beautiful. Her eyes were as blue as mine, but her hair was lighter and her skin fairer. Her cheekbones were visible but not overwhelming, and she had a good nose like my family, not the nubbins of the rather flat-faced Mongols and Hanjen. She was tall and sturdy for a woman, but was still very feminine. She could ride a horse as well as most men (who were not Mongols), but had never used a bow until I taught her. To my great relief and joy she also found me attractive and loved my company. I had no real experience with women since coming to live with my grandfather, for his wife had died long before and his only servants were two older men. When we first met, I was somewhat in awe of her and painfully shy, but she was so self-assured that she ignored my shyness and befriended me anyway chatting freely and confidently. While I had always been interested in the use or structure of things, she helped me see and enjoy their beauty. She would take us out of the way to see a view she found particularly beautiful. She would stop suddenly and point out a flower, a tree, a stream, or even an animal she found arresting. It was a whole different view of the world, and I was much amazed by it and her.

We met a scant six months before my education was complete and in that short time I was totally smitten. We pledged to be married and were greatly relieved to find that her uncle and my grandfather were not opposed and in fact seemed altogether unsurprised by it all. I often wondered later if they had planned it all along, but if they had, they did us both a great favor. We all agreed that she and I would marry as soon as I decided what I would do with myself after all this training.

When I returned home after Tsu Chi'a told me he had no more to teach me, my grandfather and I sat down to discuss my future. By now I had been longer with him than with the rest of my family and indeed felt much closer to him. Knowing my training was winding down and anxious to start my life with Paula, I had been thinking about the future, but had still not come to any firm decision. We sat in silence for a while after our meal, me weighing options for the future, him perhaps thinking of our time together. Finally he broke into our reveries.

"Karl," he began, "I cannot express how much I have enjoyed having you here with me all these years. I could not love you more if you were my own son, even if you are nothing like my own son. Still, you are a credit to him and your mother, and, to some degree, me. Now your training is over, and it is time for you to become a man and decide your own fate. It was for this that you came here and were trained. God knows you have 'learned things' as you wished. You do have some options and have no doubt given them much thought. I would only caution you not to make remaining here one of your options. I am quite old, and will likely not see it, but there is no way the Khanate will survive your lifetime. We are semujen (non-Mongol foreigners) and as such are resented by the Hanjen for our privileges under the Mongols. When they take Khanbalikh, they will not be merciful to us or the other non-Hanjen. I can't really blame them for their resentment, but I do fault their racism, a most un-Mongol trait. There is a whole world out there. I would urge you to pick a direction other than south and go."

"Grandfather," I replied, "I would have to be a fool not to see what is coming here. My future definitely lies away from Khanbalikh. I'm still not sure where to go, but I do think I should try to find the Ordu and report back to father. It was he who sent me here, and I owe him that much. I do think of them all and wonder if they are well. Besides, it would be interesting to hear what Kaidu plans to do with the Ordu—if, indeed, it still exists."

"I'm proud of you, Karl," he smiled tenderly. "You are indeed a dutiful son, and to return to the Ordu is the right thing to do. I suspect, however, that you will find you have outgrown the Ordu and the nomad's life and want something more. You will be the most educated man there—if not among all Mongols. Still, I remember

Kaidu to be a most wise and thoughtful man, there are few such men around, and you could serve far worse. You were named 'Karl.' In our family history that always meant change. Indeed, we have never had anyone in the family trained as you have been. It also has meant travel, and I see no alternative to that now. Perhaps you will lead the remnants of the family to new lands. It should be exciting."

"I don't know, Grandfather," I shrugged, "I have not traveled much except for the nomadic wandering about the Karamuren and my journey here. I have often dreamed about seeing the places I have read about—even the place from which we originally came, far to the west. It could be quite an adventure, especially with Paula by my side."

"Indeed, my boy," he chuckled, "and youth is the time for adventure. Paula is a fine strong girl, the perfect companion for adventure. I will greatly miss you, but you will soon find your way back here to gather up your bride. As to the journey home, you had best leave soon before the rains make your trip truly miserable."

Paula agreed that I was doing the right thing checking up on my family but urged me to be very careful and return to her as soon as possible. Two days later, I left Khanbalikh behind, and returned over much the same course I had come by, this time guided by maps and signposts to the still-operational yams along the way. There were a few nights I spent under the stars but most of the time the yams were still in use although meaner than I remembered them with more meager rations and rather sorry-looking mounts. Not much seemed to have changed along the way, the same small towns and villages, the same farms and huts; it was not until I approached the Karamuren from the Sungari that I saw a change. Not only had I not run into the Ordu, but also there was no sign that they had ever been here this year.

4

KARAMUREN RIVER
37TH YEAR OF TOGHON TEMUR
(AMUR RIVER VALLEY S.E. SIBERIA 1367)

It was troubling to find no sign of the Ordu along the Sungari, but as I proceeded down the Karamuren and still saw no sign of them, I became alarmed. Grim thoughts raced through my mind, another plague, an uprising by the locals, an invasion from the north, the south, or the west, a flash flood? Mongols did not panic, I reminded myself and began to sort things out. A plague never wiped out everyone, and besides we had heard nothing of any plagues in the north back in Khanbalikh. The locals had neither the means nor the inclination to attack the Ordu—besides, they liked us as much as anyone could like a pack of outsiders, for we did always treat them fairly, and we both benefited from trade, their fish for our game or herd meat. Invasion was possible, but not from the north; there was no group strong enough, not from the west. Why would they come here? The south was the only possibility, the Koryo. But even there, why would they bother to come all the way here to take out a single Ordu? Besides, I had not run into any foreign military along the way, and if they had attacked, wouldn't they have moved on afterward toward the capital? After all, they had attacked before. Of course, there were also the remnants of the Jurchids. They had actually conquered the Hanjen, but Chingis had greatly scattered and absorbed them, and it was unlikely they would be ready to do anything yet. Again, I had not seen any soldiers or signs of battle. Nor had there been any apprehension at any of the yams along the way. I closely looked at the river, but I couldn't tell if there had been a flash flood. After all, it flooded every summer and would be starting to rise soon. I continued downriver with more puzzlement than anything else. It was fairly obvious that no one had been near here with herds since at least early spring, for the grass was untouched. I decided the easiest way to find what happened would be to ask at the nearest local village. There had been a Nanai village not too far downstream from my current position. I would have to see if it was still there.

It was with no small relief when the village finally came into view. It looked much the same as I remembered it, although it seemed smaller. The Nanai summer villages were simply a scattering of conical huts that were covered with strips of birch bark. I had forgotten how "fishy" their villages smelled. Everywhere, one saw the fruits of their labor, racks of fish drying or being smoked, seines being repaired. Even the clothes they wore were made of fish skins. Not surprisingly, my approach was noted but since I was alone, I was soon ignored, as I made my way to the largest hut, which was usually the headman's hut. The headman, a large, beefy fellow, more than a little long in the tooth, was actually the same one as before, and I could see he was shocked when I greeted him by name in his own tongue. It took a while for him to realize who I was, but once he did, he received me warmly and asked for stories about the great capital. Politeness demanded that I comply before asking my questions, so I patiently described the capital for them over dinner, then asked about their health and luck with fishing, expressing all due admiration with the large sturgeon we had eaten for dinner, talked about the weather, the imminent monsoon season, then finally I felt I could ask them what had become of the Ordu and when they had last seen it.

They smiled broadly and pointed north, across the Karamuren! The Karamuren had always been our northern border. On occasion a few of us would venture across and look around, but the whole Ordu had never crossed. It must have been quite an undertaking for the river is wide and deep and swift. It seemed that the winter before last, the Ordu did not go to their usual winter camp east of the mountains, but stayed on this side near the village and braved the brutal northwest winter wind. In late winter when the Karamuren was frozen hard, they had crossed not far downstream from the village. It had been quite a spectacle, and many of the villagers had watched. All had made it safely across, headed away from the river, and no one had seen them since anywhere along the Karamuren.

The next morning, I got the villagers to help me get across the river in one of their boats while my horse swam alongside guided by his reins, which I held securely. They gave me some food and directions to another Nanai village no more than two days' ride away, where I might hear more of the Ordu since they likely passed that way. The ride was not an easy one, forcing me at times through dense underbrush, but I finally reached the village shortly after noon on the third day. Mongols rarely ride the same horse two days in a row, usually taking up to six mounts with them. I was not so equipped, however, and wisely spared my horse as much as I could. After a few tense moments, the village accepted me as a guest, mostly (I suspect), because I could speak their language. I've always been blessed with a facility with languages, and it has come in very handy. In this case, of course, my vocabulary was that of a boy, but I was quickly recalling the language and becoming quite fluent with practice, only occasionally needing to have a word explained. Of course, my hosts demanded stories over dinner. I remembered one of the silly hero tales from Grandfather Peter's books, and regaled them with that much to their enjoyment. That night the storm that had been brewing all day long finally broke and after softening us up with barrages of lightning, a torrential downpour was unleashed which continued well into the morning and then only tapered off to a steady downpour for the rest of the day. The necessary layover was very good for my horse, and it enabled me to get a feel for where I was as I began a crude map of the area north of the Karamuren. This was of great interest to my hosts, and they eagerly offered suggestions and corrections, over which they argued extensively. While all this help was probably more enthusiastic than useful, I encouraged it hoping to get some bearing on the whereabouts of the Ordu. They were fairly unanimous that I would likely find the Ordu camp near a large lake about ten days' ride to the northeast. They also suggested that I should go north up their river for about four days, then cross the mountains to another valley which heads northeast right to the lake. When the river turned north, I should continue northeast between a high hill on the north and a swamp to the south, right to the western shore of the lake. The Ordu should be on the west, south, or east side of the lake, since the north side was too swampy. They had been there early in the spring.

This last piece of intelligence, dropped in their usual offhand manner greatly excited me, and I was eager to set off. The villagers loaned me a second horse, which I promised to return, and gave me enough food for ten days. I followed their directions and corrected my map as I went along. As usual, they underestimated how long the journey would take, especially with all the rain I encountered. It took five days to get up their valley, and then it took almost two days to negotiate the crossing of the very slippery mountains to the other valley. Fortunately, they also overestimated how much I would eat, so I still had some food left some thirteen days later when the lake came into view. I couldn't see the Ordu from the lake's shore, but it was a very large lake, so I decided to ride up the lakeside of the tall hill from where I should be able to see much farther. As I climbed the mountain, I kept looking back but could see no sign of them. Finally I reached the top of the eastern ridge of the hill and could still see nothing around the lake. Blessed with a rare clear day, I started to look around and to the south, beyond a swamp, I could just make out the glassy reflection of another lake, possibly as large as this one. I went back down the hill and rode southward until nightfall, skirting around the swamp as much as possible.

The next morning, I continued south and soon reached the slope of another hill. I rode up the north side to the top of its eastern ridge, and there on the southwestern shore I could see the Ordu, for the sun was reflected off the white lime coating of the felt yurts and above them smoke from their morning fires escaped through the smoke holes and hung wraithlike in the still air. As I descended the hill toward them, it was obvious that I had also been seen, as a group of horsemen was coming toward me. By the time I got down the hill and crossed a small stream, they were upon me.

It took me quite a while to convince my "escort" who I was, but a few of the boys with whom I had played just barely recognized me, especially after I enumerated where their birthmarks were. On the way into camp, they told me that my father had died three years before, but my brother was still with them. In fact the latter was married and had children. They also warned me that there had been many changes in the Ordu, and after I had seen my family, I should report to Kaidu right away. They would tell him of my arrival. As we arrived at the camp, I could see that it did seem smaller than before. I turned aside to my father's old yurt and watched the others ride up to Kaidu's yurt in the middle of the encampment.

My brother came out of the yurt as I drew near, and we both stopped and stared at each other. He was the image of father only much younger. His children crowded out and peered curiously around him at me. Then his wife, a Turk from the look of her, came out to see and finally an older Mongol woman waded through the others and gasping her surprise, grabbed me in a bear hug.

"Kahh! My Kahh!" my stepmother screeched, "You have finally come home. Look at you, all grown, with a beard already, all that education and you smell like a Mongol, you weren't ruined! You can still ride, but can you still shoot the bow? You are not very big; did not your grandfather feed you? Are you at least strong? How did you find us? Where is your wife? Much has changed since you left!"

"Mother, stop for a minute." My brother rescued me. "Karl, you look so much like mother Christina, I thought I'd seen a ghost. Welcome! Meet the family. This is my wife, Doqus, remember her? Ussu's sister? These are my boys, Henry and John, and my daughter, Christina. Come in, come in. This is still your home."

"Kahh, you must be hungry," My stepmother could not be put off for long. "There is still some porridge left. Come, sit by the hearth, eat, and tell us all."

"Mother Yesui," I laughed, "I knew you would not change. But before I do anything else, I want to wash two months in the saddle off and get presentable, for I'm supposed to present myself to Kaidu as soon as possible."

"First," Yesui jumped up from the fire, "you must pay your respects to your father. Come."

I followed her to the little shrine she kept and there silently greeted my father's memory. I tried to see him as he was when I left, but found I could only picture my grandfather George. My memories of Father were few and tinged with sadness, while those of Grandfather were many and happy. I quietly thanked Father for sending me to Grandfather and felt sure he would not be offended if I thought about the latter for a few moments. After a while, I returned to the hearth. Doqus had readied a tub of water for me to wash and set out one of my brother's outfits for me to wear since all my things were dirty.

"You have honored your father's memory well, my son," Yesui hovered about. "To think of him and smile that way shows you are a good son, full of happy, loving memories of your father. I am very pleased with you. I feared you would have become a Hanjen in Khanbalikh."

She spat out the word "Hanjen" like it was the worst insult she could think of. But this was not the time to point out that she was more closely related to them than she was to me, anymore than that I was smiling about my grandfather's memory, not my father's. She took my soiled clothes and blatantly eyeing my privates, congratulated me on growing up completely, before going out to wash them, cackling all the way. While I cleaned up and got dressed, I reminded myself how crude her humor had always been and wondered what my poor Paula would think of her. All through my toilet, I was subjected to the rapt attention of my nephews, who stared up at me with their big hazel-brown eyes. Meanwhile, my brother tried to tell me a little of what had been going on while I was away.

It seemed that about five years earlier, Kaidu began sending some of the people away. No one was sure why, but when he had finished, almost half of the tumen was gone. He had picked up a few new members over the years, but as I had noticed, the Ordu was much reduced. Kaidu had over the course of two years personally talked to each member of the tumen who was head of a yurt or an unmarried young adult and on the basis of that interview either sent them away or allowed them to stay. There was no pattern to the division that was discernable to my brother. No tribes were excluded, age didn't seem to matter, and even health didn't matter. My father had been accepted, and after he died, Henry had also passed the test.

He supposed that was why I had to report to Kaidu, for a belated interview. He wasn't sure if my being in Khanbalikh would work against me, but feared it might, since Kaidu had not reported to the capital or even the nearest governor for some years. He had no idea what Kaidu planned to do, but here, north of the Karamuren, was out of the Mongol Khanate, so perhaps it was for safety. Henry's information was rather puzzling and obviously incomplete, so it was with great curiosity and an open mind that I went to meet the leader of the Ordu.

Kaidu was no longer a young man, but he looked strong and vigorous, his dark eyes bright and sharp. He was shorter than I remembered him but just as imposing. He was broad but not fat. His complexion was ruddy and healthy like that of most of the Ordu. He was sitting on a wooden chair set on a platform slightly above the level of the floor. I presented myself, bowing three times as I entered according to the custom, and he nodded in response. Soon some of the awe in which I had always held him came back for he seemed to be reading me with his deep, dark penetrating eyes. At his side was my old friend the shaman, Givevneu. He also watched me, but smiled at me as he had always done. Finally Kaidu broke the silence.

"So," he barked eyeing me carefully and waving me to sit on the floor, "the youngest son of my late sword maker has returned."

"I have, sir," I replied lowering my eyes with good Hanjen manners.

"Look at me when I talk to you, Ferengi!" he hissed.

"Yes, sir!" My head shot up and my eyes met his.

It had been a long time since I had been called Ferengi, but it was no insult, merely the Mongol term for all western people. We stared each other down for some minutes, until Kaidu smiled, then broke eye contact and laughed uproariously in the Mongol fashion. I continued to look at him for a while puzzled by his behavior, but Mongol laughter is irresistible, and I finally joined in.

"I like you, boy," he said, wiping his eyes. "What is your name?"

"Karl, sir," I replied.

"Kaahhr? It sounds like the song of a crow," he smiled, pleased with himself. "Perhaps I should call you 'The Crow.' Would you like that?"

"Could you at least make that 'Raven'?" I winced. "A crow is thought clever but a thief, while a raven is respected and admired."

"The Raven! That sounds impressive," he looked at me mockingly. "Do you deserve an impressive name?"

"Not yet," I replied, "but perhaps it will give me something to which to aspire."

"So be it, Raven." His tone turned serious. "But now that you are named, perhaps you can tell me what use you will be to this tumen. Have you any skill?"

"I have been trained in history, geography, cartography, navigation, tactics, engineering, chemistry, and philosophy, sir," I answered. "I can both read and write the Mongol script, Farsi, Hanjen, and our old family language."

"Very presumptuous training," he darkened. "Were you planning to become vizier to the Khan?"

"No, sir," I shook my head. "I have no interest in entering the Khan's service, those were the subjects that interested me. I really had no thought about what I would do with the knowledge, but I'm sure it will be helpful to me in the future, and I am very willing to continue learning."

"Hmmm," he mused. "We'll see. Meanwhile, whose history, what geography, and whose tactics did you study?"

"The Mongol and Hanjen history, geography, and tactics, sir," I eagerly replied.

"Mongol history is short, Hanjen endless, Mongol and Hanjen geography are constantly changing, and Mongol tactics are far superior to that of the Hanjen. Would you agree?" He smirked.

"Well," I began," I suspect that Mongol and Hanjen history are equally long, depending on how you define Mongol and Hanjen, but the latter is better recorded since they have used writing longer. As to geography, the borders do indeed change frequently, but the land itself changes much more slowly. Mongol tactics are superior if one is blessed with Mongol warriors in a fairly open terrain, but the Hanjen are very effective at siege warfare and are quite creative when it comes to weaponry and engineering."

"Why did you study philosophy?" He shot at me.

"It helps one think logically, examine motives and, in short, understand the entire picture or situation before you," I replied.

"What about religion?" he looked at me steadily. "Did you also study religions?"

"Not really," I replied thoughtfully. "My first teacher was a Christian, my next one a Muslim, then I had a Buddhist teacher, and the last never mentioned it. The first three told me about their beliefs with varying fervor, but none convinced me."

"Why?" he asked.

"The first two are too dogmatic, and I distrust anyone who has all the answers because he hasn't asked half the questions." I was warming to this subject, but puzzled at his interest. "Further, I resent the way they exclude from God's benevolence anyone who doesn't adhere to their particular and peculiar set of rules. As to the latter, it seems too fatalistic, denying that we are the masters of our fate. Its adherents seem irrationally passive."

"I thought all Ferengi were Christians," he seemed surprised.

"My Mother Christina was," I replied, "but she died when I was quite young. My father always said if Christianity had anything to do with Christ he might adhere to it, but it didn't. While I was in Khanbalikh, my grandfather George, with whom I lived, did his best to keep me free from all such 'misunderstandings of reality' as he called religions."

"You have answered well, Raven," he smiled warmly for the first time. "Or perhaps I should say you have been trained well. Some of your skills could be of great use, but it would depend on how good you are. You found us, that shows some skill, but you claim to be a cartographer. Did you have the foresight to map your way here?"

"Yes, I did." I brought out my map, which I had brought along just in case my cartographic skill was challenged. "It's a bit crude, but I think you can easily follow it. I came up from the Karamuren along this river to a village I have marked here, and then proceeding up the same river, I crossed the mountains here to this other river and followed it to that lake just north of here."

"Yes, yes," he nodded, "I know that lake, and you have also put in this lake and the rivers emptying into it. Very good, I can use you in my tumen. Would you stay?"

"Would it be presumptuous to ask what you plan to do here in the north?" I boldly asked.

"It would indeed be presumptuous to ask," he smiled, "and stupid not to, eh shaman? I rejoice you are no fool, but I must first ask you, why do you hesitate? Is it loyalty to the Great Khan? Or fear of adventure?"

"No, sir," I protested. "It is rather a fear of no adventure. It appears that you have some grand design in mind, and if it involves an adventure, I would gladly be a part of it. If, on the other hand, you merely want to become a Tungus clan leader and herd reindeer in the icy north, I would not be a part of it."

"Hah!" Kaidu roared with laughter. "Herd reindeer, indeed. No, you insolent boy, you will have your adventure, perhaps more than you wanted. Are you prepared to never see Khanbalikh or even the Karamuren again?"

"Yes, sir, but not until I retrieve my bride from there," I blurted out.

"You can get her early next summer," he shrugged. "We will remain here a little longer. But meanwhile, it is fortunate that you have come today, for you will accompany my grandson Juchi on an important adventure tomorrow and put to good use your mapmaking skills."

"Tomorrow!" I exclaimed. "Where do we go?"

"You of course remember our shaman," he began. "Some years ago, he and I began to reflect on the future of the Mongol Khanate. It was clear to us that it would soon die, and we searched in vain for a way to save my tumen. Givevneu had an idea. I saw the wisdom of his suggestion and began to pare down the tumen with his help, trying to avoid all the problems which beset the Khanate. I weeded out any who might be disloyal to me for any reason even if they had an indispensable skill like your brother, and you, for that matter.

It was disloyalty that destroyed the Khanate of Chingis. His heirs fought among themselves and soon were cutting the Khanate into weak pieces, which have fallen one by one. Next, I weeded out those who thought themselves better than others, whether because of a religious or tribal affiliation. I exempted your bigoted stepmother because she will not live much longer and, of course, she had nowhere to go. Next, I weeded out the faint-hearted, for our adventure will not be an easy one. So, what you have here is an Ordu of fearless, strong, loyal, tolerant, and undistracted Mongols. Of course, not many of us are tribal Mongols anymore, but if you recall, the word Mongol means 'the brave,' and that is why we are the true Mongols. Now as to what this journey is about, I'll let Givevneu tell you."

"I rejoice that you will be with us, ah…Raven"—he smiled broadly at me—"for have I not always said Tengri shines through your eyes making them the color of his abode."

"You honor me too much, Givevneu," I replied quietly, "for it is through your eyes that the goodness I believe to be God shines, not mine." I had always dearly loved the shaman who was so kind and patient with me. As a child I was fascinated by his appearance as well as his powers—for he had round eyes, curly hair, and a rounded head like my family had. I would tell him he had to be my relative, but he would deny it saying, "Only in spirit in this life, but surely closer in another." It was good to see him again.

"You have grown in Khanbalikh, my son," he said, "but have not become jaded. I congratulate your grandfather, no doubt a great and wise man. Your mission is simple and difficult. It is simply to deliver a message to my native village. It will be difficult, because I cannot precisely tell you where it is. I can tell you that it was on the coast of the Great Sea, and I have drawn a rough outline of the coast as I remember it. I can also tell you that you must go north and east but never south along the coast, for there is a very large peninsula that would take you far out of your way. Juchi has the drawing, and I have told him how the stars should appear when he is near my village. So, as you can see, a simple task, but a difficult one to perform."

"Indeed," I replied nodding. "Can you give me some idea how

far away this village is?"

"Not really." He shook his head. "I venture to guess, however, that it is about three months' journey on horseback."

"Will that not take us there in the dead of winter"—I was incredulous—"and is that not a rather imprudent time to head north?"

"To be sure," he agreed pleasantly, "but it is necessary to be there in deep winter to fulfill the mission."

"I don't understand." I was beginning to think it was a mistake to get involved with these people. "What possible difference does it make which season it is when a message is delivered? And, for that matter, what is the message?"

"Juchi has the message memorized," he replied. "There is no need for you to learn it as well. Besides, since it is in my native language, you probably wouldn't understand it anyway. As to the season, when and if you succeed in delivering the message, you will understand the reason for delivering it in the winter. Until then, we would prefer if you both know no more than you have been told, because our future depends on the success or failure of your mission."

"But if your people only understand their own language," I asked, "how will we communicate?"

"In the Tungus tongue, of course," he smiled. "All the northern tribes understand it well enough and if you do not remember it, Juchi does."

"Also," Kaidu interjected, "and the main reason you accompany Juchi, you must draw very good detailed maps on the journey. Maps that can be easily followed, and on your return, if you find a better route, correct the maps. Understood?"

"Yes, sir." I was beginning to be intrigued by all this. "This should indeed prove to be quite an adventure."

"A mere beginning, if all goes well," he shrugged. "But as Givevneu told you, the very future of our Ordu depends on your success. Will you take on that responsibility?"

"I will," I answered with more enthusiasm than conviction.

"Good," Kaidu waved my dismissal. "Tomorrow morning early then."

"Yes, sir!" I bowed my way out and, head swimming, returned to my brother's yurt.

5

THE FAR NORTH,
37TH YEAR OF TOGHON TEMUR
(E. SIBERIA, 1367)

After leaving Kaidu, I returned to my brother's yurt and told him the news. Yesui immediately set about getting things ready for the trip. My clothes would not be warm enough for the far north so she set about modifying some of my father's warmer clothes. Doqus helped her with this effort. My brother and I selected horses for the trip, and he promised to send back the horse I had borrowed. I checked out my bow and arrows, and Henry gave my sword a good sharpening. Things seemed to be well in hand so I set out to find Juchi.

By now it was midafternoon and leaden sky began to disgorge its cargo, but steadily rather than torrentially for a change. I found Juchi in his father's yurt and was pleased to find that he not only remembered me, but also was glad that I was going with him. He was no taller than me but like his grandfather was broad. He had Kaidu's dark eyes, but was more easygoing and fun loving. He had always been quite the tease when we were children, but he seemed not just pleased, but relieved about my coming along.

"Not just because of your fine company," he teased, "but because I was most uneasy about the mapmaking. How fortunate that you have become an expert in this most difficult task."

"More tedious than difficult," I corrected him, "but as I recall, you were never one overburdened with patience."

"Indeed!" he seemed surprised. "You remember that, do you? Well, I can assure you my father has curbed my ah…enthusiasm in your absence."

"He is to be commended, then," I rejoined. "No doubt great poems have been written about the deed. But moving on to the task at hand, did you get any partial maps of our path?"

"Sort of," he answered unfolding a piece of paper and handing it to me. "This is the area between here and the Great Sea and over here is Givevneu's drawing of the coastline near his village. I'm afraid the former will only serve us for a few days and the latter might be difficult to use. Most coastlines look the same to me."

"Well, it depends." I shrugged as I studied the maps. "Looking at his drawing, I would say we have a chance of finding it. For one thing, it appears to be on a deep narrow inlet surrounded by mountains and there is a spit of land near the mouth of the inlet where the actual village is. That means it would likely be a safe harbor for ships if it were deep enough, although I doubt if any ships would stray that far north. Also it looks like this is a southern terminus of a landmass, for you can see that the shore around the inlet tends generally northward."

"You see all that in the shaman's scratches?" Juchi shook his head. "Now, I think we might actually succeed in completing this mission. You came back just in time, Kahhr. Do you mind being called Raven? It's easier than that odd name of yours."

"I prefer it to Ferengi." I looked up accusingly. "I believe that's what you used to call me."

"I was easier to pronounce," he shrugged.

"How reliable is this other map?" I let him off the hook. "Can it be trusted or is it just a rough outline?"

"It was made by Arughtu," he replied. "He was a good mapmaker in his day, but he is older now, and his vision is weak and his hand unsteady."

"I'll probably only need to refine it a bit," I said. "But one thing troubles me. Why are we going now in the middle of the monsoon season? It won't make mapping very easy, nor will it help navigation."

"I know," he nodded, "but Givevneu said he didn't think the monsoon reached very far north, and he felt we needed the extra time to find his village by midwinter. I don't know how much he told you, but it seems it will take about two months to get to where there are no more trees and then another month to reach his village.

This assumes we can travel at a rather quick pace, with no terrain or native problems. And then we're supposed to map the path, hunt when we run out of food, endure the polite necessities in every village we enter, or fight our way out. And we still have to brave the monsoon for at least a while, followed closely by the full force of winter in the far north. Until you came along, Tengri be praised, I was supposed to do this all by myself."

"Kaidu must have a lot of faith in you," I reassured him. "You must be proud."

"Hmm," he mused, "or perhaps he just finds me expendable."

"That's ridiculous," I scolded, "You're the first son of his first son! Besides, he greatly emphasized the importance of the mission to the tumen's survival. And he wouldn't have us making maps if we weren't supposed to return. The smallness of the 'expedition' must be for speed and secrecy. Still, I just can't imagine why were going north in winter. Did you make any sense out of the message we're supposed to deliver?"

"None." He shook his head and handed me another piece of paper. "I wrote the sounds down in the Mongol script so I could read it to Givevneu's brother. Does it mean anything to you?"

"I don't think so." I puzzled over the strange note, sounding out the words. "But this sounds a little like the language of the Nivkh. Unfortunately, I never mastered it. Did you?"

"No," he replied, "we hardly ever dealt with them, so why bother? There are a few of them in the tumen, but we better not show this note around. Givevneu said we'd understand when we delivered it."

"Yes, you're right," I agreed, returning the note. "Anyway, we'll be too busy to worry about it. I had better finish getting ready for tomorrow."

I took my leave and returned to Henry's yurt. I compared Arughtu's map to mine and reconciled the two to the degree possible. While working on the maps, I asked Henry for a waterproof container for the maps and told Yesui that I would need about four months' worth of provisions or as near to that amount as was possible, since it would save time, but I could always hunt if I ran low.

Once again, I had my nephews' rapt attention as I worked on the maps. From the look of Arughtu's map, we would have to go north and a little west at first and cross more than a few streams and rivers before we could turn northeast into unmapped territory. By the scale of the map, that leg would take about eight days or so. When I finished the maps, I put them and some extra paper and ink in the waterproof bag. Hopefully, I would only have to edit the maps a little on the first part of the trip. This was especially important since the rains were continuing at the moment and showed no sign of abating. Over our evening meal, we caught up with all that had been happening in our lives. Henry asked about our grandfathers and the things he remembered of Khanbalikh; I asked about the companions of my childhood. I told of my studies, Henry of his work, Doqus of the children and the animals, and Yesui of my father. Finally I told them about Paula and was roundly congratulated by all and subjected to several ribald remarks from Yesui, but it did enable us to end on a happy note. We turned in early so I could leave at first light.

The next day dawned imperceptibly in a steady drizzle. I was ready for adventure, and with Henry's help, all was put on the horses. I made my farewells, mounted up, and leading the other horses, slogged over to the waiting Juchi. He suggested that the mapper might as well lead, so we turned north and left the Ordu. We went north retracing my path around the swamp to the northern lake. Unfortunately with all the rain, the ground was still soft and the going slower than desirable. It was almost dark when we reached the base of the hill from which I had searched in vain for the Ordu. We found a vaguely dry or, at least, well-drained spot for our first camp. At dawn, we saddled up quickly and ate our dry food on the way to save time. We went around the north side of the hill and headed north and to the west of a hill just visible in the distance. It was soon lost to sight as we entered a thick forest of tall spruce and fir trees with some birch and larch trees mixed in. Ground cover was minimal, although there were berry bushes wherever the trees thinned out and only the lodestone kept us on course as we reached the Amgun and looked for a place to cross. We followed this downstream for a while, then swam the horses across at a spot where the river broadened a bit, lessening the current. We were carried downstream, but made the other side safely. We made camp at nightfall in the woods near where we crossed the river. Now I would find out how good a cartographer old Arughtu was.

Fortunately, Arughtu's map was quite good and only needed a few minor corrections. We slogged northward through the marshy ground and finally reached the slope of a long ridge aiming northward. We made our next camp on this drier ground. The next day, we made much better time sticking to the high ground as we followed the ridge north. In the afternoon, we arrived at its end and had to cross some woods and another marshy river to get to another north-running ridge where we camped that night. We followed this ridgeline all the next day. Then we turned west and reached the western slopes of the ridgeline through a gap and followed it north the rest of the day. The next day, we crossed over a perpendicular ridge and could just see the Great Sea far to the north. We continued west along the north side of the ridge and at the end of the day reached a high point overlooking another marshy river valley. The next morning, the rain had finally stopped, but a thick fog blanketed the valley. Following the lodestone, we plunged down into it and into another larch and spruce forest, which opened into a marsh through which another river flowed northward. We crossed the river, went into another forest, and finally came out on the slope of another north-running ridge. We were able to get above the fog by going up the slope a way. We turned north again for the rest of the day, and by evening, we could not only see the Great Sea but we could smell the salt air and hear the muffled hum of the surf.

Juchi proved to be an excellent traveling companion. He was always cheerful and talkative, shared all the camp tasks, and was a much better cook than I could ever dream of being. When we weren't huddled over from the rain or forced to go single file, he would keep up a cheerful chatter, recalling things that had happened when we were children, bringing me up to date on some of our old playmates, and the many things that had happened since I had left. I told him a little about Khanbalikh and my studies, but he was obviously more interested in his stories, so I let him talk and tried to notice as much as possible about the terrain.

The following day was sunny and clear, a cold dry northwestern wind took over as we followed the coast westward around the northern end of the ridge, across a small river valley, and up along the northern end of yet another ridge, After some time, we finally came to within sight of the river which was the last bit of terrain on Arughtu's map. Once across we would be on our own. There was a hill overlooking the river, so we rode up to have a better look and get some idea what was ahead. From this vantage, we could see that the river had several channels but didn't look too deep or swift. Beyond were marsh, forest, and mountains, but the shore did turn northeast, as promised. We could see there were some villages along the river but decided it would be best to avoid locals as long as possible, although Givevneu had assured Juchi that they were almost always friendly. We decided to camp at the edge of the woods at the foot of the hill.

In the morning, we again went through a thick wood, followed by a marsh to get to the river. We slogged, waded, or swam across the various channels of the river only to find an even larger marsh on the far side, which finally gave way to another thick forest. Since the ground cover was minimal again, we made up some of the time spent wading through the marsh, and went due north following the lodestone, until the sound of the sea seemed to dim. Then we turned northeast, breaking out of the thick forest late in the day and into a thinner, more open larch and pine forest, with more underbrush, especially mosses and berry bushes. We did a bit of berry picking to top off our meal that night. By this time, it seemed we had outpaced the monsoon, for the weather was clear and dry. This made for easier mapping and more comfortable camping. Still, I began to wonder if Kaidu thought to bring the whole Ordu this way. It would be very difficult for the wagons with all the forests, marshes, and rivers. Moreover, many of the ridges we crossed were quite steep. But if he didn't plan to bring the Ordu, why would he want the mapping? I began to take more time and care with the maps, climbing trees and hillsides for better views, and making notes about the river currents and depth, the slopes of the hills, and the density of the underbrush, always with a mind to finding a path passable to wagons.

For the next sixteen days, the path was uneventful. The coast went north, east, or northeast and there were mountains and hills right up to the coast. We found the going easiest on the lower slopes of the hills up from the beach. The vegetation was sparse, just occasional stands of larches, pines, and birch especially along the small rivers we crossed, and some bushes, mosses, and increasingly, lichens. Game was sparser as well, but we still had plenty of food and only supplemented it with small game that chanced to come into bowshot. We saw natives on occasion, and they saw us, but no contact was made. They were quite busy fishing. They seemed to have reindeer, but no horses. In fact, they looked at our horses more than at us when we were near, but their expressions were hard to decipher. We mounted a watch when we camped near them, but we were never bothered.

On the seventeenth day, a direct encounter with the locals proved unavoidable. Around midafternoon we came upon a multi-channeled river, which stretched out for li in front of us. The beach proved to be the most passable terrain, so we went along for some distance only to find a large summer village right in our path. They were friendly and invited us to join them for the night. We found it prudent to agree. They called themselves Evenks, but they looked very much like the Nanai and had no trouble understanding that language. The huts they lived in were rather flimsy, consisting of laths fastened in a conical shape and covered with larch or birch bark. They insisted that they were comfortable in the winter as well, since they covered them first with earth, then with snow as it got colder. For heat they used seal oil, since wood was scarce. This was a prudent if smelly adjustment. During the course of our meal, our hosts asked about our "tribe," its proximity, and our intentions. We told them we were Mongols and that our tribe was some distance to the south. Seeing that they too had a shaman, I described our mission as taking a message from our shaman to his family far to the northeast. They were silent for a while, but finally had to ask if all the other Mongols looked as different as Juchi and I and if it was our normal practice to get our shaman from such a distance. We got around these questions by describing the Mongols as more of a group of different "tribes" than a single tribe, so it was not unusual that our shaman was from so distant a place. This satisfied them, but they urged us to hurry, because our horses would never survive a winter out in the open. Juchi and I exchanged looks at that bit of intelligence. We hadn't thought of that. While the Nanai and the Nivkh used dogsleds in the winter and we had tried them out as youngsters, Mongols always used horses—even in the winter. The steppe horse was sturdy, had a long coat, and could dig through snow to find grass. But, of course, it did not live in the far north. Shrewdly assessing our problem, our hosts suggested we continue on our journey until the snow covered everything and the rivers froze at which time we should seek out one of their villages and trade our horses for the use of dogsleds. We pointed out that we would need the horses to return to our "tribe." Surely half of them would suffice, they suggested. Would their relatives likely make such a trade? we asked. Fresh meat was always welcome they assured us, especially something different. Meat! A horse is many things to a Mongol, but only "meat" as a very last resort. We were somewhat sobered as we set out from the village the next morning.

Two days later, we again encountered a huge multichanneled river system. This one was at least sixty li wide. As before, we stuck to the beach and again encountered natives. We spent the next two nights at different villages in the estuary, the last a rather large one at the northern edge where an inlet separated a large bay from the Great Sea. They also expressed curiosity about us, and we answered consistently. In the last village there was interest in our compound bows and steel-tipped arrows. They wondered if our tribe would trade such things for food or seal oil. We said that they probably would, and that we'd pass on their offer to our tribe on our return. We thought it best to give them a stake in our safe return should things ever get tense.

After leaving that village, the coast turned east, and we followed it along for thirteen days. We stuck to the coast unless warned by the natives to go inland. The natives here looked just like the Evenks, but they called themselves either Orochel or Evens depending on the village. They were very sea oriented and either fished or hunted sea animals. They would trade with the more inland tribes for meat and furs. Their huts looked either much like those of the Evenks, or much like our own yurts only with fish skin instead of felt covering. They also were interested in trade and were most interested in our horses. After all, the inland tribes rode as well as ate their reindeer. Again we held out the promise of future trade with our "tribe" on our return. They proved to be very helpful and warned us about some sizable peninsulas that would have taken us out of our way. On the thirteenth day, we were cautioned to move inland a bit to avoid some rough terrain and another peninsula.

For the next five days, we held an easterly course across a broad plain hemmed in by mountains to the north and south, and broken up by patches of larch and fir forest with heavy underbrush. On the third day, we crossed the largest and deepest river we had seen in some time. It had a strong current but was swimmable, and we got across it without incident. Late on the fifth day, we found the coast again and followed it until nightfall.

The following day, we found the coastline turning northward again, and we stayed with it for seven days. On the sixth day, we encountered a strange valley where the wind was fierce. It roared up the valley from the sea with near gale force. We made our way across it with some difficulty and asked about it when we next found a village. It seems the wind blows landward in the summer and seaward in the winter, usually very strongly. In the abbreviated spring and fall it changes directions. It is most dangerous in winter they assured us for one can be blown out to sea. I carefully marked the valley on my map. After this, the shore turned eastward, and we turned with it for the next four days. Here we were again advised to turn away from the coast to avoid two very large peninsulas. We could see the first since the shore clearly turned south for many li, but were surprised that there was another. This second was the smoking peninsula, according to the locals. It had smoking mountains and was much bigger than the first. This sounded like the one Givevneu warned us about, so we gladly altered our course. They sent us up their river a little east of north until we came upon a larger river flowing southeast. We crossed this and turned east through a large gap in the mountains, which narrowed considerably before opening up into a large valley bisected by a ridgeline. We followed the ridge northeastward until it was cut by a river, which we crossed and then turned eastward through a narrow valley and some low hills until we reached a large lake. It took twenty-six days to reach the lake.

At the beginning of this leg of the journey, it would have been early fall back on the Karamuren. Here it was perhaps the equivalent of late fall. The nights were very cold and the days were cool. In the morning, the ground was frozen hard, and as the days went by, it took longer and longer to get soft. Small shallow lakes were frozen over, and we had to avoid them in case the ice wasn't thick enough. Anytime we were out of a windbreak, we were brutalized by the bitter cold wind. We always camped in the protection of trees or hills. The horses were having a rough time making do on the rather mean forage, and we had to ease up on them and stop anytime we found something they could eat. It took no coaxing at all for us to stay with the locals. Not only did it mean relief from the elements but also renewed directions to keep us on the trail.

The people who sent us on this detour looked something like Givevneu but called themselves the Nymyl"u. They lived in houses dug into the ground which one entered through a smoke hole in the roof. They were moving into these from their raised summerhouses, much like those of the Nanai, when we came upon them. They had some reindeer, but mostly concentrated on fishing and hunting sea animals. They used seal and whale oil for heat and cooking. Their language sounded like that of the Nivkh, but they understood the Tungus tongue, as had all the natives so far. We asked them about the An'kalym, and they turned most unfriendly not wishing to assist any friends of their longtime enemies. We assured them we were not friends of the An'kalym, but were only instructed to take them a message from our shaman. They assumed the message had to be a reprimand, and we didn't disabuse them of that assumption, so all was well again.

The Nymyl"u told us that the Chavchuvat, who were related to the An'kalym would be found along the large river north of the lake to which they directed us. I told them that the particular group I was looking for lived on the Great Sea, not on a river. They assured me that the large river flowed into the sea and the An'kalym, whom they called the Lygitann'ytan, could be found all around the mouth of the river for some distance, especially to the east.

When we reached the lake, it was definitely early winter. The lake appeared frozen over, and we camped in the lee of a small row of hills to escape the harsh wind. That night, the wind changed and a storm hit dumping about a foot of snow on us while buffeting us with gale force winds. We were unable to go anywhere but to the other side of the hills to escape the wind. Here we dug a shelter out of the snow and stayed for two days while the storm played itself out. On the third day, the wind shifted back again, and we plowed through the snowdrifts back to the other side of the hills and right into a party of natives. These were armed with spears and were eyeing us suspiciously.

6

THE AN'KALYM,
37TH YEAR OF TOGHON TEMUR
(N.E. SIBERIA, 1367)

Fortunately, the natives proved to be more curious than hostile, but they really looked like warriors, unlike all those we had seen before. Again, while they found us interesting, they were most taken by our horses. As it turned out the horses were the main reason they hadn't attacked first and asked questions later, their usual method. They hadn't seen horses before and wanted a closer look at them and whoever brought them. Looking at us they decided Juchi must be an Even, although he was strangely dressed, I, on the other hand was not easily explained. We correctly identified them as Chavchuvat, and explained that we were looking for them with the hope that they might help us find our shaman's village among their brothers, the An'kalym. This prompted an invitation to their village across the lake, which was quite frozen, they assured us.

The village consisted of a row of tents, not unlike our yurts in general shape, though they were smaller and were covered with reindeer skins. There was a large herd of reindeer grazing nearby as well a growling and yapping pen of dogs. We were ushered into the last or easternmost tent to meet the leader and explain ourselves. The headman was willing to help us find our shaman's village, but he still couldn't understand how Juchi and I could belong to the same tribe, or for that matter, why we had an An'kalym shaman. We explained again that Mongol really meant "the brave" and so was a group rather than a tribe and anyone who was brave and accepted by our leader could be a member no matter what his ethnic tribe was. This was still hard for them to conceive until one of them recalled that a group of An'kalym had mixed with the Yupigyt and were now one village. That made some sense to them, and they decided to leave it there, fortunately.

They invited us to stay with them for a while, and we thought it prudent to do so since the horses were in poor shape, we were very low on food, and we wanted their help. Our hosts soon convinced us to leave the horses with them and borrow dogsleds for the rest of our journey. They promised not to allow any harm to come to the horses as long as we returned the dogs and sleds to them before the next winter. They graciously built the horses their very own tent and promised to feed and exercise them according to our instructions. They then took on the task of honing our very rudimentary dogsledding skills. We had no idea just how complicated it was to keep a snarling, mean-spirited, hostile team of dogs from fighting each other while moving in concert in the direction desired. It took time, but we both got rather good at it, although I can't honestly say I've ever missed either the dogs, the sleds, or for that matter, the north, since.

When our tutors thought it safe to let us go, they decided to also loan us a "slave" to make sure we didn't get lost. It seems that they enslaved those captured in battle, but this particular slave had killed a member of the tribe and had become a "slave" to replace his victim (a rather unique custom). We were assured he could be relied on to get us where we wanted. They did not recognize the bay in Givevneu's drawing although they were quite taken with the idea of maps and insisted that I draw a map of their village for them. They also did not recognize the name of Givevneu's brother, but suggested that we try asking at the settlements of An'kalym around a rather large bay to the east, since they might know the man.

We set out just before the sun made its brief appearance in the south. It wasn't really dark, but more like a long twilight. We went single file with our guide in the lead, heading generally east along the northern bank of a large although apparently frozen river. Our sleds were fully loaded with dried fish to feed the dogs and ourselves, so they kicked up quite a steady spray of the powdery snow, necessitating that we leave a bit of room between us as we traveled. Our guide set the pace, and it was fortunate that Juchi and I were in good physical shape, because he was not taking his time, and we had to run along with the sled to keep warm. Turning it on its side stopped the sled. I would have thought a brake could have been devised but their solution did seem to work. Then to start up again, we would have to untangle and arrange the dogs, right the sled, and yell some sort of epithet in the Chavchuvat tongue. This yelling had to be done with authority—much like a growl—to be effective.

What little could be seen was hard to discern. The landscape was almost uniformly white, only occasionally broken up by a stand of bushes, although often these would appear clothed in a ghostly white coating of snow. The sun would appear red and low in the south and coast along the horizon for a while and then disappear into the eerie long twilight. We would usually find a village to spend the night before dark, but if not, the pale shimmering blue ribbons of the northern lights would starkly appear in the northern sky as we reached a village. Normally the activity of greeting the villagers and settling down the dogs and ourselves would keep us inside the dank smoky tents or rushing around outside briefly, but one night, Juchi hauled me out into the night to look at the stars. They were just as Givevneu had described them to him. The group of stars the Hanjen call the Northern Bushel Basket and the Muslims call the Greater Bear was in the middle of the northern sky. Below and a little to the west of the smaller similar pattern that rotates around the Star of the North, the zigzag group of stars the Muslims call the Lady in the Chair was very high in the southeastern sky, and the small cluster of stars was overhead to the south with the Starry River below it. We were far enough north, and only needed to go east.

We followed the frozen river into a very large frozen delta and across frozen inlets, then back inland to the north of a small ridge, then across a flat open plain with a small range of hills to the north where we turned more northeasterly finally arriving at a large village near the mouth of a huge bay which was mostly frozen over. This leg of the journey had taken nine days. This village was indeed peopled by An'kalym. The headman received us graciously and vowed to see us to our destination. Our guide was sent back with presents, and we were prevailed upon to stay a few days and tell stories while waiting for the coastal waters to freeze completely, since that would be the easiest route to the east. The headman was sure he had met Givevneu's brother, but it had been a chance encounter at a trading village some days to the east, and he had indicated that his village was even farther east.

The An'kalym lived in what they called "caves." These were set on the ground and framed with the jawbones and ribs of whales. Over this they layered sod and earth. The entrance was a long corridor in the winter and the smoke hole in the summer. Bones covered the middle of the floor and over this a large whale oil lamp burned day and night. There were platforms raised up on four sides of the floor and on these there were fur "tents" in which several people could sleep. Each of these had its own oil lamp for heat and light and was really quite warm—if smoky. The smell, on the other hand, was beyond the imagination. Of course, it would have been unthinkable to betray any displeasure, especially since they seemed to attach great significance to smells and were constantly sniffing each other by way of greeting. I suspect they found our smell no less repulsive than we found theirs. And by now they would be justified since a proper bath was only a fond memory for us. But they never let on any offence and were very gracious and generous hosts.

The layover was fortuitous for a ferocious blizzard hit the village on the next day and raged with varying intensity for five days. Then it took another two days to get organized for our departure. Meanwhile, every night we each had to tell stories and in turn hear their stories. They really liked the fables my grandfather George had told me but also enjoyed the Christian Bible stories my grandfather Peter had told me. Juchi's hunt and battle stories were well received as well, although they were obviously embellished. They finally told me they were relieved that I was called the "Raven" because of my wisdom evidenced in my stories. They were afraid that the name had been a mockery since I had pale skin and brown hair while the raven was very black. No, I didn't disabuse them of this interpretation. Neither did Juchi, but his smile was a bit too broad when he heard it.

We left early the next day, well before sunrise. Stars were still visible, but the southern sky was lightening to that deep blue that precedes twilight. The northern lights were still writhing slowly in the northern sky. There was no perceptible wind, but the cold was intense and penetrating. As we set off across the frozen bay, I wondered how these people went through this every year. The bay was a rather bumpy ride, but there were no pressure ridges or thin spots, and we passed inside a skinny barrier island and sped to a village on the eastern side just as the last twilight darkened into full night. We repeated this pattern every day speeding eastward over the frozen sea just in sight of the shore and spending each night in another An'kalym village. Sometimes we would pass a few villages by, but usually they were the only sign of life anywhere in the bleak unrelenting frozen landscape.

The skinny barrier island proved to be very long. It was two days before we passed it. The shore continued east for a day, turned southeast for another day, then turned south for two days before again heading east. On the second day of this heading, we found a bay similar to the one Givevneu had drawn, but the spit of land was on the western side of the bay and right at the mouth instead of a little up the bay. The headman at the village on the bay had heard of Givevneu's brother. It seems he was now the headman of a village on a bay two days' journey farther along the coast. It seemed we were surely at the end of the earth, and still we had farther to go.

And so it was that two days later just as the sun ended its brief appearance in the southern sky, we rounded a cape into a bay and headed right for a spit of land jutting out from the eastern shore of the bay a little way up from the mouth. Little twilight was left as we approached the village, but a small group gathered to greet us as we pulled in. We asked for Givevneu's brother, Naukum, and were taken to the largest "cave." He greeted us graciously, although he was puzzled that such strangers would know him by name. We told him we had a message for him from our shaman, his brother, Givevneu. This seemed to puzzle him for a while, and we began to think we might have gotten the wrong man. Then he brightened.

"You mean my brother, Blocknot!" he almost shouted. "So he has taken the drum after all. We thought he had perished long ago, after he disappeared. But who are you people? One of you looks like an Even, the other like a mystery. Where is my brother? How did he find you? Is he well? Has he become a woman? Is he with the Even now? Is he coming back? What is his message?"

We tried to answer his questions as best we could except we wanted to give him the message in private in case it was personal. Of course, some of his questions raised questions in our minds. It seems Givevneu is a title rather than a name, it means, "one who knows" and is only given to particularly wise shamans. Also, apparently some shamans "change" their sex when they heed their "call." It seemed indelicate to pursue that point, although I made a mental note to ask Givevneu about it later. We assured him that his brother was still a brother and in fact had had a few children by a Nanai wife. When we were alone, Juchi took out the message and read his transliteration much to the awe of Naukum. Apparently even the idea of writing was alien to him, and we needed to spend some time explaining the concept before we got back to the message itself. Juchi reread it to him, and he sat quietly for a time reflecting on it quietly.

"Do you understand the note?" he finally asked us.

"No," Juchi replied, "Givevneu and Kaidu, our leader, thought it best if we came to understand the note after we delivered it."

"Humph," Naukum grunted, "perhaps he thought you'd not bother delivering it. It is really very simple for me, but perhaps not so for you. It simply asks me to guide you to Kytmin through Imaklik and Inaklik as soon as it can be done over the ice with heavy loads. That will be later in the winter, perhaps thirty days from now at the earliest. We will first have to go to Pyeyek, which is about eight days away on the sleds. We should make Imaklik in one day, move leisurely to Inaklik in part of another day, and rest the dogs up for the run to Kytmin the next day. It will mean visiting with the Yugit, as they call themselves. Without one of them along, I won't cross over to Imaklik. But they have a village near Pyeyek where one of our villages is, and we have been on friendly terms for a long time now. So you will stay with us until it is time to go to Pyeyek?"

"If you will allow us," I answered, "but could you tell us what these words of yours signify?"

"Pyeyek is a large rocky hill on the coast north and a little east of here," he began in a matter of fact tone, "Imaklik and Inaklik are two small islands on the sea and Kytmin is the rocky hill on the western coast of the other land."

"Other land?" Juchi and I repeated almost in unison.

"Of course," Naukum shrugged, "didn't Blocknot tell you about it? It is a large landmass, but it is overrun with Yugit and some other kind of people farther inland. Besides, it's easier to hunt whales from here, so it's of no consequence. I don't know why he wants me to show you two the way, but I will."

Juchi and I looked at each other in stunned silence. Why would Kaidu want us to scout out another land unless he wanted to take the tumen there? But if it were a frozen waste like this, what would be the point. We might as well just stay north of the Karamuren. We'd be out of the Khanate, but in a more temperate climate. I began to wonder about this "other" landmass.

"Just how large is this eastern land?" Juchi anticipated my question.

"I don't know," Naukum shook his head, "probably as big as this land. It trails off to the east and south for some distance according to the Yugit. Of course, I've never been there."

"But why?" I asked puzzled by his disinterest.

"I have all I need here, " he replied, "why should I look elsewhere?"

"Have you heard what it's like?" Juchi asked the more practical question.

"You will have to ask the Yugit what it's like," Naukum chuckled. "Why would I ask about that in which I have no interest?"

"That makes sense." I laughed. "Excuse our curiosity."

"No need." He waved aside my apology. "You are wise to wonder about your destination. I regret I can't help you more."

We were assigned a "tent" in Naukum's "cave" to sleep and were told the routine of life in the camp and invited to join in their hunts. This we readily agreed to do since we would be their guests for some time and it was the least we could do. Naukum gave us proper An'kalym clothes for our stay. This consisted of a double layer of trousers and shirts made of sealskin with the fur side worn inside on the inner layer and outside on the outer layer. The shirts were trimmed with dog fur. The outfit was completed with fur stockings and sealskin boots. To my amazement and discomfort, they wore no hat unless there was a snowstorm. Once Juchi and I were given the storm hats, we wore them all the time much to the amusement of our hosts.

The An'kalym seemed to be impervious to the cold. While the clothes they wore were indeed warm, I could never sympathize with their complaints of how hot it was. They were also quite strong. I was amazed at the size and weight of the loads they hefted with apparent ease. I found out that they built up their strength by lifting large heavy stones that had finger holes cut into them. Juchi and I found ourselves working with these stones during inclement weather for lack of anything better to do. Our hosts, however, were artistically inclined and liked to carve walrus and whale ivory and bone. They also liked to tattoo themselves, but not excessively. The men had small circles at the edge of their mouths and the women had straight lines on their forehead, nose, and chin. Curiously, the men wore their hair shaved on the crown like the older Mongols and the women wore braids, just like all of our women do.

The food we were served was usually the meat and fat of seal, walrus, or whale. The latter two were cut into large chunks and stored in pits cut into the frozen ground. Here they would get rather smelly but not spoiled. We also were served fermented leaves and grasses with the meat and on what was considered special occasions a loaf of ground roots mixed with fat and meat. All this took quite a bit of getting used to for both of us. We shared the little of our few remaining provisions with them, and they found the dried fish and meat familiar, but were puzzled though not put off by the dried mare's milk.

Hunting in the winter consisted of seal hunting. A trained dog led the hunter to the holes seals made in the ice to breathe. The hunter would then either set a net into the hole to entangle the seal or sit on the upwind side of the hole and spear the seal when it appeared. They would also go to the edge of the ice pack and spear any seal that came by. Sometimes they would set Juchi and me up at a hole cut in the ice on the bay to fish using a line tied to a stick with a small lure as bait. The "bait" was either a piece of red cloth or a tiny carved ivory fish. We were moderately successful at the fishing but were usually mere spectators at the seal hunts.

In addition to playing with the stone weights, we also passed idle time trying to learn the An'kalym language. The language was not especially complicated until we found out that the women pronounce the same words differently. The women would use a "ts" sound for the men's "r" sound. I resolved this problem by talking mostly to the men. Juchi, being unattached and of an amorous bent, made a great effort to grasp the whole of the language. My strange looks caused some interest, but they were not offended by my claim to be attached to a woman back home. Juchi, on the other hand, was much in demand by the unattached females of the village, and from my vantage point he seemed determined to keep them all happy.

We also spent some of this layover discussing our situation. It was fairly apparent that Kaidu wanted to take the Ordu over to the eastern landmass. I saw two major questions to be answered first. One was, could it be done? And the other was, would it be worth doing? The first question bothered me particularly since I was doing the mapping. The terrain of the north was quite difficult. In fact, it was probably easiest to get around in the winter since so much of the land was either marshy or mountainous. And in the winter, the marshes, rivers, and lakes were frozen solid and so easily passable. But of course the winter would be very hard on the people and animals and the sudden blizzards could tie us down for days. Also, wheels and horses hooves are not ideal for moving on ice and snow. Juchi suggested that perhaps the wagons could be turned into sleds, and we spent some time trying to design such a hybrid. The second question could only be settled once we got to the other land and talked to the Yugit. Did the land extend far enough south for the horses to survive? And, even more important, would a group like ours have a chance to settle there? Or, would we run into another Middle Kingdom? We sincerely hoped that the Yugit would prove to be more inquisitive than our host.

At last the time was judged right by Naukum, and we set out for the village at Pyeyek. By now the days were quite short consisting of little more than twilight, with a fleeting appearance of the sun far in the south. We went north way up the bay from the village, then veered inland over a narrow flat area between some hills. Here we stopped for the night at an old abandoned village. The next day, we continued inland up a gentle slope, then back down again to the coast and an inhabited village at the end of another large bay, facing east. The next day, we went up the bay to the village just north of its mouth. We could see a large island to the east. We continued east and north along the coast for two more days, and then set out across the frozen sea losing sight of land and everything else for that matter for a while, but our guide got us to another village that night. I suppose one gets used to very minimal landmarks up here, but I found mapping completely impossible under these conditions, and only just barely could figure out the general direction we were going, for even the lodestone was proving unreliable for some reason.

The next day, we went due east along the coast to another village at the end of a peninsula. Here we had to wait out a storm that struck just as we were getting ready to leave. The storm raged for a day, but was mostly wind and blowing snow with very little fresh snow. We set out across the wide mouth of a bay to another village. After this, we hugged the coast that went north for one day then northeast for a day and finally east around a moderately high hill seemingly jutting out of the sea like an island. It was a peninsula in fact with very low frozen marshy land connecting it to the mainland. The village at Pyeyek was in a rather protected spot between the hill we had just come around and another larger higher one to the north and a third low one to the west. We tried to see the object of our quest from the hill but were either driven from it by the cold or it was too dark by the time we were high enough. Our hosts assured us we could see the island Imaklik on a clear day.

Naukum left us for a few days while he went on to the nearby Yugit village to get one of them to accompany us. The An'kalym at Pyeyek were no more inquisitive than Naukum and could tell us little more than that the land looked the same there as here at least on the shore where they had visited. I suspect that was predictable since most shores look the same—either gravel, sand, or rock. We got in some dogsled practice while Naukum was gone, but the cold made these excursions necessarily brief.

Finally Naukum returned with a young Yugit (although he called himself a Yuit) named Taukujaa. He was about my age and in appearance resembled the Mongols except for the two ivory lip plugs in his lower lip at each end of his mouth. His hair was shaved on the crown like the An'kalym. He was very cheerful and friendly and had come from a village on the other side of the icepack to visit relatives. He was very impressed that I was called the Raven since it was their "creator" and thought I was very young for such a great title. I didn't bother explaining how I got the name, but rather puffed up a bit, causing Juchi to suffer a sudden cough attack. He assured us we would be most welcome in his village. We asked him about the eastern land over our evening meal, and unlike the An'kalym, he was full of information. The land was very much broader than this land he assured us, and it extended far to the east. I found that hard to believe, but let him continue. Where his village was, the land was flat and marshy, but inland there were two great mountain ranges, one in the north and one in the south with a huge river valley in between. He had not been very far east, but there was a man in his village who had been to the mouth of a great river far in the east, which flowed north. He had only been as far south as the mouth of a more proximate "great" river, which flowed westward. I asked if there were mountains between these two rivers, but he wasn't sure. He also couldn't say how far east the near river went, but again there was a man in his village who had been quite far up it. His people only lived along the western part of the river as well as all along the north and west coast of the land. Another people lived farther inland where the weather was milder, but he knew little about them except that they were a weak, vile, thieving people. Again another man from his village could tell us more. I wondered to myself how these other people would describe the Yugit. Anyway, it would seem Taukujaa's village would hold most of the answers to our second question, and Juchi and I were eager to set out.

Naukum felt the next day would be suitable for our run across the ice, and with a few extra dogs and as light a load a possible, we set out to Imaklik. Our heading seemed to be due southeast, and we set out at a punishing pace. From seeing rivers and lakes frozen over, one might expect the sea to also freeze smoothly. This is definitely not the case, however. Our path was necessarily circuitous because of the ridges, hills, and mountains of ice we encountered. The greatest danger was thin ice or even open water, but we encountered none of this. We had started well before light, but it was quite dark by the time the island loomed ahead like a mountain barely outlined by the pale waning moon. We found a village on the near shore and were received cordially, but with some curiosity and, I would think, suspicion. It was soon apparent why Naukum wanted a Yugit along, for Taukujaa's presence did much to gain us welcome. We moved on to Inaklik the next day, all during daylight and twilight, for the first time in a long time. It was a much smaller island; actually, it also looked like the top of a mountain sticking out of the sea, but a smaller mountain. We passed around to a village on the eastern shore. Here our reception was even more cordial for Taukujaa's aunt lived here, and we were prevailed upon to stay an extra day and tell stories. Naukum thought it a good idea to rest up the dogs for the longest leg of the passage. The Yugit houses were something like the An'kalym "caves" although they seemed to have more wood than bone and were covered with sod. They were rather square shaped with a smoke hole made of a hollow whalebone in the roof (that did not double as a summer entrance) and a long entrance corridor used year-round. The sleeping platforms were left open around the central hearth. We didn't stay with his aunt, however. We had to stay in a large rectangular house called a kashim. It had sleep benches all around an open space. We had to do the storytelling in the open space and then return to our platform. During performances, the women would sit in the back and the children on the floor in front. Afterward, they would return to their houses, but most of the men, especially the unattached, would remain in the kashim for the night. there was not much privacy and with all the snoring, not very restful. Except for the shapes of the houses, this was pretty much the pattern among the Yugit we encountered.

We started off very early and were way out on the ice when the sky began to lighten. Again we encountered no thin spots, but did have to maneuver around or over several ridges, and it was well after dark when we arrived at last at a village on the other side. We were welcomed since they all knew Taukujaa, but again we had to stay over another day and tell stories. Finally we made the run to Taukujaa's village, to the northeast along the coast, one more day's journey. Here we were very warmly received, although all were surprised to see Taukujaa before spring. The next day we were "feasted" on fish and stories were demanded. Naukum repeated his whale hunt tale again, Juchi followed with a ridiculous old Mongol legend which was very well received, so I told them one of my grandfather Peter's Bible tales about a holy man swallowed by a whale, and they all listened spellbound and agreed I had indeed earned the title "Raven." It wasn't easy being gracious while Juchi suffered another coughing spell, but I managed. I was glad I had a good memory for those tales. Then it was our hosts' turn. One after the other got up and told long-winded, stretched-out silly stories, mostly aimed (successfully) as it turned out to put everyone to sleep.

The following day we could get down to business, so we prevailed on Taukujaa to introduce us to the knowledgeable men he had described some days earlier. It turned out only one of the three was in the village at the moment, a cousin of his named Ootoyuk. He proved to be very cheerful and delighted to talk about his adventures. He was the one who had been to the mouth of the north-flowing river, far to the east. There were mountains between the two rivers, but they were not too high in the north only far to the south. The north-flowing river drained a fairly flat wetland that extended endlessly to the south. The other people in the land besides the Yugit (although he pronounced it Inuit) were called the Itqilit. These were spread out in small bands that lived along the various rivers and streams and mostly hunted and fished. They looked something like the An'kalym, except for the tattoos. The Itqilit men painted their faces, but the women wore tattoos on their chin copied from the Inuit women. The Inuit would often raid the Itqilit and some would bravely fight and others would run away. The Inuit would carry off the Itqilit women as extra wives. Ootoyuk's brother had such a wife. We later found out that "Itqilit" was an insulting name (it means "lousy") the Inuit had given their neighbors.

It looked like most of our questions had been answered, but Juchi asked if he would be allowed to stay with them for a while. Ootoyuk and Taukujaa both assured him he would be most welcome, especially if he knew more stories, and so for that matter would I. When I got Juchi alone, he explained that he would best serve the tumen by staying here and scouting out the best path east to the north-flowing river, from which we could surely find a suitable place to settle. I should return and report. I pointed out that Kaidu might not appreciate me abandoning his grandson in such a place, but he brushed that aside and insisted his was the best course. I had to admit he had a point, but cautioned him not to let anyone know of our probable intentions, since he would be rather exposed and well beyond our help. I also insisted that he be back here by the following winter in case we were coming over or so I could retrieve him if we weren't. He agreed and wished me luck. I wished him the same and urged him to be careful. He laughed and reminded me that mine was the more difficult journey. I would miss Juchi, we had been alone among strangers for over half a year, and he was the best of companions. The next day, Naukum and I left Taukujaa's village and began the trek back.

7
THE RETURN, 38TH YEAR OF TOGHON TEMUR
(E. SIBERIA, 1368)

On the return trip across the sea, I prevailed upon Naukum to let us spend a night on the ice since I doubted that the carts could make it to the island in one day. He told me I would regret it, but agreed. We camped in the lee of an ice ridge to at least escape the wind. All through the night, we were assailed with shrieks, hisses, crashes, crunches, pops, and other assorted unpleasant noises, the loudest of which would inspire a chorus of "song" from the dogs. It is doubtful that I have ever spent a worse night in my life. In the morning, the smiling Naukum reminded me that he had warned me. I spent a good deal of time after that trying to think of a way to get the carts across quickly enough to avoid a night on the ice.

We returned to Naukum's village uneventfully, and I prevailed on him to speed me on my way back to the Chavchuvat village. He sent a pair of men with me, one to handle Juchi's sled and the other to return them both home. We returned by the same path to the first An'kalym village on the large bay. Here I was pressed to stay a day and tell stories and Naukum's men were replaced with locals for the rest of the journey. I arrived at the Chavchuvat village some thirty-eight days after leaving Juchi.

The Chavchuvat greeted me enthusiastically, but asked after Juchi. I assured them he was well much to their relief. They also closely looked over the sleds and dogs and agreed I had returned all in good shape. However, they strongly recommended that I stick with the dogsled, rather than try to take the horses if I insisted on returning to my "village" in midwinter. I had to admit that was logical, but I had the feeling it would be very difficult to pry the horses loose from them when we returned. They treated them like pets and showed them off to all visitors. I would have thought they would find them to be more trouble than they were worth, but indeed they doted on them. So they loaded me up with dried fish and a fresh dog team, and I started back the way I had come, retracing my steps with more ease than one would think after all this time, but I was endowed with a remarkable sense of direction. I did, indeed, make better time with the dogs than we had with the poor horses once the snow hit, but was unsure how long the snow and ice would last.

I needn't have worried. Everything remained frozen all the way back. The only problem I had was a few tense moments whenever I entered a village. The Chavchuvat were not very popular among the other natives, and I was driving one of their sleds and dressed like their relatives, the An'kalym, but all was well when they saw my face. They all remembered me and asked after Juchi and our horses. They congratulated me on realizing the sled was the best mode of travel in the winter and on getting hold of some warm clothes, even if they had belonged to the enemy. I did have to tell stories every night I stayed with the natives, but it meant I was fed and so were my dogs. This helped stretch the dried fish out for the whole trip. So it was that some eighty days after leaving the Chavchuvat I found myself breaking through the woods and approaching the river that was the last point on Arughtu's map, and there, camped on this side of the still-frozen river, was the Ordu.

Surprised, but delighted, I hurried up to them. Again I was intercepted by guards and again had to bare my head to be recognized and endure much teasing about my herd of small "horses." I hurried on to Kaidu's tent since he wanted to see us the moment we returned. I was ushered in immediately, and he ordered everyone out and sent for the shaman. He bade me sit and gave me a bowl of broth to warm up. When Givevneu arrived, he turned to me for my report. I was not surprised that he hadn't asked about Juchi, for that would be considered weak, but I put him at ease by starting off with Juchi sending his greetings and was rewarded with a barely perceptible smile. Then I gave a detailed account of the journey leaving nothing out. Using my map as a reference, I showed them where there were villages that would likely trade food, where the rivers would be hard to cross, where the forage was adequate, etc.

The two men listened intently and silently, not once interrupting me. Then I turned to the eastern land, telling them what we had found out and why Juchi thought it best to stay and scout out our path to the north-flowing river, which drained the endless plain, a most promising place for horses. I regretted that I had not actually seen the plain but had no reason to doubt the story since the Inuit seemed very open and honest, and had nothing to gain by lying.

Kaidu asked why the last part of my map was so sketchy compared to the first, and I explained how almost all landscape was lost in the coating of snow and ice in the frozen northland winter, especially when the sea freezes over. But even so, the natives were so helpful, they guided us unerringly by landmarks seen only by them. Also that leg of the journey would be best made in winter over the frozen sea just as we had done, and we thought there might be some way to temporarily convert the Ordu's carts to sleds.

"Of course!" Kaidu's eyes lit up. "We could immobilize the wheels and attach wooden runners. I've been concerned about our deliberate pace. Excellent! You and Juchi have done very well! Givevneu was right about everything. The people of the north are mostly peaceful and all were helpful. The sea crossing is possible in the winter, and the eastern land will likely have horse country. Now, Raven, perhaps you wonder how it is you found us here, rather than where you left us. It seems the miserable excuse for a Khan was reminded of our existence by one of his miscreant advisers and sent a band of soldiers to seek us out and, if possible, bring us to his aid. His world is beginning to fall around him. Some execrable Hanjen peasant has raised an army, proclaimed himself emperor, and is in the process of destroying the remnants of the Khanate. No doubt we are to turn the tide in his favor all by ourselves, or more likely act as his rear guard while he flees to Karakorum. Happily, we got wind of this and withdrew well beyond his reach and bribed the locals to forget they had ever seen us. Fortunately, we were able to gather one more harvest before we left the lake, and we are really quite well stocked for the trip."

"You realized, then, that the forage on the way would never suffice?" I asked, impressed by his planning.

"Of course," he shrugged, gesturing toward Givevneu, "our shaman had his eyes open when he came to us. I had hoped there would be some forage, but we have enough grain to feed the livestock in the absence of any until next spring."

"Perfect," I was relieved, "that is just what you'll need. I also think you should set out immediately, for it is a very long way and with the carts you cannot travel as fast as we did. Also the frozen rivers will be easier to cross than rushing ones and the frozen marshes easier than the thawed ones."

"Indeed." He nodded. "We have only been waiting for your return before pressing on, and would not have long waited for that. Do you recommend we follow your route exactly?"

"Yes, mostly," I answered. "I will mark the best route for you. You must stay near the coast even if it means crossing many rivers. Most of them were shallow, but broad and tidal where we crossed.

"No matter," he smirked, "we have anticipated river crossings, and can put together a pontoon bridge across a fair-sized river, but it would cost us a day or so to do it, so we'll try and avoid the necessity."

"I am amazed!" I stared at him. "You really have thought of everything."

"Not really." He again indicated Givevneu. "Our shaman did. Now on a more personal note, did my grandson behave like a good Mongol? Did he bring any grief on you with his bad temper? Answer me freely, it is most important."

"Juchi was a credit to the Ordu," I answered candidly. "Throughout our journey he bore all hardships and adversities without any complaint. He was cheerful and did at least his fair share of the work. As to being a good Mongol, he is no doubt even now ensuring that you have as many descendants as possible throughout the North."

At this Kaidu dissolved into gales of raucous laughter in which Givevneu and I joined. When at last he regained his composure, he thanked me again and suggested that I lose no time in getting my betrothed and rejoining the Ordu as soon as possible. He would assign me horses to replace those of my brother's I had left behind and for my journey south to fetch my bride. He wished me luck on my journey, cautioned me not to tell anyone about the Ordu or its destination, and again urged me to hurry back for I would be needed.

On leaving Kaidu, I gathered up the dogsled and went straight to my brother's yurt. After cleaning up and changing out of my An'kalym clothes, I told Henry and his family a little about the north and its winter without telling too much. I made sure the dogs and sled would be cared for and promised to show my nephews how to use them when I got back with Paula. I turned in early for a much-needed rest. The next day I copied my map and marked the best route for the Ordu and took it to Kaidu. He sent me back with the promised horses. I started to get things ready for my trip south just as the Ordu was told to get ready to move north in the morning. Even though she was busy, Doqus fixed me up with food for a few months. That evening, Yesui told me she wanted to show me something. I followed her out to one of the carts and found she had made me my own yurt. It was all finished and waiting my return with my bride. I couldn't believe she had done all that work by herself. I thanked her profusely and made her promise to live with us, much to her delight. I could see, however, that her labor of love through the winter had much weakened her. I sincerely hoped she would still be with the Ordu when I returned.

Early the next morning while the yurts were being taken down and put in the carts, I set off across the still-frozen river leading my four horses. I pulled up on a rise just beyond the last channel and looked back. The Ordu was well under way, its leading elements just disappearing into the woods. I marveled at the sight and wondered what the people of the north would think when they saw its approach. The Ordu was much bigger than any village we had encountered in the north. It would be an interesting confrontation.

I mostly retraced my path since the land was so mountainous and rough. Some seven days after leaving the Ordu, I found myself at the still-frozen Amgun and made an easy crossing, then followed it upstream, eventually picking up the trail I had taken to find the Ordu the previous summer. Retracing my path, some thirteen days later, I pulled into the same Nanai village that had directed me to the Ordu. Not surprisingly, I was recognized, profusely greeted and prevailed upon to stay with them for a day. I thought it best to do so since the horses needed a rest and I would likely be coming back this way on my return. They confirmed that some Mongols had come the previous fall looking for the Ordu, but the Nanai had denied any knowledge of the Ordu as requested, and said that the Mongols had returned south to the Karamuren and gone east along the river for a while questioning the other villages, before giving up and returning south along the Sungari. I thanked them on behalf of the Ordu. Of course, at night I had to tell stories. I was getting good at this, using dramatic pauses and emphasis to good effect. They sat spellbound and made me promise to come back through their village on my return.

I reached the Karamuren two days after leaving the village. The spring thaw had begun, and the river was frozen but with a layer of water over the ice. I thought it best to cross quickly, before it began to break up. I was just downstream from where the Bira enters the Karamuren when I crossed, so two days later I arrived in sight of the Sungari. It was flooding since an ice dam at its juncture with the Karamuren blocked its natural flow. I turned south, and as the daylight was waning, I saw a small camp nearby. There was only one cart, but a moderate number of horses, so I decided to approach it cautiously in hopes of getting some news of what lay ahead. As I drew near, I could see there were only six people in the camp, and they were preparing their evening meal. They stopped when they saw me, but since I was alone, they waited for me. When I got close enough to see faces, I was shocked to find they were all Ferengi like me. They were also surprised and called to an older man who was still in the cart.

As he came up, I recognized Paula's uncle. I was speechless, but he broke into a big smile and shouted back to the cart the magic word "Paula." And there she was standing before me. I jumped off the horse and ran to her. I stopped. We looked at each other, embraced, kissed, cried, looked at each other again, embraced again, laughed, etc., without saying more than each other's names. She was even more beautiful than I remembered her. I was so besotted, that her uncle sat us down so the others could eat without being rude. Finally, I realized that I was filthy from my trip, and this brought me back to reality. I flushed crimson, apologized profusely, and ran to the river to remedy the situation. Upon my return, I was introduced to the others and sat down to catch up on things.

It seemed that the situation in the Khanate had completely degenerated. Zhu Yuanzhang the self proclaimed Hanjen Emperor, had named his new dynasty "Ming" and marched north. Foreigners were not welcome in the new empire, so the group thought it prudent to flee while they still could. Paula and her uncle had prevailed upon their companions to accompany them this far north in the hope they would encounter me on my way to Khanbalikh. They had been concerned since no one seemed to know anything about an Ordu nearby and had feared the worst. Paula and her uncle had vowed to wait until the monsoon began and the others had agreed to wait also. I asked after my grandfathers and found that George had died early in the winter, leaving me some books (all Hanjen tomes), and everything else to his assistant. Peter found himself abandoned by most of his Hanjen "friends" and had gone off to join a tribe of Merkit Christians who needed a priest. Poor man, I thought, trapped with "barbarians" for the rest of his life. I was sorry I would never see Grandfather George again, but had to admit, it was best for him to die before the city fell to the invaders. At least he died in peace.

I told the group that I had found kin in the north, and they were planning a great adventure up there. I wanted to be a part of that adventure unless Paula insisted otherwise. She looked at me with shining eyes and said she only insisted that I take her with me. My heart leapt for joy. Her uncle had no interest in adventure or the north and planned to go on to Karakorum. He was very grateful that he had been able to see to his niece's happiness. I was touched by his confidence in me.

Of the others in the group, one young couple asked if they could go with us. They were a little older than us and felt that adventure, even in the north, was preferable to running away to Karakorum. Unsure of what to say, I asked them about themselves. It seems that they, like me, were born in Khanbalikh. Their fathers had been in the service of the Khan, but had passed away. Seeing the hopelessness of the situation, they had decided to leave. The man's name was Padraig O'Byrne. His people were from an island far to the west, but he couldn't recall its name. It seems they were all warriors, and that was his training as well. His wife's name was Mathilde, and her people were from the northern coast of France, so she was a real Ferengi. Her father had been a relative of Pierre Boucher, the great metalworker to the Great Khan Kubilai. He had not been as skilled, however, and worked more humbly. Oddly, she had not heard of my grandfather George, but Khanbalikh was very large and she had lived in the northern part of the city.

I warned them of the hardship of the north, but they were not put off. So I told them that they could accompany us, but it was not my decision whether they could stay with my kin, it would be up to our "patriarch." They were still not put off, but I asked if they felt any loyalty to the Khan. To this Padraig asked, "What Khan?" I hoped Kaidu would not be angry with me for bringing them along, but saw no viable alternative. Before we turned in for the night, Paula's uncle took her and my right hands and asked us each in turn if we wanted to be married. We both replied we did, and he joined our hands together and told us we were now married. Since I looked puzzled, he told me that a marriage was a contract between a man and a woman witnessed by a third party, so unless we objected, we were married. Who was I to question such wisdom? Everyone congratulated us, and he set up a small tent for us a little away from the rest. That night my life became complete.

The next day, I thought it prudent to set off while the Karamuren was still frozen, so we parted company. Paula's things were only enough for one horse to carry and the others had also traveled lightly. We bid our farewells and set off northward, while the others started off southward up the Sungari. The Karamuren was still frozen, but would not be for long. The water was six inches deep over the ice, and in places the ice moved under our feet. It was with great relief when we finally got across. Two days later, we crossed the still-frozen Bira and continued on to the village I had promised to revisit. When they heard I had gotten married, they had a big celebration for us. It took us a few days to get away, but we were loaded up with dried fish before we left. Paula was very impressed with my storytelling, even if she couldn't understand Nanai.

I again retraced the same path northward, but this time the pace was slower. We did much talking, some hunting, and would stop sometimes just to look at beauty. For it was early spring, and flowers were coming up everywhere. The ice and snow were melting, the days were warmer, but the nights were still quite cool. We crossed the Amgun as soon as we reached it, where it was still fairly shallow, but very cold. The ground began to soften in the day and freeze again at night, at least for a while. Then, just before we reached the coast, clouds of mosquitoes rose to assault us whenever we passed standing water. It was necessary to camp up on the ridges and go closer to the coast to stay in the mosquito-discouraging breeze. After some twenty-four days, we finally arrived at the river where I had parted with the Ordu earlier in the winter to fetch my bride.

The river was thawed and very cold but not too hard to cross. To my surprise, it was quite evident that there had been a large encampment where the Ordu hadcamped. I would have thought the spring thaw would have erased all trace of them being here, but, although grass and flowers were everywhere, there were clear signs of the camp and the livestock having been here. I felt it was only fair to tell Padraig and his wife what I had already told Paula in secret, that it was not just my kin we were joining, but also the Ordu. I explained that I was not to tell anyone, but at this point it could do no harm. They were a little hurt, I could tell, because we had grown quite close along the trail, but they had to admit I had no choice and were pleased I had finally told them. They still wanted to go along, but were concerned about Kaidu's interview. I told them as much as I could about what could disqualify them, and they were encouraged that they might pass his test.

Since the Ordu had a sixty day lead on me, I figured it would take us about forty days to catch them, unless they were moving much faster than I expected. It did seem that they had greatly depressed the game along their path, for we found little besides the occasional game bird to vary our fare. We followed steadily in their increasingly obvious wake. As the ground thawed, the cartwheels left deeper ruts. The first natives we encountered some twenty days later at the first large river delta were pleased to see me again. They admitted that the sight of the Ordu had been unsettling, but a smaller contingent had come into their camp first to talk about trade, before the whole had come into view, so all had gone well, and they were very happy with the bows and other goods they had gotten in trade. I think they were also happy that the Ordu had moved on. More to the point, they indicated that they had passed through some thirty days or so before, so they were moving faster than I had anticipated. It would likely take another forty days to catch them.

Twenty days later, we had a fairly easy time of it going through the Wind Valley. I took the detour just in case, but the wind was only at raging thunderstorm strength this time. I wondered how the Ordu had made out crossing it. Some five days later, we were near the base of the smoking peninsula and actually could see some of the smoking volcanoes in the distance. As before, the grass looked like it had been well cropped, and had not yet recovered. The north was much different at this time of year. The marshes were covered with blueberry bushes and other low shrubs. On the hillsides and riverbanks were trees and flowers. The latter were of remarkably intense color, deep and bright and pale blues, scarlet to pink reds, intense to opaque yellows, and more. It is hard to believe that anything so colorful was and would soon be again that unrelenting blinding white. And the birds vied with the flowers. Every pond was full of migratory birds, geese, swans, and ducks. Every craggy ridge was full of sea birds, gulls and puffins, especially. The beauty was quite a distraction to Paula. She would stop and point at a field of flowers, a small stream surrounded with trees, a pond, or hill full of birds and exclaim at the beauty. If anything, the long ride had made her more beautiful. She had good color from the long hours of sunlight and fresh air. Her energy and endurance amazed me. I fell in love with her all over again. I was glad we were here at this time and hoped the memory would sustain all of us through the seemingly endless winter ahead.

I felt sure we would soon find the Ordu. But it was not until ten days later that we finally caught them. They were building a pontoon bridge across the river near the Chavchuvat village. The latter were fascinated by the procedure and were all gathered on the far side to watch. The carts and animals were clustered on the slopes of the very row of hills where we had first met the locals. How different the hills looked clothed in vegetation, albeit severely cropped vegetation. As usual we were met and escorted right to Kaidu's yurt.

8

THE AN'KALYM,
38TH YEAR OF TOGHON TEMUR
(NE SIBERIA, 1368)

We had arrived late in the day, and Kaidu was in his tent meeting with the headman of the Chavchuvat village. Both were very glad to see me. I presented Paula and the other couple. Kaidu was very cordial to Paula and congratulated me on finding a fine-looking and hardy wife. He was more formal with Padraig and Mathilde and asked them to stand by in another yurt until he had the time to speak to them. As they were escorted out, I gave them an encouraging smile. Kaidu motioned Paula and me to sit, and the headman congratulated me and invited us and, of course, Kaidu to his village for a feast in honor of the occasion the next evening. He regretted he could not accommodate the whole Ordu. He complimented me on the size and strength of our "tribe" and on our choice of leaders. He had apparently been much impressed with Kaidu. He took his leave to get things ready for the feast.

"He was frightened out of his wits," Kaidu began. "He is now almost giddy with relief that we intend to move on. Unfortunately, we have made quite a mess of the land wherever we go, and he was afraid we would take all the forage from his reindeer. It is easy to see why all the villages up here are so small; the land could never support any large group. I've given him some of our grain to make up for his losses and promised to leave the day after tomorrow. I've also told him he could keep the horses, and presented him with one of our bows, a quiver of arrows and a fine-looking sword. I thought he earned it for all his help to you and Juchi. Do you agree?"

"Definitely." I nodded. "He was of immeasurable help to us. I must see that he gets his dogsled and dogs back also."

"No need," Kaidu chuckled, "they are his gift to me, and mine back to you. How did you ever keep those nasty creatures from killing each other?"

"With difficulty." I smiled, ruefully. "They are vicious brutes, but indispensable in the winter."

"We will dispense with them, however," he shrugged. "We have made runners for the wagons and have come up with a type of boot for the horses pulling the carts. Your brother can show you one. They're made of sealskin, and cost us quite a bit in trade along the way, but they should help the horses pull their loads across the ice. We won't know for sure until the winter, but it should work well. It was Givevneu's idea."

"That just might work," I said. "It never occurred to me to do something about the horses hooves. What a marvelous idea. Where is the shaman? I'd like Paula to meet him."

"He is over in the Chavchuvat village," Kaidu answered. "He is talking shop with his counterpart. He'll call on you when he returns. Meanwhile, I must thank you again. Everything was as you said, and your map was perfect up to here. Of course, beyond this point it is rather sketchy. How nice that you have caught up with us in time to remedy the situation. We cannot stay in any one place very long. It quickly becomes a quagmire. I know the final leg must be made in winter, and it is not far away, but meanwhile we must keep moving, so why not in the proper direction? I'll need you to find us places to camp some fifteen to twenty li apart in the general direction we're going. And, of course, I need you to map."

"Of course," I replied. "It is a pleasure to be back in your service."

"Good," he nodded. "Now, as to these Ferengi you have brought along. Why did you bring them along, and just who are they?"

I explained who they were and the circumstances under which they came along and how I only told them about the Ordu when it became obvious that we were following more than just my kinsmen. I also assured him that they did not know what our final destination was, but only that we were on an "adventure" and that they seemed to be fine couple who would be an asset to the Ordu, but I had made them no promise and their final disposition was indeed up to him and they fully realized it. He seemed satisfied with my explanation and sent me off to see my family. He thanked me again and promised to send the "new Ferengi" to me after his interview.

Paula wanted to wait for their interview, but I told her it was best to go and meet my family and let the chips fall where they may. We went to my brother's tent and my nephews came running up all excited to show me how they had taken care of the dogs and the sled in my absence. I introduced them to Paula, and they bounded off to get their parents. Henry and Doqus rushed out to meet us, and we were warmly embraced and ushered in to meet Yesui. She rose slowly but looked Paula over carefully, then turned to me.

"You have chosen well, my son," she began. "She looks strong. But she is not yet with child? You couldn't have been riding night and day to get back to us or you would have been here much sooner. Did not your grandfather instruct you in your duties? Are you ill or injured?"

"No, Mother." I blushed crimson, much to everyone's amusement. "I'm fine. Paula is likely not yet with child from all the riding we have done, not from any abstinence. And you know very well my grandfather taught me all I needed to know. I daresay you found my father adequately instructed."

This set her off into a gleeful cackle that lasted a little too long. I turned apologetically toward Paula, but found she was laughing almost as hard but with more gentility. I got the feeling the two of them were going to get along just fine. Yesui finally got control of herself, and she and Doqus took Paula off to show her how to set up the yurt she had made for us. I told Henry about our grandfathers and what had happened in Khanbalikh according to Paula and the others. He sighed and said it was just as well we were leaving nothing behind to worry about. That was true, there were no bonds left to tie us to our birthplace. We easily agreed on a division of the horses and the herds, for I would be setting up my own household. I insisted that he keep the bulk of both, since he had been solely responsible for them for so long and besides, I didn't want to overburden Paula so soon.

Padraig and Mathilde were brought to the yurt just then. I

was relieved to see that both were smiling when they entered, and indeed, they had received permission to stay, but in my "custody." I introduced them to my brother and my nephews and the latter took Mathilde off to help with the yurt. I told them they would, of course, stay with Paula and me as long as they wished. Padraig was much impressed with Kaidu, and felt that the Khanate might have had a different fate if he had been Khan. He was grateful that he could stay with the Ordu and that he could learn our ways from Paula and me. He was determined not to be a burden. Padraig and I had a strange relationship. I think we respected each other more that we liked each other, but that was enough. Paula and Mathilde were like very close sisters, and I was glad they had each other for it looked like I'd be away quite a bit again.

The women returned and led us to see my new yurt. It was magnificent. Yesui had indeed outdone herself. Many of our neighbors nodded in admiration, and I made sure she got all the credit. As she had promised, she moved in with us, and set to work turning Paula and Mathilde into "good Mongol wives." She thrived on the task, and I saw the sparkle come back in her eye. The three of them spent a lot of time laughing, I noticed. Oddly, it was not until some days later that I realized I finally had a home of my very own. Of course, it was a moving home, but it was indeed a home. Yesui did bring in her ongons and go through her rituals, but we were all respectful.

The big celebration at the Chavchuvat village in honor of my marriage was quite something. They brought out all of their special dishes. Most of these were repulsive in the extreme, but we sampled and raved about all much to their delight. Then, of course, we had to tell stories. Unfortunately for Paula, all was related in the Tungus tongue so they would understand it. I had to come up with a story, but was fully prepared and regaled them with one of Grandfather Peter's more elaborate Hanjen fables about a dragon, which had been turned into the northern lights. Kaidu even rose to the occasion and recounted a great hunt from his youth where he was almost killed by a bear. The stories of the Chavchuvat were hard to follow and tedious in the extreme, but at last we took our leave. Kaidu asked if I had made a point to learn these stories. I had to admit I was merely cursed or blessed, depending on one's point of view, with a good memory for tales and had a very large and as it happened, very handy repertory. He agreed that my memory was most fortuitous, and wondered if storytelling was the most prized "talent" here in the north. I assured him, that next to landing a whale, it was.

Paula was pleased that I was so popular among the natives although she hoped we wouldn't be feted again anytime soon. The next morning, I was sent ahead to look for a camp while the Ordu followed in my "wake." Oddly, the best places were along the bank of the large river we had just crossed. To the north of the river, all was marshy, impassible tundra. To the south back across the river, the land was higher, and probably more suited to us, but we would have to cross back to this side again anyway. Still, the ground was soft, and we were really tearing it up as we went.

I finally caught up with Givevneu after a few days. We kept missing each other with all my scouting duties and his shaman duties. He had met my Paula in my absence and congratulated me. He was also certain Padraig and Mathilde were good additions to the Ordu. He was concerned about Yesui, however. He could see that she was failing and was certain that she was only sustained by feeling needed by the two young women. He told me it was past her time, and I should not make her feel like an invalid or take any notice of her failing, but let her go on as she was. She would not last long into winter and was very happy being busy. He had already told Paula and Mathilde as well as Henry and Doqus and all had agreed. He was right, of course, and I made every effort to act like she was fine and joke with her whenever I saw her. It wasn't easy—she was so pale and thin. But she was happy and dearly loved Paula and Mathilde, and they her.

We crept along the river for a few days, but finally I had to lead the Ordu north to another river. We had to cross it on pontoons, then slog across to another river, and follow it upstream until it was narrow enough that we could cross it on pontoons. All this took five days and by now the nights were getting quite cold and shallow lakes would freeze overnight and thaw during the day. This meant the ground was harder at first in the morning, but not for long. Still we did start to make better time and six days later reached much better footing on a small range of hills. We worked our way slowly northeastward along this range determined to stay there until the tundra was frozen solid. While the Ordu trudged along, I was able to scout ahead and find the An'kalym village on the large bay where I had stayed a while the year before. I was profusely welcomed and had to spend the night and tell stories. I told them my tribe was nearby and willing to trade before we passed on. They said they knew they were near and were glad they were moving slowly since it would be best if they not arrive at the village until the ground was frozen. I assured them that that was the plan, much to their relief. They also needed to be reassured that we had plenty of food and would be able to trade food for food, goods for goods.

The Ordu had only been in the hills a couple of days when the first snowstorm hit. It was a fairly gentle affair—not much wind and not much snow. But things soon changed. Before we left the hills some twenty days after entering them and approached the An'kalym village, all began to understand what winter in the northland meant. There still wasn't much snow, but the brutal unrelenting icy wind soon froze all in its path. Even the large bay was apparently frozen over as we arrived at its shores. The horse "boots" worked well on some frozen lakes so it looked like all was well. The carts were fixed up for winter, their wheels replaced with the runners. Since our wheels were quite large, this left the carts quite low to the ground. Considering all the wind we would encounter that was probably best. The An'kalym recommended we not try to cross yet since our carts looked heavy. This gave us a chance to come up with a means of protecting our herds. We had greatly thinned out the goats and sheep by trading them for dried fish, but the remainder were too slow for the fast runs ahead of us. Using some of the pontoon boats mounted on runners like the carts and pulled by horses to haul the herds was the perfect solution. Padraig had thought of it, and it did much to get him accepted by the Ordu. Of course, cleaning out the boats at the end of each day was a memorable experience. The unhitched horses would have no trouble keeping up with the carts, even without wearing "boots."

Finally, the ice was thick enough and we set off across the bay. By now there was noticeably less daylight and each day was shorter as we went along. I went ahead in the dogsled to each village where we would stop to make sure we were welcome and that the ice ahead was solid. We went on like this for twelve days before we were warned of an imminent storm and were guided to a narrow valley a little inland where we would be out of the wind. The storm was brutal. Protected though we were from the brunt of the storm, some of the wind would still probe around the hills to get at us. There was also some snow, but with all the wind it was hard to tell if it was fresh or merely recycled. We were besieged for four days before it let up. Then it took another day to dig through the drifts that had piled up at the mouth of our little valley. When we finally left, we had lost several horses and there was some sickness among the old and the young. Yesui did not seem to be sick, but she looked very weak. Givevneu was much in demand.

We returned to and thanked the village that had warned us, presenting them with the meat from the horses that died in the storm. They told us there would be no more storms for at least several days—enough for us to reach Givevneu's village. Indeed, four days later we rounded the cape and entered the bay, reaching his village a little before dusk. I took him with me on the dogsled, but the rest of the Ordu was in sight, blackening the mouth of the bay as we pulled into the village. Most of the village was staring slack jawed at the coming Ordu when we arrived, but were eager to know what was chasing us thither. In the excitement, no one recognized Givevneu, but they quickly recognized me and called Naukum over.

"Has it changed?" I asked Givevneu while we waited.

"Not at all," he shook his head. "But that is the way of the An'kalym."

"They don't recognize you," I said the obvious.

"It has been a long time," he shrugged. "But I recognize my brother."

"Ah, the Raven has returned!" Naukum greeted me. "Is that your tribe coming upon us like a tidal wave? Is my brother among them? Is this your guide?"

He studied Givevneu for a moment. I could see a vague rec-ognition in his eyes, but Naukum couldn't quite place Givevneu. I decided to keep quiet, and Givevneu just smiled gently at his older brother.

"Blocknot!" he suddenly shouted. "It must be you."

With that he grasped Givevneu warmly and sniffed him in their strange way and took him off to introduce him to the rest of the village. There was much sniffing back and forth, with comments about how strange he smelled, no doubt because he was hanging around with my bizarre tribe. They were so taken up with the return of their own that the Ordu finally arrived unremarked. I found a spot a little farther down the spit for the camp and returned to the village. Givevneu's return was cause for a major celebration, and it was in full swing when I arrived at Naukum's "cave." I was invited to join, and it was some time before I could ask whether they had heard anything from Juchi.

Naukum told me that they had heard of him, but not from him. It seems Taukujaa had come back over in a boat again the past summer and Naukum had run into him at an An'kalym village in the north where both had gone to trade. Juchi had been ranging far and wide since late the past winter but had said he would be back at Taukujaa's village by early winter. Taukujaa had also mentioned that Juchi's stay in his village had not been without issue, at least potentially from the size of some of his consorts. To this Naukum added that Juchi had been no less potent during his stay with them and could claim three children born this past summer. He then chided me for not also leaving such tokens of "friendship" behind. I lamely explained that my wife would have been upset if I had, and received pitying looks from all the men except Givevneu. He seemed amused by my discomfiture.

I extricated myself as soon as possible and went back to report to Kaidu. He was much amused at Juchi's potency and happy to hear he was still attending to his job. He thanked me for keeping him informed. The next day, we moved the Ordu up the bay to the old village site. We decided to stay there until Naukum thought we could make the crossing. Our proximity gave Givevneu a chance to visit at length and bring his wife and children to meet his relatives. I wandered around a bit to do some mapping and take Paula and my nephews for sled rides. Yesui found it necessary to rest most of the time, but would shoo anyone away who tried to fuss over or wait on her. She always insisted on fixing the evening meal although she was not used to cooking with the seal oil.

When Givevneu finally returned to the Ordu, I told him about Yesui, but he assured me there was nothing he could do for her. She was only suffering from old age and a hard life, and there were no remedies for either. He then chided me for lying to his people.

"You did not sleep with any of them because you found them unattractive not because of your wife," he shook his head.

"I meant no offense," I protested. "It is true I found the tattoos repulsive, but it wouldn't matter if I had found them attractive. I will always be faithful to my wife."

"Always is a long time," he mused. "To my people such activity does not break faith, it strengthens friendships. It is fortunate that Juchi came along and behaved like a more normal man, or my people could have been insulted."

"So"—I reddened—"you think taking a pledge seriously makes me less of a man than Juchi."

"Ah." He smiled. "You do have feelings. I was beginning to think that your training had removed them. But you misunderstand me. I only said that Juchi was more normal than you, not better. I would not presume to judge your relative merits, but only made an observation. You are something of a cold, dispassionate person, Raven, at least to the eye. Because you look so unusual, it is overlooked or regarded as racial trait. I think perhaps you are just reserved, much like your father and brother. Such a demeanor may prove useful to us in the future, just as Juchi's 'normality' has been in this situation. If you wish to remain scrupulously faithful to your wife, act as though it is a clan custom or something along those lines, so it appears to be out of your control. That way no one can take offense."

"Well"—I shrugged—"I suppose it is at that. At least my grandfathers both thought it was most beneficial to be faithful to one's wife. Grandfather George said it was a small sacrifice to make to promote harmony and Grandfather Peter said it was required by his God."

"How does your wife feel about all this?" he asked.

"She told me she only ever wanted me," I answered.

"So be it then" —he shook his head—"a peculiar clan custom. My people could accept that. In any case, your marvelous talent for storytelling has swept any resentment aside. My village would be grateful if you would come tonight and favor them with one. I was unaware of this gift of yours until Kaidu told me about it after your performance at the Chavchuvat village. It is perhaps the single most respected talent in this land. It has helped that you are called 'Raven.' I, of course, did not explain the real source of the name."

"Neither did Juchi." I grinned. "But he probably bit through his tongue to restrain himself. I'll come tonight, of course."

I looked after him for a while after he left. I determined to be more sensitive to the feelings of the people we met but still remain faithful to Paula. I did feel bad that I had blamed her for my fidelity. From now on it would be a clan custom. It occurred to me that I should probably clear this idea with the other member of my "clan," mybrotherHenry.

While we were at the campsite, some of the older Ordu members died. We could not really bury them because the ground was frozen, so we dug a hole in the ice and weighting them with stone buried them at sea. Yesui still hung on, but was growing weaker by the day. Finally just as we got ready to move on, she could no longer leave her bed. We carried her into the cart, and Mathilde and Paula took turns holding her hand, as we traveled. Doqus would rush up whenever we stopped to check on her. Unfortunately, I had to go ahead each day, but I'd see her each night and get her to take a little broth. She forbade us to fetch Givevneu, insisting that he needed to see to the young, the Ordu's future, not the old, the Ordu's past.

We had stayed at the campsite twenty days, before Naukum thought it was cold enough for us to move on. Fortunately he agreed to lead us again, but we prevailed on him to take a more leisurely pace, and I think we visited and traded with every An'kalym village in the area. My reputation had preceded me, and I had to tell stories every night as well. Fortunately, I kept remembering new ones and was able to embellish the shorter ones enough to use them as well. I also was able to draw on my experiences living among them for a while to make the stories more relevant to them. In this manner it took us ten days to reach Pyeyek. We decided to stay there about five days to rest up the horses, check out all the carts and harnesses, and fetch Taukujaa for the final dash across the frozen sea.

9

THE NEW LAND,
38TH & 39TH YEAR OF TOGHON TEMUR
(NW ALASKA, 1368-9)

We had only been in Pyeyek a day when Paula came to get me, frozen tears on her cheeks. Yesui was worse than ever. I went in to see her. She was bundled up warmly, and Mathilde was holding her hand, rubbing it to keep it warm. Padraig was sitting behind her, holding her up to ease her breathing and looking glum. Yesui looked ashen, her breath was labored and shallow. Doqus and Henry came in, the former weeping silently, the latter clearly stricken. Suddenly Yesui opened her eyes, looked at us all and managed a weak smile.

"Do not look so sad, my children," she whispered. "I am much relieved to die while we are still in the old land. Bury me on the land, not in the sea. Kiss my grandchildren for me, even the ones not yet here and thank Kaidu for not sending me away."

That little speech seemed to have taken all her strength, and she gave a long sigh and breathed no more. Paula closed her eyes, and Padraig gently lay her down. Mathilde placed her hand under her blanket after kissing it. We all stood silently except for muffled crying from the women, bidding farewell, each in our own way to this marvelous woman who had been such a part of our lives for so long.

Givevneu came in quietly smiling in his gentle way and gave all in turn a comforting touch. He covered Yesui's head, and ushered us all away from her side. We all sat down a while in silence, then, at last, he spoke.

"Yesui has had her wish," he began. "She told me when we began this journey that she did not wish to end it. She wanted to die here. I think she only lasted so long because she wanted to 'train' Paula and Mathilde. You two gave her much happiness and a reason to live. Doqus, you have been more than a daughter to her, and also gave her much joy and three grandchildren. Henry, she was always so proud of you and your skill, so like your father. She bragged about you constantly. Padraig, you have been like a son to her these last months, always here when needed, tireless and patient. And you, Raven, her joy at your return was immeasurable. The excitement of making you and your bride this yurt, sustained her through a hard winter. And when you insisted she move in with you, she could have burst for happiness. You have all been wonderful to her, and need regret nothing. I know she wants to be buried on land, so we will have to do so in the An'kalym way with a few Mongol touches."

"What is the An'kalym way?" Henry asked.

"As you have seen," he replied, "the ground is too frozen to bury anyone in it, so we bury people on it, covering them with bones or stones. We place with the body things dear to the person that should accompany her."

"I know some things," Doqus said eagerly. "Her bow, her favorite stew pot, her sewing box—"

"Good, good," Givevneu interrupted. "You have the idea, but not too many things and only things that are expendable and fairly small. We should bury her tomorrow."

The next day, we went a short distance from the encampment out on the frozen tundra. We lay her with her head up facing southwest toward the Karamuren. We placed her bow, a few arrows, and her sewing box by her side, put a small packet containing her ongons over her heart, covered her with a mink cloak she had worn since she was young, and then watched as Givevneu and some An'kalym from the village arranged bones and stones around and over her until she disappeared from view. The bitter cold wind did not let up during the "burial" and made it impossible to tarry. So we sadly returned to camp.

When we returned, Padraig took Mathilde to "show her something," so Paula and I could be alone. She clung to me and cried long and hard. I held her tightly but felt more heaviness than grief. I remembered being surprised that Paula and Mathilde had grown so close to Yesui. She had been, I realized, the mother neither one had had. I comforted her as best I could, mostly just holding on to her. She finally fell asleep, and I cradled her in my arms. She slept a long time, and I dozed a little, but was mostly caught up in my thoughts. Padraig and Mathilde came back in quietly and retired. I could hear Mathilde cry herself to sleep also, while he tried to comfort her. I wondered why I couldn't grieve. Padraig and Henry had both cried at the "burial," but I couldn't. Perhaps it was because I had lost so many loved ones. Perhaps it was because I was too distracted by other events when I should be aggrieved. I was too sick to take notice when most of my family died in the epidemic so long ago. I was sent on an important mission right after I found out my father had died. And I was reunited with my beloved after almost a year when I heard that my grandfather George had died. Now, of course, we were about to cross over into a great adventure, and I had much to do. But that didn't stop Paula's grief. Even though she had only known Yesui a few months, even though it was obvious she was getting weak and would soon die, she was devastated by the loss. Maybe I was colder than even Givevneu thought. I started when I felt a hand on my shoulder.

"You have picked the perfect wife, Raven." It was Givevneu. "She is your perfect complement. I rejoice I will not live to see the day when you lose her. On that day you will feel everything you have not let yourself feel. I hope you are strong enough to survive it."

He patted me again and then left. I felt a cold chill grip me and shuddered, shivering. Paula moved a little but did not wake up. I had never thought of losing her. I couldn't think of it now either. Maybe my grief had always been mitigated because there was someone else there for me. There would be no one if she died. I shuddered again and held her more tightly. In time she woke up and was so grateful that I had held on to her while she slept and not gone off to my various duties. She felt much better and got up to fix the morning meal. Mathilde joined her, and the two chatted cheerily again as before. Padraig came up to me quietly.

"Karl," he began, "I wonder if you would mind if I went back out to Yesui's grave and played my pipes for her."

"Pipes?" I repeated, puzzled. "You mean your flute you used to play on our journey to the Ordu?"

"No, no." He shook his head emphatically. "My pipes. You haven't seen them, and not many people like them, but they are for formal occasions, and I would deem it an honor to play them for her. I played them last when I buried my father."

"Of course," I answered, touched by the sentiment. "We can all go out again as soon as it gets light.

"No, not all," he said softly. "Only you and Henry and his sons. It is the custom."

It was strange, but Paula and Mathilde didn't seem to mind, so I agreed. After our meal, I went to tell Henry and he agreed to come along and bring the boys. I also got one of the villagers to show us the way. I went to Kaidu's yurt and told him of Yesui's death and her wish that we thank him for letting her stay. He asked if she had been buried yet and I told him we had done so on land as she wanted according to the An'kalym way. He asked if he might see the grave, and I told him about our pending "ceremony." To my complete surprise he invited himself along.

As the sun made its brief appearance on the southern horizon, our little group of dogsleds set out from camp. Our guide was in the lead with Henry and the boys aboard, I followed with Padraig huddled up and cradling a mysterious bundle, and Kaidu brought up the rear on a sled handled by Givevneu. We were soon at the site and were blessed with a light breeze, bitter cold, of course, but light. Padraig had us leave the sleds a little distance away, and led us to the "grave." It looked like a little mound of snow, except that I could still see some of the bones and stones, especially on the leeward side. When we were all gathered around, he explained that the pipes were unusual-sounding instruments, advised us to be prepared, and not be surprised if the dogs howl.

With that he took some wooden things that were attached to something out of his coat, leaving the rest inside, under an arm. His coat swelled up, while there was a whining sound, then suddenly his cheeks puffed out and a haunting sound came from him. It seemed to sum up all the sadness in the world as if the world itself was weeping. The dogs did, indeed, howl, but it was not their usual yelping and yipping howl, but a long low mournful howl. When he finished, his coat whined again as it deflated, and he carefully returned the wooden pieces under his coat, and led us back to the sleds. He thanked me for letting him play for Yesui, and Henry and I thanked him for offering to do so. Kaidu was silent but thoughtful. Givevneu was charmed by the instrument and wanted to see the whole thing sometime. We returned to the camp. On the way I decided I liked the instrument and hoped he would play it again.

When we got back, Paula, Mathilde, and Doqus had a hot meal ready for all, and even Kaidu joined us. Padraig showed us the instrument, and explained that in ancient days the "bards" (a kind of poet-shaman) of his people would play them during battles or other solemn occasions. It looked like a goatskin sewn into a bag with some wooden pieces coming out of the skin, including one that looked something like a flute. Henry's boys wanted to learn the instrument, but Padraig explained it took many years to learn, but if they were serious, he would teach them when we arrived in our new land. Kaidu listened intently and asked if the music of the instrument was always sad. Padraig assured him that the battle music was stirring and had seen his people into and through many a campaign. Of course, the Mongol horses tended to bolt when they heard it, so it was not in great demand. It could sound like a demon from the darkest pit, he insisted. Kaidu asked him if he thought horses could become used to the sound. He was sure they could since his people had long used horses in battle, although not the same way as the Mongols. Kaidu said it would have to be looked into in time. We broke up and went back to getting ready for the great run to the new land.

Naukum had returned with Taukujaa again, and the latter was happy to see me, if somewhat taken aback by the size of my "tribe." He needed to be reassured that we would not compete with his people, but would continue on to go up the river that flowed north. With that he agreed to go with us, although he strongly recommended that he and I arrive at the various villages ahead of the Ordu to warn them of what was coming and assure them of our intentions. Of course, that was what we had been doing, so I readily agreed. We decided to set off well before sunrise two days hence.

It seemed to me that we would be leaving earlier than we had the year before, because the days were still getting shorter, and Naukum confirmed this. It had been a colder winter this year, and the sooner we crossed the sea the less likely we would encounter ice ridges. Of course, we would need to watch for thin ice, so it would be important for us to spread out in our dogsleds to ensure there were no thin spots. I wondered how they could tell one winter was colder than the other around here, but decided not to ask. We also got a few of the An'kalym villagers to act as outriders around the Ordu, keeping it together and on the right path. This last cost us a few sacks of grain, but was well worth it.

The first leg to Imaklik went quite well, the few ridges we encountered were quite small and only one required a bit of a detour, and it was still fairly light when we came upon it. Once we reached the shore, even with Taukujaa in tow, we had a hard time winning over the village since they could see the size of the approaching Ordu. A few gifts did the trick, however, and we promised to leave the next day. There was little choice, actually, for the shore was more like the slope of a mountain, and we were hard-pressed to find room for the Ordu to camp on the shore especially in the dark. The next morning while the Ordu was getting ready, my dogsled group set out for Inaklik and Taukujaa's relatives' village to explain ourselves before the Ordu came into view. A few more gifts and this encounter went more smoothly. Again it was hard to find room for the Ordu, but with light on our side, it was easier than on the other island. We stayed an extra day to rest up the horses while one of the villagers went ahead across to Kytmin to warn and reassure them about us. Again we started the last leg well before light in the same configuration as the first leg. Again we encountered only small ridges but did need to make a small detour north to avoid some thin ice Naukum detected. Finally the hill called Kytmin marking the other land loomed up in the east, and we led the way to the small village, just as the pale light of the rising full moon, a good omen to the Mongols, replaced the last bit of twilight. As the Ordu came up to the village, the new land seemed to be bathed in the silvery sheen of the moonlight, and in the northern sky, the Northern Lights seemed to greet us and point the way east with their shimmering undulating sheets of pale blue-green light. We had made it!

We spent the night near the village and did some trading and resting up the next day, before going on to Taukujaa's village the following day. Naukum and the An'kalym outriders took their leave, eager to return home. Givevneu and Naukum made their farewells with much grasping and sniffing. Naukum also bid me a fond farewell, wished my "tribe" and me well on our journey, and sent his greeting to Juchi. We watched them disappear to the west, severing our last link with our old land. As our vanguard pulled into Taukujaa's village a day later, I was much relieved to see Juchi, smiling and waving enthusiastically.

"I knew you'd make it," he shouted to me.

The village was all out at the sight of the looming mass of the Ordu, and Taukujaa and I reassured them at length that all was well. The biggest fear was that we were attacking, the second that the village would have to feed the mass, the third that we would stay a while and the last that we wouldn't move on, far away. It may seem inhospitable, but when one realizes that the largest villages had perhaps four hundred people, and the Ordu had over five thousand warriors, it makes perfect sense. We went through this in every Inuit village, although as time went on and we kept moving on, the word began to precede us and our reception became more cordial. Still, the first sight of the Ordu was frightening to all we encountered. I wondered what they would think of Khanbalikh, where our entire Ordu's approach would likely go unmarked.

Juchi was bursting with news, but I prevailed on him to save it for his grandfather so he wouldn't have to repeat it all again. Once the Ordu was encamped, Kaidu sent for us. Givevneu was the only other one with him when we arrived. Kaidu first embraced his grandson, and then bid him report.

"It is better than we could have dreamed," Juchi began. "I got all the way to the north-flowing river and followed it south for a while. There is supposed to be a huge endless steppe stretching south beyond the source of the river. I didn't get that far south, but all the natives in the south talk about it. No one really lives there, but some tribes do hunt there for the southern ox. There is game everywhere. The native tribes are scattered in small encampments, although they are larger than those of the Inuit. Still, imagine, they have no steel, no iron. The only metal I've seen them use is copper. A bigger, surprise, they have no horses. There are no horses anywhere around. The only animal they have tamed is the dog. They have no flocks or herds at all. They spoke of larger tribes in the south, but there is nothing like an empire or Khanate. It is much like the situation in Mongolia when the great Chingis united the scattered tribes. I passed myself off as an Inuit since I was with a group of them, so no one knows anything about us or our approach. Also, the path east is fairly easy and best made in the winter. We can cut across to the great river that flows west, follow it upstream to another river, follow that river to the mountains we must cross, and then we'll be at the river that flows north. The natives call that river the Dehcho."

"You have done well," Kaidu beamed. "I knew you were the best man for this mission, and you have borne me out. You are a credit to your father and your Ordu. I am very proud of you. I don't suppose you have made maps?"

"Well," Juchi smiled, "yes, I have. But after following the Raven's maps you may find mine crude in the extreme. But I have made Inuit friends in many villages not far out of the way, and they will happily guide us."

"True enough," Kaidu shrugged. "They will no doubt be very happy to guide us out of their country and upon their enemies. Speaking of which, are the others, the non-Inuits friendly? What is it they are called?"

"It depends"—Juchi laughed—"on whom you ask. The Inuit call them Itqilit, which means 'lousy.' The nearby ones call themselves Kutchin as a whole, but there are several tribes among them. They call the Inuit, 'Esquimantsic,' which means 'eaters of raw fish.' They are not very friendly, although they do trade with the Inuit. The nearby groups seem to adopt many Inuit ways. Still, to be fair, it is the Inuit who attack the Kutchin so one could not expect them to be friendly. Of course, as long as we stay together, no one will dare to bother us. We are far larger than any group ever seen around here. I think we will only encounter deserted villages on our way—at least among the Kutchin. The next group, along the Dehcho, call themselves the Tinneh as a whole, but again has several individual tribal names. They are more peaceful and also more timid. We will have to send out a small vanguard if we want to deal with them."

"I see," Kaidu nodded. "Yes we will use the guides, but I still want maps. Give what you have to Raven; he can fix them up for us as we go along. And put in these names of theirs, Dehcho and what is this nearby river called?"

"Again, it depends," Juchi shrugged. "The Inuit call it the Kvikhpak and the Kutchin call it the Yukanah."

"Humph," Kaidu scowled. "Which group controls most of the river?"

"The Kutchin," Juchi replied. "They fish and hunt all along it except for the mouth of the river, a few days south of here, where the Inuit hold sway."

"So be it," Kaidu said. "We will call it the Yukanah. We need to put names on these rivers and try to note the territories of the various tribes we encounter and the name they call themselves. We will only attack those who make themselves our enemies. If they let us pass in peace, we will do so. But I want to know this new land, who lives in it, and where he lives. They have no horses? What kind of game do they have?"

"Most of the same as we have," Juchi answered. "Except that their reindeer are much larger than ours, and they don't herd them. Also, their deer and bears are larger, and there is a large animal that looks like a wooly ox in the north and a less wooly one in the south. I saw the northern one, but only a skin of the southern one. The Tinneh were the ones who told me about them. It seems that there are huge herds of them in the south not only on the endless plain but also in the forest surrounding it. There are wild goats in the mountains to the north and wild sheep in those to the south. And the mass of waterfowl rivals what we saw in the lakes of the tundra on our side. We will not want for meat."

"Good." Kaidu got a glint in his eye. "Larger bears you say. Any tigers or leopards?"

"No one talks of them," Juchi shook his head. "They have lynx and wildcat and some other larger cat in the mountains, but it is tan, no spots or stripes."

"Well, we'll find out soon enough." Kaidu smiled. "We must get started soon."

We looked at Juchi's maps, trying to get a feel for the distances involved, but it was too hard to tell. He did not have a keen grasp of perspective, and his drawing was a bit shaky. Still from what he told us it would be quite a long trip, although not nearly as long as the one we had just completed. Kaidu decided to start after one day's rest, so he could properly thank Taukujaa and his village for all their assistance to Juchi.

When we set off finally, the general pattern was that one guide would lead Juchi and me on dogsleds first and another would lead the Ordu after us. The winter solstice had just passed so there was ever increasing amounts of twilight in the south. Depending on whether we went north or south we would see more or less of the sun along with the twilight. The guides thought it best to get us to the river we were calling Yukanah as soon as possible. No doubt to make sure we were well out of their territory. To that end we bypassed some villages to cut across the tundra in a fairly straight line almost due east. We did pass some low hills, but most of the way was quite flat. Six days later, we were back on the coast at an Inuit village. At least we were told it was the coast, as there was nothing to distinguish it. We kept moving with a new set of guides the next day continuing east. We stayed along the coast for almost two days before turning inland. This time it was obvious because we were going between rows of hills directly north and some distance to the south. Then we plunged through some low hills to a large valley beyond, where we came to another Inuit village. This run was seven days from the last village. On leaving this village, we exchanged guides and turned south, skirted around some hills; then we came upon a frozen river. We spent the "night" at a deserted village of wooden structures with sod roofs, on the bank of the river. It belonged to a group of Kutchin called the Kaiuhkhotana. It was a permanent winter camp, but our guides speculated that they saw us coming and expecting the worse, fled. No longer would we allow our vanguard to get much ahead of the Ordu.

We continued south along, or rather beside, this very winding river for two more days finally arriving at a much larger river. So large in fact that we thought it might be a bay of the sea again. This was the Yukanah. This time we had a fairly large deserted village at our disposal. Kaidu insisted that we not enter the homes or in any way disturb the camp, much to our guides' disappointment. They particularly wanted to destroy the camp because it belonged to another group of Kutchins, the Koyukukhotana, a fierce group they considered dangerous enemies. Kaidu was adamant, however, and since he was paying them for their time, they couldn't really argue, but they did grumble.

We followed the Yukanah eastward, staying a little north of it in the flat country or on it when there were hills. After eight days, we came to major fork in the river where our guides led us on the more northerly or left fork. We seemed to be going northeasterly and perhaps a bit uphill after this fork. After five days, the river seemed to get very wide and less sinuous, although there appeared to be many islands and, therefore, many channels. Five days later, we had lost the sun completely, but there was a long twilight. This slowed us down a bit since even our guides were hesitant to go very far with the moon only a sliver. The next day, we came to a spot where the river turns southeast, but we followed a channel to the northeast, and there on the bank was a large village with a group of natives in front armed and ready for battle.

10
Yukanah to Khanate Rivers,
1st Year of the Khanate
(N. Alaska to Athabaskan River, c.ab,1369)

The warriors were ready to fight, and their women and children were out of sight, but it was obvious that they did not expect us to attack or they wouldn't have been out in the open with their weapons ready but not aimed. Juchi and I approached them leaving the guides behind. They were dressed in reindeer skins with long tails in front and back and decorated with what we later found out were porcupine quills. Their faces were painted red; they wore jewelry and headbands and had feathers in their hair. The jewelry was of shells and bones, not metals. In fact their weapons were primitive wooden spears and bows and clubs made of antlers. There were only about forty or so of them, I could just imagine how long they would last against the Ordu.

Juchi spoke to them in the Inuit tongue, explaining that we were just passing through and meant them no harm. They told him that they had heard about us long before we drew near. It had been noticed that we had taken nothing from the abandoned villages but had passed by even if we did have Inuit among us. They called themselves the Kutchakutchin and wondered if we cared to trade with them. They normally would try to feast us, but since we were so many and they noticed that we weren't hunting, they thought perhaps we had enough food. They also wanted to have a closer look at the huge dogs we had pulling our large sleds. We reported to Kaidu who was looking them over from a distance. He doubted that they had anything of value to us, but agreed to trade. Our Inuit guides were not at all pleased, but it turned out that was only because they had brought along nothing to trade. It seems this particular group of Kutchins made little for themselves but traded raw materials at what the Inuit considered favorable terms. The raw materials were skins mostly, although we did get some of the reindeer meat to try as well. In deference to our guides, we traded no weapons or metal, just food. We didn't tarry long, leaving early the next "day."

We started up this new river (which Kaidu named the Kutcha in honor of the locals) in darkness only to find that while it was very sinuous, the land was very flat, so we were able to save some time. Even though we were going farther north, the twilight seemed to last a little longer each day as we were moving away from the winter solstice. The weather was almost always clear, but occasionally there would be a cloud cover. Although the northern lights did not shine often, the moon would give its eerie silvery light in its fuller phases. There was almost no wind except, of course, that caused by our motion. This was fortunate since it was profoundly cold, and some days it seemed that we could never warm up. Indeed, only activity would warm one, so it was particularly hard on our few remaining elderly. We had been burying our dead in the An'kalym way since reaching the new land and every several days we had another. A few very young children also succumbed, but it was mostly the elderly whom we lost.

The trip up this river went on uneventfully for thirteen days. The slope of the land gradually rose, but not uncomfortably so. We passed an occasional deserted village but no further Kutchins were to be seen. On the thirteenth day, we came to a split where one fork turned directly north. Here our guides left us, promising to send us two others. Since they had been with us so long, they were generously rewarded with most of the things we had gotten from the Kutchins. We stayed at this spot about four days before two dogsleds appeared coming toward us down the river. It turned out these Inuit also knew Juchi and were delighted to see him again. They would take us the rest of the way.

The layover was quite good for us. Not only did the horses get some much-needed rest, but also we all got a chance to rest up. A few of the men went hunting, but were not successful. Most tended the animals and the carts and otherwise took it easy. With Padraig handling all the chores, I was able to just polish up my maps, such as they were and relax. Paula and I were glad to be around each other all day for a change. She helped me name some of the features on my map. She had a good imagination for names.

Our guides took us along the river in an easterly direction for a few days, then turned us south with it, then east again, then finally south. At least that was the way it seemed, there were junctures with other rivers frequently, but our guides were certain of their path. We had turned south just as some high mountains loomed ahead of us; then we finally left the river just after the sun came back in view for a while until the high mountains in the south obscured it again. We continued south, climbing through a sort of pass in the mountains, then descending finally on another river that flowed eastward right through the mountains. It was quite frozen still, which was fortunate since the terrain was very rough here and the river ice provided the easiest passage. We followed this out of the mountains until it turned north; then our guides told us to stay north of the mountains in the foothills until we came out on the Dehcho, about eight days farther away. They went north with the river, and we went east along the foothills. Were it not for the ice, the way would have been much harder. Still we began to get occasional icy winds out of the north, and Juchi assured us that there was nothing vertical between the icy North Sea and us. We were quite relieved when we broke through the foothills and could see the Dehcho at last. From this distance, it looked huge, like a solid sheet of ice across a vast valley. As we got closer, we could see that it was a wide river snaking along a flat plain dotted with lakes. Since spring was fairly close, we decided to stay on the higher ground but turn southeast up the river and follow it to the endless steppe.

The mountains rose fairly precipitously from the plain here, so we found ourselves getting closer to the river. There were spruce forests laced with larch and aspen, but they were not impenetrable. Mostly along the river the trees were small or spread out with open spots in between. We began to see some of the promised game, although only from a distance since the Ordu spooked them up the hills into the deeper wood. Juchi's reindeer were bigger than ours and had much larger antlers. The elk were about the same as ours though. We did not turn aside for hunting since Kaidu wanted to get as far south as possible before the tundra turned into a quagmire as it thawed. We had passed some abandoned villages of mean-looking double lean-tos, but had seen no natives. We decided that if we were to meet any, we would have to send out the vanguard again as Juchi had warned us. So he and I and a few others set off on dogsleds ahead of the Ordu to try and find some natives.

It took a few days, but we surprised a small group of hunters returning to their camp carrying two of the reindeer. Since we were few, they waited for us to reach them, perhaps thinking we were Inuit looking to trade. As we drew near, they became agitated and held their weapons at the ready. As we reached them and made no move to our weapons (that they could see), they lowered theirs and welcomed us, puzzled by our attire and bewildered by my appearance. Using the Inuit tongue, Juchi explained that we were the lead elements of our tribe, which was migrating to the endless grassland to the south. We meant them no harm and only wondered what lay ahead.

They asked if our tribe was the huge one with giant dogs and sleds that had been seen coming up the Dehcho. We said it was, but again assured them we meant to pass by, and indeed had taken no game on our trek, and so were doing them no ill. This seemed to pacify them, but they pleaded with us not to go through their village, which was on the far side on the Dehcho. We told them we planned to stay on this side of the river, and follow it southeast to the grassland. Finally, they agreed to help. It seems their tribe was called the Kawchodinne, which meant 'people of the great hares,' since they originally subsisted largely on that small animal. There were scattered groups of them all about this area and more on the far side of the Dehcho. To the southeast, we would find first a related tribe called the Etchareottine, or 'people dwelling in the shelter,' since they lived along rivers and streams sheltered by willows; then we would encounter the Tatsanottine, or 'people of the scum of water' (this proved to be what they called copper). The former were a peaceful timid tribe that subsisted largely on fish, but the latter were bold aggressive hunters who ranged far and wide and took advantage of their neighbors since they had most of the copper. Farther south we would encounter the Tsattine, 'dwellers among the beavers,' in the west and the Thilanottine, 'dwellers at the foot of the head' (head of a glacier it seemed), in the east. The former were bold hunters of the forests, and the latter hunted and fished along the rivers, lakes, and the sea. They were peaceful, but great liars. Beyond them, he wasn't sure, but whoever was there was not Tinneh.

We thanked them for their help and asked if one of their men would care to join us, teach us their language, and help us pass through their country by the quickest path. They talked this over among themselves for a while and finally one of the younger ones stepped forward. He agreed to go with us to safeguard his tribe, since he was unmarried and had a brother who could look after his parents. His Inuit was a bit sketchy, but he would teach us his language. All seemed pleased or perhaps relieved with this arrangement, and we returned with our prize, one Nitsiza. He was dressed mostly in the fur of the hare for which his tribe was named with some reindeer hide touches. His face was rather flat with high cheekbones, his weapons were primitive (wood and bone), but he did have a copper knife. As we drew near the Ordu, he was either frightened or resigned, but he was a pitiful sight. We fed him, then showed him around the camp, bringing him in to meet Kaidu. The latter was pleased with our report and our guest whom he entrusted to Juchi. Gradually, as we moved on, both Juchi and I picked up his rather simple language, but as he got used to us and learned how to use our weapons and ride a horse, he wanted to stay with us.

After ten days, the Dehcho veered to the east, while the foothills seemed to continue southeast. Nitsiza told us the Dehcho would lead us to a great lake, but the plain was much farther south. Also the land around the lake was very marshy, and it was quite far out of the way. Four days later, we crossed another large river (which I named for our guide). He said it flowed into the Dehcho to the northeast. We continued south along this river for four days, then swung east up another river between mountains to its source, a moderately sized lake where we finally encountered some natives, or at least saw them flee away to the north. They were Tsattine, Nitsiza assured us. There was a strange sort of aspen growing along some of the rivers along the way. It seemed to dominate where it occurred. We had nothing in the old land quite like it that I could remember. There was a lot more spruce than we had, and much less larch. Most of the other trees looked familiar, even the ones still without leaves. It was noticeably warmer, although we did get snowed upon on occasion. The ground was appearing in patches, and the snow was getting soft during the day but hard at night. The lake was still frozen, but the ice did not appear very thick.

We turned south again arriving at the banks of a river nine days later. This river had very steep banks but proved to be frozen over still. While the higher ground was mostly dotted with spruce, the shore of the river was covered with aspen and poplar trees, making it even harder to get the wagons across. We lost a day trying to find a place where we could cross without too much difficulty. We finally found a spot where a stream joined it on our side, and there was another on the other side a little farther south. Using these two outlets, we were able to cross the river, but it was not easy, and we still had some trouble getting out of the streambed and onto the higher plain. We decided to call that river the Deep-cut River. Kaidu was fairly certain we would never cross it again.

Over the next seven days, we moved progressively south, and as we did, we seemed to move into early spring. The snow on the ground was staying soft longer, the patches of ground were becoming larger, and the streams and small lakes we passed were thawing. Early green shoots could be seen dotting the brown patches of open ground and poking through the fast-melting snow. Still we did get caught in a late snowstorm, which held us up for a while one day. It was not too deep and didn't really hold back the melt for long. We arrived on the banks of a rather large lake. There was still ice in it, but it was too thin to walk on. It was a long lake from west to east but narrow north to south. It was graced with at least two deserted villages, still the Tsattine according to Nitsiza.

We continued south and three days later came in sight of another large river. This proved to be a raging torrent of melt water with large ice chunks floating in it, so we had to stay put for a while.

We made camp on some high ground above the river and took the opportunity to convert our sleds back into wagons and retire the dogsleds. There was little snow left on the ground by now, and already grass and flowers were beginning to come up. We let our herds out of their pontoons and began cleaning everything up, especially ourselves, even though the water in the streams was quite cold. A group of the men went out to hunt. Some tried fishing. All of us were glad to be out of the bitter north into what seemed like a perfect country for us.

I decided to look around a bit and flesh out my maps during our layover, and Paula, Mathilde, and Padraig came along. It was very much like our journey to join the Ordu, and we all greatly enjoyed it. We went back up to the lake so I could get its contours right; then we followed a small river flowing from its east terminus into a larger river. This latter we followed upstream, and it proved to be the one that had halted us. As we came back into camp, we found that the hunters had been quite successful, finding elk, deer, and a very large reindeer almost the size of an elk. One of the men had seen a small herd of strange animals that were likely Juchi's southern oxen, but the way he described them, they sounded more like yaks with smaller horns and heavier fur. He had seen that a group of natives were stalking them, so he hadn't gone any closer. Several of the Ordu also mentioned seeing natives, but only from a distance. It seems they had been spying out our encampment, but had not approached, even at night. Just in case, Kaidu had doubled the guard.

I found Juchi and Nitsiza and asked the latter if he thought the locals would try to attack or steal from us. He was sure they would do neither, but were naturally curious about us and, especially, our intentions. He offered to go alone to them to explain that we were moving on and meant them no harm. He thought they might help since he no longer knew the land around here well enough to guide us surely. I asked him about the tribal organization, and he said there was none, each band was pretty much on its own, hunting, fishing, and gathering what was available and trading for what was not available with whomever they met. They would help other bands in need and would be helped in turn also. Their "leader" was not endowed with much authority. It seemed he was sort of "first" among equals, no more. He was usually the best or most skilled hunter, and if he proved to be ineffective, he would be replaced. The position was not at all hereditary, although it might happen to be by chance. I wondered if he found it difficult to adjust to our ways. He admitted that we did seem to have many more than one chief and did not really allow for argument or even disagreement with orders, but expected them to be obeyed without question. He seemed to have no inkling of the concepts of discipline, authority, and order, but in the bleak environment where he was raised, reality was harsh enough and survival was more important than order. He did have to admit we had many wonderful things, and he was prepared to compromise to get them and our easier life. For my part, I could not imagine a life without discipline and authority. It would be so uncertain, dangerous. I wondered what Givevneu would think of this, since he, too, was from a harsh climate. But more to the point, we brought Nitsiza to Kaidu to again make his offer. He thought it a good idea and bid him go but return in four days, because he wanted to move on. By the stars he could tell that we were still north of the Karamuren, and he was determined to settle well south of that on the promised, endless steppe.

Nitsiza insisted he should go alone. While he was gone, Kaidu called a sort of general assembly of all the people. It was difficult arranging this, but we spread out on a hillside that formed a wedge. We all sat on the ground, and he sat on his horse, a beautiful white stallion, in front of us. His voice was strong and clear, and I doubt if anyone could not hear him.

"For several years, I have kept most of you in the dark about my intentions," he began. "This was necessary for security reasons and because there was much uncertainty in my plans. I have always felt responsible for your welfare, and I could see only disaster in staying in the old Khanate. The options were few and not very promising on our old side of the Great Sea, but on this side there are seemingly unending possibilities. Our scouts have confirmed my optimism, or I would never have brought you here. The future looks very bright. There will, of course, be problems, but I have weeded out those who might carry the seeds of our destruction to this new land. You are all true Mongols, 'The Brave,' and here we can forge a true Mongol Khanate, in the image the immortal Chingis would approve. I have brought you here and lead you this far. The time has come for us to become a Khanate. For that you need a Khan. If you wish it, I will be your Khan, if you do not, I will step aside for the man of your choice. What is your will?"

I truly believe the earth shook with the roar of the Ordu. Swords were beaten against shields—men, women and children screamed out "Kaidu, Kaidu, Kaidu..." like a battle cry. Kaidu looked us all over drinking in the vote of confidence, a look of triumph in his eye. Then he held up his hand for silence.

"So be it then," he said. "We will be called the Khanate of the Blue Sky, after our guide, our soul, our strength, the God Tengri. We will open our Khanate to all of our new neighbors who are worthy and willing to join. We will greet all with an open hand of friendship and peace, but it will close into a fist of steel if not treated with respect. We have many advantages over these people; they have no horses, no herds, and no steel. It would be unworthy to wantonly conquer them. For now, they can join us, or not, in peace. But should they strike at us, we will utterly destroy them. No one will be allowed to treat the Mongols shamefully. Those who join us must be accepted by you as equals and trained and equipped to be Mongols. They can teach us much about this land and can be of immeasurable help to us. It is unworthy of a Mongol to be ungrateful or arrogant. Do you still want me to be your Khan?"

Again the thunderous roar shook the ground. Pleased, he dismissed us. There was much excited chattering about the new "status" of the Ordu. We had always been a mean, rough frontier group with leather armor and sparse brass ornamentation. We all had excellent arms and knew how to use them, but there was no inlay or engraving or any of the flash so common in the capital. So it was that we had long been given little respect or thought, for that matter, in Khanbalikh, the capital. Indeed, we had been all but forgotten until the Khan was in dire straits. Now we were the nucleus of a new Khanate. My brother Henry, ever practical, sought me out to advise me of a problem I should have foreseen.

"Karl," he said, "if these people have no horses, because there aren't any here, does that mean they have no iron because there is none?"

"I don't think so," I replied, shaken by the obvious implication. "I was taught that it could be found everywhere if one knew what to look for. Iron ore doesn't look like anything special, just like rock. I'm sure we'll find some. I know what to look for and I'll look for it. How much iron do you have?"

"Enough for the Ordu," he shrugged, "but if I have to outfit several thousand natives with swords, shields, and arrows, it won't work."

"For now, I'd only make arrow points," I suggested. "It takes time to learn to use a sword, but they all seem to use bows. As for armor they can use leather, like most of us do."

"That makes sense," he nodded. "But do find me some more iron, and coal. I can't melt iron ore very efficiently with wood, even using the double piston bellows. I have enough for a while, but only a while."

I had not seen any mountain that looked like it might have iron ore or coal, but then, until just recently, everything had been covered in snow and ice anyway. Perhaps I could train Nitsiza to help me find some iron. Three days later, he returned leading a small group of natives. These looked much like he did when we first found him except that they wore reindeer skins. Their language was much like his, and Juchi and I could understand it fairly well. It seemed this small group of young men had decided to join us as Nitsiza had, to get the things he had. Especially they wanted the large dogs and the magic bow with the strange tipped arrows that were stronger than stone. We explained that in order to join us, they would have to become Mongols—they could no longer be Tsattine. They would have to obey orders immediately and without question. Their very lives would be in the hands of our Khan, Kaidu. This took them aback for a bit, but they asked Nitsiza if he had agreed to all this, and when he said he had, they agreed also. I had to wonder, but we brought the group in to Kaidu, and he agreed to give them a chance.

He dismissed them and then told Juchi and me to stay.

"Because of our new status as a Khanate, I have promoted all the officers one grade. None of them have the proper complement of men yet, but I am sure we will fill out the ranks in time. I have just had a meeting with the new minghan and tumen commanders," he began, "and of course with our shaman. You two have a very special place in our Ordu, one you have earned with much hard work and no little danger. For that reason I will now also consider you both as the equivalent of tumen commanders. You have special duties, so you will not actually command a tumen for now, but that will be your rank. You both now answer only to me. Does this please you?"

We were both too stunned to do more than stammer our thanks and express gratitude in his confidence in us.

"There is more," he continued. "As I told your fellow commanders, when we find the right spot, we will start to organize our Khanate and assign tasks. Meanwhile, we must grow. I think the group our Nitsiza brought in will be adequate, but I'm sure as we go south, we will find more suitable recruits. Whole tribes would be best or at least whole bands. I realize, from what you've learned about the natives, that they are not organized as we, but if you find a group that might at least show promise of becoming true Mongols, bring me their leaders. I need you to go ahead of us again, with your group of natives, as soon as they are trained, and find me some potential Mongols. We cross the river in three days. Do what you can to train that group, leave a few to guide us, and go ahead and find what you'll find. Of course, Raven, I want maps."

Well, of course, responsibility always comes with promotion, but we were both surprised that he would trust us to find and recruit whole tribes for the Ordu. Especially after he spent all that time weeding out undesirables. We went immediately to talk to our latest recruits. They could certainly show us the way to the steppe. There were other people between our destination and us, however. These included a splinter group of Tsattine that had more or less attached themselves to the Siksika, who along with their relatives, the Kaina and the Piegans were just to the south and southeast. Farther to the east, we would find the Kensistenoug. They were not Tinneh, but their language could be understood with some difficulty. The first three were allied tribes or large bands that lived in crude wood-framed hide tents and hunted the ox or yaklike creature on the plains and in the surrounding forest. The latter group was scattered far to the east and hunted and gathered in the forest mostly but sometimes on the plains. The former were aggressive, always at war when it was in their favor, the latter were also aggressive and had pushed the former westward. They were also shrewd traders. It was quite likely that the portraits were colored more than just a bit with prejudice, but it would be the first time we encountered natives that could be called "aggressive." Perhaps these would be our recruits.

Three days later, we were packed up and on our way across the river (I had named it the Khanate River in honor of Kaidu's proclamation) on our pontoon bridge. The Tsattine and Nitsiza were much taken with the wagons. It seems that they had never seen wheels before and were amazed at the concept. Nitsiza admitted that he had been sure we would not be able to move our heavy "sleds" once the snow melted. I could see why the wheel was of limited use in the North Country, but figured it would be quite common in the south. To our surprise, none of the native peoples we encountered used the wheel, although that quickly changed. While the bridge was being retrieved, our little vanguard set off ahead. We would stay a li or so ahead looking for favorable terrain and sending back any necessary direction changes. Four days later, we came to another river requiring our pontoons to cross. We swam our horses across to check out the other side, while the pontoons were being set up. On the other side, we noticed some rapids a little upstream and went to look at them. About halfway there, a native suddenly stood up from behind some rocks and stared at us for a moment; then he turned and started to run away. We reined in and sent Nitsiza to ride after him and call to him. He stopped at the familiar language and turned back. We could see him talking to Nitsiza a while; then he came back to us with the native. We rode slowly forward to meet them.

11

THE FIRST ENCAMPMENT
AND RECRUITING TRIP, 1 K
(E. MT TO LAKE SUPERIOR 1369)

The native turned out to be little more than a boy. He was dressed in some sort of skins, and his face was painted with strange markings. It turned out he was on a "vision quest" and thought we were his vision. This was a sort of coming of age ritual for all their young men. We would learn more about it later. He was disappointed when we turned out otherwise, because now he had to continue his fast and prayers. He was impressed with our "large dogs," however, and wanted to touch them and see if they were real. Then he took a look at me and was quite puzzled. He wanted to know if I was ill since I was so pale. We told him we wanted to meet his tribal chiefs, but he said that they wouldn't assemble the whole tribe for council until the summer. So we asked about his band, and he pointed to the south, saying that they were hunting, moving toward the east about a day's walk away. He could not rejoin them until his quest was fulfilled. We asked his name, but he said to ask him after his quest. One of the Tsattine told us that the Siksika changed their names all the time, so there was no point in asking them their name. With that, our guest departed, and we went over to look at the rapids, and then returned to the Ordu. When they finally got across the river and took up the pontoon bridge, it was late in the day so we stayed on the south bank for the night. The next day, our vanguard set out toward the southeast in hopes of finding our nameless friend's band. I was impressed by his lack of fear even though he could see the whole Ordu from where we were talking.

The land was rather flat with open woods dotted with many small lakes. We could see fairly well around us, although occasionally there would be a thick stand of birch or aspen along a stream.

We were just emerging from one such stand late in the morning when we came upon a group of hunters returning from the hunt. They were hauling some of the meat on travois pulled by dogs. We surprised them since we were down wind from them. They stared at us as we approached slowly. They were visibly going through several emotions as we drew near: curiosity about the horses and our dress, and no doubt, Juchi and me; humiliation at being surprised; and contempt for our Tsattine guides. Still I saw no fear and no move to run. They were dressed in skins like the boy and were also painted but in different patterns. They wore their hair long but had a curious forelock over the center of their forehead reaching down to their nose. They wore one or more feathers on their head.

When we got close enough to talk, our guides indicated that we were part of a large tribe that was moving through their hunting ground, and we wanted to talk to their chiefs. They wanted to know where we found the large dogs and the pale man. Our guide explained that I was normally pale; there were many different peoples in the tribe, which had come from far away to the west. The "dogs" were native to our original land. The whole tribe was just behind us, but we wanted to pass in peace to the plains. One could see their thoughts racing as they looked at the horses and at us riding them. Did the horses run fast? they wondered. One of the men set off at a trot to demonstrate. Could they be used to hunt? was their next question. Of course, we replied. Might we part with some? was the inevitable final question. It would depend on our meeting with their chiefs, we hedged. With that, one of them ran on ahead while we followed with the others and sent one man back to the Ordu to advise them of our disposition.

The land became more rolling hills and began to open up a bit more as we went along. We asked if their band was on the plain, but they said not at the moment, the plain was a few more days south of their present position, but they would be moving into it as the spring advanced. We asked how far south they ranged, and they said only a few days south. Beyond that there were other bands. We finally came to a sizable encampment of the hide tents. There were dozens of them planted in a clearing along a steam. They were painted various colors and had some interesting designs on them as well, mostly stylized animals and geometric designs. A large solemn-looking crowd was watching our approach. The hunters turned their catch over to their women and led us to a centrally located tent. Juchi, one of the Tsattine, and I went in the tent while the others waited with the horses.

The tent was not nearly as large as a yurt, but was just commodious enough. This one was occupied by group of about six older men. Like the hunters, they wore feathers but many more of them in an elaborate headdress where the feathers stood up. They waited in silence until we had been seated; then they passed around what looked like a long white tube with a small cup at the far end. It seemed to be in two connected pieces. In the cup part, something was smoldering, and they would suck in the other end to breathe in smoke from the smoldering mass. It was eventually passed to me, and I could see that the cup part was made of bone and the stem part of wood. I breathed in a little of the smoke and found it foul and choking but managed to keep from coughing. Juchi also was able to breathe in some of the smoke with impunity. Our Tsattine guide, on the other hand, turned red and gasped for breath, finally settling into an intermittent coughing fit. He had taken too much. They continued passing around the tube until it was burned out, before they began to speak. By then our interpreter had recovered himself.

One of the elders was called Mahkwi Stunik. He seemed to be deferred to somewhat, but all the others also spoke. They all seemed to be named for animals or parts of animals like horns and feathers or even actions, like "Elk Swims." I'm sure they found our names as curious as theirs except for mine; "Raven" seemed to fit right in. They asked about us, our origin, intentions, relationship with the Tsattine, and of course the horses. We answered fully and honestly. They saw no reason not to let us pass if we came in peace, and asked if we wanted anything else from them. We told them that we were impressed by the bravery of their people and wondered if they would want to join our "tribe," learn how to ride our horses and use our weapons. We explained that we had much to teach them and much to learn from them and it could be to everyone's benefit were they to join us.

They thought on this a while; then one asked why we didn't instead join them, the way the Sarci had. This was what they called the Tsattine band that had joined them. The name turned out to mean "not good." We explained that we were many more and already organized into an efficient system of rule. They asked what we meant by rule. We tried to explain the Mongol system. The people select a Khan and he rules with absolute authority until his death or incompetence. They had no trouble with the way he was selected, since they also selected their chiefs in that way, but they didn't think they could accept "absolute" authority. Their authority was limited to the will of the people, and they "ruled" by means of persuasion and respect, only. The people were free to eschew them or their suggestions at any time. We wondered how they could ever conduct a war under such lack of discipline. They explained that they did not conduct wars, the war chiefs conducted wars, and they were followed because they earned the right to be followed by distinguishing themselves in battle. They didn't give orders; they simply led the men into battle. Did this not open up the likelihood of confusion and chaos? we asked. No one complained, they replied. We seemed to be at an impasse. Perhaps some of their people would be willing to submit themselves to the authority of our Khan in order to enjoy the advantages we had to offer? we asked. It was possible, they agreed, and they would not move to stop them if they did. For their part, they preferred to remain as they were. We asked them to pass on our offer to their people for us. Our tribe would be passing a little to the east of them on the next day, and any willing to join us could do so then. They agreed and filled the tube again with what looked like crushed, dried leaves or grasses of some kind. One of them lit the vile thing and passed it around until it was burned up. Then they all rose, and we left the tent, mounted up, and returned to the Ordu.

We reported the strange interview with Kaidu the next day. He was also puzzled at their indiscipline, but impressed by their courage. We all wondered if any would join us the next day. We tried to understand why they would think their system was preferable to ours but could not. I suggested that perhaps Givevneu would understand since his tribe had been ruled more like the Siksika than the Mongols. He was sent for and listened to our puzzlement.

"One always prefers that to which he is accustomed." He smiled at us. "Especially the older one gets. It is true that I adjusted, but I felt the gods sent me to you, and in my profession one always obeys the gods before all personal inclinations. The Mongols are more 'advanced' than the An'kalym in some ways, but not in any way that would make it easier to be an An'kalym. In fact, I doubt that you could live in their harsh environment with a fraction of their comfort. Similarly, they would be out of place on the steppe. It is odd that there are no horses in this land, and that alone may compel some of them to join us, but do not be offended if many or even most do not. Their way of life has worked very well for them long before we arrived and will continue to do so after we have gone. Perhaps we can come to a compromise between two very different views of rule, perhaps we cannot. We should try to learn from each other."

"But they are so undisciplined," I protested. "Imagine having to persuade everyone in the Ordu to follow each of your orders."

"In other words, my dear Raven," he answered, "you do not trust either the Ordu's discretion or your own moral authority."

"But in battle, Shaman," Juchi complained, "if orders are not obeyed, chaos ensues, disaster."

"I suspect the 'battles' of these people were much like those of the An'kalym," he replied. "They were little more than raids or skirmishes or ambushes. Of course, in a battle such as the Mongols are accustomed to fight, authority and discipline would be essential. But they most likely have never experienced anything like a Mongol battle. You must understand people in their own terms even if it means getting out of your own terms to do so. That is, if you really want to understand them."

"You are right, Givevneu," Kaidu finally broke his thoughtful silence. "But we will try to seduce recruits to our ways with our advantages. I feel a well-run Khanate is far better than the splintered system prevalent among the natives in this land. Still, they have every right to cling to it, and as long as they do not make themselves our enemies, I will see to it that we leave them in peace."

We left it at that and returned to our own yurts. I talked to Paula, Mathilde, and Padraig about the ways of the locals, and they also did not understand it, although Padraig mentioned that according to his father, his people were very hard to govern and quite naturally rebellious. I really didn't know very much about my ancestor's ways, but Paula and Mathilde were certain that their people had been ruled by kings just like the Mongols were. I wondered if we would find more organized groups farther south just as it was in our old land. It was going to be interesting to find out.

The next day as the Ordu passed the band, a small group of young men was waiting there to join us. As we passed through the lands of the Siksika and their relatives, the pattern was much the same. We would talk to the chiefs and a few of the young men would join us. Word began to get around, and some men from the bands we had missed also trickled in to join us. One entire band joined us because their shaman had seen a vision of some sort, which seemed to make joining us necessary. By the time we had passed through their territory some twenty days later, we had augmented our number by about four hundred, mostly young men. The recruits were very excited by our horses and, strangely, it was not hard to teach them to ride. They were also very impressed by our bows and our iron arrow points. Another thing they were very much taken with was our cart. They had also never seen wheels before, and they were quite amazed at the loads possible with such conveyances. They seemed to be, in general, very intolerant of kumis, and we had to limit their access to it. Similarly many of our men became too enamored of their smoldering noxious weed. They never abused it, but we found we had to limit its accessibility for the Mongols. It seemed to almost intoxicate some of them. It turned out to be a plant they called nawak'osis (tobacco) whose leaves were collected dried and crumbled up. It was the only plant they cultivated. It seems they would mix other dried leaves in with it according to the occasion. I never really got used to it and would only take polite puffs at all our meetings. Juchi got to like it, but he would only use it at the meetings with the natives, because it made him lightheaded.

When we crossed a large river that effectively took us out of the Siksika territory, we were, according to our recruits, in rarely used land. We were definitely on a steppe, and it did seem to be endless, at least from here. Much of the Siksika lands were the transition area between the forest and the open grassland, but across this last river there seemed to be only steppe. It seemed to be dominated by two grasses, neither very long. One was strange in that it seemed to send roots along the ground, which would then send roots into the ground and shoots up. The other had almost blue-green curly leaves and a tall leafless flower stalk. There were other taller grasses as well, one looked a bit like wheat, another was silvery gray, and they added a touch of variety, but the shorter grasses seemed to dominate.

We halted some fourteen days later when we came to the steep banks of another large river. There was a large bottom on both sides of the river covered with aspen, ash, elm, willows, birches, and some odd berry trees. There were some open spaces, but mostly they were wooded or covered with thickets. This general pattern prevailed on the steppe. The rivers all seemed to carve deeply into the rolling hills of the plain, and the rivers were all lined with tree- and shrub-covered bottoms. The aspens had seeds that looked very much like cotton balls and were far more abundant than in the old land. We camped on the plain above the river, cleared some of the bottomland to plant grain, and settled down to turning our recruits into real Mongols. A few more came in as time went on, and they also were plugged into the system. I did some exploring and mapping taking Paula, Padraig, and Mathilde along. Our river seemed to flow east, and we followed it both up- and downstream for a few days.

To the east, the grasses seemed to be taller, one that looked blue seemed to dominate near the river, but the one that looked like wheat dominated away from the river. The shorter grasses could be found here too, but the taller grasses were ascendant. To the west, the shorter grasses predominated except near the river where the longer ones prevailed. There were also other odd bushes, shrubs, and forbs especially in the east making quite a color variety when they flowered in late spring. By early summer, much of the shorter grasses were dry and turned yellow especially away from the river. The taller grasses seemed to hold their color better. The local yaks or plains oxen (bison) were quite plentiful—indeed they seemed to form very large herds at times as they moved about the steppe. There was also a kind of antelope and deer as well as many kinds of game birds. Our recruits were thrilled with the horses, and the mobility they afforded. They were a little hard to discipline, but they did seem to be making the necessary adjustment.

There didn't seem to be any native people to the west, but to the east we eventually came upon some villages on both sides of the river around where another river joined it from the southwest. The villagers called themselves Absaroke and lived in hide tents like the Siksika. Their language was a complete mystery to us, but fortunately one of them spoke Siksika, and we were able to communicate. They looked nothing like the Siksika, but were even taller and broader shouldered—both the men and the women. They wore their hair long and wore leather clothes and plains oxen robes. They decorated their clothes with dyed porcupine quills. Their bows were large and decorated with horn and snakeskin. They were hunters who only cultivated nawak'osis much like the Siksika.

Once the lone Siksika speaker presented himself, we asked to speak to their chiefs. He went off and after a while returned and led us to the largest tent in the carelessly arranged village. Inside we were presented to the chiefs of four of the villages. After enduring the nawak'osis ritual, we laboriously explained our mission through our Siksika recruit and their interpreter. They listened to it all in silence, then after a while lit another pipe and passed it around. When this was finished, they began to confer among themselves. Their interpreter explained that they were considering our proposal. Finally one of the chiefs spoke to us.

"Some generations ago, we lived in permanent villages in round lodges made of earth. There we grew crops and hunted the plains oxen. Then one day our ancestors had a dispute with the rest of the tribe and followed the river upstream to the mountains. Here we changed from what we were to what we are. If it is to our benefit, we will change again. But first we must see. We know the Siksika, and we do not trust them. We don't know the Mongols, and we must find out if we can trust them. We will send some men whose judgment we respect with you, and they will return to us before the fall to report what you are really like. If it seems best, we will then become Mongols. If it does not, we will remain as we are. We will not interfere with your tribe's movement in any way."

We thanked them for their wisdom and returned with about twenty of their men. Most were young, but a few were of middle age, and much deferred to by the young men. Fortunately, they also sent along our interpreter. Kaidu was impressed by the men and said they would make fine warriors. There was a little tension between the Siksika and the Absaroke, but since the former were much further along in their training, there was little contact.

Toward midsummer, Kaidu sent Juchi and me along with two of the Tsattine and two of the Siksika to the northwest to meet with the tribe there called the Kensistenoug. It was generally felt that they also might make promising recruits. It took us about ten days to find them. Our journey took us back into the forest again. They proved to be something like the Siksika and lived in the hide tent also, although it seemed a little larger and as we got farther into the forest, we learned it was made with birch bark instead of hides. They also painted themselves, but were very much into tattooing, especially the men, some of whom covered themselves with figures or designs. They wore their hair in many strange ways, all the way from wild to all but shaved off. They also had no real tribal organization, and we found ourselves moving from band to band, with about the same success we had among the Siksika, at least at first. As we got deeper into the woods, we found less and less interest. When the river we had been following reached the shore of a very large lake, we turned southeast away from the lake to try our luck with a related tribe the Kensistenoug told us about that they called the Ojibwa.

We had to veer to the east to avoid a very marshy area after which we found ourselves at the north end of a complex maze of lakes. Fortunately, the Kensistenoug, who were gathering from the lakes, a grain very much like rice, guided us around it. As we continued on, we constantly came upon lakes and "rice" harvesters, but the farther southeast we went the harvesters began to change in appearance. Everyone we met was still puzzled by our horses and our appearance, but they got around so well in the small narrow birch bark boats, that I doubt if they were very impressed. We finally were guided to one of the Ojibwa villages. It was a bit different. The "tents" were shaped more like mounds. They seemed to be covered with the ubiquitous birch bark. They called themselves Anishinabe rather than Ojibwa, which turned out to be a reference to their footwear. They wore deerskin, and the men favored elaborate headdresses of feathers, claws, fur, whatever. They also grew crops, mostly odd varieties of squashes and beans, but including a strange sort of grain they called mondamin (maize), which had large multicolored seeds in very large multiple heads on a single thick stem. They fed us some of their food while we were with them. Most of it was rather bland except for their "rice." They called it manoomin (wild rice), and it was tastier than our own.

The Anishinabe were very impressive people and would have been ideal recruits, but we had less success interesting them than any others. They were quite happy in their ways, and while they admitted our weapons looked superior to theirs, they found their own quite suitable. Also while the horse was an interesting innovation, they felt their boats were more useful in this environment. Still a few adventurous souls joined us and guided us to the shores of a huge lake, called Gichigami (meaning Great Water). At first sight we were sure we had reached the sea again, but the water was fresh and quite cold. We followed the lakeshore southwest stopping and recruiting at a few more villages, with similar lack of success. Finally, we ran out of Anishinabe territory and came upon a different people. Our Anishinabe recruits were a little leery of approaching them since there had been hostility between them in the past. They called them Napowe-is-iw, which meant "snake" and "enemy." They held back and camped while the rest of us approached the settlement.

We were received with interest and cordiality. Language was a problem, however. They called themselves Ocheti shakowin, but their language was quite different from what we had encountered so far, although it did sound a little like that of the Absaroke and they looked much like that other tribe. Fortunately one of them could speak the Anishinabe language and was able to communicate with one of the Kensistenoug recruits who had come along with us instead of going on to the Ordu with the others. The recruit was able to communicate with us since he had picked up some Mongol and we a little of his language. In spite of all the confusion we met with their leaders, puffed the burning weeds, and explained our mission. They were not much different in customs from the Anishinabe, being farmers of the same vegetables and grains and using boats to travel on rivers and lakes. They also painted themselves and used feathers in their hair for decoration. Their houses were covered with birch bark, but were large and square with deeply sloping roofs. The cup for their burning weed was of a soft reddish stone and was imaginatively worked into a stylized animal of some sort.

Much to our surprise, they seemed interested in our offer and not put off by the fact that we had recruited from the other tribes around them, including their sometime enemies. In fact, they sent runners to their neighboring bands and arranged a large gathering on the western side of a large lake (inland from Lake Gichigami) that was more central to their tribe. It would be at the next full moon—about a week and a half away. They even allowed our Anishinabe recruits to stay with us. The latter were certain there was treachery afoot, but we reassured them and mounted extra guards around our little encampment.

We made use of the time to pick up enough of their language to dispense with the interpreter chain. When it was time, we joined our hosts on the journey inland to the other lake. It took eight days to get there. Along the way we passed three other villages, and groups of the villagers joined us as we went. Lake Gichigami's shore turned east after a few days, and we continued southwest along a sort of trade path, well worn by the locals. The assembly drew a very large crowd of the Ocheti shakowin, thousands of them in fact. Their leaders met with us in a larger meetinghouse constructed of the same material as their regular houses. After the usual weed smoke inhaling, we carefully communicated our recruiting message, and our original host spoke at length in favor of our recruitment proposal.

One after the other of them rose to comment favorably or otherwise until all had done. Finally, one of the earlier noncommittal leaders came up with a very reasonable suggestion. Why not have a sizable contingent from the most willing band go with us and report back the following summer. If all was as we claimed, then they should all join us, if not, then there would be little disruption in their lives.

We were quite happy with this arrangement and assured the assembly that they would very likely all join us next year. We also asked if they knew of any other tribe that might be interested in joining us. One of them suggested a neighboring tribe that was scattered to the west of them who call themselves the Dzitsiistas, but were known to the Ocheti shakowin as Shahi'yena, because they spoke a strange language. Another suggested a group that split off from them and moved to the northwest. Our Anishinabe were familiar with them and called them U'sini u'pwawa, a reference to their cooking with stones. We thanked them and of course had to endure another round of the weed. This time I was reasonably sure the cup was supposed to be a sort of bird. I asked about the reddish stone from which the cup was carved, and they said it was found a short distance to the southwest.

We left the lake with quite a large group in tow and headed a little north of west. We crossed a moderately sized river that the Ocheti shakowin said passed by a very large camp in the south. From the description, it sounded like they were describing a city with a wall around it. They couldn't tell us much about it, though. It seems they felt it was a place of sickness, so they stayed away. We asked if the river emptied into a lake like most of the rivers seemed to, but they said that it just kept joining with other rivers and flowed south a very long way. They had no idea into what it debauched.

We split up at this point, and Juchi turned farther north to meet the splinter Ocheti shakowin group while I continued west toward the Dzitsiistas. Juchi took some of the Ocheti shakowin with him to smooth the way, but the bulk of the recruits came with me. In due course, we came upon the Dzitsiistas and found them to also be very much like the Ocheti shakowin and the Anishinabe. Their houses were covered with earth, however, and seemed to be in more permanent villages. They also made use of pottery instead of skin vessels. They, too, listened with interest in our proposal. This time the language was not too unlike that of the Kensistenoug, and we had less trouble making ourselves understood. They were impressed that a whole band of the Ocheti shakowin had joined us and thought they should also send a large group to see if all was as we said. They decided to send a group of unattached young men rather than an entire band. They promised to spread the word about us and would await their volunteers' report the following summer.

By now it was well into fall, and as we continued west, we found no other natives beyond the Dzitsiistas. They seemed to end shortly before we left the forest and reentered the steppe. The grasses here seemed very tall although they were mostly dead by now, and many had fallen. They looked like they would be quite a sight in summer. We crossed a fair-sized river, which the Kensistenoug said emptied into their lake that we had reached the past summer. They called the lake "Winnipeg," which, of course, meant "great water." There was another tribe near the lake and to the west along the banks of another river well north of our position, but we decided we would look into them the following spring unless Juchi ran into them. With our slow-moving entourage, it took us twenty days to reach "our" river (we had named it the Mongol River).

When we reached the river, we were surprised to find another tribe along its banks for some distance on both sides of it. They spotted us and sent a large force to intercept our "invasion." I detached myself from the rest and rode forward with several interpreters, not sure what we had here. As we drew near to their force without arms at the ready, they lowered their weapons and some of them approached. They looked much like the Ocheti shakowin. They identified themselves as the Numakiki and asked our intentions. I found their language similar to that of the Ocheti shakowin and used one of them to explain my mission, since my proficiency was limited. Their leader was perplexed, but promised to consult his chief and return. I told him I would like to speak to his chief. Before long he returned and said they would welcome a few of my entourage and me but could not entertain the whole party. I told him that was fine and sent the rest of the recruits upriver toward our camp while my lone Ocheti shakowin interpreter and I followed the leader to his village. The village was more of a town than a village. It had a defensive wooden wall around it. The houses were round and earthen just like those the Absaroke had described as their former dwellings. I wondered if this was their old tribe, but the language did not seem similar enough.

I was led to the largest house, and we entered it. The house proved to be more of a log hut, covered first with grasses and then with clay. There were four strong pillars and crossbeams to hold up the roof. It was quite roomy inside. The roof had a square smoke hole covered with a circular twig screen. There were sleeping compartments made of skins along the walls. They were a tall, strong and fine looking people. They wore elaborate headdresses made of sticks and porcupine quills, topped with a feather. Some of them wore tattoos, mostly stripes on their left arm and chest.

We were introduced to the chiefs of the nearest towns and after the usual nawak'osis, made our offer. They listened intently. Then after another round of the weed, they asked questions. They wanted to know, from where had we came and why?. Who had joined us and who had not? Why I looked so pale and if the other Mongols looked like me? I answered all their questions in turn as briefly, yet as honestly as I could. They passed the weed around again and conferred among themselves for a while. Finally, they also decided to send a group of observers to see for themselves. I welcomed the observers and assured them they would not be disappointed.

The observers proved to be ten mostly young men, who were quickly gathered to go with me. Before I left, the chief mentioned that there was another tribe farther upstream who should also be recruited. He would send a runner to advise them, and perhaps they also would send observers. They were called the Hewaktokto and were allies of the Numakiki. I thanked him for his help and wisdom and took my leave. I caught up with the rest of the men a day later. We were still passing Numakiki towns, and some more observers joined us. After a few more days, we finally ran out of Numakiki territory but noticed similar towns across the river. Before long we came upon a group of Hewaktokto that were waiting to join us. They and our Numakiki observers seemed very happy to see each other and chatted amiably the rest of the way. Some days later, we reached the Absaroke villages. A group of them came out to meet us and recognizing me, welcomed me and asked after Juchi. I assured them he would be along soon. I had to stop for a visit, but sent the rest along to the Ordu. My hosts told me that the Hewaktokto were their old tribe. As soon as I could get away, I hurried along to the Ordu, arriving just after my group.

Juchi arrived the next day. He had found the splinter Ocheti shakowin group. They called themselves Yanktonai, the name of one of the Ocheti shakowin subgroups. They lived much like the neighboring Kensistenoug, but still maintained their own identity. A large group of them decided to come along as observers. They had also referred Juchi to their western neighbors, the Inuna-ina. He visited them and found them most cordial. They too lived much like the Kensistenoug in an aspen forest along a river he named for them. They also sent along a large contingent. He had about two hundred observers with him when he arrived.

By now it was early winter, and there had already been a few dustings of snow when we arrived. The great fall hunt had recently taken place and had been a bit of a problem. The arrival of the Kensistenoug we had sent ahead with word of our travels had caused Kaidu to order a great hunt to ensure we had enough food for the winter. There had, indeed, been a lot of game, but the plains oxen had stampeded and broken through the circle, forcing a dramatic strategy change. It turned out that Kaidu had had quite a summer of change in our absence, and we were told that he was anxious to talk to us.

He was quite pleased with our harvest of recruits. He was also pleased with everything about the land so far. The soil was quite fertile, and the grain we planted had done well. The herds had calved more than one would have thought with all the travel and all had fattened up quite nicely on the rich grasslands. Most of the mares were showing signs of being pregnant, so we'd soon have enough horses for all the recruits. The recruits had become quite adept with the horses very quickly. They also had adjusted to our bows very well. The only problem he could see with the land was the lack of iron around here. Henry had told him about his concern and had actually scouted around the area for some but had been unsuccessful. I had not seen any on my travels east either, but had questioned our recruits, describing what the ore looked like to see if any had seen something like it. Only one, the Anishinabe Odinigun, thought he might have seen something like the stone for which I was looking. It seems there was a peninsula on the southern shore of their huge lake where they had long gathered copper. To the east of this spot there were some of the rocks Iwanted, he was quite sure. He would take me there next spring if I wished. I passed this encouraging news on to Kaidu, and he was guardedly relieved. I still felt it was inconceivable that there was no iron in this land. But, there was still more on his mind. It seems he had attended the Siksika council gathering in the summer along with Givevneu and the chiefs who had joined us. It was about this that he wanted to talk to us.

12

DOWN THE MONGOL RIVER, 2 K
(DOWN THE MISSOURI FROM E. MT TO C. IL
1370)

The Siksika council had been quite a large gathering, and Kaidu had gone with the thought that he would convince many more to join the Ordu. He and his escort had been made quite welcome, and there had been several meetings of chiefs that he and Givevneu had attended, but nothing had changed.

"They are as intransigent as ever," he said. "Nothing I or the chief who had joined us said would make any difference. They wished to remain friends and allies of ours but would not change their ways to join us. It would take a massive upheaval to move them. They are determined to retain their independence. I'm beginning to think I should form a sort of confederation with them. Perhaps they could remain as they are, but could become associated with us, as allies, I suppose. I was thinking that in exchange for our sharing our advances with them—they could send young men to be trained in our ways with the horse and weapons—we would then come to their aid if anyone attacked them, and they would send us back the trained soldiers when we needed them. Perhaps the tribe could be a sort of buffer for us. And just maybe the training will seduce away their young men one at a time. Do you think it would work?"

"It is likely best," Juchi nodded. "And the same would do for the Anishinabe and the Kensistenoug. They will never join us either. Even the Ocheti shakowin and the Dzitsiistas may not like the discipline. What do you think, Raven?"

"I've been resisting the inevitable a long time." I shrugged. "We cannot expect these people to change as radically as necessary to adopt our ways. To be honest, I think only the Ocheti shakowin and, perhaps, the nearby tribes along the Mongol River are likely to make the adjustment. Their chiefs seem to have more authority. We might have better luck in the cities they talked about."

"Cities?" Kaidu jumped up. "There are cities in this land?"

"So the Ocheti shakowin implied," I answered. "They said that there was a large walled settlement in the south along a river we crossed, but they avoided it because of sickness."

"A city!" Kaidu smiled. "We must investigate this as soon as possible. Winter would be the best time. You can go by dogsled as soon as there is enough snow. Do you think you could find it?"

"I suppose so." I nodded. "But what sort of contact would you want? If they are, indeed, cities, would they be as friendly as the bands have been? Would it be best if we were discreet?"

"Of course," he agreed. "Don't go until you can communicate suitably with one or two of the Ocheti people and take them along. You two stay out of sight, but send one of them in to find out what they are like. We must not tip our hand too soon, we might have our first enemy."

We left pleased at the interesting assignment, but not pleased that we'd have to leave the Ordu so soon again. I went back to Paula and the others and told them the news. I also told Henry about the possible iron ore I'd be checking out next spring. He reminded me about coal again and the fact that he had only once worked with iron ore, and wasn't sure about the blast furnace design. I sketched it out for him as it had been explained to me and was reminded that we would need to turn some of the coal into coke and find some limestone also. The latter would be no problem, since I had seen limestone along our path and would likely find some nearby. Coal remained a problem, however, and I was determined to address it in the spring.

Juchi took over giving language lessons to the two Ocheti sha-kowin volunteers, leaving me a little time for Paula and my maps. I decided that the following spring when I went to look for the iron ore, she would come with me. I had been over much of the path before, and it was quite safe. At any rate, I would need to bring along some carts and furthermore was tired of being separated from her most of the year. Padraig and Mathilde would also come along. We should make quite an eyeful for the locals.

Once our river was frozen enough, our small party moved out over the ice in three dogsleds. Nitsiza had also volunteered to come along as well as one of the Tsattine, Saya. From what the Ocheti shakowin told me, I thought it best to follow our river downstream, for they were sure it emptied into the other river near the "city." The river was alternately broad or narrow with cliffs or large deciduous tree-covered bottoms as we went along. Some evergreens could be seen along the slopes up to the plains, but the plains were treeless. On the second day away from the Ordu, the Absaroke River joined the Mongol from the south. It was several times wider, but we had just emerged from a gorge, which had considerably narrowed "our" river. The Absaroke was dotted with small tree-covered islands so it was probably shallower, also. Perhaps one day we could explore that river. Of course, the Absaroke villages were in this area, and we stopped by for a visit to try out our Ocheti shakowin on them. They could make out every few words, so it was clear I would have to learn their language, also.

Our river twisted and turned a bit but tended generally eastward for four days before turning south, east, south again, and east again over the next four days, and finally generally south. Of course, along this stretch we passed and had to visit the Hewaktokto and Numakiki towns. The latter could make out about half of our Ocheti shakowin. I promised I would learn their languages before spring. They were very interested in our dogsleds and asked a lot of questions. Not long after the river turned south the latest time, I was attracted to what looked like three black parallel lines on a cliff over the river. We stopped so I could look at it more closely. It proved to be a bit of a scramble up to the lines, but we were rewarded when they proved to be three seams of coal. They were only about a foot thick, and they were bituminous coal, good enough for our needs, and potentially suitable for coking. I took out a small amount and carefully marked the spot on the map. There was quite a large bottom just downriver from the coal, so we could probably move the Ordu down to here, as long as the Numakiki joined us, since they had villages both north and south of this site. The site itself did not look like it had been settled in the recent past. I was sure we'd find even more coal in the area.

We continued on our way, and five days later, the river veered to the southeast after a little switchback, taking us out of Numakiki territory. The river continued generally in that southeast direction for the next six days. During this leg, we encountered a group of villages with mound dwellings much like those of the Numakiki. We stopped to see who they were and found a completely different people. They spoke an utterly incomprehensible language. We did make out that they called themselves, Ariki. They were a fine-looking people, although they had a curious hairstyle. They had two bones sticking up like horns on each side of the crown. Perhaps they were imitating the plains oxen. With much difficulty we got across the idea that we wanted to learn their language and got one of them to go along with us to that end. His name was Hishkowits, a young man of perhaps seventeen years. We passed more of their villages for much of this leg, and then the river shifted to the east for two days and then back south again. We could see that ours was quite a river, for all along the way rivers and streams of all sizes joined it from both banks. It was quite a chore mapping this river, and I was glad we would be retracing our path on the way back so I could check my map. Also the high cliffs seemed to recede farther away as we progressed and by the time we turned south were fully replaced by more gentle slopes with occasional bluffs. Game was plentiful along the way, especially deer, but we had brought along enough food and did not want to tarry.

For the next seven days, we went generally south and a little east, and again we encountered Ariki villages. Hishkowits helped us pass by without wasting too much time, although there was again much interest in the dogsleds. We finally ran out of Ariki villages, and then the river turned sharply east, continuing in this general direction until it emptied into the other river, or the other river emptied into it depending on one's point of view. Had we continued uninterrupted, this last leg of the trip would have taken about eight days. As it happened, however, after two days, we were surprised by an arrow ambush. We quickly shifted to the far side, in this case the north bank, of the river to seek cover until we could see what we were up against. Fortunately, no one was hurt for the attackers underestimated our distance, or overestimated their bows. Once under cover, we tried to see who had attacked us, but they remained out of sight. I must admit I was quite incensed when the first arrow skidded across the river ice short of its mark. Everything had been so peaceful so far that I had become complacent and oblivious of danger. So, on further thought, I should have been grateful to our unseen attackers. The moon was a mere sliver that night, so we set up a small ambush for our adversaries. We made a campfire and bundled up some rocks to look like sleeping figures, then moved the dogs a distance away downwind and lay in wait. No one took the bait, however, and we spent a cold miserable night for nothing. We decided to go overland along the north shore at a more careful pace to avoid any more surprises. Late that day, we saw a settlement on the southern shore of the river and hid in a shallow ravine while one of our Ocheti shakowin, Wanbli Sapa, went over to scout out the town. He left behind all his more modern weapons, taking only an old stone and wood war club. He went straight across the river to the town, making no attempt at concealment. From what we could see, the town was larger than any we had seen so far, but it was not walled, and the houses were quite similar to those of the Ocheti shakowin, with the same steeply sloping roofs, but they appeared larger.

He went right into the town before anyone took notice of him, and we lost sight of him among the houses. There then followed a lot of commotion and noise from the town, but we could not see what was going on. We decided to wait until dark and then go over to investigate. As soon as it was dark enough we (except for Nitsiza who stayed with the dogs) slipped across the river making use of whatever cover we could. It proved unnecessary, however, for there were no sentries. Our other Ocheti shakowin, Wakinyan Cetan, moved stealthily into the town while the rest of us hid behind the riverbank. He soon returned with the disturbing news that Wanbli Sapa had been taken prisoner. He would have likely been killed by now except that there was tremendous disagreement about the situation. It seems that since he boldly and freely walked into the town, there was a sizable group who felt he had to be treated as a guest and should be honored for his courage. Another group felt that he had insulted the town by striding contemptuously in as if they were not worth fearing. A third group felt it didn't matter how he fell into their hands, he was a prisoner and should die. A final group felt he should simply be thrown out of town with the garbage since he was one of their "poor relations" from the north and not worth all the fuss. It was this last group that most angered our spy, Wakinyan Cetan. He was prudent enough to do nothing for the moment until the argument was settled. He explained that these people were related to his people. They were called Hotcangara and could be found from here all the way up to just south of where his people lived. They had all been one people in antiquity, but his group had moved away because of all the sickness and had flourished in the North Country. The Hotcangara were arrogant and treated all other people with contempt. I asked about the sickness, and he said it was a wasting disease that was accompanied by much coughing. It sounded like a disease the Hanjen called lao (tuberculosis), a fatal lung ailment, but I couldn't be sure. Wakinyan Cetan returned to the town to await developments.

While waiting, I looked around the town a bit using what little light came from the town. It seemed to have about forty or fifty of the long houses. There were extensive fields that had apparently been cultivated. It would seem there were about six to eight hundred people in the town, but still, it was hardly Khanbalikh, or even the small towns in the old Khanate I had passed through on the way to and from the old capital. I decided that if we could get Wanbli Sapa back, we would just go on to look at the so-called "city" but not bother entering it. Finally a grim-looking Wakinyan Cetan returned to us. "The fourth faction won out," he reported darkly. "We must be avenged."

It took a while to get him over this idea. First, we got him back across the river, so we could wait for Wanbli Sapa; then when he returned, we managed to convince them that we were only a scouting party, not a war party. The next time we came, it would be as a war party, and they would have their revenge with interest. This seemed to satisfy them, especially since the whole Ordu would be descending on their antagonists. In fact, they were very excited at the prospect, spending the rest of our journey fantasizing about the looks on the Hotcangara's faces when the Mongol horsemen surrounded them. We continued on to the "city" traveling as inconspicuously as possible. At this pace, it took us about four days to get to the junction of our river and the one from the north. The latter was a bit larger, and we gave it the name "Missi Sipi" by which the Ocheti shakowin knew it. It meant, of course, "Great River." It was quite an impressive river, about two li wide, and fortunately, it was frozen—greatly simplifying crossing it. Once across we were in a very large bottom, which had been cleared and heavily cultivated. We left Nitsiza and Saya with the dogs near the riverbank, and the rest of us moved forward on foot. It was late in the afternoon when we set out from the riverbank toward what looked like a village to the south of our position. It was indeed a village and not a very impressive one. We continued toward what looked like a hill to the southeast of our position about four or five li away. As we drew near, we passed between two more villages before reaching what had looked like a hill. It was too regular to be a natural hill but seemed to be a truncated earthen pyramidal mound that was topped with a platform on which was a wooden building. It was deserted at the moment, so we climbed up the mound to have a look. It was too dark to see anything inside the building, but it was probably some sort of temple. There were a few other smaller pyramidal mounds also topped with wooden structures around a flat open area like a square. From our vantage point, we could see some fires from settlements. There appeared to be a large one to the north with several smaller ones to the south and east of it. There was a scattering of smaller ones to the west and east of our position, with the eastern ones being farther away. To the south, there seemed to be a profusion of settlements, but we could not tell where they were separated from one another from this perspective. There also seemed to be more of these pyramidal mounds. We decided to move south for a closer look.

We found a fairly settlement-free area east of our first mound, so we went south along that corridor. About nine li south, we came upon a town about the size of the one that had detained Wanbli Sapa, although it also had one of the pyramidal mounds with the building on top. Six li farther south we came upon the "city." The moon had risen by now, and although it was still waxing it gave enough light that we could see a truly high pyramidal mound with a wall around it. We approached from the northeast, and because of the dim light, it took a while see clearly. We crossed a small river and came upon a group of four pyramidal mounds of various sizes about a large open area. Just south of this was another small river and across it the largest pyramidal mound we had yet seen. It seemed to be about a hundred feet high and also appeared flat on the top. We couldn't see a building. There was a high wall made of large logs set on end and with square bastions at regular intervals along the wall. Still, it was open at the north or river end, which was strange. We could not get any closer since it was manned with lookouts and we did not want to be seen at this point in time. We went east along the river and crossed it well out of sight of the bastions.

The wall proved to come to a point in the south about two and a half li from the river. We could still see the high pyramidal mound over the wall from our vantage, but nothing else. There were a great many houses scattered on the western side of the "citadel," and there were more mounds surrounding squares on both sides of the citadel. Some of the mounds were conical rather than pyramidal in shape. We continued around the city to the west noticing that there were even more settlements to the south. When we finally cleared the city, we turned back north, noticing another large settlement to the south and another pyramid center to the west. We moved northward as quickly as possible not wanting to be caught in the open in daylight. Just as the sky was beginning to lighten, we heard the low welcoming growl of the dogs. We immediately recrossed the Missi Sipi and found a convenient ravine in which to rest up from our night's work. I quickly sketched out a map of the area before turning in. There had to be at least twenty five thousand people in that complex. I wondered what Kaidu would want to do about them.

Late in the afternoon, we set out back up our river again on the north side, out of sight of the river. We found two towns on this side of the river on this more northerly course, but managed to avoid them. They were on a river that ran parallel to our river and encouraged us to veer back to the latter. Once we were beyond the point at which we were attacked, we sped back up the still-frozen river the same way we had come. The return took about forty-five days and proceeded without incident. Along the way, we stopped at Hishkowits' village, and with the Ariki we had learned and the Mongol he had learned, we were able to make our pitch to his chief. He was much surprised by our proposal and wondered what we had to offer. We showed him our bows and arrows and tried to explain our horses. He considered for a while and finally sent Hishkowits with us to see if it was all true. This was beginning to look like a pattern. It was still late winter when we got back. The river had remained frozen the whole way and didn't start to thaw for another ten days. As soon as we returned, we reported to Kaidu about the city and the rude reception we had received at the Hotcangara town. He thanked us for our report and told us to rest up for a while, he would talk to us more later. I told Henry about the coal seam and showed him my sample. It turned out he had never made coke before, so I had to show him how to make a coke oven. It was fortunate I had a good memory for detail; it was becoming essential.

The kidding and foaling was beginning, so we thought it best to wait until spring had fully arrived before setting out on our iron expedition. I was anxious to hear what all of our recruits thought about the Ordu. They were all very excited although some of them seemed more interested in retaining their settlements and independence. While I was gone, Doqus had presented Henry with a daughter, and Mathilde had presented Padraig with a son. Quite a few others among the Ordu had also given birth in the new land making us feel all the more at home. Paula had still not become pregnant but with me away all the time it was no wonder.

Finally Kaidu called Juchi and me to meet with him. We found him with Givevneu but otherwise alone. The two had been conferring when we came in, but stopped and greeted us as we approached.

"Our shaman tells me he has learned much from his Siksika colleagues," Kaidu said. "He has learned about the medicinal properties of various local plants. More to the point, he was humble enough to learn. The Siksika are an admirable people; they remind me of the old Mongols, before we got into all the trappings of empire. I, too, have learned from them. I will again attend their council this summer and offer them the sort of confederacy we spoke about earlier. After all we don't want to become a roving horde. It is best that we remain scattered until we need to come together for defense. We still need to train their young men, so that when we call on them, they will be ready. From now on this will be the proposal we will offer. Of course any who wish can still join us outright, but if they prefer, they can remain our allies only and maintain their separate identity. What do you think?"

"Most prudent." Juchi seemed relieved. "I would like to return to the Kensistenoug, the Inuna-ina, the Yanktonai and the Anishinabe with that proposal. I think they may warm to the idea, what say you, Raven?"

"I would add the Dzitsiistas to that group also." I nodded. "But why not let me talk to the Anishinabe since I must go there anyway in search of iron. That still leaves the Absaroke, Hewaktokto, Numakiki and Ocheti shakowin. I think they are all ready to become Mongols en masse."

"Aren't they all rather large tribes?" Kaidu asked. "Do you really think they will all want to join us?"

"I do," I replied. "The groups who have been observing us are very enthusiastic. If they all joined us, they would very likely outnumber us six or seven to one, so it would be quite a job absorbing them all. But I think you will find them to be fine Mongols."

"They are all impressive people," Kaidu agreed. "They seem to be fearless. They took to the horses as quickly as the Siksika. They are also a rather refined people. They remind me of you, Raven."

"I am honored by the comparison," I replied. "But Juchi informs me that they are much better looking than I am."

"Indeed?" Kaidu looked at Juchi. "Does that mean you finally decided to marry?"

"No, not yet." Juchi grinned. "But perhaps this fall, if you promise not to send me off to scout any more cities."

"That brings me to the final problem." Kaidu turned serious. "I feel we should send an ambassador to this city you found, but from your report I have no reason to believe he would be received with respect. I have decided to wait until next year, and then we will send an army to make sure they receive us correctly. That should give us enough time to turn all these recruits into Mongols. Also, I have decided to move the Ordu farther down the river. After harvest this fall we will move down to your coal seams, provided the Numakiki do join us and do not object. I will leave an outpost here. You should both be back before then. Good luck on the recruiting and on finding the iron."

With that we left and getting together our expeditions, set out in different directions. Juchi with a small entourage of Kensistenoug and a few others moved northeast, while I with Paula, Padraig, Mathilde, and a group of Absaroke, Hewaktokto, Numakiki, Dzitsiistas, Ocheti shakowin, and a few Anishinabe including Odinigun, set off downstream to the east.

13

THE SEARCH FOR IRON ORE, 3 K
(E. MT, ND, MN, WI, MI, 1371)

This was undoubtedly my favorite trip so far in the new land. We set out at a leisurely pace to accommodate the wagons to some extent, but really so we could enjoy the beauty of the steppe in spring. As we moved east and spring became summer, we were greeted with a remarkable variation of flower size, shape and color. I'm fairly sure that white and yellow was the predominant color, but we also saw many shades of reds, pinks, oranges, blues, and purples. I had never seen the Mongol steppe, but I doubt if it was any more beautiful. The only thing wrong with the steppe was the weather. There didn't seem to be anything like a good orderly monsoon season. On the contrary, it was very changeable. It would be a clear, windless, warm day in the morning, and before midday, the wind would pick up, huge black clouds would come out of nowhere, pelt us with hail, endless barrages of lightning would crash all around us, and then it would be quite cold, and it cleared up again. Sometimes we would see dark clouds and lightning, but there would be no wind or rain and it would stay humid. Some days it would be clear and pleasant but then would become very windy all day with no other change. Still, there were enough good days to make the journey memorable, and it was wonderful having Paula with me for a change.

The second day of our journey, I noticed some hills that I thought might have coal and stopped to look wondering how I had missed them all the other times I had passed here. There was indeed coal, but only the poor quality brown coal. Still, it gave me renewed hope that we'd find more coal around here somewhere. It took twenty days to reach my coal find of the past winter since we had to stop at all the villages along the way. I had learned a decent amount of their several languages much to their delight (although I did occasionally mix up a few words of the very similar Hewaktokto and Absaroke), and I told them about the new confederation option. They, however, seemed intent on joining us outright. Everyone was most interested to see that I wasn't the only "pale" Mongol.

The coal was easier to reach from the steppe, and we dug out a fair amount of it to take with us. Wanbli Sapa, one of the Ocheti shakowin who had come with me, finally had to ask why I wanted black rocks that were neither hard nor sharp. He had heard of a black rock that was sharp like flint, but a bit too brittle. This was surely not that. I didn't know at the time what he was talking about, but later found out he was referring to obsidian. It was only used for decoration in the north, but quite differently far to the south. I promised to show him how I used the coal when we made camp. That night, when the fire was strong enough, I put in a piece of the coal for the locals. They were quite amazed that the stone would burn and glow red-hot. They wondered how I knew about this rock if I had never been here before. I explained that we had such rocks in our old land, the world was after all one, we had the same stars overhead, many of the same trees and animals and the same earth. Odinigun wondered if the iron ore I was looking for would also burn like the coal, I assured him it wouldn't but I'd show him what it could do if we found it and got it back to the Ordu.

The land was rough near the Mongol River, with many tributary rivers breaking the plane of the steppe and cutting deeply into it. As we moved away from the river, the terrain sloped gently downward; the grassland was dotted with small lakes full of ducks and other water birds. We would hear the birds well before we could see the lake. Ten days later, we reached the area where the grass was getting taller. It was in full height this time and could easily hide a man. We could still see over it on horseback but not by much. It looked like a taller version of the grass that seemed bluish green, but the stems varied in color from almost gray to dark red. There were also patches of a tall golden brown grass and a tall green grass, but the first grass clearly prevailed. When the wind blew, it looked like waves on a multicolored sea. Paula was quite taken by it and would often stand up in the cart for a better view. Two days later, we entered the country of the Dzitsiistas and soon crossed the river we had named for them.

One of the Dzitsiistas who had returned with us rode ahead to gather the tribal leaders, while another, Motsoyouf, led us to the gathering place. Pine trees dominated this forest, but there were quite a few oaks and maples also as well as a tree that looked like a very large linden tree with huge leaves. Odinigun told us that his people took ziinzibaakwad (maple syrup) from the maple in early spring. I asked him what he meant, and it seemed they would score the bark and the sap would flow from the tree. They would collect the sap and boil it down to produce a sweetener. He promised to give us some to taste when we returned to his village. At length we arrived at the gathering place and were received with much interest. The Dzitsiistas in our entourage were beset with questions while the rest of us and the carts and the horses were observed carefully but politely. Motsoyouf had to let everyone get on his horse and let everyone touch the carts, but we were not so put upon. I could see they were especially curious about Padraig and the women. The former's height coupled with his reddish hair and beard, and the latter's strange clothes and appearance fascinated them. There was also some interest in Mathilde's baby since he had the reddish hair like his father. I suppose they also really didn't think there could be any more people like me.

Finally the chiefs gathered, and Motsoyouf and I joined them. We passed the weed around, and then the chiefs asked for Motsoyouf's report. He told them all that he had seen and learned and how much it would benefit them to join us. He certainly wanted to be a Mongol, and so did all the others who had gone. Once again, one after the other of the leaders spoke his piece, a few in favor of joining, a few against, most not yet sure. Finally, it was my turn. I told them of Kaidu's confederation offer. They could stay here and live as they have sharing with us their knowledge and experience and receiving ours in return. Their young men would train with us and return to them or stay with us as they wished. If they were attacked by anyone we would rush to their assistance and destroy their enemy as though he had attacked us. For their part, they would not initiate any hostilities with their neighbors and would send us back their already trained young men should we go to war.

Predictably, this set off another extended round of talk, much more favorable this time. They finally agreed to the proposal, although it was not unanimous. They did wonder if all their neighbors had agreed to ally with us in this way as well. I told them that Juchi would be talking to the Kensistenoug, the Inuna-ina, and the Yanktonai group that had moved away from the Ocheti shakowin and I would be talking to the Ocheti shakowin and the Anishinabe. I would send word to them about the outcome of those meetings. This satisfied them, and they promised to send a large group of their young men to train and anyone else who wanted to join us. I detailed Motsoyouf and the other Dzitsiistas with us to lead them back. It turned out to be quite a group. Not only a few hundred young men, but also about a hundred and fifty others, mostly relatives and friends of those who had decided to stay with us. I dashed off a note to Kaidu and gave it to Motsoyouf to deliver. He was familiar enough with me by now to ask what it was. I tried to explain writing to him, but he couldn't quite figure out what I meant. He was a bright fellow, so I promised to teach him when I got back. He was quite pleased with this, so I told him to learn as much Mongol as possible by the time I got back. I decided to teach him the Uighur script. If I tried to teach him Hanjen, we'd both go mad, besides, only a few of us in the Ordu knew the language.

The rest of us turned east to meet the Ocheti shakowin. Once again I sent one of them to ride ahead and announce our arrival. Meanwhile, I asked Wanbli Sapa and Wakinyan Cetan how they thought their people would decide. They told me that they were almost certain the entire tribe would join, especially after they heard how the Hotcangara had insulted them. I suggested that would not be the best reason for joining us. They assured me it would only serve to convince those who were wavering.

In due course we arrived at the same place on the west bank of the large lake (which I had named Ocheti) where I had met with the chiefs the year before and was ushered into the same large house before the same group of chiefs. The chief who had come with us last year, Tatanka Ska Koda, had also returned with us to report to his colleagues. After the usual weed, he was called upon to speak. I could not really understand the language well enough yet, so I had Wanbli Sapa serving as interpreter. Tatanka Ska Koda spoke at length to the chiefs, telling them all about us. He definitely had his eyes open during his stay, for he told them about everything there was to tell, favorable and unfavorable. When he finished, each of the chiefs who wanted to say something did. Finally I told them about the confederation option. Tatanka Ska Koda next said he thought it best that the whole tribe become Mongols. He had noticed that others who had joined still maintained their identity and spoke their own language, but had become and were accepted as Mongols, which after all meant "The Brave." And were not the Ocheti shakowin "brave"? One older fellow with bright intelligent eyes then asked me what it was "The Brave" was planning to do that required bravery. I explained that we had traveled a long distance through an unknown country braving the long bitter winter of the far north to find a new home and establish a new Khanate. We wished to unify all the tribes into a great nation that would be both strong and peaceful. We would be the best of friends and the worst of enemies. A younger chief wanted to know if it were true we would punish the village that had treated Wanbli Sapa shamefully. I assured him it was—we would send an expedition there the following year once we had fully trained our new army. He then rose up and said he wanted to join that army. It turned out, Wanbli Sapa translated army as war party since they had no word for it. In any event, it was agreed that the whole tribe would join us en masse in the fall. Meanwhile a large group of young men would go back to the Ordu to train.

I again dashed off a note to Kaidu and gave it to Tatanka Ska Koda to deliver. He was honored and too polite to ask what it was. A few days later, he led a group of almost three thousand young men and several hundred others west, while the rest of us continued northeast. About four days later, we arrived at the shore of Lake Gichigami. Those who had not seen it before were quite impressed. Even though we were at its narrow end I could still see how huge it was. We found Odinigun's village a short distance along the north shore of the lake, and he gave us some of the Ziinzibaakwad to taste as he had promised. It was really quite sweet, more so than honey, and with a rather unique flavor, hard to describe. I also prevailed on him to get us some of their rice since I wanted the others to taste it. While one of his relatives was fixing us the rice, he went on to try and arrange a meeting of the Anishinabe chiefs.

We were there a few days before Odinigun was able to tell us that the chiefs, or at least some of them, had agreed to meet with us at a place called Mooningwaneking two full moons hence. The moon was waxing, so that would probably be about forty or so days away, but he pointed out the additional time would ensure a better turnout. I asked where the meeting place was. He said Mooningwaneking was a sacred place, and it was an honor that I would be received there. It was an island off the southern shore of the lake about ten days away from his village. But we could not go there until it was time, so he would take me to see the stone that looked like dried blood. He would also be able to show us a great "manidoo" on the way.

We set off back down along the northern shore of the lake and swung around to the southern shore, then headed east again. The woods began to change a little as we went; there was more variety, with spruce, fir, and hemlock joining the pines and aspen joining the maples and lindens. The oaks seemed to be reduced. The woods made the going a bit rough with the carts, and we found ourselves hugging the lakeshore. This took us a bit out of the way, and it was twelve days before we saw the sacred island of the Anishinabe. It was one of several islands. It looked quite long and narrow, and it was a bit of a distance offshore. We would get there by boat, it seemed. I decided I'd leave the others behind for that meeting. I did know how to swim, but cold as that water was I wasn't sure it would matter.

It was quite hilly on this part of the lake near the island, with cliffs coming up close to the shore, and it continued to be so for a few days' journey. Then the hills receded, and we had to slog through a small marshy patch before again the hills approached the lake. Soon the lakeshore flattened out again, but then we had to weave our way among trees, slowing us down considerably. We finally arrived at a village near a small river. Here Odinigun prevailed on us to leave the carts in the village's care while we continued on horseback or boat, because we'd never get the carts to where we wanted to go. I thought horseback would be best, not having too much faith in the light boats. He led us up the river, first south quite a way, then back west for a much shorter distance, finally stopping near dusk at what looked like a large rock. He proclaimed it to be the great "manidoo" he had promised to show us. On closer inspection, it was a huge lump of apparently pure copper. It was about three feet wide, two and half feet long, and nearly two feet tall. It was quite irregular in shape and was mostly dark from oxidation, but with a little rubbing I could see it was copper. A remarkable find, but I was curious why it was considered a "manidoo" which I understood to mean a kind of spirit or demigod. It turned out they thought it was responsible for the smaller pieces of copper that they had found nearby and had been using for many years. They honored the large chunk so that it would continue to give them the smaller chunks. It was fairly obvious that it would be inappropriate to take a piece of the chunk, so I merely congratulated them on their good fortune in finding the "manidoo."

We camped nearby, and I asked Odinigun if his people ever melted the copper to shape it into things. He said it wasn't possible to melt it; they just hammered it into the desired shape with stone hammers. It seemed they had no metallurgy at all. I wondered if there was any copper ore in the area as well as native copper. I described the ore to him, and he said he thought we could find that kind of rock just a little to the east; he was sure he could find it tomorrow. Of course, we didn't really need copper unless I could find some tin or zinc, but it would be good to know if there was any ore.

The next day, we returned down the river until it turned north; then we crossed it and continued east into the more rugged hill country. I had to admit he was right about the carts, between the irregular grades and the trees, we would probably have to build a road to get through here with them. Of course, this made me wonder about how we'd ever get the ore out if we did find it, but I decided it would be best to find it first, then worry about getting it out.

Late in the day, shortly after crossing a small river that flowed east, Odinigun stopped and showed me a hillside that had been cleared by a rockslide a few years ago and had not yet been fully reforested. Sure enough, there was copper ore. I took a moderate amount and put it on one of the horses. When we camped that evening, I asked Odinigun that if I needed a lot of this rock, what would be the best way to get it to the carts? He suggested that I leave the carts at the western end of Lake Gichigami. His people could easily carry the rock to the river we had just crossed, then transport it by boat to the carts. I suggested it would be too heavy for the boats, but he disagreed strongly. I asked Padraig to carve a model of a Hanjen wheelbarrow for me with a moving wheel if possible. He was quite accomplished at woodcarving and assured me he'd be finished with it by the next day.

Before we set out, Padraig presented me with a perfect model, and I showed it to Odinigun. I explained that just as the wheels enabled the carts to carry heavy loads, the wheelbarrow enabled men to carry heavy loads more easily. He was fascinated, but thought the model was too small to carry much of a load. I explained that it was only a model just as they made small model boats; a large one would hold a large amount. Would not that be better than carrying heavy loads on one's back? They would not fit on a boat if they were as big as I had demonstrated. I explained it would be best to have one at each end of the boat transportation. He was no fool and finally grasped what I was talking about, even though the whole idea was quite new. He had to admit the wheelbarrow might come in handy for moving rocks like this, but since the Anishinabe always lived on the water, it would not be of much use in their daily lives. He was right, of course, but I hoped to encourage some changes in their lives.

Some three days later, we arrived at another not-yet-healed rockslide, and there was indeed quite a vein of hematite. I took as much as I thought the horses could carry and asked Odinigun if he thought his people might be willing to get more of these rocks for us. He asked what they would get in return, and I suggested iron goods like arrowheads, axes, knives, etc. He thought they might be interested, but wasn't sure. What if our people dug out the rocks, would they help us carry them to the carts? Perhaps they might be willing. Then I had an inspiration. What if we gave them all the copper they could possibly want? Well, that was a good offer, except that they already had quite a bit of copper. I had a feeling our meeting on the sacred island was going to be a frustrating one. What could we offer the Anishinabe that they would want badly enough to join us. I had brought along some steel tools, perhaps if they saw the advantage of steel over their stone implements in a demonstration, I might make some headway.

With the remaining time, I scouted around to see how much iron ore there was here, and it seemed to be all along a group of hills that ran east for quite some distance, many li. Lake Gichigami was not too far from the hills, perhaps only fifty li, and even better, there was a lake less than thirty li to the north that was drained by a river that flowed into Lake Gichigami. I carefully mapped the area and asked to return along the lakeshore so I could map it as well. He agreed up to a point, for there was a very large peninsula jutting deeply into the lake that would have taken us well out of our way. We cut across the base of the peninsula, which proved to also have copper ore along a range of hills that likely extended from the one farther south where Odinigun had shown me the copper ore. Finally, we got back to the carts with six days to spare before our big meeting. We moved back along the shore and arrived opposite the island the evening when the moon had just become full.

The next morning, I wrapped the steel tools I had brought along in a piece of felt and carefully boarded one of the birch bark boats. I was seated in the middle with Odinigun, and there was a rower in front and in back of us. The boat seemed to have no trouble with all the weight and indeed our rowers easily propelled us the distance to the sacred island. We landed and were led to one of their good-sized houses. We entered and found a large gathering of older Anishinabe men suffused with an air of wisdom and dignity. I was seated and maintained a respectful silence. The burning weed was passed around as usual until spent, and then the man in the center addressed me.

"You have moved among our people in peace," he began, "and asked us to leave our home to which the sacred miigis shell guided us to join your strange-looking tribe on the plains. A few of us have indeed joined you, and they are free to do so, but if we leave our lake, we will surely die, for so our legends have told us."

"It was wrong of me to ask you to leave your ancestral home," I replied. "Our leader in his wisdom has come to see that it would be better if you remained in your home according to your customs. Still we would be your allies and would like to help you and have you help us. Our leader has proposed that we be joined in a confederation among equals. If any of you wish to join us outright, they are most welcome, for it is obvious what a fine people you are. However, for the rest, we ask that you send us your young men as you can spare them so that we can train them in our army. Therefore, should anyone attack you, we will quickly fall on them and destroy them, and should anyone attack us, your young men would be able to help us. We could also exchange goods. You have rocks that are of great use to us; we have implements I think you would find helpful."

At this point, I unwrapped the tools and passed them around. Old as they were, they were strong enough to heft the tools with ease and could see the potential. Each one methodically examined each tool in turn. Finally they asked about the rocks I wanted, and Odinigun explained where they could be found. I passed around a small piece of the iron ore to them. They were clearly puzzled that I would trade such wonders as these marvelous tools for rather unimpressive-looking rocks. At length, one wanted to know why we wanted the rocks, and I explained that with much effort and special procedures we could turn the rocks into the tools he was holding. They wanted to see this. But I explained I didn't have the necessary equipment or the other raw materials I needed, but I would show Odinigun when I got back to the Ordu, and he could return and tell them about it if they wished. I was beginning to think the Anishinabe would also join us. But no one was asleep in this room.

"The trade is good," one of them said. "It benefits us both and harms neither. However, why should our young men join your army to defend us, when they have been most successful in doing so without any such training? What can you teach them about fighting in the forests? Are you not a plains people? Should not you learn from us?"

I had to admit he had a point. Mongol tactics are most effective on an open field. We rarely encountered woods such as these in the old Khanate. So I suggested that perhaps we could learn from each other. We would send some of our army to train with them, and they could send some of their young men to train with us. That way there would always be some of each group that could effectively come to the aid of the other. I explained that at least two of their western neighbors had joined us, and it was possible that the Kensistenoug would also join. They were surprised that we had been able to talk to all of the latter in so short a time since they were scattered over a very large area both to the east and the west, north of the Anishinabe. That rather surprised me, but I explained that Juchi, whom a few of them had seen with me the year before, had gone to them with the confederation offer while I had taken the more southerly route here.

At length, and it was indeed at length, most of the day in fact, they agreed to confederate with us. They decided that young men from the villages west of the lake would train with us, and we could send our men to the same villages for training. Since we had effectively removed all their potential enemies from that area, it would be safe to leave it less protected. Should we manage to induce their neighbors to the south and southeast to join us also, then young men from these areas could also be sent. Meanwhile, they would pass on our offer to their relatives and allies in the east, the Potawatamink and the Ottawa if I wished. I thanked them and asked them to by all means extend our offer to their allies. Finally, I asked them about their southern neighbors.

It seemed that to the south were the Hotcangara who had spread there from farther south and to the southeast were the Menomini-wok ininiwok, a tribe vaguely related to them but whose language was difficult to understand. They occupied both shores of a long large lake that could be found not far from where I had gathered the rocks I wanted. I blanched that I could have taken Paula so close to a potentially hostile group. I asked if this tribe was friendly to them, and they said that there was trade between them but little else. I promised to contact them as soon as possible but was not sure about the Hotcangara since we were already planning to punish one of their villages for mistreating one of our men.

We passed around the weed again, and we finally got back just before dark. I gave the news to the others, and they admitted that they had become worried since I was gone so long. The next morning just before we left, one of the chiefs, Gagewin, came across and asked to see the ore again. He looked at it a while and said he was sure we could find more of it on a line of hills beyond the marshy area on the western end of the lake. He promised to send me a sample as soon as he got back; it would probably be waiting for us when we reached Odinigun's village. I decided that was worth the detour, and Odinigun was happy to return to his village because he wanted to bring some of his relatives back to the Ordu with us.

It was the perfect time to arrive at his village—right after the rice harvest. We spent a few days there while Odinigun organized his relatives, most of his immediate family actually. Meanwhile, Gagewin had kept his word and sent some of his men with a boatload of iron ore. We loaded it on the wagons, and I left the others and went back with the men to see how much ore was in the hills and to pinpoint it on my maps. If this source panned out it would be a lot more convenient than the other, at least immediately, and the other would serve as a backup. The hills proved to be almost one hundred eighty li northwest of the lake, through a marshy area. They were beyond the marsh, and the ground to the west seemed to be firmer. I sent a couple of the men back to tell Odinigun to lead the carts back to Lake Ocheti and I would meet them there. I wanted to assess the size of this lode and also decided it would be best to find a better way into these hills. The ore extended throughout the row of hills. It would take us a long time to use this up. The hills ended before a group of lakes, which I passed to the south. I then turned west to avoid the western edge of the marsh and eventually swung around it finally reaching the northwestern shore of Lake Ocheti. It was about a two hundred and seventy li journey. I continued on to the western shore of the lake until I reached the appointed rendezvous point. The western shore of the lake was less marshy than the southeastern shore. The carts had not yet arrived.

Once the carts reached me, we turned southwest from Lake Ocheti. Most of the journey brought us back into the high grass, interrupted only by many small lakes. At this time of year, late summer, the grasses had all flowered and now many shades from crimson through copper and gold to straw colored the gently rolling steppe. When the sun shone on it and wind stirred it, the beauty was breathtaking. We crossed a good-sized river that was surrounded on both sides by heavily wooded bottoms. The river was conveniently low at this time of year making an easy passage for the carts. This was again Dzitsiista country although well south of where I had contacted them before. We stopped at a few of their villages along the way. They had heard of us, of course, and we were well received. We had met some of the village chiefs at the meeting earlier, and they were most cordial. I decided to name this river for them also, the South Dzitsiista River. We stopped by my coal seam and found the place quite a bevy of activity. A group from the Ordu was working the vein. They told me they had already sent quite a bit back and were holding the rest here since the Ordu would be moving here soon. It was early fall when we arrived back.

14
CONSOLIDATION AND EXPLORING
UP THE MONGOL, 3-4 K
(UP THE MISSOURI RIVER, SD, MT, 1371-2)

When we got back, I immediately showed Henry the ore. He had built a blast furnace, but it wasn't quite right, so I showed him what was wrong. He had done better with the coking oven and had produced some pretty good-looking coke. He had also found limestone some distance upriver, but not very much. We decided to wait until the move downriver to fire up the blast furnace. Meanwhile some of the recruits had shown interest in his work and he was training them. Others among them had shown interest in other skills of the Ordu and were becoming very much integrated. The training of the army had been going very well. Although the recruits didn't look much like Mongols, they rode like Mongols.

The only problems were the kumis and nawak'osis. The locals had never used and had no tolerance for alcohol, they would quickly become intoxicated and some had been injured in falls and fights. The Mongols had never used and had no tolerance for the nawak'osis; many became addicted to it and wasted much time smoking it. The locals felt the Mongols were abusing the nawak'osis and the Mongols made fun of the locals for not being able to hold their kumis. Kaidu had no intention of letting this nonsense ruin all his plans, however. He forbade use of nawak'osis except at meetings and kumis except at celebrations. He also limited the amount of either that would be available. Of course, rules were broken occasionally, but punishment was swift and harsh and without discrimination. I was rather glad I had missed all the excitement.

Juchi finally rode in a few days after I did and we both went to see Kaidu. He had wanted to wait and see us together. Juchi had been able to get some of the Kensistenoug to agree to join up in confederation, but had found out as I had that they extended very far to the east and had a very loose organization. The bands in the western part had agreed to join, but the eastern bands were still not sure, they would let us know. The other tribe that lived between the Kensistenoug and the Dzitsiistas, the Inuna ina, were very much like the Dzitsiistas and had agreed to join in confederacy since they had heard that the latter had joined. His only problem with them was delicately trying to explain how it was we hadn't asked them first. The Yanktonai splinter, who the Kensistenoug called the Asinipoituk, had only agreed to confederate like the Western Kensistenoug, and that reluctantly. They looked just like the Ocheti shakowin but dressed and lived more like the Kensistenoug whom they seemed to emulate.

I reported on my successful mission. The two tribes (the Anishinabe and the Dzitsiistas) had confederated and the other one, the Ocheti shakowin, had joined outright. The Anishinabe had offered to contact two allied tribes in the east and extend our invitation to them. I had found two sources of iron ore, both quite extensive; I had also found copper ore, but no tin. There was also no good coal so far, only the veins of brown coal I had found the previous winter and the hills containing brown coal near our old camp. We had not yet found much limestone either, but I was sure we would around here somewhere. The Anishinabe had agreed to provide us with the iron ore in exchange for iron tools, and had offered to train our men in forest warfare.

Juchi offered that he had seen quite a bit of limestone in the Inuna ina lands and was sure they wouldn't mind sending some. He also strongly urged we take up the Anishinabe on their offer to train us in forest warfare because it looked as though the whole eastern part of the land was forest and Mongols were not used to fighting in the forest.

Kaidu thanked us for our efforts and accomplishments. He agreed that we should hear what the Anishinabe had to say about forest warfare, but felt that we would have to build on it, since it was most unlikely that they would be able to fathom the Mongol scale of warfare. Still, he would send one of his best tacticians to learn from them, and adapt it to our needs. He outlined the accomplishments and problems that had occurred in our absence. He was confident he had handled the problems and was very pleased with the accomplishments. The recruits had managed the more complex Mongol maneuvers with remarkable skill and he was sure we'd be able to march on the Hotcangaras the following fall. The herds had greatly increased and the harvest had been excellent again. Further, many of the recruits had shown interest in learning important skills and had proved quite capable.

Meanwhile, since the Numakiki did not object, we would move downriver to my coal seams within a few days, and then go out for the fall hunt. The latter was quite different now. A herd of the plains oxen was located and then our hunters would come at them from all sides, taking down as many as we needed in a running "battle." Other game would be taken as it presented itself, or someone got the urge to hunt. He urged us to rest up this winter because he wanted us to explore westward in the spring and return by late summer for the fall campaign.

We were both glad we could stay put for the winter but not exactly thrilled at the long trek we'd have next year. The move downriver was fairly smooth. There were no major rivers on the north side of our river, and anyway, all the rivers were low at this time of year. The biggest problem was the steepness of the descents to the rivers from the plains. This required a bit of planning, but since I had already come this way and found the easiest passages for the carts, it was not difficult. The site we chose looked as though it had been settled at some time in the past. There were remnants of postholes and vague outlines of houses just visible on careful study. One of the Numakiki said that it was likely one of their old abandoned villages. We set up camp quickly, and most of the men went out on the fall hunt. I stayed behind to help Henry set up the blast furnace. I was quite anxious to make sure our iron problem was solved and didn't want an oversight to set us back again. Just as we were ready to get it fired up, the rest of Ocheti shakowin started coming into camp. To our surprise, they had a cart full of iron ore with them. The clever Anishinabe had not only mined it all summer long, but had made copies of our carts and brought them to the Ocheti shakowin. The latter had been able to hitch the carts up to horses when their people had ridden back to get them. There would be several more carts along presently.

I congratulated Odinigun on his people's initiative and trust. He reminded me that I had left the iron tools with Gagewin, and he probably felt he was just paying us for them. We got the furnace going, and it worked perfectly. The newly arriving ore was also reduced to iron over the rest of the fall. As Juchi had promised, the Inuna ina brought in a load of limestone, and the coal seams continued to produce. I finally had to blast away some of the over-laying rock with some gunpowder. This created quite a stir in the camp and required quite a bit of explanation. I had been hoarding our gunpowder supply until I located a source of saltpeter, but this really helped the coal mining. I used the occasion to see if anyone was familiar with saltpeter, but while they all thought it looked like salt, they agreed it was quite different and not at all familiar to them. I wasn't surprised, since it only occurred in the hot and humid areas of the old Khanate, and I had learned that it was never found in temperate areas.

Once the iron production was running smoothly, I got down to teaching reading and writing to any takers. Motsoyouf and Odinigun were in the first group along with several of their fellow tribesmen; also a few from each of the other tribes were interested as well. Some did not persist, but most did, and to a few that seemed to have a facility for drawing, I taught mapmaking. Paula and Mathilde helped with teaching, and a few of the native women also learned. Padraig could just barely read, so he confined himself to training the warriors with swords, which were finally becoming available.

Fall slipped into winter and Paula finally told me what had been apparent for a while now, she was pregnant. She had held off saying anything since she was afraid she might miscarry, a problem in her family. The child should arrive before I went west in spring, she assured me. I mentioned her fears to Givevneu, and he gave me some sort of concoction for her to take. He had gotten the formula from one of his local colleagues, and it had worked for another woman in the Ordu. Paula used it, and sure enough, in late winter she presented me with our first-born, a son. I named him George after my favorite grandfather.

Juchi finally married that winter. He had been smitten by a winsome Kensistenoug girl, whose ponderous name was Wahsakapeequay, and had finally persuaded her father to let her go. Kaidu was very pleased that he had married a local girl, and a few other such marriages also took place, not only between the Mongols and the locals but also between the different tribes. It was inevitable, of course, for we were now the minority in our huge camp.

With spring, the herds kidded and foaled again, the plains turned green, the sky was filled with migrating birds, the bottom was cleared and planted after the floods, and Juchi and I got ready to leave. We had decided to return toward our old settlement, now a small permanent mostly Siksika camp. Then, one of us would follow our river upstream, and the other would follow the Absaroke River upstream. We would then come back east and hopefully pick up another river that flowed into our river south of our new camp. My best mapmaking pupils would go with Juchi, and I'd take the others. I charged Odinigun with keeping the iron ore coming and made sure the furnaces were in good shape before I left.

It was almost mid spring when we left. Eight days later, we came to the junction where we would split up. Juchi decided he wanted to explore the Absaroke River, so after cautioning him not to go too far south by the stars and admonishing my apprentice mapmakers to do their best, I continued on to our old camp. We were welcomed profusely, and a couple of the Siksika joined us. For the duration of the trip, they were called by the Mongol names Iron Arrow and Felt Lodge. Both names changed again later on. Wanbli Sapa had come along with me as had Nitsiza. One of the Tsattine had gone with Juchi, as had Motsoyouf, my most promising mapmaker. Woksihi and Mahohivas (both also Dzitsiistas), Shingabaossin, an Anishinabe and Pesaquan, a Kensistenoug were the apprentice mapmakers with me. Doqus' brother Ussu also had joined me. We must have been quite a sight.

We followed our river almost due west from the camp for four days. I had been along this course the year we arrived as far as the first major river. It joined our river from the north, but shortly turned northwest. I had named it the Little Sungari since its tan color reminded me of that much larger river. Our river soon turned south and then more southwest. The river was more channeled and more swift throughout this bend and beyond, it widened and its bottoms were quite extensive and heavily timbered. Occasionally, we would see an island in the river. While the short grasses predominated on the steppe, the land was hardly flat. There were hills, mountains and buttes, some quite high, constantly interrupting the steppe. Game was plentiful and frequently in sight, but rarely in bow shot. There were antelope, plains oxen, deer, and an odd-looking mountain sheep with big curved horns. There were also large colonies of a type of ground rodent. It lived in holes dug in the ground and many stood up on the rim of the holes to act as lookouts scolding whatever approached with what sounded like a small dog's bark. The going was easier along the bottoms because the steppe was getting increasingly rough and broken.

After six days, the river made a steep loop to the south to meet a good-sized river flowing due north, then straightened out and turned due west again. At this point we came in sight of a high hill at the eastern end of a row of hills. Iron Arrow called it Mouyistsi-mokam or Hairy Hat, and said it was a well known lookout point the Siksika used when they hunted in the area. It was covered with evergreens on the top and rather steep and free of trees on the sides. I was surprised to hear that the Siksika ranged this far south. I asked him if he had been here before, but he had only been to the lookout, not down to the river. On the other side of the river, the land looked rather bleak. It was dotted with dark scantily treed buttes. They looked black from this angle or perhaps just dark brown, but I could see lighter sandstone with it also. They were cut with deep ravines that were heavily wooded. I wondered if Juchi was fighting his way through country like that.

We soon found the bottom getting too narrow and sometimes underwater, so we had to scramble back up to the plateau. This slowed us down considerably since there were so many ravines, but it also introduced us to a strange-looking plant. It was composed of flat padlike pieces apparently stuck together at random. The pieces were green, but otherwise there were no leaves or stems. The pieces were also covered with a formidable array of thorns. This strange plant was blooming and had a very pretty, large yellow flower. Felt Lodge said that the plant yielded a very good fruit in the late summer and was also found farther north. It was, as well, a handy source of water. We also found a similar although more cylindrically shaped plant with red or greenish yellow flowers and a small, round-shaped one with light red to purple flowers. I had never seen anything like them in the old Khanate. The grasses were different here as well. The most common one was a fuzzy gray-green pungent-smelling grass that grew in tufts and sometimes looked more like a bush. There were also some blue-green grasses and a green threadlike grass, but the smelly one was most common, and the horses were constantly releasing its aroma for us as we passed.

The land had another surprise for us. The soil was seemingly dry and hard, and then it rained. It wasn't much of a rain, but it turned the ground into a sticky mud, and along the slopes, it was dangerously slippery. We found it best to wait out the rainstorms, which were fortunately infrequent. The wind on the plateau dried the soil out rather quickly, but made the slippery slopes even more dangerous. Four days later, we got another surprise. We climbed up out of another ravine, and far in the distance was a range of snow-capped mountains extending both north and south of our position. They seemed to be blue from this distance and appeared to jut out starkly from the plain, for we couldn't see their base. They were probably the southern extension of the mountains we had traversed far to the north during our memorable trek to our new home. I had the feeling we wouldn't be going across them, but we should at least get to them.

Two days later, we came upon another north-flowing river just after the bottoms opened up again enabling us to go along the riverbank. I decided to cross our river and have a look at the other river, since the former looked fordable here. It was fairly shallow but was also rather swift, and I was more than a little wet when I got to the other side. The north-flowing river proved to be clear, unlike most of the other rivers we had come across, and it had a good-sized tree-covered bottom of its own, so I mapped it for a short distance upstream and named it the Paula River. There were a great many of a small ground bird, a bit larger than a pigeon, of a rather dull coloration. I got back to the others just before dark and dried out from my second dunking by the campfire. The bottom on the north side was wider and deeper and was also cut by a stream that seemed to flow from the northwest. We rested up an extra day at this pleasant site, and a few of the men went hunting.

The next day, the bottoms quickly narrowed, and our river turned northwest just after another river joined it from the south. Shortly before dusk, we came upon a dark cliff about 500 feet high on the north side of the river. This marked the entrance to a strange canyon in which we rarely had much room between the river and the walls. The walls of the canyon were multihued with large horizontal white streaks sometimes interrupted with perpendicular dark streaks. These were eroded into massive, strange, heroic shapes, rounded, pointed or squared. On the second day, we came upon what looked like a stone wall on either side of the river, which, after extending up a few hundred feet, merged into the smooth cliff face. The stones were of varying sizes and shapes but overlapped so as to appear to be intentionally placed. Having seen the Great Wall, I had to admit this one was more impressive. From the looks of the breach the river had made in it, it was no more effective, however. The only game we saw along here was the mountain sheep. Finally, the river opened up into extensive tree-filled bottoms again just before turning generally southwest. At this point, we were again treated to a view of the blue snow-capped mountains ahead. They ran in a line from southeast to northwest and seemed to be in multiple rows as far as I could see. A formidable barrier!

We made particularly good time the next day, following the river southwest along its broad bottoms. Then in the late afternoon, we came upon a junction with another river from the northwest. It was about the same size as our river and was as silty and turbulent and may indeed have appeared more logically to be our river, but we decided to cross it and continue southwest with the clearer, more swift river, since that was the general direction we wished to follow. It turned out that a much-later expedition found the other river was not quite as long or impressive farther upstream. We eventually named it the Tungus River for the tribes that lived north of the Mongols.

The next day, a loop in the river forced us north enough so that we found a small river flowing parallel to our river. It likely flowed into the Tungus. We followed it until it turned north through a pass in the ridge that bounded the broad bottom in the north. We returned to the Mongol. The following afternoon, the bottoms began to narrow again and finally showed signs of becoming another canyon. We camped for the night among the trees near the river. Before dawn, we were awakened by the horses and rose to find them under attack by a huge bear. We quickly fired arrows at him and that drew him angrily toward us. Arrow after arrow found its mark but did not stop the bear as he furiously rushed at one after the other of us. Finally, he seemed to weaken and tried to break off contact, but thinking him too dangerous I pulled my sword and, while Ussu drew his attention, ran him through on his left side. Fortunately, he fell in the act of turning back to me. No less than forty arrows had pierced the bear, some surely mortally, but none had been able to drop him. This was a formidable animal. In the morning light, it appeared to be of immense size with a silvery sheen to its back. The Siksika called it Nitapi Kaiyo, which meant real bear, and they assured me that they had seen bigger ones and recommended we bring along spears next time we want to hunt bear. Measuring the length of the bear's arms and the size of its claws, I decided long spears were called for. Meanwhile, we fashioned rude spears by securely fastening our knives to spear-length poles. This turned out to be a very wise move.

We had barely started out when the horses started to shy away from our path and protest nervously. Hafting our "spears," we dismounted and started forward just as another huge bear charged us. He snapped most of our makeshift spears like twigs but not until they had found their mark, especially Iron Arrow's which resulted in a flood of blood and the fall of the giant. We repaired our "spears" this time using stouter shafts, before continuing. The Siksika insisted on bringing along some of the bear meat assuring us it was quite good. They also took the skins and the claws. The latter were apparently used for decoration.

I decided we had had enough excitement for one day, and we climbed out of the bottoms and onto the plateau above. This made travel easier, albeit drier, for there was no water worth drinking here. We made a few trips back down to the river along the way for water, but camped up on the plateau for safety. The next day before we had gone very far, we could see what looked like a mist in the canyon, and soon we began to hear a dull roar like distant thunder that grew louder as we continued. Near midday we saw it: about two hundred feet below us the river poured over a precipice almost ninety feet high. The spectacular sight held us in awe for some time. Even the locals were impressed. Eventually, we continued our journey, remaining on the plateau. Just before we stopped for the night, we heard again the sound of a waterfall and pressed on to find a smaller drop only about twenty feet and from a rather crooked cliff. As we got closer, we could hear a louder roar and continued on to find yet another waterfall gently curving about a li and a half from bank to bank, falling at least fifty feet straight down and sending billows of foaming mist way down the canyon.

The following morning, we continued on our journey and found two more falls. The first was only a six-foot drop, but the second was at least a thirty-foot drop. Beyond this, the river was at the level of the plateau, and the terrain was hilly but fairly open except for the aspen-lined riverbanks. We seemed to be surrounded by mountains from the east to the northwest. By midmorning, we crossed a river that emptied into our river from the west. The latter had by now turned south only to bend into some lazy turns gradually shifting it to the southwest again. We climbed a higher plateau where we could see and thus avoid all the turns in the river. Two days later, we seemed to be entering the foothills of the mountains, the river was narrower, and the high plateaus were closing in on either side. Late the next day, the river swerved south and just slightly east. The following day, we passed through another hemmed-in area; then the plain opened up again much like it had been above the falls. This area was watered with many creeks, and streams and beavers had dammed up most of them. There seemed to be a remarkable concentration of the creatures here. There was also a sizable herd of the plains oxen in the open country south of the river. The beaver lakes attracted moose, elk and deer. Unfortunately, the bears were also in residence here. We had to set a double watch each night and keep the horses close to us. One night a type of small leopard—or more likely a lynx—was chased off.

The next three days, we followed the river slightly east of south. Our river's banks narrowed again as ever-higher fir- and pine-coated mountains gradually began to hem us in. Still the land sloped gently up from the river to the mountains, which then rose starkly and abruptly. The evergreens probably made them look blue from the distance. The following day, the river seemed to veer to the southwest again, and after some thought, I decided to follow it a little farther. Toward midafternoon, we cleared a small rise, and right before us was a large ring of conical tents open on the east, facing the river. We had also been spotted, but while it caused a commotion, no one moved for his weapons. Felt Lodge said that his people had occasionally come into contact with these dark, stocky people, but he didn't know what they were called. Since they didn't seem hostile, but rather seemed unsurprised by our advent, I decided to go on into their camp.

15

The Western Mountains, 4 K
(The Rockies, MT, ID, WY, SD, ND, 1372)

As we entered the village, the people seemed quite friendly and tried to talk to us. Their language sounded rather nasal and was full of choking or gagging sounds. None of us could make it out. They switched to making gestures with their hands and arms and led us to understand that they wanted us to wait with them until someone came from another camp. They called themselves Ga-i-gwu or Ka-i-gwu, the sound was somewhere between a "g" and a "k." They wore their hair long and used body and face paint sparingly. They wore deerskin and used plains oxen robes when it was cool. They served us something of a feast, followed by the ubiquitous nawak'osis. They again tried to use the signal communication system in combination with their words, but we couldn't quite get what they were saying.

The following day, the one we were waiting for arrived, and everything became clear. He could speak Siksika. It seems that Juchi's group had encountered elements of their tribe some distance to the east and a little south. Juchi had already recruited them and had left one of my mapmakers to guide them east in the late summer. Word had been sent to the mapmaker that we were here, and he would no doubt be on his way to meet us. The whole tribe was planning to join us, so taken were they with the horses. Late in the evening, Pesequan rode into camp. He had been fairly close when he heard we had come and quickly hurried to meet us. Juchi had followed the Absaroke upstream and had run into some villages belonging to a tribe that called itself Na-i-shan-dina. They spoke a language that Japasa, the Tsattine accompanying Juchi, could understand. They told him there were more of their bands to the southeast and a great tribe to the west farther upriver which they called the Beshilt-cha. They would do whatever the Beshiltcha did. Juchi decided to continue along the Absaroke and found the Beshiltcha who proved to be the Ka-i-gwu. They called the Na-i-shan-dina, the Tagui. He brought along one of the latter to act as interpreter through Japasa, a fortunate move since they had a very strange language. He had continued stopping at the main Ka-i-gwu villages along the river up to a large lake, which seemed to be its source.

It seems the Absaroke River's lower half contained huge bottoms with vast herds of game. They had also found coal along one north-flowing river that joined the Absaroke River. The bottoms narrowed about midway into a long canyon, and there were rapids, but then it opened up again for most of the rest of the river until it entered its source mountains to the southeast. The going was quite rough along that part, but the scenery and the lake were beautiful. They had also found hot springs and hot mud and intermittent springs that gushed hot water high into the air at regular intervals. Juchi had decided to continue southwest to a great salt-water lake the Ka-i-gwu had told him about. There were also a couple of tribes along the way for possible recruitment. Pesequan was going to lead the Ka-i-gwu and any others Juchi sent along back up the Absaroke River, since there was so much game, and it was a fairly easy way, except for the bears. I was surprised that they had such an easy run of it, since the land south of our river looked so bleak, but the bears, we knew all about and traded stories. It turned out Juchi had a lot more trouble with them. They had lost a horse and one of the men. Abishabis, a Kensistenoug, was mauled, but not too seriously. That was fortunate—for he was Juchi's brother-in-law. I made a quick copy of Pesequan's map, figuring I could try to reconcile it with mine later.

I decided that it was too soon to turn back east, so we would continue along our river to its source. Pesequan showed us where three rivers join to form ours, and we were told that the westernmost one was the longest. The eastern branch actually joined the main river below where the other two joined. But it and the middle branch drained the same mountains as the Absaroke River. Pesequan stayed with us while we were among the Ka-i-gwu, and the one that spoke Siksika, Guipago, agreed to go with us. He told us that there were

other tribes to the northwest and the west of them, but they were
not often in contact because of the high mountains between them.
I asked if there were any passes through the mountains, and he
said there were, but they were not easy. After a few days of slogging
through the marsh all the beaver dams had made out of our river's
upper reaches, we all agreed a mountain pass sounded interesting.

While it hadn't seemed a steep trek, it was obvious that we
were at a much higher altitude than our Ordu's camp. Not only
were the nights quite chilly for high summer, but also we all tired
more easily. We abandoned our river in a ridgeline and moved west
along a maze of creeks dotted with extensive beaver handiwork,
finally reaching the higher, drier ground leading into the pass. The
pass wasn't particularly difficult, and we found ourselves following
a creek down from the pass into a narrow valley whose river flowed
northwest. We followed it for a while and ran into a group of natives who were returning from a hunt. Guipago went up to them,
spoke to them for a while, and then returned to us. He said that they
were Tagui, not their sometime allies, but a similar people who had
also come from the north and lived in brush lodges along the rivers
and hunted game. He seemed rather contemptuous of them, but I
let it pass. As we drew closer, Nitsiza said that they looked like his
people. He went up to them with me in tow and began speaking to
them in his language. They understood him with some difficulty
and me with even more, but we were able to communicate. They
called themselves Dine instead of Tinneh, and their legends did place
them in the north originally. We explained our mission and, after
looking over our weapons and horses, proclaimed themselves ready
to join. We told them to get their people and follow the Ka-i-gwu
down the Absaroke River in the late summer. We had to explain to
them just where the Absaroke River was, of course.

They urged me to come to their village and speak to their chief.
It took the rest of the day to reach it, and Guipago had a point, the
houses did look like piles of brush. The people were a little taller
than the Ka-i-gwu. They wore their hair long with a leather band
around their forehead, to keep it out of their eyes. They wore no
feathers or other adornments except earrings and dressed simply in

leather. The chief explained that they had no organization beyond the village and his authority was limited. He would send runners to the other nearby villages and tell them of our proposal, but he could make no promises. I thanked him and urged him to send any who were willing to join us down the Absaroke River in the late summer. I made sure he knew which river I meant.

Our trip to the village had led us to a river flowing west through a broad valley. We continued along this river and came upon a few more Dine villages where we repeated our pitch with varying results. Eventually, we came upon a different sort of people. Guipago called them the Grass House people and did not appear to think much of them, either. He did know a little of their language and was able to interpret for us. We were brought before their chief.

Their chief was wearing a headdress of ermine skins, rather crudely put together and wore a necklace of bear claws. Otherwise he looked just like the Ka-i-gwu chief, same clothes, same body and face paint. They also passed around the nawak'osis. Guipago told us that the Grass House People ranged far to the south almost to the Great Salt Lake. They were greatly scattered into small bands like the one we were visiting. I repeated our offer of horses and peace in exchange for confederation, adding that their neighbors, the Ka-i-gwu, would be leaving their old haunts and joining us in the east. The chief was surprised and asked Guipago if it was really true. He confirmed it, of course. Next the chief, whose name was Uriewiki, wanted to know what we meant by confederation. I hated to think how all this was being translated by Guipago. It took quite some time to explain the concept, but it helped when I mentioned that one of my colleagues was even now presenting the same proposal to their fellow tribesmen in the south. He decided he would confer with his fellows and go along with their decision. Meanwhile, he agreed to help us get to another tribe to the north although they were enemies. He fervently hoped I would convince them to go east also.

The next morning, we were presented with Trehero. He would guide us to the enemy. Along the way, we tried to learn each other's language. I discovered that his people call themselves the Nomo, while the more southerly bands call themselves the Newe. We went north up the valley to another larger river, which also flowed north for a while before sharply turning west. We followed this river westward. The going was very rough. We were constantly scrambling up and down tree-covered slopes. The footing was so uncertain that we often had to dismount and lead our horses. Below us, the river we followed was often a churning, foaming rush carving its path through solid rock. Only rarely could we get down to the river. Nights were remarkably cold for summer, and then the days were sometimes quite hot. If it rained toward evening, it would turn to snow after dark, and all would be frozen the next morning. The trees gradually changed from spruce, fir, and pine to all fir, then all pine. The pine was a very fragrant one with an almost copper-colored bark. After a few days of this, we arrived at a different-looking village. There were either conical or pyramidal earth-covered mounds scattered along an open area between a creek leading to the river we were following and the forest carpeting the mountain we had just descended. There was only a scattering of people in the village, and these were startled to see us approach from the woods. Trehero went ahead with his arms outstretched to show he wasn't armed, and we followed slowly a little behind.

The men in the village had fled, but only to come back armed. They hesitated, then listened to Trehero and finally put away their weapons, welcoming us to the village. It seemed the majority of the band was fishing at a temporary settlement on the river since the salmon were running. They sent someone for their chief, who was supervising or participating in the effort. The people wore clothes of deer and rabbit skin, but also used cedar bark. The women wore hats that looked a bit like baskets. I was surprised that none of these fishing people thought to use fish skin for clothes like their counterparts across the Great Sea. The mounds proved to be pit houses. One entered them from the smoke hole on a notched log, which was imbedded in the ground and at a slight angle. The pit was about four feet deep, and the roof was of layers of wood covered with pine needles, grass, and earth. The houses were quite large, easily accommodating a few families.

At length, the chief came in and Trehero acted as interpreter.

The tribe was called the Nimipu, and the chief was named Ollikut. We endured the nawak'osis, and then I presented him with the usual offer of confederation or complete merger, as they wished, in return for our advances and help. He explained that he could only speak for his own band, and, frankly, he wondered how useful the horses were in the mountains. I explained that the horses had gotten us through to him, none the worse for wear, and could prove essential to them should the salmon run fail as it inevitably did on occasion. They would find the horse would greatly improve their hunting success. He agreed that I had a point and for his part would prefer the confederation offer since he didn't want to leave his beautiful mountains. I had my own thoughts about that, but I readily agreed and suggested he contact the other bands and perhaps a number of their young men could accompany me back. He sent out runners to the neighboring villages and suggested that I go with him to a more centrally located village where several of the chiefs might be able to meet me.

The next day, we set out along the river (at least the river was often in view). Ollikut was impressed by the way the horses were able to handle most of the climb, and when one of the men set off after and bagged a deer—he was even more impressed. He was also interested in our iron arrow points, and our long-range bows. Five days later, we arrived at a village near where another smaller river joined the one we were following (I had named the latter the Nimipu River, since they lived along most of it), which turned sharply north. We were shown to a very ample pit house in which there was a large gathering of very dignified-looking men. We were served roast salmon and some sort of cooked tuber, then the nawak'osis was passed around, and finally we got around to talk. They listened to my proposal, faithfully passed on by Trehero. Ollikut then spoke in favor, reminding them of the great hardship they had suffered the last time the salmon run had failed, and telling them about what he had seen of the horses' capabilities. While the young men who accompanied me would be missed during the fishing season, it was also true that they ate the most anyway.

As usual, they all took turns commenting, and Trehero did his best to keep up with the commentary. Most seemed to favor the confederation idea, but a few were puzzled about why we would want to help them, wondering if perhaps it was all a clever trick. I reminded them that if a reasonable number of their young men accompanied us, they would far outnumber us, and if we meant ill, they would surely be able to punish us. We simply wanted to bring peace and security to our new land. Almost all of them were in favor of confederating and urged me to wait a while, and they would send young men from most of the villages. I asked if the Great Sea was nearby, but they said it was still far away, over mountains and dry plains and more mountains. I asked about the people between them and the sea. They said there were some people to the north of them called the Salst, to the west one found their relatives, except that they had pointed heads! That wanted some looking into, but it was late summer, and I couldn't afford to tarry long enough to look in on these people. I asked the Nimipu if they would invite their neighbors to join us, after their young men returned next summer. They readily agreed to do so, if all was as we promised. These people were no fools.

I asked our hosts if there was an easier way south and west than the way we came, and they suggested we ascend along a very large river a little to the west. It drained a large plain in the south, where one could find Trehero's people. First, we would have to cross this river I had named for our hosts. To that end, I looked it over and found it was too deep to ford and too swift to swim. This brought us to their boats. I suppose my experience with the Anishinabe should have given me more faith in the things, and these looked more substantial, being carved out of a whole tree, but they didn't look very stable at all. Still, there was no other way across, so we got our hosts to ferry us across the river two at time with our horses swimming behind, held with long tethers. I figured if they were too close behind and pulled suddenly, the boat would quickly flip over. We made it across safely, and one of the Nimipu told Trehero that I would probably like the boats of the coastal Salst. They were huge and could carry the horses aboard. How was that possible? I wanted to know. It seemed that there were huge trees on the coast because it rained all the time, and the locals carved them into huge boats. It was necessary in any case because they used them on the sea. My informant had no idea if they traded with anyone across the sea, but he did know that they hunted sea creatures. I wondered just how seaworthy these "huge" ships were and was sorely tempted to find out, but it would have to wait for another time.

While we waited for the young volunteers to drift in, I went over to look at the other river we would be following. It took most of the day to reach it. We scrambled up one pine-covered ridge, moved across a saddle to another, and there, far below, was the river. It appeared greenish where it wasn't white. I couldn't see anything that approximated easy going anywhere near this river. Our hosts admitted that the easy part was well up the river, so I asked if there was an easier way to get to the easy part, and they agreed on what would surely be an easier route. They suggested we follow the stream that joined their river just as it turned north. Near its source, it opened up quite a bit, and we could cross the ridgeline to the east and follow the river on the other side of the ridge down a broad valley to the easy part of the other river. They called the other river the Kimooenim, so I kept the name, figuring I couldn't think of anything pleasant to call it at this point.

After a very unpleasant cold night above the Kimooenim, we returned to the Nimipu. The young men were still trickling in. I decided that rather than wait, I'd have a look at the new proposed route, just in case it was even worse. The route was a bit of a scramble up a pine-covered slope, but not bad, and there was even a bit of a waterfall the first day. Late the second day, the canyon did open up into a pleasant valley leading up to something of a plateau. The pines thinned out and grassland took over. That same gray-green pungent grass predominated here. I decided to stay here and sent one of the Nimipu back to guide the others here when they were ready. I also sent along a note to Ussu telling him to move everyone within three days of getting my note. Any stragglers would have to take their chances.

Meanwhile, I decided to look around a bit after resting the horses a day. Pine-covered mountains on the west and south and northeast hemmed in the plateau, but the southeast was still open over a gentle slope. Over the slope, I found a herd of the plains oxen and another river. It was well dammed up by beavers, no doubt making the land near it marshy. The aspens along the river had been thinned out by all the construction or flooded out by its resulting lakes. I could see that the river flowed south, and the plateau seemed to continue in that direction out of sight. For demonstration purposes, I went down and bagged a few of the oxen for the Nimipu. They were very impressed with the ease of the hunt and immediately set to work on the carcasses. There were only about a dozen in my company, so they set up poles to dry out strips of the meat over low fires and prepared the rest for us to eat. They were particularly pleased that I didn't want the skins, and they prepared them for curing also.

I took a couple of the men with me and went over to have another look at the Kimooenim River, for my map. We went back to the western end of the grassland, and then plunged up the slope of a ridgeline. Once across the ridge, there was a moderate slope in which two small rivers drained a wooded valley. They seemed to flow south or southwest. Continuing west, the slope rose a bit, then plunged down dramatically to the still-churning river far below. I looked for a vantage point so I could get a good view of the river and finally had to climb a tree. As far as I could see in both directions, the river flowed through a steep canyon. I decided we had made the right choice after all. We spent the night in the more sheltered valley, and while cold, it wasn't as windy. The next day, we moved south along the valley, swerving east to avoid another deep canyon made by a smaller river and finally climbed up another slope. At the top of the slope, I could see a large stretch of grassland to the south, but I knew it wasn't the one where I had left the rest of the men, for that was farther east. We descended to the plateau and moved eastward across it to another ridgeline, crossing it at a pass carved out by a small stream. We camped on the plain on the other side and the next day returned northward to our camp.

We got several more of the oxen and one of the bears, and just as the last of the meat had been dried, Ussu came up with the rest of the men and the volunteers. There were at least three hundred of the latter. A small group of them was from the Salst tribe, which had been trading with the Nimipu, when word came of our offer. They came along to see if there was anything to it and were very impressed by the horses. We bagged a few more of the oxen so everyone would have a good meal before we started out. The next day, we started south. On the third day, the valley narrowed into a canyon, but we managed to scramble along it for the rest of that day and most of the next until we stumbled out into the plain again. Actually, the plain sloped gently down to a midsized aspen-lined river along which we could see a settlement of the Nomo. I sent Trehero ahead to reassure them about our intentions, for we surely looked like a very serious Nimipu raiding party.

We were received nervously, but they had heard by now of our offer, and some of their young men were getting ready to go east with the Ka-i-gwu in the late summer. Perhaps some would want to accompany us instead. I was not at all loathe, but did not want to wait around, so I told them we would be following the Kimooenim upstream and any recruits could join us along its banks. They had their own name for it, of course, and they said it was about a day's walk to the south. We had arrived at the village late in the day, so I sent some of the men to bring in some game, since we were, after all, among "confederates," and it wouldn't do to eat all their food. The men bagged a good number of the ubiquitous oxen, making quite a feast for our hosts. This was politic since my entourage outnumbered the village.

We crossed the river (which I named the Nomo River) in the morning and, joined by a handful of their men moved south, reached the Kimooenim late in the day near a waterfall. We followed the river upstream moving first southeast, then east, then south, then east, then north, east again, and finally northeast. The country around the river reminded me of the upper reaches of our Mongol River. The banks sloped up either gently or dramatically to a higher plain, dotted sparingly with buttes of varying sizes and shapes. On both sides we could see tree-covered mountains in the distance. Once we turned north, the mountains were much closer on the south side of the river. Besides the grayish green grass, which was more like a shrub here, there was also a blue-green grass that grew in tufts and occasionally there would be a few flowers, generally white, yellow, or blue in color. We also encountered some forbs and other brush. About midway on the course of this river, we came upon a truly spectacular waterfall. The major fall was over two hundred feet, and there were also smaller falls leading to the main one. The Nomo called them Pah-Chu-Laka, which meant something like "thrown waters leaping." I hadn't been naming waterfalls, but I went ahead and put their name down for it, in part to make up for using the Nimipu name for a river that was obviously just as much theirs. We were joined by small groups of men almost every day along the way. While everyone had brought along enough dried fish for a month's journey, I always had a few outriders on our northern flank looking for game. They were usually successful, bringing in oxen, deer, or antelope almost every day. We followed the river upstream about twelve hundred li over eighteen days, passing first Nomo and then Dine villages.

Above another falls, the river turned east and disappeared into the mountains. We left it and moved northeast into the hills and out of the grassland. At least the forest wasn't all pine as it had been in the west. Here there were mostly fir trees with spruce, hemlock, and larch to keep it interesting. Trehero was leading us to a pass through the mountains south of the Absaroke River, so we wouldn't be going back along ground already covered by Juchi. Two days after leaving the river, we turned sharply east, then southeast along a wooded valley. The second day, we found ourselves climbing up across a saddle between two mountains and on the other side descended to a large patch of grassland totally surrounded by mountains. Cutting through the plain was a wide, island-filled river flowing south. Our guides insisted it was the very Kimooenim we had left four days before. We had taken a short cut. I tried to get an idea from them how I could connect the two river segments on my map, but I couldn't vouch for that segment until many years later. We followed the river upstream, past a line of very high mountains all with rugged snow-covered peaks, reaching its apparent source, a fair-sized lake dotted with a few tree-covered islands and teeming with waterfowl, the next day. To the west of the lake, the shore was covered with trees going partway up the lower slopes of the line of high mountains. The slopes were quite steep, and in fact the mountains seemed to rise very steeply from the plain. To the east, the mountains were lower, snowless and thinly treed, except for bare patches on the highest ones. The Nomo called the western range Teewinot, which meant something like "mountain with many peaks." They considered this area the top of the world. I thought it would be impolite to tell them about the very high land west of the old Khanate. Besides, I had never been there, so I couldn't be certain it was any higher. In any case, this was a beautiful spot, and I have never forgotten it. Also, the hunting was quite good in the little plain, mostly elk, oxen, and antelopes. Still, I imagined (as I later confirmed) winter would be quite long and very cold on that high plain.

Here we came to the need to make a choice. I emphasized the need to stay near water, but my guides were of two minds. One group wanted to turn east and follow a river southeast, then swing north and follow one of the tributaries of the Absaroke River to the latter to get back to the Mongol. They admitted they had never been that way but had heard about it. The other group wanted to go north to the lake that was the source of the Absaroke, pick up a river that rises in the hills east of it and follow it to the same spot in half the time, without making a long trek through a semidesert with rarely enough water this time of year and most of that bad. They also had never been their way. To save everyone's face, I asked if all agreed that the second way was shorter. They did, so I opted for that route.

We went around to the north side of the lake and continued upstream along a river that emptied into it. At one point, there was steam rising from the river and on looking into it, there seemed to be a hot spring emptying into it somewhere. The whole river wasn't hot, just this one part. The river split to pass on both sides of a small hill, so we took the northern end, which turned out to drain a fairly high mountain. We crossed it and continued around the foot of the mountain, crossing another river, and coming up to the shores of a small lake. This deflected us eastward, across yet another river and through a small pass between two hills. Once through the pass, we could see a spur of a very large lake to the north. I went up a hill for a better look and could see that it was indeed a good-sized lake also dotted with a few islands and teeming with waterfowl, like its counterpart three days to the south. We went around the southern end and camped midway up its eastern shore.

The next day, I sent most of the men out to hunt waterfowl, and, while our Nomo "guides" looked for the pass we were supposed to follow east, I went around the lake to look at the Yellow Canyon Pesequan had told me about. It would also give me a chance to make sure his map and mine meshed. I wanted to get back by evening, so I took a few horses with me and hurried along around the lakeshore. There were a few small clear spaces, but mostly the terrain was open wood consisting primarily of fir trees. All around were rugged bare or snow-capped mountain peaks, with trees covering the lower slopes. Quite a few streams flowed into the lake, but I only found one that flowed out of the lake. It was on the north shore, and Pesequan had done a good job of indicating it. His rendering of the east shore of the lake was not very accurate, but that was because he had passed along the west shore and it was a big lake. There was a fair amount of steam or mist visible beyond the western shore of the lake, no doubt the hot springs Pesequan had mentioned, and that might also have made his mapping more difficult. I followed the river downstream to the northwest. A steaming creek among others joined it. I could hear the falls before I could see them, and as I turned eastward with the river, I could see the mist rising. I moved along the rim of the canyon for a better look. It was an impressive sight, the falls dropped at least a hundred feet into the canyon, but the canyon walls were not yellow. As I went farther along the rim, I heard another roar from a waterfall. Continuing along, I found the highest falls I had ever seen. The drop was at least three hundred feet into a long deep canyon. This time the canyon walls did look yellow, especially in the sunlight. It was quite rugged here; Juchi's party must have had quite a climb up to this level. The yellow was from sulphur, whose smell was noticeable in this area. It was past midday, so I couldn't tarry and enjoy the sight. I collected some of the sulfur, then hurried back arriving at camp late in the day to a feast of waterfowl. The "guides" had returned and were certain they had found the right path.

We set out early, quickly climbed the low hills east of the lake, and soon picked up a small stream. It led us to a small river, which was, indeed, flowing east. Two days later, we were descending out of the trees into another plain covered with the gray-green pungent grass. Soon, the river we were following was joined by another river from the south, and then after passing between two buttes it turned generally northeast. We followed it through increasingly arid land for three days. Along this difficult stretch, the pungent grass gave way to scrub especially a particularly offensive-smelling one with small spiky leaves. The river became increasingly less potable as alkaline streams joined it. There were also quite a few dry streambeds, and almost no game, just a few antelope. On the third day, we came upon large north-flowing river, which while an improvement on the one we had been following, was also quite silty. On crossing it we could see more clear streams were joining it from the east. They were draining a pleasant-looking row of mountains.

I didn't want to go back north to the Absaroke River since it would take me out of the way, so I decided to continue east and try to pick up another east-flowing river to lead us to the Mongol. I had marked the mouths of many rivers that emptied into it from the west and was sure I could find one of them. The hunting was better on this side of the river, so we camped for a day along a clear stream and bagged a fair number of the oxen so everyone could eat their fill for a change. The next day, I decided to send one of my mapmaker apprentices, Shingabaossin, to follow the river we had just crossed north to the Absaroke River so we would have a better picture of this country. I sent about fifty of the Nimipu with him along with both of the Siksika, Iron Arrow and Felt Lodge, so they could get back home and help with hunting along the way. The rest of us moved east into the mountains. We crossed the mountains in two days. They were covered with spruce, fir, and pine, and were rocky and rough, but pleasantly cool and full of clear clean streams.

We left the mountains and found ourselves back on the butte-dotted prairie, much like we had found along the Mongol far to the north. Small rivers and streams flowed in all directions, but the only river we found flowed north. I sent another of my apprentices, Mahohivas, the Dzitsiista, along this river to map it. Again I sent some of the volunteers and two horsemen with him. The plains were full of the oxen, so I was sure they wouldn't go hungry. Three days later, we came upon a strange-looking butte rising starkly out of the plain. It looked like it was made of columns of stone packed together. It rose from an elevated platform at least a thousand feet in the air, and we had been seeing it for some time as we approached it. We camped below it for the night, and while the men were hunting, I tried to climb the east side for a look. I couldn't get very high up, but I did get a good view, and I saw a river that did seem to flow generally northeast. The river was not far from the base of the butte, so I called it the Column Tower River. We followed the river northeast for a day, and then it swung a little south of east passing north of a little row of mountains separated from a much larger range of mountains by a narrow patch of grassland. The mountains were covered with a dark green tall pine tree making them appear almost black from a distance. Here we found some villages of Juchi's Na-i-shan-dina. They had heard about us from their relations along the Absaroke and were breaking up their villages to move to join us. I invited them to come with us. Next, we came upon some almost empty Numakiki villages. They had also heard about us from their relatives along the Mongol and most had already moved east to join us. The few stragglers came along with us.

The Column Tower River led us generally southeast for five days before joining a larger northeast-flowing river that seemed to drain the black-looking hills. This river proved to be the South Numakiki, which finally led us to the Mongol River some three days later. This passage took us through a steppe grassland just like on the eastern side of the Mongol. We swam or waded across the low and sluggish Mongol and continued up the east bank past empty Numakiki towns to the Ordu, reaching it four days later. The camp was huge, with the hide tents and earthen lodges surrounding the felt yurts for some distance. The volunteers were clearly struck by the sight,

as well as the huge formations of horsemen performing maneuvers
on the plains east of the Ordu. When I reached camp, I learned that
I was the first one back, but others had been reported approaching
from the north, my mapmakers, no doubt, but still no word from
Juchi. I was a little concerned for him since his return passage was
south of mine, and it was said to be much drier there, but then he
wouldn't be encumbered by all the volunteers I had, so he shouldn't
have too much trouble. I went to report to Kaidu.

16

THE FIRST HOTCANGARA CAMPAIGN, 5 K
(CAMPAIGN AGAINST THE "CHIWERE" SIOUX,
MO, IO, 1373)

Kaidu was very pleased with my report and the new recruits. He would have to assign some of the men to remain behind to train them while we were on campaign. Looking over my maps, he was surprised at the size of the Mongol River and intrigued at the size of the land. He, too, wondered if the pointed-headed Salst traded across the Great Sea. He doubted it, since he had never heard of any pointed-headed traders from across the sea all the time he was in the old land, but it would be interesting to know if it was even possible in their boats. Meanwhile, all had gone very well in my absence. The army was fully trained and ready to go. He had sent Donduk, his second in command, and a group of soldiers to the Anishinabe to learn forest warfare according to their practice. More warriors from the confederated tribes had come in for training. Game seemed to be endless, and the herds thrived on the steppe. Henry had more iron ore than he could use and had about a dozen apprentices he was training. Kaidu thanked me again and wanted to see Juchi the moment he got back into camp.

My son had grown in my absence and had already been riding with Paula. She was radiant in motherhood. Henry was very busy and very happy. The furnaces were in good shape. More coal had been found across the river. There was much excitement about the camp over the upcoming campaign. Padraig was particularly pleased with his sword students, and Kaidu had put him in charge of a minghan, quite an honor. I worked on my maps, played with George, and watched for Juchi. The first of my mapmakers to come in was Shingabaossin. He came in the day after I did. He had reached the Absaroke River six days after leaving us. He had been

delayed going through a rough canyon, but after that the land had
been pleasant and full of game. The wide bottoms of the Absaroke
River particularly impressed him. He found Juchi's Na-i-shan-dina
at the junction of his river and the Absaroke and had named it
for them since Juchi's expedition hadn't named it. Two days later,
Mahohivas rolled in. His river had made a wide arc, first turning
northeast, then northwest. It turned out to be the river with coal
along its lower reaches, which Juchi had called the Coal River. He
was very enthusiastic about the river, it had been an easy trek, and
they had eaten well.

Finally, three days later, just when I had decided to go look for
Juchi, he was seen approaching from the south. Greatly relieved, I
went out to meet him. He was glad to see me and relieved to be
back. We compared notes on the way into camp. He had seen the
salt lake, and there were Newe villages all around it. He had made
a little headway with them—at least they agreed to send some more
observers. South of the lake he found an aggressive, rough-look-
ing tribe. They had quickly grasped the potential of the horse and
joined en masse. They were called the Ute and spoke a language
similar to that of the Newe. He sent them to join the Ka-i-gwu
and the others up the Absaroke Valley, since he knew it was an easy
path. The area around the lake was very dry and water became a
real problem forcing him to go out of his way to stay along rivers
and streams. The country was very rough, and game was quite
scarce along the way. He constantly found himself in steep winding
canyons, especially along a river that flowed south into the river he
finally followed upstream back east. This last river was surrounded
by a steep breathtaking canyon, which extended far to the west. He
also found another tribe in its shadow, the Hopitu-shinumu. They
spoke a language enough like that of the Newe and the Utes that he
could just barely communicate through them. They were not at all
interested in joining us and only wanted to be left in peace. They
raised vegetables and mondamin like the forest tribes, but also raised
cotton. It was a type of cotton with longer fibers than that in the
old land, and Juchi brought some back with him to show us. One
of the Hopitu-shinumu, Talaswaima, came with him as a guide and

stayed. He followed this river, which he had named the Hopitu, northeast ever uphill through seemingly endless canyons of varying depths lined with either tenuous toeholds or broad bottoms to its source in a ridge with high snow-capped mountains. After a short rest, they plunged over the mountain range finally descending to the plain along a river that flowed northeast.

This river he had followed many days to reach the Mongol. The river was joined by another from the northwest and became very broad and shallow, with many channels and sandbars, sparsely lined with trees but full of waterfowl, including a white crane like the one back in our old land. A few days after the merger of the rivers, he found yet another tribe. It seemed the tribe was related to the Tanish we had run into along the Mongol two years before. They had heard about us from their relatives last year and had already sent observers. They were called Chahiksichahiks . The river was named for them since they ranged all along it. Woksihi showed me his maps while Juchi reported to Kaidu, and I worked on a reconciliation with my maps for much of the rest of the day.

Finally, two days later, Kaidu called a meeting of the commanders. He announced that we would march the next morning. Because of our recruits we now had three tumen (of ten thousand men each), and would soon have the makings of a fourth. He wanted to take all three, so we would only be able to take three horses each. No matter, though, for food and fodder were both plentiful all along our path. We would send scouts out in advance to locate the first Hotcangara village along our river. We would surround the village and demand its surrender. If they refused, they would be annihilated. Two of the commanders were assigned to remain behind to run the Ordu and help train the new recruits. Juchi and I would be in Kaidu's entourage since we had not trained with the troops in some time.

Near dawn the next day, the Mongol army assembled. Each tumen was assigned a banner made of feathers from a raptor. From now on they would be known as the Eagle, Hawk, and Owl Tumen. The commanders were given a special headdress made from the appropriate feathers. Each minghan commander (of one thousand) got a smaller headdress and the jagun commanders (of one hundred) an even smaller one. The arban commanders (of ten) got two feathers, and each of the soldiers got one feather to wear on their helmets. Kaidu rode before the troops. He had an elaborate headdress made of eagle feathers and wore a cloak made from the hide of a white plains ox. The men began to cheer and beat their swords on their shields. I was amazed; he had truly achieved a melding of Mongol and local tribal customs. He stopped in the middle, turned, and started to ride south. As a man the whole army moved with him. I was told later that while Kaidu wanted all the tribes represented in each of the Ordu, he had to make an exception for the Inuna-ina. They considered the owl an unlucky bird.

For twenty days, we moved steadily covering about a hundred li a day. We only stopped for a day when we reached the end of Tanish lands. Scouts were sent out on both sides of the river to find the first Hotcangara village. The next morning, we started up again, moving along the north bank at a slightly slower speed. On the second day, the scouts began coming in. The nearest village was on the southern bank of the river within a day's ride. The army crossed the river and continued on for the rest of the day. That night there were no fires in camp, and sentries were posted up to three li away. The next day, precise marching orders were given to bring all three tumen to the village from three sides at the same time. The Owl Tumen had the longest march, but since the village was only nine li away, we would all be in position by late morning, when the Hotcangara would be harvesting in their fields.

The surprise was complete. The first sound they heard was the horses hooves, looking up they saw thousands of horsemen silently riding toward them through their fields, out of the surrounding hills and up from the riverbank. In terror they fled to their village only to find they were surrounded and still the horsemen rode on. The commotion, panic, and despair must have been truly frightening. Then as a man the army stopped. The screaming stopped, and those who dared, looked. One of our soldiers, Wanbli Sapa, of course, went forward to deliver the ultimatum. Obviously, they didn't have a chance, and they knew it. They were so relieved to have a choice that they almost happily surrendered. I wondered what Kaidu was going to do with over a thousand prisoners, and I soon found out. First they had to feed us. Next they had to show us where their other villages were. Any treachery and they would be annihilated. If they cooperated, who knew?

That little piece of hope was enough to send them scurrying to do our bidding. Since they had surrendered, the army was not allowed to abuse them, but they still fawned all over us. The next day, we left them to continue their harvest until our return and went on to the next village, which was some distance to the south. Here the scene was repeated with the same result. We continued taking a village a day until the sixth day. As we approached that next village there was no sound. Assuming a trap, we sent in one of the Hotcangara guides, but he returned to announce that the village was deserted. Again we sent our own scouts out, and they reported that the next several villages were deserted, but they eventually discovered that there was a large concentration of Hotcangara warriors marching toward us about two days' distance to the east near the southern bank of the Mongol. Kaidu was pleased: at last, a battle!

The enemy was scouted out and found to be advancing steadily but not very quickly. There seemed to be about twenty thousand warriors armed with their primitive bows and war clubs. We checked out the terrain and set our trap. There were forests of oak and a strange tree something like a wing nut, all along this part of the river that had been only partially cleared for fields. That meant there were extensive clearings punctuated with smaller or larger forests. The land was hilly with deep river and streambeds affording ample opportunity for concealment. As the lead elements of the fiercely painted Hotcangara cleared a small hill, they saw across an open field before them a small force of our horsemen. They yelled and rushed. The horsemen stood their ground, fired off a few arrows, then rode away toward the west at an easy pace. The Hotcangara rushed after them in headlong pursuit. Meanwhile, we had been looking for the rear of the force and finally found it some twelve li from the front just struggling out of a stand of trees. Forming a broad U around their straggling rear, the Hawk Tumen began to fire into their rear and flanks at range forcing them to rush forward to get away. By this time, the forward elements of the Hotcangara had "chased" our troops across a wide plain. Suddenly, the troops turned, and over a hill to the south, the Eagle Tumen and, up from the riverbank in the north, the Owl Tumen appeared, forming another U. Arrows began to rain on the dismayed and by now tired Hotcangara. A few rushed their tormentors and some tried to find cover but most turned and ran back along the only open corridor, east. The two "U's" channeled the Hotcangara into the trap finally meeting to surround a milling mass of panicking, despairing, and frantic Hotcangara in a huge clearing. They would rush first one side of the circle, be driven back, rush another side, and again fall short, and all the while, arrows rained down on them. Finally, they stopped charging and we ceased firing.

There were perhaps several hundred of them left alive and many of them were wounded. Again Wanbli Sapa moved toward them to see if they had had enough. They were exhausted, frightened, and totally defeated. There was no fight left in them. Some had fought bravely and many had not, but they had been badly led right into a trap. Some had managed to escape to the river before the trap had closed, but the majority littered the battlefield. We had lost no one, but had a few wounded. The men had performed all our maneuvers flawlessly and had shown great discipline. Kaidu was very proud of them. He was disgusted with the defeated enemy, however. He considered them unworthy foes for his army. He had the prisoners disarmed and dismissed, not allowing us to treat their wounds. We spent the rest of the day picking up our arrows. We had a good supply, but we didn't want them coming back at us.

Again the scouts were sent out, while the army continued east. They rejoined us to report that all the Hotcangara villages along the southern bank of the Mongol were deserted, those farther back from the river were also deserted. They had seen some of them fleeing across the Missi Sipi in great numbers. Kaidu ordered the army to cross over to the north side of the Mongol. The scouts went ahead as usual. One soon came back badly wounded. The Owl Tumen was sent north along the west bank of the Missi Sipi, the Eagle Tumen spread out west along the north bank of the Mongol, and the

Hawk Tumen was sent on a long sweep west of the Eagles. When the Owls and Eagles were in position, they began to move in a wedge northwest, away from the juncture of the two rivers. The terrain was much like that south of the river, open fields alternating with varying sizes of forests over rolling hills broken by streambeds and punctuated with deserted villages. More scouts came in and reported a large concentration of warriors lying in wait along a riverbank in the north, about thirty li from our lines. Smaller groups were watching for us along the way.

Kaidu ordered the wedge to be rolled up with the Owls replacing the Eagles along about half the front and gradually forming a double line with their right flank along the Missi Sipi. The Eagles formed a double line to their left. More scouts came in and reported that the concentration of warriors was heavy, but limited and our lines already overlapped it. Kaidu sent word to the Hawks to put themselves in the rear of the enemy, making use of whatever cover was available, and to attack them from across the river as soon as they were in position. The rest of the troop moved forward at a steady pace. As we went we would occasionally see a man jump out of cover and run madly north. We stopped within bowshot of the riverbank, behind which they were massed, and waited. I was certain they would start to shoot at us and thus give themselves away, but they maintained remarkable discipline, and no sound came from the riverbank. Soon I began to think they had fled, but events proved that wrong also. The trees had been cleared in this area, and there were at least two villages in sight among extensive, mostly harvested fields.

Suddenly, the far bank of the river was alive with the Hawks. They soon began firing on the massed enemy across the river from them. Odd screams and war cries emanated from the Hotcangara and in confusion some climbed up the embankment and rushed our position. Others tried to rush the Hawks across the river; still others ran to their boats and tried to flee. All those that rushed us were quickly cut down, and we advanced to the embankment. Those that tried to cross the river were mostly cut down in route; only a few managed to reach the other side and be cut down there. Those that fled in boats had the best chance although many of them were also hit. A few of them managed to get off some shots, and some of our men were hit, a few seriously. This time Kaidu was more impressed by the enemy. As he put it, they had shown some cunning and bravely tried to ambush us even though they were badly outnumbered and clearly outarmed .

Among the Hotcangara wounded was one of their war chiefs. He was patched up and brought before Kaidu. Wakinyan Cetan acted as interpreter. Kaidu told him that he would be sent back to his people along with the other wounded, but this would be the last time. He was to tell his people that they must either surrender or die. We would return the following year, and if we met any hostility from them, we would annihilate them all. This year we would be content with clearing this side of the Missi Sipi. This chief, Tayhah nea, looked at Kaidu with a mixture of shame and hate. He angrily replied that he was no messenger, especially for dogs like us. Kaidu laughed at his bravado, but warned him not to press his patience. He was brave and deserved one more chance, but only one more chance. Kaidu's eyes narrowed and gave Tayhah nea a truly brutal look. The latter backed down and agreed to take the message. He was put in one of his boats and disappeared down the river. The rest of the prisoners were released with the same warning; If any of them dared attack us again, they and their village would be destroyed. They fanned out in several directions except for a handful that wanted to join us. I had no idea what Kaidu would do about them, and he surprised me by telling them to return to their villages and get their whole villages to join us and then they would be accepted.

We rested a couple of days and gathered our arrows while our scouts looked in vain for any sign of further hostility. Then we moved out westward along the northern bank of the Mongol back to the Ordu. We encountered a few villages along the way, and all were either abandoned or obsequious, bringing us basketsful of their vegetables. The presents were accepted, but Kaidu's ultimatum was repeated to them. Whole villages could join us the following year; any hostility would be severely punished. Almost all of them wanted to join and were disappointed that they had to wait. It was obvious that Kaidu didn't trust them and wouldn't until things had been resolved with the whole tribe. In fact, they were not really a united tribe but rather, a very loosely connected group of towns and villages. As it turned out, only the ones nearest to the Ocheti shakowin even called themselves Hotcangara (others called themselves Iyakhwa, Watota and Niotachi), but we continued using the name for all of them for convenience. It was only fear of us and some of their more fiery war chiefs that had caused them to unite against us.

On the third day after our return, Kaidu called Juchi and me in to see him. He said we were quite fortunate to have done so well. While the men performed flawlessly, it was the poor tactics of our enemy that had made our fight so one-sided. They had made the mistake of fighting us in the open when close at hand there were forests of oak and other hardwoods that would have given them cover and inhibited our movements. Surely they would realize that soon and become a more effective foe. That was why he had decided to try to win them over instead. We were invincible on the open plain, but in the forest, we could have trouble. He was very grateful that we had urged him to take up the Anishinabe on their generous offer to train us in forest warfare and was anxious to hear what Donduk had learned. Meanwhile, he was glad we had gotten so many recruits and hoped we would find more next year. Yes, he was sending us out again in the spring. He wanted Juchi to explore eastward beyond the Anishinabe, and he wanted me to explore southward along the plain, beyond where the Mongol turned east. The Hotcangara were by far the most numerous tribe we had yet encountered, and those farther south might well be even larger. It was quite prudent, therefore, for us to increase our numbers as soon as possible.

He was going to set up the three tumen as Ordu in separate camps. One would be left at our current camp, another would be across from the mouth of the river that Juchi had followed back this summer (the Chahicks) and the third would be at the point where the river turned east in Hotcangara territory. These would be set up on the way back. He would leave the Owls at the bend under his eldest son, Kuyuk, Juchi's father. He and the Eagles under his youngest son, Tului, would take the middle position, and the Hawks under Mangku, his second son, would stay in the old camp.

The recruits and the training would be done at the middle camp. Juchi and I would also stay there. My brother Henry would stay at the old camp with the smelter, until he could locate closer to the source of his ore. Meanwhile, as soon as his apprentices were ready, they should set up in the other Ordu. Further, he wanted any of my mapmakers not needed by Juchi and me to fan out next spring and fill in some of the blanks on our maps. He hoped I would get a few more mapmaker trainees this winter. The two new camps would be set up before the great fall hunt. Finally, he wanted to set up a yam system between the camps, but felt that they would be too vulnerable to attack at this time, since there were still undisturbed Hotcangara villages well north of the Mongol, but once all the Hotcangara were dealt with, it would be a very good idea. For the short term, the camps would only be a hard four-day ride apart.

So it was that riders were sent to get the appropriate yurts and tents moving south from the old camp and we left the Owls behind to set up camp at the bend and continued on to the site for the middle camp. I went on to the old camp to get Paula and give the furnaces a final check. Padraig was in the Eagle Ordu, so he would still be with us, and he accompanied me back to help. On the way we ran into the caravan of carts, herds, and men moving south. Some of the recruits that had accompanied me east the past summer were among them and greeted me enthusiastically. Paula and Mathilde had everything packed and loaded on carts by the time we arrived. I checked out the furnaces, told Henry what Kaidu wanted him to do, bid him and his family goodbye, and we headed south for the Eagle Ordu. We arrived and set up our yurt, and then Padraig and I joined the fall hunt.

The fall and winter passed pleasantly. I gave reading, writing, and cartography lessons, took George and Paula for rides on horses in the fall and on the sled in the winter. The recruits in camp were trained and the permanent ones, the Ka-i-gwu, the Dine, and the Utes were incorporated into a fourth tumen along with some of the earlier recruits. It was called the Falcon Tumen and was put under the command of Borgurchi, one of Kaidu's best commanders. Donduk had returned and was in the process of passing on what he had learned from the Anishinabe to the unit commanders. Kaidu had decided to try to get enough recruits from the forest tribes to form a tumen of forest soldiers, with a Mongol cadre among them, under the command of Donduk. Some of the men who had distinguished themselves on the recent campaign were promoted and given leadership positions in the new squadrons. Among these were both Wanbli Sapa and Wakinyan Cetan.

More people from the confederated tribes kept trickling in to stay, not just to train and leave. This was especially true of the Siksika, the Dzitsiistas, and the Kensistenoug, but even some of the Anishinabe and their allies decided to stay with us. From all these, Kaidu was able to fashion not only a forest tumen, the Kestrels, but a fifth plains tumen, the Cranes. Also a second forest tumen, the Ospreys was being organized late in the winter. The forest tumen would only have one horse each while eventually the plains tumen would have five. Of course, our herds were not quite that large yet, but they were thriving and multiplying in this ideal environment.

The people in our new land were much given to ornamentation, and they were quite imaginative. It was remarkable what they could do with something as humble as porcupine quills. They would dye them different colors and sew them into geometric designs on clothes. They were very interested in some of the ornaments of the Mongols, especially the gold ones. There was no gold around here, so far, but Henry had shown his apprentices how to work the copper I had brought back, and there was great demand for copper copies of the gold ornaments. And before long, the more creative of the apprentices were making ornaments of their own design, some very intriguing. I made a note to look for gold and silver on my journeys, since it would no doubt be put to good use. I was never much for ornaments, myself, but Paula liked them and so did Mathilde and Padraig. Another thing that had become quite clear was that there was no sign of silk anywhere. We Mongols had a limited amount of it, of course, but it would not last forever, and we had come to depend on it. There was some interest in it among our recruits, but we could hardly share our supply with them. It became obvious that we would have to try to get more from the old land unless we could find it farther south. I wondered if that was why Kaidu was sending me south in the spring rather than west again.

17
EXPLORING SOUTH, 6K
(THE CADDO TRIBES, KS, OK, 1374)

With the coming of spring, it was time for Juchi and me to get ready our separate expeditions. Among my cartography students, were a Nimipu and a Salst, Kulkulstuhah and Tahhachet, respectively. Since they had to return to their tribes to report anyway, I prevailed on them to follow the Mongol upstream until it turned south and map their way along one of its tributaries and on back to their homes. They both agreed, pleased that I had such confidence in them. They were both determined to return with more recruits in the fall, and I urged them to fill in some of my blank spots on their return. Trehero, my Nomo guide, had also shown some talent for mapmaking and had agreed to return home along the more southerly route through the drier country, which we had avoided the year before. He also said that he'd be back in the fall and promised to look for new way back. Shingabaossin and Pesequan would accompany Juchi, the former all the way and the latter would map the northern shore of Lake Gichigami and as much else in that area as time permitted. Mehkwasskwan, my best pupil and a Kensistenoug, would finish mapping the river that emptied into Lake Winnipeg and would continue on to map the areas around the lake. Mahohivas would spend the summer mapping the other tributaries of the Absaroke River. Woksihi would go back up the Chahicks River Juchi had followed the year before, map the northern tributary, and try to follow another river back to the Mongol. Of my other students, two Inuna-ina, Watang'a and Desthewa, and Anawangmani, an Ocheti shakowin, would accompany Juchi and fan out as soon as Shingabaossin felt they were ready. Ahmukikini my first Siksika student, Chiwat, a Dine, and Pakonkya, a Ka-i-gwu, would stay with me.

A few soldiers would also accompany each of us; I took along a few Ocheti shakowin and Juchi a few Anishinabe. Talaswaima, the Hopitu-shinumu, wanted to come with me, and Kai Otokan, a Siksika, wanted to go with Juchi. I picked up a few others in the Owl Ordu, including Hishkowits, who had decided to join us. We both set out in mid spring, again admonished by Kaidu to return in time for the fall campaign. My group moved easily down to the Owl Ordu giving the ice a chance to clear the river. The river was still swift and deep, so we crossed on the round hide boats of the Numakiki (many of whom had moved to the Owl Ordu) much as we had crossed the Kimooenim the year before. I decided that the Anishinabe boats were better than these or those of the Nimipu. Once across the Mongol, we moved a little west to return to the plain, as there was an almost continuous forest in that spot. To that end we followed upstream a good-sized river (I named the Owl River, in honor of the nearby Ordu) that joined the Mongol just above where we crossed. It seemed to be bordered by forested bottoms, so we went up the slope and came out on a more open country with scattered stands of trees. We turned a little west of south. We passed a couple of abandoned Hotcangara villages in clearings along this river.

On the second day, we crossed a small tree-lined river that flowed southeast. Two days later, we came upon larger tree-lined river, but this one had been largely cleared on both banks a little distance upstream from us, and on the plain above the cleared river bottom, we could see what looked like a Hotcangara village. The houses, however, looked more like the earth lodges of the Dzitsiistas or the Nimipu, although I couldn't see them clearly enough from this angle. Using the trees to screen our approach, we got closer for a better look. We could just see some of the people on the far side of the river. The men wore only breechcloths and shaved most of their heads except for small ridge in the middle that had been dressed to stand up like a horn. The women wore their hair braided and either had robes on or were bathing in the river. Hishkowits told me not to worry; these were the Chahiksichahiks whom Juchi had encountered last year. I decided to go back downstream out of sight and cross the river, gain the plateau on the far side, and then approach the village in full view, so no threat could be perceived. The river was not at all easy to cross, and we were swept downriver quite a distance. So it was twilight by the time we approached the village.

We were seen, of course, but the openness and deliberateness of our approach, gave them pause, and they waited patiently for our odd party to enter. They were very puzzled by our horses and our appearance. Hishkowits spoke to them in his language, which was close enough to theirs, and we were warmly welcomed. They had heard rumors about us from Hishkowits' people and had been wondering if we'd come. We were ushered into the chief whose name was Sharitarish. He seemed to be in complete control and did not rely on anyone for advice. Once he decided he could understand Hishkowits and me satisfactorily, he ordered everyone out except for us. He then had his women serve us a meal and passed around the weed before we talked. The house was an earth lodge of the Nimipu type, but access was by means of a long tunneled ramp rather than a roof hole. The inside was also about three feet into the ground, but was square shaped with rounded corners. The lodge was fairly large, with a fire pit in the center and beds around the walls except for some sort of shrine at the part of the wall opposite the entrance.

As soon as the weed was burned up, our host asked if we were the people who had destroyed the Pashohan. Hishkowits explained he meant the Hotcangara, and I admitted that we were. He wanted to know why we had done it, and I replied because they had attacked us without provocation and had treated one of our men shamefully. He thought we had perhaps been too severe, and I explained that we only killed the warriors that attacked us. Finally, he wanted to know why we had come to his village. I explained the usual, and he listened intently. He asked for the alternative to joining us. I replied either war or peace. They did not have to join us, and as long as they didn't impede our movements, we would not interfere with them. After some thought he told me that for his part he would prefer to remain independent but trade with us especially for the interesting horses. I explained that we didn't trade horses but would give them only to our allies and confederates. He grudgingly agreed that that was prudent and explained that his people were already a confederacy of villages extending for some distance to the north and west. I replied that I knew of his people; some of them in the northwest had already sent observers. Perhaps he had heard of this. He had not and was more than a little miffed. He asked Hishkowits what his people had decided to do. He replied that they were still considering. Sharitarish then told me that there was a related tribe to the southeast with which his group was friendly. It would be best, he felt, if my proposal was presented to his confederacy as a whole, and pending that outcome, to their neighbors. He would also need to make some discreet inquiries as to why his fellow tribesmen to the northwest had not informed him about us.

I thought that was a good idea and congratulated him on his wisdom and diplomacy. Hishkowits gave me a look before he passed on that last bit. Our host promised to set up a meeting of the confederacy at a village some distance to the northwest in about a moon. Meanwhile, he suggested I try to learn much more of his language. I agreed and asked for the extended services of an instructor. He agreed and we were assigned a man named Tahirussawichi as an instructor and one of their houses for our stay.

The next day runners were sent in several directions (mostly north and west), and I took language lessons while my men went hunting, much to the edification of our hosts. I sent my apprentices to map the river on which the village was located. Like most of the local languages, this one was not at all simple to learn, although my smattering of Tanish helped. One would assume there would be more similarity among languages than we had found in this land. Although many were similar in some respects, distance seemed to effect vocabularies and especially pronunciation. I wondered how many more such languages we'd find. Still, I had a good ear and picked this one up fairly well over the next fifteen days. I regretted not having mastered the Tanish language, since it would have made things easier, and promised myself I would spend the coming winter learning more of the local languages. In the Ordu, Mongol had become the second language of all of our recruits, mostly because so many of our things had no name in the local languages. They had all learned the language quite well, but still retained their own. I suppose this had made me a little lazy about learning new languages.

While we were in the village, I noticed that these people had the most complex religion I had yet seen in the new land. All of the other tribes had shamans much like ours and were on the whole more spiritual or even more mystical than we were, but while they had special prayers and chants and several different demigods or spirits they honored, they believed in a principle God much like ours. The Chahiksichahiks, while their beliefs were not unlike the others, did seem to give much more power to their shamans, who were more properly priests. They were much given to ritual of dance, songs, and poetry. The more I could understand their language the more I got the impression that they were worshiping heavenly bodies, especially the sun. They had a young girl in the village, who was being lavished with attention. Tahirussawichi told me she was dedicated to the Morning Star and would have a prominent role to play in the ceremony for the Morning Star on the solstice. It was just as well for the sake of my mission that I didn't ask what the ceremony entailed. I learned some years later what the fate of the child had been. It seems on the solstice, they strip the girl and paint her half white and half black, then tie her to a wooden frame out in their fields. When the morning star rose, the shamans would murder the child with arrow, knife, and fire; then all the males in the village would shoot arrows into her body, and it would be left to fertilize the fields. I have often wondered what I would have done had I been interested enough in rituals at the time to ask what they planned to do. I remembered being puzzled that the Nivkh would capture and raise a bear cub for a year treating it like a pet and lavishing it with food and attention; then on their given day they would ritually kill it. But to do that with a human child would have been to me at that time, unthinkable. I had much to learn about our neighbors. Indeed, by the time I learned the truth about this practice, I was only mildly shocked.

Once I was comfortable with the Chahiksichahiks language, I suggested to our host that perhaps we should move on to the village where we would meet with the chiefs. He agreed, although he felt we would be early. We set out the next morning, and nine days later, we came to a very wide river, but Sharitarish told me we didn't have to cross it yet. We moved northwest along this river to near its source, crossed over it, and continued north to an east-flowing river. From my maps I thought this was the Owl River and asked if it continued east to a larger river. Sharitarish explained that it joined a larger river about a days' walk to the east. That river joined a still larger river far to the east. We would be crossing both rivers to reach our destination. We crossed the first river, then continued north a few days before reaching the second river (the Owl), which we followed upstream another day before crossing it just below the village. We were early, but not by more than two days. I spent the time mapping the area. The village was already crowded, but more people were arriving all the time. Some came on foot, but many arrived by dugout boats, much like those of the Nimipu. They used face and body paint, but no tattooing, and all were skimpily dressed, but ornately decorated. Some had what looked like red-stained duck down stuck on their horn-shaped hairstyle. Most wore gorgets of stone or shell. Some had necklaces of small shells, leading me to ask if the ocean was nearby. They told me it was quite some distance away yet to the southeast. I was surprised that it was to the southeast, but then I didn't realize there would be another Great Sea. My disparate group aroused quite a bit of interest, especially me. In fact, only the horses were more of an attraction.

Finally, we got around to the meeting. I was ushered into a particularly large one of their houses that easily accommodated the group of chiefs. There seemed to be a time-honored order in which the chiefs sat, so I asked Sharitarish where I should sit, and he placed me closest to the entrance. The nawak'osis was passed around, and at length Sharitarish spoke. He explained that he had called the meeting to present me to the chiefs since I had a proposal for a new alliance. He explained that I was from the tribe that had destroyed the Pashohan, but that they had invited the disaster by insulting us. He further explained that if they joined us we would share the wondrous animal that gave us remarkable mobility, greatly enhancing the hunt as he, himself, had witnessed. He added rather testily that the same offer had been made earlier to some of the villages in the northwest and no council had been called. He then invited me to explain my offer fully.

I spoke to them at length, explaining that we had come to their land to bring peace and unite the tribes. Some had joined us completely and others had confederated with us. The Pashohan or Hotcangara had attacked us, or we would have never destroyed them. As it was even they would be given one more chance to mend their ways. If they receive us graciously this fall, we could make peace, if not they would be annihilated. I thanked them for receiving me so graciously and assured them they had nothing to fear from us, even if they did not join. We could not, of course, aid people who might one day turn that aid against us, but we would take no action against them unless they broke the peace. On the other hand, I pointed out the advantages of joining us, not only the horse, but also iron weapons. At this point I passed around a knife, and I could see they were impressed.

One after the other commented, most favorably, including Starapat, the chief of the village that had received Juchi the year before. He apologized for not calling a meeting explaining that he first wanted to make sure all was as we said. Still, I could see there was an unspoken concern among them. Finally, one of them got to the point. He and his colleagues were chiefs among their people, like Kaidu was among us. If they joined us, they would no longer be chiefs, they would be subordinate to my chief, or, even worse, to several chiefs. It was a heavy price for them to pay to bring my innovations to their people. I explained that as our confederates they would lose no power. Their young men would train with us, but then return to them, only to be recalled when absolutely necessary. Similarly, they could call on us should some other tribe be attacking them, and we would rush to their aid. They could remain in their villages as chiefs, or join us and be leaders and still get all benefits. If their young men trained with us, another chief pointed out, they would likely choose to remain with us. One could not long be a chief of a village with no young men. I was impressed that he had so easily seen through Kaidu's stratagem, but I kept up the fiction, pointing out that while indeed some of the confederated tribes' young men had joined us, certainly most had not. Surely most of their young men would feel the same obligation to return. I could see that they were not so sure, but would be embarrassed to admit it. After a bit of silence, Sharitarish told the assembly that the benefits were worth the risk, and for his part, he would send his son among the young men from his village to make sure at least one would return. This stirred them all up, and one by one they all agreed to confederate.

They wanted to send some men right away and more in the fall, so anxious were they for the horses. I agreed and detailed Tahca Ushte, one of the Ocheti shakowin soldiers, to lead them back to the Eagle Ordu. I also requested that Tahirussawichi (whom I had taught some Mongol) go along to interpret. Then I asked about their allies to the south. They told me that I would have to talk to them myself, but they would, of course, send a guide with me to make the necessary introductions. Their allies called themselves the Kitikiti'sh, and their language was very similar to that of the Cha-hiksichahiks. I was presented with a charming young fellow who was called Pitalesharo. He would lead me to the Kitikiti'sh.

The next morning, Tahca Ushte and Tahirussawichi remained behind to await the recruits while the rest of us accompanied Shari-tarish back to his village on the way to the Kitikitish . I urged the others to return along this river and sent Ahmukikini along to map it. We retraced our path to Sharitarish's village, and I named that river that joined the Owl after him, for all his help. We regained his village and, after a suitable feast, took our leave and continued downstream. Within two days, we arrived at our first Kitikiti'sh vil-lage. Instead of earth mounds, the houses looked like grass mounds. And the number of them was remarkable. There must have been about a thousand clustered along the bank above the cleared river bottom. The houses were about fifteen feet high and about twenty-five feet in diameter. Inside, there were wooden beds around the sides with painted hide curtains for privacy. There was no smoke hole, but the smoke would vent through the grass roof. Each house had an open arbor with a raised wooden floor where the people spent the day and another arbor where they stored dried meat and vegetables. There were also raised platforms, smaller than those of the Hotcangara, but also capped with a building, which turned out to be a sort of shrine, attended by shamans, or perhaps it would be more correct to call them priests. The other major difference was that the people were heavily tattooed. Enough, in fact, that their skin looked darker than that of the Chahiksichahiks. Otherwise, they were just like them, same scant clothing and same decorations. I had no trouble communicating with their chief, Nar-hax-to-wey. He decided it would be best to call a meeting of the chiefs, just as their neighbors had. They were not spread out as much and could get together in about twenty days. Again we would go on to a more central village about five days' walk downstream.

I used the time to explore around a bit. There were some mountains to the southeast, and I spent a few days looking around for minerals. I found some coal but nothing else. The mountains were heavily wooded with pine joining the hardwoods on the higher slopes. Mapping was not easy. I also found some strange animals. One looked like a very large rat. It could hang from a tree limb by its tail. Pitalesharo told me they weren't fit to eat. Another odd creature looked like a fat fox with a ringed tail and a dark band over its eyes. Pitalesharo assured me that it was also not fit to eat. Of course, he didn't think fish and birds were fit to eat either, so who knew, but I wasn't hunting anyway.

In due course, we went to the meeting, and it had the same result. They had the same misgivings, but reluctantly came to the same conclusion, and they also suggested that I make my presentation to the principle tribe of the neighboring Hasinai confederacy to the south, the Kadohadacho. If I could win them over, all the other tribes of the confederacy would also join. They promised to send one of their men with me to guide and introduce me. One of the chiefs, Howitscahde, introduced me to his son, Isadowa. It seemed they couldn't send just anyone to present me to the Kadohadacho. Meanwhile, I had to detail another of my Ocheti shakowin, Ptehe Woptuh'a, to lead their young men to the Eagle Ordu.

We went downstream southward along the Kitikitish River (I had decided to name it for them) for four days spending each night at another village of the Kitikiti'sh. We stayed west of the river in the open prairie rather than negotiate the woods on the east. On the fifth day we reached the juncture of the Kitikitish with a larger river from the northwest. Once across it, we could be in Kadohadacho country (so I named it after them). Crossing the river would require boats, so we went upstream until we found a village. It was not Kitikiti'sh, but rather one of the related tribes. Some of the people had oddly shaped heads, flat in the rear and sloping in the front to form something of broad point on top. It gave them an unsettling appearance, and I was hard-pressed not to stare. I wondered if this was what the Nimipu meant about the pointed heads of the Salst. Isadowa said that the deformation was intentional, achieved by means of a rigid crib board when they were babies. Not all of the Kadohadacho indulged in the practice since it was derived from tribes in the east and caused the babies much discomfort. I asked him how it is the Kadohadacho became preeminent, but he didn't know. He said it was always that way. Even though his people were not members of the Hasinai Confederacy, they, too, respected the position of the Kadohadacho, and deferred to them. It sounded like I would be meeting the closest thing to a king this land had to offer so far. We were taken across the river in the dugout boats, then continued south passing some of the Kadohadacho villages.

We arrived at another river joining the Kadohadacho from the southwest that was fordable. I named it for Isadowa. After the Isadowa joined the Kadohadacho the latter turned more east, and before long we could see a very large town on the bluff above the river bottom. As we climbed the bluff, a large crowd assembled to gawk. I could see no difference between these people and the Kitikiti'sh, either in their appearance or their houses, except for the occasional deformed head. There were more mounds, and they were much higher, but otherwise, I could not detect their preeminence from appearances. We went to a large open square in the middle of the town and crossing it came to the base of one of the mounds. Isadowa went up the ramp to a large house on its summit. While he was gone ever more of the townsfolk gathered to observe us. Finally, he returned and beckoned me up the ramp.

The house on top the ramp was taller and wider than any I had seen so far, but otherwise it had the same layout. The chief, Owixa, was of middle age, perhaps forty from the look of him, the youngest chief I had yet seen. He had a muscular build and was heavily tattooed on all exposed skin. He wore an elaborate headdress with feathers, shells, and fur and wore a beautifully carved shell gorget. A cloak made of brilliant feathers lay to one side. He bid me sit down, and one of his servants handed him an elaborate container for the nawak'osis. The stem was covered with the green neck feathers from one of the local ducks, and the bowl was carved into the shape of a kind of sea creature from its tail, perhaps a seal. After the weed was burned out, we sat in silence a moment.

"You are a strange-looking person, riding on the back of a strange-looking animal," he began. "Your people have united the tribes of the north and scattered the Pashohan across the Great River. You have even seduced away our relatives to the northwest. And now you come to seduce me as well. Yours is a small tribe made numerous by alliance; this is a large confederation made numerous by relation. Why should we be joined to you? Do you think we should fear you? Your animals would not help you on our rivers and in our forests. Your weapons are good, but against our numbers, they will not help you. Do you think you can conquer us?"

"No, of course not," I replied evenly, although I was surprised at the hostility. "We are not bent on conquest. We are new to the land, and we have many advances that we would be happy to share with those who will ally with us. We do insist on alliance, because otherwise our advances could be turned against us. But alliance is not domination. It would be an alliance among equals. You would rule in your land, and we would rule in our land."

"It seems to me that you rule over a lot of land already." He eyed me suspiciously. "How much land do you intend to rule? Will you cross the Great River after the Hotcangara and continue? Just what are your intentions?"

"We wish to explore the land." I was impressed by this man's keen grasp of the situation. "And find out who our neighbors are and what their disposition is toward us. If we are received courteously, but our overtures are rebuffed, we have no quarrel. If we are insulted, our honor demands a response. The Hotcangara are the only people we have attacked, and even in their case, we are willing to make peace. We are no threat to any people who receive us in peace. We offer alliance to mutual advantage or peace and respect. It is others who choose war."

"It is no great thing"—he shrugged—"to offer peace to a people whose warriors you have all but destroyed. The Pashohan are not fools. They will make peace if you let them. You have already divided them and taken many of them into your tribe. You will greatly enlarge your numbers with them. How do I know that you will not then march them down here to attack me if I decline your alliance?"

"It is not our way," I protested. "We want to unite or ally with all the tribes in the land and produce a people that thrive in peace and strength."

"Young men need wars." He studied me. "If you achieve your design, your warriors will become weak from peace. Then anyone could destroy you. Besides, it may well be that this noble intention is held by your chief, but what will happen when he dies? Perhaps his successor will have different ideas. Nobility never lasts for long; it is always replaced by either weakness or tyranny. Which will it be for your people?"

"Your views are pessimistic." I shrugged. "And at the same time, history would support you. But it need not be that way. If your people join ours, they would have equal say in our next leader, for we all choose him. Besides, yours is a great and powerful nation. If we turned on you, even if we prevailed, we would be too weak to rule anything. But do not fear that peace begets weakness, for peace only prevails in the interior, never on the borders. Our young men will always find challenges. This is a big land."

"You are clever for a young man." He almost smiled. "I can see why your chief sends you to seduce us. Still, if we do confederate with you and send our young men to train with your warriors, we will kindle the flame of our own destruction. I am well aware of how seductive power is. Our young men will feel a new power as your warriors. I have heard about your battles in the north. They are spoken of with awe. It is undeserved awe, but it is awe, nevertheless. If we send you our young men, they will not return, and we both know that. So your alliance would mean our destruction. Why should I willingly destroy my tribe and my position?"

"It need not be that way," I protested. "Some may stay, but most will return. It has been that way with the others who have confederated. Your people are very sophisticated and may find our people too rustic. The people who joined us are much more primitive than you. It is more likely that you would absorb us if you joined than the other way around."

"You are much too clever," he chucked gently. "I will do this much. I will send with you my younger brother. He is very shrewd and will stay with you for a year. At the end of that year, return here with him, and I will decide what to do."

With that he sent an assistant to get his brother. Meanwhile, I agreed and complimented him on his wisdom. Soon, the assistant returned with a man about my age. He was only lightly tattooed, but seemed to be darker than his brother. He also had a rather large, hooked nose. His only ornament was a gorget made of obsidian cut in a star pattern. He seemed to walk oddly, and my attention was drawn to his feet. His right foot had only a heel, but he held himself proudly, so I assumed that it was a battle wound. He was presented to me as Adihanin, and his mission was explained to him. He agreed immediately and turned to look me over. I thanked his brother, and Adihanin and I both went back down the ramp again. Many of the gawkers were happy to see Adihanin and waved to and chatted with him. He told me that he would need a day to get ready for the trip and took us to a large guesthouse to wait for him. Isadowa assured me that this was a very positive response and that from all I had told him about our people, surely Adihanin would report back favorably. I asked if he knew anything about the latter, but he said he didn't. I would have to find out about him on my own.

18

SOUTH TO THE SEA AND THE SECOND
HOTCANGARA CAMPAIGN 6 K
(OK, TX, AR, LA, MO, IL, 1374)

While waiting for Adihanin to get ready, I wandered around the town with Isadowa. There seemed to be a lot of activity, but occasionally I'd see a leader wield a stick to urge on anyone he thought was being indolent. The Kadohadacho society seemed to be rather stratified. On the top was the Xinesi, the main chief; then each village had a Caddi or chief; then under these were the Canahas, who were elders or assistants; then there were other elites who didn't govern. These latter were the announcer (Tanmas), the warriors (Amayxoya), the pages (Chaya), and the shaman (Conna). The Xinesi was also the high priest, and he had many ritualistic duties added to ruling. In fact, their religion was very much integrated into their governing, a rather unsettling combination from our Mongol point of view. I wondered what Kaidu would think about them. In any case, they were much less independent and uninhibited than the tribes we had previously encountered. I wondered if they would even fit in.

Talaswaima surprised me by telling me that his people had traded with the Kadohadacho. I asked him how that was possible, for from what Juchi told me it was a brutal journey. He said he didn't know the route, but he knew the goods. His people got salt, shells, and bow wood from the Kadohadacho and traded cotton and turquoise in exchange. The latter was a cloudy blue or green stone with or without dark veins. It was highly prized in the old land—just below jade (a soft, pale green stone) among the Hanjen and above all in Tibet. He pointed out cotton and turquoise on some of our hosts. It was obvious that trade existed between the tribes, but one would not have expected it to cover such distances when everything had to be carried on people's backs. The bow wood came from a medium-sized crooked tree covered with inch-long spines.

At length, Adihanin arrived with a fairly small bundle and an odd-looking club. The latter was made of wood and rather flat with obsidian embedded on each side. It was quite sharp, making it more like a sword than a club. I asked about it since it was new to me, and he said it was a gift from his father. It turned out that his father was something of a wandering merchant from a tribe far to the south. I asked how it was that his brother had become Xinesi with foreign parentage. He said that his brother had no foreign parentage. His mother had been a latter wife of the previous Xinesi, and he had given her to his father as a great privilege and mark of honor. In fact, he really wasn't related to his brother at all, since the latter also had a different mother. Furthermore, his real name was Tezcatlipoca. His father gave him the name some years ago. It was from his father's language (Nahual) and meant Smoking Mirror, their name for obsidian. He would prefer to be called Smoking Mirror in our language.

We spent a day getting Smoking Mirror used to riding a horse. He took to it quickly, and one could see a thrill in his face to be liberated from his ungraceful gait at last. I wanted to visit some of the other tribes in the area, but he thought it unwise to go east because the tribe there tended to ambush strangers unless they were carrying trade goods and gave a signal well in advance of their approach. We could visit the tribes to the south and west, if I liked. I really didn't want to waste time making the pitch to the tribes of his confederacy, since they would only respond to his "brother's" decision. He said that there were other tribes in the south beyond his people, along the shore of the Great Sea. So, I agreed to visit them. I was excited at finally reaching the sea, and adding it, or part of it, to my map.

We moved south for several days until we reached a river Smoking Mirror called the Red River (it was reddish, so I kept the name). We stayed in Kadohadacho villages each night along the way, for the area was quite populous. The terrain was prairie dotted with stands of oak trees. The bottoms along the Red River were rather different. They had forests that were mostly oak but also had a gum tree larger than the one in the old land, and an odd-looking tree that I thought was rather like a hemlock, but it was nothing like the trees in the old land. It thrived even when surrounded by water and although a conifer shed its leaves in the fall. Its wood was very resistant to water—making it popular for dugout boats. We followed the Red River downstream southeastward as it carved a broad valley through a range of hills. The valley had been fully exploited. We first skirted the eastern limits of the Hasinai, after whom the confederacy had been named, then those of the Hais. At some mysterious point, we left the river and, keeping the hills on our west, turned south. Two days later, we approached a mean-looking village nestled inconspicuously in a small clearing. There were perhaps a dozen "houses" that consisted of raised platforms covered with thatch roofs and open on the sides. The villagers were tattooed, but otherwise sparsely clad and ornamented, and they wore their hair long and loose. The men were armed with only spears and spear throwers. They seemed to know Smoking Mirror and greeted him profusely and enthusiastically. Their language was a complete mystery to me, but he had no trouble chatting with them.

At length, he turned to me and said that we were among the Ishak. They lived by fishing and raising a few crops. They were widely scattered between this village and the Great Sea and far to the west. Their most illustrious chief was currently at a village some distance to the southwest. The various bands were independent, but would likely follow his lead if I cared to recruit him. I got the impression I was being tested. Smoking Mirror had betrayed none of the arrogance one would expect a member of his tribe to have toward this pitiful group, but it was obvious he thought I would pass up any alliance with this tribe. To his surprise, I agreed to seek out the chief and expressed to him the hope that the man would join us.

We turned southwest and moved out of the trees into a steppe consisting of the bluish-looking grass and a tall cordlike grass. As we continued, the latter grass began to predominate and was sometimes so tall that we could barely see over it. We would occasionally come upon a village, and always the villagers seemed to know Smoking Mirror and were happy to see him. I finally asked how it was they all seemed to know him. He replied that he had visited them before with his father who had traded with them over the years. I asked if they would have received us as well without him along. He said that would depend on whether we looked threatening, whether they thought they could beat us, and whether the fishing was bad. He then told me that the people in the east refer to the Ishak as "man eaters." It seemed that while most of the people, including his own, engaged in ritualistic cannibalism on brave captives, the Ishak also indulged when other sources of food failed. It was fortunate that I did not usually betray emotion because a wave of nausea engulfed me at that moment, but no one knew. I wondered what Kaidu would think about this piece of information. Why was it, I wondered, that such a repulsive practice started? I supposed one could understand cannibalism to avoid starvation, but ritualized? How could such an idea have arisen?

"Do not your people"—Smoking Mirror read my silence—"sacrifice captives?"

"No," I answered matter-of-factly, "we only sacrifice animals, and that rarely."

"Do not your priests demand it?" He seemed puzzled.

"We have no priests," I answered. "We have shamans, and they only treat the sick and give advice, they make no demands."

"Really?" he marveled. "How strange. And the tribes who have joined you?"

"They are the same." I shrugged. "Or, at least, they seem to be. We've had no trouble with any of them so far."

"You may find things a little different should you succeed in recruiting among the southern tribes," he said.

He was right, of course. The Mongols in general and Kaidu in particular would not tolerate human sacrifice or cannibalism or any sort of a powerful priest class. I wondered what Kaidu would do about it. To change the subject I asked if Smoking Mirror's father was still alive. He was and off on a trading expedition in the south. Might we run into him? I asked. He replied that his father was in the far south in the land of his people, the Tolteca. With some more prodding, it turned out that his father's people were the descendants of a great civilization whose city fell to some wild desert tribes who scattered them into a high valley in the mountains, where they were greatly esteemed for their skills and even ruled a few of the cities. Since I thought the Great Sea was in the south, I asked if this land of his father's was across the sea. But it turned out that while the sea was south of our current position, the coastline eventually turned south for some distance, then turned east, north, east, south, and east again. But he had no idea how far the coast continued.

In due course, we came to a large lake and a fair-sized, but still mean-looking village. The chief's house was on a somewhat raised platform and larger that the others, but of the same design and material. As usual, Smoking Mirror was enthusiastically greeted and ushered right to the chief, who also welcomed him warmly. The chief was heavily tattooed and wore a shell gorget and a feathered headdress. We were motioned to sit on woven reed mats. Some nawak'osis was produced, and we passed it around until it was burned up. Then Smoking Mirror told the chief about my offer. The chief had a few questions, but in the end decided to send his oldest son along with me to see if all was as I said. Since I didn't understand the language, I wondered if that was at Smoking Mirror's suggestion, but actually it was the most prudent course for them to follow. We spent the night, and the next day, Smoking Mirror asked if I wanted to see the sea. He said it was at the southern end of the lake and recommended that we go by boat, for the land was quite marshy. We set out in two boats very ably handled by our hosts. The lake was quite large, perhaps forty-five li long, from north to south, but much less from east to west, except at the southern end where it widened. It took us much of the day to reach the southern shore of the lake, and then we followed it to the river, which drained it into the sea. We beached the boats and climbed over some dunes to reach the shore. It had been some three years since I had seen the ocean and smelled the salt air. The surf was gentle, the waves almost imperceptible. The coast stretched out from east to west as far as I could see. We joined the others on the beach for a meal of shellfish they had collected and prepared, then spent the night on the dunes above the beach.

We spent the next day returning to the village, and so we had to accept their hospitality for another day. It was still only midsummer so I wanted to visit the next tribe to the west. Smoking Mirror explained that to the south and west of the Ishak, there were only similar widely scattered tribes with vaguely related languages and absolutely no central organization or authority. Unless I wanted to visit each band, I would be wasting my time. I asked if there were any celebrated chiefs, like the one we had just visited, who might sway the others. He said there was one such chief, but his village was some distance away. He asked if I was sure I wanted to try. I replied that I was. He seemed to be studying me for a moment, but finally agreed to take me.

We crossed the river at the northern apex of the lake with the aid of the boats, then moved due west crossing a few good-sized rivers and gradually turning southwest. We came upon a huge bay, fed by two major rivers, and finally some twelve days after starting, reached a second smaller bay and the village we were seeking. We had come upon fewer settlements except around the large bay, since most of the villages were nearer to the sea. We did encounter an occasional hunting party and always everyone knew and liked Smoking Mirror. Again, we were ushered into the chief's presence. He was virtually indistinguishable from the Ishak chief, except that he was of taller stature. His only adornment was a necklace consisting of a lump of the turquoise surrounded by shells. He wanted to ride out and hunt the plains oxen with us to see if indeed the horses were all that valuable. The next day, we set out and, finding a herd, culled enough to greatly impress him. He decided to send a small contingent with us to report back to him.

These people did not have a specific name for themselves, but used the name of their village as their name, and that would often change. Smoking Mirror told me that there was a similar group to the south, and there was among them also a noted chief if I wished to visit him. I did. This journey was much like the previous one except that it was mostly due south. After ten days, we entered the village. The chief had just returned from a raid in the west, where he had apparently covered himself in glory, and was a bit puffed up. Even so, he also warmly welcomed Smoking Mirror, heard us out, and decided to send his younger son with us. I knew we had to start back if I wanted to return by fall, but I asked if there was a tribe farther inland in the north, and indeed there was, again much like the others, but this time possessing two esteemed chiefs. Both would be on our way back.

On our way north, I suggested we follow the coastline for a while at least, so that I could map it. Smoking Mirror looked on my mapping efforts as a bizarre hobby or ritual, but finally as he saw the coastline appear on my map, he understood what I was doing. So he began helping by telling me things about the terrain. He said that the river we had crossed to reach the last chief's village would lead one to Talaswaima's people. It was flowing from the west when we crossed it, but apparently it originated far to the northwest in some mountains. Talaswaima was excited that he had crossed that river, but he said it was not the one his particular band lived on, but a very "sacred" river nevertheless.

There were narrow barrier islands all along the shore, and Smoking Mirror knew how long and wide they were, so I could draw them in. We came to a large bay, and some of the locals ferried us across the narrow mouth. Smoking Mirror was able to fill in the details of the bay. The next bay was much larger, but he felt it would be better not to cross it since the river at its head would lead us to the first chief of the inland tribe. It seemed the people of this tribe called themselves the Titskan watitch and were very widely scattered all over the plain inland, living mainly on the plains ox and whatever they gathered. The river at the head of the bay was a large one, so I named it the Titskan for our target people. The river led us at first northwest, then mostly north, then a little west, where we found the village some ten days after leaving the last chief. By this time, the river was little more than a sluggish stream bordered with mud.

The village was all of the conical hide tents, much like those of the Siksika, except that they were smaller and not decorated. The village was not as clean either, for there was refuse and snarling dogs all around. They were shorter than the Siksika and were armed mostly with spears, but also with bows. Some had leather armor and shields; some had leather helmets adorned with ox horns or feathers. They looked quite fierce, and their welcome was friendly but wary. They were very interested in the horses. The chief was named Sanukh. He was fairly young and expressionless enough to be a Han. He was wearing a gaudy feather headdress. He produced a rude pipe and looked at us expectantly. Fortunately Smoking Mirror carried some of the nawak'osis with him and produced a pouch with which he filled the pipe. After we passed it around, he made my pitch to the chief in still another incomprehensible language. Sanukh wanted to try out the horses on the oxen, so we staged a demonstration for him on a nearby herd. He was very impressed. He also wanted to try out one of our bows and arrows. He was again very impressed, but only the glint in his eyes gave it away. He told us he would join his worst enemies to get his hands on these things. He announced that he would pack up the whole band and follow us back.

Indeed, the next day as we left, the whole village was dismantled, and they set out after us. Smoking Mirror told me that it was most likely the second chief, Kwesh, would also join up. The rest of the tribe would likely follow the next year. He went on to say that his confederated tribes were in contact and friendly with the Titskan watitch, and would not impede their joining us. This leg of the journey took eleven days. During the course of it, the dry shrub land gave way to rather dry grassland, frequently cut by very low rivers and dry streambeds. Some of the latter would spring into life on rare occasions when a rainstorm passed upstream. Kwesh's village was on a fairly respectable, although easily fordable, river (which I named after him). The village was somewhat larger than Sanukh's, but otherwise identical. Kwesh was more animated than the other and smiled at Smoking Mirror in greeting. The interview went as before with Smoking Mirror again providing the weed and doing all the talking. The result was also the same. Kwesh wanted a demonstration and afterward was ready to follow us north.

Smoking Mirror congratulated me on my recruiting success, but I pointed out that it was he who had done all the talking. He smiled, but rejoined that it was I who had made all the promises. I asked him if the Titskan watitch were also cannibals. He said they were only if the oxen gave out. That was a relief; we would have to find a way to get them to permanently eschew that particular practice. He continued to help with my mapping pointing out which rivers we crossed corresponded to the ones I had marked near the coast. Some eight days later, we finally came to a river with a forested bottom that he insisted was the Red River. He told me it was the path his father would follow to get from Talaswaima's people to the Hasinai. It was still quite a river, but we were able to swim across without incident. The prairie began to be dotted with copses of oaks, and we began to run into villages of the Kitchai (another of the Hasinai confederacy) at first and then, the Kadohadacho. We advised all we met of the two bands in our wake, and they promised to speed them on their way.

Five days later, we reached the Kadohadacho River, well above the town where I had spoken to the Xinesi. The river was much easier to cross at this time of year. We continued on, passing through the lands of first the Yatasi (another member of the Hasinai), and then the Kitikiti'sh. Ten days later, we arrived at the Owl River, which we had followed away from the Mongol River in the spring. We followed it downstream and reached our outpost at the mouth of the river a few days later. I advised the commander of the coming bands and suggested that he send a group to meet them. We crossed over to the Owl Ordu on the Numakiki boats, and I reported to Kuyuk. He relieved me of my recruits and observers and turned them over for training. He promised to make sure the approaching Titskan watitch were guided into camp. He asked if anyone could speak their language, and Smoking Mirror, who insisted on staying with me, found one of the Chahiksichahiks volunteers who could speak the language. He was sent with a group to meet the Titskan watitch. I went on to meet Kaidu who was already in route south. We ran into him a day's journey north and turned to join him. I sent Talaswaima on to the Eagle Camp to tell Paula I was back and well. Smoking Mirror had been rather quiet in the Owl Camp, just looking around at everything. At the sight of the Ordu on the march, he was awed. They were quite a sight, four of the plains tumen in full battle array on the march. When we camped that evening, I reported to Kaidu. I couldn't find Juchi.

Kaidu was pleased that I finally made it back and listened intently to my report. He decided that he wouldn't worry about the overly organized religion of the Hasinai Confederation unless they joined us outright. If they only confederated with us, we would not interfere with their rituals, but we would also not adopt them. The more primitive tribes I had recruited would likely give up their cannibalism since there was always plenty of food. Besides, the more primitive tribes tended to slavishly imitate the Mongols, making them easy to assimilate. He wanted to meet Smoking Mirror and thank him for his assistance, but first he wanted to bring me up to date. It turned out that Juchi had returned from his expedition several days earlier. He had spent a long time visiting and recruiting among the central and eastern Kensistenoug and then went on to their eastern neighbors, widely scattered nomadic bands that were apparently related to the Kensistenoug and spoke a similar language. These did not have a specific name for themselves, but called themselves after their chiefs. He wandered among these bands until he reached the sea. At this point I had to see the maps Shingabaossin had made. It seemed there was a long narrow bay cutting deeply into the northeastern shore of the land. This bay was likely part of the northern sea, but how was it connected to the sea I had found in the south?

In any case, Juchi had crossed the bay and found more, similar bands of natives on the other side. He continued south again encountering the sea. At this point he turned back west, through more of the same sort of bands until he finally arrived among a more organized tribe. They also spoke a language similar to the others and called themselves by the name of their village, but they had permanent villages, and the villages had a central meeting area. He had recruited them at a general meeting, and they had insisted that he first speak to their "grandfather" tribe, the Leni lenape. This proved to be a large tribe to the south along a river he named after them. This tribe was split into three or four subgroups. He met with the chiefs of the northernmost subgroup. It seemed they had a tradition that they had come from the far west across the sea and then over a mountain range and many great rivers until they reached their present location. The scattered and more organized tribes all around were split off from them in antiquity. The Kensistenoug and Anishinabe who were with Juchi were not amused by the contention, but prudently did not create a scene. The Leni lenape had agreed to send a group of observers with Juchi to check us out. They very much approved of the idea of uniting the tribes. Upon leaving them, Juchi's group had been ambushed by a strange tribe in supposed neutral territory. The Leni lenape called the attackers Mingue, but that just meant stealthy or treacherous, a euphemism for enemies. The attack was beaten off but not without cost. Several of the party were badly wounded and a few subsequently died.

They were later attacked again while camped by another group related to the Mingue, with more losses. Juchi had also received a minor wound. There were a few more scattered attacks but with less effect over the next several days until they finally got out of the hostile territory. They found themselves on the southern shore of a large lake among a tribe vaguely related to the Anishinabe called the Twanhtwanh. They were hated enemies of the Mingue, whom they called Notowega (snakes), so they willingly guided them to the nearest village of the Potawatamink, the allies of the Anishinabe. Needless to say, Kaidu wanted to annihilate the Mingue and sent Juchi to train with the forest tumen that had now grown to four. He decided that a punitive expedition would be mounted the following fall, after forming a few more forest tumen. Also the Potawatamink and the Ottawa had agreed to confederate. The Twanhtwanh and a related tribe, the Kiwigapawa, had sent along observers and definitely wanted to be part of any attack on the hated Notowega. Kaidu wanted me to also train with the forest Ordu rather than go on any expedition the following spring.

With his dark mood, I found myself feeling sorry for any Hotcangara who might cross him this fall. He had me bring in Smoking Mirror. The two measured each other quietly for a while, and then to my surprise, Kaidu asked him if he had lost his foot in battle. Smoking Mirror admitted that he had, but had taken a head in exchange. Kaidu grunted and nodded, then invited him to join us for the fall campaign. He thanked him, but asked if I would be on the campaign, for he wanted to stay with me. Kaidu was puzzled (as was I) but replied that, of course, I would also be along. When we left, I asked him why he wanted to be in my company, and he said because he felt he had measured me sufficiently that he could trust me, but was unsure of the others. Indeed, he stayed with me throughout the campaign and rest of the year.

We picked up the Owls, and they and the Falcons and Cranes crossed the Mongol to sweep the southern side, while the Eagles and the Hawks swept the northern side. Each village received us in peace and humility. No resistance was to be found all the way to the Missi Sipi. At that point, a few of the Hotcangara were sent across to the city to see what the rest had decided. They returned with an older chief, Munche Khanche, who identified himself as the "Peace Chief." The people of the city had elected to have peace and wanted us to spare them. Kaidu explained that they must surrender and join us or be wiped out; there was no longer room for compromise. He asked if they would be considered slaves. Kaidu said they would not, but they also would not be trusted with either horses or our weapons, until they had proven themselves worthy of that trust. They would have to feed us while we were among them. Also, he would appoint a governor to rule over them until they could be trusted. And if they proved not to be worthy of trust, they would cease to burden the earth with their existence. The old man nodded and returned to the city.

We could just barely see him conferring with the other leaders for a while. There seemed to be a lot of discussion. Meanwhile, the men had already begun setting up the pontoon bridge to cross the river. The next day, the old man returned again to announce that those in the city had accepted all our demands. Unfortunately, the war chief had refused to capitulate and had left the city with some of his supporters and gone north to rally some of their related bands. When the bridge was finished, the Eagle and Hawk Tumen crossed over. Meanwhile, the Falcon Tumen crossed to the north side of the Mongol. The Hawks were deployed on the north side of the large city complex, and the Eagles were deployed along the east side. A strong force went with Kaidu to look over the city. Smoking Mirror and I were in the force.

The "city" was more like a huge cleared bottom with scattered ceremonial centers surrounded with villages of varying sizes, which in turn were surrounded with fields. The main center was in the south central part of the bottom. As we went along, large groups of the Hotcangara stood silently and unarmed watching us. I asked Smoking Mirror if he expected any treachery, but he said he didn't, since the Hotcangara were usually faithful to their word, unlike some of the tribes in the south. I stored that piece of information for future use, but continued to study the Hotcangara for any sign of defiance. We entered the palisaded ceremonial center from the north across the stream. There were smaller mounds on either side of the huge one and a very large open area in front of it. There was an earthen ramp leading up to the mound from the square. There was a platform at the top of the ramp, and another ramp lead farther up the mound to a sort of temple. There were more mounds around the large open space. There were also some strange round flat stones which I noticed but was too preoccupied to ask about. I found out about them later when I encountered them again. To the west of the palisade, there was a circle of about fifty erect logs over four hundred feet in diameter with a taller log near the center of the circle. It seemed that the circle was used for marking the solstices and star paths. The elite of the city stood silently in the square to meet us. Their main distinguishing characteristic was their adornments. They wore capes made of shell beads and wore copper and mica accoutrements. Kaidu did not speak to them, but we just looked everything over and then returned to the Ordu and camped in the northeast corner of the bottom. We set up a strong guard just in case, but nothing happened in the night.

The next morning, Kaidu appointed Tatanka Ska Koda, the Ocheti shakowin chief who had joined us, to be his governor. He detailed a large force to ensure his orders were carried out. Meanwhile, the Falcon Tumen set up its headquarters on the north side of the Mongol while the Crane Tumen set up on the south both right across from the "city." The Hawks recrossed the Missi Sipi and started back home. The Owls crossed over to replace them. Finally, I found out what we were waiting for. Out of the woods to our north came shouts and cries of battle. We backed up to leave a large open space in front of us and before long, groups of Hotcangara warriors began to emerge from the forest and head in our direction. We waited calmly for them to get into bow range, then began cutting them down. More and more emerged, and it became obvious that they were being driven toward us by another force. Finally, the main force emerged, and seeing us, charged. We fired into them until they got close, then rode back a little, turned, and fired into them again. They stopped and looked for cover, and we moved back toward them and fired high into the air showering them with arrows even in their shallow cover. In confusion and panic some broke for the river, but were cut off and cut down.

At last from the woods there emerged the forest tumen. Advancing from tree to tree, they poured a flanking fire into the remnants of the enemy. No quarter was given, or, to their credit, requested. When no more stood, the men moved methodically among them dispatching the wounded and recovering our arrows. Among the dead was the Hotcangara war chief, the same Tayhah nea whom we had encountered the year before. Among the forest tumen was Juchi. He had been leading one of the two new ones, the Foxes. In overall command was Donduk. Expecting trouble, Kaidu had sent them south from the Anishinabe lands to make sure the northern Hotcangara surrendered. Along a broad front, they had visited all the villages until they ran into Tayhah nea and his contingent. The latter never had much of a chance and tried to retreat to the east only to run into another tumen closing from that direction. Between them they funneled him right back into Kaidu's trap. The forest tumen would continue visiting the remaining Hotcangara settlements in the east to make sure there was no more resistance. Kaidu ordered me to join Donduk for the rest of the campaign. I had the feeling there was a reason for this. Smoking Mirror stayed with me.

19
END OF THE SECOND HOTCANGARA CAMPAIGN,
6 K
(IL, OH, MO, IO, SD, 1374)

When I reported to Donduk, he assigned me to stay with him as part of his staff. Two of the tumen, the Kestrels and the newer Bears, were well to the east of us. Juchi's Foxes would continue south along the Missi Sipi River and the Ospreys would go a short distance east and then move south also. We would stop when we ran out of Hotcangara territory. So far, the Hotcangara had been quite cooperative. Even the ones in the north, who protested our "unprovoked" threats, did not want to fight us. Of course, when ten thousand warriors surround one's village of at most two thousand people, it is no disgrace to surrender. Their northern settlements were quite scattered and mostly small, and although they were in contact with each other, they did not seem to be in much contact with the group we had fought and were quite surprised at our aggression. Once the tumen got farther south, however, it was different. Most were expecting us, but from the west or south, not the north. The majority surrendered, but some resisted, and a few tried to flee. Most of the latter were on the battlefield north of the city. The former were strewn about in their now-destroyed towns. Only five towns had resisted. The largest town in the north was among them. The tumen had reached the townabout eight days previously and were attacked before they had fully surrounded it. The siege was brief, however, since everything was made of wood or straw and was quite dry this fall. A barrage of fire arrows forced the villagers from their palisades into our arrows and swords.

Each of the tumen had a mapmaker with them, so when the campaign was over, I should be able to piece together a good picture of the Hotcangara country. Meanwhile, I could just observe. While each member of the forest tumen had a horse, they were only used in open country, to arrive at a jump-off point, or in the unlikely event of a retreat. Otherwise, they were left behind with one man holding six horses. The horse holder was usually a boy too young to fight, but old enough to hold onto six horses no matter what happened. The warriors would then move forward silently on foot through the woods. When a good forward position was found for the horses, they were sent for and brought up. At night, they would always be close at hand. It made good sense to do it this way. I was amazed how silently the men glided through the forest even with dense underbrush. The towns we encountered were usually surrounded before they knew we were there.

We moved east for two days before turning south. We soon came upon a fair-sized town along a river. It was already surrounded when I arrived. It did not resist, although they protested that they were not allied to the city. The pattern was repeated as we moved south. After five days, we began to run into scouts from the Fox Tumen. The Missi Sipi had turned east, so we moved farther east to accommodate them. Three days later, we came to a very wide river flowing sluggishly westward. We moved upstream and soon came upon another fairly large town. We surprised and captured a hunting party, on its way back to the town. The land was all cleared around the town, so it was impossible to surround it on foot. The horses were brought up, and the men broke out of the forest and surrounded the palisade. This was a bit complicated since it was built on a bluff above the broad bottom along the river, but by moving along the riverbank both up and down stream, the Hotcangara caught below the town fled back to the town and were allowed to do so by our deliberate advance. Once inside the palisade, we sent their hunting party to deliver our surrender demand. An intense-looking older man in chief regalia left the palisade and approached our lines.

Donduk and the staff moved forward a little to meet him. He looked us over dourly and asked who was our "war chief." Donduk was indicated to him by one of the Ocheti shakowin. He then raised his war club and rushed him screaming a battle cry. Before anyone else could react Smoking Mirror cut him off and struck him down with his strange swordlike weapon, cutting deeply into his head much like a heavy sword might. Meanwhile, the Hotcangara warriors rushed from their palisade, and our men began the usual archery maneuver (fire until they got close, retreat a short distance, fire again, repeat until they started retreating, then move forward firing until none were left). The enemy soon retreated back inside their palisade. While we readied the fire arrows, Donduk thanked Smoking Mirror for his quick reaction and asked if something had tipped him off as to the old man's intention. He replied that the man's eyes were full of arrogant defiance, and even though dressed as a peace chief, he was obviously a war chief. Donduk thanked him for his insight and turned back to the battle.

The fire arrows soon had the town ablaze, and the light wind fanned the flames. In time, the Hotcangara started pouring out of the opening or over the palisade and into the waiting arrows and swords of the attackers. When all resistance stopped, the men moved about the fallen, dispatching the wounded and recovering arrows. Once the fires burned themselves out, the town was inspected, and to our surprise there were few remains inside and no sign of any women or children. It looked like our attack had been expected, and they had sent their dependents away. But where had they sent them?

Donduk decided to cross the river using the boats the Hotcangara had left on the shore. First he wanted to check up on the other tumen, and he sent out messengers to them, while we camped near the town for the night. A strong force was placed near the boats on the shore just in case, and, indeed, there was attack in the night. It was likely aimed at destroying the boats, but had been easily beaten off with little loss to either side because of the moonless night. By morning all the messengers had reported back. The Foxes were heading toward us and, in fact, were already filtering in. They had met no resistance all the way down to the point where this river enters the Missi Sipi, and the town at that point assured them there were no Hotcangara allies on the far side of the river. They had then turned upriver to find us and had met no resistance in the two towns they had found on their way. The Bears had run into the river northwest of us and, like us, found a town that needed to be reduced. They then turned east and soon encountered another town that would not surrender. Finally, they ran into the Kestrels and started back toward us. The Kestrels had met very little resistance but instead had run into a seemingly different tribe (although they spoke a similar language) along a large river that flowed into this one from the north. They called themselves the Wazhazhe, and the Ocheti shakowin in the tumen also insisted that these were no more Hotcangara than they were.

Donduk decided to cross the river with the two tumen at hand, have the Bears take up a position right where we were now, and have me go to the Kestrels and look over these Wazhazhe. If I felt they were Hotcangara, I could make use of the Kestrels to take their surrender or destroy them. While the Donduk's Ordu began crossing the river, Smoking Mirror and I began following the river upstream. This led us at first southeast, then sharply north across a huge bottom that had been extensively exploited. We could see two large rivers emptying into this one on the far side. The second day, we ran into the Bears and soon passed the first of the cities they had destroyed. The river then led us east and toward late afternoon we came upon the second destroyed town. The smell was such that we pressed on almost until dark to escape it.

"Raven, am I correct in assuming your people never take captives?" Smoking Mirror asked while we ate a light meal.

"As a rule, we kill all those who resist us," I replied. "We found it tends to discourage others from resisting also."

"But that means you also kill women and children." He frowned. "Had there been any in that town we attacked, would not they also have been killed?"

"Yes," I admitted, "that is our way. But surely you see that if we spared the women and children, the men would be more likely to fight? Whereas, if they knew any resistance on their part would forfeit the lives of their loved ones, they are more likely to submit."

"But what if you find the women and children of that town when you cross the river," he persisted. "Will you then slay them?"

"Not unless they admit to being of that town," I suggested. "And even so, they could be spared since they didn't actually take part in the resistance. It would be up to the commander's judgment. What do your people do when you take an enemy village?"

"Well"—he shrugged—"such an occurrence would be rare. Most of our battles are mere skirmishes. The men not killed are taken captives and sacrificed to the Sun. The women and children are sometimes made slaves, but usually adopted into the tribe."

"Do you consider ritual torture and murder or slavery preferable to a quick, clean kill?" I pressed.

"The sacrifice honors the Sun and the captive," he replied evenly. "The slavery is not harsh and usually ends in adoption. Death is merely death."

"Among the Mongols," I continued, "slavery was almost always permanent. Kaidu considers owning slaves as owning the seeds of our own destruction and forbids it. In any case, we do not attack anyone without provocation. All we meet can either join us, confederate with us, or remain independent of us in peace. It is only if they attack first that we turn on them."

"In theory, what you say seems more than just," he rejoined. "In practice, however, your attack on the whole Hotcangara nation, because of a minor and harmless provocation by one simple town only loosely connected to the others, is rather extreme. The rest that followed was in response to your provocation. Do you equate roughing up and throwing out a stranger with surrounding a town and giving them the choice of surrender or death?"

"It is possible that we overreacted"—I shrugged—"but in order to establish oneself and gain respect sometimes that is most expedient. Besides, they could have just surrendered."

"No war chief of the Hotcangara would ever condone surrender without a fight." He looked at me as though I were mad. "And if he did, he would not long be a war chief. They had to respond to your challenge and admittedly, your destruction of the considerable force they sent against you established your people as a force to be respected. Add to this what I have seen, a huge army, divided into both plains and forest divisions, with superior weapons and mobility and led by very brave and able commanders. If you keep absorbing all the scattered tribes in the north, there is nothing that can resist you in all the land. I'm glad you are led by a man like Kaidu, but who will succeed him?"

"It is interesting," I mused, "that your 'brother' had the same question. I would guess that one of Kaidu's sons would succeed him. But I really can't say. He will make known his preference to the tumen commanders, and they will choose a successor when he dies. It need not be the one he recommends, but with his prestige it most likely will be. Then the choice is presented to the Mongols, and they either agree or not. At the moment most of the commanders are from the old land, but in time they will not be and things may change."

"What about you, Raven?" he smiled. "Will you be Khan one day?"

"No"—I laughed—"even if such a thing were likely, I wouldn't want it."

"Really?" He also laughed.

Late the next day, we arrived at the camp of the Kestrels. They were on a rise above the river bottom within sight of the river we had been following and the one that joined it from the north. On another rise to the north of the broad cleared and harvested bottom was the town of the Wazhazhe. We stayed with the Ordu that night and I went in to see the commander, Togun, a cousin of Kaidu. He told me they had been ordered to set up the Ordu right here for the winter, but to cooperate with me should I need them. It seemed that as soon as the other forest tumen were finished, they would also winter to the north of here in Hotcangara country. Meanwhile, more intense training was in progress in the north among the Anishinabe, the Dzitsiistas, the Kensistenoug, and newly allied Potawatamink and Ottawa to raise more forest tumen. He also mentioned that large numbers of my western tribes had come east to train at the Hawk Ordu. They would remain there for the winter. I would have a large pile of maps to reconcile when I got back.

The next morning, Smoking Mirror and I set out with a small escort to visit the Wazhazhe town. A high palisade that was open along a narrow corridor surrounded the town. The houses were much like those of the Hotcangara and the Ocheti shakowin. The men shaved their heads except for a small lock in the back. They wore a breechcloth and leggings with slipperlike shoes. Their women wore a sort of tunic like dress that fastened on the right side. They practiced limited tattooing. Both of us were viewed with some curiosity as we went to the chief's house. I still hadn't learned the Ocheti language, so I needed an interpreter. It was fairly obvious that these were not the Hotcangara and extending our hostility to them would have been unjustified. The chief was named Hehlashishe and was dressed as a peace chief. I explained that we had no quarrel with them and instead would welcome them as either members or confederates, explaining the usual at length. He explained that their organization was a loose one, and he could only speak for his town. I pressed for a meeting of the various chiefs, perhaps at a central location. He agreed to try to arrange such a meeting, but it would take time. I asked if I might stay and learn his language while we waited for the meeting. He agreed and assigned me one of his men to help learn their language. I sent word to Togun of the situation and my intention to try to recruit.

We were assigned one of their houses and brought food as honored guests. The language was not as complicated as I feared it would be, and both Smoking Mirror and I learned it rather easily over the next several days. After a few days, Hehlashishe informed me that he had arranged a meeting of the chiefs, at a town about six days' journey up the larger river. It seemed their tribe was on both sides of the river for some distance upstream. I decided to name it after them, since they were more worthy than the Hotcangara, who lived farther downstream. We set out for the town the next day. We crossed the river to the east of the town (which I decided to name for Hehlashishe) and continued east along the Wazhazhe. The terrain remained hilly, with broad bottoms along the rivers. The trees were of the same hardwoods, the oak and odd nut-bearing tree, that seemed to predominate along the southern half of the Mongol River. Just before we reached the town, however, we ran into what looked like larger versions of the beeches and maples found in the old land. The Wazhazhe River twisted about quite a bit, but led us generally east and a little north. During one of the northward swings, we came upon the town. It was fairly large and located above a huge bottom cut by many small rivers and streams.

We were ushered into a large meetinghouse and after the inevitable weed burning, I gave them the usual pitch. I had to explain the attack on the Hotcangara at length, but I threw in the fact that their other "relatives," the Ocheti shakowin, the Numakiki, and the Hewaktokto, had joined us outright. One of my escorts was one of the Ocheti, and he was also questioned at length. The questions were good ones about whether they had lost their identity, were treated poorly, still respected their chiefs, etc. He answered very positively, to their satisfaction. Next, I was asked about the disposition of the defeated Hotcangara. They thought that was fair. Finally, one of them wanted to know who Smoking Mirror was. When this was explained, they decided to also send a group of observers to stay with us for a year and report back the following fall. They also mentioned that there was another related group to the east of them, farther up the Wazhazhe, who were called the Amani yukhan. If I wished, they would inform them of my offer. I did wish and thanked them.

The next day, I set off back down the river with a small army of observers in tow. When we got back to the Kestrel Ordu, they had set up camp and already had their fall hunt. Togun told me that the other tumen were back across the Wazhazhe and were either on their way or already established in winter quarters. They had swept the southern shore of the river and found more Hotcangara-like people, who insisted that they were not Hotcangara, as well as another strange tribe. Juchi had tried to recruit them and was rebuffed by the former, but the latter had sent along some observers. The last of the "real" Hotcangara were either rounded up and returned across the river or dead. Togun kept most of my recruits but thought it best that a couple of them go on to the Eagle Ordu with me. He issued me a few extra horses to speed me back. We cut straight across to the city taking five days for the trip. I visited Tatanka Ska Koda in the city and asked him how the governorship was working out. He said he was honored by Kaidu's trust, and so far the Hotcangara had been peaceful if unfriendly. He wasn't sure if he'd be able to win them over.

The pontoon bridge was still up, speeding our crossing of the Missi Sipi, but even as we crossed, they started taking it down. We continued up the Mongol reaching the Owl Ordu in seven more days. The Titskan watitch bands had arrived and were already riding horses and learning our ways. Both Sanukh and Kwesh greeted me in Mongol; the former almost smiled. Both were anxious to know if Smoking Mirror was going to join, but he said it was up to his "brother." We continued upstream and eight days later finally got back to the Eagle Ordu. I greeted Paula and George first, got Smoking Mirror settled in with us, and then went on to report to Kaidu.

Kaidu had already received dispatches from Donduk and Togun, so he knew most of what I reported. He was glad that the Wazhazhe had sent along some observers. He asked me what I thought about them. I said that they were a lot like the Hotcangara, more so than the Ocheti shakowin. Still, they would likely confederate and might join. I also mentioned their willingness to pass on our offer to their related neighbors to the east. Finally, I mentioned Tatanka Ska Koda's misgivings about winning over the Hotcangara. He said that in the spring a group of them would be sent to each Ordu for preliminary training. Also a large contingent of them would be brought along on the campaign the following year. They would soon get the chance to prove themselves. He then handed me a pile of maps and said all my mapmakers had made it back to the Ordu and were at my disposal for debriefing. He wanted me to coordinate all the maps rather than anything else, and I should report back to him when I was finished.

When I got back to my yurt, I started looking over the maps. Smoking Mirror wanted to see them and grasp their significance more fully. I showed him the route we had followed from the time he had joined me. He was soon fascinated and wondered how we had come up with such an idea. I had to admit that it came from the Hanjen. He asked about them, and I tried to explain a little about them. He wanted to know where they were, and I showed him the route we had taken from the Karamuren to the Mongol. Grasping the distances and the nature of the terrain involved, I think he gained a new respect for us. Then he wanted to know where my people came from. I dug out an old map my grandfather George had given me. It was crude, and I knew it wasn't too accurate in the old Khanate, but it was all I had of the Far West, and I tried to show him from where my people originally hailed. He spent quite a while contemplating the map, and finally said it would likely take years for me to return to my people. I explained to him that it had taken my ancestor three years just to reach Karakorum from the west, but anyway they were no longer my people, and I couldn't even speak their language. We did still learn the book language, but we all spoke Mongol at home not the other language. Grandfather George knew some of it, but I had never learned it. I didn't ever remember my father speaking it either.

While I worked on the maps, Smoking Mirror kept pouring over them and asking questions. Meanwhile, I called in each of my mappers in turn to discuss their efforts. Tahhachet had returned to his Salst by taking the Tungus River, the first river that joined the Mongol after it turned south. It was the one that had looked as though it might be the Mongol since it was so muddy. It led him north for a while before turning west and was joined by many smaller rivers. He eventually came upon another river that led him to the north end of a large lake. He had circled the lake to get it all on the map, then followed a good-sized river from the southern end of it to his people. He had continued to map the river (which he named the Salst), until it was time to return. It was quite a river, snaking through the mountains. He said it eventually emptied into the sea, but, of course, did not get that far. He had brought a larger group of recruits back with him since the tribe had decided to confederate. He had followed another river (the South Salst) back. It eventually led him around another lake and onto a new pass through the mountains and to a small river (the Small River), which brought him to what turned out to be a southern tributary of the Salst. He followed the tributary (South Fork) back upstream until it ended in the hills; then continuing east, he found a small river heavily dammed by beavers (Beaver River) which finally led him back to the Mongol well above the falls. His maps were quite good. He had a very sure hand. It was a shame he didn't have much imagination.

Kulkulstuhah had taken the river that joined the Mongol right at the falls (Great Falls River). He followed it upstream until it turned north, and then took a southern tributary (Shining River) to its source. Over the mountains he found a north-flowing river (Sparkling Cold Seeking River), so he followed its southwestern tributary (Dark Boiling Creek) to its source. Again over the mountains, he found a west-flowing river (Bright Burning River) that emptied into Tahhachet's South Fork River. He followed it to a tributary that joined it from the south (Sharp Bitter Root River) that led him to another pass. Across the pass, he found the Churning White Water River, which eventually led him to the Kimooenim River downstream from where the Nimipu joined it. He mapped it up to the juncture and beyond to fill in my map. His people had also decided to be confederated with us, so with a large group of recruits, he returned up the Nimipu, taking the river (White Mountaintop River) that joined it from the north just where it turned west when we were following it. It led him to another pass over which he found a broad open valley with a river flowing north and west (Great Open Place Among the Mountain's River) which finally led him to the Mongol well above the Three Forks. His work was also quite good. It was a shame he had too much imagination.

Trehero had returned up the Absaroke River to the Naishandina River and followed it up to the river we didn't take the year before (Wind River). The country was indeed quite dry. He followed it to the large open place we had been the year before and then followed the same path we had taken the year before to the Kimooenim. His tribe had also chosen to confederate, and he led a large group up a tributary (North Branch) that joined the Kimooenim from the north just as it turned east not long before we left it the year before. It led him to a pass over which he found the source of the middle branch (Little Mongol—I changed it to Merkit) of the Mongol River. Recognizing the Three Forks when he reached them, he followed the third fork (Tiny Mongol—I changed it to Tatar) to near its source, then picked up the Absaroke and followed it back.

Woksihi had mapped the North Chahicks River to its source,

which turned out to be quite near that of the South Chahicks. He also did some mapping around the mountains at the source and of some tributaries of both rivers. Mahohivas mapped all the unexplored tributaries of the Absaroke River as far as the Naishandina. He named the two major ones the Horn and the Feather. The rest were mostly small intermittent creeks. Mehkwasskwan mapped the entire Inuna River from its source to Lake Winnipeg, then mapped the land around the lake, a marshy land of many lakes and streams. Pesequan mapped all around Lake Gichigami, as well as the Wooded Lake to its northwest; then he mapped the north shore of another large lake east of Gichigami and connected to it by a waterfall and a short river. He named it for the Ottawa who live there.

Shingabaossin had mapped for Juchi, and I had already seen his maps, but his three assistants had been sent on special mapping expeditions in the far east and had returned much later. Watang'a had mapped along the northern shore of the deep bay they had found. He saw and mapped two very large islands offshore, although he couldn't finish the second one because his party was attacked by the locals, a strange tribe who painted themselves red. The land continued north beyond the second island, but it was too late in the year to continue mapping, and he returned. Desthewa had mapped the southern shore of the same bay. He found a large peninsula cut by another bay and a generally rough irregular coastline. There was a long narrow island near shore just north of a very large wide peninsula with a very narrow neck. He had eventually run into Anawangmani, and both had returned through the North Country. Anawangmani had been sent east the last time Juchi touched the shore. He had also found a very rough irregular shoreline cut with many bays and rivers.

The mapping was a little sketchy during the running battle with the Mingue, but once past them it looked like there was another large lake south of the one named for the Ottawa. It was connected to the latter by a short river with a small lake in its middle. Shingabaossin had been able to fill in most of the lakeshore missed by Pesequan. At its western tip, it was connected by a strait to yet another large lake to the south and west, that the locals called Lake Michigamaw.

The western shore of this lake was well mapped by the forest tumen during their sweep of the Hotcangara. Much of the area swept seemed to be the same mix of open prairie and woods that I had seen in the land of the Chahiksichahiks. They had also found two tribes between the Wazhazhe and the southern shore of Lake Michigamaw. They were somewhat related to or allied with the Twanhtwanh and were called the Iliniwek and the Shawunogi. They had been quite pleased that we were destroying the Hotcangara and had sent some observers to look us over.

Smoking Mirror had known nothing about the northeast and northwest and was amazed how far it extended. He had traded with his tribe's neighbors to the east, but had not penetrated very far in that direction. Most of his travels had been to the south and west. He was very enthusiastic and wanted to learn how to make maps himself. He also wanted to learn to read and write. Once again, it looked like I would be giving winter classes. I took the finished maps to Kaidu, and he poured over them. There was a very large blank area where the Mingue were, but we could not be sure how numerous they were or how much of that blank spot belonged to them. I suggested we ask any visitors from the flanking tribes where their territories ended and any other information they might have about the Mingue. He agreed, and we found representatives of most of the tribes in camp. It seemed that there were at least ten separate tribes of Mingue, but no one agreed just where they were. Their numbers were obviously exaggerated and, of course, they were all taller than Padraig and fiercer than the huge western bears. One of the Leni lenape, however, insisted that they also fought among themselves. That piece of information was of great value. It looked like they would not be too hard to defeat since they were not united. I suggested we line up as many forest tumen as we had and sweep eastward from the lake as far south as we reached and take out as many as we found until we reached the Leni lenape borders. Kaidu said that that was what he had in mind and was glad I had some strategic ability since I would be leading one of the tumen. He wanted me to report to the training camps in the spring. The attack would begin in early fall. My first military command!

20
THE MINGUE CAMPAIGN, 7 K
(IROQUOIS CAMPAIGN, MN, WI, IL, IN, OH, PA, NY, 1375)

The winter passed busily with classes. Once again Paula and Mathilde helped with the reading and writing classes. It seemed that Padraig and Mathilde would be leaving us in the spring. He had been made commander of a new plains Ordu that would be set up along the Absaroke River, at its juncture with the Coal River. Paula and Mathilde were going to miss each other, but it was quite an honor for Padraig. Toward the middle of winter, Paula announced that she was again with child. It would be born while I was away in the early fall. I got Givevneu to give her some of the herb mixture she needed and to promise to keep an eye on her for me. George was already quite a rider, at least on small horses, and he was working with a toy bow and arrows. We did manage to make a run up to the Hawk Ordu to visit Henry. We waited until the river was frozen and went up on the dogsled, much to George's delight. Nitsiza had also come along, so he wouldn't forget how to use a sled. Actually he was quite taken with a young Siksika girl who lived there, and we saw none of him until the return trip. There was quite a bit of intertribal marriage and that, as well as the Mongol tolerance, had done much to eliminate tribal animosities. Still, there were occasional problems, especially with misunderstandings about various taboos. The Mongols' taboos were no exception to the confusion. But great pains were taken to discover and honor each other's prohibitions with as much goodwill as possible. Of course, kumis remained a problem. These must be the only people in the world who didn't have some sort of alcoholic beverage. Talaswaima said his people used some sort of sacred plant that gave them visions. I suspected it was likely the mukamur of the Tungus tribes of the old land or something similar. Smoking Mirror said that the southern tribes like his father's people had a strong drink, but it was made from the juice of a tall barrel-shaped plant with spines on it called the maguey. He was not impressed by the kumis and thought the southern drink was stronger. I wondered what he would think of the "burnt" (distilled) wine and the chiu lu" (distilled spirits) of the Hanjen.

Henry had made a special surprise for me. Having heard that I would be in command of a tumen, he found out that it would be the Wolf Tumen and made me a helmet with a very realistic wolf's head on it. He had found the time to become very artistic since he had so many apprentices. Some of his students, including his two boys, were also producing excellent work. I praised him lavishly and could see he was quite proud.

In early spring, Padraig, Mathilde and their children set off for their new Ordu, the Antelope. Paula, George, and Smoking Mirror accompanied me to the training ground where I would take charge of the newly forming Wolf Tumen. The training ground was in the old Ocheti shakowin village near Lake Ocheti. It was a lovely spot, and Paula enjoyed it. It was also very nice to have her with me for a change. A few more mapping expeditions were sent out to flesh out some blank spots. Shingabaossin was sent to map the western borders of the Mingue and, if possible, the northern borders as well. Pesequan was sent with Watang'a to map the northern shore of the land above where the latter left off the year before. Desthewa and Anawangmani were sent to map the shore south of where the latter left off the year before. They were to stop if they met any hostility, but both groups would have a sizable escort. Mahohivas and Pakonkya were to map the rest of the Wazhazhe River, then cross it and map the southern side as far as they could go among friendly tribes. Again a mapper was assigned to each tumen.

The training went quite well. The men had to get used to the horses and our bows. The greater range of the latter necessitated aiming changes. They got used to our various arrows also. The armor-piercing one was puzzling to them, since none of them nor anyone they knew of wore metal armor, but it was always a good idea to be ready for anything. Some of them took to the sword, but many preferred to use axes, and Henry had made quite a few steel axe heads for them. The maneuvering was probably the hardest thing to teach them. They had no trouble moving stealthily through the woods, but reaching a certain spot at a certain time took quite a bit of training. It was fortunate we had plenty of time to train them. By midsummer, however, I could wait at a clearing in the forest and almost the whole Ordu would poke through the surrounding trees at the given time. They were as ready as they would be.

Word came to move to the jump-off point. I sent Paula and the other women and children back to the Eagle Ordu with a strong escort. She was quite large, but still had some time to go before the baby came. I told little George to take care of her and made her promise to look up Givevneu when she arrived. We all left at the same time, they heading west, and we heading southeast. There were three other new forest tumen as well as mine. These were the Deer, the Moos (we had begun calling the large elklike animal by the name given it by the eastern tribes), and the Otter. My tumen was assigned the northern flank at the southern end of Lake Michigamaw. The other Ordu were placed on a line to the south of us about seventy-five li apart. The friendly tribes in our immediate path were already advised of our approach and assured we would bother neither them nor their game when we passed. All of them had given indication that they would likely confederate with us, and, indeed, the observers they had sent the year before were among the Ordu. They wanted to send more, but we didn't really want any untrained and undisciplined auxiliaries along.

Smoking Mirror was still along with me. He had sent word to his brother through one of the returning Kitikiti'sh that he would return in the winter after the current campaign. He had been observing and taking part in all the exercises, and, although he now had a steel sword, still used his own. It was hard to say how he would advise his brother, he never gave any indication, and I thought it would be rude to ask. He stayed by my side throughout the campaign and even wore a wolf's head like my other minghan commanders.

A copy of Shingabaossin's map of the western "borders" of the Mingue was waiting for each of the tumen commanders. There didn't seem to be any special terrain problems in the area covered by his map. We all moved forward on the given day, about eight days after we arrived. Juchi's Foxes were to my right. The people through whom we would be passing were the Iliniwek. We passed through their country as quickly as possible, remaining on horseback and making long marches. It only took us three days to clear them and begin encountering their eastern neighbors, the Twanhtwanh. These had a very large contingent among us and more were kept from tagging along only with great difficulty. It took four days to clear their land. Toward the end of the third day, we came to the large lake where Juchi had found the Twanhtwanh the year before. I decided to name it Lake Twanh after them since they had been such help. The land near the western end of the lake was rather marshy, but farther south, along a slow meandering river, it was more like a swamp. Assured no one lived in the swampy area, we hugged the lakeshore until the land became more solid.

As soon as we cleared the marshy border of the Twanhtwanh, we changed over to the infiltrative advance. This, of course, slowed us down considerably, but would help us avoid ambushes. Word soon came of a palisaded town ahead. It was isolated along the bank of a small stream that emptied into the lake. I brought up the horses to expedite surrounding the town. The palisade was quite high, at least thirty feet, and it was impossible to see over it from our position. The townsfolk were doing some late harvesting and were obviously not expecting us. They were no taller than any other tribe we had encountered, but they did wear very little clothing for being so far north. The men's hair was all shaved except for a thin line in the middle of the head, from forehead to neck, dressed to stand up like bristles. Just as the horses were brought up, a heavily laden hunting party could be seen approaching the town from the east. This caused some excitement, and further covered our getting mounted up. I waited until the party was almost to the palisade before ordering the encirclement. The men streamed around the village in a large arc. The stunned Mingue stood for a moment, then ran back to their town. Once we had surrounded the town, I sent one of the Twanhtwanh, who could speak a little of Mingue language, forward to deliver the usual ultimatum.

I could see that their palisades had platforms on the inside, for their warriors were visible above it. When my man finished the ultimatum, he was promptly pierced with several arrows and fell. I was furious, but quickly overcame the fury, and gave orders. We were out of their bowshot, but they were not out of ours. First, I had the men shoot three volleys of arrows high over the palisade, then two volleys of fire arrows, then more regular arrows. I thought they might be able to put out a regular barrage of fire arrows, but with a little softening up, and overkill with the fire arrows, and enough deadly hail to keep them from putting out the fires, it should get out of control. Indeed, it was obvious that the fire was spreading fast. A gentle breeze off the lake fanned the flames, and soon even the palisade was smoldering. In desperation, the warriors clambered over the palisade and tried to rush us, only to be cut down. Even their women and children poured out of the palisade opening and headed for our lines armed with sharp sticks and stones. These also were cut down. When resistance seemed over, the men advanced carefully, and as expected when they got close enough, some of the apparently lifeless warriors sprung up to the attack. This cost us a few men, but only a few.

We recovered our arrows and took the rest of their harvest, before moving on a little to camp for the night. I sent out scouts to reconnoiter and set up sentries. Nothing happened in the night, but the next morning one of the scouts did not return. The others reported no less than three towns nearby. One was quite small and a short distance ahead. The other two were to our south and to our southeast. The missing scout had gone south, so we went south. Late in the day, we arrived at the palisaded town. It was larger than the one we had destroyed. There were fields all around the town that had not been fully harvested, but no one was in the fields. There was a lot of noise coming from the town, and only a few warriors were visible on the palisade. Their attention seemed to be directed inward, with occasional glances outward.

Not wishing to waste any more men on ultimata, I ordered the men around the town. As we broke out into the open, the lookouts finally noticed us and tried to raise the alarm. By the time we had surrounded the town, the noise died down, and the palisade began to bristle with warriors. I used the same strategy with the same effect. The warriors spent less time on the fire, however, and rushed us with an odd sort of frenzy. They screamed wildly and seemed to need more arrows than one would expect to cut them down. Some even got close enough to be cut down with sword or axe. This was also true of the women and children, even the rather small children, who rushed us like rabid dogs. I was quite taken aback by this and asked Smoking Mirror if he had ever seen the like. He admitted that he hadn't seen anything quite this extreme, but sometimes after the Hasinai warriors had partaken in the flesh of a captive, they did fight with extra ferocity. A sickening thought occurred to me, and when the fire in the town burned itself out, I went in and found the charred, dismembered remains of a captive, still tied to a stake. I couldn't tell, of course, but I had a feeling it was our missing scout. Again, I felt a wave of fury and only with difficulty overcame it. We paused long enough to bury our dead (including what was probably our scout) and retrieve our arrows, then set off to the east to the next town.

We reached it a little before dark on the next day, and we camped for the night. Before first light, we had surrounded the town, and as the Mingue lookouts squinted into the early dawn, they saw our force emerge from the woods into the cleared fields encircling the town. Before I could order the first barrage, a lone man emerged from the palisade and came toward our line. He was unarmed and held his hands up to demonstrate the fact. As he drew near, I could see he was an older man, but I was on my guard, fully prepared for some sort of treachery. I found one of the Ottawa who could speak the language of a tribe related to the Mingue. The old man looked at our horses and us; then his eyes returned to me. It was obvious he was bewildered by us in general and me in particular. I told the interpreter to deliver the ultimatum. He did, and again the man turned to me.

"Why have you come to my village with this ultimatum?" he asked. "What have we done to warrant destruction at your hand?

Who are you? You are not one of our neighbors."

"You are a warlike, belligerent people, whose very existence is an affront to the Blue Sky," I answered coldly. "Your people and your relatives to the east attacked our peaceful expedition last fall and must answer for the outrage. As to who we are, we are the Mongols, the Wolf Tumen of the Khanate of the Blue Sky."

"My village attacked no strangers such as you last fall," the old man rejoined. "If we had, we would accept the consequence of our actions. You cannot hold us responsible for the deeds of distant relatives only some of whom are even loosely allied to us."

"You can always surrender the town," I said. "Otherwise, you must share the fate of your towns to the west."

"What was that fate?" he asked.

"Annihilation," I answered.

"If we surrender, what will become of us?" he wanted to know.

"You will have to join us," I began. "Of course, we could not trust you, at first; you would have to earn that. But in time and in the absence of treachery, you would become Mongols. We would require a group of your warriors to accompany us, and eventually we would appoint a governor whose orders you would have to obey without question."

"You would not kill any of us or make us slaves?" He seemed surprised.

"No," I answered. "You have until midmorning to bring us your decision."

He returned to the town, and the men got ready to attack. They seemed to be sure the Mingue would never surrender. Smoking Mirror asked me if I thought there was some similarity between the language of the Mingue and that of the Kadohadacho. I couldn't see it, but reminded him that he was much more familiar with it than I was. Still, I couldn't imagine how a people this far removed from his could speak a related language. I asked him what he thought the chief would decide to do. He had no idea, but suggested that I not enter the town if it did surrender, just in case they did plan treachery. He was right, of course, but I hated to order someone else to take such a risk.

Before long, the old man returned to our lines, again holding his arms up to show he was not armed. He reported that the town had agreed to surrender and would send out the young men requested. He then invited me to visit the town. I prudently replied that I had to move on. They would be left alone for now, and should any other group of Mongols approach, they should say that they had already surrendered to the Wolf Tumen. We gathered up the men and proceeded north to the small village. They also surrendered quickly after one of the Mingue explained the situation to them. We continued eastward with occasional excursions to the south and accepted the surrender of several more towns before we came to another large town that killed the Mingue who delivered our ultimatum. This upset the others from his town, and they wanted to take part in the attack, but I told them, they were on probation and would have to obey orders or else. The town suffered the same fate as the others that had resisted. The demonstration was also instructive for our Mingue guests, who were shocked at how totally we destroyed the town at such minimum cost.

The shore of the lake was taking us farther north, so I thought it wise to contact Juchi to see if he was covering me well enough or if I had to stretch farther south. We made contact, and it turned out he was still a little to the west of me, but he was covering my flank pretty well. While he had been slowed by the need to reduce six of the towns, the tumen to his south were shifting north due to running into a mountain range free of any Mingue or anyone else except for scattered hunting parties from the Amani yukhan. To the south, the tumen had found a small group of Mingue towns that called themselves the Honniasontkeronon. These had offered no resistance at all. The group we were currently fighting our way through called themselves the Yenresh, or people of the long tail (a reference to a medium-sized panther-type cat). Their resistance varied along the line, but all the tumen had seen some action. Donduk ordered that we keep in contact with neighboring tumen every day.

On the sixteenth day of the campaign, we reached a town that our Yenresh said belonged to a different group of Mingue, the

Atirhagenrat. They also surrendered, as did the six other towns they had on this side of the lake. We found that the lake ended in a river at its northeast tip. The river flowed northward over a broad band of waterfalls and on to another large lake. I called it Lake Mingue, since they seemed to surround it. The Atirhagenrat said that most of their villages were on the northwestern end of Lake Twanh, across the river with the falls. I sent some of them to contact their other villages, promising them destruction on our way back if they didn't surrender. The next town we encountered was of yet another group of Mingue. They killed the Atirhagenrat we sent with the ultimatum, so we had to destroy them. This seemed to be the pattern with these people, and of the eight villages I encountered, only one surrendered. It seemed they called themselves Oneniute'ron'non. Few of them surrendered to the south either. Juchi only got two of seven to surrender and only five of the rest surrendered. The next group of Mingue were the same, only a total of six of the towns surrendered, none to me. This group called themselves the Kwenio'gwen and, while less numerous than the last group, were no less fierce. Our losses were beginning to mount. One of my minghan commanders was killed fighting this group.

Our more southerly tumen were also encountering a very fierce group, the Kanastoge. These were the ones who had first attacked Juchi. They turned out to be living in a very broad valley along a wide shallow river. They had no real tribal cohesion owing allegiance only to their town. Only one of their towns ended up surrendering. Not as far south, there was a small group called the Awenro'ron'non, who surrendered all of their few towns.

The next group we encountered surrendered almost half of their towns. They called themselves the Ononta'ge. They were almost as numerous as the Oneniute'ron'non, but less bellicose. The next group was another small one, but only a few of their towns surrendered. They were the Tiionen'iote'. The last group we encountered was the worst. They resisted savagely; only four of all their towns could be induced to surrender. These called themselves the Kaniengehaga. We were much relieved when we finally finished them and found the northern neighbors of the Leni lenape along an east-flowing river that proved to empty into the Leni Lenape River. They sometimes called themselves the Mahican, that meant People of the Wolf, making my tumen quite a hit among them. This leg of the campaign had taken us to late fall, but the Mingue were destroyed as a threat.

Our losses were not as inconsequential as in the Hotcangara campaign. I had lost about seven hundred dead and twice as many wounded. The other tumen's losses were comparable. One of the southernmost tumen, the Kestrels, had almost four thousand killed and wounded. The Bear Ordu set up camp at the eastern limit of Mingue territory on the bank of the river (I named it for the Mahicans since they controlled its lower end) that flowed east to join the Leni Lenape River. The seriously wounded were left with them so they'd have a chance to recover or at least die in peace. The Osprey Ordu set up camp near the eastern end of Lake Twanh, right in the middle of the river that connected the two lakes. The rest of the Atirhagenrat had decided to surrender also, but we were a little suspicious of them. It also turned out that there was yet another group of Mingue on the north shore of Lake Mingue. These called themselves the Wendat. It was too late in the fall to make an attack on them, so Donduk ordered the Atirhagenrat to contact them with a surrender demand they could think over during the winter. Donduk further decided to remain as governor so he could keep an eye on them as well as the rest of the Mingue. The Otter Ordu was placed at the headwaters of the Wazhazhe River, not far from where two rivers join together to form it, and the Moos Ordu was placed on the western border of the Yenresh tribe, not far from the first of their villages to surrender. This would enable them to come quickly to aid the other Ordu if needed. Meanwhile, the Mingue were charged with burying their dead and keeping all four of the Ordu fed for the winter. The rest of us started back. The Kestrels returned to their old Ordu, as did the Foxes. The Deer and my Wolves went to the old camps of the Bears and Osprey. I settled them in, put my second in command, Temur, in charge and went on to the Eagle Ordu. It snowed off and on most of the way, but the new fully functional yam network made it an easy trip.

Smoking Mirror wanted to return to the Eagle Ordu with me and take his leave of Kaidu before returning home. I asked him what he thought of the Mongols after being with them for a year. He said we were good warriors, but our main strengths were our superior weaponry and the horses. Our tactics were more logical than innovative, and the forest tactics were quite typical of the southeastern tribes. We would not easily conquer them, but we would in the end, from sheer force of numbers. He thought it little short of miraculous that we had been able to unite as many tribes as we had, and turn them into a cohesive, disciplined army. He was particularly surprised that we were so successful since we seemed to do nothing for our gods. He couldn't imagine how they could be so benevolent to us when we all but ignored them.

I assured him that Kaidu made the requisite sacrifices to Tengri and the more devout Mongols made appropriate offering to their lesser gods. Also the locals who joined us continued to honor their gods, but we just didn't let it interfere with our orders. He then said that he had never seen me offer any sacrifices at all in the year we had been together. Did I actually feel no obligation to the gods? I tried to explain that my "tribe" believed in a god that did not need sacrifices. We offered him our work and strove to do the best we could at it to honor him. He said that I sounded like an artisan. I told him about our family history and explained that I was the first one who was not a swordsmith. He then said he understood. His father revered the god of the merchants, Yacateuctli, the Lord of the Nose. Smoking Mirror also served that god even though he was not exactly a merchant.

I went with him when he took his leave of Kaidu. He thanked him for his hospitality and the openness with which he was received. He told him that he was fortunate to be served by me, and he was grateful that he had been allowed to remain with me throughout his stay. Finally he said that he would tell his "brother" that he should confederate with us, or, at the very least, remain at peace with us, for we could easily destroy the Hasinai. He then thanked me again and took his leave. We gave him the horse and weapons he had been using as a gift.

Kaidu was pleased and told me he hoped the Hasinai would

confederate. I reported on the campaign, fleshing out the dispatches Donduk had sent. He was satisfied with the campaign, but regretted that it had been so bloody for us. Of course, the elimination of a large hostile force was necessary, but it would behoove us to mop up the following year instead of taking any new ground. The various mappers had come in, and I would be able to flesh out my maps further. All of the major tribes we had contacted the year before, except for the Hasinai, had either confederated or joined us. Actually only the scattered, primitive southern tribes had joined us, the rest would only confederate. Still, the ploy was working, and more and more of the confederates were joining as individuals, if not as tribes. It looked as though we would not only be able to replace all of our losses, but we would be able to raise at least two more tumen. Kaidu did not want to take on the southeastern tribes for a while.

I told him that the main flaw in our strategy was our dependence on the weather. While we had been lucky to have had a fairly dry fall to aid in our fire arrow attacks, it was quite likely that the damper southeast would need another approach. I suggested that he let me try to find a source of saltpeter or, failing that, petroleum. With the former, I could make gunpowder, and if Henry could make a cannon, we could make short work of the palisades even if it was raining. We could also terrify the enemy with the rockets the Hanjen used to make. From the petroleum I could distill the clear burning liquid that was used in the Hanjen fire thrower. He thought the saltpeter was worth looking for, but considered the fire thrower too dangerous as an offensive weapon, but an excellent defensive weapon. If we ever went on the defensive it would be useful, but he had seen too many accidents with it on offensive operations. He told me to look for both, but especially the saltpeter.

Paula, meanwhile, had presented me with a daughter. She wanted to name her for her friend, Mathilde, and I thought it a good idea. The delivery had been easier than the first, and both mother and child were fine. George was only a little interested in his sister, but was especially thrilled with the miniature replica of my helmet that his cousin, Henry, had made for him. Mathilde had written that their Ordu was in a beautiful spot, and they hoped we could visit them if

time permitted. Padraig had sent out his mappers toward the west
to contact the tribes beyond the Salst and the Nimipu. They would
winter there and return in the summer. Perhaps that prospect would
help draw us there? I was interested in the western shore tribes, but
whether I could go there in the summer would depend on whether I
had found any saltpeter. I decided to see if any of the newer recruits
from the eastern tribes were familiar with it. None were familiar with
it until one of the Wazhazhe tasted it. He was certain he had tasted
the "salt that cools the tongue" before. He said it was in a cave in
the northern part of the tribal lands. He was sure he could take me
there in the spring. I had not heard of it being in a cave before, but
it sounded more promising than the miserable method of making
it artificially with rotting vegetation and ash.

The maps were interesting. The men had been again rebuffed
on the large island off the northeast coast, but to the north of it, the
very rugged coast gradually turned westward. They eventually ran
into people that sounded like the Inuit from the description. They
had been allowed to map the coast and found it occupied by them
until it plunged south into a very deep bay. At the southern end of
the bay, they had run into Kensistenoug. They would go back to
finish mapping the coast the next spring. Great rivers cut the central
part of the eastern coast. At the mouth of the Leni Lenape River
was a group of islands, one very long and narrow, and the others
much smaller. They named the largest island Montauk for the main
group of villages on the island. All along the mainland coast to the
south of the Leni Lenape River, there were barrier islands broken
occasionally by channels. The interior coast was very marshy on both
shores of the back bays. After some distance, they arrived at the tip
of a peninsula jutting in to narrow the mouth of a broad bay. They
followed this up to another great river, on both sides of which lived
the Leni lenape. Since it was a great river, but there was already one
named for the tribe, they decided to name this one the Raven River.
That was flattering, but not very politic. I changed the name to the
Chingis River. Beyond the bay, they again found barrier islands and
again came to a peninsula and a huge bay. They followed the western
side of the peninsula all the way up to the mouth of the same wide

river along which the Mingue had been found. They had not named this river yet, so I named it the Kubilai River. At this point, it was late fall, and they went to the Bear Ordu to winter and sent their maps west with the dispatches. They would continue the following spring. Shingabaossin had finished mapping most of the northern side of Lake Twanh and filled in some of the area farther north of it. He would start mapping the area occupied by the Atirhagenrat and the Wendat and fill out what he had missed during earlier expeditions the following spring. South of the Wazhazhe River, the lands of the Amani yukhan seemed to extend to the foothills of a chain of mountains running from northeast to southwest. Mahohivas and Pakonkya had made it as far south as one of the two great rivers we had noticed joining the Wazhazhe from the south. Along it they had run into the strange tribe Juchi had found the year before. They had reluctantly decided to confederate. They called themselves "Tsoyaha Yuchi" which apparently meant "Children of the Sun from Faraway." It seemed they believed they were descended from the sun and traveled from "far away" to arrive at their current location. They did not consider themselves related to any other tribe. We decided to call them Tsoyaha, and they were quite happy with that name.

21
Gunpowder and Cannon, 8K
(SD to OH and Back, 1376)

In late spring, I set off with Paula and the children back to the Wolf Ordu. Over the winter, Henry and his men had fashioned helmets with appropriate effigies for all of the Ordu commanders. The helmets for the leader of each Ordu had a larger effigy with a widely open mouth (I wasn't sure if there was a message there). The second tier of commanders had effigies with closed or (if appropriate) snarling mouths. The third tier had the same effigies as the second, but made out of copper. I took the ones for my Wolves with me. Everyone was very pleased with them, for they were quite well crafted. I decided to have the fourth-tier commanders, the arban commanders, wear the actual wolf heads over their helmets, since higher ranks no longer needed them. Temur had done an excellent job in my absence. The Ordu was back up to full strength and in fighting trim. Still, there would have to be quite a bit of training for the new recruits. There was also a group of about a hundred of the Hotcangara in camp to be trained. They were distributed around and kept under close scrutiny. Making sure all was in order, I again turned the Ordu over to the able hands of Temur, and, with Paula and the children and my Wazhazhe guide, set off to find the saltpeter.

I had brought along with me all the sulfur I had gathered in the Yellow Canyon just in case I found any saltpeter. I also brought some of the same sort of iron tools I had given the Anishinabe in return for their iron ore.

The Wolf Ordu was in Hotcangara territory on the eastern bank of the Missi Sipi River some distance north or upstream from their city. We had renamed the city Murenbalikh (River City in the Mongol tongue). This was, of course, an insult to the Hotcangara, but was intended also as a test to see if they were prepared to fully accept their defeat by accepting our name for their city. It was too soon to tell at this time, and I certainly didn't trust them. In fact, the next leg of our journey would take us through their territory to the Deer Ordu, so I made sure we had a strong escort. We passed a few of their towns but did not stop or even pause. Paula wanted to see the towns but appreciated the imprudence of doing so. The Hotcangara we came upon were not overtly hostile, nor were they even vaguely friendly. I did begin to think they were resigned, but I remained on guard.

We stopped at the Deer Ordu for a couple of days. Their commanders were all resplendent in their new helmets and expressed gratitude for them to Henry through me. I promised to pass it on to him when I saw him later. Chagatai, the commander of the Deer and a nephew of Kaidu, brought me up to date on events in the east. A renegade group of the Mingue had become bandits, attacking small groups of our men as well as any of their own people who had accepted the situation. Donduk cleverly ordered the Atirhagenrat to wipe them out as a proof of their loyalty. They went out in force and pretty much ran the renegades to ground virtually annihilating them. It seemed they didn't like them anyway and took to the task with some relish. Meanwhile, the Wendat had sent spies to check us out and see if our threat should be taken seriously. What they heard from their relatives convinced them they should cut a deal, and they sent a group of their chiefs to visit Donduk in early spring. Donduk had ordered the scattered Mingue towns of the eastern groups including the southern one that had resisted us so bitterly to relocate between a group of small lakes not far south from Lake Mingue and the Mahican River up to where the Bear Ordu was camped. This would put them directly between two Ordu making it easier for him to keep an eye on them and at the same time protect them from any opportunistic attacks by their neighbors. Once they were removed, he sent word to their neighbors to freely move into the evacuated areas. They lost no time in doing so. The groups that had not resisted were left intact, and the Yenresh were consolidated near the eastern end of lake Twanh. It looked like all was in control there.

When we left the Deer Ordu, we moved southeast through the lands of first the Iliniwek, then the Shawunogi before reaching the country of the Wazhazhe. We, of course, had to stop at any villages we encountered and go through the usual formalities. Paula and the children attracted a lot of attention probably because the locals couldn't believe there were any more like me, especially women and children. Paula enjoyed seeing the towns and villages and admiring the crafts the women showed her, and showing off and fussing over each other's babies. George was all over the place having the time of his life. I had to go through the weed burning and meet with the elders. Paula would wrinkle her nose when I returned from these meetings, lest I forget the noxious smell clinging to me. I guess she never did get used to it. At length, our Wazhazhe guide brought me to the cave. It proved to be a limestone cave, and indeed there was a large deposit of saltpeter on its floor. It must have formed from seeping through the limestone, but I had no idea how or from what. In any case, while I gathered up as much as the horses could carry, I got my guide to get together the chiefs of all the villages which might have caves like this near them.

It took a few days to get the group together, but was well worth it. They passed around the iron tools and agreed they were worth having. I explained carefully what I wanted from the caves and passed around a bit so they could all be sure. One of them told me that there were more such caves across the Wazhazhe River as well and offered to send word to the chiefs of the villages near those caves. I thanked them all and asked them to take great pains to keep the saltpeter dry and deliver as much as they found to the Kestrel Ordu, the most convenient location to them. After the meeting, I hurried to the Kestrels myself. It took several days to get there because we had to stop at any villages along the way and go through the usual. By the time we reached the Kestrels, even Paula was getting a little tired of it.

Once at the Kestrels, I briefed Togun, their commander. He was excited that we would be able to use gunpowder again, for he had seen it in action in the old Khanate when he was young. I sent dispatches to Henry to send more iron tools and to Padraig to send me some more sulfur from the Yellow Canyon. Then I set up something of a factory at the Ordu. I got some of the men preparing charcoal. Although there were several different gunpowder formulae, I was mostly interested in the exploding formula, the best to use in cannon. Besides, we didn't have any arsenic, and I always considered the use of it as typical Hanjen overkill. I made up as much gunpowder as I could with the sulfur at hand, showing a couple of handpicked men how to make it. They would stockpile the saltpeter and charcoal until we got more sulfur from Padraig. A special building reinforced with stone was erected near the center of the Ordu to hold the materials. The finished gunpowder would be sent to my Wolf Ordu and to the Eagle Ordu, the most central locations. Meanwhile, I would take all I had made with me to the Hawk Ordu and see if Henry could make me cannon, or at least the more primitive fire sticks. We loaded the powder on horses rather than wagons so I could make better time, and set off for Murenbalikh under very strong escort.

Tatanka Ska Koda greeted us warmly and assured me the city was safe and the Hotcangara reconciled. Still I insisted on an escort as I showed Paula the city. We crossed the Missi Sipi on the pontoon bridge, which had been set up again after the spring floods. All the river bottoms were green with growing crops. I sped on the Owl Ordu and called on Kuyuk. I told him about the gunpowder and asked if he had heard anything from Smoking Mirror. He had not, but there were so many recruits that he had had to send large groups of them to the three nearby Ordu for training. He didn't know if there were any of the Hasinai among them, but there were many different tribes represented. It occurred to me that Smoking Mirror might know where I could find sulfur more conveniently than the Yellow Canyon. Since he could now read and write, I wrote him a note asking if he knew where it could be found and enclosing with it a small amount of it in case he wasn't familiar with it. Kuyuk had set up a yam system to connect us with our confederates the Chahiksichahiks and the Kitikiti'sh, so I sent it to the latter asking them to deliver it to him. If we could get a good reliable source of sulfur, I could even make some of the sorely missed matches we had grown used to in the old land.

We took our leave and went on to the Eagle Ordu where I briefed Kaidu. He was glad I found the saltpeter, but told me to be very careful in making the cannon. He had seen them explode horribly when flawed and didn't want to lose Henry and me to an experimental cannon. I assured him we'd detonate from a safe distance. It was almost late summer by the time I arrived at the Hawk Ordu. Henry assured me that he had sent a large shipment of tools for the Wazhazhe. He was willing to try to make a cannon but had no idea how. I explained the shape and thickness and suggested he not make it very long or a particularly large caliber for now. We settled on about two feet long and about three inches thick with a caliber of about four and a half inches. It would have to be of cast iron since I had found neither tin nor zinc to make bronze or brass. I decided to start with some solid stone projectiles at first just to see if it would work at all. I fashioned these and some very long fuses while Henry worked on the cannon.

The finished cannon was a beauty. Henry was justifiably proud of his effort. Once it had completely cooled, I carefully checked it for any cracks or thin spots, but found none. We loaded all on a wagon and went well away from the Ordu to try it out. We found a promising spot, and I wedged the cannon against some rocks, loaded it with powder and one of the rock projectiles, and attached one of my very long fuses. We checked around to make sure no one could be in any danger from it; then I lit the fuse, and we took cover. The cannon erupted, and the projectile flew with great force for some distance. I ran up to examine the cannon carefully. It was unharmed and still showed no cracks. I fired off my remaining rocks playing with the trajectory and different amounts of powder to get a feel for what the gun could do. After each shot, we both carefully examined the gun for any cracks, but it remained sound. I congratulated Henry and told him to make two or three for each tumen and some extras if possible.

While he had that task before him, I showed his apprentices how to make hollow shot to fit the cannon and odd-sized ones for use as thrown bombs. I got some other men started on making solid shot out of stone. Still others I had gather and make stone and pottery chips and store them in containers for shrapnel shot. I showed another group how to make the Hanjen fire arrows using a little gunpowder. These were more effective than the older Mongol fire arrows. Finally, I converted some of my gunpowder to burning powder and made some rockets. These would have to be battle rockets rather than festival ones since I didn't have the ingredients to make colors. Even so, I fired one off for the Ordu much to the amazement of the non-Mongols. I made sure each new cannon was fired at least once and checked for flaws as soon as it was ready. The locals eventually got used to the "ground thunder," as they called it.

By early fall, I was getting low on gunpowder, and still there was no sulfur from Padraig. I sent another dispatch to him, but the rider had just set out when an answer to my note to Smoking Mirror arrived. With it was a bag of sulfur. In his note he said that there was a very large supply of sulfur in the lands of the Ishak, and they would be glad to trade it for almost anything we might offer. He suggested dried ox meat would be the best commodity. Meanwhile, he was sending more sulfur, but he would need us to send him the promised meat for now, and I could send anything else I thought the Ishak might be able to use for further shipments. This was ideal since we always had a large supply of the dried ox meat on hand in case of need. I sent a dispatch to Kuyuk asking him to send several horse loads of the dried meat to Smoking Mirror and asked him to route the promised sulfur to the Kestrel Ordu. I sent the Kestrels a dispatch advising them of the coming sulfur and asking them to send me a few wagonloads of their saltpeter. I thought it best if we had a good supply of gunpowder here in the Hawk Ordu so we could test the new cannon and make more of the bombs and fire arrows. I got some men to make a stone-reinforced building to house the gunpowder just like the one at the Kestrel Ordu. I used some of the sulfur to make matches and sent them with a note about our progress to Kaidu. Finally I sent another note to Smoking Mirror thanking him for his help in getting us the sulfur and inviting him to come for a visit so I could show him how we used the sulfur.

Finally, in mid fall with the first snows already dusting the plains, a wagonload of sulfur came from Padraig. I sent him a dispatch thanking him and explaining that I realized how hard it was to get it from the Yellow Canyon, but urged him to get more the following year and send it on to the Hawk Ordu. I had gotten some of the men to make and powder charcoal so when the saltpeter arrived all was ready. I showed a couple of picked men how to make the burning and the exploding gunpowder, and, at Paula's suggestion, showed a couple of the women how to make matches. With everything under control, we returned to the Eagle Ordu in early winter. When we got back, Paula informed me that she was again with child. I should have noticed by now, but had been so caught up in my work. I apologized for missing the obvious. I promised myself not to miss such a thing ever again. I did make sure she consulted with Givevneu again.

I went in to see Kaidu to report on all that had been accomplished. I suggested that it would be a good idea to train some men to handle the cannon, perhaps giving them a distinguishing helmet or insignia since it was dangerous work. He thought that a good idea and suggested that my brother might come up with an appropriate helmet. He also said that he had an old gunner in the Ordu. His name was Kabul; he was about sixty years old, but still quite sharp. I thought it odd that he had a Mongol gunner, since they usually left that to the Hanjen. He said Kabul's mother had been a Hanjen and her brother a fine gunner who had taught him all he knew. In any case, he didn't want me teaching gunners next spring; Kabul would do that. He wondered if Smoking Mirror had given any indication of his brother's intentions in his note. I replied that he had not, but he couldn't be too hostile, since he let us get sulfur. I mentioned that I had invited Smoking Mirror to visit and find out for what we used the sulfur so I could find out how his tribe was leaning. He thought it unwise to let them see the power of the gunpowder unless they were with us, or they would surely cut it off. I suggested I could just show him the matches, and he thought that best. He gave me the latest efforts of our wandering mappers and sent me off telling me he might have a task for me next spring.

The maps filled in more of the blank spaces. Shingabaossin mapped the rest of Lake Twanh and all of Lake Mingue as well as the rest of the river that led from the latter to the deep bay they had found two years before. He had named the river the Wendat since the group had been quite cooperative. He also filled in the area between the lakes and his earlier more northerly passage. Pesequan and Watang'a had spent the whole time mapping the very large bay they had found the year before. They had tried to map all the rivers that emptied into it up to the fall line, a daunting task. It looked like quite a bay. Their notes said it was full of shellfish, fish, and waterfowl. The locals never went hungry. They were apparently related to the Leni lenape, although not closely enough to be friendly to them. They used the village names to name the rivers resulting in the following odd names: Tauxenent, Potomac, Cuttatawomen, Onawmanient, Rappahannock, Mattapony, and Mummapacune among others. I wasn't too sure these were the best choices, but no doubt the locals would approve. Mahohivas and Pakonkya had finished mapping the land of the Tsoyaha. They mapped all of the first and most of the second of the two large rivers that joined the Wazhazhe from the south and had named them the East and West Tsoyaha rivers. At the headwaters of the East Tsoyaha, they had run into the southern extension of the chain of mountains we had encountered during the Mingue campaign. They had found a chiefdom consisting of several towns about halfway up the West Tsoyaha River. They were not overtly hostile, but would not allow them to continue mapping the river. Looking at my completed map, I thought we should first explore the mountains between the Tsoyaha and the coast. I wondered how Kaidu would see it and when he would want us to begin our exploring. Padraig's dispatches said that his mappers had not yet returned to him from their expedition to the western coast, so he would be sending out scouts to try and find them the following spring.

I had barely finished the maps when Smoking Mirror showed up. He said he had planned to come in the spring since he found our winters a bit rough, compared to what he was used to. Nevertheless, my note had piqued his curiosity since he had only heard of the yellow substance being used as a medicine. I asked if his brother had made a decision about joining us yet. He said that his brother had decided not to join or confederate, but he would cooperate with us and in no way impede our movements. Also, he would not stand in the way of any of his people who might want to join us. I was a little disappointed but not entirely surprised. He had been the most hostile of all the chiefs I had interviewed on my journeys. But at least he would not impede us. Still, I wondered how Smoking Mirror felt.

"My brother is more interested in his own position," he began, "than in the welfare of his people. Or at best, he confuses the one with the other. He sent me to look you over because I have seen much and been among many different people. He was sure I would be able to find you no more threatening than any of our neighbors. He was quite angry with me for not fulfilling his expectations. Of course, I would never lie to him, and he knows that. He fears you and will not raise his hand against you. I suspect that before long some of the members of the confederation will split off from him and join you. For my part, I will join you, and serve you in any capacity except against my own people."

"I am sorry about your brother," I told him, "but delighted that you have joined us. I can show you both things we do with the sulfur. Kaidu was concerned that your brother would impede our getting the sulfur if he knew what we used it for."

"He has given his word that he would not obstruct you in any way," he replied. "Besides, you get the sulfur from the Ishak, and they could easily send it to you from the west through your new allies. In truth, the Ishak and the others to their southwest have expressed their desire to join you as long as they need not move to the cold north. My people are now surrounded by yours on three sides. I have been doing some "trading" to the east of our tribe, the fourth side, and have been asking questions and spreading some information about you. Directly to our east, there are three groups. In the south, around the mouth of the Missi Sipi River, there are the Pantch. North of them are a group of cities that are subordinate to a city called Natchez whose chief is referred to as the Sun. North of them are the Taunika, who are more of a confederacy like the Hasinai. They make and trade salt in competition with us. North of them are the Chikasha and then Hotcangara. Except for the Hotcangara, these groups speak somewhat similar languages but are hostile to each other and to some extent the Hasinai. East of them away from the river are two other groups related in varying degrees to these four and definitely related to each other, speaking a similar tongue. These are the Pansfalaya in the south and many different chiefdoms in the north and east. The former are a generally peaceful group who live in towns and raise crops. They have chiefs in each town and are only tenuously connected to each other. The latter include some violent, restless, and warlike people, living in palisaded villages and always attacking their neighbors as well as more peaceful settled people determined to avoid conflict. The majority falls in between the two extremes, but in general is more warlike than the Pansfalaya. I suspect one of them will eventually attack the tribe you call the Tsoyaha before long or perhaps even the Hotcangara group south of the Wazhazhe that you left undisturbed. Or perhaps the Hotcangara will attack the Tsoyaha. They have in the past. Some of them have even passed through the Taunika to attack us."

"Do they know what we have done to the Hotcangara and the Mingue?" I asked. "Would they really dare attack us?"

"All the southeast knows what you did to the Hotcangara and the Mingue." He shrugged. "They speak of little else around the campfires, but some of the chiefs would rather die fighting than be forced to live in peace with anyone. You may well get the Pansfalaya to confederate with you, but I'm sure your next campaign will be against one of the other chiefdoms, and it will be at their provocation."

"Well, our mappers were told to avoid their 'country,'" I said. "But I don't remember any mention being made of them by the Tsoyaha. Of course, Juchi interviewed them during the Hotcangara campaign, and they were fairly quick to agree to send observers. Perhaps that was why. What about the other groups?"

"Ah!" He smiled. "I took the liberty to speak to our three immediate neighbors on your behalf. The Pantch and the Taunika have sent observers. I left them at the Owl Ordu along with a small group of my Hasinai. The 'Sun' would not give me an audience since I was only the son of a lowly merchant. I'm afraid you will have to visit him yourself. Perhaps this spring?"

"If Kaidu agrees," I replied, "I'll be happy to try. But meanwhile, we must go see him and report on your recruiting efforts."

We went to see Kaidu and told him all. He was amazed at Smoking Mirror's initiative and very grateful for his information. Dispatches were prepared and sent to the Kestrels and the Cranes, the two Ordu nearest the Tsoyaha, advising them of the possibility of an attack on the latter. The two new forest tumen, the Martens and the Wildcats, were put on alert to move south across the Wazhazhe River in the late winter and set up camp between the West Tsoyaha River and the Missi Sipi. We would not start anything ourselves, but we would be ready if anyone else started something. As for my visiting the "Sun," it would depend on whether we had to move against anyone. If we didn't, then I could visit him and the Pansfalaya as well. As for visiting the other chiefs, I should only do that with very strong escort. Kaidu thought it would be worth the trip if a large group like the Pansfalaya could be induced to confederate. Also, I could finish mapping the Missi Sipi.

At this point, Smoking Mirror brought out another surprise. He had finished mapping the southern coast of the land all the way to the Missi Sipi and had mapped the Missi Sipi from its mouth almost to where we left off. Kaidu and I were both very impressed, and Kaidu insisted on raising Smoking Mirror to the rank of minghan commander, detached from command for special assignments. He wanted him to accompany me the following spring, if possible, and perhaps go on beyond the Pansfalaya to the tribes farther east. He told me to get Smoking Mirror an appropriate helmet as though he were in my tumen.

I sent word to Henry to make the helmet and meanwhile showed Smoking Mirror the matches and the gunpowder. I used one of the matches to light a small trail of the "black sand," as he called it, and he was truly amazed. He wanted to know how we ever figured out such a thing, and I had to admit we didn't, it was the Hanjen again. I explained about a cannon and promised to show him what it could do in the spring. Meanwhile, I did demonstrate a rocket for him.

He said he would very much like to meet the remarkably inventive Hanjen, and he was sorry we hadn't brought any with us. I suppose, after all, it was an understandable sentiment, but I cautioned him not to say such a thing to the other Mongols.

"The Mongols despise the Hanjen," I explained. "The Hanjen always looked down on the Mongols as barbarians. Besides, even with all their inventive abilities, they were unable to prevent the Mongols from conquering them."

"Do you hate the Hanjen?" he asked.

"No," I admitted. "I learned too much from them to hate them. Still, they can be a corrupting influence. They corrupted and finally destroyed the Mongol Khanate in the old land. They can be too clever, to the point of being conniving."

"Yes." He nodded. "I have known such people. Every tribe has a few. They are very dangerous while being very helpful. The sun shines and burns; the river quenches thirst and drowns; the fire warms and burns. So it is. Still, I would like to see these people and their cities."

"Well"—I smiled—"if we ever decide to get back in contact with them, I'll bring you along."

I added Smoking Mirror's efforts to the master map with his help. He was quite fascinated by it all and hoped to be able to travel to the northwest part of the land sometime. The winter passed fairly uneventfully until Paula presented me with a second son. We called him Ignace, her father's name. He was a fine healthy boy. All the children seemed to thrive in the new land. It was a wonderful place, there were no epidemics, and in fact, there did not seem to be anything like the sickness we would see in the old land. I supposed it was because the people were not so concentrated in small areas as were the Hanjen. But I really didn't know why the new land was so salutary. At any rate, both people and herds flourished.

22
RECRUITING IN THE SOUTHEAST, 9 K
(SD TO MS TO KY, 1377)

The following spring, we all went up to visit Henry. He had Smoking Mirror's helmet ready, and the latter was quite pleased. I showed him what the cannon could do with rock projectiles and explained that one could also shoot solid iron shot, hollow iron shot, and shrapnel. He again wanted to know if all this was Hanjen invention, and I had to admit it was. The gunnery classes were beginning, and Kabul was taking to his task with great enthusiasm. His recruits were from many different tribes, but I noticed there were no Mongols among them. Somehow, that didn't surprise me. Old feelings die very hard. Henry had designed a special helmet that covered the ears for the gunners. Considering all the noise, that was probably of some help. The helmet also had a small cannon standing upright on the top. It made them feel very special, the least we could do for them considering the danger of their job. Indeed, there were already some injuries before we left.

Smoking Mirror and I set off in late spring after dropping Paula and the children back off at the Eagle Ordu. We picked up a moderately sized escort at the Owl Ordu along with a large group of returning Chahiksichahiks and Kitikiti'sh, and a smaller group of Ishak. We also brought along a wagonload of dried ox meat for the Ishak. En route, we passed large groups of the same tribes as well as a few whole bands of the Titskan watitch on their way to the Owls. Once we got into "confederate" country, progress slowed considerably as we had to stop and visit each town we encountered. We finally reached Hasinai territory, but still had to visit the towns. At length we got to Smoking Mirror's city and stopped to call on his "brother."

The Xinesi was cordial if not friendly. He seemed to be reconciled, but not at all happy about the situation. He was even rather brusque with his "brother" which I did not expect. We left as soon as politic, and I asked Smoking Mirror if he had anyone he wanted to take back to the Ordu with us on our return, but he said he didn't. He was only close to his parents, and his mother had died a few years before, and his father was still in the south. I asked him how that happened, and he said it was because he had often accompanied his father and had not been around to form any strong friendships with his fellow tribesmen. His "brother" had never been close, but had always been good to him, and he was sorry they had become estranged. Things would only get worse, he was sure, because the western tribes of the confederacy wanted to confederate with Mongols instead of remaining with the Kadohadacho. Also, about a hundred of the Kadohadacho had gone off with this year's group of Kitikiti'sh recruits. Being a priest as well as a ruler, the Xinesi was sure he had offended the Sun in some way and was frustrated in his efforts to set things right. He fully expected that the Sun would turn on the Mongols eventually since we didn't honor him properly. He hoped he could hold his tribe and confederacy together until then so they would not be swept away with us.

All that reminded me of the sort of useless threats my grandfather Peter used to make against me in particular and the "godless" Mongols in general. I'm afraid I was as unimpressed with the Xinesi's expectations as I had been with my grandfather's threats. I supposed it was natural enough to hope for divine intervention when all else failed, but usually quite futile. Still, it kept him from despair, so it was a comfort to him. I had always been amazed at the lengths people would go to avoid admitting that they were wrong.

Smoking Mirror thought it would be good for me to call on the Taunika and the Pantch as well as the Natchez "Sun." I agreed, so we continued down the Kadohadacho River and followed it through the Yatasi lands southeast to the lands of the Taunika. We found their main city on the bluffs above the point where the river empties into the Missi Sipi. Their houses were rectangular, made of thatch and spread out over a considerable area. They also had temples on mounds like the Kadohadacho. The people almost all had the grotesquely deformed heads like I had seen among the Kadohadacho. They wore their hair long and neither greased nor dressed. They practiced extensive tattooing, and the women seemed to have very black teeth—a staining done on purpose which they found attractive. They wore clothing made from the bark of the mulberry tree. It was definitely not silk, and they did not seem to be familiar with silk or the silkworms, although they had the right tree. They also wore robes of feathers or furs if it was cold enough. They were very active farmers, cultivating the usual large mondamin grain as well as beans, squash, melons, and a very large flower that yielded many nutlike seeds. Their language was quite melodious without being singsong. It was pleasant to hear, even if I couldn't understand a word. Of course, Smoking Mirror could speak the language.

Their leaders were very cordial and glad that Smoking Mirror had brought me along. They were particularly interested to be reassured that if they confederated with us, we would rush to their aid if they were attacked. It seemed they had suffered incursions from the Chikasha, one of the more warlike chiefdoms as recently as the previous year. In the past, they had been raided by the Hotcangara, and they were quite happy that we had subdued them on the west side of the Missi Sipi and earnestly hoped we would destroy them on the east side as well. They would send observers and wait to hear their report before making their final decision, but all seemed quite favorable.

We moved on down the Missi Sipi River for several days before crossing to the eastern bank and climbing up the steep bluffs to the widely scattered houses of the town of Natchez. The "Sun's" house was raised about ten feet on an earthen mound. It was quite large, about ten feet high by forty feet square, and made of mud mixed with straw and covered with an arched grass roof. Across a very large open space from it was another rather circular mound surrounded with mud walls on which was their temple. On the roof of the temple were wooden effigies that looked like birds. The people all had the deformed heads and, if possible, were even more tattooed than the Taunika. Their faces, arms, and legs were covered with blue, black, and red tattoos. Only the warriors were allowed to mark their trunks, however, and this only according to their exploits. The women wore their hair either braided or bundled in netting made of thread from the mulberry bark. The men cut their hair so it formed a sort of crown around their head with a few hairs left long on the top with which they tied feathers. They wore mostly deerskins and used hide and feather robes if it was cold. They also made ribbons and belts by weaving the longer hairs of the plains oxen.

We found the "Sun" inside his house, seated on a raised platform with some of his women and elders in attendance. My appearance and especially my blue eyes impressed him. He wondered if we also worshiped "his father" the sun as did most of the local tribes. I told him we instead bowed to the Blue Sky, Tengri. Unable to impress me, he asked about my reason for visiting, and I gave him the usual recruiting message. He wanted to know if what he had heard about our destruction of the Hotcangara was true. I replied that it was, but it was caused by their provocation rather than by our aggression. He asked if we would truly leave them in peace if they did not join us. I assured him that we would, but, of course, we would also not protect them from any tribe that was not allied with us. He explained that it would be unthinkable for the "Sun" to be subordinate to any other group, no matter how powerful, but as the sun shone on all, he would in no way impede us or in any sense be guilty of a "provocation." I thanked him for his time and his neutrality and assured him that we and our allies would remain at peace with him as long as he remained so with us. Before we left, he wanted to know who our nearby allies were. I told him who had joined and who was thinking about joining. He was sorry to hear that we had not dealt with the Chikasha as yet, for they were his worst enemies. I said that we would deal with them in turn as necessary, and we would keep him informed as our alliance grew among his neighbors.

As we left, we were given an escort to make sure we left their territory unharmed. When the escort departed a few days later, Smoking Mirror told me he was glad that they had not joined and he hoped they would eventually provoke their own destruction. I was surprised at his hostility and asked him about it. He said that they were such a pitifully small tribe of absolutely no consequence and yet they had the temerity to put on such airs and haughtily dismiss their neighbors, almost any of whom could easily destroy them. He then explained their rather stratified society. It seems the bulk of the people were called "stinkards," above them were "honored people," then were the "nobles," and above all was the "Sun." I reminded him that the Kadohadacho were also rather hierarchical, but he said that their ranking was according to duty and responsibility not because of which ranking their mother happened to belong. It seems one's mother's rank was the determining factor in the tribe. We learned later that certain activities such as sacrificing your child during the funeral of the "Sun" could gain one a class promotion. Somehow that didn't warm us up to them at all.

Eventually, we came upon the Pantch. They lived in houses much like those of their northern neighbors but had smaller and more scattered villages. Their land was rather swampy, and we found it necessary to leave the horses and most of our escort in one of their villages and go the rest of the way by boat. They also flattened their heads and tattooed their arms, legs, and faces. They wore their hair long and tied and the men tied a piece of lead to the end. The men wore little more than a breechcloth and the women little more than a skirt, but they were much ornamented, wearing rings, bracelets, earrings, gorgets, arm bands, and even bangles of copper, shell, and other things hanging from belts and other articles of clothing. They were quite artistic in their basket making. They also raised the mondamin grain, beans, squash, melons, and an odd sort of yellow root that looked like a small yam and was tastier than it or the squash. They also hunted and ate a creature something like the crocodile of Sungjen lands, but much larger. Its meat was an acquired taste. They subsisted more on fish than any other meat. They used a dart propelled by their blowing it through a long hollow cane tube for bagging small game and birds.

They also had a rather stratified society with the same orders as their neighbors, but the distinction was not as noticeable. Their leader was also called the "Sun," but I found him much less haughty than his counterpart to the north. I was surprised that they had the same system if they were unrelated, but this "Sun" insisted that the others had adopted and corrupted his system. They would also send observers and were willing to confederate if they reported back with favorable impressions. They sincerely hoped that they would be left in peace by all their neighbors. I told him that we would see that they were undisturbed if they confederated, and in fact, we would be visiting their neighbors to the east, the Pansfalaya, next. He said that the Pansfalaya were no threat to anyone who left them alone; it was the far ranging Chikasha that plagued them the most along with the occasional ambushes by the Ishak. I assured him that the Ishak would no longer bother them without our permission now that they were our allies, and we would probably make some contact with the Chikasha and the other eastern chiefdoms later this year. He was happy to hear that and told me they would send word as soon as the decision was made.

We returned to the horses and began to move eastward out of the marshy river delta toward the lands of the Pansfalaya. Not long after we entered their territory, we came upon a large plain over which were scattered groups of houses as well as individual houses surrounded by fields. One of the houses was raised up on a mound. As we drew nearer, a group of locals came toward us playing on a sort of reed flute with one of their number being carried on another's shoulders. They had the distorted heads and were heavily tattooed like their neighbors. Their clothing was also much the same. They wore their hair long and loose. Their heads and faces seemed to be broader than those of their neighbors, however, and at the time I wondered if that was also an artificial distortion (it wasn't). In due course, the man being carried came up to us and proved to be the chieftain of the town. He welcomed us as having come openly and in peace and invited us to his house.

The chief's house was the one up on the mound. It was an oval-shaped thatch house, not very different from that of his neighbors. It turned out they favored a more substantial mud-reinforced house in the winter. A group of elders were waiting in the chief's house, and we burned some weed, as usual, before we got on with it. After I gave the recruitment speech through Smoking Mirror, the chief informed me that he was not like the "Sun." He exercised a more limited authority and would not order his people around. He would advise them, and they could accept or reject his advice. Further, he was only the chief of this particular town and had no authority whatever beyond it. I assured him that we were quite used to the system, having encountered it very widely all through the north. Was there perhaps an occasional meeting of chiefs, where matters of mutual interest were discussed? There were no such meetings to his knowledge. I asked if it would be possible to set one up, so I could talk to the chiefs, and they could pass on our offer of confederation and peace to their people, and the people could then decide the merits rather than me visiting each of their towns and talking to each of their chiefs. He consulted with the elders at length and finally they decided it would do no harm to ask the other chiefs if they would agree to such a meeting. I thanked them for their wisdom and asked them to please do so. They agreed, but warned me it would take a while and asked if I wished to stay with them while I waited. I said I would be honored to do so and promised to learn their language while I waited.

We were assigned a few houses, and I sent the men out to do some hunting so we wouldn't become a burden. Their fields were quite extensive, however, and there seemed to be no shortage of any food, except perhaps meat. Smoking Mirror started giving me language lessons once we were settled in. It was a very different language again. I could see no similarities with the others I had learned so far. Smoking Mirror said that the much-maligned Chikasha spoke virtually the same language, and the people farther east as well as the "Sun's" people spoke a similar language. We wandered around the town a bit while we waited. The people worked their fields extensively, but also found time to play skill games, especially one where one person rolled a flat wheel like stone (much like the ones I had seen in Murenbalikh) and a few others threw very long poles at it. I can't recall if the object was to knock down the stone or merely get it to stop at your pole. They also used the hollow cane blowgun weapon to hunt birds and squirrels. They rather prized squirrel meat. The bird most hunted was a sort of pigeon that roosted in huge flocks in certain areas.

They seemed to have three different kinds of the mondamin grain that ripened at separate times. There was a short version, which matured quickly and would be eaten boiled. Then there was a type with a thick husk protecting each seed. They soaked these in a solution of wood ashes and water which ate away the husk and freed up the seeds which they would either eat as they were, or dry and grind up into a kind of porridge. The last kind they would usually dry and grind up to make their flat breads. They also grew peas, beans, squash, and the other plants just like their neighbors. They also gathered different sorts of nuts, berries, and roots. There was a sort of grape in the area, but they used it for food, not wine. Far be it from me to give them any such ideas.

After we had been with them a while, I noticed that they didn't seem to have a temple nor did they seem much given to religious ceremony. There was what turned out to be a tribal ossuary. It was attended by an odd group of older men with very long fingernails. They were referred to as "buzzard men" and treated with some deference. We found out that their name and their fingernails were due to the noisome task they had taken on themselves. They placed their dead up on a scaffold to decay a certain length of time, and then the "buzzard men" would pick the flesh off the bones utilizing their long fingernails. The bones would then be placed in the ossuary. I suspected there was some horror in the deference they enjoyed.

One day the chief came by to invite us to a great ceremony. We, of course, agreed and much of the evening was spent with singing and dancing. They made their dancing music with drums, rattles, and a sort of rasping instrument. The singing was more chanting than melodic. The dancing was rather energetic, and the dancers were frequently replaced through the ceremony. The next day, the scene of the dance proved to be something of a field where a kind of contest was held. The field was about two hundred feet long and a hundred or so feet wide. At each end there were two long pieces of cane stuck in the ground and tied together. There were about forty young men very painted up and wearing a ringed animal tail tied to the appropriate spot. They each held two sticks about three feet long with a sort of rude small basket at one end. They formed into two groups and a shaman threw up a small ball made of deer hide, which they endeavored to hurl through the tied sticks at each end of the field. There was much parrying and thrusting with the sticks and passing about of the ball and tripping and bumping and falling, but all seemed to be quite in earnest. The shaman connected to each side spent the contest making incantations and arbitrating disputed scores. When one side was finally declared the victor, two teams of women took over the field and played just as hard as the men. When they finished, there was a general feasting. It was an odd but entertaining spectacle. I wondered where they got such an idea.

It seemed that all of the Pansfalaya belonged to one of two groups, the Imoklasha and the Inholahta. These groups always played against each other in the game. They also only married out of their group, so it wasn't really a source of disunity. Strangely the Imoklasha were considered the "peace" group and the Inholahta the "war" group. This was only in the sense that members of those groups would initiate either peace or war, but, of course, all of them could participate in any wars. Most of their wars were with their relatives the Chikasha in the north, their neighbors to the east, and less often, to the west. While the Pansfalaya were, just as the Pantch had suggested, a peaceful people, they were not afraid to fight. They told me that they preferred to ambush their attackers on their land rather than carry the battle to their antagonist's camp. This was so that they would only kill warriors, not women and children. They also frowned on torturing prisoners, but would quickly dispatch those condemned to death and enslave the others. They were a most unusual tribe, and I hoped they could be induced to join us.

At length, the chief announced that the large majority of the chiefs would be willing to hear me out. They wanted to meet with me at Nanih Waiya, their most sacred site. All were sure I could not lead them astray there. It seemed that they believed that they emerged from the ground or an underworld at that particular spot. Since the Mongols used to think they descended from the union of a wolf and a man, I wasn't about to comment on their legend. The site was about ten days' journey to the northeast, and we would meet at the next new moon. I decided we might as well get started since the new moon was about sixteen days off, and we could take a rather leisurely pace, and I could look about for any useful minerals. A young man named Thliotombi was sent with us as a guide.

About all I found on our journey was a very rich soil and forest not unlike those on the west of the Missi Sipi. The land was virtually flat except for the sloping bluffs above the very many broad river and creek bottoms. These were heavily wooded unless the Pansfalaya had cleared them. They tended to clear very wide swatches of the river or creek valleys and spread their houses and fields widely. Their "towns" were quite large in area if not in population, but there did seem to be quite a lot of them. Smoking Mirror was convinced that they were as numerous as his own Hasinai Confederacy. We reached the town closest to the appointed spot with a few days yet to spare. I asked the local chief how near their eastern neighbors were, thinking that we had come some distance to the east, although mostly to the north. He said that their lands began across a river about three days' journey east. I would have liked to recruit them as well, but the summer was waning, and I needed to get back by early fall. Besides, they were supposed to be a collection of vaguely similar tribes spread over a very large area and divided into numerous independent chiefdoms, and it would likely take some time to talk to all of their leaders.

Finally, on the appointed day, we went to Nanih Waiya. It proved to be a mound along a creek. There was a large crowd of Pansfalaya waiting for me there. We sat on the ground in a huge circle, for there must have been a hundred chiefs. Beyond the inner circle, there was a larger group of elders. A few pipes were fired up and passed around before we started. I stood up to give my pitch so I could project my voice far enough to be heard by (at least) most of the chiefs. They listened politely, and a few of them asked some questions. Most of these were the usual ones, but one wanted to know if we would recruit the Chikasha or just destroy them. I told him that because we had been warned that they were very warlike, we would send a strong force to them to determine their disposition toward us. A small embassy such as mine would be at risk, and we never foolishly risked our people. Of course, if they attacked our allies or us before we made contact with them, we would destroy them. He seemed satisfied by the answer, but another wanted to know how long it would take us to reach the lands of the Chikasha from our land. I replied that we had two large forces a few days' north of their frontier and a third across the Missi Sipi from them. Several more such forces were in striking distance of them, since they had been identified to us as a potential threat by some of their neighbors. Of course, one of our Ordu would be enough to deal with them since they were not really very numerous. With the questions answered, the chiefs retired to their respective groups of elders and conferred for a while.

Late in the day, we got back into our circle, and one of them told me that all had decided to present my offer to the people of their towns. The people would choose to either join us, confederate with us, or remain independent of us. He wanted to assure me that whichever choice was made by the individual towns, all wished to remain at peace with us. He also wanted to make sure I realized that the various towns might choose any of the options, and their choice would only be for their particular town. Was such an arrangement acceptable to us? I told him that we welcomed their decision to be at peace with us and were quite used to having individual towns or villages of a tribe join us to varying degrees. I went on to tell them that having lived among them for many days, I was very impressed by them and could assure them that our people would be honored to have them join us. I thanked them for their time and consideration. I could see that something was still troubling him, but thought it rude to ask him directly. After another round with the weed, we broke up. Those chiefs I had met before personally took their leave of me, but I could tell that they really had no idea how their people would choose. There seemed to be something on their minds also, but they didn't bring it up either. I noticed one of them talking to Smoking Mirror, however, and could see them both look in my direction. At length Smoking Mirror rejoined me and I asked if there was something wrong.

"In a way," he replied enigmatically. "Our hosts are puzzled that you are of such great rank and yet are so emphatically unadorned. Even I, your humble subordinate, am decently tattooed, wear ear-plugs and gorget as well as bracelets, but you—nothing."

"Do you mean that one's rank must be proclaimed with bangles and scars?" I protested. "That's ridiculous. I've always detested cluttering myself up with such ornaments like a Hanjen matron."

"Do I look like a Hanjen matron?" he asked pointedly.

"I'm sorry, my friend," I replied sheepishly. "It is just my preference. What others wear is their business. I don't mean to impose my taste or submit to anyone else's."

"While that seems quite fair of you," he observed, "it does not make your task any easier. Appearances are quite important in this area, and except for your generally odd appearance, you don't really look special. The farther east we go, the more difficult things will become. You can't expect a chief to receive someone decked out like a commoner just because he looks strange."

"You mean to suggest"—I stared at him—"that I should get tattooed, cut up my ears, and hang copper all over myself to impress some petty chieftain."

"Well," he hedged, "at least go with the copper."

I was disgusted, but decided to think about it a while and talk it over with Paula and Givevneu when I got home. Meanwhile, I decided it would be best to move directly west to the Missi Sipi staying out of potentially hostile country. Once across the river, we could move directly north and link up with the Cranes. They would know what was going on, and I could finish mapping the river. Thliotombi decided to go with us for the adventure, and I thought it wouldn't hurt to have one of them along who could report back, perhaps reassuring them of my rank. We stopped in Pansfalaya towns along the way so that as many as possible would be able to see us, and we could answer any further questions they might have. Eventually we left them and came upon a Taunika village. We were well received and helped along to the river. Here another village ferried us across on their dugout boats. We worked our way through more of their villages, finally leaving their country and entering the unmapped area between them and us. We were warned that Chikasha raiding parties were in the area, so I switched us over to infiltrative advance. I kept us close enough to the river so I could map it, but into the woods enough that we couldn't be easily seen.

After a few days, our vigilance paid off. We could see a few boats approaching the riverbank below us. The band beached the boats and started climbing up the bluffs near us. We laid low so we could get a better look at them, but Thliotombi assured me that they were Chikasha. Smoking Mirror whispered that he knew a way to make them return once they got up on the bluff. I told him to do so then, because while we could have easily wiped them out, I thought it im-portant that we not initiate hostilities. After all, if they were headed for a tribe who was not our ally, we had no quarrel with them. At the same time, I didn't want to risk any of our men in a vain attempt to parley with a war party. Neither did I want them to pass by and later ambush us. As they drew near, I could see that they were all painted red and black. Their heads were deformed and their hair worn something like the Mingue, shaved on the sides with a nar-row roach left on the top from front to back but also with a fringe left above the forehead. The hair was greased to stand up, and on the top they had attached feathers, other parts of birds, or a single finger-sized shell. Their ears looked very odd, and we later found out that they cut the outer rim of the ear and stretch the freed flap of skin by winding copper wire around it. They also wore rings in their noses and some had bracelets made of beads or shells. They did not seem to be very heavily tattooed, at least, from what I could see through all their body paint. They wore only breechcloths, belts, and headbands, and carried bows, arrows, javelins, shields, and either clubs or axes. One of them, the one right behind the leader, carried a bag that looked like a stuffed owl skin with what could only be described as reverence. When Smoking Mirror judged them to be close enough, he made a chirping sort of noise like a bird. The band froze and listened carefully. He repeated the sound, but in such a way that it sounded just like bird might. The group all exchanged glances and without a word went back down to the river, reembarked in their boats, and paddled furiously back across.

I pressed Smoking Mirror for details. He said that his father had taught him the trick many years before. He had discovered their fear of the bird one day while he was hiding from one of their war bands. The actual bird was heard calling, and the band returned home immediately. Apparently they viewed it as a bad omen. His father listened very carefully to the bird and imitated the sound until he had it just right. Once Smoking Mirror struck out on his own, he taught it to him. From his description of the bird, it was something like a sparrow only with a longer beak. I never did see one.

Late in the day, we came to a spot across from a large landing site. The bank was full of boats and we could see a fair amount of activity all on the far side. There was a rather steep bluff on both banks, and we could see what must have been a trail on the other side. There were a number of "southern" Hotcangara in the area but no more than would be normal for a landing site. There were women and children among them, so it was likely they either meant us no harm or were unaware of our presence. Still, we decided to camp a little way farther upstream and keep them under surveillance. In the morning nothing had changed. There were the same casual comings and goings we had seen before, so we moved on. We found two more such landing sites farther north, but the first was the largest. We saw a few of their settlements on the bluffs above the river, but there was no sign of them or anyone else on this side.

Several days later, well north of the point where the Wazhazhe joined the Missi Sipi, we finally ran into elements of the Cranes. They were quite surprised to see me, and I was rather surprised that they weren't much farther south. I sped on to the Ordu and found it no more than four days' ride south of their original position. The commander of the Cranes was Khassar, another nephew of Kaidu. He said that they had been much farther south, but were recalled because of a revolt among the Hotcangara. The revolt had been crushed long before they reached their original camp, but they had not been informed and were just now returning to their earlier position. The southern group of Hotcangara who claimed to have no association with those in the north had attacked the Tsoyaha in concert with the revolt. So the Cranes were on their way to make sure that none of them escaped across the river. I fleshed out his map of the river and pointed out the landing sites, suggesting that they take or destroy the boats left there. He thanked me and urged me to rejoin my Wolves, for they were south of the Wazhazhe along with the Kestrels, Deer, Foxes, and the Otters. The Falcons were a day behind and would help the Cranes seal off the west bank of the river. Kaidu was with the forest tumen and in overall command of the Ordu. The quickest way to join him would be by boat.

He was right, of course, and I had no choice, but I still didn't like the boats, especially for doing more than just crossing a river. I dismissed most of my escort, and the rest of us got into boats for the journey downstream. A few of the Cranes familiar with the river went with us. We camped each night on the west side of the river since we weren't too sure of the northern Hotcangara either. On the third day, we reached the place where the much cleaner Wazhazhe joins the muddy Missi Sipi. The current wasn't too strong in the fall, and we easily crossed over near the shore, putting in when we saw some of our people. They proved to be elements of the Foxes, and they took me to find Juchi.

23

The Third Hotcangara Campaign 9 K
(KY, MO, AR, TN, MS 1377)

Juchi was glad to see me, but hardly had time for idle chatter during a campaign. I gave Shingabaossin the corrected map so he could fix up the tumen map and told him to make extra copies of the new parts and send them to the other tumen on campaign. It seemed that Juchi's Foxes and the new Martens were strung along the northern limits of the Hotcangara territory. The two plains tumen were sealing off the western escape, and the Otters, backed by some Tsoyaha irregulars, were sealing off the eastern escape route. My Wolves, the Wildcats, the Deer, and the Kestrels were forming a line along the southern limits of their territory and would then drive them up and into the waiting line in the north. As the eastern line narrowed, the Otters would reinforce the northern line. It turned out that the spies had found a few cities and many smaller towns. The southern line would reduce the towns and cities in their path and drive any escapees into the trap in the north. Kaidu wanted to destroy them all without giving them the usual ultimatum, but Givevneu had convinced him that he should give them a chance since it was likely all were not involved in the treachery. We decided that it would be best if I crossed back over the river and rode with the plains tumen downriver and cross back when I came upon the Wolves. They were to be the left flank of the line. I supposed these things happen, but it was frustrating to have to retrace my steps. If I had dawdled a bit, my tumen would have come to me. In any case I would find Kaidu along the southern line.

I took my leave and gave the bad news to my escort. I took the copies of the map for the southern tumen with me, and we went back down to the river. The boats and men were still there waiting to see if there would be any dispatches to take back to the

Cranes. They ferried us back across the river, and we camped for a day waiting for the Cranes to come down. They quickly mounted us up and brought us along with them. Since they were behind schedule, Khassar was making forced rides of about ninety li a day. This would have destroyed the horses, since the going was not easy through the woods, except that the Plains Ordu each had about six horses per man and by changing horses four or five times a day, they were able to handle the rush. I showed Khassar where the Taunika villages began so we would stop short of them, and as we got near some six days later, I stayed with the lead elements so that I could reassure the Taunika that we weren't after them. We had made no pretense of infiltration on this ride, but had gone crashing through the woods making enough noise to scatter anything in our path. Occasionally we could see boat activity on the far side of the river, but no one ventured over to our side.

When we were close enough to the Taunika, my escort and I went ahead alone to them. I explained the situation, and they were very grateful that I had come. They had heard that a large force was on the east side of the river a little farther upstream. I sent a message back to Khassar that all was explained and that the Taunika would happily help in any way they could. I suggested that they might pick up any fugitive Hotcangara they found on the river. I also told Khassar that I would be crossing back to the east bank and, therefore, would be out of his hair. We each kept two horses and swam them along behind us as the Taunika ferried us across on their boats. I only took Smoking Mirror, Thliotombi, and three others with me. As we reached the other side, the Taunika there were also greatly relieved to hear the reason for the invasion. They had guessed that the invaders were Mongols since they had horses like I had, but they were very nervous to have such a large force so near and had been making quite a few sacrifices in their temples, just in case the Sun Gods were angry with them.

I was a bit puzzled to hear them refer to the sun gods in the plural and remarked on it to Smoking Mirror. He said that they have an image of a frog and a female, which they collectively view as representing the sun. He had no idea where they got such an idea, since their neighbors had images, but not as representations of the sun. The people of Natchez and his Kadohadacho used a sacred stone to sacrifice to the sun and as such it represented him, but he was male and not a frog. Of course, he added, Ayo-Caddi-Aymay, the Kadohadacho god, was more than the sun; he represented the sky, the stars and the moon as well. He felt the Mongol god Tengri was an underdeveloped version of Ayo-Caddi-Aymay. I sincerely hoped that Tengri would never achieve such "development" either. Their cult was excessive.

We went along the bank to the north and finally came upon my Wolves about a day later. They welcomed me back enthusiastically and commiserated with me for missing all the action. I found Temur and told him to remain in command since he had led them all this way. I could see a light come into his eye and knew I had made the right decision. I did ask him to bring me up to date as we moved forward, and I would then go on to find Kaidu. He said that some of the Hotcangara had revolted under a disgruntled war chief, Wabokieshiek. He had tried to win them all over to his revolt, but only got a few thousand. They left their villages so as not to invite reprisals and tried to gather up enough strength to attack one of the Ordu. That failing, they decided to march on Murenbalikh and kill our governor and his staff. They hoped some sort of victory would rally the rest of the tribe to their cause. As it happened, we were informed every step of the way, and they were crushed between the Wolves, the Deer, and Kestrels. The Falcons moved across the river to protect Murenbalikh, but weren't needed. All this did delay the present campaign a bit though. I praised Temur for his victory and for his subsequent march around the Hotcangara to his present position. He puffed up a bit and smiled a little, justly proud of his accomplishments. I took my leave of him and went off to find Kaidu.

I found Kaidu among the Wildcats, the only new tumen in this line. He was glad I had rejoined them and anxious to hear about my trip. I briefed him on it and brought in Thliotombi to meet him. Once he had gone, Kaidu asked if all of them had the weird heads. I told him that all the southeastern tribes I had met so far did, as did some of the Hasinai. But I told him how easily the Pansfalaya would fit into the Mongols otherwise, and the head deformation might go the way face painting had with the tribes that joined us. Over the years, the Ocheti shakowin had become more Mongol than the Mongols as had some of the others. The only way one could tell them apart was because they were taller, (and, in my opinion, better looking). One generation could end the head deformation. He was glad to hear that since he found it somewhat distracting.

He brought me up to date on what had happened. The southern Hotcangara had been in constant touch with the rebels and lain low all summer long not disturbing the Tsoyaha or the Ordu at all. They had even come out to trade with the Tsoyaha who informed them that they were now confederated with us. A few days later (the very day the revolt began), they attacked the same village with whom they had traded, killing a few dozen of them. Kaidu couldn't believe anyone would challenge us in such a way, but they had. Now he wasn't sure what they were up to, since we had been steadily advancing and had yet to run into any of them. Some elements of our line would reach their first settlement in about two days. I asked if anyone was watching our rear as we advanced since there were potentially hostile forces there, especially the Pansfalaya's relatives, the Chikasha.

"By Tengri, the horses!" he shouted. "Thank you Raven, you have saved us a humiliation. Send in dispatch riders immediately."

I ran out, grabbed a few riders and ushered them in to Kaidu. He dashed off notes to each of the commanders, and the riders rushed off. Then I told him that I felt it would be unfair to take over command of the Wolves from Temur this late in the campaign, so I could remain with him. His eyes narrowed, and he looked at me searchingly for a moment. Then he said I never ceased to amaze him and dismissed me for the moment suggesting, almost as an afterthought, that I help my brother-in-law Ussu, the commander of the Wildcats. I was surprised to hear that Ussu had been made a commander, since he had never betrayed much intelligence all the time I knew him. When I found him, he was quite relieved to see me.

"Raven!" he shouted. "Have you come to take over?"

"No, of course not," I replied. "Just to help you. You don't want to give up your first command, do you? It is quite an honor that Kaidu selected you."

"No, no." He shook his head emphatically. "It was most certainly an accident. Kaidu's nephew Jebei was the commander. He was badly wounded by one of our own men during training, so I've only taken over until his recovery, which is taking a long time. I had to lead the men across the Wazhazhe myself. If you hadn't trained all those map people of yours, I would have never found it. Then there were no boats and spring floods, and to add to the humiliation, the Martens were across days before us. I didn't realize there was a ford. Then I had no idea what to do all summer long and had the men scattered all over the place hunting when the campaign started. This entire affair has been a disaster. Why do you think Kaidu is with us?"

"Well, you're in a central location," I groped, "surely he's with you so that he can maintain overall command."

"Oh no," he insisted. "You don't know about the march down here. We were supposed to lead it, but it took so long to get the men back together that the Wolves lead. Then I got way behind the Wolves and in the way of the Kestrels. It was so hard to be sure where we were in the forest, even though all we had to do was follow the West Tsoyaha River upstream until it turned east. I kept thinking each meander was the turn, and then I missed the real turn and went too far southeast. Ever since Kaidu has been with us, I must run all my orders through him. That is, he runs all his orders through me. He won't even let me give any orders. You must take over before my humiliation is discovered."

"Better yet," I suggested, "I'll act as your second in command, and give all the orders in your name. You can just sit on your horse and look dignified until we come to attack; then you can lead. No one is braver in battle than you."

That was not an exaggeration either. He was fearless in battle. When we were small, if someone told him there was a tiger in a bush, he would rush in to do battle. Fortunately, we were only teasing him or he would not have still been among us. There was no question of his bravery, but he was not very bright and completely indecisive about mundane matters. He was pitifully grateful that I would help him out. I had a feeling that this command would be his last. It didn't take Kaidu long to realize what our arrangement was. The men began to move with confidence, the leaders with authority. The tumen moved as one man relentlessly northward with a strong detached force guarding our rear. It was amazing how totally a weak commander can ruin a good army. Before long, Kaidu no longer rode with us, but moved among the other tumen in the Ordu as well.

We came upon our first town around midday. It was not very large but did have a palisade covered with a clay whitewash, a few houses on mounds, and a large open area in the center. Eerily, it was completely deserted. We set it on fire, then left and continued north. When we started our northward march, each tumen had to cover about seventy-five li, but as we progressed northward the Otters' westward progress enabled us to close up our lines as we enabled them to close up theirs, and by the time we reached the first settlement, we were only covering about forty-five li.

The next settlement was also deserted. It was not large, but to our west, the Wolves found a large city on the bluff above the first landing area I had seen. It too was deserted. All along the line the Hotcangara settlements were empty and there was no sign of them. The third settlement had no palisade but was also deserted, and it too was fired. Finally, as we approached the fourth settlement, a few of our men paid the price for hastily assuming it, too, would be deserted. Again there was no palisade, and the arrows seemed to be coming from their houses, so these were quickly set ablaze with fire arrows. Those who were flushed out were mostly quickly dispatched, but a few got away. It turned out that they were merely a rear guard, no more than a hundred of them. We pressed on northward, by now our front was only thirty li wide. Word was passed along that the other tumen had also finally encountered some rear guard action.

I began to have misgivings about the ease of this campaign against what should be a desperate foe. I called in Smoking Mirror and Thliotombi and asked them about this group of Hotcangara. They confirmed that they were not afraid to fight and were very likely preparing a trap. They would retreat if in an untenable position, but only to fight later when they deemed the odds better. The several towns had been known to band together and defeat larger forces than their own, although never a force as large as ours. Thliotombi mentioned that they were probably waiting for word from their head shaman before they attacked. The shaman supposedly could make it rain, ward off witchcraft, and predict the future. He thought they might have hesitated since the Mongols were from the west and all witchcraft came from the west in their beliefs. I asked if he shared that belief, but he said that the Pansfalaya had not adopted the beliefs of their neighbors. He added that they consider fire very sacred, a manifestation of the Sky God. I thanked them and went to see Kaidu.

"I think we're being lured into a trap," I said when I found him. "This has been too easy, and I'm sure they are planning a very unpleasant surprise for us before we reach their last settlements."

"I'm sure they are"—he shrugged—"but what of it? What can they possibly do to us that we couldn't handle?"

"I don't know," I admitted. "But I have an idea. Why not have three of the Ordu in our line stand fast and send the Otters around to the north line with the Deer replacing their position? Then we could have the north line close in on them from an unexpected direction and thwart their plans."

"I like the plan," he nodded. "You do have some strategic potential, Raven. Get the tumen mounted up. We'll pull the three remaining in the southern line back to the last creek whose banks had been cultivated and spread them out a little. That will give them some open fields of fire. And we'll send the others as you suggest. Send in a dispatch rider. I'll send the northern line the orders. You get the southern line in position."

I ran out and sent in the rider, then ordered messengers to send up each tumen's horses, and told Temur, Chagatai, Togun, and Ussu to mount up their Ordu and pull back to the last creek. Kaidu decided to move around to the northern line and went to make sure the Otters moved quickly. He put me in charge of the southern line. By nightfall the southern line was in position and Chagatai was moving his Deer in the Otters' wake. I kept thinking about what the Hotcangara were planning, but I figured, or rather, hoped that our stopping would either embolden them to attack, or confuse them into capitulating. Either result would be to our advantage.

The air had been quite still since I joined the campaign, and the march had been rather uncomfortable and oppressive. Still it had not rained, although the sky was overcast. Suddenly, a fresh cool dry wind picked up, gently, at first but with increasing force out of the north. The sky began to clear, and we very much enjoyed the change. Before long, we began to smell burning wood, vaguely at first, but growing stronger. The land was fairly flat here, with little more than low hills offering no real vantage point. I sent one of the men to climb the tallest tree he could find to try and see if the whole woods were on fire. I pulled the men back to the south side of the creek after first having them clear away anything that might burn on both sides of the creek and pile it at the edge of the wood line north of the creek. The man up the tree could see nothing but smoke. I sent word to Temur and Togun of my discovery and suggested they do as I had. Togun congratulated me on my keen grasp of the obvious, but Temur was more polite merely assuring me that he had things in hand.

The wind-driven smoke began to reach us in earnest. We dismounted and moved the horses back over one of the lines of little hills, but in easy reach and well guarded. We began to choke on the thick smoked and had to breathe through wet rags. Our firebreak seemed to be holding, although occasionally some of the grass on the far side of the creek caught fire and quickly burned out. The line at the edge of the wood where we had piled up combustibles became quite a conflagration. Some of the trees fell forward, but did not cross the creek. An occasional ember blew over to our side of the creek, but our men quickly ran out and extinguished it. It was fortunate for us that the Hotcangara had cleared so much of the creek valley for their fields. As the fire began to die down, I realized how close we had come to disaster. Had we been where we would have been if we continued north, we would have been hard-pressed to outrun that fire. It sort of made sense, a sacred fire to burn out the western "witches"—very clever of them.

I had the men lie low and wait out of sight for the advance of our foe. As I expected, they couldn't even wait for the fires to cool, but could be seen approaching gingerly through the smoldering ruin of the forest all along our line. When they reached the settlement clearing, they could see that the woods on our side were not burned, and they began to hesitate, peering toward us suspiciously and talking among themselves. They were out of earshot, but I wished I could have heard them. I wonder what they thought had happened to us, since we were not charred remnants in the wood, the fire had not gone as far as they expected, and they could see no sign of us. The warriors began to accumulate in the hundreds across the creek in front of my position, but none moved to cross. Finally, one of their leaders raised his javelin and let out a sort of scream then rushed across the creek. His cry and gesture was repeatedly his fellows who then followed closely after him. As soon as he got close enough to see us, we opened fire. The first volley was devastating. Not only did very many fall but also the rest were seized with panic and routed completely. I ordered up the horses only to discover that the force guarding them was under attack from the south and was repelling it only with difficulty. I reinforced them, we mounted up and I sent Ussu with the rest of the men to pursue the fleeing Hotcangara. They had no chance in the charred woods, virtually devoid of cover, against our mounted warriors and the slaughter was great. Ussu stopped only because it was getting dark and he didn't want any of the enemy escaping through our extended lines.

Meanwhile, the force behind us fought stubbornly, and I got the idea to use Hotcangara strategy against them since the wind was still blowing strongly from the north. I had the men set the underbrush on fire in front of them, and before long, the fire spread south. Seeing the danger, the attackers fled, and I mounted up our men and joined Ussu. I made sure we were in contact with our neighboring Ordu, that our line was continuous, and that our rear was covered before we turned in. The Wolves and the Kestrels had also been attacked from the rear, and their pursuit of the Hotcangara was delayed until they noticed my ploy and copied it. The attackers were not Hotcangara. I had seen enough to recognize them as Chikasha. They would pay for their imprudent alliance.

The next morning, we took up the pursuit of the Hotcangara again. Soon we came upon their last settlement. Our northern line was emerging from the woods to the north just as we breached the charred remnants of woods on the south. Between us was their last city. It was quite large and palisaded, but not large enough for all the refugees. All around the wall there were circles of warriors surrounding women and children. Cut off on the west by the Missi Sipi and hemmed in from the north, south, and east, they had consolidated for their last stand. We concentrated our forces and held our ground while one of the Tsoyaha delivered the ultimatum from a safe distance. One of the warriors rushed him but was cut down immediately. They were asked if that was their final answer. Their faces were a study in fear, anger, defiance, bewilderment, and despair. For a while they made no move; then one of their elders put down his weapons and stepped forward. I moved up a little so I could hear him.

"When we are attacked," he began, "we retaliate in kind, avenging our losses. Sometimes we kill more than we lost. But we have never all but destroyed a people in retaliation for a raid on our allies. What sort of beasts are you to send a whole nation into the spirit world? Have you no fear of the Creator? Does not his light shine on us as well as you? Why have you done this evil thing? What kind of witchcraft turns back the sacred fire?"

"Anyone," Kaidu coldly replied through the interpreter, "who dares attack an ally of ours forfeits his right to exist under the Blue Sky. We don't need witchcraft to defeat a minor force such as yours, just better tactics. For now, you may surrender and try to earn back that right, or die where you stand. The choice is yours."

"How would we earn back that right?" the elder asked.

"By living in peace with your neighbors under our protection and under our orders," Kaidu answered sharply. "You would be allowed to hunt and farm in peace for a year. Then your young men would come to us for training, and in time, you would become part of our 'tribe,' or, should you attempt any treachery, we would finish you off. None of your neighbors will miss you, and neither would the Blue Sky regret your passing. You have until the sun is directly above us to decide."

The man seemed older as he returned to his people. They had all heard, of course, but there was still some discussion of the matter, and much disagreement from the look of it. In time we could see that they were splitting into two groups. Even many of those in the city began to come out. Most of the women and children and many of the men formed one group, and these dropped their weapons and moved toward the interpreter. The other group contained many of the older people, the majority of the remaining warriors, all of the elites, and even a fair number of the women and children. All these filed into the city and stared out at us over the palisade with hatred and defiance. The elder was with this group. Word was passed that this group wished to die. Once the other group had passed through our lines, the remaining Hotcangara yelled their defiance. Some even jumped down from the wall and rushed us. Few of these got even halfway to our lines. The city was quickly fired with barrages of fire arrows, and finally the rest of them came out to be cut down. It was an impressive show of bravado, but a stupid one as well. As the old saying went: "Courage combined with arrogance is always fatal."

We gathered up our arrows and finished off any wounded. Then we tore down the palisade. The remnant of the tribe was left to rebuild the city we had just destroyed except for the palisade, since that would keep them in easy reach and defenseless. The Martens set up camp near the Missi Sipi above the large boat-landing site, the Wildcats were detailed to destroy the Chikasha, and the other Ordu returned to their camps.

Since Jebei was still not recovered, I was sent to lead the campaign, and Ussu was reassigned to the Owl Ordu. When we finished, we were to camp on the West Tsoyaha River at a point more or less due east of the Martens. I asked Thliotombi if he could guide me to the Chikasha towns and he agreed. It took us four days to clear the last of the burned forest. I switched to infiltrative advance, and it was three days later before we reached the first of their villages. It was deserted. They had two types of houses and some storage huts strewn all along a creek in a haphazard fashion for some distance. The houses included both a summer and a winter variety. The former were made of wood and cane and covered with a kind of whitewash. The latter were of mud daub in a round shape with thatch roof. They had a small door and a winding passageway leading into a central room cut about a foot into the ground with a hearth in the middle surrounded by decent-looking benches, beds, and stools made of cane. They had taken all of their food with them, so I had the men burn the village.

We found and burned a few more deserted villages; then suddenly we came upon an incongruous palisade between two creeks. It was not a solid palisade, but there was space between the logs so that the warriors could fire at us and still have some cover. It was obvious that they didn't understand the range of our bows or the usefulness of our horses. I had about a quarter of the men advance slowly toward the palisade on foot and had the rest of the men ride around the barrier and pour an enfilading fire into them at range from the flanks and rear. We were able to screen our movements with the terrain, and, with their attention focused on our advancing bait, they were completely surprised by the flank attack. They did not run immediately but tried to find cover and return fire. Some tried to charge but did not get far. Soon the trap was closed behind them, and we fired into them until none were left. We picked up our arrows and dispatched the wounded before continuing.

Before long we came to their main city. It was not palisaded, and we soon had it surrounded. One of their chiefs came out to ask why we had attacked them. I was amazed at the gall. I reminded him that his people had attacked us in the rear during our campaign against the Hotcangara. At this point their lives were forfeit and bravado or senility was no excuse. He asked if we would allow the women and children to leave the city. I told him that either all surrender or none surrender. He cursed me and returned to his people. We began sending fire arrows into anything that looked like it might burn and eventually they made their charge. Even some of the women and children were armed and screaming as they rushed us. With the usual drill, almost all were cut down en route to our lines, but a few made it close enough to be dispatched with club, axe, or sword. When the fire had burned out, we finished off any survivors in the town and again picked up our arrows. The remaining Chikasha villages surrendered as we approached, except for the last one. I ordered those left to take whatever food they had and march northwest. I settled them near the Missi Sipi about a day's march north of the Martens. During the winter, a few strays who had slipped through our lines rejoined the Chikasha camp, but they never revolted and in time gave us some of our best warriors.

Thliotombi wanted to return to his people and tell them what he had seen, and I thought it might help our case, but just to be sure I asked him what he thought about us. He said that except for the fact that we were so ugly, he felt very much at home with us. Since I had established that he was not one to pull any punches, I asked him if he thought his people would be more likely to join us now. He said that much would depend on how each town's shaman viewed the matter. They could see the future, he assured me confidently, and would know if joining would be the best thing for them. Of course, he added, each individual would still decide for himself, and he for one wanted to join us, ugly or not.

I asked him if he thought I might be able to set up a meeting with the various chieftains of the people to the east of his people. He said that it would be easier to call a meeting between a wolf and a panther. The chieftains were of varying power, and all were very jealous of their power. They would not even consider doing anything in concert with their neighbors except attack a third. I would just have to visit each one separately. I asked if there were any groups that were particularly large and perhaps more prestigious. He said that there was a prominent chieftaincy not far from Pansfalaya frontier that was ruled by a people related to his, at least in language. His town usually traded with them in the winter, since they always had a rapacious appetite for luxuries, so it would be no problem to suggest that they give us an audience. Since his horse was a gelding, I let him keep him. Perhaps the horse would help tip things in our favor, but it was hard to tell how the shaman would view us. Mystic types were completely unpredictable.

I settled the Ordu in its camp just as the almost-recovered Jebei joined us. I turned them over to him and started back to the Eagle Ordu. I caught up with Kaidu in the Owl Ordu and brought him up to date. He praised me lavishly for all my service in the recent campaign and shocked me by promoting me to his council. It was a largely honorary position, but it carried with it rank above tumen commanders. At the moment only Donduk and Givevneu were in the council. It was a heady honor and wholly unexpected. He had given Temur command of the Wolf Ordu. He was very proud and greatly appreciated it when I sent him my commander's helmet. It was only fair, of course, but I would miss the Wolves. I suspected that the "promotion" would mean quite a few more journeys. Juchi had been put in overall command of the eastern Ordu that was still keeping an eye on the Mingue. Donduk was recalled to the Eagle Ordu. Togun was put in overall command of the Ordu in the lands south of the Wazhazhe River while remaining in command of the Kestrels. Wanbli Sapa, the first local raised to the rank, replaced Juchi as commander of the Foxes. He was assigned a second in command who could help him with administration, but he was quite sharp and wouldn't need help for long. Both Juchi and I were quite happy for him.

We got back to the Eagle Ordu in late fall. Paula and the children were fine, but she was disappointed to hear that I would likely have to leave again for the southeast, since she wanted to visit Mathilde. Still, she was proud of my promotion and hoped that it might mean I would be with the family more. I didn't have the heart to tell her that it was probably just the opposite. Once I had all the maps in order, I went to see Givevneu. I found him in his yurt earnestly studying some notes of his. As always he smiled broadly as soon as he saw me.

"Raven!" he said warmly. "Who would have thought that that refugee from Khanbalikh would become the third council member? Of course, who would have thought back then that there would be a council?"

"Why do you suppose," I asked, "Kaidu would give me ranking above all his own sons? Might they not resent it?"

"In answer to the first question," he replied, "he gave you the rank because he has come to trust you completely. In answer to the second question, not really, because you will never be the Khan, and if they resent you, neither will they."

"I never expected to be the Khan"—I shrugged—"after all, I'm not one of Chingis' descendants. How could anyone think I would be the Khan?"

"Ambition can lead down many paths," he said thoughtfully. "You would not be the first person to reach for what was never meant to be his. However, it is obvious that Kaidu is convinced that you would always put the good of the Khanate above your own personal benefit. It seems that when you refused to displace Temur from the command of your tumen and then took pains to save the face of your poor, overstretched brother-in-law, it became clear to Kaidu that you had no personal ambition. Of course, I told him that long ago, when you came back to us from your first mission. It is a mark of your family; the same is true of your brother. I wonder if it will be also true of your children. Time will tell."

"Ambition and jealousy are what destroyed Chingis' Khanate," I said. "If one doesn't learn that from our history, one is incapable of learning anything. I rather hoped that Kaidu's screening process would have eliminated such elements from the Ordu."

"They did at the time"—he nodded—"but ambition can rear its ugly head at any time. People seemingly free of it can become enmeshed in it. Power is very habit forming and very exhilarating. The Khan has absolute power. Kaidu knows how to use it and hopefully will make the right choice among his sons to succeed him. But it would be naive to think that there will be no trouble throughout our history here. I hope there will be none in my lifetime. I'm sure there will be none in Kaidu's. But if all his sons can live in peace under one of their number, it will be a surprising thing."

"But they are all fine men," I protested. "Surely they wouldn't destroy the Khanate to take it over."

"You are a student of things." He shook his head. "I am a student of people. The only hope is if most of them do not outlive Kaidu. Fortunately, that is possible since he is a most vigorous man."

"I can't believe" —I was discouraged—"that we came all this distance at all this trouble to repeat the very mistakes that forced us to flee in the first place."

"I can see why Kaidu had so much trouble accepting you as you are." He laughed. "You are so practical that you can understand nothing else. Blind ambition is so called because it is blind to anything but itself. But don't be discouraged. Continue to serve Kaidu as you have. leave intrigue to others. Just be true to yourself. Do what you feel you should do. I know you will make the right choice."

"Was it a mistake to come here?" I asked.

"No, of course not." He shook his head. "We had no choice, once we knew it was possible. Besides, I think we may do much more good than harm here. I don't want to dishearten you, Raven, just make you aware of certain realities. Don't judge others' motives by your own. I'm glad you're a member of the council, and so is Donduk."

I was pleasantly surprised to hear that Donduk approved of my promotion, but was disquieted by the rest of Givevneu's insights. Kaidu's sons had always seemed so noble, that I couldn't imagine them being petty. I talked it over with Paula, and she echoed Givevneu's advice to be myself and not worry about intrigues. She added that knew she made the right decision to tie herself to me, and the rest would lead us where it might, she would not trouble herself about it. No wonder I missed her when I was on my journeys.

24
MY FIRST COUNCIL MEETING AND MORE
RECRUITING, 9-10 K
(SD TO AL, 1377-8)

Before winter settled in, we had my first council meeting. Kaidu reviewed the three campaigns. He felt the Northern Hotcangara would not revolt again, since surely the last of their hotheads were dead, and none of those who had trained with us had joined in the conspiracy. In fact, it was they who kept us informed of the whole scheme. Still, we would keep the Ordu in their country just in case. The Southern Hotcangara and Chikasha campaigns had ended them as any sort of threat. The former were reduced to about one fair-sized city, the latter to barely enough people for a town. If the Southern Hotcangara gave us any more trouble, we would move any survivors north of the Wazhazhe. If the Chikasha remained quiet, perhaps it would be possible to preserve their unique identity. He did like the fact that they had tried the sneak attack and was amused at the method I chose to repel it.

He then announced that word had come that the Taunika and the Pantch would both confederate with us. Some elements of the Hasinai also had sent word that they wished to leave the Kadohadacho and confederate with us. I mentioned that Smoking Mirror had said that would happen. I urged that we accept them, adding that separating from the Kadohadacho might dilute their excessive religious cult, since the latter were the principle proponents of it. No word had come from the Pansfalaya, but I would perhaps be meeting with some of their eastern neighbors in the spring. I explained what I had heard about them. Since they had an elite ruling class in each city and apparently did not cooperate among themselves, but were rather rapacious and much given to show, it had been suggested that I would make a better impression if I wore a lot of "finery" and brought them gifts. I thought it would be better if I didn't since it would give the impression that we approved of stratified societies and accepted their values. I was open to suggestion, of course.

"In the time of Chingis," Kaidu began, "any Mongol could come up to him and speak his mind. Any Mongol could rise through the ranks to the highest positions. There was no real 'elite' until we conquered the Hanjen in their so-called Middle Kingdom. We let ourselves get corrupted into forming classes. Of course, we considered the Hanjen beneath our lowest classes and didn't trust them at first. But in time we did accept them and, before long, listened to their intrigues and destroyed ourselves. That will not happen here. Any elites you encounter must come to know that they will have no standing among the Mongols unless they earn it. They will receive no deference, no bribes, and no compromises. If they confederate, we will not interfere with them openly, but their young men will be exposed to our ways and will likely adopt them. In time they will find themselves alone in their towns. If they refuse to join us, but promise to live in peace, we will not be naive enough to trust them, but will recruit spies and watch them very carefully. We will not prevent any of their people from joining us on their own, nor will we return to them any who do. In time I expect they also will find themselves alone in their towns. It is the 'elites' who are our enemies. The Hotcangara revolts were led by them, and with good reason. They have lost everything, but the rest of the people have only lost the burden of the elites. I think we have fully isolated them, but I don't expect them to fade away. I wouldn't be surprised to hear that they were trying to get the Southeastern towns united against us."

"Would it perhaps be better," Givevneu asked, "if we did not risk Raven on any further recruiting expeditions to such stratified societies?"

"Indeed," Donduk added, "would we not be sending him to certain death?"

"It is not completely free of risk." Kaidu shrugged. "But Raven is a curiosity and as such commands interest. Also, the elites may be craven, but they are not stupid. Surely the lessons of the north are not lost on them. Besides, I would not ask him to go anywhere he was not willing to go, and I trust his judgment completely. Indeed, Raven, if you think it best, we will send you with an army."

"A small escort would be enough," I said, "enough men to rout a sneak attack and conduct a fighting retreat if necessary, perhaps a few hundred men. It would also be a good way to convince them of my 'status' so I would be received in the cities, without bedecking myself with annoying bangles."

They all had a good laugh, and Kaidu told me to pick up an escort from the Wildcats next spring. Since all these people had no general name, but only called themselves after their cities, we decided to refer to them as the Southeastern towns, unless I could come up with more specific names, or there proved to be unrelated groups beyond them. My maps indicated that there was only a limited amount of land left in that area unless there was a large peninsula at the extreme position. Perhaps I would be able to find out the following spring.

In the east, the Mingue had remained very quiet and had been most cooperative. It would be interesting to see if they would continue to do so under Juchi's scrutiny. They were still a considerable, if divided, force and so should remain under watch, but they did not have an elite class, and their women, who had a lot of clout among them, greatly favored peace with us. The Leni lenape and all their neighbors had agreed to confederate with us, as had the northeastern groups. Since most of these latter also had no real group name, but many village names perhaps we should call them the Northeastern Bands. To the south of the Leni lenape, the groups all around the large bay, had also agreed to confederate. They seemed to be related to the Leni lenape and also were named for their villages, so we could call them the Great Bay Tribes. South of these, our mappers had found yet more Leni lenape relatives on an inland from a large sound enclosed by a thin line of very narrow barrier islands. This group sent observers to the Bear Ordu and would decide later about joining us. There was a group south of them that was not related to them, but our mappers had not yet contacted them.

The odd, unfriendly red-painted group on the island off the northeast coast was finally contacted through the good offices of one of the Northeast Bands that was friendly with them. They call themselves the Beothuk, and while they looked more like the Inuit than the Northeastern Bands, they spoke a very strange language. They would prefer to be left alone. The Inuit bands in the North Country were not really recruited since we would prefer not to renew our acquaintance with the icy north, and they could do quite well without us. The same held true for the various Tinneh bands in the far north. Some of them had joined us, and occasionally a few more come, but we would not actively recruit them either.

The mountains to the east of the Tsoyaha and the west of the Great Bay Tribes contained a nation called the Tsalagi. We had no reliable information on them. The Tsoyaha claim than they lived in caves and ate people, and the Leni lenape claimed that they drove them south into the mountains during their migrations long ago. In other words, we would have to find out about them for ourselves. Perhaps I would be able to visit them the following year as well.

No hostilities were foreseen for the next year, but a few new tumen would be formed in the spring. These would consist of five forest and three plains tumen. The Turtle and Goose Ordu would be encamped on either side of the Kubilai River not far from its mouth on the Great Bay. The Panthers would be placed near the eastern coast at a point roughly midway between the Great Bay and the deep bay at the mouth of the Wendat River. This would be near a river the mappers had called Kennebec after the band living on it. The Pheasant Ordu would be placed on the East Tsoyaha River well upstream near the mountains. The Beaver Ordu would be placed just north of the point where the Kadohadacho River joined the Missi Sipi. This last Ordu would have extra horses and be trained as a plains tumen as well as a forest tumen. The three plains Ordu would include the Horse, the Duck, and the Cormorant. The Horse would be placed on the north bank of the Red River well west of the Hasinai lands, but just north of the Titskan watitch areas to facilitate their joining us. The other two would be on the west bank of the Mongol River, the Ducks at the point where the Chahicks River joined it and the Cormorants at the point where the Black Hills River joins it.

We did not use any of the gunpowder in the recent hostilities since the foes didn't warrant it. Kaidu thought it best to use it only when necessary so as not to waste it. In time, when training was complete, there would be an artillery section in each tumen, fully equipped with cannon, rockets, and the several kinds of shells. Of course, all Ordu were already equipped with the new fire arrows. Also, everyone was pleased to have matches again.

Givevneu reported that still there were no epidemics among the Ordu in the new land. The tribal shamans he had spoken with had no knowledge of any such things, claiming that they never happened in the land. He was a bit concerned about that, but his own people also never had had anything like an epidemic in their history, so it was possible that epidemics were merely a curse of civilization, and would occur later on. I mentioned that the Hanjen had shown that epidemics were caused by agents of infection rather than by civilization—although the one may foster the other. He said that, of course, agents caused them, had not he many times fought against the ke'let that attacked the Ordu in the old land? Perhaps the ke'let had not yet found us. It was a wonder and we were growing into a great people.

Donduk said that he was certain the Mingue would give us no more trouble. He was not sure how much use we would be able to get from the Northeastern Bands. They were fairly small and widely scattered in the north, and larger and almost sedentary in the south. Most of their time was understandably spent looking for food, although the southern groups did raise some crops. They had sent some young men to us, but almost all had refused to return to their band. Still, there was no hostility, and he had maintained large stores of grain to ensure that any who needed it could get it from the Ordu. The Leni lenape and the Great Bay Tribes, on the other hand, needed no help at all. The former had sent trainees and most of them had returned home. The latter would begin sending men this spring. He expected it would be the same with them. Perhaps, if time permitted, I should visit them also.

I reported in depth on my journey of the past year, touching on the Xinesi's impotent hostility, the aloofness of the "Sun" and his people and the traits of the Pansfalaya that made them ideal recruits.

I mentioned that we would hear this winter whether I would be welcomed at the large city Thliotombi had mentioned. In any case, I would revisit the Pansfalaya and try to visit the Tsalagi as well as any of the Southeastern towns that would receive me. If possible, I would try to finish mapping the coastline, or at least get some idea of its extent.

The meeting broke up and we were told that we would meet again in early spring before I left. I told Paula that it looked like I would be gone again, this time leaving earlier and returning later that usual. I suggested that she spend the spring and summer with Padraig and Mathilde. That helped cheer her up. I had hoped I would be able to visit them the following year also, but events made that impossible. Padraig's mappers had never returned, and he had sent another group to find out what happened. If they did not return in the spring, he would have to send a large force west. We made it up to visit Henry once the river froze. The children really enjoyed the sled ride. Doqus and Henry both thanked me for helping Ussu. I exaggerated his role in the running battle a bit for them. They agreed to send young Henry and Christina along with Paula to visit Padraig and Mathilde.

In late winter, I took Paula and the children back up to stay with Henry until they went west. I returned home and, after the uneventful council meeting, set out south with Smoking Mirror. When we arrived at the Owl Ordu, we were told that a visitor was waiting to see us. We went to the yurt where he was staying and found a rather older man who was tall and thin with very dark skin and a big hook of a nose. He was wearing a cotton tunic bound with a colorful belt. His long black- and gray-streaked hair was tied back off his shoulders. He wore no ornamentations at all. Smoking Mirror was shocked to see him.

"Tlacuectli!" he exclaimed. "Is it really you? When did you come? How did you find me?"

"My son, your manners." He chuckled. "You have not introduced me to your pale friend."

"Raven"—Smoking Mirror turned to me—"this is my father, Tlacuectli. He is back from his homeland at last. I have so much to tell him."

"It is an honor to meet you, Tlacuectli." I smiled. "Your son has told me many wonderful things about you. Perhaps I should leave you two alone to catch up with each other."

"No, no." Tlacuectli shook his head. "Stay with us. I was sent by Tezcatlipoca's 'brother' to win him back from the evil influence of the pale witch. But from what I've seen, he made the right decision. You don't make a very convincing witch."

"I don't think I've ever been called a witch before." I laughed. "Should I be flattered?"

"What it means," Smoking Mirror interjected, "is that the Xinesi feels powerless on your account."

"Indeed," Tlacuectli agreed, "his world is falling apart around him. He curses the day you came to visit him. His confederation is shrinking, and his prestige has evaporated. I didn't have the heart to tell him that he is viewed with pity by the rest of the Hasinai. He's been making sacrifices of captives to the god whenever he can. He's afraid to attack any of your confederates so he's had to attack the people of the Natchez towns. I hope the rest of the Kadohadacho put him away before he does something foolish."

"I'm sorry to hear that." Smoking Mirror shook his head. "He is a very proud and stubborn man, but he was very good to me. I hope he will stop resisting the inevitable and come around."

"You have not seen him recently," Tlacuectli said. "His frustration has driven him mad. He wanted me to kill Raven and you if you resisted me. Imagine, kill my host and my own son. He will only find peace in death. But after listening to him, I felt I had to warn you. Besides, I only returned there to see you. And once I found out where you were, I followed."

We sat down, and Smoking Mirror brought him up to date on all that had happened, even showing him the maps and how he had learned our writing. Tlacuectli was interested in the writing, since his people as well as other people spread out to the south and east of his use a form of picture writing. It sounded like a rather more graphic version of Hanjen. He claimed that his people's pictures could be recognized to some degree, unlike the sample I showed him of the Hanjen characters. He felt that our script was definitely easier to learn. He was quite taken with the maps and gave us a rough idea what was south and west of our maps. He insisted that there was no connection between the eastern and western seas. The land along the east coast went south, then southeast from our map's end. There was then a large peninsula jutting out northward into the sea, and after that the land continued eastward as far as anyone knew. The western sea came close to the eastern sea beyond the peninsula, but he was certain they didn't join. He described the cities in his high valley and hoped we would both come down for a visit soon. Much had changed since Smoking Mirror had last been there. I was surprised that he invited me as well, but told him it would be unlikely that I could make such a trip for a while, since my duties were rather demanding.

He asked if we'd consider trading the horses and iron implements or even the marvelous matches. But I explained that we could only give horses and iron to our allies. The matches could be traded, but would be dangerous to transport over large distances. Besides, what would his people have for us? He opened his pack and took out some brightly colored feathers, some pieces of a rather inferior jade, some of the turquoise Talaswaima had pointed out, a large quill filled with gold shavings, and some little beans. I had to admit feathers were popular with the locals as would be the jade, turquoise, and gold. Actually, the gold would probably be well received by the Mongols also. The beans seemed an odd trade good. At this he laughed, and told me to wait a bit. He took some of the beans, ground them up to a fine powder, dissolved the grounds in hot water like a soup or a thick tea, added some strange ingredients, and then presented me with a small amount of a dark liquid. It was very aromatic, rather bitter, and oddly stimulating.

"What is it?" I asked.

"Chocolatl," they both answered together. Tlacuectli added, "It is highly prized by all people in the south and perhaps you can see why. It is even used as a medium of exchange. It only grows only on trees in the jungles along the coasts and is not easy to harvest. The city that controls a grove of such trees is wealthy indeed."

While the bean tea was good, I was surprised that it was used as an exchange medium since it was consumable. We had learned that many of our locals here in the north prize a bead made from a type of shell as a form of exchange, which was, in a way, no stranger than gold or silver coinage, except that it was perhaps more accessible to the general population, at least along the coast. We had not really found any need for currency since everyone received what he needed as long as he did his fair share. Still, I wasn't too sure what we could practically trade with the southerners that they would want. I suggested that Tlacuectli look around for whatever was not proscribed that he thought might be useful in the south. He said he had a few ideas and would like to set up trade between his people and us. I wished him luck and excused myself so he and his son could talk in private for a while.

I went to see Kuyuk. I mentioned to him Tlacuectli's interest in trading and recommended that it be allowed as long as it didn't include iron or horses. He agreed and added that perhaps we should send some people along with him as helpers to spy out the land and report back. I had to admit that was a good idea, but wondered if Tlacuectli would see through it. The next day, we took our leave of Tlacuectli and the Owl Ordu and continued on our journey. We finally reached the Wildcats by mid spring. Thliotombi had left word that the city would receive me but to wait until his return before setting out for it. Since we had a little time, I decided to visit one of the nearby Tsoyaha towns.

The town was palisaded on three sides but open on the fourth since it was a steep cliff overlooking the West Tsoyaha River. Their houses were made of wood and plastered with reddish clay, the whole thing covered with bark or wooden shingles. The women didn't seem to use face paint very much, but the men did. There was little tattooing and no head deformation. The men wore their hair in the roach style like the Chikasha, although some of the older men favored a turbanlike headdress. They were not heavily ornamented, but did wear colorful sashes, decorated with shells. They were tall and not as dark as their southern neighbors. They reminded me more of the Ocheti shakowin. We returned from the town, and Thliotombi was still not at the Ordu, so I went to visit a small chiefdom on the middle reaches of the West Tsoyaha. These proved to be a scattering of small villages on both sides of the river with no clear capital, but one town, Koasati, that claimed some sort of preeminence over the others. It's chief, Hildis Hadjo, welcomed me, and I found they spoke a language close enough to the Pansfalaya that I could understand it. They, of course, knew what had been going on and had fully expected a visit. They were willing to confederate simply for protection, since various enemies had pressed them hard in recent times and their cities had been declining. I assured them that the Wildcats were close at hand and could be quickly brought up to help them in need. Again I returned to the Ordu, and this time, Thliotombi was there.

He greeted me warmly and told me that he was delayed since he had been trying to get a more definitive decision from his people as to whether or not they would join. He had been surprised that there was disagreement among the shamans as to whether they should join. He admitted that he had been certain they would all see the same thing when they looked into the future, but they hadn't. The predictions included certain death if they joined, certain death if they didn't join, we would bring them great pestilence, we would save them from great pestilence, we would attack them anyway, we would save them from a great invasion, and finally, it didn't matter if they joined us or not, since we wouldn't be around long enough to affect their future. In any case, they wanted to confer with me at the holy hill again.

Before we set out, I advised Jebei that the little chiefdom had decided to confederate with us and would be sending some of their young men for training. He should send word to the Tsoyaha of their new status and perhaps set up a yam system through the Tsoyaha country to them. We set out toward the southwest to see if any one had moved into the lands of the Chikasha. Not surprisingly, we did find the area occupied with a few new towns. The new residents were not Chikasha, but called themselves Shaktci homma, or the Red crayfish people. They were indistinguishable from the Chikasha and, indeed, had been their western neighbors, but assured me they were much more peace loving and wouldn't dream of attacking us, especially since I was accompanied by a force strong enough to destroy them. I gave them the usual recruiting speech, and they promised to give it much serious thought. Thliotombi told me later that they would join if the Pansfalaya joined but not otherwise.

We moved on south into Pansfalaya country and enjoyed their warm hospitality in each town we encountered. Still, the majority seemed to be quite noncommittal. At length, we reached the holy hill and found a very large gathering of chiefs and elders. If any thing, it was larger than the original one. The majority of the shamans had been at the shrine for some days. They had purified themselves, starved themselves and in general tried to open themselves up to the spirits to arrive at a consensus about the future of the people if they became connected with us. They had finally achieved that consensus and were prepared to advise the assembled chiefs and me what it was. Their spokesman would be the eldest. He proved to be one Kiliahote, a remarkably wizened, skinny, wrinkled specimen, with very dark skin for a Pansfalaya and deep-set black shinning eyes. When he spoke, his voice was remarkably deep and powerful for such an ancient.

"Hear me, my people," he croaked in an almost sepulchral tone, "the spirits of our ancestors have spoken to us from the mound of our birth. The strangers from the northwest will bring us both good and evil. The good is readily apparent in the marvelous beast that serves them and the hard metal they make from stones. They will bring peace to the land and all will thrive. Then one day, they will bring great pestilences to the land and many will die. Whole towns will disappear in death. Only the strongest will live. But in the end those who survive will be stronger and will again flourish. So when the truly great evil comes out the rising sun, we will be able to drive it away and we will not die. The spirits would have you join with this people so you may live."

The hush on the crowd was palpable as the old man took his seat. I looked at the shamans to see if he had indeed spoken for all of them, but could find no hostility, no dissent. I wondered what pestilences we would bring to the land. If we had brought any with us, they should have broken out by now, for we had already been here some years. I hated to think we would bring death to the land and wondered if I could or should try to stop it. After all, the sage said that it would in the end make the people stronger, so they could resist the evil out of the rising sun. What evil could come from the east? Was there a large island offshore peopled by a powerful race that would one day fall on us? Or was the whole thing a hallucination brought on by starvation, which just happened to favor us? I would have to talk to Givevneu about this; perhaps he could make some sense out of it. My grandfather George would call it a lot of nonsense and my grandfather Peter would call it witchcraft, but I long suspected there might be something to all this mystical stuff, not a lot, but something. Time would tell.

Meanwhile, the chiefs each got up to proclaim their desire to join us, not as confederates but as full members. They wished to remain where they were, of course, and hoped we would send people down to train them in our ways as soon as possible. I have to admit I was overwhelmed by it all. At best I had thought that perhaps a few of the towns would confederate and perhaps a few of the people would join us as had Thliotombi, but the whole people, a tribe larger than the Ocheti shakowin, joining us was more than I dared dream. I assured them that they could remain in place and we would happily send down people to train them. I dashed off a detailed dispatch to Kaidu telling him of our good luck and urging immediate action to cement the relationship. They played one of their "ball games" and served a feast to mark the occasion. The men with me from the Wildcat Ordu mentioned that the Tsoyaha also played this game and it was catching on in the Ordu, but they were not good enough at it to take on the Pansfalaya just yet. I rather hoped the game wouldn't become a source of friction, but it didn't seem to among the Pansfalaya.

After a few days, we took our leave and started due east toward the great city. In two days, we crossed the river that marked the end of Pansfalaya land. I had already named a large river in the midst of their land for them, so I called this one the Union River to commemorate their joining us. Late the next day, we began to come upon some very small scattered farming hamlets. The people were scantily clad and hard at work in the fields. They viewed us with some temerity and were much relieved when we not only didn't bother them but also made an effort to avoid their fields. Early the following morning, we came upon a bluff overlooking a fair-sized river on the eastern bank of which were several towns and villages and one large city in view. We moved along the bluff in full view until we reached a point opposite the city. Then we descended the bluff and moved across the river.

As we came out on the eastern shore, a procession came out of the city to meet us. The procession was led by people blowing on a kind of flute much like we had seen in our first Pansfalaya town. The chief, however, was borne in a litter. He wore a rather elaborate copper headdress and was heavily ornamented with copper and shells. He had a robe or cape made of shell beads. Those carrying his litter were also heavily ornamented as were the entourage bringing up the rear. This last group was armed with long javelins and carried shields. There was some head deformation among the group, including the chief. The chief's litter was ceremoniously set down before us, and the chief addressed us. He introduced himself as Steek-cha-komico, welcomed us to the city and tried to present me with some gifts. I explained that I was not allowed to give or receive gifts, but would accept his hospitality while I explained my mission. I could see that he was disappointed that I wouldn't be giving him any gifts, but the size of my entourage gave him pause, so he led us back into the city. There were three fairly large mounds and a number of smaller ones surrounding a large open space. On top one of the large mounds, some sort of ceremony was in progress, very likely of a religious nature. We were led to another of the large mounds, and the chief was carried up it in his litter. I dismounted and followed him with Smoking Mirror and a few of the soldiers. The house on top the mound was quite large, very much like the house of the Great Sun of Natchez. The interior was much like those of the Pansfalaya only more ornate.

We were seated, and after the usual weed burning, I gave the usual talk. I was surprised how similar their language was to that of the Pansfalaya. I asked Thliotombi about it later, but he insisted that they were no more closely related to his people than were the Chikasha. The chief listened intently to my spiel, then asked if we would join them in a brief raid on a neighboring group of towns in order to demonstrate the advantages of their joining us. I replied that we had not been sent to him to help him attack his neighbors, just to offer him the possibility of joining us or not. We would make the same offer to his neighbors, if they were willing to hear us out. Furthermore, if he did join us, he would not be allowed to attack any neighbor without permission from the Khan. Also, should he not join, while his neighbor did, any attack on them would be considered an attack on us, and we would descend on him and destroy him. He said that we would not have asked him to join if we didn't need him, so we would have to prove to him that he needed us before he'd join. I told him that he had seriously misinterpreted our needs and his value to us. Indeed, we were doing him a favor allowing such a small group as his to join us. We had no intention of proving anything to him; he would have to take or leave the offer either on my word alone or by sending representatives to observe at one of our Ordu.

He asked me to withdraw while he conferred with his advisors. So we went back down the mound and looked around the city. There seemed to be centers for artisans around the city. There were potters, bead makers, hide tanners, and even food handlers in specific areas. There were yards for the disk-shaped stone game on the north side of the city near some large buildings. There was a sweathouse on the southern end of the town as well as the temple shrine. There were larger houses in the northeast corner, which were probably for the elite, while more humble abodes were found in the other areas. Finally we were called back to the chief.

"If I joined you," he asked, "would I be second only to this Khan of yours?"

"No," I replied, "but you would be allowed to stay in charge of this city, as long as you discharged your responsibilities worthily."

"Do you expect me," he thundered, "to give up all my authority and subject myself to the whims of your Khan?"

"I did not come here with any particular expectations," I answered. "I merely present you with our offer and you can either accept or reject it."

"Well then," he nearly shouted, "I reject it!"

"As you wish," I was impassive. "Do you wish to remain at peace with us?"

"Do you dare threaten me in my own city?" he choked at me.

"No," I remained calm, "I just want to know what your intentions are."

"Peace, then." His face contorted. "For now."

"Fine," I said. "I should warn you that your neighbors to west and north have joined us and any attack on them would be considered an attack on us. We will advise you if any of your other neighbors decide to join us."

With that, I turned and left, never pausing or looking back until we had cleared the palisade. I halfway expected him to attack, but he didn't. I decided to move south and visit another scattered group of chieftains who also spoke a language similar to that of the Pansfalaya.

25
MORE RECRUITING IN THE SOUTHEAST, 10 K
(AL, GA, FL, 1378)

We went down along the riverbank past the towns and villages that were allied to the large city. We cleared their area not long after their river joined the Union River. I decided to call their river the East Union River rather than name it for their city, since it was likely they would not join. Some three days later, we began to encounter more of the small farming hamlets and again took pains not to disturb their fields. As we approached a small, palisaded town the next day, a small group came forward to meet us. They were elaborately garbed, but no one was being carried. Their leader was a bit older than me and of a somewhat haughty demeanor. Still he greeted us politely and asked us our intentions. I told him I wished to speak to the principle chief of the area in order to present him an offer of unity with us. He replied that the head chief was in a large city some distance east of his town. He would be glad to contact the chief for me and present my proposal. I thanked him for his kindness, but insisted that I would have to present my own proposal if the chief was willing to hear it. If he was not, we would like to continue on to the coast in peace. His hauteur disappeared as he worried about what he should do. Finally, he offered to send someone to see if the chief would receive us, and we could meanwhile camp here outside his city. I agreed that he should send the messenger, but insisted on continuing south. If his chief would receive me, he could send messenger to intercept us, and we would detour to his city. Meanwhile, we would continue south along the river.

The next day, we passed a few more towns and, late in the day, came upon another larger river joining ours from the northeast. We crossed the river and camped on its banks. We followed it into a fairly wide and marshy delta, which forced us a little farther east until we finally came in sight of a bay. It was longer than it was wide, and there was quite a lot of fishing and shellfish gathering in progress all around it. The settlements around the bay were small and scattered and without walls. They also seemed to have some sort of allegiance to the chief upstream. They were quite friendly and shared their food with us. They said that the main city was called Alba ayamule, and it was quite some distance up the river. It was an odd name, since it meant, "I clear the thicket" in Pansfalaya, but perhaps it had some more subtle meaning to them. In any case, I decided to name the river Albayamule for the city, since its subjects were so friendly. We reached the mouth of the bay and found it was protected by barrier islands. We had just begun to turn east along the coast when a messenger who announced that the chief would receive us in his city intercepted us.

I decided to continue along the coast for a while, before turning north toward the city. The messenger was concerned since there was a large city ahead that was not subject to his chief. We came upon a smaller bay with a river at its head and more small villages all around it. The next day, we found the city that concerned the messenger. It was at the head of another bay. It was an odd bay with a very long narrow peninsula jutting out from its east end and almost closing it to the sea. Beyond it were more of the barrier islands. It looked like one would need to take frequent soundings in order to use this for a seaport. The bay seemed to drain several rivers, but the town was at the mouth of the first one. As we drew near, a procession came out with flutes, armed guards, and a litter-borne chieftain. None seemed to have the misshapen heads, but all were heavily tattooed and bedecked with copper and shells. They also spoke a language very similar to Pansfalaya and called themselves Pensacola, which also referred to their long hair. Their chief was named Hopthole Mico. "Mico" meant chief in the similar languages of the South-eastern Towns. That was why it kept cropping up in the names of their chiefs.

The interview went no better than the one at the first city, however. Again it was obvious that gifts were expected and again the chief wanted us to help him attack one of his neighbors. When

I refused, we were ordered to leave the town at once and get out of the lands it controlled. I asked just how far his lands extended, and he claimed to own all the land south of the river I had named Albayamule. I told him we would follow the river (I had decided to name it the Pensacola since I couldn't think of anything else) that ran past his town upstream until we reached the city of his northern neighbor who was awaiting us. This changed his tune a little, and he asked if we were planning to join them. I replied that we merely were going there to make the same offer we had just made him. We would not attack him or join in any attack against him unless he provoked it. Once we left the town, the messenger ridiculed the chief's territorial claims, assuring us we would be out of their lands by the next day.

The river led us northward for two days, then swung north-eastward. Several smaller rivers joined it, but we continued to follow the main stream. All along its course, we would find farming hamlets and cultivated fields. Our guide claimed that his master, Tustenuckochee, controlled all these hamlets. We would occasionally encounter a town, and our guide would go in and confer briefly, then catch up while we continued on our way. Eventually, some five days up the river, our guide insisted that we must move north now to reach Alba ayamule. Four days later, we came upon the city along the bank of the river just below its junction with another river. The city was large and palisaded, but not as large as the first city we had encountered on this trip. Even that city was not nearly as large as Murenbalikh, but it was the largest we ever found in the southeast. As usual we were met by a procession. Tustenuckochee was close to forty years old from the look of him and decked out in the usual finery. He seemed more dignified than haughty, however. He was heavily tattooed and wore copper wire in his ears like the Chikasha as well as copper nose ornaments. He had a cloak of some light tan–colored animal pelt.

He greeted me formally and invited me into the city. Again the language was enough like Pansfalaya that I could understand him. We followed the procession back to the city. It proved to be the usual open square, with several building-capped mounds surrounded by the more humble abodes. We stopped at the most pretentious mound, and our host was set down. He gravely indicated that I should follow him, and we went up the mound to what appeared to be a temple rather than a house. Inside were large carved figures made of wood. There were baskets full of inferior-looking pearls. Along the walls were ceremonial weapons made of copper. I was uncomfortable in the temple and wondered what he was up to. He bid me wait and went into a second room screened by a curtain. I looked around a bit while waiting. The images seemed to be warriors with some animal, mostly avian, features. The weapons looked like axe heads and spear points.

At last the chief came out of the other room and led me out on the terrace in front of the temple. He bid me sit on a mat to one side of the entrance, and he sat on another. An attendant came out of the temple carrying a dark liquid in a large shell. He brought it to the chief who took a deep draught, and then he brought it to me. I took a taste, it was exquisitely bitter and fairly close to vile, but tolerable and at least a change from the weed. I did find I began to perspire profusely from the drink. The attendant passed the shell between us again until it was finished. The chief seemed to be watching me for some sort of reaction to the drink, but I couldn't fathom what he expected. Considering some of the things I'd had to eat and drink on my journeys, it wasn't half bad.

"What are your chief's intentions?" he finally broke the silence.

"To unite the various tribes throughout the land in peace," I replied.

"Why?" he asked.

"We have seen petty divisions destroy our people in our old home," I suggested, "we don't want that to happen here."

"When people move," he said, "they usually take over a finite area to build a new home. Your people seem to want all the land under the sun. Why?"

"We only want to unite the people in peace," I returned to the theme. "We are now but a small part of our people, for whole tribes far larger than ours have joined us. I am simply exploring the land

and asking those groups that I meet to either join us, confederate with us, or just remain at peace with us. We only force the issue when we are attacked."

"So if I tell you," he studied me, "to leave us in peace, you will?"

"Yes, we will," I assured him. "As long as you leave us in peace."

"And if someone vaguely connected to me," he pursued, "should perform some act that you would judge to be hostile, you would descend on me as you did the Hotcangara?"

"Not if you eschewed that act," I replied.

"What if I was not aware of it?" he continued.

"Are you not kept informed of your subjects' activities?" I feigned surprise.

"Do you really think," he seemed affronted, "that any leader could be aware of all the actions of his subjects?"

"Well, if those actions could affect the common good," I continued the tack.

"Did our neighbors ask you to join them in an attack on us?" he changed the subject.

"Perhaps," I answered, "I wasn't interested in who they wanted us to help them attack, since I didn't come here to attack anyone, only offer alliance."

"And has anyone allied with you?" he asked.

"The Pansfalaya have joined us," I replied, "and the small group of towns, in some way under or allied to the town called Koasati, along the large river to the north has confederated with us, but the rest of the people in this area are not very interested in our offer."

"Is there a ruling class among your people?" he changed the subject again.

"No." I looked at him steadily. "Anyone can rise to leadership among the Mongols."

"How many Mongols look like you?" he switched subjects again.

"A handful look like me," I returned.

"How many of them are leaders?" he shot back.

"Two of them," I answered. "One leads an Ordu, and I am on the Khan's Council. We both joined the Khan shortly before we left the old land and earned our promotions."

"It may prove"—he seemed thoughtful—"that yours is the better way. But it is not our way. We cannot join you as you are now organized. The elites rule our people and keep everything orderly and organized. The people are accustomed to it and thrive under it. Mine is the largest territory you will find, and it is no accident."

"I can see that you are a cut above your neighbors," I said, "but only because you don't suffer from their blind arrogance. The Pansfalaya are organized much like we are, and they are a far larger people than yours."

"They are a large group," he conceded, "but they are all independent and disorganized."

"No longer," I rejoined, "you will soon find them organized into one or more tumen, just like we are."

"But you assure me," he persisted, "they and you will not fall on my 'paltry' domains unless provoked."

"That is true," I agreed.

"Good." He rose. "We will live in peace with you, and you may continue on your journey. The guide will remain with you until you leave our areas to ensure that no one disturbs you."

I thanked him, and we descended back down the temple mound. I mounted up, and we left the city. We had not gone long before I found myself retching uncontrollably. Thliotombi asked if I had drunk the Assi-lukutshi. I said I had been given a dark liquid to drink, and he explained that it usually made one retch immediately. He was impressed that I had held it in so long. I told him that the chief had not betrayed any problem, but he suggested that the chief drank it all the time and was probably used to it. I decided that was not quite enough provocation for war.

Since I was interested in mapping the coast, I asked our guide, Itchhasu, if there was a direct route back to the coast that would pass through some other chiefdoms. He said there was a large river in the east that would lead us to the coast, but we should first visit the ancient town of Coosa, up a tributary of the Albayamule River, near the city. I agreed as long as he would show us the way. He said he wanted to join us, if we'd allow him. I wondered if he was a spy, but figured it would do no harm since we often had observers along anyway, and they were little better than spies initially. The trip to Coosa took us four days up the tributary, which flowed generally south into the Albayamule. I decided to name the river Coosa, for the town.

Coosa was not fully palisaded, although there was a partial one on the eastern edge of town. The town was fair sized with a large open square with a pole in its center topped by a bird effigy. There were a few mounds capped with the usual large houses, as well as a very large "hot" or winter house around the square. The rest of the houses seemed to be organized in groups of four around an open area. The four houses included a winter house, a summerhouse, a grain storage house, and a warehouse. Some of the poorer townsfolk managed to concentrate all these things in one or two buildings. The people looked and dressed just like the Alba ayamule people but were quite busy with various pursuits, and little note was taken of us at first. Then a group was hastily thrown together to determine our intentions. Since these were peaceful, we were brought into the center square, and a bit of a crowd began to gather. At length Tustennugee, the chief, came down from his mound to greet us and lead us back up to his house. He was not young, perhaps sixty years old, and was missing quite a few teeth. That along with the strange dialect necessitated our using Itchhasu as interpreter. In time I got so I could get a little of what was being said, for the language was also related to Pansfalaya. The chief seemed a bit distracted and frequently lost tract of the conversation. Some of his replies were to questions not asked. Assistants attended him, but they did nothing to help the matter.

We finally rose to leave with nothing resolved, but the chief assuring us our chief had made a wise decision to accept his daughter's hand in marriage. We were shaking our heads in disbelief as we descended from the house, but were intercepted at the square by a much younger man who apologized that we had been taken to see the "old" mico. He explained that the older man was his father and had become much confused in old age. He thanked us for coming to visit them, but he knew all about our recruiting drive, and his people were not interested. He did hope we could live in peace with each other, since war had not been kind to his people in recent times. I assured him we would, indeed, remain in peace with his town and wished him better fortune in future campaigns unless they were against our allies.

As we left, Itchhasu apologized and insisted that the old Mico had been quite sharp the last time he had seen him, some five years earlier. I suggested we move on the river that would lead us south now. We moved due east for some four days until we reached the river. The terrain was different here. We had to go a little north to find a pass through a steep ridgeline, and the country beyond was rather rough and uninhabited except for hunting camps. The river marked the return of the little settlements we had become used to, and as usual we made every effort to avoid their fields. After two days along this river, we came to the town of Kasihta, the leading town of another chieftaincy. The town was much like Coosa as were the people, and the language was just as hard to follow. We were met since we had to cross the river to the east side to reach the town. We were well received and treated politely, but again there was no interest in our offer at all. As we left, we were given some of their grain stores and told how far downstream we would find the next town. Since they were so pleasant, I decided to name the river for their town.

We kept finding towns of varying sizes along the river all claiming to be independent and none wishing to join us. Finally, as the riverbank began to get marshy, we came upon a town that spoke a language more like the Pansfalaya. They called themselves A'palachi and seemed to have a sort of confederacy of towns in the area. They were rather warlike and were expanding eastward by force of arms. At first they thought we might be induced to join them, but were not put off when I refused since I had nothing to prove and had no quarrel with their neighbors. The chief was named Kushiksa, a tall strong man a little older than me. He engaged us in an archery contest, and we did quite well. He was impressed by our arrows as well as our steel weapons, but I explained he'd have to at least confederate with us to have access to them. He asked what that would entail, and when I explained, he was hesitant about losing some of his warriors for the summer, especially if they'd have to go way north through hostile territory. I suggested they would have to go no farther than the Pansfalaya lands. He seemed to be wavering, so I asked him to send a trusted man along with us who could report back to him as to whether it would be to his advantage to join us. He liked that idea and called in his younger brother, Schakchu. The latter was eager for the adventure and suggested we return after we visited the town they were fighting so he could join us.

The town they were fighting was a few days up a river east of the Kasihta at the southern end of a lake. The town was fairly large and palisaded. I could not detect any difference in appearance or language between them and the A'palachi. There was a difference in their leaders, however. Their chief was not at all interested in my offer and was angered that I had made the same offer to his current enemy. He ordered us away from his lands. We returned to pick up Schakchu and went on down to the coast. The land was increasingly marshy, so I went on down to the coast by boat with Smoking Mirror and Schakchu, in order to finish mapping. I sent the men eastward paralleling the shore until a point where dry ground reached the shore. A guide was sent along to make sure they didn't get lost. Meanwhile, we reached the sea and found more of the barrier islands along the coast. We paddled along the coast toward the east, putting in on the beach at night. It was amazing how calm the sea was inside the barrier islands, almost like a protected bay. The coast led us northeast for a while before turning east and finally southeast just as we met the troop. Schakchu assured me that there was a large peninsula in the south that was rather marshy, especially at the extreme southern end.

I asked about the locals on the peninsula, and he said that nearby and for some distance south I would find a people he called the Nukfila. They were spread out in many groups of farming towns and cities that were not really connected to each other except occasionally by marriage, or temporary alliance. South of the Nukfila were the Calusa, who also did some farming but mostly exploited the sea and swamps. These were united under a great chief. They were also very aggressive and would likely attack if we tried to visit them. The Nukfila might be more open to a visit, however.

We moved along the coast for a while and soon found the ground quite marshy again, prompting us to move along the beach. The heat soon drove us back into the marsh and the shade of the trees. These were mostly a type of palm. At last we came upon a small village, and they directed us to the principle town, somewhat inland to the southeast. It was called Ossachile, and the people called themselves either that or Yustaga. The town was palisaded and had a central square and mounds for the chief's house as well as the temple. The houses were rectangular and made of wood with cane mat roofs and rather open to catch any breeze. Understandably, in view of the heat and humidity (it seemed to rain every afternoon), the people dressed skimpily, only a loincloth for the men and a short skirt for the women. The skirt was woven from a type of fibrous moss that seemed to hang from the trees. There was some ornamentation, including bracelets of beads, copper, or bones, and pieces of copper and shell dangling from their belts. They had tattoos on their chests, arms, and thighs only, and these were blue, red, or black. They wore their hair bound up on top their heads with a type of netting or a piece of ropelike material. They often fastened feathers to their hair binding and many carried fans made of feathers. The rather odd habit they favored was growing their finger and toenails long and filing them to a point. Schakchu said that it was for battle. They would gouge their opponent's foreheads to blind them with their flowing blood. I made a mental note to avoid hand-to-hand combat with these people.

The language proved to be a problem. There was a vague similarity to Pansfalaya, but I could not understand it at all. Fortunately, Schakchu could speak the language and acted as our interpreter. They were intrigued by the idea of sending along an observer, but that was the extent of their interest at the moment. There seemed to be a decent road of sorts that was used for trading, and I was assured it would take me to the other major towns. I was glad enough for the road, but I did want to map the coast, so I prevailed on the Yustaga to guide one of my mappers south along the coast as far as was safe while I led the men along the trade road.

The road took us east for some distance through several small towns that would not even send an observer along with us. Then it intersected with a larger road that went north and south. We turned south on this road and after passing through some rather mean little villages came to a wide, languid river, meandering generally southward along the road. Eventually the road crossed the river, or, at least, ended on the west side and started up again on the east side. Not long after crossing the river, we came upon a fair-sized town of people calling themselves the Potano. They seemed to be part of a group of towns and directed us to the principle town. These people were exactly like the Yustaga from all appearances, although Schakchu claimed their language was a little different.

The principle town was larger than the others, and its chief was indifferent to us and our mission. Still, he did not mind our passing through his territory and even suggested that we talk to his relatives and sometime allies to the east, the Utina. This entailed an eastward detour on another trade road, but eventually we came to the principle Utina town, and they did agree to send an observer along. The observer, ponderously named Dulchancheyin, guided us south to the next major chieftaincy, the Ocale. This group was also indistinguishable from their northern neighbors, although they were a bit friendlier. Their chief seemed rather thoughtful over our proposal and decided to send along his oldest son, Katcili, a lad of about fifteen years, to expose him to the ways of diplomacy and to broaden his horizons. The boy was very excited about his mission. We were turned east again to visit another group who called themselves the Acuera, just across a river from the Ocale.

The Acuera proved to be a smaller, more scattered group, with generally poorer, smaller towns than the Ocale. Interestingly, Katcili showed no contempt for these people, but greeted them warmly and was equally well received. It seemed that they had formed an alliance in the last few years, and it had been quite beneficial to both. The Acuera chief also decided to send his oldest son, Athore, along much to Katcili's delight since the two were good friends. We were now turned back again to regain the trade road and follow it south. This lead us through a few independent towns of varying size, but no interest in our proposal. A few of them rather rudely urged us south without even hearing me out. Eventually we came to a river that flowed north, and along its banks, we found another major chieftaincy, the Urriparacushi.

We were guided to the chief town and brought to the chief. He was a rather grave man, of perhaps forty or so years. He informed me through Schakchu that his coastal tributaries had warned him that we were coming. They had intercepted our expedition along the coast, but had let them continue once they explained themselves. He trusted that we were not a group of exiles looking for a new home. I reassured him through Schakchu of our intentions and gave him the usual recruiting speech. We piqued his curiosity, and he also decided to send an observer. He chose his younger brother, Helicopile, a man about my age. The latter was a bit reluctant to join us, but agreed. We found out later that he had just gotten married.

We crossed the river and continued south. We passed through a few more of the Urriparacushi towns before again encountering some independent towns. One of these sent along an observer. After a while, we came upon a river flowing southwest, and Helicopile informed us that it would lead us to a large bay on the coast. We followed it and soon came to a town of another chieftaincy, the Tocobaga. We were ushered along to the principle town, which was rather large and palisaded. There seemed to be some difference with these people, however. In appearance they were the same, but they seemed to live in large communal houses with the end of one of them walled off for the chief. The house was quite open on the sides, but was covered with palm fronds woven together. Indeed, they seemed to use the whole trees as pillars and then weave the fronds together for a roof. Further, logs were used as half walls and reed benches held up by logs cut two feet long and painted blue, red, or yellow. The language was different enough that Schakchu had to use Katcili's help to interpret.

The chief came out of his enclosure to meet us. He was a heavy man of middle age and had also been expecting us. Our mapping expedition had been in their territory not long ago and had continued around the bay. He had warned them not to go south of the bay, since the Calusa would likely kill them. He expected they would be back soon. He listened intently to our proposal and asked a few questions of the observers from the northern tribes. Word had filtered down along the trade route that there was a new very powerful tribe in the north that controlled the copper sources. They had also heard that we traded tools made from a new harder metal for such things as a kind of salt. He was anxious to trade salt for the tools. I explained that we weren't interested in regular salt since we had all that we wanted from our confederates. We were interested in the salt that cools the tongue. He didn't know anything about such a salt, but promised to ask about it. I told him that he would have to at least confederate with us in order to get the steel tools and showed him my sword so he could appreciate the value. He was quite impressed and decided to send his nephew, Uti, a lad of about twenty, along with us.

We moved on down the river to the bay, and as we started south along it, the mapping expedition came into view. They had switched to boats to map the coast and Skenne-mok, the mapper, proudly presented me with his effort. He had done a good job. There were two more chieftaincies around the bay before one got to the Calusa. They had ventured a little too close and had been pursued by some of the latter in boats. They had managed to elude them and return to the last chieftaincy. I went ahead and visited the two groups. The first was called Mocozo and the second Ozita. They were just like the Tocobaga in every way, and they also agreed to send along observers. I asked the Ozita chief about the Calusa. He said that at times they trade with them, but only if they initiated it. He had no idea why they were so hostile, but they kept to themselves and he had never been in one of their towns. He suggested that I go to the east coast and talk to the people there. They weremuch more approachable, and some of them might be on good terms with the Calusa, although he was sure that was not likely. He recommended that I just forget about them.

Since Skenne-mok was an Ishak, I decided to send him to map the rest of the coast that we had missed. I told him to stay along the coast but avoid the towns until he got near the Pansfalaya land and then go inland and make contact with them. The Pansfalaya did not live along the coast, but were friendly with the tribes that did, and the latter would make sure he got to them safely. I sent a few men with him who were also quite good with the dugout boats. I told them to meet me at the Wildcat Ordu in the fall. The rest of us moved east threading our way through swamps, marshes, and lakes. There was a trade road, but it was not as well used or as easy to follow once we left the Mocozo lands. We did encounter some villages, but they were poor-looking collections of round grass huts with tiny entrances. The people were friendly and had large culti- vated fields. We traded them some dried meat for fresh fish. After six days, we finally came to the coast. It was completely protected by a long chain of barrier islands. We turned south and eventually came upon a small bay or inlet and on its bank a town.

The people called themselves the Wacata. They lived in the same sort of grass huts we had seen inland and were also very friendly, although their language was different enough to encumber com- munication. They shared with us a kind of walrus without tusks that they considered a delicacy. They were not really organized, but were a loosely allied group of towns with similar interests. They would be happy to join us if we ever spread down this far. They did not deal with the Calusa, but they were on good terms with their southern neighbors, the Hobe. We continued south to look in on the Hobe. They proved to be just like the Wacata, even to the point of agreeing to join if we ever reached them. They suggested we visit their southern neighbors the Tekesta, who perhaps did deal with the Calusa.

The Tekesta were about three days' journey south of the Hobe. They looked much like them in general, but wore more adornment including necklaces, bracelets, and hanging decorations mostly con- sisting of shells, wood, and fish spines. They were not very friendly, but were put off by our numbers and appearance enough not to at- tack. We had a terrible time communicating with them, but finally

our Ozita observer, Yehowlogee, was able to talk to them in halting
Calusa. They brought up their chief, Emolda, and he listened carefully to our offer. He replied that the Calusa were the strongest people
he knew of, and until that changed, he would be a fool to ally with
anyone else. Of course, if we destroyed them, the Tekesta would be
happy to join us instead. However, we did not have enough men,
and he didn't think our large dogs would help us against them. I tried
to explain that I wanted to talk to the Calusa, not attack them. Our
offer was also open to them. I asked if he could arrange a meeting
between some of the Calusa chiefs and me. He gave this a lot of
thought and finally said that he would try. While we waited, I sent
a mapping expedition along the coast in the remarkably seaworthy
Tekesta boats, with a few of them as guides.

26
MORE SOUTHEASTERN RECRUITING, 10 K
(FL, GA, TN, 1378)

While we waited for the Tekesta chief to return from the Calusa, we looked around a bit. I thought it prudent to set sentinels and make sure we had a clear line of retreat should the Calusa decide to attack instead of talk. The Tekesta's main town was on the mainland, but they also had a village on a large barrier island. Since the barrier islands were mostly sand and the mainland was much more solid, I decided to stay just north of the main town. There was a wide cleared area inland from the town, and the pine forest beyond the clearing was not really impenetrable. Once our position was secure, I tried to find out about the Tekesta. They mostly exploited the sea, as did the Calusa, although they did do a little planting. I asked how far to sea they went in their boats, and they said to the large islands. I asked about the islands and was told they traded with the Lucayo on the eastern islands and the Taino on the southern islands. It was hard to get a fix on how large the islands were or how populous the Taino and Lucayo were. I wondered if these might be the eastern threat the Pansfalaya shaman had warned about. I asked about the Taino and Lucayo people, and from the description they did not seem either particularly warlike or much different from the Tekesta. It took a few days to reach either island by sea, so I thought I had best wait until I had talked with the Calusa before looking into these island people.

At last the Tekesta chief returned, and with him was a large contingent of Calusa warriors. They did just outnumber us, but I was sure we could handle them as long as there weren't more of them trying to flank us. I kept the sentinels in place and moved forward with the interpreters to the Tekesta chief and the Calusa leaders. These also began to move toward us leaving the warriors behind.

Once we were close enough, I dismounted. They eyed the horse and me for a time, and then finally spoke.

"Is it a dog or a deer that carries you about?" one of them asked.

"Neither," I replied. "It is an animal native to our original home far in the west. We also have dogs and deer there—this animal is different. We call it a horse. We have not found any in this land."

"Why do you look so strange, but your warriors look normal?" another wanted to know.

"My original people live farther west than my current people, the Mongols," I explained. "You would find the original Mongols strange also, but now most of our people are natives to this land. We would also invite you to join us."

With that I launched into the usual pitch, explaining the advantages of joining us and how many of the northern tribes had already done so and several of the southern tribes were sending observers to check us out. Perhaps they would also like to send along an observer. They explained that they were not the principle Calusa chief, but only his representatives. Such a decision would be his. They would not take me to him, since he forbade it, but would explain our proposal to him and return with his answer. I asked how long it would take, and they said six days. I asked the Tekesta chief if his people could take me to the largest of the offshore islands and back in six days. He said not really, but anyway we would need to take trade goods in order to make the trip worth the effort, and there was hardly enough time to gather any. I asked when he might make such an expedition again. He replied that perhaps toward the end of summer.

I was disappointed that I couldn't get to the islands to reconnoiter, and I could hardly leave one of my mappers with these people until the end of summer. It would have to wait for another time. Meanwhile, I had the men do some hunting and fishing so we would not be such a burden on our reluctant hosts. We were able to bag enough for us and still have plenty for our hosts. This did serve to warm them up considerably, perhaps all the way to frosty. My mapper returned the next day. He had been able to get to the point where the peninsula turned west. He had found a long string of islands extending to the southwest but had only been able to map the first one before attracting undue attention from the Calusa. The Calusa chiefs returned in four days with the chief's reply. He sent his younger brother, Chekika, to go with us as an observer. He was of moderate height, good build, and nearly nude. He wore a scant cover of his manhood made of braided palm fronds. From its belt were hung crab claws and fish spines. He had a necklace of shell beads and a bracelet of fish teeth. His ear lobes had been pierced and distended by a wooden plug decorated with shells. I delicately asked if he had anything for a cooler climate, but he didn't. I figured we could get him an animal skin along the way, or get something more suitable in the north.

As we began our trek north, Smoking Mirror and I tried to learn the Calusa language from Chekika with the help of our Ozita observer, Yehowlogee. It was not an easy language, although Smoking Mirror thought it was vaguely reminiscent of Pansfalaya. In the course of learning the language, we asked Chekika about his people. His brother, Cuchiyaga, was a chief much like the Sun of Natchez. He seemed to have fairly absolute power over his own town as well as over all the other Calusa towns. He said there were almost a hundred Calusa towns, but I suspect he was overstating it a bit. It seemed Cuchiyaga's house, the temple and some other leaders' houses were all on top mounds, just as it was among their northern neighbors. In the swamp towns, the houses were built on pilings above the water. They did cultivate a little but mostly hunted and fished in the swamps and on the sea. They traded with the Taino and the Lucayo much like the Tekesta did. They traded fish, pearls, and amber for various fruits and vegetables. He also said that the islands were very large, especially those of the Taino. In fact, the Taino only controlled the eastern and central parts of the largest island, which he insisted was longer than this peninsula, although it was not very wide. The western part of the island was home to a primitive people called the Ciboney. They were not worth contacting in his view. He was a bit vague on numbers also, but insisted that there were more Taino than Calusa. The Ciboney and Lucayo were not quite so numerous. He said that the Taino were good fighters but not especially belligerent. He was sure that the Calusa could conquer them if they wanted to do so. But their island was too full of mountains and forests for their taste. I thought it had to be a large island if it had mountains and forests, we'd have to see.

We passed through the villages of the Hole and the Wacata again, then came upon a people called the Ais. They were much like their southern neighbors the Wacata, although there were far more of them. They had much regard for the Calusa, and the presence of Chekika among us did much to warm them to us. Their villages were all along a very long sound, protected from the sea by a few very long, thin barrier islands. They made a fuss over Chekika and told him they would go along with his brother's decision about joining us. I asked Chekika what his people had done to the Ais to inspire such fear, but he claimed it was merely their strong feelings of loyalty to his brother. Yehowlogee later insisted that the Calusa attacked all along both coasts of the peninsula and ate any captives. Schakchu confirmed that they had even attacked his people on rare occasion, but it was more of a raid, with few casualties. They would more often send trading expeditions. He didn't know about the cannibalism, but said most of the people in the area dismember their fallen foes, perhaps that gives the impression of cannibalism.

North of the Ais, we found a group called the Surreche. They agreed to join if their stronger neighbors did. They were just like the Ais only not as numerous. Still they had several towns on both sides of the northern limits of the same sound on which the Ais lived. It was wider at this point, and the barrier island was much more substantial, forming a fair-sized peninsula extending into the sound some distance from the barrier island. It took a few days to map this mess, even with help, so I set the men to hunting and fishing and shared the excess with the Surreche. North of this, we began to encounter people more like the Acuera in appearance. They were more likely to be tattooed, and the houses were of the pole and mud daub variety. The villages were very small and scattered, however, perhaps for more efficient use of the cultivated fields. They were quite peaceful and friendly, also much like the Acuera. They promised to join us if their neighbors did. They mentioned that there was a large north-flowing river a short distance inland, so I sent one of my mappers to cover it for us and meet us at its mouth. It took us six days to reach the mouth of the river, and then we were met with the challenge of crossing it. It was wide and rather deep for summer. Once across we found ourselves on a swampy island. Fortunately, we found a village on the island, and they guided us across another river to the west and on to the mainland. I had the bulk of the men find a dry campsite while I took one of the native boats and a crew and mapped the area. The locals called themselves Saturiwa and lived in small villages all around the mouth of the river. They were so helpful and friendly, I named the river for them. They also picked up my mapper and guided him to the main encampment. They too promised to join if their more powerful neighbors did.

The river was very wide farther upstream according to the map, and the whole area around its mouth was swampy. As we moved north, we found more rivers and islands all along the coast. The islands were much larger than the barrier islands to the south and proved to have villages on their landward sides. Again the locals were friendly and in every other way also indistinguishable from their southern neighbors. I kept the bulk of my escort inland to avoid the wetlands while I and the other mappers got the coastline and island complex down from boats. We were on a large island called Tacatacuru when we ran into Pesequan and Watang'a . They had been mapping their way south from the Great Sound and were delighted to see me after all this time. We immediately sat down to compare maps. From the mess on their maps north of my current position, I was very glad I ran into them. They were surprised at the large peninsula in the south and rashly offered to finish mapping its southern end. I explained the circumstances and told them to return to the nearest Ordu for now. Perhaps they could map the large islands off the coast the following year if all went well. That prospect excited them, and we copied each other's work while I asked them about the coastal people. They said that they were much like the people on this island. The language was a bit different, but they couldn't understand either one anyway. Just south of the Great

Sound, however, they had found a different sort of people. Their language sounded something like that of the Amani yukhan. At least it seemed that way to Watang'a who had befriended one of them at the Turtle Ordu the past winter, and they had tried to learn each other's language. I thought that was odd, but since that particular family of languages stretched from both banks along almost all of the Wazhazhe River to the Missi Sipi River from the Kadohadacho River to its source with much of the land between, it was possible. They said that these people lived in small fishing villages along the coast under powerful chiefs. The chiefs held sway over varying numbers of towns, and in general were peaceful. Farther inland, however, the chiefdoms were larger and more warlike. Once they got near a large river they named the Etiwaw, they found the people were just like the ones on this island. Since the coast was mapped, I decided to turn inland along the nearest river that would lead me northwest into the country of the Tsalagi so I could contact them and anyone else on my way there before fall. If time permitted, I would look into the tribes farther north that spoke the strange language and were warlike.

It was a relief to leave the coast and head for some mountains. This coastal trek had been singularly uncomfortable. The humidity and the heat were reminiscent of the sweat baths the locals favor. Even some of the streams and rivers were tepid. Our hide clothing was totally unsuitable for the area. Most of the men stripped down to the mere basics, of course, but I was left longing for cooler clothing since I learned long ago to protect my light skin from the sun. I vowed to get some cotton clothing before ever venturing here again. As it turned out, I was wrong, it was worse once away from the not infrequent sea breezes. On the other hand, the rivers and streams were deliciously cool at the end of the day.

Pesequan and Watang'a accompanied us as long as we were headed north. We got back to the main force and continued along a little inland. The first large river we came upon seemed to come from the west, rather than the northwest, and the locals confirmed this. They were a pleasant people, called the Wahili by their neighbors. Since "Wahili" means south and there were quite a few people farther south, one had to wonder. They were heavily into painting themselves, at least when receiving guests. They were occasionally tattooed and also had the long sharp fingernails like their southern neighbors. They often wore strings of shell beads around their necks, wrists, arms, and legs. Their small houses were rectangular and made of rough-cut pine planks with palm frond roofs. Their furniture consisted of cane mats, often fringed with colored fabric. They were as dark as the Pansfalaya, but seemed to be taller. The language was related to Pansfalaya, but not closely, and we did have some communication problems. Their towns were only loosely connected to each other in a sort of defensive coalition, but each one remained independent, and none would acknowledge that there might be a principle town among them.

We visited several of them as we moved north, and a couple of the towns sent along observers. Finally, we came to a river that the Wahili insisted would take us northwest and in the process past many "great cities" along the river. It was a good-sized river, and the banks were rather marshy, but it did seem to be flowing out of the northwest. I decided to name it for the Wahili, since they predominated along the coast here and had been cooperative. Not far from where we came upon the river, we found a sort of well-worn path. Unfortunately, it led north and south along the coast. It looked a lot more solid than the ground on which we had just traveled, and I was sorry I had not found it sooner. I sent Watang'a and Pesequan to map it southward until they found some tie in with my map, and told them to then return north along it to their winter quarters. I warned them to be careful, since it was always harder to map interior roads than coastlines. They were pleased with the challenge. I sent along one of the Wahili observers to help them with the locals. It seemed that it was another trade road, long used by the locals. Some of the men reminded me that there were more narrow versions of the trade roads in the north, and, in fact, I had followed one south through the peninsula earlier in the summer. I asked why there wasn't one along this river and was told it was because they didn't trade with their interior neighbors, since there was often hostility between them, and they were some distance away. There was a bit of an inter town trail, however, and we made use of it when we could. We visited a few more Wahili towns over the next few days before we finally ran out of them and entered a sort of no-man's-land between them and their neighbors.

Eventually, we began to come upon small farming communities just like we had seen farther west. As usual we took pains not to disturb their fields, and they gave us a little produce. We soon came to a river flowing into ours from the north. On a bluff above it on the west side was a medium-sized palisaded town. I crossed over to visit it with a small group while most of my men stayed on the south bank of the Wahili. Since I left the army behind, I was met (with some temerity) by the town's leader. He looked more like the people we had encountered along the Kasihta. The houses were also much like those, although a bit meaner. There did not seem to be much wealth here, at least in terms of the decorative bangles the locals seem to prize. There were some feathers and furs and some shells, but not much else. We came upon another of the trade trails, which obviously led to the town from the south and seemed to continue on to the north. In any case, the town was called Ukwunu, as were the people here about, and it considered itself the principle town. There were a few more towns up the smaller river, which I named for them. The chief agreed to send an observer along. I was sorry I couldn't map the trail, but I asked about it, and they said it split not far from their town both to the north and the south and led to many great cities. It seemed odd that they weren't more prosperous, if this was such a crossroads.

We continued upstream, only to find the river turned us south-west for a couple of days before turning us again more sharply northwest for a few days. Along this leg we ran into the outlying villages of another people. They also had a principle town and chief. It was called Altamaha, and proved to be a large palisaded town. Again the people were totally indistinguishable from those along the Kasihta, and indeed they claimed to trade with them along their own road, which apparently hooked up with the main road in the south and continued north along the Wahili River to some other towns of theirs and their northern neighbor. Also like the people of the Kasihta, they were not interested in my proposal.

The river seemed to turn us more to the north beyond the city, but we stuck with it since the parallel trail made the going easy. The other towns in league with Altamaha called themselves something like "Yamasi" in their odd dialect. From our limited knowledge of the language, we couldn't figure out what it meant. Whoever they were, they were not interested in us. At last one could detect some ascent in our progress. We climbed out of the river bottom onto a fairly broad plateau. The ground was more solid and the river more narrow and swift. The trees changed to mostly oak and the nut-bearing tree that looked something like a walnut tree, with some pine trees around clearings. The air was a little fresher, but only a little. There was a strange swampy patch along the path where several creeks joined the river in a level spot and, with some help from beavers, made a watery mess. Fortunately, the path led us to the west of the mess, but the resultant mosquitoes that night were not appreciated.

Not far above the little swamp, we began to run into some of the outlying farming hamlets of yet another city complex. In a few days, we came to the main city whither the other towns had directed us. It was called Okimulgis in the local dialect. That meant "boiling water" and perhaps referred to rapids or a hot spring of which we were not aware. The city was quite large at one time, spread out for some distance on the east bank of the river. We crossed over to find that only part of it was now occupied, but enough to make a fair-sized town of it. They called themselves Ahitchita but were again just like their neighbors to the south, except that they had some impressive mounds under their temples. One had to be fifty feet high. They had cut steps leading up the mounds out of the native clay soil. Their houses and general appearance were just like those of their neighbors, however, as was their response to our offer. The town did appear to be a major crossroads for the trade trails. There was the minor trail we were following, which ended there, but then there was a larger one going east and west and another large one heading northwest.

We followed the one heading northwest for a few days since

it paralleled the river, but then it veered westward after crossing a north-running trail. I decided to send a mapper, Zhawaesh, an Anishinabe, to finish mapping the river while I continued up the northern trail. There was a continuing gradual rise in the terrain, and the trail made it much easier for us. The settlements were fewer and smaller along the trail, but it was definitely taking us north. After two days on the trail, we came upon a trail heading east and west, and I sent a man down to the river to make contact with Zhawaesh, while we continued north. He rejoined us several days later with a copy of the latter's work in progress. A few days later, we ran into Zhawaesh, himself, waiting for us along the trail. He had been able to travel more quickly than us since he had been given enough food so that he didn't have to hunt. The river split up as he neared its source, so he took the easternmost branch, and it led him to the trail. There was also an abandoned village here, but there was no sign of attack.

The trail split into two a day later. One fork led northwest and the other northeast. We turned northwest. Over the next several days, the country got wilder, the air fresher, and the settlements ever fewer and smaller. We were definitely wending our way through some foothills and low ridgelines. The road looked as though it was not heavily traveled, and we had to improvise on occasion to stay with it. Eventually after passing through a line of mountains, we came upon a moderately sized palisaded town surrounded by cultivated fields, but no farming hamlets. Our approach was noted with alarm and soon the palisade was bristling with armed warriors. The men were pleased at the prospect of finally seeing some action, but I wasn't here to fight, so I approached with a small group. On seeing my approach, a group came out of the town to meet me. They looked much like their southern neighbors and also spoke a similar dialect. It took us a while to understand each other, but finally I was able to give the usual recruiting speech. The town chief, Checote, was actually quite excited at the prospect of joining us, especially in view of our promise to come to their aid if attacked. He was concerned about how far away our nearest outpost might be. I explained that at the moment it was about seven hundred and fifty li to the west, but that as more people joined we would set up more Ordu and would no doubt get closer to them. As it was, we had allied tribes who were less than three hundred li to the west of them. Of course, I then had to explain what a li was and how many days it would take to travel three hundred of them. I actually told him six days on horseback and fifteen on foot. Considering the terrain that was probably a bit ambitious, but it was possible.

The chief asked us to wait a bit and went back into the town to confer with his advisors. While he was gone, I noticed that there were trails heading north, northwest, and south as well as the east one we were on. I asked one of the people the chief had left with us where the north road went. He said that both it and the northwest road led to several other fortified towns on this side of the foreign invaders. I asked if he was referring to the Tsalagi. He was. He didn't know what they called themselves but they were huge, ugly, and fierce and ate their captives. Where had I heard that before? He also assured me that they were part snake and were very evil. He wasn't too sure how far away they were, but it wasn't nearly far enough. The chief returned and said that they would join us and would send runners to the towns between them and our allied tribe to urge that they also join us. I thanked him and told him that I would be traveling northward along the road and would welcome one of his people to join us and help us recruit them. He readily agreed and picked out a young man to go with us.

We followed the trail northward through a broad valley between two ridgelines. The ground was rough, but there were cultivated fields all around the palisaded towns weencountered as we continued up the valley. All the towns were quite eager to join after I gave my pitch, although the last one wanted to make sure we'd plant an Ordu in this valley as soon as possible. I had to explain that it would depend on whether we felt it was necessary. When we left and continued north, they sent a runner after us to warn us that there were only the snake monsters in that direction. I thanked them for their concern, but informed them that I had every intention of talking to them. I could see that the boy from the crossroad village was quite nervous, but he didn't ask to be sent back, and I didn't suggest it.

We came upon a river flowing west, and I sent Zhawaesh with a small escort to see where it went while the rest of us crossed the river. There had been a palisaded town here at one point from the looks of the ruins, but it had been quite a while ago. By now it was early fall, and the air was clear and dry in this most pleasant valley. A day later, we came upon a small, palisaded town surrounded by fields. It didn't look appreciably different from those in the south. As we approached, the people in the fields stopped and looked at us curiously but made no move from their work. From the town came a small delegation. I stopped the men and moved forward with a few men. The men were much like the Mingue in general looks, but they wore their hair long and tied in the back. Some wore tattoos and some nose ornaments. They were dressed in deerskin and had some copper, shell, and feather accents, but were not heavily adorned. The language sounded something like the Mingue dialects, but since none of us could speak them, I couldn't be sure. Finally, we were able to find one of them who could speak the language of the Tsoyaha, and we found one of them in my troop. With that settled, we went into the village to confer.

Needless to say, the Tsalagi were not especially large or frightening, nor did they resemble snakes in any way. I couldn't say whether they were cannibals. The houses were rectangular and large about sixty by fifteen feet. They were made of wood and covered with clay and had a thatch roof. They also had smaller winter houses looking much like the hot houses of their southern neighbors. We went into a large round "town house" that looked like an earthen mound. A small door led through a narrow passage to a large open room with seats around a fire pit. Since it was not cold, there was only a small fire to give off light. They passed around the weed and then began to talk. There was quite a crowd in the room, both men and women, mostly older, but a few young. The chief was cordial, but it soon became apparent that he was no absolute ruler. They all listened to what I had to say; then both men and women would comment in turn on my proposal. They seemed to be trying to reach some sort of consensus on the matter. They batted the issues back and forth at length and ad nauseam until, in the end they decided to send an observer with us, the young man who spoke the Tsoyaha' language. His name was Kollee. I thanked them for their decision and asked if there was a principle town or chief that would be able to speak for all their people. They informed me that while there were some great towns, which were revered because of their historical significance, the leaders of those towns could only speak for themselves, each Ani' Yun'-wiya (their real name for themselves) had to make his own decision.

One of the "revered" towns, Itsati, was nearby, so I decided to visit it and any towns between, before returning home. It took seven days to reach Itsati, mostly because of the long meeting at each of the three towns along the way. They had each decided to have Kollee report to them after he reported home, and they would decide based on his report. Zhawaesh caught up with us on this leg of the journey. It seemed that the "border" river joined a broad river that flowed southwest. My men insisted that it was the same West Tsoyaha River that flowed by their Ordu. From what we had mapped of it, it did seem possible it was. Our journey took us along a south-flowing river to a north-flowing river, which we followed to a wide west-flowing river, which everyone was certain was the West Tsoyaha, again. We followed this river upstream to a north-flowing river, which in turn led us to Itsati. I decided to call the "border" river the South Aniyunwiya River, and this river the Itsati. The town was quite large, stretched out along both sides of the river, with each house surrounded by its own fields. Since Kollee was with us, we caused no alarm but did draw a fair amount of curiosity. Kollee led us to the "town house" which was arguably near the center of the elongated town. It was like those in the other towns except that it was quite a bit larger.

I was received by the chief, Ostenako, and given a meal. Then we all repaired to the town house and went through the usual. This time, however, there was a much larger crowd, and we had to suspend the meeting and take it up again the next day. There seemed to be a lot of disagreement this time. There was a group that wanted to send an observer, a group that wanted to have nothing to do with us, a group that thought we were probably just spying on them and would attack later, and so on. It looked as though consensus would not be achieved. Then Ostenako spoke again.

"These strangers are not like our neighbors," he began. "Any nation that claims to be as large as they do, cannot be lightly dismissed. At the same time, since we know nothing about them but what they tell us, we can hardly throw our lot in with them. If they were going to attack us, it would be foolish to send in such a force and lull us with promises of alliance rather than a few scouts to spy us out. I feel it is best to send one of our own with them to see if their words are true and their intentions are friendly. If you agree I will send my son, Utasite with them."

This set up quite a stir and not a little protest since he was one of the town's best ball game players and would be sorely missed. The discussion continued into the night, but more were coming over to Ostenako's view, and in time all those of other opinions remained silent, and it was agreed. Ostenako then promised to send his most influential men to the other towns in the valley and speak on my behalf if Utasite returned with a favorable report. I thanked him profusely, since I couldn't take too many more such meetings. I asked if the Ani' Yun'-wiya only lived in the valley. He told me that other groups lived to the east of the mountains and farther north, he could also speak to them if I wanted, but it would probably be better if I made my own presentation to them, since they spoke a different dialect and no one in Itsati knew the language. There did seem to be a dearth of linguists among them.

We took our leave and, with Utasite in tow, went back down the Itsati River to the alleged West Tsoyaha River. We followed it west for a while, then turned southwest for ten days, then west for six days, then finally north. It was indeed the West Tsoyaha River. It was quite a broad meandering river full of islands. On some of the larger islands, there were towns and fields. These proved to be a people more like the southern people, than the Ani' Yun'-wiya. They had heard all about us from their neighbors downstream whom I had recruited in the spring. They also wanted to confederate since they were afraid of their neighbors. It was mid fall by the time we got back to the Wildcats. Skenne-mok was waiting for me with his map of the rest of the coast. I went on with Smoking Mirror, Thliotombi, and most of the observers, after first outfitting most of the latter with some suitable winter clothes. We sped along the yam system but arrived at Murenbalikh too late for the bridge, necessitating a boat crossing. Finally we got to the Eagle Ordu in early winter, mercifully just before the first snowfall.

I checked in first with Paula. She and the children were back and well and had greetings and maps from Padraig. A hostile coastal people had killed one of his mappers, and he would be mounting a punitive expedition the following spring as soon as the passes would allow. He had sent Kaidu a long dispatch explaining the situation and suggesting that we try to set up an Ordu on or near the west coast. I went on to report to Kaidu. He thanked me for my efforts and personally greeted and welcomed all the observers. He urged me to rest up for a few days, and then I could report when we had our winter council meeting.

27
Council Meeting and The Iyehyeh
Campaign 10-1 K
(SD to VA, NC, 1378-9)

I worked on the maps while waiting for the council meeting. Padraig's mappers had reached the coast at the mouth of the Salst River. From the map it seemed that there was a rather flat, barren or desert area beyond the mountains where the Salst and the Nimipu lived. Then there were more mountains and forests near the coast. They had also marked a waterfall on the river. They had not gone too far along the coast to the north, but had gone some distance to the south before turning back. It appeared to be no smoother a coastline than the eastern one. I wondered if he had any word on whether they traded with the Hanjen.

At last the council meeting was called. Kaidu brought us up to date on Padraig's dispatch. It seemed that the mappers were attacked when they moved north from the Salst River. One was killed and the other badly wounded, as were several of the escorts. They managed to get away, but could not go far because of the wounded. They were attacked again, but had found a strong position and had repelled the attack. Still they were in bad shape, and decided to retreat to a more "friendly" tribe inland. The more "friendly" tribe, seeing their condition, also attacked them, and only a few were able to get away. Quite a few of the horses had been killed, but none were captured. The survivors managed to get back to the Nimipu before winter, but a few more died of their wounds. The following spring, they met the second group Padraig had sent out, and together they returned to scout out the tribe that had turned on them and the more northerly tribe. They also had a running battle with the latter, but got away and returned to the Antelope Ordu. We know exactly who they were and where they were, and they would be destroyed next summer.

Considering the problems, he thought Padraig's suggestion to put an Ordu on the west coast was a good idea and had decided to implement it. The newest plains tumen, the Salmon, would be sent west with the Antelopes for the campaign and would remain behind on the best spot near the sea. We would also set up a yam system to keep them in touch. We would eventually put an Ordu in the valley of the Nomo, but the population could not support it at this time. All had gone well in the east, and we had organized a forest tumen, the Snakes, made up heavily of Mingue and quartered them to the south of the Great Bay some distance inland along a major river that emptied into the Great Sound. We also had established another forest tumen, the Pigeons, among the Pansfalaya. It would remain dispersed among them for now but could come together quickly if necessary. Eventually it would become a more formal Ordu and be placed on their eastern border. Finally, the Wildcats would be moved up the West Tsoyaha River next spring to a point to be determined by me, since I had just traversed the area. I suggested the southern bank of the South Aniyunwiya River.

I then gave my report on the southeastern tribes. If all those that sent observers allied with us, we would completely surround the elitist chiefdoms of the southeast. The long peninsula had shown some promise, and I passed on what I had learned about the islands offshore. I thought it would be good to look them over if we could win over the Calusa. I mentioned that the east coast had been completely mapped, except for the southwestern part of the peninsula, and all the coastal peoples except for the group below the Great Sound had been recruited. Then I told them about the prediction of the Pansfalaya shaman and asked them what they thought. Everyone looked at Givevneu.

"It must mean," he said thoughtfully, "that one day the ke'let will find out where we have gone and will come after us. It may be our ke'let will hurt them, too, although I wouldn't have thought so. But I can't imagine what evil would come out of the east. Perhaps there are more lands there?"

"Well, according to the Hanjen," I said, "the world is a sphere, and if one went far enough east, one would return to where he started. But, of course, no one could travel that far because of the huge ocean. In fact, from what I had learned from Smoking Mirror's father, there seems to be a second ocean. This land is not just a very large island but seems to extend very far to the south separating the western and eastern seas."

"The world is a sphere?" Kaidu asked. "Why would they say that? It always seemed to be flat to me."

"The Hanjen are good at noticing things," I answered. "They noticed a curvature in the surface of the water. When a ship sails away the hull disappears before the mast. If the earth were flat, that would not happen, it would all just keep getting smaller."

"The world always seemed flat to me," Givevneu added, "but I can't say for sure, for when I make my spirit journeys I travel in a kind of tunnel, and cannot see what is around me."

"I never gave it much thought," Donduk shrugged.

"What did your grandfathers think of this spherical earth idea?" Kaidu asked.

"Grandfather Peter said it was heresy, or something like that," I replied, "but Grandfather George said he trusted the Hanjen powers of observation. He said that, while they were spiritually inert, they were keen observers of the natural world."

"I remember George," Kaidu was thoughtful. "He was a true artist of a sword maker. It was a tragedy when he stopped making swords. Your father was quite good, but not as good as your grand-father. He was very innovative and resourceful. There was nothing he couldn't do with steel. If he accepted the spherical earth, there's probably something to it. So what do you suggest will be coming from the east?"

"I don't really know." I shook my head. "It would depend on just how large the world is. Just as this land turned out to be here, perhaps there is another land beyond, unless…"

"Unless what?" Kaidu demanded.

"Well, if the world is a sphere," I said, "then the far west could be the near east. In other words, my original people could be across the eastern sea."

"The Ferengi?" Donduk looked incredulous. "But they are worthless fighters, with no concept of tactics. We could wipe them out as easily as the Hotcangara. The only reason we didn't conquer them was because the Khan died, and we had to return to elect his successor."

"That was a long time ago," Kaidu frowned. "It is a mistake to think they didn't learn from their defeat. Remember, the Hanjen regularly scattered the Mongols until the great Chingis organized us into an invincible force. And even then the miserable Hanjen eventually managed to drive us back out of their Middle Kingdom. Never underestimate your enemies, and never rest on your victories."

"That is true," Donduk nodded. "But let them come, we'll be ready for them."

"I don't think they were talking about the near future," I interjected. "After all, first we're supposed to bring death on them; then they should recover in time for the eastern threat. But, of course, they could be mistaken about it."

"I wouldn't be so sure of that," Givevneu said. "These people are very mystical, and much in tune with the realm of the spirits. I have been very impressed by their shamans and their understanding of the spiritual realm. In fact, it has had a salutary effect on our Mongols. They, too, are becoming more mystical."

"You know how I feel about religions," Kaidu said darkly. "Why haven't you warned me about this earlier?"

"No, no." Givevneu shook his head. "Religions are simply public displays of cult that give exaggerated power to a priestly elite. Mysticism is a personal, private, individual relationship with the spirit world. It presents no danger. It is, in fact, the same sort of piety you display, Kaidu, but perhaps on a more intense level."

"Ah." He was visibly relieved. "As long as I don't find a priestly class telling everyone what he must do and exacting a large tribute for the information, I don't really care what people believe in."

I brought up Smoking Mirror's father again and passed on what he had said about the great cities in the south and about starting up trade with us. I mentioned that Kuyuk had thought it a good idea to send some spies back with him to look over the land, but I didn't know if he had, since I didn't see him when I passed through the Owls on the way back.

"He mentioned sending them when he was here," Kaidu said. "He was here to ask about the west, of all things. When I told him about the coming western campaign, he asked if I would appoint his second son, Ogedai, head of the new Ordu. It was an odd request, but I granted it since he has been serving under Kuyuk for some time and he should know if he was ready to command."

"Well, if he's anything like his brother Juchi," I said, "he would make a great commander. I'm afraid I don't remember him at all."

"He is some four years younger than Juchi." Kaidu shrugged. "He would have been a toddler when you left. He was always more quiet than Juchi, and I don't really know him well either, but Kuyuk assures me that he is ready for the position. I'll put Padraig in overall command of the campaign and if he feels Ogedai can't handle the job, he can replace him."

"Is there something I can do," Donduk asked, "besides growing old and fat?"

"I don't want to send you west." Kaidu frowned. "It is a very hard journey and you are too valuable to lose."

"Perhaps you could send him to organize the Pansfalaya," I suggested. "Since the whole tribe has joined us, their country could become a training center for the southeastern tribes that ally with us. No one can train men better than Donduk and the southeast is very important to us and could be a hot spot with all those hostile chieftains nearby."

"Would you like that assignment?" Kaidu asked.

"Yes," Donduk beamed.

"It's yours then," Kaidu said. "Now what about you, Raven. I think you should finish with the southeast and the east. Contact those tribes you missed this past summer."

"As you wish," I replied. "I also think it would be helpful to map the trade roads in the southeast, since they could come in very handy for moving troops quickly should any hostilities break out. Perhaps we could disguise our mappers as traders carrying copper, which is quite popular for ornaments."

"Good idea." Kaidu nodded. "Give the orders."

With that we broke up until the spring. I wouldn't have to leave quite so early next year, since I didn't have as much ground to cover. I thought I'd go directly west and south from the new Snake Ordu and visit the various tribes between them and the mountains. Meanwhile, I decided to look around a bit and see if what Givevneu said was right. I had to admit to myself that I had been so busy running all over the land or caught up in my projects that I really hadn't noticed what was going on in the Ordu. The Eagles probably had more of the original Mongols than any other Ordu. I nosed around a bit, listening in on conversations, renewing old acquaintances and visiting some of the ones I didn't know at all. There had been some changes. The Mongols had moved away from many of their sillier superstitions and seemed to be more thoughtful and deep and less hearty and crude. They had also taken to the sweat baths favored by the locals. This had a very salutary effect on the smell of the camp, and even though I preferred taking normal baths, I did try the sweat bath and found it quite invigorating. The Mongols had also encouraged their boys to undertake the spirit quest like the locals did and insisted it made them much better men, more insightful, more aware of and in tune with their surroundings. They urged me to send my boys when they were old enough. They had also taken to using feathers for decoration in addition to their various bangles, but not excessively. The locals, on the other hand, had moved away from body paint and tattoos and had begun to look like clean Mongols. It looked like a very good compromise between the two was developing.

I suggested to Paula that perhaps this year Mathilde could come and stay with her since Padraig would be gone on campaign. She loved the idea and wrote to her suggesting it. She wrote back accepting and mentioned that Padraig would have to leave in late winter to reach the mountains at the best time. And he wouldn't be able to return until the following year. It would be quite a trek, with two Ordu in such a wild country. I hoped he picked his route very carefully. The new Salmon Tumen had already joined up with the Antelopes in the fall, and they took pains to make sure they had plenty of food for the campaign with a truly legendary great hunt. All had been very busy drying all the meat before winter set in. I was sorry I couldn't be on that expedition, but felt it was in good hands with Padraig.

We visited Henry in the winter as usual, and I looked in on the gunpowder and shell works. One of the Anishinabe apprentices, Migizi, seemed to have a real creative flare and had been experimenting with smaller more portable cannon. I told him about the handgun my grandfather had made for me and took him back with me to see it. He was quite excited about it, and I let him borrow it to see what he could come up with as a modification or improvement. The gun was good for piercing metal armor at close range, but was not very accurate at any distance. I found the bow a superior weapon in this land since no one wore metal armor.

Mathilde and her children arrived in early spring. She had seen Padraig off some two weeks earlier. Fortunately, it had been a rather mild winter in their valley, and there was not the usual heavy snowfall. Padraig had already set up a yam system to the Nomo; the Nimipu and the Salst and would continue it as he went beyond their lands so he would remain in touch. A large detachment from the Ox Ordu had arrived at the Antelope Ordu to guard it while the men were on campaign. Morale had been quite high when they set out. The men were confident of complete victory.

The spring council meeting had little new to discuss. Kaidu promised to keep us informed as to the western campaign, although it might prove difficult in my case. He urged Donduk to return in the fall, if possible, or at least send a report if not. He wished us luck on our assignments. We set out a week later and traveled together until we reached Murenbalikh. Donduk stayed there a few days to visit while my group continued on our way. We visited the Kestrel Ordu and looked over gunpowder production. All was well. We continued up the Wazhazhe visiting the river towns on our way. I finally got to visit the Amani yukhan, the Wazhazhe's eastern neighbors. As reported they were virtually indistinguishable from the latter, except that their dialect was different enough to give me some trouble. They had been drifting eastward to fill in the vacuum left by our

Mingue campaign. We stopped by the Otter Ordu, and I was told that the area was full of coal deposits. I urged them to try to get a fix on how much was here, where it was, and how it could be best transported. While at the Ordu, I copied the maps they had made of the area between them and the Turtle Ordu. The Ordu mappers had not been idle, but had been fleshing out the countryside between them. I was very glad they had shown such initiative and urged them to continue and to send updates to the Eagle Ordu at least once a year. Oddly, they had not established a yam system toward the east, but only toward the north. It seemed they thought it best to wait until they were sure there was no hostile force in the mountains to the south that might prey on the exposed yams. I thought they were being too cautious, but could hardly fault them for such prudence. We would have to rough it.

We followed the Wazhazhe to the point where it was formed by its north and south forks and took the north fork until we came to a river that would lead us east. The country was quite wild here, forested hills and mountains cut by rivers, streams, and creeks. Understandably, the land did not look like it had been cultivated or even settled, although we did find signs of hunting parties and camps. The river took us into some hills where we picked up another river that flowed east through a ridgeline and into a broad but hilly valley. We crossed the valley and plunged through a series of passes through line after line of mountains until finally we came out in a broad flat valley which led us eastward to the Kubilai River. Along this valley, I could see the charred remains of some of the Mingue villages destroyed in the campaign four years before. When we reached the Kubilai, we found a Leni lenape settlement. It seemed that they had been spreading west into the valley. We turned southeast along the river and followed it to the Turtle Ordu. The river was quite broad and full of islands, but also quite shallow. There were a few more Leni lenape settlements on the way to the Ordu.

The Leni lenape were a fine-looking people, tall and slim. The younger men wore their hair in the roach style like the Mingue, the older men let it grow long. The women wore it long but braided. There was some tattooing of animal shapes, and the men painted their faces, chest, and legs. The women used red paint on their eyelids, cheeks, and ear rims. They dressed in deerskin, breechcloths for the men, and skirts for the women. They tended to be heavily ornamented with jewelry made of stones, shells, beads and animal teeth and claws. The men wore a small skin pouch around their necks, which turned out to hold nawak'osis and assorted charms. Their villages were not palisaded, but strung along a creek or stream a little up from the river. Their houses were bark-covered frames of various shapes with a single door and a smoke hole. They had tiered platforms made of tree limbs covered with skins as furniture. They were very friendly and generous even offering us their wives or daughters for the night. I demurred, of course, but Smoking Mirror was quite happy to oblige, as were most of the others. We finally arrived at the Turtle Ordu in early summer.

We went on down to the Great Bay at the mouth of the Kubilai. It was quite a sight, although one would have to sail it to get a real feeling for it. From the map, it was much more long than wide. The Bay tribes were just like the Leni lenape in appearance and customs, and they reaped quite a harvest from the bay. Crabs, oysters, and a huge and delicious fish were most heavily exploited, but there were quite a few other kinds of fish also. Apparently in early winter, the bay teems with waterfowl, especially ducks and geese. In addition they also raised crops of the mondamin grain, beans, squash, and melons. I must admit the Bay tribes looked quite well fed. We cut across to a river the mappers had named Potomac for a village at its mouth. We crossed over to the west side and moved south along its course until it turned east; then we continued due south to avoid all the marshy peninsulas that bordered the Great Bay. We would occasionally come upon a village. More of them seemed to be palisaded along this path, and the people seemed to be more tattooed, but otherwise they were also the same as the Leni lenape. All the major rivers we crossed were tidal and fairly easy to cross. Eventually we came to the Snake Ordu on the north bank of the large river that had been named Hokomawanank. The commander was Khurumsi, a Mongol about twenty years older than me. He suggested that while we were there we go on down to look at the Great Sound. It was very shallow, but quite broad, about nine li across. We went over to the barrier islands and crossed over the sand dunes to see the sea but were soon driven back by a constant high wind that blew parallel to the shore.

The Great Sound tribes lived in small, scattered villages along the western shore of the sound and inland along the rivers and streams. They also were much like the Leni lenape, and they exploited their sound like the Bay tribes exploited the bay. The language of all these people did vary somewhat, but since I didn't know the Leni lenape language, I couldn't say how much. I thought the language was something like Anishinabe or Kensistenoug, but not enough that I could make it out. They were pleasant, peaceful people and had joined us mostly out of fear for their interior neighbors. The Ordu had not yet made any contact with the interior people, but had done some scouting and found them to be living in towns, mostly palisaded, often with mounds and ceremonial centers and surrounded with extensive cultivated fields. It was uncertain if there was any sort of state organization. About all the Sound tribes knew about them was they were huge, fierce, etc. I decided it would be best to have a bit of an escort when I visited these people, so I took a hundred men from the Snakes. The Ordu had been established in the area between our allies and the interior people, so we didn't have to go very far before we ran into them.

As usual in the southeast, we first came upon farming hamlets. These were impossible to distinguish from their counterparts in the south. The farmers of the first hamlet were alarmed at seeing us and fled into the woods. We made no move against them, of course, and as usual I made sure we did not disturb their fields. As we drew near their little group of houses, I saw there was an old man who had been left behind. He sat defiantly in front of one of the houses awaiting his fate. I wondered if he was disappointed when we left him alone and passed by. A few of the men in the woods began to appear at the edge and give us a more puzzled look as we continued on our way. There was something of a path on the western side of the hamlet, and we followed it to yet another hamlet. The result of our approach was much like that at the last hamlet, although more of them tarried at the edge of the woods this time. We passed through a few more hamlets until we finally reached a well-used path through the forest. We followed this for some distance when suddenly the men urged me to stop. They felt something was wrong. Smoking Mirror also felt something was going on. We dismounted and began melting into the woods when suddenly the air was filled with arrows. There were a few wounded, but we had narrowly avoided walking into a trap. Still, we weren't safe yet. We formed a bit of a line in the woods on both sides of the trail and returned fire when we could see a target. Finally there was a yell and a rush. Here the men's discipline paid off handsomely. They picked their targets carefully and made their shots count. The attack was quickly repulsed, but I could see that they were trying to surround us, so I had the men pull back keeping the enemy in front of us.

They rushed a few more times to try to hold us, but we repulsed them each time. At last we were close enough to the edge of the woods, and I had the men mount up and ride about a hundred yards beyond the woods. We then turned and poured a memorable barrage into our pursuers as they rushed us across the open field. Again they quickly retreated, but I could see we were greatly outnumbered, and I couldn't be too sure that we weren't being flanked while we dallied with our pursuers. I got the men going at a good pace that we could keep up without tiring the horses. We went back through the hamlets, and this time everyone stayed out of sight. I sent out scouts to make sure we weren't being flanked. We reached their last hamlet, and the scouts reported that the enemy was still behind us, but the flanks and front were clear. We were almost to the woods beyond the hamlet, when suddenly what looked like a drainage ditch erupted into archers firing into us. The range was only fifty feet and the effect was telling. Horses and men fell. We returned fire and made for the protection of the woods as best we could. Once there we began to get the upper hand, and they retreated out of range. We secured our wounded and dispatched any horses that couldn't keep up, then hurried back toward the Ordu.

It was during this ignominious retreat that Smoking Mirror pointed out the arrow in my back. It had not penetrated far because of my leather armor, but I had been too busy to notice it. He got it out and placed some sort of poultice he carried with him on it. We paused for a short time to treat the badly wounded, and I sent out scouts to keep an eye on the enemy and to get help from the nearby Ordu. The scouts soon came back reporting the continuing advance of the enemy, so we mounted up the wounded and as many others as possible, and the rest formed a fighting rear guard. Just before nightfall, a strong force from the Ordu overtook us. They took over the rear guard duty and guided us back to the Ordu.

Only about twenty of the men were unscathed, forty-two were killed or soon died of their wounds. I sent a dispatch to the Turtle Ordu to join us immediately. It was possible that one Ordu was enough, but I couldn't leave a frontier Ordu unprotected while we were on campaign. Meanwhile, I sent out scouts to find out exactly who had attacked us. While they were gone and until the Turtles arrived, we licked our wounds, and I sent a report to Kaidu. I looked over the weapons available to the Snake Ordu. They had a large supply of rockets, but still no cannon or shells. The rockets would likely come in handy. Later, I asked Smoking Mirror how he had noticed something was wrong before we were attacked. He said that the woods had sounded different, smelled different, and felt different. He found it difficult to explain, but the rest of the men had noticed it too, so I had a lot more to learn. We went into the woods, and Smoking Mirror pointed out the nuances for me, and I began to get the idea, but I'm still not sure I would have noticed. Needless to say, anytime any of the men felt odd about the path before us from then on, I took it very seriously.

It took two weeks for the Turtles to reach us. The Goose Ordu had come along as far as their new site, on the bank of a river called the Powhatan for a town farther downstream. They would be nearby if the campaign proved more difficult. The scouts reported back that from the obvious appearances, the trails of the attackers seemed to lead north of west, but after careful study, it looked like our attackers had melted less perceptibly southwest after first leading us to another tribe. The scouts had thought it odd that the trail ended abruptly at a river close to the other tribe's farming hamlets. Filtering near the main town, they could see no signs of a recent campaign. There were no celebrations, no walking wounded, no groups of heavily armed men. They returned to where the trail ended and picked up the faint southwest trail right to the town we had been approaching when we were attacked. Here they found all the signs they were looking for. They had been holding a weeklong celebration, quite a few men were obviously wounded, and the approach we had taken was heavily guarded. They discovered a path from the southeast that was not guarded, however.

It was tempting to just rush them frontally and crush them as we found them, but it was irresistible to totally surprise them instead. I sent half the Snakes on the phony path northwest making sure they made no secret of their movements. They were to try to make friendly contact with the town to which the enemy had tried to lead us. I then took the Turtles and all the rockets downstream along the Hokomawanank, then southwest across the Secotan River until we picked up the uncovered trail, then northeast along the trail. The scouts kept reporting the path unprotected as we steadily drew near the enemy. We reached the edge of the woods still unnoticed, and I spread the men out for the rush to surround the town. We exploded from the trees and into the fields. Anyone caught in the open was cut down, but cries soon alerted the town, and those in the fields rushed headlong toward the town. After the initial charge, we began to fan out just out of their arrow range and soon had the town completely surrounded. I sent scouts to make sure no surprises would be coming from the surrounding forests.

The scouts flushed out a few sentries and brought one of them to me. We tried to communicate, but I couldn't make out his language at all. One of the Turtles, an Amani yukhan, was able to make some sense out of his language. I remembered that Pesequan and Watang'a had mentioned that they thought the people here spoke a language that sounded like Amani yukhan. The sentry (his name was Datha) said that his people were called the Iyehyeh, and the ruler of this town was a woman. A stranger from the west had warned their people that we had come to kill them and had been trying to unite all the local people against us. Their ruler had married the man and put him in charge of their army. Some of the other towns besides those under the chieftainess had also joined. I asked him if he had any family inside the town, but he said his family lived in one of the outlying farming hamlets. I told him we would spare the hamlets as long as the people remained there and did not take up arms against us. He would also be spared if he led us to the other towns that had joined against us. He agreed, although not with much enthusiasm.

There was no point in giving an ultimatum, since I had no intention of sparing this town, so we commenced the usual fire arrow barrages, and soon the town was in flames. The people tried to sally forth against us, but the narrow passageway through their palisade made them leisurely targets. Then they began to jump over the palisade in numbers, but many were injured by the jump and again made easy targets. Finally they cut down a large section of their palisade for a final rush. I massed the men at the point, and the rush did not get far. As the resistance ended, we dispatched any of their wounded outside the town, then went into the town to look for any survivors among the ashes. There were none. Datha pointed out the ruler of the town, but couldn't find the western stranger. I noticed that the ruler and some of the more ornate (copper and shell bangles) dead had the misshapen heads. I also noticed that some of them, especially the ruler, were very tall. It was odd to see a tall woman in this land. The warriors were oddly painted. Their faces were red with one eye circled in white and the other in black. It was weird, but hardly frightening. They also seemed to fix their hair in many strange ways. Some wore their hair variously shaved; others grew it long and molded it into fantastic shapes with grease.

Word came the next morning that a group of the enemy was seen approaching from the northeast. I set up a little ambush party for them in a small depression near the town and hid the rest of the men in the woods. They came rushing out of the woods in obvious flight only to be stopped dead in their tracks at the sight of the smoldering ruin of their town. They conferred hurriedly and turned toward a path leading west. At this point, the ambushers rose and poured a withering fire into their flank. Meanwhile more men came out of the woods and blocked their path; then the Snakes burst out of the wood behind them. The end was quick for them. The western stranger was not among them either, however.

The Snakes had made contact with the town to the northwest. They called themselves Cheroenhaka and proved to speak a language much like the Mingue dialects spoken by many of the Snakes. They had gotten along famously, and the town had agreed to send along an observer, one Histek. He was about my age but was scarred from several wounds. He wore his hair long with copper ornaments dangling in it as well as from his ears and neck. He wanted me to know that his town would also be contacting the related towns about our offer. I asked if his people were related to the Tsalagi or Ani' Yun'-wiya as they called themselves. He was not familiar with them, however. I tried out a little of their language on him, but he could not follow me at all. Smoking Mirror insisted he could tell the similarity and was sure he could quickly pick up Histek's language.

I decided to move on to the next town and sent scouts with Datha to see if we were expected. From what he was able to tell us, the chieftainess we had just eliminated ruled over three nearby, but smaller towns, as well as many farming hamlets. The towns that had allied with her were the chiefdom to the west of her towns and two others to the southwest. The western one was the largest, consisting of eight towns most of which were larger than the one we had just reduced. I decided that I might be playing it a bit close and sent a dispatch to the Goose Ordu to send a large force to the Snake Ordu so that I could take the rest of the latter with me. The scouts returned to report that the other three towns belonging to the chieftainess had been abandoned. I sent the scouts west toward the largest chieftaincy and started the men after them. This time I had scouts in all directions with orders to report back at least once daily. I would not be ambushed again.

28
THE IYEHYEH CAMPAIGN CONTINUES, 11 K
(NC, SC, 1379)

We moved on to the two abandoned towns and set them on
fire. As usual we did not bother the hamlets or the fields. About a
week later, we were moving toward the western chiefdom with great
caution. I sent scouts out in all directions, and they reported back
frequently. Every body of water was checked for telltale breathing
reeds. Every depression, copse of trees, field of crops was checked.
We were advancing in infiltrative formation through the woods, so
I also constantly checked the wind direction and the dryness of the
forest in case they might try fire. The winds remained fairly light,
however, and the woods were well soaked from downpours every
few days. We began passing the outlying hamlets and found these
completely abandoned. Finally the scouts began to see signs of life.
The rest of the Snakes had been seen a day's march behind us. And,
the enemy was massed in the woods just beyond the next hamlet. It
was difficult to get a precise figure on their number since they were
hidden in the woods. The crops in the fields around the hamlet had
been cut down and removed so that there was a very large open space
around the hamlet's houses. There was also a group of the enemy
conspicuously lounging around the houses that were supposed to
lure us into the clearing, so we could be trapped in the open. Not a
bad ploy, but surely they knew we used scouts and would discover
the trap. I questioned the scouts carefully, but they were certain they
had not been seen.

The men were quite adept at moving silently through the woods,
so I decided to teach the enemy a lesson. I sent the majority of the
men straight ahead into the woods to infiltrate unseen to the edge
of the clearing and wait. Then I sent several hundred men in a wide
arc to surround the enemy forces ahead of us. With them I sent a

bunch of rockets they were to set off behind the enemy at my signal once they were in position. I went ahead with the bulk of the men. We reached the edge of the clearing, capturing or killing the scouts they had posted to watch for us. We lay in wait until the word came that all were in position. I then shot a screaming arrow into the air. Immediately the woods all around the clearing were rocked with the explosions of rockets. The enemy poured into the clearing in fright as more rockets roared through the woods behind them crashing and exploding into the trees. As their fear became panic, they rushed toward our position, the only direction free from rockets, across the open field. Alarmed at their numbers, I only waited until they were a hundred feet away before we rose up and poured arrows into them. Sheer numbers and total panic keep them coming, however, and soon our front line was hacking away with sword and axe, while the rear lines shot over our heads. Many of them had dropped their weapons in their initial panic or we might have had more problems. As it was, we were getting hard-pressed when the rest of the Snake Ordu came up on their left flank and along with the rocket men began pouring a withering fire into their flanks and rear. Some managed to filter back through the woods from where they had initially fled, fewer managed to fight their way through our lines, but the vast majority were slaughtered in the very pen they had prepared for us.

We did not pursue immediately, but dispatched any of their wounded and treated our own. We left their dead in the field, but buried our own. Our losses were not negligible, but paled in comparison to theirs. I sent the wounded back to the Ordu under strong escort and, with scouts all around, moved on toward the first town. We reached it at dusk and found it abandoned. We spent the night in the town, then set it ablaze the next morning before we left. Datha said that the chieftain's town was still some distance away. The scouts continued to report no signs of life, and we continued to find and burn the towns of this chieftaincy. Finally the scouts reported seeing enemy movement again. This time they were distributed all over the woods around the next town in our path. They had made great efforts to camouflage themselves, but our sharp-eyed scouts had found them out. The easiest thing to do would be to set fire to the woods, but they were still too damp for that. I decided they were probably still not used to the rockets, so I sent the men to form a huge circle around their positions.

When the circle was complete, we began firing the rockets into their positions. By far the majority panicked and fled to the town, but a few did hold their positions and took some of our men with them as we advanced. One of them almost got me, but he misjudged his lunge and just missed me. He didn't get a second chance. Smoking Mirror was struck in the arm by an arrow, and Thliotombi was badly gashed by a war club. We finally cleared the woods and surrounded the town. Datha said that this was the chief town. It was quite large, but was not palisaded. An attempt had been made to barricade it somewhat, and the efforts were continuing as we approached. I immediately ordered the fire arrows launched. They attempted to contain the ensuing fires, but to no avail. Without further ado, they rushed us. We fired into them as we backed away, but without the horses some of them reached us anyway, and there was more hand-to-hand combat. Still, there were not enough of them, and we mercilessly finished them off. The chieftain was not among the dead, and neither was the western stranger.

We patched up our wounded and buried our dead and then marched into the woods toward the next town. The scouts reported it abandoned except for some elderly. I ordered them removed and the town razed. A few of them made feeble attempts at attacking us and were cut down. The rest were placed outside of the town with whatever food they had with them, but without any weapons. I'm not sure if I did them a favor. We continued on to the next town and found it also abandoned, as were all the other towns of this chieftaincy. We moved on to the next chieftaincy. It was not one of those allied against us, and the scouts reported no hostile activity from them. I halted the men at their first hamlet and continued ahead with a moderate escort. The people of the hamlet ran when we approached, but stopped when we didn't pursue and watched us from the edge of the woods.

We passed into the woods along a well-worn path toward the

town. I was too wary not to bring along scouts and had them ranging all around us. We passed through a few more hamlets, then finally came to a palisaded town. Just as we were clearing the woods, a procession came out of the town. Men blowing a kind of flute or beating a drum led it. The sound was more shrill than musical, but it did draw one's attention. Behind the noisemakers was a heavily ornamented honor guard. All of these were carrying long javelins and small ornate shields. They were quite tall and had the misshapen heads. Behind them was a litter borne by taller, more ornate, but unarmed guards. In the litter was a heavily ornamented woman. She was in a reclining position on the litter, but was bedecked with copper, shells, and pearls in the form of bangles and wore a feather cloak that was mostly green. I had not seen any green birds, except for the green-headed duck, but this was a lighter green than that, and the feathers were larger than those would be, although not by much. I eventually learned that the feathers were from a parrotlike bird that lived in large flocks here in the eastern part of the land. Once we reached them, the musicians let up, the guards stood to one side, and the litter bearers set down their burden. The woman rose and came forward to meet us. We dismounted and I stepped forward. She was taller than me and about ten years older. She had the misshapen head, but was quite graceful and dignified. Smoking Mirror had already managed to pick up the language from Datha, so he acted as interpreter.

"I thank you for coming in peace," she began nervously and per- haps, hopefully. "I am Si'wi, the chieftain of this group of towns."

"I am called the Raven, ambassador of the Khanate of the Blue Sky, and I always come in peace," I replied, "but I have not been so received by your neighbors. Still, I have been told that this chiefdom was not a part of the attack on us. Do you then wish to be at peace with us?"

"Most certainly," she answered earnestly. "I am glad that you have been correctly informed about us. We did not approve of the attack on you and felt that we should hear you out, before believ- ing the wild story of the stranger. You are indeed an odd-looking person, and your 'deer-dogs' are remarkable creatures, but most of your followers look normal. You crushed the forces arrayed against you and destroyed the towns, but spared the fields and the hamlets. You could have attacked us, but took the time to learn that we were not involved and came to us in peace. What are your intentions toward us?"

"If you mean to receive us in peace," I began, "you need merely listen to my proposal. I offer you three alternatives. You may join us, becoming subject to our khan; you may ally with us, remaining independent, except that you must send your young men for training with us and you cannot make war on your neighbors without our permission; or you may remain as you are. In both the first two cases, you will be under our full protection, and we will share our weapons and horses (the 'deer-dogs') with you. In the third case, you will be left alone, and we would be willing to remain at peace with you and trade anything except weapons and horses. Of course, we would not protect you and should you attack one of our allies, we would destroy you."

"The western stranger said that you destroyed or enslaved all his people with no provocation," she returned to her misgivings. "Is that true?"

"No," I replied, "it isn't. There was provocation, but one could argue that we overreacted. In any case, we only destroyed those who resisted, and those who didn't resist were not enslaved, they were merely joined to us without giving them a choice. If we overreacted, it was because we misunderstood the nature of their organization. We thought they were united under one chief, rather than somewhat splintered. As it turned out, they were the first to resist us, and destroying them helped establish our credentials. Such shows of force are no longer necessary, and we take pains to separate our enemies from our friends or the neutral."

"Do you really want me to tell her that?" Smoking Mirror was shocked.

"Well, why not?" I returned. "It's the truth."

"You continue to amaze me." He shook his head, before translating.

"A most straightforward answer," she smiled. "I think I can

deal with you. Please come into the town as our guests, and we will discuss these options of yours in more detail."

We followed the procession back into the town. It was much like the others. The houses were made of bark strips in a rectangular shape with a vaulted, barrel-shaped roof, much like the Mingue houses, only much smaller. The town was laid out much like those in the south, with a large central court for their games and a couple of mounds with structures on top. We stopped at one of these, and a heavily bedecked man bowed to all and led the way up. He was introduced as Yensigri, the chief of this particular town. We were seated and the usual nawak'osis was passed around. It was followed by a reddish liquid. It wasn't the awful black drink, I hoped, but I tried it with some trepidation, only to discover it was a type of fruit wine. They were sparing of it, so they didn't become intoxicated, but it was the first time I had seen such a drink here. Smoking Mirror said it was pleasant, but little more than water. It didn't seem as strong as kumis, but since I very rarely had wine, I really couldn't be sure.

I was questioned at length and quite intelligently about our people and their ways, and the subtleties of the choices I had given her. I also asked about her people. It turned out that she ruled as an absolute monarch, with total, unshared authority. She also said all of the other Iyehyeh chieftains had the same power over their towns. They did occasionally fight each other, although more often they fought their unrelated neighbors. Her people had been skirmishing with their western neighbors, the Tsalagi. I explained that I had already recruited the southern branch of that group and planned to visit the others after I had finished with the Iyehyeh and whatever tribe was directly south of them. She said that there was a great chieftaincy south of them called Kofitachiki. It covered a huge area and was ruled absolutely just like them, but they were a different people. I told her that I had already recruited among the groups to the south of them with very mixed results, and if they were of that sort I would probably do no better with them, but I was obliged to try. She then warned me that the western stranger had also planned to get them to join against us, but she didn't know if he was successful. She did know that the two largest Iyehyeh chieftaincies had not joined the conspiracy. I would find them to the south of hers. I told her that my information indicated that there would only be two more chieftaincies to reduce, and both were relatively small. She said that she knew of them; they were to the southeast, not far from this town. There were others farther east, however, and she didn't know what their disposition was. I asked if the stranger was one of the Hotcangara elites, and she nodded affirmatively.

Before we broke up, she told me that she could not join us outright, since she felt it would be too much of a change for her people, but she would consider allying with us and wanted to send a man with us to report back about us. I was amused at the idea that enslaved people would find freedom too much of a change, but made no comment on the arrogance. I agreed to take along her observer, but warned her that until they actually allied with us, we would not come to their assistance. We would pass on that they were considering it, however, and that might help. She thanked me and pressed us to spend the night, but I demurred, since I was anxious to get back to the men. We hurried back and arrived just before the last light failed.

The scouts were waiting to report on the enemy. It seemed that the closest chieftaincy, consisting of only four towns was completely abandoned. The next morning, I sent the scouts out again and split the men into three groups. They would each ride to and destroy a town, and we would meet again at the last town. The positions of the towns suggested this maneuver, but I urged the scouts to be vigilant so we weren't caught while we were divided. Everything went according to plan, and we were all at the last town by nightfall. We spent the night there, then set it to the torch in the morning. Meanwhile, the scouts reported that the last chieftaincy was also deserted. It had five towns, but they were aligned in such a way that we could easily stay together while we burned them. Two days later, we reached the last of their towns. While we were burning it, the scouts reported that a small group was coming through the woods toward us from the northeast. I sent them out again to make sure this was no more than a small group. Before long the group came out of the woods and moved slowly toward us.

I could see that they were armed, so I took along enough men to wipe them out if they tried anything, and I moved toward them. As we drew near, I could see that they did not have the characteristic war paint, and then one of them laid down his weapons and approached alone. He was much like the other Iyehyeh elites in appearance, although he was not heavily ornamented. He was not a young man, and the journey could not have been easy for him. When he got close, Smoking Mirror and I dismounted and approached him.

"I am Sawen, from the chieftaincy to the northeast," he said. "I come in peace."

"Are you part of the conspiracy against us?" I asked harshly.

"No." He shook his head emphatically. "We did not join it. I offer myself up to you in exchange for my people. You may do as you like to me, but spare my people."

"If you are not part of the conspiracy," I asked the old man, "why should I want to harm you or your people?"

"We were told you would kill us anyway," he said simply. "I hoped it wasn't true, but I didn't know."

"Well, now you do." I was getting annoyed. "Where is the vile Hotcangara who has been spreading all these lies?"

"He is southeast of here," he said, "concentrating those he has won over."

"Can you tell me with any certainty," I asked, "who else has not joined him?"

"I know that my eastern and southeastern neighbors have not," he replied. "But I don't know about the others."

"Are your northern and northwestern neighbors," I continued, "the ones we destroyed?"

"Yes." He nodded. "And, of course, the one north of them and this one and the one northeast of here."

"If your information is so complete," I said sarcastically, "why didn't you know we didn't harm the far western Iyehyeh chieftaincy?"

"I did," he replied sheepishly, "that's why I dared to come to you."

I gave him the usual recruitment speech and urged him to pass it on to his neighbors. I also suggested that he pass the word that those who are not arrayed against us have nothing to fear from us. We would be continuing toward the southeast and strongly suggested that anyone not against us make it known to us. He readily agreed and asked if he could send an observer with us. I agreed and he assigned one of his men. He sent some of the others off on the run to spread the word, and then he turned back more slowly. I was glad he had come and hoped he could sway some of the others not to join the Hotcangara malcontent.

We continued toward the southeast behind a full screen of scouts. Our path was along a river, and the ground was getting increasingly marshy as we went along, so I decided to move a little north of the river. This only worked for a while, and soon we seemed to be in a swamp. The scouts reported that there was higher ground a little to the north. We found a small narrow passageway between the muck and followed it for a few days. Then we came up against more swamp along a river right in our path. I decided to send out the scouts in all directions to look for anything, while we stayed put. The hunting wasn't too bad, but it was fortunate we had brought along enough food with us. I was sure we were somewhat close to the coast, unless I had miscalculated the distances or directions we had traveled.

While we waited, one of the scouts brought in another small group from one of the chieftaincies, among whom was their chief, Keranhere. He had gotten the word and wanted to assure us of his good intentions. He remembered some of our men passing through the year before and again this spring and had no quarrel with us at all. I gave him the usual talk, and he also appointed a representative to go with us. He also told me that the sea was a distance that I interpreted to be about one hundred twenty li to the southeast. The swamp ahead of us was not very wide and beyond it was a town. It was also not against us and would receive us cordially should we go there. He didn't know where the enemy was, but assured us they were not in the northeast.

We saw him off and some of the scouts began to trickle in. Those who had gone to the southeast confirmed what the chief had said about the terrain and the town. I decided to wait until all the scouts were back before crossing the swamp to the town en masse. Meanwhile, I went on to the town myself with a small contingent. All was as the chief had said, we were well received, and they sent along an observer. They also sent word to the coastal towns, which also eventually sent observers. They were able to tell us that the enemy was somewhere in the swamps, because they were not along the coast, and they had heard that the Kofitachiki had not joined them. I returned to the camp the next day.

The only scouts who hadn't reported back were the ones who had gone west. Concerned, I sent two others after them, urging extreme caution. The next day, they returned with the others. It turned out that they had found the enemy and had been trying to figure out how many there were. It looked like they were little more than a frightened band of perhaps a thousand fugitives. They were hiding in the swamps hoping that we either wouldn't find them or would give up because of the swamps. Well, it was true that I didn't like swamps, but I wanted the Hotcangara renegade. If he got away, there was no telling how much trouble he could make, especially among the less than friendly southeastern towns.

I pared the men down to a few thousand. We left the horses and stealthily slipped into the swamp and surrounded the fugitives. They had not set any remote lookouts, or if they had, they had run off. Once they were surrounded, we crept closer and, picking our targets, shot a barrage of arrows into them. Virtually all of them who were exposed at all were struck with several arrows. The rest either crouched behind cover or ran in panic into more arrows. We crept closer and took out anyone who presented a target. They tried to return fire, but any of them who rose to shoot was quickly hit several times. We were finally close enough that we rushed them. We cut them all down. Only five of our men were wounded badly, and about twenty more were lightly wounded. We recovered our arrows and finished off their wounded as usual. Among the dead, Datha pointed out the chieftain of the large chieftaincy we had reduced and the Hotcangara. The latter was not as tall as the others and didn't have the misshapen head. Even in death, his face was a mask of hate, but I didn't recognize him.

As we slogged back out of the swamp toward camp, I was still not satisfied. There had to be more of them somewhere. No less than nine towns had been abandoned along our path. They must have held more than that pitiful group. Besides, there had only been a few women and no children among them. There had to be more of them somewhere. But where were they? Until I found them, I could not dismiss the troops. We crossed the river back toward the town I had visited. I sent their observer to reassure them that our presence was not hostile. We turned south along the dry ground and headed toward the coast. We had not gone far when the observer returned with some extra food and offered to guide us to the next chieftaincy to the south by the driest path. That was an irresistible offer.

He led us past a small town allied to his and on across a marshy river until we finally came upon the hamlets of the next chieftaincy. He guided us to the principle town, and there we were met as we approached. Word had preceded us, and they also had an observer ready to send along as well as observers from their neighboring chieftaincies. I accepted the observers and tried to ascertain the extent of their boundaries for my maps. They were a bit vague on that score, but it was clear that there were no more Iyehyeh chiefdoms besides this group in the immediate vicinity. To their south along the coast were the Cusabo. They were the neighbors of the Wahili through whom I had passed the year before. The latter had promised to pass my proposal on to them, and my mappers had been told to reiterate it when they passed through this year. So it was time to move inland. There were two major rivers on my map between my present location and the Wahili that I had followed inland the last year. These were the nearby Sewee and the farther south Cusabo. There were also some smaller rivers, but these two looked to be the principle ones. Our hosts claimed that the Cusabo River drained the lands of the Kofitachiki. The Sewee would also take me to a portion of their lands but would also lead me to more of the Iyehyeh chiefdoms, two nearer small ones and then two larger ones.

I decided more could be accomplished by going up the Sewee, so I asked our observers to take us by the driest route up the river.

We went through another chiefdom and were given fresh fish as we passed through, no doubt to urge us on. Eventually we came to some hamlets containing a slightly different-looking people. They looked like a compromise between their northern and southern neighbors, with the southerners getting the better of it. They were unadorned and only lightly tattooed. They stood watching us as we passed waiting for us to make a move, and no doubt well aware that we did not disturb their fields. These people had only one town on this side of the Sewee, and our guides led us to it. We made no attempt to hide our approach, and the town was obviously prepared for the worse as we broke through the woods into the clearing. I left the men and rode ahead with a small escort. I was met by a small contingent from the town. They were fully armed and somewhat decorated and tattooed, but it was obvious that this was no major town. The leader was a grizzled veteran who had probably earned his position the hard way. He showed no fear as he stepped forward alone. His language was a little hard to follow but enough like the other Pansfalaya-related languages that I could make it out.

"I am Thlacco, mico of this town," he announced.

"I am the Raven, ambassador of the Khanate of the Blue Sky," I announced.

"You have a heavy escort for an ambassador." He scowled. "Do you mean to attack us?"

"No, we never attack without provocation," I replied. "Do you mean to provoke?"

"Not intentionally." He studied me. "Are you the people who scattered some of the speakers of a strange tongue to the north?"

"We are," I answered. "Would you happen to know where the rest of them have gone?"

"Yes, I do," he replied. "It is no concern of mine if I tell you. They are among the people upstream from us."

I thanked him for his help and told him about my offer. He said he could not speak to that since he had no authority. I would have to talk to the great chief of his people. If I wished he could send word to him and could catch up to me with the reply. That sounded like another subtle attempt to urge me on, but I thanked him for his help and agreed. He assured me that I would not need my huge escort if the great chief agreed to meet me. I told him I wouldn't bring them with me if I were invited. I asked for a guide to speed me on to his neighbor by the quickest path, and he eagerly agreed, ordering the man to stay with us until the messenger from the great chief made contact with us. The man was not thrilled with the prospect, but the mico was not one to be quibbled with, and he fell in with us.

The next day, we were again among the Iyehyeh hamlets as we made our way to the first town of this chiefdom. I sent out the scouts again just in case. At dusk they reported back that the first town was nearby, but there was no apparent hostility and all looked normal. We camped in the woods that night with a double set of sentinels anyway. The next morning, we came out of the woods and approached the town. They sent a small delegation to meet us. No one was on a litter. There were just some of their warriors, heavily armed, but not adorned. Their leader was lightly adorned but didn't have the misshapen head. I stopped the men and drew near with a small escort. They looked a bit nervous to me.

"I am Iswan, chief of this town," he announced. "Have you come in peace?"

"That depends," I replied coldly. "Do you intend to surrender the fugitives you have taken in from the north?"

"We have no fugitives here," he almost shrilled nervously.

"I don't care where they are." I eyed him darkly. "I want them turned over to me at once, or we'll consider you to be at war with us also."

He excused himself for a moment so he could consult with his "advisors" in the town. While he was gone, I sent the scouts into the woods and had the men surround the town. This last gesture had the desired effect, especially after the men started testing their bows. Iswan came out again only this time accompanied by a woman.

"I am Pi'ri, the chieftain of these people," she began. "We have granted refuge to our neighbors. I could do no less, for their chieftain is my husband's brother. I cannot turn them over to you, but can guarantee they will give you no further cause to pursue them."

"You don't seem to understand." I showed no warmth. "You either give them up or we destroy you with them. It was not a request—it was a demand. The Mongols do not allow people to ambush them or attack their peaceful embassies. They must step forward and accept their fate, or we will impose it on them anyway."

"I can't turn over these people to die," she protested weakly.

"Whether they die is up to them," I replied. "Are you prepared to sacrifice your own people for them?"

"You don't intend to kill them?" she grasped the straw.

"As I said, that depends on them," I said testily. "It has nothing to do with you. You must turn them over to my justice, or withhold them to certain death for them as well as your people."

"They are scattered among my towns," she said, "but I will have them brought to you here if you wish."

"Fine." I remained cold. "But first send out those in this town."

"As you wish," she almost whispered as she turned and slowly returned to the town.

There was a lot of commotion in the town, including some wailing and shouting. I began to wonder if they would fight, but before too long a slow procession started out of the town toward us. They were unarmed and unadorned as if they expected to be enslaved. I had them line up about five deep and looked them over. There were only about three hundred of them. The elites were easily distinguished since they were taller than the others and all had the strange heads. I separated these out, then spoke to the others.

"You have forfeited any right to choose your destiny," I began. "You will all move north to the first Iyehyeh chiefdom that attacked us. There you will toil and raise enough crops to feed yourselves as well as the nearby Ordu. You will be assigned a governor to rule over you with absolute authority in the name of the Khan. Should you disobey or in anyway offend the governor, you will be destroyed without mercy. Should you prove to be trustworthy, you will become a part of the Mongols. If you prefer, we will kill you all now instead. That is your choice. What is your decision?"

It would not be an exaggeration to say the people's relief was palpable. They eagerly accepted the offer. I told them to retrieve their belongings and proceed north under a small escort of my troops. I sent along a message to Khurumsi to pick a man to be governor. Then I turned to the elites. There were only about fifteen of them, and as I icily looked them over, their arrogant defiance began to change into a more appropriate fear. My first inclination was to wipe them out on the spot, but I decided to wait until the others trickled in before doing anything with them. Meanwhile, I had them placed under close guard.

The chieftainess sent out runners to get the others and invited me into the town to discuss the usual offer. I refused to meet with her until all the fugitives had been turned over and urged her not to hide any of them from me. Smoking Mirror was fairly silent during all this, but finally he took me aside to confer.

"Do you plan to kill their elites?" he asked.

"I probably should," I hedged, "but not before I have them all."

"You are thinking"—he nodded—"that they are the ones most likely to cause trouble in the future?"

"Yes," I agreed. "I don't want to have to come back here with another army to destroy them all over again. I'm afraid that they are too arrogant to change, and the world would be better off without them."

"Perhaps." He shrugged. "But if I may make a suggestion, why not exile them to the west, perhaps have them create their own settlement, where they would have to do all the work? There is nothing like honest work to erase ideas of privilege."

"It's an idea," I considered. "Perhaps if we only killed off the chieftain, or perhaps assign them a governor also. We could put them next to the Chikasha, south of the Wazhazhe River. They all have those heads, so they should find each other attractive. It might be a sweeter revenge."

"I thought so," he smiled, rubbing his still-healing arm.

As the fugitives filed in from the countryside, I continued to cull out the elites and send the others to the north under escort. Eventually all were accounted for, and I was left with about a hundred of the elites. I agreed to see the chieftainess and gave her the usual talk, but also warned her of the dire consequences of any treachery on her part. I think it was mostly in fear that she decided to send along an observer. We moved on to the neighboring chiefdom and found a large group of refugees already gathered to be turned over to us. These were divided up as usual, and careful inquiry led me to believe that we had them all at last. I sent the elites north with the Turtles to be sent on by the long northerly route since it was more secure. I told Siban, the commander of the Turtles, to send them under strong guard all the way. I also gave him dispatches for Jebei to explain what was coming to him and to Kaidu to explain my decision. I sent the rest of the Snakes back to their Ordu with the last of the other fugitives, keeping only an escort of a hundred men, a group of scouts, and all the observers. The chief of this chieftaincy also sent along an observer. We continued on to the next chieftaincy, farther up the river.

29

MORE RECRUITING, THE COUNCIL MEETING AND
A FAMILY TRIP 11-2 K
(SD TO MS, 1379-80)

Just as we had entered the next Iyehyeh chieftaincy, a Kofita-chiki messenger approached us. Their ruler had agreed to see us, and the messenger would guide us to him. Our other guide asked to be excused since he had completed his mission. I agreed, but it put me on my guard, although I recalled his initial reluctance to go with us in the first place, and, indeed, as it turned out no treachery was planned. Our guide led us across the Sewee River a little west of south. After passing through many small farming hamlets and past a couple of towns over the next four days, we finally arrived at a very large palisaded town. It had outgrown its palisade, and there were many houses outside the wall, making it look like a city within a city. The locals stared at us as we approached. The people and the houses were much like those we had seen to the south, as was the city. It was not as large as the unfriendly city just east of the Pansfa-laya, but bigger than the city of Alba ayamule. We were brought to a large mound, and Smoking Mirror and I were led up the ramp to the large house on top. The chief greeted us at the top of the ramp. His name was Menawa. He was not as tall as the Iyehyeh chiefs were, but he was taller than I was. He was a large man and quite strong from the look of him. He was perhaps forty or so years old. He wore his hair long and was liberally decorated with copper and pearls. He was moderately tattooed and wore a cloak of the same green parrot feathers I had seen on the western Iyehyeh chieftainess. We were seated, and the nawak'osis was passed around.

He listened politely to my pitch, but then said he could see no pressing need to give up his position for the safety we offered, since he didn't feel particularly threatened, especially if we were good to our word to leave them in independent peace. I assured him we were and told him that most of his eastern and northern neighbors had sent observers and if they joined would be under our full protection. He said his tribe was peaceful and only attacked those who first attacked them. Remembering the grizzled mico we had met earlier, I wondered about that, but said only that he would get no unprovoked attack from us. We left and began to retrace our path back to the Iyehyeh country. I wondered how long it would be before we ended up at war with the Southeastern tribes, especially if they found themselves surrounded by our allies.

When we came upon the first Iyehyeh town some five days later, we were greeted by a delegation. It was a modest one, but included the local chief. He welcomed us warmly and told us he would entertain us for the night and then guide us on to the head chief who was waiting to hear us out. True to his word, we were set up in the large square town house near the center of the town and a great feast with much spirited dancing and general noise making ensued. Their singing tended to be chanting much like that of most of the people in the land. Their music was equally uninteresting, but the dancing was quite energetic. The food was quite good and abundant. There was even a group of women left for us to make use of were we so inclined, all apparently unmarried, unlike some of the Leni lenape women we had been offered earlier.

The next day, we were guided to another town for another feast, and the next day to yet another town and feast. This continued until the fifth day, when at last we came to the head chief's town. His name was Pirere, and he came out of his town with much pomp and ceremony: musicians, guards, litter, escort—the whole routine. After some flowery speeches, he led us into the town and set us up in the town square. He took Smoking Mirror and me up a mound to his house. Here he introduced us to Heresewi, the chief of the large chieftaincy to the northeast. They had thought it most convenient if I addressed them both at the same time, since they were related and generally acted in concert.

I thanked them for making things so convenient as well as for the most generous hospitality they had extended. I congratulated them for not getting involved in the recent "unpleasantness" some of their neighbors had pursued to their great harm. They expressed their understanding at our justified wrath and commended me for showing mercy to the remnant. They wondered if I had any immediate plans for the lands recently abandoned by their reckless cousins. I replied that only the lands nearest our Ordu would be kept for the refugees, any tribes that ally with us could take the rest. We, of course, would hesitate to strengthen potential enemies. The maneuvering at an end, I gave them the usual pitch, and they asked the usual questions and in the end agreed to send along observers. I urged them not to attack any of their neighbors until all had decided whether they would ally with us. We would, of course, keep them informed.

We continued northeast along the Sewee River, moving ever higher in elevation through the foothills east of the mountains. I consciously avoided the remaining Iyehyeh towns of the chieftaincy so we wouldn't be delayed by any more feasting. We eventually entered into a sort of no-man's-land. It was overgrown as though it had once been settled but then abandoned, making it quite a tangled mess to pass through. By now it was early fall, and we would occasionally run into small hunting parties from both the southeastern tribes and the Iyehyeh. We were friendly to all and even told them of any game we had seen on our way. Eventually we reached the mountains. There we came upon a small settlement of Ani' Yun'-wiya along a stream. As a frontier town, it was understandably fortified, but the workers in the fields seemed to take no notice of us as we drew near. Just as we reached the palisade, a heavily scarred old warrior ambled out to meet us. To my dismay, we couldn't understand each other. Although there was a similarity to the Ani' Yun'-wiya dialect I had learned, it was too vague to enable us to communicate. He seemed to realize the problem and sent for someone in the town. An older woman came out and was able to act as interpreter. She introduced herself as Wahnewauhi, and the chief as Collanah.

"My brother is married to one of the Ottare speakers," she explained, "and I learned the language from him. The chief asks if you are the western strangers who visited the Ottare last year?"

"We are," I replied, assuming the Ani' Yun'-wiya I had met were called Ottare.

"How is it," Collanah wanted to know, "that western strangers approach from the south last year and from the east this year? Are you lost or are you now from those directions?"

"Neither." I tried not to laugh. "We were simply recruiting allies and exploring in those directions."

"We heard about your recruitment among the Ottare," Wahnewauhi translated. "There has been much discussion among all the Ani' Yun'-wiya, especially since you planted that huge town south of the Ottare. The observers returned and spread the word about you with much enthusiasm. Still, there is much doubt among the people and little desire to change our ways. On the other hand, there is no denying you are a powerful people and would make a formidable ally or enemy. We think it best that you go to Kituhwa, and there meet with a representative group of our people to answer their questions."

I was not exactly looking forward to a large meeting of these people after my experiences with their "meetings" the previous year and had no idea where Kituhwa might be, but could see no alternative to agreeing to go. I had the feeling we might end up doing this annually for the next several years before they committed. Still, they were an impressive people and would make a great addition to our Khanate. So, we would go to Kituhwa. Our host said it would take two weeks to get there unless we were used to the high country, in which case it would take less. He sent out runners to announce our arrival to the other towns and prevailed on us to spend the night with him and start off in the morning. I agreed and over our meal asked what his dialect was called and if it would be helpful if we learned it before we reached Kituhwa. He replied through Wahnewauhi that his language was called Atali, and while it would be helpful to him if I learned it, it wouldn't do much good in Kituhwa since they spoke yet another dialect. In any case, I shouldn't be concerned since there would be interpreters at the meeting.

The next day, we set off toward the west with a young man to guide us. Collanah would not be going to the meeting, since he felt it was more important to guard the frontiers. Of course, Wahnewauhi couldn't come along either, so we would have to do the best we could with our guide, Unaduti. He led us generally westward for about six days threading us through mountain passes and across valleys. Almost every night, we were put up at a different town, and the next morning some of the townsfolk joined us on our trek. As we continued into the mountains, the palisades began to disappear, and the houses of the towns tended to be spread out along a creek or riverbank. On the sixth day, we crossed a high pass and descended on a narrow river valley. The river flowed northwest, and we followed it for two more days. The valley got a little wider, and then we came upon a very large settlement spread for many li along a loop of the river. It could only be described as a patchwork of fields spotted with groups of houses, much like Itsati, but larger and a lot longer. After wandering through the settlement for a while, we finally came to the meeting or town house.

The house was quite large, but I could see from the huge crowd that it was probably not large enough. It had apparently been decided that my party would be housed in the town house and the meetings would be held in the ball playing field. Since it was fall and the crops had been harvested, we would be meeting during the day. Most of the young men would be out hunting, so they would not be present except for the observers who had gone with me the year before. I suggested that my escort might as well do some hunting also, to keep them busy and help provide for us. This gesture was appreciated, particularly by my men, who were not especially keen on sitting through myriad boring speeches. Smoking Mirror alone preferred to stay with me since, incredibly, he was fascinated by such meetings.

The next morning after a light meal, we repaired to the playing field while the men set out for the mountains to hunt. There was a real throng waiting for us at the field. They had been divided into three groups according to their dialect, and interpreters were prepared to translate to each group. I was put with Ostenako and the Ottare, since I spoke that language. We both greeted each other warmly, and Utasite and Kollee also came up and sat with us. We had to wait for the weed burning, of course, and then the chief of Kituhwa rose up and greeted and welcomed everyone and told them why they were there. After a few more remarks, he called on me to make my proposal. I did so at length, trying to anticipate as many of the usual questions that I possibly could. My remarks were translated into the other dialects, further slowing down matters. Finally, I was finished.

Of course, I really didn't think I was finished, but I sat down anyway. One by one people rose up to comment or ask questions or both. It was all very polite, some of the questions were trite, but others were quite probing. They were especially interested in the understandably suspicious appearance of the Wildcat Ordu on their frontier. I innocently explained that they were there to protect our allies from the Southeastern tribes should they become hostile after refusing to join us. Of course they were no threat to the Ani' Yun'-wiya, since they had not made a decision. Otherwise I hedged when I had to, answered the trite questions as if they were insightful and in general tried to keep the tone polite and friendly. Needless to say, one day was not enough for everyone to make his comment or ask his questions, nor were two or three days enough. In fact this went on for a week. It was their custom to never deny anyone his say, no matter how long, how often, or how irrelevant. At the end of the week, I was exhausted, and we were no closer to a consensus. Despite many favorable comments especially from last year's observers, the only thing they could agree on was that they should send a larger group of observers along with us. They would meet again to discuss the matter the following year. I told them that I might not be able to return the next year, but they didn't think that mattered as long as someone else came to answer any questions. I couldn't think of anyone who deserved such a job, but decided to let Kaidu decide. I thanked them for their time and consideration and took my leave.

As we left, I dismissed my escort, securing a guide to lead them back to the Iyehyeh lands, from where they could return to the Snake Ordu and on the way see what the Iyehyeh were doing. I sent a mapper with them to map the route and included a full report on my recruiting efforts for Khurumsi. The rest of us would proceed through Ani' Yun'-wiya country to the Wildcat Ordu. The large group of observers would also go to the convenient Wildcats during the winter after providing for their families. As it happened, Ostenako, Utasite, Kollee, and many of the other Ottare were going in the same direction as we were. In fact, Ostenako informed me that this river we were on was the same one that flowed by his Itsati. And, indeed, some five days later, we reached his town. He insisted on entertaining us and assured me over the meal that his people would eventually join us, even if it took years. We continued on our way retracing our journey of the year before until we finally reached the Wildcat Ordu, six days later.

Jebei greeted me warmly and handed me a pile of dispatches. I told him about the large number of Ani' Yun'-wiya that would soon be descending on him and told him about my summer. I gave his mapper a copy of my map to bring them up to date. Then I sat down to the dispatches. True to his word, Kaidu had tried to keep me informed about Padraig's campaign. Padraig had quickly wiped out the tribe that had turned on our first expedition, but the tribe on the coast proved to be more of a problem. They had seen his approach and had taken to the sea in large boats. He destroyed all they left behind and moved north laying waste to their settlements. He eventually reached another tribe, and they proved to be friendly in light of his numbers. He continued up the coast to a large bay, contacting a few more tribes. He circled the bay and sent a mapper to a large island just off the coast. Three more tribes, one of whom also had settlements along the coast, inhabited it. He sent more mappers up the coast and returned to look for the rogue tribe. The other coastal people insisted that they hadn't seen them and that there were no other islands offshore where they could hide.

He tried to set some traps for them to lure them ashore, but there was no sign of them, so he spread about half his men along their territory to wait for them and sent the rest south to look for them. Finally a large flotilla of their boats approached one of their razed settlements from the sea. A small group of our men was on the shore to tempt them in, but instead, they held their position a little offshore, and one of them who was wearing a strange mask stood up and yelled and screamed at our men while making threatening gestures. No one could understand him, but eventually one of the men dropped him with a well-aimed arrow. The rest of the men shot at the men in the boats, but the latter quickly withdrew again, and only a few were hit.

Finally a few days later, Padraig was approached by a shaman from another tribe who wanted to mediate the "dispute." Padraig informed him that there was nothing to mediate; the tribe had forfeited any right to come to terms by attacking his men. They would all have to die, and should come ashore and take their punishment like men. The shaman withdrew and before long the flotilla reappeared along the shore and tried to fight from their boats. The exchanges were quite uneven, however, since our bows had greater range. Again they withdrew and again the shaman approached to announce that we had killed at least as many of them as we had lost, and so the blood debt was satisfied, and we should now negotiate. Again Padraig rebuffed the man and warned him not to return again unless he was prepared to reveal the whereabouts of the fugitives. He also had the man discretely followed and found their hiding place, a cove on the large bay. He left a small screen of men along the coast and sent the others to surround the cove. Before he left, however, a lone boat pulled up to the shore and discharged a lone passenger. Through interpreters the man identified himself as the chief of our enemies and offered himself in exchange for his people. He was quickly cut down without comment, and the boat was allowed to leave unmolested.

Padraig then hurried to the cove and found the men had surrounded it as much as possible. They waited in silence until the boat was seen returning from its mission. As soon as they had stepped ashore, a barrage of fire arrows set their boats aflame, and more arrows cut down anyone who tried to get in them, a few more showers of arrows, a final rush, and it was over. The neighboring tribes were horrified at our ferocity, but the lesson was well taken and no other tribe caused any problem.

Since territory was important to the locals, the Salmon Ordu was set up in the lands of the destroyed tribes. Half would remain on the coast and the other half on the Salst River near the waterfall. The neighboring tribes were showing the men how to build their ships (dugouts made from huge trees), and how to fish on the ocean as well as the rivers. Padraig would start back with the Antelope Tumen in the spring. He would leave Ogedai in charge of the Salmon. Meanwhile, he had dispatched a mapping expedition southward along the coast to return by spring and was awaiting the return of the northern mappers, which should be soon. Kaidu also mentioned that there were more details about the people and terrain and, of course, maps for me to pour over on my return.

I started back with the usual group and some of the more adventurous observers. We reached the Eagle Ordu just as it began to snow. Winter was early that year. I settled the observers and stopped to see Paula before reporting to Kaidu. Mathilde was still with her, and I congratulated her on Padraig's successful campaign. When I presented myself to Kaidu, he gave me Padraig's maps and told me to return the next day for our winter meeting, so I wouldn't have to repeat myself.

At the winter meeting, Kaidu briefed us on Padraig's latest dispatch. The northern mappers had returned, and there was no report of problems. He had ascertained that the coast people did not cross the sea in their boats, but did hunt sea animals from them, and trade along the coast in them. Knowing nothing about boats, he couldn't say if they were seaworthy enough to cross the ocean. They were smaller than the Hanjen ships that plied the ocean, but larger than the Hanjen riverboats. Many of the tribes he had contacted had sent observers to the Salmon Ordu, and a few of these would accompany him east in the spring. None of the tribes had joined outright, however, and a few had opted for independence with peace. He also reported that contact had been made with many of the inland tribes, and most of these had also sent observers.

The group of observers I had brought with me the year before had returned home, but no response had been received from their tribes. There would be no new tumen this year, but the Deer Ordu would move to a location at the northeastern frontier of the Pansfalaya, to be in a position to help either them or the towns along the southern extreme of the West Tsoyaha River. No other changes were planned. The Hotcangara had become increasingly cooperative, and he felt we could soon move some of the Ordu stationed among them to the frontiers. Still, in light of the renegade I had encountered, it was still too soon to trust them. The Mingue, on the other hand, were fully integrated and had given us no trouble at all.

Donduk reported that the Pansfalaya's training was coming along well, as was that of the Saktchi Huma. A small coastal group of towns had also made overtures and had observers in the Pigeon Ordu. A larger group of the A'palachi had come in to observe, just before he left to return here. There was still no decision from them or any of the others on the peninsula.

I reported on my efforts, the crushing of the Iyehyeh coalition, the Hotcangara who had started it, the contacting of the others, and the problems with getting a consensus from the Ani' Yun'-wiya. I passed on their request for a representative to sit through another general meeting next fall and answer questions. I described the meeting I had endured and observed that while the meeting would be a trial for our representative, the Ani' Yun'-wiya were worth cultivating.

Givevneu had no new developments to report, except that since he was getting rather old, he had taken on an understudy to learn all his lore. The young man was one of the Dzitsiistas, named Okuh-hatuh. He had made his Spirit Quest and had seen a vision of "a fat fishlike creature with whiskers and long fangs" that told him to go to the shaman of the Mongols.

"It was obviously a walrus he saw," he said quietly, "my dream symbol for myself. The message was clear—I must prepare a successor. He is very bright and will easily fill my role one day when I must leave it. I hope when I return, it will be to this new world rather than the old one."

"Nonsense," Kaidu growled. "You are younger than me or Donduk, and we are not yet ready to groom replacements. You'll have to put up with us for a long time yet before Tengri gives you rest."

"We will see." Givevneu smiled. "In any case, it doesn't hurt to be ready. After all there is much lore to be learned to be a shaman. One is born to be a Khan and over time merely proves his mettle."

No doubt wishing to change the subject, Kaidu said that Donduk should return to the Pigeon Ordu the next year, since he thought some of the peninsula tribes would at least ally with us. He felt I should look into visiting the islands off the coast of the southeastern peninsula. He thought I could take copper and perhaps matches along making it something of a trading expedition to induce the Calusa or the Tekesta to take me there. Of course, if they were hostile by then, I should abandon the idea. In any case I could go back to the Ani' Yun'-wiya for their fall meeting. He realized it would be dreadful, but I was the only person in a leadership position who understood the language. He promised not to ask me to go back again. I planned to hold him to that promise. He also said that he was quite pleased with Juchi's administrative efforts in the east, and he thought it would be good to send him to explore the lands farther west along the Hopitu River he had explored some years ago. He understood that there were many great cities there, and he didn't like the large blank spot on our maps in that direction. He felt Juchi should go west along the Red River to reach them since that was touted to be a major trade route and perhaps return along the river I had crossed far to the south that Smoking Mirror claimed arose in that area. I said that it would be a wonderful idea and that he should be encouraged to take his time, perhaps setting out with trade goods and a two years' supply of food, since merchants were always welcome, and food was often scarce from what Talaswaima had told us. Talaswaima should go with him, of course, and could also teach him the language of his people. I wasn't sure, but I thought he was currently with the Horse Ordu. Perhaps Juchi should go there this winter so he could jump off in early spring. I really envied him that expedition, but it made more sense to send me southeast and him southwest since we were already familiar with those areas. Dispatches were prepared, and we were dismissed until spring.

I gave Paula the bad news, but suggested that she and Mathilde might go part of the way with me. We could go as far as the Pigeon Ordu together. It would give Paula a chance to see more of the land and would give Mathilde a first look at Murenbalikh. They were all excited about the adventure, and it would still give Mathilde plenty of time to return to the Antelopes by late summer when Padraig would be getting back. With that settled, I looked over Padraig's maps. The coast north of the Salst River was more rugged than that to the south of it. North of the deep bay, the coast was really wild. Mountains met the sea, creating a tangled maze of bays, inlets, and islands. The mountains were the northern extension of those I had partially crossed a few years ago. I wondered how long it would take the mappers to reach the mouth of the Yukanah River we had followed so many years before. It would be fascinating to see the coast unfold. I was also looking forward to the results of the mappers that Padraig had sent south along the coast. There was still a vast empty spot on the map, and I couldn't blame Kaidu for wondering what was there. Meanwhile, other mappers had been filling in a lot of smaller blanks in already explored directions. The northerly mapping was slow because of the short season. The mappers had named the very large bay cutting deeply into the land Inuit Bay since that people lived around most of it. They had still not reached the mouth of the Dehcho. They were mapping from boats because the land was impossibly marshy in the summer. Elsewhere, many more rivers had been mapped, nearly all of them in the lands we controlled and quite a few in the lands we didn't control. The land was really beginning to take shape and was proving to be very large.

The winter passed uneventfully. We made the usual trip to visit Henry. I looked in on the artillery school, and Kabul said that he had already deployed some of his students and should have a unit in each tumen by the following summer. He was very proud of his students and wanted to show them off for me in spite of the cold. They were really quite good, and I praised them all effusively. Migizi had had mixed success with the handguns, but he was determined and had even enlisted one of Henry's boys to help him. Henry thought it a waste of time, but was loath to discourage any creativity. He was also touched by Migizi's enthusiasm. I encouraged him since I felt he would eventually be successful.

In early spring, Juchi sent me a note from the Horse Ordu asking if I had any idea why his father was trying to get all the silk we had brought with us from the old land. I replied that I had no idea. The Owl Ordu did get rather hot in the summer, but one would think that cotton would suffice. Unfortunately, I didn't give the matter any more thought. Instead I got everything ready for our trip. I arranged to have a load of copper waiting for me at the Pigeon Ordu. Donduk would accompany us all the way to the Pigeons this year so we would take a leisurely pace. The spring council meeting brought up nothing new, and we got started south while there was still ice in the river.

We reached the Owl Ordu and Donduk visited some old friends. I went in to see Kuyuk to ask about the spies he had sent with Tlacuectli. He seemed a bit vague as though he was not too impressed by what they had seen. I asked if Tlacuectli was in camp, but he said he wasn't expected until fall. My acquaintances in the Ordu seemed a little distant, but I thought they were just preoccupied and gave it no thought. As we left, Paula asked if I had noticed all the gold ornaments people were wearing in the Owl Ordu. I had to admit I hadn't. She wondered if they had found a mine nearby. I doubted that since there were no mineralogists among the Mongols besides me. I asked Donduk if he had found anything odd among the Owls, but he hadn't. Smoking Mirror reminded me that his father had brought gold with him to trade and must have found something to trade it for, since it was most unlikely he would give it away. He also pointed out that most of the gold was being sported by the original Mongols, not the newer ones. I still can't believe I didn't make the connection between silk and gold, but I didn't until much later.

The women enjoyed exploring the now fully pacified Murenbalikh. It had grown larger and even more fields were under cultivation. We visited the Kestrels and the Deer on the way to the Pigeons. The gunpowder factory was in full swing, and we had quite a stockpile. They were making shipments to all the other Ordu. The Deer had enjoyed the milder winter in their new location much farther south than their original one. They were also looking forward to the possibility of more action in the near future. When we reached the Pansfalaya lands, the women and children evoked much curiosity from them, and they in turn found it difficult not to notice the misshapen heads. They were familiar with the practice since they had met Thliotombi, but a whole town of them took getting used to. I took them all down to the coast, since the coastal towns had also joined us, and the children got their first look at the ocean. Finally I reluctantly said goodbye, and they returned home while I went east with a small escort from the Pigeon Ordu.

30
THE LUCAYO AND THE TAINO, 12 K
(FL, BAHAMAS, HISPANIOLA, 1380)

The copper sent down for me to take was in thin sheets, apparently the preferred form. There was a fair amount of it, but remembering that it had to cross an open ocean I pared it down to a few horse loads. I kept it hidden away since I didn't want to be trading my way to the southern end of the peninsula. The first leg of the journey was along the fringes of the lands loyal to Albayamule. These people had been friendly before, and nothing had changed as we circled their little bay and continued east. Some of the people had deserted to the Pigeon Ordu, but no one seemed to mind yet. The next lands we passed through were those of the town called Pensacola that had not been too receptive to our overtures. We only stopped to camp, and I kept sentries vigilant, but there was no disturbance. The proximity of the Pigeon Ordu and the size of my escort were enough to give anyone pause.

Once we left their lands, we found a number of smaller settlements of people who mostly utilized the sea but also planted some crops. All were friendly, and I recruited among them, but could get no commitments or even observers. Eventually we came to the lands of the A'palachi. I sent word to Kushiksa of our arrival. He came to meet us. He said that he wanted to confederate with us, but he felt he should bring his difficulties with his northeastern neighbor to a conclusion first. Since we insisted on approving any hostilities among our allies, he thought it might cause a problem.

"How long has this quarrel been going on?" I asked.

"Some four or five years," he answered pleasantly.

"Do you have any particular reason," I pursued, "for thinking you will be able to bring it to a conclusion in the near future?"

"Yes, I do." He beamed. "As soon as enough of my men have

completed training with you, we should be able to wipe them out."

"That is not our intention"—I was irritated—"when we train your people. They were accepted with the understanding that you would join us. We will not help you conquer your neighbor, unless you join us and he attacks you fully aware that you have joined us. We go around recruiting promising no duplicity and no involvement in old quarrels. I will have to send word to have your people dismissed."

"Surely you are overreacting," he protested. "Does your Khan really care what happens to this miscreant neighbors of ours?"

"Our Khan very much cares if he is being used," I said darkly.

"You can't expect me to give up." He reddened. "My own father was killed by them."

"If you wish," I suggested, "you can ally with us, and I can tell them that you have. If they still wish to fight you, we will help you wipe them off the face of the land. If they choose peace, however, you must honor that. We do not tolerate duplicity, and it is instantly punished once discovered. If you want personal satisfaction over your father's death, issue a personal challenge to whoever killed him or ordered him killed. If they accept, your satisfaction is in your hands. If they refuse, they admit they are cowards and all will despise them."

"Very well," he said after a long pause. "I accept your suggestions. Consider us your allies."

"I will go to your neighbors then," I said, "but remember, there can be no further provocation from you or your people. The others must freely make the decision to fight us. Is that understood?"

"Yes," he reluctantly replied.

I wasn't at all sure of his resolve, but decided to go ahead and see the neighbor again. The situation might be fluid enough to induce them to join us also. That would be truly interesting. Just in case there might be some misunderstanding, I sent word that I was coming to confer with them and bringing my escort with me since they had not been too friendly during my last visit. I also sent out scouts to make sure we weren't walking into a trap. Shortly after we entered their territory, the scouts flushed out a few of their scouts. These were brought to me, and I asked them separately what their leader's intentions were. One said he was sent to make sure the enemy was not with us. The other said he was sent to see how many of us there were. I told them to look us over openly and report back to their leaders. I also told them to warn their leaders that hostile activities against us had already been shown not to be prudent.

Our scouts flushed out a few more of their sentries as we continued, but there was no ambush. As we broke through the woods and approached their first town, I let the sentries go. They ran ahead to the town and soon a small procession came out to meet us. It consisted of the usual fanfare: musicians, guards, escorting elites, and a litter bearing the same chief I had talked to earlier. He looked as haughty as ever as he alighted from his perch and approached me.

"I already told you," he sneered, "that we were not interested in joining you. What do you want now?"

"Your neighbor"—I remained impassive—"the one you've been fighting for several years, has decided to join us. Therefore, it is only fair that we warn you any further hostilities initiated by you will result in your destruction. If you wish to now end your quarrel, you may. The A'palachi will not be allowed to initiate any hostile action against you."

"Humph!" He grimaced in disgust. "The cowards are hiding behind you now?"

"Not really." I shrugged. "If you wish to cease hostilities, Kushiksa challenges whoever killed his father to single combat. If you want us to destroy you, that won't be necessary."

"How should I know who killed him?" he reddened.

"I'm sure he bragged about it," I replied. "On the other hand, Kushiksa was willing to fight whoever ordered the killing."

"I didn't order anyone in particular to be killed." He was becoming agitated. "We fight these skirmishes and some kill and some are killed. Surely you realize that?"

"I don't really care," I continued. "If you want to end hostilities, send out whoever might want to take credit for the slaying to do single combat with Kushiksa. Otherwise, we will assume you wish to fight our ally and, therefore, us. Surely you realize it is better to risk losing one man than to guarantee losing all of your people?"

"How do I know," he nearly shouted, "that will be the end of it? What will prevent them from starting something and claiming we did?"

"Once people join us," I layered it on, "they have no further thought of petty squabbles. One can go from one end of the land to the other with no fear for his safety from any man. Adventures never dreamed of await those courageous enough to grasp for them. Besides, one of our Ordu could annihilate all of your towns in two or three days. Two of them could be here in two weeks if I called for them. In other words, you are far too insignificant for the A'palachi to notice now that they have joined us."

"Can they really get here that soon?" He was visibly shaken. "Wouldn't their advance be resisted?"

"No one has ever interfered with the advance of an Ordu." I smiled grimly. "If you ever saw one coming toward you, you would hole up in your towns and pray to all your gods that it was merely passing through. Resisting its advance would not even occur to you."

"How would the single combat take place?" he asked quietly.

"I'm sure you can arrange it to your mutual satisfaction," I replied. "I can send your terms to him and he will reply. From now on, your people are at peace. That should make the exchanges simple."

He wanted a well-witnessed duel at a specific clearing near their mutual frontiers. It would take place in about a week. I returned to Kushiksa with the news and the proposal. He agreed and withdrew to get himself ready. I left a small group to make sure all went as advertised and continued on my journey. Kushiksa was a fine warrior in superb condition, and I found out later that he had prevailed against the other chiefdom's champion although he was seriously wounded and took a while to recuperate.

We wended our way through the peninsula, on much the same track I had followed two years earlier. I renewed old acquaintances on my way and pressed those who had sent observers for a decision on alliance with us. To my amusement I found that all they were waiting for was to hear that one of their neighbors had joined. Once the Yustaga heard that the A'palachi had allied with us, they also joined. That induced the Utina to join, which, in turn persuaded the Ocale and so on, all as confederates. The chiefs who had initially rebuffed my overtures now all cheerfully sent observers. This continued until we reached the Hobe. They as well as the Wacata and Tekesta would only join if the Calusa joined.

When we reached the Tekesta, I asked them to contact Cuchiyaga, the Calusa chief, for me again and also expressed my interest in visiting the large islands with some trade goods. The chief said that he had nothing to trade at this time and wouldn't want to go empty handed. I explained that I had copper to trade and would gladly pay for transport to the islands with some of the copper. That piqued his interest, but he next said he couldn't take all my men. I replied that they would not be going; only a handful would make the journey. Now he wanted to know how much copper I had. I didn't say until we had agreed on the transport price. Once that was settled, he wanted to start right away, but I wouldn't go until I had heard from the Calusa. He had to admit that was best.

Eventually, word came from Cuchiyaga in the form of his brother Chekika, who had gone with us as an observer during our last visit. He was delighted to see us again and wanted to take us to meet his brother. He would only take Smoking Mirror and me, of course, so I told the men to go do some hunting and fishing while we were gone. We rode a moderate distance inland and then switched to boats for the rest of the journey. At dusk we would pull into a nearby town for the night. Each town seemed to be marked by a huge pile of shells. The houses were wooden with thatch roofs. The sides were largely open, and the floor was a few feet above the ground to accommodate flooding. The houses had furniture made with woven mats. The Calusa seemed to have an artistic bent as their tools and weapons were imaginatively carved and decorated with beads and shells. They were also much given to bangles made of wood and inlaid with shells, tortoise shell, beads, and bones, and sometimes were even painted. They also carved animal heads with moving parts attached with leather strips, and odd part-animal and part-human figures. After a few days, we arrived at a moderately large town. It had a few of the flat-topped mounds with buildings on top, and we repaired to one of these.

Chekika proudly introduced his brother, Cuchiyaga. The latter was taller and more powerfully built than the former. He was also even more heavily bedecked with ornaments. He carried a flat war club that was studded with shark teeth in rows along the edges. Their spear and arrow tips seemed to be sharp bone fragments. He bid us sit down and the usual weed was lit and passed around. He thanked us for our hospitality to his brother and felt from Chekika's report that we were a great and powerful tribe well worth cultivating. Still, he felt quite secure in his environment and doubted if our horses or weapons would do him much damage here. I pointed out that we were more interested in an alliance with him to mutual benefit than we were in attacking him. I agreed that he would have little need or use for the horse, but he could surely see the value of our iron for tools and weapons.

He agreed that the knife his brother had brought back with him was quite sharp and seemed to hold the point better than bone, but they had done quite well without it for many generations. I suggested that as experts in warfare in a swamp area, they would have much to teach us and would be held in esteem in our Khanate, much as the Anishinabe were for teaching us forest warfare. He was intrigued that we had to learn forest warfare since we had proved so devastating at it. Would we actually set up one of our Ordu here in the swamp if he allied with us? I said that we would more likely put it on the northern fringe of the swamp, so that we could still make use of our horses while learning to fight in the swamps. He wanted me to again go over the confederation option. I did so at length also pointing out honestly that while it had caused some of the tribes to lose people, the happier ones had not lost a man. In fact, some of them had to expand to accommodate all their people. I suggested that his people would likely prefer to stay with the tribe and prosper under confederation.

He next wanted to know why we were interested in the offshore islands. I answered that it was mostly out of curiosity. We wondered what the people were like and wanted to offer them confederation also. He asked if I had any idea how many islands there were. I replied that I did not. He said that there were two very large islands and two more not as large and a host of smaller ones. They ran in a line from west to east from some distance south of the peninsula. There was also a group of smaller flatter islands east of the peninsula. These were more sparsely populated by a weak offshoot of the island tribe. The latter were divided into many chiefdoms led by chiefs called caciques. The chiefdoms were either loosely connected with each other or, more rarely, at war. They usually settled their differences with a gamelike contest with a black spherical object. This object was hard but bounced, and they would bounce it around a field. It sounded vaguely like the game the southeastern tribes all played, although the ball was larger from the description, and they didn't use sticks to propel it. I mentioned the latter game, but he insisted that this one was very different. Only a few would play on a side, rather than the whole tribe, and it ended when one side had scored the agreed-on number of scores.

I asked about the tribe on the western end of the large island, the Ciboney. He said that they did not plant crops but only hunted and fished. They lived on the tiny islands offshore or on swamp hummocks inland. They had no real organization but lived in family groups. They lived in areas where the Taino would not live, since the latter relied heavily on their crops. There was no point in trading with them since they had nothing to trade, except for some pearls, and who needed them? They also lived on the western edge of the second large island. I asked what the Taino planted, and he said it was mainly a kind of root called yoca that they made into a flat bread called cazabi, although they also raised other tubers, the mondamin grain (which they call ector), beans, squash, and the fiery pods used for flavoring. I pointed out that the Calusa did little planting and mostly hunted and fished. He pointed out that the swamps were hardly suitable for planting crops. I agreed, but suggested that it was odd that he seemed to have no use for the Ciboney since they were more like the Calusa than the Taino were. He rejoined that the only problem with the Ciboney was that they had nothing worth trading and therefore were of no use to the Calusa. It was a long trip to the islands and had to be worthwhile in order to be under-taken. I had to admit that he was right, but was still curious about the Ciboney. I asked if the Taino and the Ciboney were enemies, but he said that they had nothing to fight about since they lived in areas of no interest to each other. Or, at least, the Ciboney lived in areas of no interest to the Taino, and the latter were too strong for the former to attack.

He finally decided that he would think on the confederation option while I was visiting the south islands and would give me his decision when I returned. Chekika led me back the next day along the same route. I asked him if he thought his brother would join us, but he wasn't too sure. He hoped he would and intended to urge him to do so. The Tekesta were glad to see me return so they could launch the trading expedition as soon as possible. The boats we would be using were fairly large, easily accommodating twenty or so men. I took Smoking Mirror and eighteen others with me while the Tekesta included twenty men. We would be taking two boats, so I split my men and the copper between the boats. The boats had a crude sail made from a kind of bark that was used when the wind was favorable. The basic mode of propulsion was the paddle. We would all take turns paddling in shifts of ten. There was a strong ocean current offshore that flowed north, and the winds tended to blow southwest, so we would get little help from either and would have to paddle toward the southeast in order to reach our first stop, a small island to the east.

We left before dawn and seemed to be going at a good clip. It was impossible for me to measure the distance we were traveling or the speed, but from the compass I could tell that we were heading southeast at first. Once we hit the current, we were sharply pushed toward the north, but our furious paddling kept us on a generally eastward heading. Somewhere along the way, I suddenly realized that this was the first time I had ever been on the ocean out of sight of land. The sea was fairly smooth, so I wasn't uncomfortable, but still the idea was a bit disquieting. Fortunately, it was soon my turn to paddle, and I got too busy to dwell on the matter. We finally broke free of the current and our "pilot" felt that we had held our course fairly well and only needed to continue eastward to reach the island. Toward evening we could finally just make out the long shore of the island ahead. We reached it just before dark, and some of the men set out to get water while the rest of us set up camp. I looked around a bit while the light permitted. The "island" seemed to be a small group of islands. The one we were on was several li long but only a few hundred feet wide. To the northeast was a shorter but wider island that might have been connected to our landfall, but I couldn't tell. To the southeast there was a longer and wider island. The three islands seemed to form a lagoon of sorts that was also dotted with islands heavily covered with mangroves. Our landfall was more like a barrier island. I could just see some distant campfires, and the Tekesta said that the island was inhabited, but that the locals weren't worth bothering with since they wouldn't have much to trade.

The next morning, we set out south along the shore, turned around the south end of the island and headed southeast to our next landfall. The ocean water was very clear and shallow enough that we could see the white sandy bottom below the boat as we paddled. There was no noticeable current here, and neither was there much wind except that generated by our motion. Occasionally, fish with wings could be seen flying above the surface of the water. We caught one of them, and I could see that they were more like long fins than wings, but they were remarkable, and I had never seen anything like it before. As the sun sank low in the west, we finally could see the shore of a large island before us. We came ashore and quickly set up camp. The island was inhabited, but not near our landfall. The Tekesta said that we would go visit the locals the next day. It would give us a welcome rest and perhaps we might find something worth trading.

The next day, we rowed around the northern end of the island and turned south along the eastern shore. We went along the shore for some distance passing some settlements, until we finally turned in toward the shore near the southern end of the island. We beached the boats and went inland along a trail until we came to a moderately sized village. The houses were circular and made of cane with thatch roofs. They were arranged around a large open space in the middle. There was a large lake or lagoon beside the village. The people were lighter skinned than the Tekesta, but not by much. They were also quite nude except for some elaborate and colorful feather accessories. To my surprise, even the women were nude and none were self-conscious either. They were very friendly and welcomed us heartily. As usual I aroused some interest, but so did Smoking Mirror and some of the others. Their language was a complete mystery, but the Tekesta could speak it and interpreted for us.

They called themselves Lucayo, and they were a bit more loosely organized than their southern neighbors were. They cheerfully fed us, and I traded a little copper for some bright pink feathers that came from a cranelike bird with an odd-shaped beak. I gave them my usual recruitment speech, and they said they would be delighted to join us if we could protect them from the cannibals. I asked them where these cannibals of theirs were. They said the cannibals were from the south and had chased them from their homes along a chain of islands to the southeast. I asked if they meant the Taino on the large islands. They shook their heads emphatically and said that the Taino were related to them and peaceful. The southern cannibals were tall and dark and vicious. Of course, I was used to the hyperbole reserved for enemies, but I knew better than to argue. I told them that as soon as we could get established in the area, we would protect them from their enemies. They were very grateful and wanted to shower me with presents. They promised to send some of their men to the mainland for training and to spread the word among the islands.

The Tekesta were not too pleased that I had turned the trading trip into a recruiting trip, but only complained a little. They didn't want to be held up while I went to every island. I assured them I would only recruit when we happened to encounter people. The Lucayo slept in a bed they called a hamaca. It was a piece of woven cloth made of heavy cotton twine, hanging loosely between two poles in the houses. It was quite comfortable, and I got one from them. The next morning we departed heading due east. Not far offshore, the bottom of the sea fell away becoming too deep to see, and then about midday we could see the floor again. Late in the day, we came to a long chain of small islands leading a little east of south. We continued along the chain until it was almost dark and then put into one of them. This particular island was not inhabited, but there was water, and we could see campfires on a nearby island. The next morning, we continued along the chain that seemed to be turning a little more to the east. The water near shore was a remarkable light blue-green color, becoming more blue away from shore. Late in the day, we reached a large island and went along its shore until dusk when we put in near a large group of locals who had just returned from fishing. Again we were cheerfully received and fed, and I traded more copper for pink feathers. I recruited again and got much the same enthusiastic reaction. I asked the Tekesta about these alleged cannibals, but they knew nothing of them, except what the Lucayo had said. These Lucayo also promised to send young men to the mainland for training and to spread the word about us.

We left early again the next morning turning due southeast. The water remained relatively shallow as we headed for our next landfall. This proved to be a very long narrow island with a small peninsula jutting out from the southern half. We headed for the southern end of the island, so we had to detour a little to miss the peninsula. We arrived at a settlement late in the day and again were warmly received. Trading and recruiting went just as before. It occurred to me that we had been gone six days already and were still not at the large islands yet. I asked the Tekesta why they had told me two years before that we could get to the islands and back in perhaps a week when that was obviously not true. They replied that since we had copper to trade, we were going to the greater chiefdoms in the eastern large island called Aiti. The western large island called Cuba could be reached in less time, but Aiti was better for trading. Besides, we could always visit Cuba after Aiti if I wanted. I had to admit that my intention was to see as much of the islands as I could, but wondered how much longer it would take to reach Aiti. They said three more days.

Indeed, the next day, we again headed southeast passing over deeper water briefly this time before coming to another long thin island blocking our path. We slipped around its western tip and camped on its southern shore. The following day, we again headed southeast finally reaching a large island and skirting around its eastern tip near a small island before stopping at a settlement on its southern shore. Our reception was the same, and they too were receptive to recruitment although they urged me to recruit the chiefdoms on Aiti also. The next morning, we set off toward the southeast again crossing over some really deep water. We could see large fish and sea turtles during this passage. The Tekesta said that sometimes they saw whales along here, as well as along the coast of their peninsula. I told them about the people who hunted the whales along the coast of the western sea, and they were truly impressed. They merely scavenged beached whales. Around midday we could see clouds ahead. As we went on, we could see that they shrouded mountains that grew ever larger as we approached. We passed to the east of a long flat island and headed for shore near the mouth of a small river. The river was full of boats heading upstream toward a large town. We joined them and put into shore with them.

The town was rather large. There were a few hundred of the houses arranged around the large open space in the middle. Our reception was friendly, but a bit more formal than on the islands. We were taken to the house of the chieftain. He came out and welcomed us, ascertained that we were there to trade, and put a few houses at our disposal. He invited us to join him for our evening meal. I noticed that he and some of the others wore what looked like gold ornaments. At the evening meal, the chieftain wore a feather cloak and a woven belt of cotton trimmed with gold. He sat on a carved wooden seat. They also used the nawak'osis, but they rolled up the broad leaves of the plant tightly to smoke it instead of grinding it up and using pipes. They called this rolled-up leaf form tobaco. Our meal was a sort of stew with some of the fiery condiment. It took some getting used to but was quite tasty. The meat in the stew was something like rabbit in texture and appearance, and some of the vegetables were familiar except for an odd sort of tuber. They also served a kind of flat starchy bread to dip into the stew. I asked if the meat was rabbit, but found out it was agouti, an odd creature that looked something like a rabbit except for the ears. Some of them were kept as pets.

I told my host about the Mongols, since he asked and broached the subject of his joining us. He listened intently to the offer but replied that such a decision was not his to make. I would have to see his cacique, Hatuey, who alone could make such an alliance. He said that this Hatuey could be found inland about two days' journey to the south. My Tekesta interpreters weren't too upset with this since they wanted to trade there anyway. The chieftain went on to say that there were five caciques on this island, and perhaps I should talk to them all. The Tekesta were not pleased with that prospect. I asked if there was a central location where I could meet with all of them. He said that each cacique was fairly independent and had to be approached diplomatically with presents and lavish praise. I replied that it was neither our custom to give presents nor to praise people we didn't know. Surely these caciques would understand that. He wasn't sure they would, but promised to send a message and try to smooth my way with his cacique. He in turn could decide how or if to contact the others.

I thought that since they had gold, they wouldn't want copper, but they liked it because of its color. It seemed that they really didn't prize pure gold, but preferred a form of it they called tumbaga. It looked like some sort of alloy, but at the time I didn't know with what. I later found out it was a copper alloy of gold. In any case, they readily traded gold for copper. I only took a little, however, since it is rather heavy, and we didn't have that much use for it. They also had some strange-colored feathers, which I knew would be popular back home. I also got some of their cotton cloth.

The next morning, we were awakened before daybreak by a dreadful wailing coming from all around. Our Tekesta guides told us it was just the way they greeted the sun. Indeed, once the sun rose, the wailing gave way to happier shouts and wild dancing. Then the chief quieted them down and gave everyone his assignment. I wandered around a bit and found extensive fields just beyond a screen of trees surrounding the village. They were mostly growing the plant called the yoca. The plant was a kind of bush that had long thin leaves and long thick roots. They grated the roots, then put them in a long tubular basket type of container called a matapi. This was attached to the roof pole at the top and to another pole on the bottom. The bottom pole was then bounced by children to squeeze out the juice from the grated roots. It seemed that the juice was poisonous until it was boiled down into thick syrup. I could see why this thing never caught on in the mainland. They also made attractive, imaginatively decorated red and white pottery and carved figures and shapes in stone and shell. There seemed to be much reverence given to what looked like a piece of shell in the form of a cone. It turned out that their principle god, Yocahu, was what sounded like a volcano god from their description. I was surprised to hear that there were volcanoes on these islands, but was told that the volcanoes were on smaller islands far to the east. They would also put a face on the base of the volcano to depict their god. They said that Yocahu had given them yoca. They also had a female goddess called Atabeyra, a fertility figure, and a dog god called Opiyel-Guaobiran, who guided the dead to the next world.

I got a chance to see them practice the ball game they called batey. The field was about one hundred feet long and forty feet wide. Stone markers surrounded it. Some of the players wore a carved stone belt to help them propel the ball farther. The object was for a team of three or so to bounce the ball from one end of the field to the other without using their hands or arms. Meanwhile the other team would try to prevent them from doing so and instead get the ball back to the other side. The ball itself was black and hard but did indeed bounce, especially on a hard surface. It was a curiosity, but all they could tell me was that it came from the south. Around midmorning we set out for the town of the cacique Hatuey.

31

RECRUITING THE TAINO, CALUSA AND ANI' YUN'-WIYA 12 K (HISPANIOLA, CUBA, FL, AL, MS, TN, NC 1380)

The trip inland took us along a narrow path through hills covered with a dense tropical wood. The trees were largely mahogany and oak, and some of them were truly huge. We seemed to be wending our way through a mountain range from all the climbing, but the tall trees made it impossible to see anything except for a lot of colorful birds and quite a few flowers. We crossed a good-sized river and again seemed to be climbing into mountains. We camped among this second group of hills the first night and were treated to a remarkable variety of animal sounds all night long. Apparently there were no bears, wild cats, or even wolves on the island to concern us. There was, however, a significant array of insects, and I was glad I had the hamaca on which to sleep instead of the bare ground. The next day, we came to a spot cleared by a landslide, and I could see that we were approaching a huge bay. It seemed that the northwestern tip of the island was a peninsula. I found out later when we finally mapped it that there was an even longer peninsula at the southwestern tip, but from this point what looked like the southwestern tip, but proved to be a large island, seemed to be about the same size as the northwestern tip.

We arrived at the cacique's town near midday. It was along a stream that led to a river that emptied into the bay, a short boat trip away. The town was not unlike the first one although it did seem to be larger and had three of the ball playing fields. The largest was lined with monolithic stones that must have been difficult to set up; the smaller ones were lined with smaller stone markers. There were players practicing on the smaller fields as we came into the town. We were ushered to the cacique without ceremony since we were "mere" merchants, and he got first choice. He turned out to be a man of average height and heavy build. He wore a feather cloak and headdress, gold ear ornaments, and a necklace of various semiprecious stones (jasper, carnelian, amethyst, jade, and amber among others). He was pleased with the copper and traded gold and feathers for it. He invited us to join him for an evening meal and assigned us a hut for the night.

We finished trading and looked around a bit before the evening meal. In the center of the town near the chief's house, there was a carved wooden chair trimmed with gold. Behind it was a large monolithic slab with curious petroglyphs. The glyphs seemed to be faces rather than designs. At the evening meal, we were joined by the cacique's "court" a group of leaders who had specific responsibilities. All were heavily adorned with feathers, gold, beads, and gemstones. Each was introduced to us in turn. The stew featured fish this time, and we were served in large shells. The flat bread was in a large decorated basket on four legs. The basket also had a large decorated lid. After eating, the women brought in some large jars, but the chief asked if there was any business to attend to before they were passed out.

A few of his retainers brought up some minor things. When all had spoken, I brought up the subject of joining us and perhaps arranging a meeting with the other caciques on the island to also invite them to join us. He listened politely, but said that there was peace already on the island, and he didn't think they needed us to keep it, since they were all allied by marriage. I suggested that we could help by destroying the cannibals that the Lucayo feared. He replied that they only attacked the small islands far to the east, not his island. I asked if they had any problems with the other islands, and he said that they didn't, but if they did, they would settle them with a ball game. I suggested that at least he should send along an observer, who could report back on us and perhaps being more familiar with their needs could best tell how we could be of help. He said that he could hardly ask one of his people to leave these beautiful lands for the harsh mainland. Getting desperate, I recounted part of the vision of the Pansfalaya shamans, the part where joining us would save them from the great evil that would be coming from the east. That got his attention, and he asked the retainers for their comments. Most of them were quite vague, but one said that perhaps his younger son, Aracibo, could go with us and report back. The young man was not yet married and could be spared. Besides, he was a bit adventurous and had visited some of the nearby islands already.

The young man was called for immediately. He approached very respectfully and stood silently before the cacique. The latter told him that his father thought he might be willing to go on an important mission. He said that he would be greatly honored to do so. The cacique then explained that it was to go to the mainland with the pale stranger and stay with his tribe for a year carefully observing everything and then reporting back as to whether any advantage would come from an alliance with them. Aracibo thanked him for having such faith in him and asked to be excused so he could get ready to go. When he left, the cacique congratulated Aracibo's father for having such a brave son. He hadn't thought the young man would be willing to go. That settled, the jars were passed around. They proved to contain a very weak alcoholic beverage, like a beer. I found it unpleasant, but not nearly as much as I did when I found out how it was made. It seems that the women thoroughly chew up pieces of their flat bread and spit the mass into the jars, which are then "aged" a few days. Fortunately, I didn't have much that night, or I might have never recovered when I found out about it. The others drank large amounts of the stuff and started talking or singing loudly, and some began to dance wildly to the music of drums and rattles. It was finally ended, and we retired for the night.

The next morning, we were again treated to the wailing before sunrise followed by the celebration after sunrise. No one could ever say these people take the rising of the sun for granted. Aracibo presented himself to us after we ate our morning meal. He had all he would take with him tied up in his hamaca. We set off on our return trip back to our boats right away. Two days later, we were setting out to sea again. The Tekesta had every intention of visiting the western island called Cuba, since it would be the easiest way to return. We would have to fight the offshore current for a while, since it flowed between the islands, but once we cleared the channel, it would speed us westward along the northern shore of the island. For a change, the wind was also favorable, and we easily made it to a village near the eastern tip of Cuba well before dark. The village was smaller than the others, but we were well received and cheerfully fed and put up for the night. The next day, we set out again and arrived late in the day at a larger town. The ruler here was a cacique, and he also traded gold and feathers for copper and entertained us that evening much as Hatuey had.

At the appropriate time, I made my recruitment speech and received the same polite disinterest until I pointed out that Hatuey had agreed to send an observer. Aracibo proudly confirmed this, so the cacique felt he also should send along an observer. Carefully ascertaining Aracibo's rank, he and his retainers settled on one of the latter's younger sons, Armaketo, to be their observer. He was dully brought in and eagerly accepted the assignment. That dealt with, the jars of beer were served up. We set out again the next morning and continued trading our way along the north coast until we reached the point where we would turn north. I had tried to map the coast, but a long reef kept us well offshore for much of the eastern end of the island. Still, since they were so friendly, I was sure I could send some mappers to the islands with the returning observers the next summer. There were a lot of islands of varying sizes all along the north coast of Cuba. It was once we had passed a particularly long narrow one that we put in to shore for the last time.

By now, both Smoking Mirror and I were getting fairly comfortable with the Taino tongue, and Aracibo and Armaketo were beginning to learn Mongol. I asked them about the other large islands. They said that to the south of the eastern end of Cuba there was an island called Xaymaca. It was a beautiful island with mountains and trees and a lot of flowing water (rivers perhaps?). To the east of Aiti was Boriquen. It also was a beautiful island with mountains, trees, and water. There were nine caciques on Boriquen, and all of the chieftaincies were older and more revered than those on Aiti. There was a great ceremonial center on Boriquen also, but neither of them had seen it. In fact, Armaketo had not even been to the central part of Cuba, let alone nearby Aiti. Aracibo had been as far as eastern Aiti, eastern Cuba and to Xaymaca, but not Boriquen. Neither had visited the islands of the Lucayo or the mainland. Actually, except for merchants and people like Smoking Mirror, most of the people in the land, much like the Hanjen, didn't wander very far from home.

When we left Cuba the next morning, we went a little west of north and spent the night on the northernmost of a group of tiny islets. The next morning, we paddled north until we hit the current, then cut our way slowly westward across it while it propelled us northward. Before dark we arrived at the Tekesta village on the large barrier island. The next morning, word was sent to Cuchiyaga that I had returned, and runners were sent to gather up my scattered escort. A few days later, my escort had begun trickling in, and Chekika arrived to take me to his brother. He invited the two Taino to come along with us. Chekika spoke the Taino language rather well, and I was sorry he hadn't come with us. He would have made a much better interpreter than the sullen Tekesta. Chekika was amused that I was now using the hamaca to sleep on at night, but the two Taino lads understood completely and were very glad they had brought theirs with them. He had no idea what his brother had decided about joining us, but he could tell me that he had consulted with several of the town chiefs as well as the shamans.

We finally arrived at Cuchiyaga's village and were taken right to him. He welcomed us all and passed around the weed. He asked the Taino if they had been sent as observers and reassured them that they would be treated well by us. Turning to me, he spoke at length and eloquently about his people. The niche they exploited made them a very close-knit and interdependent people. It also made them very different from their northern neighbors. Differences had bred hostility and caused much bad feeling over the years. This in turn made the Calusa what they were today, a proud, self-sufficient race of warriors, ready to look anyone in the eye as equals. I had come to them as an equal, offering them a partnership among equals. My people had treated his brother with kindness and respect. openly showing him all there was to see of our tribe. There was some resistance among the village chiefs and the shamans to us, but he had decided to confederate with us. And he would be happy to share with us the secrets of swamp warfare.

I thanked him for his decision and assured him it was the best one for both his people and mine, as both would greatly benefit from the alliance. I promised we would set up an Ordu at the northern end of the swamp, so we could learn the swamps while his people learned to use horses and to use our weapons and tools. I further invited him to send more observers to our Eagle Ordu or to come himself if he wished. He replied that he would be a poor leader if he left his people, but he would visit the new Ordu once it was set up and help with the training. He recommended that we set it up in winter, for it was the driest season with the most pleasant weather for northern people. The swamp warfare training would be best commenced in the rainy season, for that was when it was most difficult and most effective. I thanked him for his advice and told him I would send a message to Kaidu containing all his suggestions and urging that the Ordu be set up this coming winter. He was pleased and asked Chekika if he would like to stay with me. He replied that he would if I would accept him. I quickly assured him that I would he honored since he would be most helpful. I envisioned him taking up great responsibility one day and further cementing our alliance with the Calusa.

We started back right away, and by the time we reached the Tekesta, my entire escort had reassembled. They had bagged a fair amount of game and fish, and the Tekesta were quite grateful for our generosity with it. I sent out riders with dispatches for Kaidu and Donduk, telling them briefly of the islands and the alliance with the Calusa and strongly urging that Donduk come here for the winter and set up a new Ordu, instead of returning to the Eagle Ordu. I promised to find an appropriate site on my way back to the Pigeon Ordu. Meanwhile, I passed on the news about the Calusa to the Tekesta. They were surprised, but reluctantly agreed to also confederate. As we moved north, the Hobe, Wacata, Ais and Surreche also joined.

We turned inland to look for a site for the new Ordu. It had to be near the swamps but not in them. There had to be suitable land for crops and grazing nearby. Chekika was very familiar with the swamp fringe area and was able to take me to several potential places. The non-Calusa in the area were either in scattered small villagers or our allies, but I made certain all were in accord with any site I might select. We finally settled on a bit of high ground near the center of the peninsula. It was about forty-five li northwest of the huge lake that dominated the southern swamp, and there was a large lake just north of the site. The soil was fair, at least good enough for grazing, but there was better soil near at hand. It looked like a perfect site, and Chekika assured me that this high ground was never flooded, even during the great storms that the Taino called hurakan. From his description, the hurakan sounded like a typhoon. I had heard about them, from my grandfather, especially the one that destroyed Kubilai's invasion fleet off Yapon uls. They never reached Khanbalikh while I was there, however, so I wasn't personally familiar with them. It seemed they struck between the summer and winter solstices, and could totally destroy a small island or do serious damage to the larger ones as well as the shore of the mainland. It seemed they could strike anywhere along the eastern and southern coast, but usually just hit the peninsula and the southern coast. It was nothing to worry about, Chekika assured me, because they always knew when one was coming in plenty of time to get away. I was sure they did.

I left part of my escort to get the Ordu site ready and continued northward. I told the groups who had confederated with us that the Calusa had also joined and they were all very glad to hear it. They seemed to hold them in great respect and didn't want them as enemies. It was late summer by the time I reached the Pigeon Ordu. Donduk greeted me warmly and gave me a pile of dispatches. He thanked me for suggesting he spend the winter setting up a new Ordu. Kaidu had agreed to my suggestions, especially since Donduk had included his own hearty endorsement when he sent on my dispatch. He had been growing weary of wintering in the icy Eagle Ordu, then summering in the hot, humid Pigeon Ordu. He was ready to stay in the warmer areas all year round. I told him we would miss his wisdom in the council meetings, but he said he would send lengthy reports, and he and I could always talk things over when I was nearby.

The dispatches told of Padraig's return to the Antelope Ordu and promised I'd have maps of much of the western coastline waiting for me. Juchi's trek had led him to the Hopitu-shinumu again, and he found them still unwilling to ally with us, but most willing to trade. He had visited among them and their southern neighbors, the T'han-u-ge for much of the summer before moving on to their western neighbors, the Shi'wona. These people lived in large towns made of bricklike mud. They were farmers and hunters and generally peaceful. He had also found a few more isolated bands of Dine along the way, and as their relatives had done, they joined us outright. He would report back more later. It looked like he was having quite an adventure. I wondered if he enjoyed getting back to exploring. I still had to go to the fall meeting of the Ani'-Yun'-wiya, so I couldn't tarry, but I told Donduk about the new Ordu site, and he made ready to leave for it with a cadre of instructors. The Pigeon Ordu would be commanded by an Ocheti shakowin, Mato Anahtaka, who had been Donduk's second in command for two years. The new Ordu would be called the Alligator Ordu.

I headed north to the West Tsoyaha River and then east along it to the Wildcat Ordu. Jebei was most relieved to see me, since Kaidu had told him he would have to go to the general meeting of the Ani' Yun'-wiya if I didn't arrive in time. He was aghast at the prospect. Most Mongols have no time or patience for meetings, especially when no one was in charge who could just bark the meeting to a close when it had gone on long enough. I couldn't say that I was looking forward to it either, but hopefully this would be my last one. Utasite had come to the Ordu to lead me to the meeting. I asked him if things looked any better for a decision this year. He said that at least there were more in favor of joining, since all of the observers had returned filled with enthusiasm for the alliance. He had tried to convince his father to at least ally his town with us if the others wouldn't, but Ostenako wanted to give consensus one more chance.

We gathered up Ostenako on the way to Kituhwa as well as quite
a few others. I had only brought Smoking Mirror with me, and let
the rest of my entourage stay at the Wildcat Ordu. As before, the
town was crowded with chiefs and elders and quite a few others.
We were a day early and stayed with Ostenako's group in the town
house. The next day, we formed at the same place, and the chief of
Kituhwa, Ushesees, made a few opening remarks, explaining to the
assembly why we were gathered, and passing on that the observers
who had visited with the Mongols had all been well treated and
returned filled with praise for their hosts. I was called on to make
a few remarks. This time I briefly outlined the choices for alliance
with us and told them which groups had joined us and which had
sent observers since the last time we had met.

One of the chiefs wanted to know which groups had refused to
join us. I enumerated them, the Southeastern towns, the Natchez,
the Kadohadacho, and the Hopitu-shinumu. They only knew the
first of these and admired their cultural advances, but little else.
Another chief wanted to know why they had refused our overture.
I explained that the first three groups had very stratified societies,
and in our alliance, the ruling class would lose much of its power
over the rest of the tribe. Since they had to make the decision to
join us, it was no surprise that they refused. The last group lived in
a barren, mountainous region far to the west. Their isolation had
made them leery of strangers. As they would get to know us better
through the trade links we had established just this year, perhaps
they would join us. I found out later that Smoking Mirror was not
pleased that I had lumped his people in with the others. He told
me that it was his brother's excessive religious zeal and our apparent
lack of it that made him want no part of us, not the Kadohadacho
society, which he insisted was not nearly as stratified as that of the
Natchez. I apologized profusely, although I didn't think I was off
the mark, but his friendship meant too much to me to risk it splitting hairs.

Another chief wanted to know if any tribe had left us after joining us, or, worse yet, had ceased to exist. I told him that none had
tried to end our alliance, only one of those conquered had revolted,

and their own people had warned us about the revolt in time to thwart it. No tribe had ceased to exist, even among those who had joined us outright. They continued most of their customs, and in some cases the Mongols adopted them as well. Anticipating the next question, I added that all tribes retained their languages, but most also learned Mongol, especially if they wanted to learn our writing system. There followed a few questions about writing. They had heard of the marks that give speech and were impressed that we could convey all of our words with the marks, not just some of them as they did with their pictographs. Their observers had keen eyes, and I spent quite a while explaining Mongol and other tribal customs and practices that they had noticed. In fact, as the day wore on, I felt I was teaching a course on all that I had seen in the new world and half of what I had seen in the old.

As expected, one day was hardly long enough. I had to answer questions most of the second day as well. Then the comments began. For the next three days, one after the other, chiefs, elders, women, warriors rose up to give their views. Occasionally, there would be a question for me, but mostly they just gave their views. It looked like all the towns near the Wildcat Ordu were in favor of joining us. The towns near the eastern frontier were at least partially in favor of joining as were those on the western frontier. The towns to the north seemed the least inclined to join. Near the end of the fifth day, I got up and passed on my observation of the apparent division among them. I then asked if the northern towns had sent any observers to the Ordu. They had to admit that almost all the observers had been from the southern, eastern, and western border areas and the rest from the center. I then suggested that perhaps if the northern groups sent observers this year, all would be settled, and they could confederate as a group.

This caused quite a bit of discussion among the groups, and finally one of the northern chiefs rose up and agreed that I had made a good point. Every village and town must send a trusted observer so they would be able to make an intelligent decision on the matter. Other northern chiefs rose up and echoed the man's view. Then Ostenako rose up and said that as a people he felt they had not treated my people fairly. They had had two years to send observers and make a decision regarding the alliance. He would not blame the Mongols for thinking that the Ani' Yun'-wiya were toying with them. He did not want to lose the advantages of alliance because a few towns had been too self-involved to do as they should have.

These remarks brought on quite a bit of grumbling from the northern group, so before things had a chance to deteriorate, I got up again and said that the Mongols had been patient with the Ani' Yun'-wiya and would continue to be because we thought highly of them and felt it was a small sacrifice to make if it might result in them joining us. No group would make a better addition to our ranks, and if they needed another year of observation to make their final decision, we would wait another year. That mollified things somewhat, and Ushesees rose up quickly and suggested that if all were agreed, we would adjourn until next year with the under-standing that any town that had not yet done so would send an observer to our nearby Ordu and a final decision would be made at the next meeting. There was no disagreement, and the meeting was adjourned. Ushesees later thanked me for my soothing words and admonished Ostenako for his harsh words. The latter replied that his people were ready to join us now and greatly resented the delay caused by the northern intransigence. Ushesees reminded him that they had always been the slowest to change, and taking three years to make such a change was not really excessive.

I thanked Ostenako for taking our part and urged him to be patient. Since he had already said he wanted to join us, there was no reason he couldn't go ahead and send his young men for training. This cheered him up considerably, and he assured me that his town would join us next fall with or without the rest of the tribe. I asked Ushesees about his town's feelings since I had not heard him express any opinion on joining. He said that as host for the meeting, it would have been bad manners to take sides in the discussion. Besides, his was the principle and first town of the people; therefore, he would abide by the decision of the people. If most joined, Kituhwa would join with them, if most did not, neither would Kituhwa.

On the way back, I asked Ostenako where his people had

come from originally. He said that they had drifted down along the mountains from the north over several generations. Before that, they had come from the west. I told him what I had found in my travels westward. Except for the eastern plains, the land was harsh, dry, and mountainous. It could hardly have supported all the different people who claim to have come from there. He just said that all their traditions put them in the far west originally, and that was all he knew about it. I mentioned that his language seemed similar to that of the Mingue far to the north. Did he know if they were related? He couldn't say since tradition was silent on the matter, but the intransigent northern towns would likely be able to tell me more, should they ever agree to join. They had changed less over the years than the southern towns had and may have retained the old stories more accurately.

I got back to the Wildcat Ordu, picked up my retinue, and started back west. We moved rather quickly along the yam system and arrived back at the Eagle Ordu in late fall. I settled the observers, looked in on Paula and the children, and reported to Kaidu. As usual he presented me with maps and dispatches and told me look it all over before the winter council meeting in two weeks. I looked over Juchi's dispatches and maps first. He had traveled up the Red River to a lake near its source and then turned north for some distance to what turned out to be the Kadohadacho River. He found another band of the ubiquitous Dine at this point. He followed the Kadohadacho upstream through increasingly dry, rugged country. He left the river when it turned sharply north and followed a trail to a south-flowing river where he found one of the T'han-u-ge towns, called P'e-a-ku'. He named the river for the town since it was quite a large town. They were more polite than friendly, but were happy to trade. With guides he was led west to another south-flowing river and another T'han-u-ge town. He went north along the river (which he named Thanuge) until the next and last town when he was guided west again to a shallow, west-flowing river, which was so dotted with ruins of abandoned towns that he named it the Ruin River. He followed it to the Hopitu River, and all along it, he found a very large band of the Dine. Farther down the Hopitu River, he found the Hopitu-shinumu. He spent the rest of the summer getting the various rivers in the area mapped and the remaining inhabited towns marked. From what he was able to gather, there had been far more people in the area at one time, but the weather turned colder and drier and almost all left, moving south, while first the Hopitu-shinumu and then the Dine filtered in from the north. His mappers reported finding many more abandoned towns, some quite large. He would slowly continue down the Hopitu River as long as the weather permitted and send his next dispatch in the spring. I wondered what he would find.

Turning to Padraig's dispatches and maps, his mappers had gone some distance north and south along the coast. In the north, they had found it necessary to take to boats because the coast was so rugged. Mountains seemed to spring right out of the sea, forming deep-sea canyons. The coast seemed to run a little west of north and was dotted with innumerable islands. The natives all along the coast exploited the sea. To the south the coast was not as wild. The tribes along the coast were generally not given to agriculture, but the climate was pleasant and certainly wet enough for crops, at least as far as they had gone. They seemed to have gone as far south as the Owl Ordu, if the scale was right. I wondered how far they would be able to get before running into problems. Juchi planned to go as far as the coast if he could, and perhaps he would meet Padraig's mappers.

At the council meeting, Kaidu went over everything that had transpired in the west and said that all seemed to be in order there. He expected Padraig to come down in the spring to report in person. Juchi might be back by next fall or, if delayed, not until the next year. The mappers had done a remarkable job of filling in the blanks on the map in the east and in the near west, but now that we were getting the shorelines in the west, it would be good to fill in the western blanks as well. He felt the landscape would make it more difficult, so all mappers should be well provisioned and escorted, and stay near water sources. We had no need to map any deserts they might encounter, except, as you would map a lake. He asked me to discuss the events in the east.

I went over what had happened during my journey and enumerated all the groups that had confederated with us. I explained
that the Lucayo had joined us, but until we had a base on one of
the larger islands, we wouldn't be able to do much to help them
against their enemies, except train them. Should we manage to win
over the Taino, I thought we should train an Ordu to operate at sea
in the large boats of the Taino. Then we could make short work of
the marauders, or, better yet, recruit them. As it stood now, we had
allies all along the eastern coast and almost all along the southern
coast. The few tribes on the peninsula not already allied had sent
observers and would likely join by next year. Of course, most of the
Southeast Cities had not even sent an observer, but the coastal groups
had joined along with the peninsula tribes. The tribes between the
Ani' Yun'-wiya and the Sound Tribes (the Iyehyeh and Cheroenhaka)
had sent observers, but no final decision had yet been made. I then
explained what had occurred at the latest general meeting of the
Ani'-Yun'-wiya. I said that I was fairly sure they would confederate
the next year and that would likely cause their hesitant neighbors
to join also. The bulk of the Southeastern towns would never join
us, however.

Givevneu reported that his apprentice was progressing quite
well, and he would soon take over much of the work in the Ordu.
Still, the health of the people was good; no ke'let had found us yet.
In fact, flocks and people were expanding so quickly that he was
concerned that they should spread out a bit more since ke'let were
always attracted to large groups. Kaidu suggested that since the largest group of us was an Ordu, it shouldn't be a problem. The cities of
the Hanjen would surely be far more inviting to them than a mere
Ordu. Perhaps, Givevneu allowed, but he wasn't so sure, since they
had found the original Ordu before we left the old land.

Kaidu thought that the time had come to consolidate. He
would not send me anywhere next year, unless I wanted to visit the
infamous fall meeting of the Ani' Yun'-wiya again. Otherwise, he
wanted me to supervise the efforts of the mappers from here and be
on hand should he need me for any special assignment. I thanked
him for the break. Much as I had enjoyed all the adventure, I was

growing weary of all the separation from Paula and the children. George was already the age I was when I first left the Ordu to begin my education. Kaidu dismissed us until Padraig arrived next spring. I rushed home with the good news.

32
PEACE THEN DEATHS, 13-5 K
(SD, MT, 1381-3)

The next three years were wonderful for me. My family was always by my side. I began to teach George some of the things I had learned in Khanbalikh. He was a bright boy, eager to learn, and a joy to teach. Mathilde did learn to read and write, but otherwise showed no further interest in book learning. Instead she became quite intrigued with medicinal plants and eventually grew quite skilled with them. Ignace also learned to read and write, but was much taken by metalworking, and eventually we let him stay with Henry to learn the skill. During this time, Paula also presented me with two more children, first, another son, Theodore (after Paula's uncle) and a year later, another daughter, Ludmilla (after Paula's mother). The children were all quite healthy and strong.

Padraig came to report and brought his family with him that first summer. It had been some time since I had seen him. The responsibility of running an Ordu had matured him. He was quieter and more thoughtful than the wild warrior I had met so long before. We went back with him for the rest of the summer and much enjoyed the rugged setting of the Antelope Ordu. He had established a group that would play that strange instrument of his. He had gotten the horses used to it and insisted the music had frightened the enemy in the west. He had the men play some of the battle airs, and I could see how one might find it frightening, but I really liked it. We spent a lot of time exploring, with Padraig showing us the sights. My family got to see the Yellow Canyon where we gathered sulfur, and I showed Paula the strange sights around the beautiful lake that was the source of the Absaroke River. We were amazed at all the geysers and hot springs in this cool high mesa. Padraig said that it became quite snowbound during its very long winter. Indeed summer was the only time to come here. We ran into some Nomo hunters while we were there, and they were quite taken by our families. They were awed at my younger children's blond hair and Padraig's oldest son's red hair and kept touching it.

Padraig's mappers never actually met up with Juchi, but they both trod the same ground. The west coast became more arid as they went south and eventually turned into a very long, bleak, and rugged peninsula with few people and little water. It took them another year to map the whole of it. The coast east of the peninsula was also rugged, but had more water and many more people. The coastal people all seemed to be fairly peaceful fishermen and gave the mappers no trouble at all.

To the north of the Salmon Ordu, the people also exploited the sea, but were much more warlike. A few punitive expeditions had to be undertaken by the Ordu to free the mappers or avenge their deaths. Finally, a reconnaissance in force was used to finish mapping the hostile area. The coast eventually turned west except for a southwest interruption along a peninsula ending in a long string of islands extending in an arc westward back toward the old land. Then the coast turned north again. It was several years before the entire coast was mapped to where we had crossed. It was a huge land, but nowhere was it closer to the old land than where we had crossed. The Salmon Ordu had become quite adept at using the large boats of the local people and found them indispensable in patrolling the coast and keeping the peace. Less progress had been made with recruitment until Padraig took a hand and sent his own recruiters to the various tribes. Ogedai claimed his time was taken up subduing the warlike northern coastal tribes. Padraig was concerned about it, but wanted to believe Ogedai and never passed on his concerns to Kaidu. Eventually most of the tribes in the area confederated, although two more had to be wiped out.

That first fall, Smoking Mirror earned my undying gratitude by going to the annual meeting of the Ani' Yun'-wiya. After another several days of discussion at length, they all agreed to confederate. He still insisted that he enjoyed the meetings and all the free and open debate, but I began to wonder when he returned with a daughter of Ostenako as his wife. It was a bit embarrassing to me that I had never noticed anything between them when I was there, but it wasn't the first time I missed the obvious when it wasn't relevant to my mission. In any case, she was quite a handful, very bright and outspoken. She quickly learned to read and write and became quite close to Paula. Smoking Mirror changed her name, Katalsta, to Mazatl after they were married. Apparently name changing was quite typical among the Ani' Yun'-wiya, especially in connection with momentous events.

As I expected, the tribes east and northeast of the Ani' Yun'-wiya also confederated with us that winter. The following spring, we moved the Goose Ordu south to the frontier on the Sewee River. We also established the Manati (the Taino name for the tuskless walrus-like animal) Ordu in the northern part of the peninsula, coincidentally completing the surrounding of the Southeastern tribes should they get restless. They still refused to deal with us, even though we now surrounded them and our trade routes bypassed them. Some of their people joined us as individuals, but not one city ever did. Later events took care of them with much less compassion than we might have shown. The Taino from Cuba, Aiti, and Xaymaca confederated with us the second year, and we set up Ordu on Cuba (the Dog) and Aiti (the Parrot). As I had suggested, these were trained to use the large Taino boats, although we eventually got some horses over to the islands and started up herds there. Boriquen resisted us for some time, but after a few years, they began to confederate one cacique at a time. The cannibals on the smaller eastern islands were first badly mauled in a punitive expedition, then many years later won over as allies.

Juchi returned the second year (14 K). He had followed the Hopitu River westward through a remarkably wide, deep, and rugged canyon. He was finally forced to climb out of it and follow it along its northern rim for much of its length. The river turned south as it escaped the canyon and wound its way through a semidesert until emptying into the sea at the top of the gulf formed by the long narrow peninsula and the mainland. The people along the last part of the river were largely hunters and gatherers living rather meanly, although they did some cultivating. Most of them were amenable to joining us, but only if we could set up an Ordu nearby. To this end, Juchi went back up the Hopitu River for some distance to a river that joined it from the east well below the canyon. He went up that river and eventually found a very different tribe. They called themselves the A'-a' tam and lived in the cubical adobe rooms much like the Hopitu-shinumu. They also managed to do quite a bit of cultivating by means of extensive irrigation unlike their western neighbors. They were spread out in villages on both sides of the river (which Juchi named the Ahatam after them) as well as for some distance to the south of the river. Since times had become more difficult for them recently with a prolonged drought, they were willing to send observers with Juchi and to spread the word of his offer to their other villages. Ultimately, they did confederate as did their western neighbors, but it took a few years of observers before they did.

Farther up the Ahatam, Juchi found yet another tribe that also lived in the cubical adobe houses, but piled on top of each other in two or even three stories. They had large villages, but they were not very full. They called themselves the A'shiwi and had also suffered much from the drought. They were involved in trading with their neighbors and in extensive agriculture also aided by irrigation. The drought had hit them first and hardest (according to them), and their once-large and numerous towns had been reduced to mere shells. Even so, their shell villages extended from a river that emptied into the Ahatam from the north (he named it the Ashiwi) for quite some distance to the south. Their situation was so desperate that they were happy to join us, and a large group went with him while runners were sent to their other villages to spread the word and perhaps follow in his wake. He found yet another band of Dine (who quickly joined us) near the headwaters of the Ashiwi.

East of these people, he came upon two more groups. The first was called the K'eres. They lived in a fairly compact area along a river that flowed into the Thanuge from the west. He named the river the Keres for them. They also lived in the adobe cubes and also irrigated their fields. East of them along the Thanuge River, but south of the T'han-u-ge were a fairly similar people called the Ti'wan. Both of these groups were in contact with the T'han-u-ge and were rather put out that he had taken so long to get in touch with them and that he brought along all the A'shiwi. Still, they too had been hurt by the drought and also agreed to send along observers. Both of these groups eventually confederated, as did the T'han-u-ge. Even the Hopitu-shinumu began confederating one village at a time as the drought continued unabated over the next few years. It was some time before we were able to set up an Ordu in the area, however, since there was so little dependable water available. Ultimately, we did establish the Coyotl (the Nahual name for the yellow prairie wolf) Ordu along the middle of the Thanuge River. Juchi made noises about going even farther west and contacting the coastal tribes, but he never got around to it.

That second year was truly a great year. There was no trouble anywhere; the harvests were all phenomenal due to very favorable weather (except in the southwest), and a new Ordu (the Pelican) was established on the lower reaches of the Ishak River. Smoking Mirror's "brother" died during an attack on the Natchez, and with his passing, the Kadohadacho quickly confederated with us, joining the rest of the old Hasinai confederacy that had already joined. This meant that only the Natchez and the Southeastern tribes still refused to join us.

The following year was quite different. First of all, spring was cold and rainy on the plains, delaying the planting considerably. Then in late spring, a vicious windstorm struck the Eagle Ordu, doing a lot of damage and injuring quite a few people. We had seen these odd storms before, but this was the first time one had struck an Ordu. Next, a freak hailstorm destroyed most of the Owl Ordu's crops, and a prairie fire forced the Cormorant Ordu to flee across the Black Hill River and watch as half of their crops were consumed. Then a typhoon struck the Alligator Ordu, wiping out their crops as well as drowning many of their animals and causing quite a few injuries. Fortunately, there was ample grain in storage to make up for all these problems, and Juchi and I spent a lot of time traveling to the various Ordu with relief supplies. The eastern Ordu had fared quite well, but an early freeze caught them by surprise and damaged some of their unharvested crops. But these losses could be made up. Late that fall, we suffered an irreparable loss when Givevneu died.

He had been fine all day and had just sent his assistant to treat an injured yam attendant, when he suddenly got a strange look on his face and went to see Kaidu. Kaidu called me in and told me that Givevneu had just told him that it was time for him to die, gave him some final advice, and asked him to see that no one disturbed him until evening and that he be buried somewhere on the plain east of the Ordu, away from the river, standing up and facing northwest. At dusk, we went to his yurt and found him lying on a rug with his arms folded over his chest. We wrapped him in the rug and took him out on the plain and buried him as he had asked and covered the place carefully so no one could tell where it was. Kaidu was devastated by the loss. Not only had Givevneu always been an exceptional shaman, but also he was always there with thoughtful, insightful, invaluable advice. It was he, after all, who planted the idea of this new land in Kaidu's head and gave him a goal toward which to strive over the frustrating last years along the Karamuren. I, also, would miss him. He had a remarkable understanding of people and what motivated them, which was a great help to me. His open, friendly manner, and cheerful mien did much to brighten up the Ordu. He would be desperately missed. But he was not the last loss that year. In early winter, word reached us that Kaidu's second son, Mangku, died quite suddenly at his post in charge of the Hawks. Then word arrived that Donduk had died peacefully in his sleep at the Alligator Ordu. The strain of dealing with the aftermath of the typhoon was too much for a man his age. The loss of Donduk, his loyal lieutenant from his years in the old Khanate, was even harder on Kaidu than that of his son. For the first time, he confided in me, he felt old. For the first time, he began to look old; the strength and vigor was gone from his step, the fire from his eye. It was sad to see.

The following spring, it was reported that one of our trading expeditions had been taken captive. They had been trading in the cities on the Tolteca high plain and were on their way back when they were seized by one of the coastal cities of a people called the Huaxteca. It was not clear if they had been harmed, and no one knew if Tlacuectli was among the group. Smoking Mirror was concerned about his father and warned me that the Huaxteca were not known for being kind to their captives. Kaidu recaptured a bit of his fire and told me to organize a punitive expedition to punish the city. I ascertained from Smoking Mirror that their cities tended to be large and fortified so I thought that I would need the Horse and the Pelican Tumen with a full complement of artillery. Since the Huaxteca were along the tropical coast, it was thought best to launch the attack in the late fall, after the rainy season. I sent messages to the two Ordu and made sure that they had an ample supply of powder and shot for their cannon and that they would be ready to move out in early fall.

I went up to the Hawk Ordu to make sure a steady shipment of powder and shell would follow us to depots I planed to set up. While there Henry presented me with a suit of scale armor. The scales were small and quite finely wrought, and I was quite touched that he would make such a complicated thing for me. He also presented me with a helmet to go with the armor. It was rather strange. It looked like the head of a snake with its mouth opened wide. He admitted that it was an odd design but told me that it had been very strongly suggested by Smoking Mirror during our winter visit when Henry had shown him his work in progress. Doqus meanwhile presented me with a sort of banner made of black feathers (from my namesake bird). It, too, had been suggested by Smoking Mirror. It was very nicely done, and I complimented her on the work, but I had never seen anything quite like it before and found it very puzzling. When I got back home, I asked Smoking Mirror about it.

"Henry and Doqus have exceeded my expectations," he laid it on. "I must send them a note thanking them. Meanwhile, I have here a couple of things that go with the ensemble."

He handed me a cloak made of the feathers of the green parrot of the east coast and a sort of headdress made of some of the gaudy feathers we had gotten on the large islands. The work was quite well done, but I had long resisted wearing feathers and what passed for finery in the land and was not too thrilled about the prospect now. My long silence before I stammered my thanks was just a bit transparent.

"Isn't it time the Raven wore feathers?" he teased.

"Why now?" I tried to be polite. "And what have feathers to do with this odd snake helmet?"

"Everything." He grinned. "It will make you look like Quetzalcoatl."

"Who?" I asked.

"The Plumed Serpent," he continued. "In the last days of Tollan, there arose a leader named Ce Acatl Topiltzin. He promoted the cult of Quetzalcoatl and added the name to his like a title. A rival faction dedicated to the cult of Texcatlipoca and led by a man named Huemac drove him out of the city. After many wanderings, he found himself on the coast and despairing of his situation. He told his followers that he would return on his birth year and then threw himself on a pyre. He was instantly turned into the Morning Star, Tlahuizcalpantecuhtli."

"And I thought the Mongol legends were ridiculous." I was disgusted. "The Hanjen have been recording the appearance of the Morning Stars for millennia. I can assure you, none of them have just made their appearance in the last few generations."

"The fall of Tollan was about two hundred years ago," he said. "But it doesn't really matter whether the transformation actually happened. It's just that Quetzalcoatl is associated with the brightest Morning Star, and, therefore, the east. And over time the man Ce Acatl Topiltzin has become confused with the god Quetzalcoatl."

"Where did they ever get the idea of a Plumed Serpent anyway?" I asked. "Surely no one has ever seen such a thing."

"Well, I don't really know," he mused. "But Quetzalcoatl is a wind god, a rain god, or an earth god depending on who you ask, and may be a combination of a serpent god and a bird god."

"I'm beginning to think that you are as unimpressed with gods as I am," I said. "I hope I haven't corrupted you."

"My father corrupted me long before you came along." He laughed.

"At any rate"—I returned to the main point—"why should I pretend to be this Plumed Serpent god? You know we don't really

encourage excessive cults, and Kaidu would probably be most displeased at the idea. Besides, even with all the costume, why would
they think I was a god? I have been viewed as strange in this land,
but hardly as a god. I think it would be better if we went as who
we are."

"I just thought it might make it easier." He shrugged. "It should
at least give them pause. Besides, the cult of Quetzalcoatl discouraged
human sacrifice, so I thought you might be able to use presumed
authority to end the practice. It is quite widespread in the south,
you know. Also, this does happen to be Ce Acatl's birth year."

"I think the idea is to wipe out the kidnappers," I said. "Convert-
ing them won't really be necessary under the circumstances."

"The city in question is deep in Huaxteca territory," he rejoined.
"You may find you have to fight your way to it. The Huaxteca prize
war and are not likely to let an army pass by without challenging it.
Now, of course, if you are the god's incarnation on a special mission,
they are less likely to interfere. Especially if I go as Tezcatlipoca."

"How would you manage that?" I asked.

"My name in Nahual is Tezcatlipoca." He grinned. "My father
called me that when I lost my foot. You see Tezcatlipoca is usually
pictured with a piece of obsidian instead of one of his feet."

"So,"—I was amused—"you wanted us to go as two rival gods
united in the holy purpose of reducing the den of kidnappers. Do
you have an obsidian foot for the occasion?"

"Indeed." He whipped a wedge of obsidian out of his pack and
strapped it onto his foot stub.

"I'll tell you what"—I couldn't disappoint him—"we can put on
our costumes when we meet with the Huaxteca, but we won't actually
claim to be gods, we'll just let them draw their own conclusions."

"Excellent." He bowed ceremoniously.

"One thing I don't understand." I paused. "How could this be
the birth year of someone who died two hundred years ago?"

"The Tolteca calendar repeats itself," he explained. "It has a
fifty-two-year cycle, and the years are named either Rabbit, Reed,
House, or Flint and numbered one through thirteen. The order is
One Rabbit, Two Reed, Three House, Four Flint, Five Rabbit, and

so on. Ce Acatl means One Reed, and this is the year One Reed in the Tolteca calendar."

"I thought Ce Acatl was the man's name." I was puzzled.

"It is." He nodded. "Tolteca names are usually partially one's day of birth. The days are named after one of twenty-day signs again numbered one through thirteen. The years are named for the first day of each year, which coincidentally is always one of the four signs I already mentioned."

"But that's not enough days," I calculated quickly. "It only gives you two hundred and sixty days' worth of names. What about the rest of the year?"

"The cycle is repeated," he explained, "until you have three hundred and sixty days. Then the last five days of each year are unnamed and uncounted. There is also a solar year consisting of eighteen months of twenty days each named after the gods appropriate to the season. For example, the first one is in late winter and is dedicated to the gods of rain to whom the appropriate sacrifices are made to ensure that the rains come in the spring. The two calendars match up every fifty-two years."

"What would you sacrifice to rain gods?" I was curious.

"Children," he said simply.

"Children!" I was aghast. "Every year? Whose? How many? How old?"

"It depends"—he shrugged—"on the city, the priests, and the situation. If the rains were good the year before and the priests don't foresee any godly anger, there would only be a few. They are usually quite young and belong to the people of the city. After all, it is no sacrifice to offer someone else's child. It is deemed quite an honor, and the child is assured a place with the gods. There is rarely problem getting victims."

"Doesn't it bother you?" I found him just a bit too dispassionate.

"It is none of my affair," he shot back. "The country to the south is a harsh, dangerous place. Vicious storms lash both coasts, mountains rain down fire and ash, and the very earth itself shakes. Yet the land can be very bountiful giving great harvests every year.

Much time and effort is taken up with ensuring the bounty and preventing the danger. For them, the price they pay is not too high. Perhaps if I had grown up among them I would agree."

"But children"—I couldn't let it go—"not even your brother sacrificed children."

"True." He met my eye. "But is the life of a child worth more to you than that of an adult? When we destroy a town, we make no special allowance for them that I recall."

"No, I suppose not." He had me there. "It's just that ritually killing your own child seems unthinkable. In war, there is no ritual involved, just expediency."

"Before your people came to this land," he said, "children were never intentionally killed in battle and women only rarely. Both were instead taken into the tribe first as slaves, then eventually as members."

"That is more humane,"—I nodded—"but dangerous. How can they forget who killed their fathers and husbands? What's to prevent them from turning on their humane captors in the end?"

"I never heard of such a turning," he replied. "But I suppose it is possible. Still, our people find child sacrifice no more shocking than killing every man, woman, and child in a town. Yet, when you ordered it, it was done."

"I suppose," I mused, "one does what he thinks has worked before, and much depends on what was first tried."

"An astute observation." He smiled. "Perhaps the spirit of Givevneu lives."

It was stupid of me to be shocked about child sacrifice. After all, it was a small step from adult sacrifice. I wondered why it ever started. There had been a story about a sacrifice of someone's child among Grandfather Peter's stories connected to his religion, but it seemed to me that it was stopped just in time. In any case, we weren't going south to persuade anyone to abandon their religious practices; we were going to destroy a town. As to their two calendars, they were no worse than the Hanjen attempt to reconcile the lunar and the solar calendars by adding extra months whenever necessary. The Hanjen calendar was more accurate since it did take into account the extra day every four years. Personally, I preferred my old ancestral calendar. It ignored the moon and allowed for the extra day making it as accurate as the Hanjen calendar. Of course, it was rather difficult to explain why the twelve months were either 28, 29, 30 or 31 days long. There was no logic in it that I could see. Of course, we had long ago forgotten the year count or the months and days for that matter. But the idea seemed less complicated.

Toward the end of summer, all my preparations were ready, and I was about to take my leave of Kaidu when word reached that he had been thrown from his horse and badly injured. One of the rattling snakes had startled his mount while he was lost in thought. He was carefully brought back to his yurt, and Okuh-hatuh did what he could for him, but he never regained consciousness and died in the night. He had not indicated who should succeed him, but the older Mongols felt that he would have wanted his oldest son Kuyuk to take over. He was sent for and asked to be Khan. He refused a few times, in the time-honored tradition, but was "talked into" accepting. The new Khan was presented to the Eagle Ordu, and all acclaimed him. The nomination was sent to the other Ordu, and they too acclaimed the accession. I suppose the unanimity was more from numbed shock over the loss of Kaidu than any great faith in Kuyuk. To be fair to the man, he could hardly have replaced Kaidu. He did immediately declare that he wished Juchi to succeed him, and that was a very popular action and built up a lot of goodwill, since Juchi was very well known and esteemed.

What can one say about Kaidu. He was completely responsible for all the Khanate of the Blue Sky. If it continued to prosper, it would be because of the solid foundation he laid. It was he who turned a casual remark about another land into the whole focus of his and his forgotten Ordu's existence. He had the vision to cull that Ordu into fighting trim and relentlessly drive them into the unknown. His was the spirit that brought us all together and held us all together. How ironic that he died the same way his hero Chingis had died after accomplishing almost as much in much less time with far less bloodshed. Would we ever see his like again? Not in my lifetime.

We buried him near Givevneu just as he had mentioned he wanted to be. Again the spot was disguised according to the custom. When a decent interval had passed, I went to see Kuyuk and told him about the upcoming campaign and asked if he still wanted it to take place and me to lead it. He replied that he certainly did, and in fact, he wanted to expand it. I was to consider all the Huaxteca as enemies of the Khanate and either accept the surrender of or destroy all their cities and villages. To that end, he told me to order the Owl, Cormorant, Crane, and Beaver Tumen to follow me south as soon as possible. I should keep him informed of my progress, and he would send new instructions as events warranted. I should consider it likely that I would be gone for more than one year.

I was a bit surprised that he would want to conquer the Huax-teca as a whole instead of just punish the kidnappers, but I assumed he had his reasons. I explained the new situation to Paula, and she understood that such a thing might happen, but was glad we had had so much time together. She suggested that if the campaign did drag on for more than a year, perhaps she should send George to be with me. I promised to send for him as soon as I felt it would be safe for him to join me. Meanwhile, I sent out dispatches to the four Ordu advising them of their new orders and giving them route maps to ensure that they would not all be covering the same path and run into fodder problems. I sent instructions and route maps to the Horse and the Pelican Ordu also and instructed them to set out at once for our base camp and depot on the north side of the Thanuge River near its mouth. They were to send out scouts to the south as soon as they arrived, I would probably get there soon after them since I would be traveling with only a small escort. I also sent word to the Kestrel and Hawk Ordu advising them of the change in the scope of the campaign and ordering them to start sending loads of shot and shell to our base camp depot as soon as possible, and keep them coming. I took my final leave of Kuyuk, and, with Smoking Mirror and my escort, started south.

33

THE HUAXTECA AND TOTONACA, 15-6 K
(NE MEXICO, 1383-4)

It took almost two months to get to the delta of the Thanuge, and I made use of the time by having Smoking Mirror teach me the Nahual language that was so widespread in the south. The Pelicans and Horses had already been at the delta for several days by the time we arrived. The scouts reported that the first Huaxteca villages were still some days' march to the south, just across a moderately sized river. The villages near the Thanuge were all confederates of ours and eager to help. Those who had already trained with us were allowed to come along. I set up a small garrison to guard the depot, and with most of our supplies started across the Thanuge on a hastily constructed pontoon bridge. From the scouts and Smoking Mirror, I learned that the Huaxteca were organized into towns of various sizes with varying numbers of smaller villages subject to them. The towns were usually at war with each other as well as their neighboring tribes. The largest towns were along the coastal plain and in the south, but smaller ones could be found for some distance inland among the foothills and even into the mountains. I decided to first deal with the coastal plain and hit the mountains later when I had all the other tumen with me. I spread the tumen out a bit over several li, and we headed south with our scouts in advance. We arrived at the "border" river a week later. We crossed at first light along a broad front, and I sent minghans to each of the nearby villages our scouts had found, while I proceeded to the largest nearby town with about four thousand men. We came upon the town near midday and quickly surrounded it while remaining out of their bowshot.

To my surprise, rather than a negotiating committee, a shower of arrows flew out from behind the town's low wall. They all fell harmlessly in front of us. Next, a group of warriors jumped over the wall and rushed toward us. The men calmly cut them down with arrows. The survivors retreated back to the town. Noticing thatch roofs on their houses, we let loose a shower of fire arrows and quickly set them ablaze. There was no wind, but the town seemed to be all aflame. Still, there was not the usual last desperate rush. Undaunted by the fire, they remained behind their wall waiting our attack. I brought up the cannon and trained them on one side of the wall. The plain shook with the barrage, and the mud wall disappeared in a cloud of dust along with the warriors behind it. The rest of the people of the town threw down their weapons and marched toward our lines. When they got fairly close, they fell to the ground and awaited their fate. They were short but rather thick of stature, reminding me of the Mongols. Their heads were misshaped, and there was a fair amount of tattooing. Many of the men wore a sort of "armor" made of quilted cotton and carried a round shield made of braided reeds. The men seemed to have a tube stuck in their nasal septum, in which they wore feathers. There seemed to be a great deal of feather ornamentation, especially yellow and red ones. Many of them were also bedecked with trinkets and jewelry of gold, silver, jade, turquoise, and shells. Otherwise, the women wore skirts and the men loincloths, capes, and leather bands, all decorated to varying degrees. Many of the men wore their hair in dangling locks dyed yellow or red and favored a strange conical hat. They were a sturdy, brave, and impressive-looking people.

I asked Smoking Mirror what usually befell them in a situation like this, and he said that the warriors expected to be sacrificed to our gods while the women and children expected to become slaves. I approached the prostrate group and asked if any of them understood Nahual. One of them got up on one knee, but kept his head bowed. I instructed him to translate to the others for me.

"It is not our custom to sacrifice captives," I began. "Nor is it our practice to take slaves. You must decide for yourselves your fate. You have two choices. Either you join us without any reservations and serve our Khan loyally or you die here and now on the field of battle. If you choose to join, and later betray us, you will suffer an ignominious death too horrible to contemplate. So choose well and choose carefully. Those who wish to join us may go back to your town and rebuild it; we will appoint a governor for a time to make sure you remain loyal and to take care of your needs. Those who wish to die remain on the field, and I promise you a quick death."

My words were translated, and the people began to steal furtive glances up at Smoking Mirror and me. He had donned his foot, but I was just arrayed in my armor with the snake helmet. A murmur began to pass among the people, and soon the majority of them got up and returned to the town with the heads still lowered but casting nervous glances back to see if we would follow them, or perhaps to see if we were real. I asked the translator to tell the remaining few to stand up and face their deaths proudly. They rose, raised their hands to salute me, and died singing some sort of battle hymn punctuated with shouts. I asked the translator if he chose to live. He replied that he did, and I assigned him to help the new governor, Inoli, an Ani' Yun'-wiya. He was one of my more patient men, ideal for the job. I sent along with him a small contingent of guards one of whom understood the Nahual tongue. I urged them all to learn the Huaxteca language as soon as possible. We set up camp outside the town and waited for the others to report. Most of the villages had surrendered immediately, but two of them fought and were wiped out. Since I had all the cannon, there were some moderate losses.

We moved inland a little to the next set of towns and subject villages. The results were much the same. Again, they didn't negotiate first but immediately attacked, we fired their roofs, they resisted anyway, we blasted one side of their protective wall with cannon, and they surrendered. Again, only a few of the unfortified villages resisted. I asked Smoking Mirror why they didn't negotiate first, but he only said that he had always heard they were rather warlike, indeed that they thrived on war. We continued in this way clearing a band about thirty li wide south of the border river. Finally, the other tumen began coming in. I sent the Horses and the Pelicans to deal with towns in the western highlands since they were more used to the dry rugged western land, and I strung out the others along a broad front to sweep the coastal plain south of my cleared band. I gave each tumen about sixty li of front to clear and positioned them in order from the coast inland, the Otters, Cranes, Owls, and Cormorants. I stayed with the Owls since they had the newest commander, Tsakaka-sakis, a Hewaktokto, who had just replaced Kuyuk. The northern part of the coastal plain was split in two by a small ridge running parallel to the coast. There were a few villages on the lower slopes of the ridgeline, but it still managed to impair communications and movement for a time, especially at its southern terminus where it spread out toward the west. Fortunately, there were no real problems in dealing with the Huaxteca along this stretch as we reduced or accepted the surrender of each of their towns and villages.

From the reports, the trend was continuing as we moved south beyond the ridgeline, although the towns were getting larger, more populous, and better fortified, and their villages were getting more numerous in what appeared to be a very broad river valley. We had advanced some forty-five li into the valley, when the scouts reported that a large body of warriors was up ahead. They were waiting for us in a broad open area, not in ambush. Such folly was hard to understand, but was not unexpected given all the Huaxteca bravado we had witnessed so far. The plain was in the path of the Cranes, so I joined them to see the spectacle. We reached them near midmorning. They were arrayed in ranks in the open field. There were about ten thousand of them, all in line with no reserves held back. We approached and rapidly fanned out to surround them. We then advanced to just out of their bowshot and waited to see if perhaps this time they would talk first. They stood for a while in solid ranks with the most gaudily attired in front. Some of these were dressed in headgear designed to look like an eagle with feathered armor and even eagle feet around their ankles. Others were decked out to look like some sort of spotted lion or lynx creature. It turned out that there were special military orders among all the peoples in this area dedicated to the eagle and the spotted lion (it was called ocelotl in Nahual). One of them began a sort of chant, and then they all started singing one of their war songs, and then with a shout, they rushed us. Our usual tactics cut them to ribbons, with little loss on our part. Since this was a pitched battle initiated by them, we took no prisoners, but left them all dead on the field, their finery covered with their blood.

Eventually we reached the town that had sent out the army, and they surrendered without any further ado. Their ruling class had been wiped out, but they seemed to be more at a loss than relieved. They were greatly confused when we didn't take them as slaves. Since the town was intact, I decided to have a look at it. The houses seemed to be either mud or wood with thatch roofs. The town had a central court around which were ball courts (where they played a game similar although more elaborate to that of the Taino) and platforms holding temples or the chief's house. These were made of elaborately painted blocks of stone with wood and thatch roofs. The paintings were in very bright colors and featured warriors, gods, rulers, or mythical beasts. The figures were quite well executed and animated, although some were anatomically preposterous. They had a real talent for using color. Many of their houses were also brightly painted, as was their pottery. The overall impact was quite cheerful. That was until we looked into the temples. These looked and smelled like charnel houses, with dried blood and gore smeared everywhere. There were piles of sculls and what looked like human skin that had had been dried. Smoking Mirror told me that the main Huaxteca god was Xipe Totec. This was a sort of spring god, connected with rain and planting. Then he told me that the usual sacrifice was accompanied with flaying of the victim, and the priest would wear the skin to symbolize the earth putting on its new skin of green in the spring. I mentioned to the town's new governor, Kahkewaquonabe, an Anishinabe, that he was not to allow any more of their bizarre religious practices. Also in the temple we found a small pile of their "books." These were written on a kind of bark paper in vibrant colors. They used the picture writing Tlacuectli had shown me long ago. The books dealt with astronomical observations and heroic legends—rather dry stuff.

It didn't look like Smoking Mirror's idea of us being mistaken for gods was working very well. Those that didn't fight to the death were given some pause by our appearance, and it may have caused more of them to choose life, but this was not as easy as he thought it would be. Although, to be fair, it might have been different if their leaders ever came out to talk to us before choosing to fight. The other strange thing about them was their refusal to act in concert with each other or at least resort to subterfuge to gain some advantage. It never happened; however, they always fought in the open or behind their town walls or later their citadels, and we never had to face more than one town and its villages at a time. Word began to drift in from the west that the same sort of thing was occurring with the mountain Huaxteca, although they did on occasion resort to ambush in the more rugged mountain passes. The terrain made progress a little more slow, but the cannon assured success against the towns every time.

We eventually got a clearer picture of the large river valley. It was formed by two major rivers joining just before they reached the coast. The northern one rose in the mountains in the west and snaked its way through the coastal plain generally east and south. The southern one turned out to drain the southwest limits of Huaxteca territory and be joined by many tributaries on its way to its rendezvous with the northern river. Between the two, a little west of their juncture was a fairly large lake. The land near the coast in this area and for some distance to the south sported vegetation as lush as that on the large islands of Aiti and Cuba, while previously the terrain was little different from that at the mouth of the Thanuge, more dry and tending to scrub vegetation, although increasingly responsive to irrigation as we moved south. It was obvious that these people heavily exploited the land, but again as in the north, there were no herds at all. They only domesticated a small breed of dog and the large pheasantlike bird. There were some deer, but no other large animals except for the rare incursion of the plains oxen. Of course, there were a lot of fish and other seafood to exploit, as well as a great deal of waterfowl, but one had to wonder how they could support so many people with so little meat. Even when they resorted to cannibalism, it was more ritualistic than predatory and thus rather limited. They seemed to thrive on mostly a combination of beans and the mondamin grain.

As we neared the rivers, the towns got quite large and the resistance even more fierce. Still, they really didn't have a chance and merely suffered even greater losses. One town on the southern bank of the northern river had to be completely wiped out. They never surrendered, even though we blew away their wall one side at a time, and then had to kill off the survivors as they ran at us from their burning houses. I had their temple blown up and completely leveled the town in hopes that such resistance would not recur. The only towns we were able to take without a fight were those that sent their armies out to meet us. Along the coast there were a few towns surrounded by lagoons that thought themselves to be safe from us, but cannon and rocket fire reduced them. The former exposed them to direct fire; the latter frightened them into surrender. The Cranes conducted that particular siege, and I sent a note of commendation for their commander, Khassar, for his clever use of cannon and rockets in a potentially difficult situation.

The Owls at this point were besieging a large town just south of the southern river. There had been no response to our siege when I arrived on the scene. I suggested that we send a Huaxteca forward to demand surrender in our name. A peasant was found and sent to the town with the message. In due time he returned with the unusual response that the chief of the town would come out to meet our leader. Since there was some risk that it was a trap, I insisted on meeting him. Smoking Mirror also wanted to come along and suggested the time had come to wear full regalia. I reluctantly put on the feathers and rode forward a bit with Smoking Mirror. From the town a pair of figures started forward. As they drew near, I could see that both were heavily tattooed and ornamented. Feathers and bangles hung all about them. They both had the nose tube and the dyed hair we had seen before. When we dismounted and stood before them, they gasped, exchanged looks, and sunk to their knees, bowing their heads to the ground.

"Do you come to surrender?" I asked in Nahual.

"Who are we to resist the gods?" the chief replied in the same language.

"Such considerations did not deter your neighbors," I replied.

"We are at your command." The chief kept his head on the ground.

"I am appointing a governor to rule in the Khan's name," I began. "You will obey him in every way without question. If any harm comes to him, you will all be destroyed. If you prove loyal and faithful, rule will return to you after a time. If you accept this, there is no changing your mind later. You will be held to this under pain of death. Do you still accept?"

"The gods command, their servants obey," the chief said.

"So be it," I said with finality and dismissed them.

I appointed Wihio, a quick-witted Dzitsiista who had long impressed me by his common sense and uncommon grasp of a situation. He also had a flair for language and already had a working knowledge of Nahual. I explained the situation to him and warned him to be careful. It was clear that they thought we were gods, and I wasn't at all sure that was a good idea. In any case, he should try to run the town like an Ordu, brooking no insubordination or questioning of his decisions. He could allow them to continue with their various cults, but was not to allow any human sacrifice. Their army should be sent out to accompany us as we move south. He could pick a strong guard to be with him. All should remain alert and keep me informed. If this "god" idea was as unwise as I thought it was, I wanted to know before we made the same mistake again. I sent him off, and we camped for the night outside the town. The next morning, their army marched out of the city to join us. Although they were on foot, they really didn't slow us down since we had them move directly south in a group while we had our men spread over a large area. The name of this first town to surrender completely was Panuco.

We continued southward receiving a few more towns' surrenders after sending in one of the Panuco warriors to demand surrender or after reducing their citadel positioned near the town and manned exclusively by warriors. A few times the unfortunate messenger warrior was cut down by the town, and we had to wipe them out, and a few times even the reduction of the citadel was not enough to induce surrender of the town. The citadels were just walled fortresses with supplies, but little else. It was a strange idea since an army could easily bypass the citadel and attack the town if he so desired. The Panuco warriors were quite loyal and fearless, making me regret even more that we were unable to win over more of the Huaxteca. I sent word that if any towns chose to talk before they fought, I should be sent for. It was only partially effective. Along the coast, the fighting was bitter and the slaughter great. In the mountains, there was little talk as well. Only inland along one of the tributaries of the southern river (the Panuco) did we find much willingness to talk. Smoking Mirror and I found ourselves shuttling between the Owls and the Cormorants and occasionally the Cranes. The Otters found them-selves on a narrow strip of land between the sea and a huge lake or lagoon. It was not heavily settled, but again the vegetation was lush and the resistance stiff, making for slow going.

In the west, the Pelicans and Horses had finally worked their way through the Huaxteca and had encountered elements of a less organized people speaking a language similar to that of the A'-a'tan and calling themselves the Ralamari. Since there were a few A'-a'tan among the Horses, communication was possible, and they agreed to send observers, spread the word about us among their neighbors, and help us find the remaining Huaxteca towns. They proved to be invaluable. Remarkably, they were able to run seemingly with-out effort over vast stretches of very rough terrain. Soon they were used instead of couriers to send messages between the two tumen, although they still sent couriers to report to me. The Ralamari also knew exactly where to find the Huaxteca towns, warned the Ordu about ambushes, and guided them around the traps. With all this help, the Ordu soon made very good progress and even had a few towns surrender after token resistance. By late winter, they were at the headwaters of the Panuco, and turning east back toward the coast. They had run into a people that lived in rather mean villages or towns and spoke another strange language. One of the Ralamari could speak their language, so communication was possible. They called themselves by the name of their village or their leader. They were hostile toward the Huaxteca whom they claim had displaced them. They were lighter skinned than the Ralamari, and lived by hunting and primitive agriculture. They had no tribal organization, but claimed that some people related to them lived in great cities farther south. Smoking Mirror said that they were elements of the Otomi. A few of them agreed to send along observers.

Near the southern end of Huaxteca country, we came upon four major towns that ruled over large areas. Two were near the coast, Tuxpan and Tuzapan, and two were well inland, Uexutla and Xiuhcoac. Tuxpan was very near the coast on a river, while Tuzapan was some twenty-five li up the river from Tuxpan but a little south of the river itself. Xiuhcoac was along a tributary of the Panuco that flowed north into that river. Uexutla was north and west of Xiuhcoac away from its river. The Otters found themselves fighting it out with Tuxpan. It was the town that had captured our merchants and had refused to surrender or even talk. It required a devastating bombardment before they finally gave in. The town was beyond repair and had to be abandoned, but the survivors admitted that the merchants had been sacrificed to their gods shortly after capture and their goods taken by the leaders. One of the survivors was of the priestly class and was executed in retribution for the murders. The rest were simple folk and were spared and resettled. Tuzapan, surrounded by the Cranes, agreed to talk, but it took us a few days to reach them. Because of the delay, a few hotheads had sortied out of the town and been quickly cut down. One would think it would have been a night sortie, but it was in broad daylight, with full regalia and song. When we arrived, the chief came out and as usual fell to the ground at the sight of the "gods" and apologized profusely for the hotheads. This was the largest town to surrender so far and, as it turned out, was on their southern frontier. South of their lands, beyond a row of hills were another, unrelated people called Totonacs.

The Owls reached the town of Uexutla and surrounded it with part of the tumen while detachments were sent out to deal with their subordinate villages. Resistance was bitter in the villages, and a large force attacked from the town as well. They never had much of a chance, but continued attacking out of the town in uncoordinated rushes. In the end, a pitiful band of survivors surrendered, and, since the town was too large for them, they were settled among the villages that had surrendered. The Owls also confronted Xiuhcoac. There was a citadel on a hill on one side of the town. The Owls had their Huaxteca auxiliaries guard the town while they surrounded and reduced the citadel. The defenders fought to the last man. Once the Owls moved over to surround the town itself, a negotiating team quickly came out to discuss terms. There was no need for an appearance by the "gods" as surrender was swiftlyselected.

A few more frontier towns had to be mopped up, and by early spring, we had completed our conquest of all the Huaxteca towns. I had been sending Kuyuk weekly reports of our progress along with maps of the area. His replies were generally encouraging and congratulatory. Since it took about a month to send dispatches to Kuyuk, his replies were understandably irrelevant until the one that arrived just as we were going into camps to rest up from our campaign before most of us would return. It said that by the time I received the dispatch, I would likely be finished with the Huaxteca. At that point I was to send the two most damaged tumen back home. The rest should prepare to sweep through the people south of the Huaxteca, the Totonacs. Since their terrain was heavily tropical, the Alligator and Parrot Tumen would be arriving soon to assist. He suggested that I leave two tumen among the Huaxteca and proceed against the Totonacs with the remaining four.

I was completely floored! I couldn't understand what provocation the Totonacs had made, since I had heard nothing. I showed the dispatch to Smoking Mirror. He had a rather knowing smirk on his face as he read the dispatch.

"I'm not surprised," he said handing it back to me. "I had the feeling Kuyuk planned to conquer this land, with or without provocation. The Huaxteca indiscretion was simply an excuse. What do you intend to do now, Raven?"

"Why, what I'm ordered, of course." I was puzzled by the question. "Do you feel that Kuyuk is attacking the Totonacs without provocation?"

"I do." He nodded. "But I bear them no affection. They are an insufferable lot, parading their wealth around and claiming to be the founders of the great old city in the high valley, Teotihuacán. I'll be happy to help you crush them, but only because I despise them, not because it is somehow 'justified.'"

"What do mean 'justified'?" I didn't understand his point. "It is a direct order to be obeyed, not a suggestion to be bandied about or 'justified.' What are you talking about?"

"Never mind, my friend." He shook his head almost sadly. "Of course, you will obey your orders, and I will help you."

He continued to bewilder me on occasion by questioning orders from Kuyuk, but in time it became moot. He didn't seem to grasp the concept of a Khan with absolute, unquestioned authority. I rather hoped his strange ideas didn't catch on with the men. But he was always faithful to me and without question most knowledgeable and helpful whenever he was with me.

I looked over the tumen and decided to send the Otters and the Pelicans back. I told the Horses to remain where they were on the Panuco River and set up camp. I had the Owls set up camp near the "border" river (I named it the Tuzapan) and the rest of us set up in the mountains on the frontier waiting for the replacement tumen. It was obvious Kuyuk had thought this out carefully, even sending us the most appropriately trained Ordu to deal with a tropical campaign. I wondered who had been keeping him informed and just what he planned for us to do ultimately. I would find out soon enough. I had barely gotten everyone in position when elements of the Parrots and Alligators began filing in. Among the latter was Chekika, the younger brother of the Calusa chief. He had risen quickly in the ranks and was a minghan commander. I was pleased to see a number of the fierce Calusa among the ranks. I put everyone into line, and we started south.

Oddly, the area closest to the sea was not always lush jungle, but there was a large band of it inland for some distance. The Parrots and Alligators dismounted and along with the Huaxteca auxiliaries began filtering into the jungle. I placed the Cranes and the Cormorants west of the jungle in what began as scrub plain but was soon replaced with rugged foothills and then precipitous mountains. The jungle cities tended to surrender after token resistance. Some of them claimed to be subordinate to other cities, but we insisted that they decide their fate on their own, and most surrendered. In time, the resistance began to stiffen and become more creative. Bravado was less important to the Totonacs than survival. It was here that the Parrot and Alligator Ordu proved their worth. Only once was an ambush undetected in time to thwart it. Because of terrain considerations I sent Smoking Mirror with the Parrots and Alligators while I stayed with the Cranes and Cormorants. We had fewer towns to contend with, but they were hard to reach and more easily defended. Still, a few rounds of artillery generally broke even the most stubborn resistance, but our losses were mounting. The Cormorants were getting the worst of it since they were in the far west and had to deal with the most rugged mountain terrain. I began to think we would need to develop a mountain Ordu to deal with this. Fortunately, most of the Totonac towns in the mountains were not large. The Cranes covered the area between the mountains and the jungles. There were some very large towns in this area and more than one of them resisted fiercely. In the end they all fell. One of these, with the impossible name, Tlatcauhquitepec, sent out a delegation to demand an explanation for the aggression. I disingenuously explained that they had somehow offended our Khan, and he demanded their complete submission to his rule or they would be destroyed. They appeared bewildered by my words, but after discussing it among themselves, they asked what would become of them if they did submit. I told them the usual, and they agreed to surrender. I hated to admit it even to myself, but I was sure Kaidu would never have ordered me to attack these people.

The scouts reported that we were nearing the Totonac frontier, so I went east with the Cranes to deal with the coastal plain, which the Parrots and Alligators had bypassed. Meanwhile the Cormorants mopped up along the confusing frontier along which it was hard to tell the tribal affiliation. I also had them garrison the more important mountain passes so that we wouldn't have to fight our way through them should the high valley of the Tolteca be our next target. The coastal plain also had some large cities. One of these, Cempoalla, surrendered without a struggle. It was quite a sight. The houses were plastered and some were covered with vibrant colors.

Much of the population turned out to see my staff and me enter. The men were slightly taller and more slender than the Huaxteca, but also resorted to tattooing and piercing their nose septa. They also pierced their earlobes and wore large ornaments there. Some even pierced their upper or lower lips for ornamental plugs like the Inuit, but more elaborate. They wore the usual loincloth, but also wore colorful cloaks. Many of them used the jaw of a strange fish with lateral rows of teeth as a sword and used the carapace of a large sea turtle for a shield. The women wore long brightly colored skirts and some wore cotton vests. In the center of the city was a huge walled square containing large temples, a ball court, and the residences of the city chief and the priests. All were made of highly polished and dressed stone and shone brilliantly in the sun. Oddly, the chief claimed that he was subordinate to the chief of Cotaxtla, a city well to the south of his city. He told me that my forces presented a more immanent danger than those of his master, so he quickly changed allegiance. This made me wonder about his sincerity, but he gladly accepted our appointed governor and sent his army to march with us. By early summer, we reached the limits of Totonac lands along the coast. Smoking Mirror joined me to report that the jungle Totonac towns had also been dealt with successfully. I asked him about Cotaxtla. He said that they had resisted most tenaciously and had to be virtually wiped out. He said that they had been about the strongest of all the Totonac cities.

I sent my final report to Kuyuk and wondered how much time we would have before the next campaign, unless this was all he wanted. Smoking Mirror assured me that he would order us to continue, and he hoped that it would be toward the cooler drier west and the Tolteca valleys rather than the steamy south and the Olmeca jungles. We didn't have long to wait. Barely a week after I had sent off my last report, our marching orders arrived. He was really quite good at calculating the length of these campaigns. This time he wanted us to ascend the mountains into the high plain and take the towns in the first valley, to the east of the valley of the Toltec cities. He suggested that I leave the Parrots and Alligators among the Totonacs and send back the most mauled of the other two tumen. The

Antelopes were on their way and should arrive within a few days of this message. I was surprised that he would send the Antelopes since they were the only Ordu in that part of the land, but had to admit, they were quite well versed in mountain campaigns. Also, it would be good to see Padraig again. I decided the Cormorants needed to return and moved the Cranes into their positions to replace them. I dismissed the Huaxteca but kept the Totonac auxiliaries, and sent scouts toward the target valley to reconnoiter while I waited for the Antelopes.

34

TEXCALLA, HUEXOTZINCO AND CHOLULA, 16 K
(PUEBLA-TLAXCALLA VALLEY, MEXICO, 1384)

Padraig and the Antelopes arrived within days of the departure of the Cormorants. I could hear them long before I could see them. Padraig had the men marching to the sound of his pipe instruments. Fortunately, they stopped before getting close enough to spook our horses. As he drew near, it appeared that he was very introspective and that something was troubling him. Not wishing to pry, I welcomed him warmly and expressed gratitude that his tumen had been sent since we had some difficult mountain terrain ahead of us. He smiled wanly and assured me his men were up to any challenge. We rode together in awkward silence toward the camp I had set up at the base of the mountains. Once in camp, I asked him into my tent and showed him the maps of our route up to the plateau. A little life came back into him as he studied the maps, but only a little. Finally, I had to ask.

"What is wrong, Padraig? Is all your family well?"

"Yes." He nodded. "They were all well when I left. But tell me, how well do you know our new Khan?"

"Not well at all. He is not his father, but he does seem to be decisive. Why do you ask?"

"Ogedai is up to something with the Salmon Ordu and Kuyuk approves, but won't tell me what it is and, in fact, forbade me from making any contact with the Salmon Ordu. He said it was too far away for me to lead adequately, and so he was putting it completely under Ogedai's command."

"But most of the Ordu are independent, and you always did give Ogedai a lot of latitude. Do you see this as a demotion?"

"No, not at all. I was only to advise Ogedai since he was inexperienced. But even from the beginning, I thought there was an excessive amount of dispatch sending between Kuyuk and Ogedai, even for father and son. Now, that Kuyuk is Khan, the dispatches have been replaced by wagons carrying sealed goods between them. It is, of course, none of my business—but why the secrecy? Why does no one know or admit knowing what is going on?"

"Goods? You don't suppose he is trading with the old land?"

"No, I thought of that. We have nothing they would want, and I can't imagine what we need from them. Anyway, the boats of the Northwest tribes are seaworthy, but I doubt they could travel that far, or carry enough goods to make the trip worthwhile. Besides, we are Mongols and left the old land because we had no future there."

"That is all true, but the Hanjen would trade with anybody, and so would the Koryo. We have some gold and silver and they have silk. It wouldn't take much of a ship to transport such non bulky items."

"Silk! But we don't need silk. The local cotton is wonderful, much better than the Hanjen cotton. But anyway I haven't seen much silk around. If he were getting it, wouldn't he wear it?"

"As to needing silk, trade has nothing to do with need and everything to do with want. As for not seeing any, he could be hoarding it. Not long after Smoking Mirror's father started trading with the Owl Ordu, Kuyuk's old command, gold ornaments appeared in profusion, and silk began to disappear. Paula mentioned it to me, but I never gave it much thought before."

"But even if he is trading with the Middle Kingdom, why the secrecy? I had thought we were leaving all the intrigue behind us."

"I don't know, unless it is because he knows most of us realize his father would not have approved. But perhaps I'm beginning to understand the reason for this campaign."

"Have you been sending gold back to Kuyuk?"

"I have sent any plunder salvaged from the destroyed towns. That is the custom. It has included quite a bit of gold so far."

"So, then, you are on a plundering expedition?"

"Plunder is only part of my mission. I suspect he will want me to conquer all of the large cities in this land. It could take years."

"There is no want of those wishing to participate. All the tumen are excited about joining the campaign. Kuyuk has assured them that they will all get the opportunity."

"All of the tumen?"

"So he told them."

"But there are at least thirty of them. Only nine have come so far."

"Thirty-two. At least four more are on the way to you now. They should be here by the time you finish with the cities on the first plateau."

"Then we will be here for years!"

"Probably."

I called in Smoking Mirror to share Padraig's information. He was not at all surprised, since he had already suggested as much, but was too polite to be smug. In fact, he seemed more sad than anything else. I told him he was far more perceptive than I, but that did not cheer him at all.

"I have finally come to know," he said, "who planted the idea for all this conquest in Kuyuk's heart. It was my father, Tlacuectli. If we are ordered to leave his town alone, it will be certain."

"His town?" I asked.

"Chalco," he said. "It was subjugated by Huexotzinco some years ago and lately has been engaged in a long war with the Tepanecas. We have already been ordered to take Huexotzinco along with the other cities that share its plateau. I suspect we will next be instructed to take every town in the great valley called Anahuac except Chalco. If we are, I will know it is all Tlacuectli's work. This will bring me shame. It is one thing to avenge wrongs or invite people to join you in peace, it is another to conquer them simply because they are between you and your real objective. As I told you before, we were justified to some extent in the Huaxteca campaign since we had to reach a town in the south and the northern towns would not permit us to pass. The Totonacs did nothing to deserve our attack, except for being obnoxious. And now we attack the people of the plateau. They are a proud and brave people. Many will die before they surrender. They deserve a better fate. So do some of the other towns farther along our path. But to think that the instigator of all this destruction was my own father."

"That would explain why Kuyuk seems to know so much about this area," I said. "We will know soon enough, I suppose. But, if you do not want to take part in this campaign, I will be glad to give you some other duty."

"No, my friend." He shook his head sadly. "I made my choice a long time ago. One does not leave his tribe because he dislikes the new chief. I know I am helpful to you and will stay as long as you want me. After all, you have not changed at all. I've come to understand you completely, even when I don't agree with you. Also, the next Khan will likely be better."

I thanked him for his loyalty, for he was invaluable. Once all the Antelopes had had a chance to rest up from their long journey, we started up the mountain passes. Our path was along the well-used merchant trail, but it was not easy. Often we had to dismount to get up the steeper parts. There were a few losses of horses and men on this trek. Visible for much of the trip was a huge mountain (it was called Citlaltepetl locally) to the south, its peak covered with snow, even now in the summer. It was revered as the first part of the land to be touched by the rising sun. There were a few small towns along the trail, but these offered no resistance and agreed to recognize the Khan as their ruler. I had the feeling they would have agreed as much to any passing army. The trail continued to climb into the rugged mountain range and eventually, after several days, brought us to a rocky, almost treeless pass. The wind whipped around us driving clouds past us like a misty blizzard. Once through the pass we debauched into a bleak volcanic plateau. A few shrinking lakes broke up the severe landscape. It took almost three days to cross this plateau. On the second day, we passed a quiet volcano standing like a sentinel before the largest lake. Again there were only a few small villages on the plateau whose people also pledged eternal loyalty to the Khan with as much sincerity as had the people in the mountains. Needless to say, I didn't leave any governor with them.

The merchant trail led us into another pass, which brought us to a town called Zautla. The town was not inclined to resist us and readily accepted a governor and a small garrison. The town's name meant "jar" in Nahual, and there was quite a pottery industry there filling the air with smoke from kilns. The people were only partially Nahual speaking, mostly the ruling classes. The rest spoke another tongue we had encountered before and had began to encounter more and more as we went along, Otomi. I engaged H'donwe, a young man who spoke both languages, to go with us as an interpreter. He insisted that the Otomi speakers were the original inhabitants and the Nahual speakers the upstart invaders. Smoking Mirror was not amused by the assertion, although I noticed he didn't actually refute it.

Beyond Zautla the trail led us through a jagged, rough series of ravines. This slowed our progress considerably, but we eventually reached a town on the far side called Ixtacamaxtitlan. It was situated on very high cliffs choking off the narrow valley through which we were traveling. These people proved to be willing to let us pass on unmolested as long as we didn't make any demands on them. Unfortunately, I couldn't do that. I explained to them that we could hardly leave such a position behind us if it was hostile, so they would either have to join us or we would have to destroy them. They pointed out that their town would prove most difficult to take. I had the men send up a few rockets into the town and had some of the men quickly scramble up the nearby cliffs and haul a few cannon up with them. Once these began to lob rounds into the town, the surrender was quick. I garrisoned the town strongly, even leaving a few cannon. I then ordered the town's army to go with us, to prevent any treachery.

We followed a small river upstream to our target plateau. I waited a few days so that all our train could catch up and we could rest up a bit. I sent a few scouts out to look over the land and see if we would be opposed. They soon came back to report a small force encamped nearby. I sent one of the Ixtacamaxtitlan auxiliaries to them to demand their surrender. He returned bearing a few of their weapons. This was their way of declaring war. I set up sentries and sent the scouts out again to make sure this group wasn't part of a trap. They reported that the small force was unsupported, but a larger force was encamped on a large open plain a day's ride away.

While they were watching it, more warriors were joining it, but they weren't sending any out. They didn't seem to be too interested in posting sentries either. A few of the scouts remained to keep an eye on the camp. Meanwhile, I sent the Antelopes on a wide sweep that would bring them behind the large camp, and I took the Cranes directly to the nearby group.

They, too, were in a large open spot surrounded by forest, and as we came through the trees into their view, they formed up into a massed front and waited for us to get into position. We quickly rode around them, surrounding them. This puzzled them and they began to form a confused circle facing outward toward us. With a yell, they rushed at us. Most wore the quilted cotton "armor" colored yellow or white and were armed with the obsidian-lined club, although a few used bows and some even used slings. These last were the only ones that did any damage, since their missiles alone reached our lines. The rest were cut down in a merciless rain of arrows. I sent in the auxiliaries to finish off the wounded, gather up our arrows and, at Smoking Mirror's insistence, burn the dead. We continued on most of the way to the large encampment. The next morning, we filed into the plain on the side opposite the camp. With much drumming and horn and whistle blowing, they began to form up in massed ranks behind banners sporting a golden eagle with wings stretched out. Meanwhile, I set up my cannon in front of each of the massed ranks. Once they were ready, they sent one of their leaders up to present us with the ceremonial weapons. Smoking Mirror and I accepted in full "god" regalia. Our appearance and the presence of the horses made a deep impression on the presenter, but he swallowed back his fear and handed us the weapons wordlessly. We took the weapons, cut them in half with our swords, and handed them back to him. He accepted the pieces and hurried back to his lines.

There was a heated discussion on his return, but nothing came of it. Just as they started the din before their charge, the Antelopes began driving through their camp behind them and wiping out all their rear guard and camp followers. They had already started to rush us, however, before any of them became aware of the attack in their rear. As soon as they were close enough, we began tearing large gaps in their ranks with the cannon. The shock left them milling around in confusion long enough to get a second round. This shattered the attack, and they turned to flee only to find the Antelopes cutting off their retreat and arrows pouring into them from front and rear. Only a few were allowed to escape; all the rest were cut down where they stood or as they ran. I deliberately hadn't completely surrounded them, so that the survivors would spread panic and make the task easier for us.

I looked over the battlefield. The oddest thing about it was all the feathers. It was as if we had slaughtered a huge flock of very gaudy birds rather than an army. Otherwise, those still recognizable as human wore the eagle and ocelotl costumes we had seen before or other complicated costuming or more often just the quilted cotton. Again, Smoking Mirror prevailed on me to burn the dead warriors in a large pyre. This delayed us a while since there were so many, but it meant a lot to him. He mentioned that they would also have appreciated a piece of jade in their mouths, but he thought that practice was not as important since they had died in battle. I decided I didn't want to know about what all that was.

Again I sent the scouts out and they reported back that much of the more open countryside had been abandoned. The roads and pathways were clogged with people fleeing us. Many of them were heading to one or another of the large cities on the plateau, but others were hiding in the woods around the periphery of the plateau or hurrying across the mountains to the great central plateau called Anahuac. The first major town we came to was named Texcalla. It was not abandoned, and we quickly surrounded it. The scouts reported no army marching to its relief, and, in fact, no army was marching anywhere on the plateau. Everyone was holed up in the larger cities and towns. There did seem to be a lot of courier activity around the strongest city on the plateau, Huexotzinco, some distance to the southwest. Once we were in position around Texcalla, a delegation came out from the city. It consisted of an elaborately garbed man flanked by two older men and escorted by a small group of guards. As Smoking Mirror and I went toward them with an equal guard, he explained that the man was their chief and the older men were his advisors. He and I were in full regalia, and they found our appearance quite unsettling. The three principles left the guard behind for the final approach. We dismounted and approached them.

"It is true then," the chief began, "that Quetzalcoatl and Tezcatlipoca have ended their feud and come from the north and the east riding large shaggy deer to conquer the center of the One World? Our seers did not foresee your reconciliation or your return, or we would not have dared to oppose you. Perhaps a suitable sacrifice and gifts for all your warriors would turn away your wrath."

"You seem to persist in misunderstanding our purpose," I replied. "We are not interested in sacrifices or gifts. The Khanate of the Blue Sky is expanding to encompass your plateau and all the cities and towns on it. If you do not submit and accept a governor to rule until you prove yourselves to be loyal, we will destroy you all and your city."

"Would it be presumptuous," one of the older men interjected, "to ask what the Khanate of the Blue Sky is?"

"It is an understandable question," I had to admit, "and one not yet asked of me during this campaign. A Khanate is an empire ruled by a Khan. A Khan is the title of a Mongol ruler. The Khanate is called the Blue Sky because the Mongol god, Tengri, is symbolized by the blue sky."

"Might one further inquire," the other older man wheezed, "who the Mongols might be and whence they have come."

"The Mongols are 'the brave,'" I snapped. "They come from many tribes in many lands. If you prove worthy, you too may become Mongols."

"Enough questions." The chief silenced his advisors. "We cannot resist your forces in battle. We accept your directives without question. Appoint your governor, and we will honor him in my place and obey him without question. I only ask that you accept us into your 'Mongols' and end the war between us. I place my own fate in your hands."

"Your fate and that of your city depends on you," I replied. "If, indeed, your people obey and respect our governor, they may become Mongols, you may regain your position as head of your city, and we will withdraw our governor and his garrison. If there is any treachery or disobedience, you will all die horribly and your city will be totally destroyed. Do you still choose to submit?"

"We do," the chief said.

I appointed Michikinikwa, a Twanhtwanh to be governor. He had been part of my entourage for some time and had always shown courage and good judgment. He needed both for this job, and he did not let me down. I gave him a few hundred men as a garrison and as usual had the Texcalla army (or what was left of it) join me as auxiliaries. At this point, I dismissed the Totonaca auxiliaries, but kept the rest. The chief pressed us to visit the town so that we could see "our" temples. The town had a rather new look about it, and it turned out it had been founded only several years before. "Our" temples proved to be subordinate to that of Mixcoatl, the main deity in the city. Otherwise, they were the usual charnel houses attended by the usual disgustingly filthy and bloody priests. We did not tarry. We quickly subdued a few smaller towns near Texcalla, then marched toward the main power on the plateau, Huexotzinco. This city dominated much of the plateau and had also spread its influence west into the valley of Anahuac. I assumed that once I took it, most of its subordinate towns would surrender also. As we entered their territory, the scouts reported deserted villages between the city and us, but a very large army was gathering before it. Again the scouts looked in vain for a trap or any support or reserve forces. There was only the army and behind it the city. We approached the city like a malevolent dust storm across the dry treeless plain. We camped for the night in sight of the city and posted sentries. Again there was no sneak attack in the night.

The enemy formed up their ranks and waited patiently for us to get into position. Their force was half again larger than ours, so I decided on the old Mongol entrapment strategy. I left the Antelopes behind and had them split in two and withdraw to the right and left just out of sight. I sent the auxiliaries well to the rear to await my call, and then I went forward with the Cranes presenting the enemy with a force apparently only about one-third the size of their own. We stayed well away from them and set up our cannon before the largest masses of them. We kept the artillery horses at the ready to pull away the cannon quickly. The men remained mounted with bows at the ready.

Before long, the masses before us began to move forward. Huge drums roared drowning out horns and whistles and the shouts of the warriors. Masses of figures led by the most gaudily attired surged toward us with no attempt to dress lines or keep ranks. Our horses and men remained unmoved by the spectacle. As soon as they reached cannon range, the first volley ripped gaping holes in their ranks. Frenzied, they rushed on oblivious to the destruction. A second volley shuddered into their lines, but again they surged forward. I gave the signal and the cannon were quickly hitched to the horses and pulled back to the first fall back position. As soon as the enemy was in arrow range, we fired a few volleys into them and withdrew following the cannon to the rear.

We set up the cannon about two li behind our original line. We kept stopping and firing a volley of arrows into the enemy every hundred paces or so as we moved to the new line. In spite of their mounting losses, they kept coming after us. Again the cannon got off two rounds into them before withdrawing again about another two li. Once more, the men poured arrows into the now-ragged ranks. Occasionally one of their missiles (usually a stone) found our ranks. We again conducted a fighting withdrawal to the next cannon line. When we reached our third line, I held the cannon fire and had the men pick off the by now totally scattered warriors as they drew into arrow range. Eventually some of their leaders saw the problem and began holding the by now winded men back out of arrow range to reform masses. As soon as their masses were large enough, I had the cannon open up on them again. Their frenzy spent, they began to falter, and some broke to the rear, while others continued forward, and more were still coming up. To add to the confusion, the Antelopes appeared on their flanks and rear firing arrows into them.

There was a moment amid all the confusion when I could see they were defeated. It was as though there had been a short pause in the action, giving them a chance to notice the hopelessness of their situation. I could see their battle madness giving way first to surprise, then fear, and then panic. Some still stoically rushed forward only to fall to our arrows, while the rest turned and ran to the rear. But it was too late for them. A few more rounds were fired from the cannon, but then the men put away their bows and charged, hacking away at the fleeing enemy with sword, axe, or club. I sent for the auxiliaries to clean up behind us and again brought the cannon forward. Very few of the enemy reached the city walls, and they were those who had either not advanced with their fellows in our wake or had not advanced very far—in other words, the least brave. We surrounded the city and set up cannon at each gate in the wall just before dark. The funeral pyre of their dead lit up the night with an angry red glow. A lightning storm far to the north enhanced the unsettling spectacle for the people in the city.

The next morning, a delegation came out from the city. It consisted only of old men with a few guards. As we approached, they prostrated themselves before us and begged mercy for the city. They identified themselves as the former ruler's advisors. He, the great, all conquering Xayacamachan and all the leaders of the people were dead. There were only a handful of men in the city. It could not be defended, and they were surrendering it to us. Even now they were removing all the valuables from the town to present to us. If they were not enough, perhaps we would consider taking some of them as slaves, or as sacrificial victims. I told them that we were not interested in slaves or sacrificial victims, but would take their treasure for our Khan. I appointed a governor and gave him a few hundred men and as usual took what was left of their army with me. Then I ordered the elders to go to each of the towns subordinate to theirs and urge them to surrender to us immediately. They agreed, but explained that the subordinate towns only paid them tribute and supplied warriors; they were not slaves and could refuse to submit. I told them that as long as they returned with the answer, no harm would come to them no matter what that answer was. They departed at once.

The auxiliaries remained outside the city cleaning up the battlefield under close supervision, while the Ordu went into camp just south of the city. I sent the scouts out as usual, but they reported back nothing of note. Eventually, the elders began returning from their mission. Most of them reported full and total submission to us, but a few towns wanted to think about it for a while, and Chalco wanted to know what we planned to do about the Tepaneca army that was even now fighting them. I sent them back a message that if they joined us, we would protect them, if they refused, we would destroy them before the Tepaneca had the chance. Of course, I had not yet been ordered into the Anahuac Valley, but since Chalco paid tribute to Huexotzinco and I was sure we would be ordered into the valley, I was curious as to what their response would be and couldn't resist. Also, I wondered if they were aware of us from Tlacuectli. Significantly, the next largest city on the plateau, Cholula, surren-dered immediately and invited me to take possession of "my" city. Smoking Mirror explained that the principal cult in Cholula was to Quetzalcoatl, my godly alter ego. I sent Padraig and the Antelopes to clear up all the small towns we had missed on the plateau while I took the Cranes toward Cholula, accepting the surrender of any of the still-inhabited towns between Huexotzinco and it.

Cholula was southeast of Huexotzinco, and there was quite a scattering of towns between and around them. A lone snow-capped volcano marked the eastern border of the plateau while two very high and also snow-capped volcanoes formed a very stark western border. The locals called the north one Iztaccihuatl and the south one Popocatepetl ("White Lady and Smoking Mountain"). The latter was indeed smoking but not erupting. As we approached Cholula, we could see what looked like a mountain in its midst. It proved to be the temple mound. It was by far the highest such mound I ever saw in all my travels. I cannot imagine how long it took them to build it, or, for that matter, why they built it. The city was ruled by two priests, and they prevailed upon me to climb up to the temple and see "my" representation. It was a nicely worked image, but not much of a likeness. From the look and smell of the place, it was obvious that human sacrifice was quite common here in spite of Smoking Mirror's contention that Quetzalcoatl did not approve of it. I asked the ruler-priests why they did such things to "honor" a god who opposed the practice. They insisted that they had been guided by a vision to take up the practice and, indeed, the victims were honored to be sacrificed, but, of course, they would do as I wished. I wished the practice abandoned and told them to clean up the stinking temple, and henceforth only sacrifice fruits of the soil. Smoking Mirror never said a word but wore an irritating smirk most of the day.

While we were still in Cholula, a courier came from Kuyuk. The message confirmed all our suspicions. The Oxen, Osprey, Otters, Wildcats, and Beavers would soon join us. We were to send back the Cranes, then proceed into the Valley of Anahuac and take all the cities. Only Chalco was not to be attacked if it resisted. The others, especially those on the western side of the large lake in the valley, were to be shown no mercy. I was instructed to be particularly leery of the ruler of Azcapotzalco, Tezozomoc. I shared the note with Padraig, who had just rejoined us, and with Smoking Mirror. The latter explained that the Tepanecas, whose leader was Tezozomoc and whose principal city was Azcapotzalco, ruled the cities on the western side of the lake. It was he and his allies that were trying to take over Chalco. They would prove to be the strongest foe in the valley and perhaps should be an early target.

It was in Cholula that I found out what Kuyuk was doing with silk. Some of the highest classes were draped in it when they presented themselves to us. I asked where they got it, and they said it was a very costly material spun by the gods in the western sea. A Chalco merchant had acquired it only after a long and perilous journey. They had paid dearly for it, but mostly with gold, which seemed to be all that these sea gods wanted. Smoking Mirror blanched at his father's pitch, while Padraig rolled his eyes in disbelief. I managed to keep a straight face and thanked them for the information, adding that I had seen the material before. They offered it to me, but I declined. More silk turned up in the plunder from Huexotzinco, and we continued to see it occasionally (only draped upon the wealthy) as we went along. Meanwhile word reached me from the coast that Tlacuectli had passed through on his way southeast to trade with the Olmeca and the Maya. He was carrying silk and making no secret of it.

The tumen began to arrive in late summer. They were quite spent from their long trip, and I gave them a few days to rest. Meanwhile, I sent back the Cranes and gave the Antelopes the garrison duty on the plateau. Padraig set up his main garrison in Huexotzinco since it was most centrally located. Word of the surrender of all the remaining towns once subject to Huexotzinco came in while the troops were resting. Even Chalco responded to what proved to be my empty threat and invited us to accept them into the Khanate, and coincidentally help drive away the Tepanecas.

Just before we started to move west, we received a curious caller. He was named Acamapichtli and was the Cihuacoatl (a sort of religious leader, although the word meant "snake woman") of the Tenocha, a group that served the Tepaneca. He had been sent, bearing gifts, by Tezozomoc to greet us and thank us for destroying the might of the Huexotzinco once and for all. The One World was a better place now. Having accomplished this worthwhile task, would we consider allying with him to remove similarly unpleasant groups from the Valley of Anahuac? He suggested we could sweep the eastern and northern shores of the central lake while he finished off the south. Then, he would be honored to help us administrate the valley while we went on to greater things. Of course, he would like to have a look at our marvelous weapons whose reputation had reached him and perhaps we would give him some as a present to cement our eternal friendship. He was also prepared to offer me one of Tezozomoc's daughters for a wife. One had to admit, this one could have ruled in the old land.

Acamapichtli seemed to be much less equipped with guile, and I pried a few bits of information out of him. His town's service to Tezozomoc was necessitated by their position on one of two adjacent islands in the shallow waters off the western shore of the lake. The other island was also in Tezozomoc's service. The people on both islands were from a tribe called the Mexica, not related to the Tepaneca, and although the tribute they paid Tezozomoc was harsh, they had proven to be valuable mercenaries for him. Tezozomoc had named his son, Cuacuauhtzin, to be Tlatoani (ruler, although the word meant "speaker") of all the Mexica and had allowed them to conquer and receive tribute from Xochimilco, a town on the southern shore of the lake, as well as three towns on a peninsula that extended into the southern part of the lake from the eastern shore. The picture was becoming rather complicated, but I told him that his mission as defined by Tezozomoc was in vain, but he could spare his own people any harm from us if he could convince them to join us freely, before we come into conflict. I explained that if they did that, his people would not be harmed, and he would be left to rule, but subject to any orders from our Khan. I offered that such orders usually consisted of sharing surpluses in time of famine and providing warriors in time of war. He replied that he would discuss our offer with his council in the southern island (Tenochtitlan) and reply when our troops reached the first of "his" cities. He assured me that the northern island, Tlatelolco, was the seat of Cuacuauhtzin and was fiercely loyal to him, since he was his father's military commander. I thanked him for his honesty and information and sent him back with Tezozomoc's gifts untouched.

The hunting in the southern lands had not been very good. There was nothing bigger than deer to hunt and the large pheasant and small dogs were the only domesticated animals. I had sent word with the Cormorants that we be sent the dried strips of the plains oxen that had become a staple among all who hunted the animal. The five new Ordu had brought some with them and more would be on its way. That proved fortunate because the hunting kept getting worse, except for all the waterfowl on the lakes. Once all the troops were rested, we started on our way. The road would lead us right between the two volcanoes.

35
ANAHUAC, 16 K
(VALLEY OF MEXICO, 1384)

It was early fall when we left our camp near Cholula. Because of the relative narrowness of our trail, I had the tumen leave one at a time a day apart. I went with the first one, the Oxen. I had scouts out in every direction, but so far nothing untoward had been reported back to me. Not far west of Cholula, we entered a mostly oak forest. The hardwoods soon gave way to pines as we ascended the slopes between the two volcanoes. It was growing quite cold as we climbed, so I thought it best we camp among the trees, for some protection from the wind. The next morning, we left the trees behind us, and before long clouds were also below us. Above was only the cold, open, sparsely grassy pass and the two snow-covered volcanoes. Eerily, a localized storm dropped fresh snow on the southern peak, but the pass remained clear. As we neared the crest of the pass, the wind began to probe us with icy fingers. The cold made breathing difficult for many of our auxiliaries and some of the Oxen as well, but I had been through far worse and found it rather invigorating. Smoking Mirror did not enjoy the passage at all and looked on my cheerful demeanor as quite inexcusable. We regained the tree line on the other side in time to camp that night. The following day, we descended the western slopes of the volcanoes and turned northwest reaching the city of Amecameca by dusk.

This city had been a tributary of Huexotzinco and had already agreed to join us. The leaders came out to greet us and invite us into the city. I went in with a few of my staff and some guards but had the rest of the Ordu camp outside the city. I informed my hosts that we would be expecting their army to join us on this campaign, and they quickly agreed, although they pointed out that it had been somewhat reduced by the unpleasantness outside of Huexotzinco.

In truth, I was able to secure very few warriors from that plateau, since so many had fallen in battle. It presented no hardship, however, since I only had them along to prevent them from making any mischief in my rear. Well, to be fair, they were handy for doing the dirty work after battle. We waited for the other tumen to join us, and then I left behind a small contingent to "protect" the city before moving on.

Beyond Amecameca, the pine forest gave out, and we crossed an old barren volcanic flow eventually reaching another newly allied city, Tlalmanalco. The next day, we reached Chalco (which was actually a group of four cities very close together) near the eastern shore of the southern finger of the central lake. Oddly enough, even though the lake was continuous and pinched by the shoreline into three sections, the locals saw it as divided into five parts. This southern finger was called Lake Xochimilco in the western part and Lake Chalco in the eastern part. It was all fresh water, nourished by gushing mountain streams and natural springs, and was used extensively for what were called chinampa. These were a sort of artificial island used to cultivate food and flowers. The people made the rectangular islands by pounding stakes into the lakebed and lashing them together with vines. Then mud and reeds were dredged from the shallow lakebed onto the "island" until a planting surface was achieved above the water line. The chinampa were taking over much of the shoreline of the southern part of the lake and were very productive. The central and largest part of the lake was called Lake Texcoco. It was mostly clear, fresh water in the south, becoming increasingly muddy and brackish in the north. There were also chinampas in the southern part of this "lake." The northern part of the lake was called Lake Xaltocan in the south and Lake Tzumpanco in the north. Its water was brackish and of a reddish hue. It could not support the chinampa, but teemed with waterfowl and rather small fish.

The leaders of Chalco made us welcome. The people also were glad to be finished with the long war with the Tepaneca and greeted us as deliverers. Their enthusiasm was enhanced when they realized we required no tribute of them, just the usual men in time of war and food in time of famine. And, of course, they would not be allowed to fight any wars on their own. They genuinely seemed war weary, and I could almost see why Tlacuectli went to such lengths to free them of war. I asked them only for a token force of their best warriors for auxiliaries and again posted a garrison with instructions to train the remaining Chalco warriors in our ways of battle. Smoking Mirror had not been to Chalco for some years, but he remembered his father's house, and took me to meet his relatives. His father had three other children, all younger than Smoking Mirror, but all young adults. They were so different from Smoking Mirror in both appearance and demeanor as to seem not even vaguely related. Still, they were all cordial and expressed delight to see him again after such a long time. They were all merchants or married to merchants and were quite excited that the Mongols were making the One World safe for trade. We didn't stay long.

The lake was dotted with islands that often had independent cities or towns on them. This complicated our task a bit, but I quickly got the Beaver Tumen to equip themselves with dugout boats while the rest of us marched west along the southern shore of the lake in a broad swath making sure we visited each city and town between the lake and the mountains to the south. The scouts were quite busy, and they reported that the Tepaneca army was withdrawing from the southern shore of the lake and moving northward along the western shore. In due time, we reached the Mexica tributary called Xochimilco ("Flower Garden") the apparent inventors of the chinampa. They opened their city to us without a hint of resistance, but could say nothing of the intentions of the Mexica. By now the Beavers had their boats ready, and I ordered them to deal with the island cities in this southern part of the lake. The largest of these were Xico and Cuitlahuac. Neither resisted once we explained there would be no tribute. We sent their armies to assist the Beavers.

By mid fall, we had reached the southwestern edge of the lake and turned north. At this point, we were approached by another delegation from Tezozomoc. Cuacuauhtzin, his son and military leader, led this one. He came bearing more gifts and to welcome us into Tepaneca territory. The nearby towns had been abandoned for our army's convenience. His father invited us to take them over.

Then perhaps my staff and me would come to Azcapotzalco as his honored guests and take our pick of his daughters and those of his nobles to cement our very necessary alliance. He had gotten wind of an evil conspiracy involving several neighboring people and felt that if we worked in concert, all their plans could be thwarted. It had come to his attention that the perfidious Tarascans were marshalling their forces to invade from the west. They had enlisted the aid of the evil Mixteca from the southeast who had designs on the very plateau we had just taken. Moreover, they were bribing the wild Chichimeca to raid from the north to further destabilize the situation. All this was inspired by the diabolical ruler of the godforsaken Alcolhua, a vile, untrustworthy race that occupied the eastern shore of the lake. This demon, Quinatzin, was determined to rule all of Anahuac because he claimed some vague relationship with the great Xolotl, Tezozomoc's own grandfather, who had once ruled the entire valley. His intention was to get us to weaken ourselves by destroying the Tepaneca, then stand back and watch while we were cut apart by the invaders. After that, he would first side with the victor, and then turn on him at the right moment.

He suggested that instead of playing into Quinatzin's hands, we seize the initiative and first help him destroy the evil Alcolhua; then while he protected our rear from the Chichimeca, we could divide our forces and take the battle to the both the Tarascans and the Mixteca before they were ready to attack. A great victory was assured, but should we need any help, he would surely rush to our aid. We could trust him completely.

The man had to be a genius to come up with such an imaginative story. If, indeed, we were total strangers who knew nothing of the situation, we might be drawn into his plans. But Smoking Mirror quickly informed me that the Tarascans were rulers of a small basin far to the west, the Mixteca fought among each other as much as the Huaxteca did, the Chichimeca always raided into this valley, and, indeed, most of its inhabitants had some of their blood in their veins, and, finally, Quinatzin was the direct descendant of Xolotl (also a Chichimeca), while Tezozomoc was related through his mother. I really hoped I would get to meet Tezozomoc; he was truly unique in this land. I thanked Cuacuauhtzin for all his information as well as his kind offer, but said it did not coincide with our orders. Since his father was so determined to ally with us, he would no doubt be willing to swear his allegiance to our Khan and turn over his army to me. Any moves by neighboring tribes would have to be dealt with as they occurred, since we could only invade other lands when we were instructed to do so. If this resulted in greater casualties, it was out of my hands. There was, of course, no need for potential allies to desert towns in our path. After all, we might get the impression that we were looked upon as invaders. While he had been able to deliver his message with an appropriately grave air, he was unable to answer my points, and said he would have to report back to his father. I assured him that he would find us closer when he returned, since I planned to continue north. I kept the gifts this time, to send on to Kuyuk, but offered nothing in return.

As we moved on, the first of the Tepaneca towns we reached was called Tlapan. It was completely deserted, as were the next two, Huipulco and Coyoacan. These were all good-sized towns, and their complete abandonment seemed rather haunting. As we left the last town behind, we were approached by another embassy. This one came from the south. The Tlahuica, a people living just south of this valley beyond the bordering mountains, had heard about us and wanted to make peace while it was possible to get good terms. The chief of their principle city, Cuauhnahuac, offered me his daughter, as well as many gifts to form an alliance with them. I told the embassy the usual conditions for joining us and held their gifts pending their acceptance of our conditions. I promised to return them, should they reject our conditions and leave them in peace until instructed otherwise. I couldn't wait to write Paula about all these marriage offers I was receiving. No doubt she would have something to say about them that would make Yesui proud. I could almost hear the latter's cackle.

The scouts were spread far and wide and no reports of activity came in from the west, the far north, or the southeast. In time our scouts reported back that there was a large concentration of warriors in the forests to our immediate north, around a hill called

Chapultepec ("Grasshopper"), and an even larger concentration trying to conceal themselves a little beyond them, farther north. Finally, I was going to encounter a trap. I immediately assumed the first group was supposed to resist us stubbornly, then fall back, first in order, then in apparent panic. We would then follow them in loose order, and suddenly the reserve force would spring up and the fleeing force would turn and join them to crush our now strung-out line. Unfortunately, they hadn't taken the speed of the horses into account or our superior firepower. Still, it was nice to find a slight challenge. As it turned out, it was even a better trap than was apparent. The Mexica were supposed to cross the lake by boat at night and cut off our retreat or fall on our rear as events warranted. I received a message from Acamapichtli outlining his orders and suggesting that he instead come over and join us. I thanked him for the intelligence and congratulated him on a wise decision, but told him to stay at home and defend his island from any Tepaneca assault. It was then that his messenger told me that while the Tenocha, his Mexica, would join us, the other Mexica, the Tlatelolca, would remain true to their Tepaneca overlords. Indeed, he had not mentioned anything to them about our offer. I told him to feign a departure but return to his city, since we would consider any boat traffic on our front to be hostile.

Remarkably, Tezozomoc wasn't content with setting his little trap; he had to make sure I went into it to his best advantage. Again Cuacuauhtzin came to see me. This time he came to announce that Tezozomoc had indeed decided to join us. He was sending a large gift to us by boat that very night. He regretted to report that a group of Chichimeca had infiltrated into the woods around Chapultepec spring, but he had sent his army south to crush them, and they should fall on them in the next few days. Of course, should we be impatient, perhaps we would want to drive them north into the Tepaneca army instead. We were closer after all. He also heard that the evil Alcolhua were marching on Chalco, and perhaps we should send some of our forces to meet that threat. Further, it had been reported that the vanguard of the Tarascan invasion was already at Tecaxic (a city to the west just over the surrounding mountains).

We may want to send some troops there. In any case, his father was readying Azcapotzalco to receive me and promised an unforgettable reception.

I decided that it was best to respond in kind so Tezozomoc would treat us with a little more respect in the future. I told his son that I was glad his father had decided to join us, and I was looking forward to meeting him and enjoying the reception in Azcapotzalco. I thanked him for the gifts he was sending by boat and promised to have porters ready to meet the flotilla, perhaps at Huipulco, since it had the better port facilities. I appreciated the explanation for the strange activity near Chapultepec, and we would indeed flush the invaders out the next day. I also thanked him for warning me about the Alcolhua and the Tarascans. Since I had nothing more to fear from the Tepaneca, I would, indeed, send forces west and east to meet these threats and continue on with only one of my tumen. He seemed relieved at my words and left quite happy.

That evening I had rafts loaded with combustibles strung out across the "mouth" of the southern part of the lake and had the Beavers in their boats at the ready. Meanwhile, I had the Oxen, the Osprey, and the Otters march loudly and conspicuously west, then quietly drop the Otters off to cover the west flank while the others made a wide arc north and east around the two forces before us. I advised the Beavers to move north on the lake when they were finished with the Tlatelolca. Keeping only the Wildcats with me, I moved north into the "trap" while it was still dark. Near midnight, the lake was lit up by the flaming rafts as the Beavers made short work of the prospective infiltrators. As soon as we were near enough to the enemy, I had rockets shot off through the forest and over the hill. The result was complete panic as the Tepaneca streamed to the north. We followed cautiously, since I didn't want a general engagement until first light. Very few of them remained in the woods to attack us as we moved through their position. We halted near their second position and waited for dawn.

As the rising sun lit up the scene, no sign of the enemy was apparent. The land was broken with ravines and lightly forested, but occasional vague movement would just catch one's eye. We waited patiently and soon the Beavers formed their boats just offshore and began lobbing arrows into anyone visible to them. Next, the Otters came into view along the western flank, and finally with a lot of screams and shouts coming from the north, I assumed the Oxen and Osprey were in position. Unable to wait any longer, the Tepaneca rose out of their concealments and turned to fight their way north. It was the logical thing to do, but in battle one does not always use logic. It certainly made our work easy. My Wildcats attacked them in the rear, the Otters and the Beavers harried their flanks, and they rushed into the oncoming Oxen and Osprey. The slaughter of the enemy was staggering, but the close fighting cost us a fair number of casualties as well, very many wounded, and over a hundred dead.

We surrounded their next major town, Tlacopan, but they quickly surrendered. Once more we received a messenger from Tezozomoc in the person of one of his advisors. This was an old man dressed in silk and feathers but hard to understand since he had no teeth. Tezozomoc did not disappoint me, as he greatly lamented the terrible misunderstanding that led our great people into conflict. He swore allegiance to the Khan and offered to come at once and bow down before me, his representative. He would empty his treasury to send to the Khan and begged us to accept his abject surrender and if possible spare their great capital, Azcapotzalco, from the quite understandable but perhaps misguided wrath of my army. I explained to the old man that we never gave terms. All hostile cities were given the opportunity to surrender or be destroyed once we surrounded them. If they surrendered, they would lose their treasure, but otherwise be spared. The people of the cities had nothing to fear from us if they treated us honestly; otherwise their fate would be on their own heads.

Tezozomoc and his immediate family fled Azcapotzalco, and it surrendered immediately. The other Tepaneca towns and cites quickly sent their most distinguished representatives to pledge their allegiance to us and offer us whatever it would take to convince us to spare them. I had each Tepaneca town fill a few wagons with their treasures and sent them to Kuyuk. I felt that a general looting was not called for since they had surrendered. Among the surrendering cities was Tlatelolco, whose leader, Cuacuauhtzin had fallen with his troops. They, too, had to fill a few wagons for Kuyuk. Tenochtitlan was accepted into the fold, and Acamapichtli remained their leader. I put Tlatelolco under his governance and confirmed their other possessions, except Xochimilco, which had already been given its complete independence. I was sure we would hear from Tezozomoc again.

North of the Tepaneca lands, there was a scattered loosely organized confederation of towns centered on Xaltocan an island city in the southeast corner of the northern section of the lake. The people in these towns were Otomi speaking, and the towns were simpler or more primitive than their southern neighbors were. Still, the people were brave and did put up some resistance before bowing to the inevitable. They were heavily tattooed and had the disconcerting habit of dying their teeth red, black, or both. This part of the lake was full of inhabited islands, and the Beavers were quite busy paying each of them calls. Beyond the lake, we went as far north as the old city of Tollan, greatly revered as the capital of the Tolteca. The city was a ruin, inhabited by a sorry-looking band of ruffians. They scattered at our approach leaving us to examine the ruins alone. It was not a large city, and it really wasn't that impressive, aside from some rather large carved stone figures of warriors, but Smoking Mirror went about in reverent awe. I didn't feel it was worth a garrison, so we withdrew. By midwinter, we were at the end of the Otomi "territory" and about to enter that of the Alcolhua.

Word reached me that the Chichimeca Teuctli had presented himself to our leading elements, and he wished to speak with me. The title meant "Lord of the Chichimeca," but Smoking Mirror told me that it was an old title of great prestige that was used by the descendants of Xolotl, who had once ruled over most of the Valley of Anahuac. Its current holder was the same Quinatzin, of whom Tezozomoc had warned us so often. He resided in the city of Texcoco on the eastern shore of the lake in the shadow of the great mountain named for the rain god (Tlaloc). He was a much-admired warrior and had been nicknamed, Tlaltecatzin (Earth Flattener), so we might find him ready to fight.

We caught up with Quinatzin at one of our camps on the shore off Xaltocan. He was waiting in the commander's tent as we came up. He rose to meet us. He was a fine-looking man, about my height, but with a broader build and definitely older. He wore the hard look of an old soldier. I knew Kaidu and Donduk would have taken an instant liking to him. He was dressed in the quilted cotton armor with a few ornate touches of feathers and an oversized shield with an intricate pattern of feathers worked into it. He wore the plug in his lower lip but otherwise little jewelry. He had been attended by some of his warriors, but they had been detained outside of the camp under guard. He still carried his obsidian club, but held it like a cane. He studied me silently for a time, and then shifted his gaze to Smoking Mirror. We returned his look steadily and wordlessly.

"You are men, not gods." His frown deepened. "One of you is a strange-looking man, but a man all the same. I fear no man. I stand before you ready to defend my people. We will not bow before any mere men."

"Bowing is not necessary among the Mongols," I replied stiffly, "integrity is. We never claimed to be gods. We serve the Khan of the Mongols. He has sent us to bring the people of this valley under his rule. You may either join us in peace and maintain your lives and positions of power, or you will all be killed and your cities destroyed. No one yet has proven our match on the battlefield. Do you wish to try?"

"You do not fight with honor," he returned. "You use strange animals and weapons. You harness the thunder and hail of Tlaloc. You use sorcery and magic to strike terror into whole armies, who fall before your mercy only to be cut down like reeds. You take no prisoners to honor the gods, and you will bring their punishment down on us. You do not even spare the weak or the old. You have brought a great evil into the navel of the world."

"You are a fool." I remained indifferent. "What honor is there in using inferior weapons when you have superior. Would you hunt deer with a club instead of a bow or fish with a bow instead of a net? Do you face the cougar armed only with your teeth and fingernails? There is no honor in war. Such thoughts are unworthy of a warrior.

Our weapons have nothing to do with gods or magic. They are simply weapons quite well known in other parts of the world. As to our practice of war, it is our custom to make war against us so horrible as to render it unthinkable among our opponents. In the long run, it saves lives and time. We do not sacrifice battle captives or anything else to our gods, and they are yet to betray any displeasure with us. We have only triumphed in all our battles."

"Your words are hard," he replied. "Time will tell whether you ignore the gods of this land to your peril. For my part, I would spare my people as much death as possible, but cannot deliver them to slavery. Therefore, I propose a contest of honor. You and I alone will fight to the death. If I win, your armies will leave this valley forever. If you win, my people will serve your Khan."

"When I was a child my grandfather told me stories of such gestures. No doubt it would suit your needs to have me accept. Should you win, the valley is yours, should you lose, it no longer matters to you. Unfortunately, I cannot accept your proposal. I can meet you in single combat, if you wish, but it will mean only whatever its outcome, nothing more. I am not in a position to bargain with you. My orders are clear, and I must carry them out or die trying. If I should die, my second in command must take over and carry out the orders. If you wish to change my orders, you would have to appeal to the Khan himself, and we would not be able to wait for that appeal. You will have to choose war or peace on our terms, here and now."

"What evil brought you here?"

"Orders."

"If the cities surrender, you will not destroy them?"

"We will not."

"You will not enslave the people?"

"We will not. Surely you have heard how those under us in the valley have fared. Why should we treat you differently?"

"Your treatment has not been consistent. You have done no ill to some cities and exacted tribute from others. Some towns were merely threatened, others were destroyed."

"We have destroyed few towns in this valley. Only those that resist are destroyed. Those that send an army against us must pay plunder. Those that join us in good faith suffer only the temporary loss of their army. We have been most consistent, your information is flawed."

"Will you spare the cities any tribute if they expel all who would resist you?"

"That would depend on how many that would be. We will not be toyed with. We have already played enough games with Tezozomoc. I was led to believe that you were cut of a different cloth."

"Did not Tezozomoc agree to join you only to have you destroy his army and besiege his cities?"

"Tezozomoc is the most remarkable man I have yet to meet. He seems incapable of telling the truth about anything. Did no one tell you what really happened across the lake? How can you rule your people with such poor intelligence?"

"Tezozomoc owes me allegiance. He came to me and reported your not honoring his offer of peace. He asked me to release his cities of their allegiance to me so that you would not destroy them. It was he who suggested I offer you single combat."

"I hope I get to meet this man; he really fascinates me. Since he's wanted me to attack you from the time I first reached the shores of the lake, I'm not surprised to hear he wants you to die while leaving your army intact. Tell me, is he now on a recruiting expedition?"

"Why yes, he offered to rally the Otomi cities in the north and the Mixteca in the southeast to help drive you out of the valley."

I told him then about all of Tezozomoc's messages to me and suggested he confirm my story with Acamapichtli. He was at first stunned, then furious. He vowed to see to it that Tezozomoc died a horrible death. Meanwhile, he agreed to ally his cities with us while he went to see the Khan himself. He wanted to challenge him to single combat, or, failing that, cut a better deal for himself and his heirs. I agreed to send him to Kuyuk.

With Quinatzin neutralized, all resistance had ceased in the valley. So far, only the Chalca were being trained to form the nucleus of an Ordu. I decided to have the Beavers train the Mexica even though I wasn't sure about them or anyone else in the valley. The northern people, except for the Hotcangara, seemed much less devious than these people, and one generally knew where one stood with them. Here, however, I always had the feeling that given the right set of circumstances, they would turn on me without the slightest compunction. To be fair, they had been given little choice in the matter, but I did feel we were an improvement over their several previous overlords, and in time, they should grow to appreciate that. I decided not to train or arm any others for now, except those on the coast.

For once, I had finished a campaign in less time than allotted, so I decided to act on my own and sent the Oxen and the Osprey to replace the Horses and the Owls among the Huaxteca. Quinatzin would thus be able to travel with a most formidable escort most of the way to Kuyuk, and I'd be giving a much-needed break to the Horses and Owls, both of whom were no doubt quite weary of garrison duty. I also told the commanders of the Oxen and Osprey to explore the possibility of raising a native tumen from among the Huaxteca. I sent the Otters to replace the Alligators and the Parrots among the Totonacs. The Totonacs were much less damaged than the Huaxteca, and tumen were well on the way to being developed. I asked the Parrots to leave a training cadre behind to continue training them in the jungle tactics. I would keep the Beavers and Wildcats with me for the present. I split the Wildcats into two groups to guard the north and west. The Beavers watched the south and patrolled the lake. We heard again from the chief of Cuauhnahuac to tell us that his and the other Tlahuica cities and towns would join us as allies and invited me to visit. He also advised me that Tezozomoc had been trying to recruit them in a grand alliance against us, but had not met any success. I sent them a messenger thanking them for the information and invitation and promising to visit them as soon as practical. Meanwhile, I dismissed the auxiliaries from outside the valley and ordered the valley auxiliaries back to their towns but to remain in a state of readiness should events warrant. I sent scouts out in all directions and recruited some spies among the Chalca merchants to find out what Tezozomoc was up to.

Smoking Mirror prevailed on me to see another old sacred site of great importance in the valley. It was a city that was once even greater than Tollan, although the Tolteca did eventually rule there for a time. This was now called Teotihuacán (Place of the Gods) since the "fifth" (current) sun had been created there. Although I was not at all interested, he regaled me with the legends about the several suns. I wasn't listening. We followed a river upstream from the lake into a smaller valley. Here was a small Alcolhua town, and gradually appearing from among the overgrowth were the ruins of a great city. Aside from the great structures in the city's center, there were clear signs that it had been a sprawling city with stone houses and laid out streets. Only the foundations remained, but they were so extensive that this city could have been large enough to accommodate many thousands of people. I had never seen a city to rival it anywhere before or since in the new land. The center of the city was remarkable for its scale alone. There was a central square of no great size, but it was surrounded by pyramidal platforms, including a large one, on the north side referred to locally as the Pyramid of the Moon. Opposite this was a long (almost six li) straight and wide (about fifty paces) paved street leading south to a very large ceremonial center. Along its way was an even larger pyramid (The Pyramid of the Sun). As one climbed its considerable height, one lost sight of the stairway below giving the sensation of climbing into the sky. The top was not very large, but likely at one time sported a temple of some sort. The ceremonial center included a temple dedicated to Quetzalcoatl including some interesting representations of him. One couldn't help but wonder what sort of people these were, and how they happened to build such a large city and what happened to it. Smoking Mirror had no answer to these questions worth writing down.

Not long after my visit to Teotihuacán, a courier arrived from Kuyuk. More tumen were on the way and should be arriving by early spring. Meanwhile, I was to take the surrounding cities of note to the west, north, and south, especially Tecaxic in the west and Cuauhnahuac in the south. In the spring, I was to march west and take all the cities as far as the western sea. Juchi was being sent to take the Mixteca areas to the southeast under separate command. He would step off from Cholula also in the spring with an Ordu of three tumen. I would only need two. A fourth would be sent to Juchi in the summer so he could continue on to conquer the Zapoteca. After I worked my way west to the sea, I should then take the coastal people between there and the Zapoteca. If I felt I needed them, I could keep as many as I wanted of the five tumen I now had. More instructions would be given later.

I asked Smoking Mirror if he now wanted to give up, but he wouldn't leave me yet. He said he had always wanted to visit the western lands, and this was as good a time as any. I was glad that Cuauhnahuac had already joined us, but I would have little time to clear the surrounding area by spring. It would not be a restful winter.

36

FROM ANAHUAC WEST TO THE COAST, 17 K
(FROM MEXICO CITY TO THE PACIFIC COAST,
1385)

Since I had so little time to clear the surrounding area, I decided to split my forces. I had the Beavers under Smoking Mirror move north, and I went west with the Wildcats. I took along a group of auxiliaries from among the Mexica, so I could get a better feel for them as well as the newly trained Chalca, fully outfitted like Mongols. I integrated the latter into the Wildcats and sent a cadre of the Wildcats to train some auxiliaries from among our new allies, the Tlalhuica. A group of Alcolhua would accompany Smoking Mirror and the Beavers as auxiliaries. We wouldn't organize the Alcolhua into tumen until Quinatzin returned from his visit to Kuyuk, and I was satisfied that they could be trusted. I sent Smoking Mirror northeast toward the independent town of Tulancingo while I crossed the mountains to the southwest toward the town of Tenancingo. He would then head west and north, and I would head north bringing us together again somewhere around the town of Atlan. Late winter was a bad time to begin a campaign over mountains, but at least we would not be expected.

We threaded our way through the cold mountain passes, grateful for the lush covering of pines to deflect the wind. Fortunately, we only had the single row of mountains to cross before we found ourselves in the valley named for Tecaxic, the city at its center. It also had a lake in the center, and a snow-covered volcano (Tolotzin) brooding over it. We entered the valley through the southern highlands coming upon the town of Ocuilan. Taken by complete surprise, they surrendered without a fight. We hurried on to Tenancingo. It was a fairly large town on a river near the southern terminus of the valley. A few tried to escape the town by means of the river, but it was sluggish at this time of year, and our arrows found their marks. It, too, surrendered. I set up a garrison and took their army with us as auxiliaries. We now turned north up the valley in a broad band, demanding and receiving the surrender of all the small towns. Eventually we arrived at something of a fortress town, Teotenango, in the southwestern foothills of the valley. It was occupied and refused to surrender. We quickly surrounded it and brought up the cannon. A few massed salvos breeched the eastern wall, a few more softened up the town, and the slaughter commenced. The lesson was not lost on our auxiliaries.

No further resistance was encountered until we approached Tecaxic. There a small force tried to engage us, but then quickly fled north into a forested area. Sensing a trap, I sent half the Ordu around the forest to the north between it and the city and moved slowly toward the wood with the rest of my forces. Once everyone was in place, I had a large number of rockets fired into the woods. The resulting panic exposed the trap, and we moved in to flush out the rest. Those streaming toward the city found a formidable barrier to their retreat. Not many got away, and we took no prisoners. We now moved on to Tecaxic. As we neared the city, a delegation came out to meet us. It consisted of five men and a retinue of attendants. This proved to be the Tlatoani and the Council of Four, the rulers of the Matlatzinca, a grouping of cities centered on Tecaxic. All five prostrated themselves before us and begged for mercy on their people. I bid them rise and explained their options. Since they had resisted us, they would need to fill some wagons with reparations, and I would have to appoint a governor to make sure they remained true to their word. Further, they would have to give me what was left of their army. If all went well, they would be returned rule of their cities as Mongols. The alternative was, of course, we would destroy them and their city. They accepted my terms with gratitude. It seemed that they had been warned that I usually tortured anyone who surrendered to death, but had taken heart from reports filtering in from the south. It turned out that Tezozomoc had tried to recruit them, but they trusted him less than they feared us. I set up a governor and a garrison and continued north.

As we neared the central lake, it became clear we would have to cross a good-sized river, known locally as the Lerma. On the far side of the river, there was an army prepared to contest our crossing. They had cleverly removed all boats from our side of the river, and the river was a bit too deep for fording under fire. I sent a group of men to fell trees for dugouts and pontoon planks. Meanwhile, I brought up the cannon and set up a defensive perimeter in case they might try an attack. While some of the men worked feverishly on the pontoon bridge, I had others keep the enemy off guard by feigning attacks and scouring the lakeshore for boats. In a few days, all was ready. Under cover of darkness, we put most of the bridge into place. Then, at first light, we fired cannon and rockets over and into the enemy while the last few boats were put in place and the first contingent raced across the bridge and fanned out to surround the enemy. Some brave soul among them noticed what was going on and got any who would listen to rush the bridge. This unsupported attack was quickly beaten back with heavy losses.

We ceased firing and prepared to bring the cannon across, once most of the Ordu was in place in an arc around their position. As soon as the smoke cleared and they could see their situation, they reacted variously. Some dropped their weapons and ran in whatever direction seemed to suggest safety. Some tried to withdraw in good order toward the lake. Some dropped to the ground in submission. And some turned and tried to fight their way north toward their city. Only those who reached the lake and launched the boats they had hidden there escaped. The rest were wiped out. Then, while our lead elements rushed to surround the main city, Xiquipilco, I had the auxiliaries take up the pontoon bridge and bring it along with us. We were barely in position before a sheepish delegation approached us from the city. This time it was one leader with a few advisors. Again, all prostrated themselves and begged for mercy. Once more, these people represented a group of cities this time they called themselves the Mazahuaca. I was irritated at being held up by them and told them that if they delivered all the cities in their group to me with no further trouble, they would be spared the destruction they richly deserved. But still, they would have to fill many wagons with riches, obey my governor without question, and turn over what was left of their army to serve as auxiliaries.

They immediately agreed, and it proved quite beneficial, since their league consisted of quite a few towns north of the lake. I left the wagons for them to fill and continued north. This proved to be little more than a march since we met no resistance for some days. Even after we left Mazahuaca territory, the scattered nonaligned towns surrendered without a fight. We did lose a few scouts to roving bands of warriors, and we wiped out the few of these we could find, but they were not associated with any towns, so retaliation was impossible. This was a wild rugged country with forested mountains cut by ravines and only occasionally, valleys. In one of these valleys, we finally reached Atlan. It was not much of a town and offered no resistance. I sent out men to the few surrounding villages, and they also quickly surrendered. I sent out mappers and eventually realized that this river was a tributary of the Panuco, which watered the Huaxteca lands. The mappers also ran into Smoking Mirror's scouts downstream and sent them on to me. A few days later, he and I ran into each other at almost the same spot. His campaign had met more but less organized resistance than mine. A few smaller towns were destroyed, and several cities were now lacking armies, but all the northland was in our hands. The Otomi we had contacted during the Huaxteca campaign had joined us as had most of the Ralamari. He had run into elements of the Ralamari and had cleverly organized a yamlike communications system with them. He felt they would prove invaluable in this rugged mountain country and would help ensure that our new allies would remain loyal. I immediately extended his system to cover the area I had just taken in the north as well. The Tecaxic valley was better served with horses, however. I sent the Beavers back to the Anahuac Valley while the rest of us set off for Tecaxic, which would be our base for the campaign in the west. En route, word finally reached me that the new tumen had arrived and would be waiting for me at Tecaxic.

It was already spring by the time we regained Tecaxic. The Deer and the Foxes (Juchi's old tumen) were camped around the city, and their scouts met us well before we were in sight of the city. When I reached the city, Chagatai and Wanbli Sapa, the commanders of the Deer and Foxes, met me. They assured me that the men were ready and eager to get started. They had already taken the liberty to send out scouts, and there were no hostile forces in the area. I thanked them for their efficiency and told them we would move out in two days. Smoking Mirror and I decided to keep most of the auxiliary forces with us for the campaign and called on the Tlalhuica to send their army.

Not long after the Ordu commanders had left, I was informed that there was a messenger from Cholula to see me. I bid him to be shown in. To my surprise it was George, my oldest son. He was now fourteen years old and looked every inch the Mongol warrior. He saluted me properly; then we embraced. He first assured me that all were well at home and then said that Juchi had sent for him while en route from the northeast, and he had accompanied him all the way to Cholula. He then was sent to give me Juchi's message. It was to be an oral message, but he had written it down in the old language, and since only our family understood it, Juchi didn't mind.

The message was long. It seemed that Juchi was quite unsure of his father's intentions. He had, therefore, kept only those he trusted around him and sent the others off on one-way missions. He recommended that I do the same. His suspicions were aroused by a number of things that had happened since Kaidu had died. First of all, there was this campaign. It was pure aggression, and Kaidu would never have ordered it. Next, there was the fact that first I and then he were sent to lead separate elements of the campaign, effectively removing us from the seat of power and putting us in harm's way. Meanwhile, a veil of secrecy had descended over the Eagle Ordu and his "observers" there had been transferred far away. He had advised Paula to move to the Hawk Ordu and stay with my brother Henry as long as I was away. He would try to send the Antelopes back as soon as possible and suggested that I urge Paula to stay with them.

But there was more. His "observers" had managed to get word to him about several developments before they were sent off. First of all, there was a large store of silk at the Eagle Ordu. It was under guard and only for Kuyuk's use. There was also a large store of gold under guard. The gold was being sent to the Salmon Ordu, and the silk was being sent from the Salmon Ordu. The Salmon Ordu had an even more impenetrable veil of secrecy over it, but he had managed to pierce it a little. It turned out that they had been trading with the old land. At first, they had sent a fleet of the ocean-going coastal boats over to the old land with a few old timers who knew the coast of the old land well enough to steer them to a major port. They wound up in Koryo and had set up trade with some merchants there. Since then, the latter had sent their larger ships across the western sea to enlarge the trade. The Salmon Ordu was now little more than a trading center. Ogedai kept a sizable guard with him and fortified the position with a walled fort, but sent the rest of the tumen as well as the local warriors south to conquer all the tribes along the coast unless they agreed to join us.

Add to all this the fact that even though Kuyuk had designated Juchi as his successor, he had not once contacted him since Kaidu died until he was given orders to join this campaign. And this message was precisely that, an order, prepared by a staff member and signed by Kuyuk. He was also ordered to keep in touch with no one except Kuyuk during the campaign, since I would be in a different theater and preoccupied with my own efforts. It was for that reason that he had hit on the stratagem of taking my son with him and sending him on to me with a message. The boy was old enough to be on campaign, and he knew he and I could trust him. He urged me to be very careful what I said and to whom I said it.

To say the least, this was a very disappointing message. It seemed that all the intrigue from the old land had found us even before one generation had passed. As usual, I had missed it completely, too ready to think the best of everyone, too slow to get suspicious. It was naive of me to think that everything would be different in the new land. The truth was that everything depended on the Khan. I wondered if Juchi would finally succeed his father and if he did, would he return things to Kaidu's ways? Time would tell. Meanwhile, I didn't really think my family was in any danger, but even so, suggested to Paula in my next letter that she go on with Mathilde and Padraig should he return to his base before I got back. I also thought it best to destroy Juchi's letter. I decided not to burden Smoking Mirror with this message and told George to forget all about it and never mention it again. He was a bright boy and understood the situation immediately. Juchi had not paid any attention to him all along the trip until they reached Cholula when he called him ostensively to greet our old family friend, Padraig, and give him news of his family, which he had left with Paula. George realized that great caution was necessary and never mentioned anything about the message to anyone. He did mention to me that there was a rumor in the Eagle Ordu that Ogedai had been named as second in line after Juchi, since the latter would be on campaign. After passing on this piece of information, he really did forget all about the intrigue and happily immersed himself into the campaign. I tried to do so also, but the situation hung over me like a cloud.

Keeping busy was helpful, however, and I was very busy. The terrain of the western lands was quite varied. In the south, there were thickly wooded mountain slopes plunging down through dense humid forests into a deep tropical valley cut by a very long river called the Mexcala. Farther north, the mountains ascended to a high plateau made up of a series of large shallow basins often surrounding a lake and separated by a rings of low hills covered with pine and fir forests on their higher slopes. Farther north there was the valley made by the same Lerma River we had encountered in the Valley of Tecaxic. This was bordered farther north by more arid lands giving way ultimately to more mountains. The basin land was called Michoacan (The Land Where There Are Fishermen) by the Nahual-speaking people, and indeed, the lakes and rivers did abound in fish and waterfowl, and the surrounding land was quite fertile, much like Lake Texcoco in Anahuac. I decided I would make a three-pronged assault of the land. I would send the Foxes down the Lerma to clear its entire length of all resistance. I would give them the pontoon train and the Alcolhua and Mexica auxiliaries. I would send the Deer to the south to move west in a wide band through the upper slopes and foothills north of the Mexcala River. I gave them the Tlalhuica auxiliaries, who would at least be used to a similar terrain, and some of them even claimed to know the area.

I would take the rest of the auxiliaries and the Wildcats and proceed due west into the high plateau and the basin country where most of the Tarascans were supposed to be. We would all stay in contact and be ready to come to each other's aid if necessary. I figured I would see most of the resistance. I sent the Foxes and the Deer to their jump-off points, and with the scouts well out in front, we all moved west. The great snow-capped Tolotzin brooded to my south until we crossed the rim of mountains and lost sight of it. The first few towns we came upon on my front offered no resistance. The inhabitants were Otomi-speaking people with no particular allegiance to anyone. They did inform us that the Tarascan Kingdom was the only well-organized people in the area and, although not particularly large yet, were rapidly advancing because of the prowess of their warriors. They also mentioned that the Tarascans called themselves Purepecha. We encountered several more such towns in the wooded hills before eventually coming to a shallow basin and our first Tarascans or Purepecha.

This was in the persons of four messengers sent by the leader or cazonci. Their appearance was a bit unsettling since they seemed to have no hair anywhere on their bodies. It turned out they shaved or plucked it all for cosmetic reasons. They spoke Nahual conveniently enough and demanded to know our intentions. I explained their options as usual, and they said that our imminent destruction was in our own hands and withdrew. As usual, I had scouts out but losses among them began to mount and those returning spoke of running into Purepecha scouts, requiring extra vigilance. They also reported that a large concentration of enemy was moving inexorably in our direction. It was still some days away.

Due to the terrain, I decided to steer the battle to my best advantage. I found a very large basin and set up an obvious camp at its western end. I set up all the auxiliaries as bait with a few of my Ordu troops among them to keep them brave. I waited until the Purepecha were close enough that I could predict when they would reach my position and could get a good fix on the size of the force. Seeing that I would be greatly outnumbered by them, I sent a note to the Deer and the Foxes to send me most of their tumen (leaving some men behind to watch the auxiliaries) and have them time their arrival at the basin at just the time I calculated the enemy would arrive. I then had most of the Wildcats withdraw into the woods on the slopes above and behind our camp. I made sure that the Purepecha scouts got close enough to see how small my force was, but not close enough to see the Wildcats behind us.

In a few days, right on schedule, the Purepecha were clearly visible to our west marching right for our position. The size of their force was, as reported, over thirty thousand warriors. As they drew closer, some of the auxiliaries grew restive and began to show inordinate interest in the rear. I found it necessary to remind them that the Wildcats were in the rear and would cut down any of them they found fleeing the battle. This did wonders to return their attention to the front. Most of them had seen the cannon in action, and we set these up to receive the first enemy rush. The auxiliaries were torn between a desire to be behind the cannon for safety and a fear of the noise the cannon made. Their nervousness made me wonder if they could bear any of the enemy assault. I decided to bring up the Wildcats before the attack. I waited until the enemy was about a li away, however, before doing so.

They were really too close to pull back when the Wildcats came into their view, but to their credit they showed no such inclination. They halted when they were about a hundred paces from our perimeter. Even with the advent of the Wildcats, it must have looked to them like they outnumbered us at least two to one. They dressed their lines a bit, and with a blood-curdling scream, they rushed our position while shooting arrows and stones at us. The first barrage from the massed cannon ripped into their leading elements disintegrating most of their leaders and causing some wavering in the attack. This enabled us to get off a second round before they reached our lines. Those that did reach our lines had a blank almost frenzied look to their face and were no match for the Wildcats. They did make some inroads into the auxiliaries, however, and I was glad to see the charging Foxes and Deer explode out of the woods to the north and the south and throw the enemy into complete confusion. Still, they did not panic, but fought steadily and desperately giving no thought to retreat. They had no chance really, but they did do some damage. They were excellent archers and slingers who found some marks among us. More than a few arrows and stones bounced off of my armor. Smoking Mirror was grazed along his cheek, leaving quite a scar. George was knocked off his horse by a well-aimed stone, but only ended up with a few bruises. Quite a few of the auxiliaries were killed or wounded, and many of our soldiers and horses were among the casualties.

In the end, the Purepecha all lay dead, although some of our auxiliaries wanted to return home with prisoners and were quite upset that we would not allow it. I found out later that they wished to sacrifice them to their gods. In spite of some wavering, the auxiliaries on the whole had acquitted themselves quite respectably in the battle. Many had shown a ferocity and determination in spite of considerable losses. Others had to be goaded into action and took no initiative. I decided that it would be best if I had them stay with me. I congratulated the brave and warned the sluggards that if they continued to show so little interest in fighting, they would have to accompany us for the entire campaign.

Since all had taken part in the battle, only the wounded were excused from cleanup detail. There was quite a bit of gold ornamentation among the leaders, but most of the Purepecha fought naked with only black and red paint and tattoos to protect them. I could see from the booty collected that they knew how to work metal. While there were no swords, they had knives, spear points, and axes of some sort of copper alloy. It was not as strong as steel, but it was much better than the obsidian blades used by everyone else here in the south. It took a few days to gather up and burn all the dead. When we were finished, I sent some men with the booty and the seriously wounded back to Tecaxic. I sent a message to the governor to receive the wounded with honor and send the booty to Kuyuk.

We rested up a day before continuing west. The Foxes and the Deer returned to their areas. They had encountered little resistance so far, except for the town of Acambaro on the Lerma, which the Foxes had to reduce. The scouts reported no further military activity ahead of us, although they still had a few encounters with enemy scouts. We met no further resistance as we advanced toward the Purepecha capital, Ihuatzio, but it took us quite a while to visit each of their small and scattered towns and villages on the way.

By late spring, we were approaching the central lake called Patzcuaro and the cities along its shores, including Ihuatzio. The lake had a sort of bicornate shape with the rounded horns pointing east. Ihuatzio was in the center on the eastern side between the horns. We bypassed the other cities and headed right for it. It was not fortified, nor was it particularly large, but it did have a fair-sized ceremonial center. The leadership of the capital came out to meet us and prostrated themselves before us. The cazonci had not been with his troops but had remained in the city to meet his fate. He identified himself to me and expressed a willingness to be sacrificed to our gods, since they had proven superior to his, Curicaueri (some sort of fire god). I explained that we didn't sacrifice anyone to gods, not even cazonci. He could save me a lot of time if he would surrender all the towns and villages under his command and fill a few wagons with valuables to atone for his resistance. I would then set up a governor and garrison to rule here until his people had shown themselves worthy of becoming Mongols. Any treachery would be punished swiftly and with no mercy. He could stay here, assist my governor and perhaps succeed him. The alternative was, of course, an ignominious end for him and his people. He quickly chose submission and sent runners to advise all those previously subject to him that they were now subject to the Mongols. He then invited me into his city.

The houses in the city were of wood tightly notched together with high-peaked roofs greatly overhanging the walls of the house. The ceremonial center was on a huge raised platform of dressed stone. On it were houses of wood and temples of dressed stone. The cazonci and his top advisors lived in a huge wooden house in the center. It was of two stories with a high-peaked curly cornered roof. It had a cedar doorway and a terrace made of cedar slabs. All visible wood on the house was carved with mostly curly designs and heavily lacquered. Among the usual temples there were some rather curiously shaped platforms called yacatas. They were stepped and consisted of a circular element attached to a rectangular element by a thin neck. They were faced with very nicely dressed and perfectly fitted stone slabs. It turned out they were funerary monuments to past cazonci. The current cazonci regaled me with tales of the great Purepecha hero chief, Tariacuri, who founded the "empire" and was his ancestor. He had lived in Patatzequa (The Place of Temples) at the southern end of the lake, but his family had moved to this more central position. Ihuatzio meant "Place of the Coyotl" in their bizarre language. I had noticed that there were islands in the lake with towns on them, and I asked him about them. He said that the first Purepecha had settled on the islands for safety, but as time went on, they conquered the surrounding lake and the whole area.

I asked him what remained of his army, and he admitted that it was little more than his personal guard and those few that had missed the general muster, perhaps a few thousand warriors at most. I told him that they would have to accompany me on the rest of my campaign, but I would leave a sizable garrison here to protect our new subjects. In time, we would raise and train a local tumen if all went well. He assured me of his complete cooperation and sent for the commander of his guard to give him his new assignment. I picked Bimiibatod Omasus, an Anishinabe and the second in command of the Wildcats, to be governor. I had him keep half the tumen as a garrison, spread them about the province, and set up a yam system for communications. I left with the rest of the tumen after sending messages to the Deer and the Foxes to continue on to the coast where we would rendezvous eventually.

I took the Purepecha auxiliaries with me. The accompanying auxiliaries now outnumbered the half tumen, but only if they acted together, and that seemed unlikely. Anyway, everyone wanted to be part of a winning army, and there was no trouble. It took us several days to clear the remaining Purepecha land, but eventually we reached what they considered their western frontier. There was really no difference in the terrain, but they had not seen fit to expand this far. Small wonder, actually, there were only more small villages which raised crops, fished, and hunted birds enough to feed themselves, but no one else. There was some fair craftwork, but on the whole they were barely worth noticing. All we met offered no resistance and assured us that they would henceforth obey all Mongol pronouncements. Since they were most unlikely ever to hear any, that was just possible, but who cared?

Word filtered in from the Deer and the Foxes that they were only encountering occasional towns worthy of the name. The Foxes had found a large lake (called Chapala) at the end of the Lerma with a few sizable towns around it and had to destroy a couple of them. Wanbli Sapa mentioned that the Mexica were proving to be ferocious fighters, but the Alcolhua were more deliberate in their attacks. Still, both had shown courage and skill and had been most helpful. The Deer had found it necessary to travel along the river since the humid forest had given way to a more arid valley. This river was called the Tepalcatepec and flowed eastward to join the Mexcala River just as the latter turned south to the sea. They had encountered a few larger towns also, but little or no resistance, until they reached the town of Tepalcatepec. This town resisted to the end and fought desperately. Chagatai commended his Tlalhuica auxiliaries for their bravery also.

From the maps that were coming in to me, it seemed logical to shift our lines a little to the north. There was a river (the mapper named it after the lake) flowing northwest from Lake Chapala, which looked like a good focus for the Foxes. The rest of us would have move a little northwest to cover the rest of the land. We found ourselves roughly following a parallel river we called the Ameca after a town along its upper reaches. The Deer had the more difficult unrelenting mountainous terrain. We all found that there were independent towns of varying size in each valley, very few of which were inclined to resist us. This made the trip easy but boring. By early fall, we had all reached the sea. I had the men rest a while and went up the coast to meet with the Foxes.

They had reached a fairly populous region near the mouth of the Chapala River. There were several large towns in the area, but only one of them decided to fight. It was called Tepic and was the largest of them. By the time I reached them, the town was a smoldering ruin and the dead were being burned. The Foxes and their auxiliaries had been much reduced by the campaign. They had encountered the most resistance and had been ambushed a few times. They had also left a lot of men in garrisons along the way. I told Wanbli Sapa to stay here with the rest of his men and make sure the lines of communication back to Anahuac remain intact. He should also do some training of the local forces with an eye to setting up a new tumen eventually. I sent the Mexica and Alcolhua auxiliaries back home. When I returned to the Wildcats, there was a message from Kuyuk. He had sent the Pigeons and the Snakes to join me at the mouth of the Mexcala River early next spring. I should dispose of the other Ordu as I saw fit, although I should continue with some force along the coast to the Mexcala. If my mappers were correct, the Mexcala was almost twelve hundred li from my present position, and I was supposed to reach it by next spring.

I hurried back to the Wildcats and sent them back to join the rest of their Ordu in the Purepecha lands. I told them to make sure that a good line of communication was established between Ihuatzio and the incoming tumen. I reluctantly dismissed all the auxiliaries except the Purepecha and the handful I had picked up on the way to the coast. The others had been with me a long time, and I didn't think they had another campaign in them. I went on ahead to the Deer and ordered the auxiliaries to follow me south. The Deer were encamped near the mouth of a small river and had been exploring the coast to the south while they waited for me. I commended Chagatai for his initiative and gave him the bad news of our orders. I decided to keep the Tlalhuica auxiliaries since they were almost a tumen and they and the Deer had had the easiest campaign so far. My auxiliaries showed up in a few days, and we began to march south along the coast in a band extending well inland.

37
EAST ALONG THE SOUTHERN COAST TO THE COIXCA, 17-8 K
(W & S MEXICO, FROM THE RIO AMECA TO THE RIO GRANDE, 1385-6)

It was the perfect time of year to traverse this area. In the summer, it would have been both too hot and too wet. In the late spring, the rains began and continued through the late fall. But it was now winter, and although some of the rivers were still high, we were able to cross them with our pontoon bridge. The terrain was fairly open, mostly shrubs, rather than trees, except in the mountains where there were pine and fir trees. The people were few and widely scattered along the first part of the trek, generally along the river valleys. They offered no resistance, and many joined us willingly and guided us to their neighbors, unaware that we already had maps of the area. Eventually, we came to a fair-sized town in the hills called Cuautitlan. Unaware of our cannon, it thought itself invulnerable. It wasn't. On a river not far from the coast, we encountered sizable town called Cihuatlan, which offered no resistance. It was large enough to warrant a governor and garrison. This required establishing a communication link back to Ihuatzio and, if possible, back up the coast to Jalisco where the Foxes were set up. It would require a yam network, but not a lot of men. I left this charge to the governor and took the Cihuatlan army along with me. I kept up a link with the garrison by setting up further yam stations as I went along.

At the ideal spot for the first such station, just some ninety li from Cihuatlan, was a town called Tzalahua. It was on the coast at the eastern end of a small bay. East of it was a long narrow lagoon separated from the shore by a long thin strip of land. The town exploited both the sea and the lagoon. It did not choose to resist us and readily accepted a governor (it was too large for a mere yam station) and a garrison. They did not have much of an army, but I took it with me anyway. The bay looked like it would make a good seaport, although this spot was not particularly convenient to any of the population centers. There were a few more towns inland, especially along a good-sized river farther east, but we met no further resistance, and I only left a governor and garrison at two of them, Coquimatlan, in the hills along the river, and Coahuayana, near the coast on another river. The rivers had been named for these two towns by the mappers.

The next major river also had a town on it for which it had been named. Oddly, the town, Coalcoman, was far inland, well into the hills. The mappers had decided to map some of the river valleys along the coast and had gone far up this one. It was a pleasant valley, dotted with smaller towns and villages, but the upper reaches of it were cooler and drier, much more comfortable. The head of the town remembered the mappers as being mere curiosities when they passed through; he never suspected that an army of conquest would follow in their wake. I tried to mollify him, assuring him it was more amalgamation than conquest, but he was no fool. The town had something of a real army, so I had to take them along and leave a governor and garrison. The leader was distressed at the small size of the garrison, but I pointed out that reinforcements could be sent for swiftly, if needed.

The rest of the way to the Mexcala River, the towns were too small to leave a governor and no resistance at all was encountered. This was fortunate, since it was spring by the time I arrived at the river and elements of the Snakes and Pigeons were already waiting for me on the far side. They had thrown a pontoon bridge across to speed me over the large river and were worried that they would have to remove it before I arrived if the rain continued swelling the river. An intermittent rain two days before had yielded to a steady downpour the day we arrived at the river, and I lost no time getting everyone across. The Ordu had set up camp about a day's ride east of the river on the higher ground at a town called Xiutla, which they had already taken without a struggle. I could just imagine the look on the faces of the townsfolk when they found themselves surrounded by two tumen. Especially since the tumen were the tall, fierce Snakes and the deformed headed Pigeons. The Ordu had also taken the liberty of visiting all the towns and villages within a day's ride and accepting their surrender. Since Xiutla was the most centrally located town in this area, I gave it a governor and a garrison. I made it a large garrison, about five hundred men, since they would have to keep an eye on several towns as well as keep open the lines of communication to both the west and the north along the Mexcala.

Khurumsi, the leader of the Snakes, and Mato Anahtaka, the leader of the Pigeons, told me that they had had to fight their way along much of the length of the Mexcala. They were guided to it by the Tlalhuica, who led them to one of its tributaries named for Alahuitzlan, a town on its upper reaches. It surrendered once surrounded, but the other towns along the river almost all had to be reduced. The larger towns were all independent of each other even though the people seemed to all speak the same language. It was an odd tongue called Chontal, but they had a Tlalhuica guide who spoke the language. There were more of them to the east of the Alahuitzlan River, but they would have to wait for another day. Once on the Mexcala, the resistance was even more desperate. The towns were again not organized into any sort of nation, and often they spoke completely different languages. It had been necessary to keep an irritating number of interpreters on staff, and after messages ran the gauntlet through them, one could only hope there was a resemblance imparted. They found out eventually that someone had told the locals that we tortured to death all those we captured. I detected the hand of Tezozomoc. Finally, as they drew close to the point where the Tecapaltepec River joined the Mexcala, resistance began to fade, since my forces had already passed nearby, and the locals knew the truth. The language babble only grew worse, however.

Khurumsi and Mato Anahtaka had heard that Juchi had met fierce resistance against the Mixteca (or Tya Nuu, as they called themselves). Their land was very mountainous, and progress against them had been quite slow. They had also heard that he was continuing his campaign during the winter. Otherwise, they were quite removed from any gossip from the Eagle Ordu, or at least, they didn't share it with me. From the morale of their men, however, I was quite sure that all were either unaware of or unconcerned with Kuyuk's intrigues.

We got moving eastward along the coast in a broad band. The Pigeons took the steamy coast, the Snakes the cooler highlands, and I took the alternately cool and steamy middle with the Deer and all the auxiliaries. None of the towns we encountered offered much resistance. The people lived in small low houses made of wood or mud with thatch roofs, and the leaders' houses were only marginally more impressive, perhaps surrounded by a plastered fence and painted. This was odd because it was a rather well-off area. There was extensive agriculture and trade, some game in the hills, plentiful seafood from the ocean, and gold and copper mines. They should have been able to live better than they did.

The first organized resistance we encountered was when we crossed into what turned out to be a loose confederation of a people who spoke the same language. It was called Cuitlatec and was the virtually the same language spoken by the people the Pigeons and the Snakes had encountered when they first reached the Mexcala River. The Snakes reported that they were encountering a different people on their left (north). These other people were called the Tepuztec and offered no resistance and, in fact, eventually sent us a large contingent of auxiliaries. The Cuitlatec, however, withdrew their armies before us leaving us almost empty cities. The scouts reported that they had pulled back to the far side of a flooding river some thirty miles from their western "border" and fortified the far bank at a point some fifteen miles from the river's mouth to contest our crossing. It seemed odd that they would only fortify one small part of the river, but it was on my general path, and the country was rather wild to the north, and the river rather wide to the south, so it made some sense. I told the Snakes to ford the river far upstream and move south to get behind them and cut off their retreat. Meanwhile, I moved right for their position with the other tumen. When we arrived the next day, we set up the artillery opposite them and at night laid down our pontoon bridge.

At first light, we shelled their positions with cannon and rockets, enabling our men to start across the bridge. The barrage caused the enemy to pull out of their positions and form ranks in battle lines just beyond the cannon range. I crossed over to look at them while the men brought the cannon over. They were armed with bows, slings, and clubs, wore the usual padded cotton armor, and carried shields. The Ordu fanned out to surround them on three sides and began firing arrows into them. They advanced in a line to their bowshot range, only to see us pull away again while firing into them. Their losses beginning to mount, they again withdrew, only to find us following after them and still firing into them. They tried to take cover, but the high arrow trajectories found them easily. At last, the Snakes came up on their rear. They rushed toward them trying to fight their way out, but they pulled back out of their range, and the rest of us moved after them. Desperately, they ran toward the Snakes, but the latter remained out of their reach, while pouring withering barrages of arrows into them. Meanwhile, we kept them boxed in and cut them down from the back and flanks. This continued until they were all down. We sent in the auxiliaries to finish off any of their wounded and recover our arrows. The dead were relieved of any valuables and burned as usual. There were very many of them. We suffered only a few wounded, and a couple of the auxiliaries drowned when they fell off the bridge. The scouts reported no other activity on our front, so I split the Ordu up again, and we continued our march east.

Not long after we resumed our march, the scouts reported the approach of a large contingent of Cuitlateca: women and servants bearing gifts, but no soldiers accompanied them. Smoking Mirror and I, along with a suitable escort, went forward to meet them. They were led by a group of perhaps twenty old men, simply clad in cotton mantles, followed by a larger, more diverse, highly ornamented group of men, a very large group of young women, and finally the heavily laden gift bearers. There were no soldiers, escort troops, guards, or even weapons in the group. We waited for them on a small rise, with my escort in battle line with bows ready, just in case. When the leading elements reached me, all of them stopped and fell to the ground. I spoke to them in Nahual, and one of the elders rose up to speak. It was a crude version of Nahual, but I could make it out.

"You speak a tongue similar to that of the Coixca. But they are in the northeast, and you come from the west. Also you look nothing like them. Who is it that has defeated us? Are you the scourge from the north we have been warned of?"

"We are Mongols. Some of us are from the north and others from the west. We are only a scourge to those who resist us. Those who do not, have nothing to fear."

"You have destroyed our armies, and we are at your mercy. What are your demands? We are prepared to fulfill them and only beg you to spare as many of our people as your gods will allow you to spare."

"Are you elders the leaders of your people or their spokesmen? You do not look like leaders."

"We are the high priests of our gods. They told us to come before you in their name to plead for our people. The leaders are also here just behind us."

"Your fate is in your own hands. If you surrender to us and offer no more resistance, you will live. I will appoint a governor, and he will reside along with his garrison in your principle city. You will obey all his orders without question. After a time, should you prove worthy, you will be allowed to join us as fellow Mongols and resume authority over yourselves. Any treachery at any time will be brutally punished. Meanwhile, for resisting us you will have to fill several wagons with gifts for the Khan and what's left of your army will have to accompany me on the rest of my campaign. Otherwise, there will be no further requirement of you except food in time of famine elsewhere in the Khanate and warriors in time of war. The alternative would be that we would kill all of you and destroy your cities. What do you choose?"

"A most generous choice. I am certain we will accept, but must confer with the others. Would that be permitted?"

"Of course, but only for a short time."

He quickly conferred with the other priests, and then they went and spoke to the leaders. Very soon, he returned to me praising my generosity and asking for the privilege of escorting our governor to the principle city. Meanwhile, he told me that the young women were for our troop's "amusement" and the gifts were a personal tribute to me. I replied that as this was now our new territory, we would have to set up a communications system leading to the principle city, so we would all go in that direction, and they could certainly come with us. The young women were free to amuse or not amuse the troops as they wished, and I never accepted gifts for myself, but they could put their gifts in wagons as a start toward the necessary reparations to the Khan, although his taste ran heavily toward gold. That exchange and his subsequent translation got quite a few strange looks from the leaders. Some of the women departed, but most actually chose to stay and service the troops. I supposed they had all been slaves and had nothing better to which to return. The gifts were mostly textiles, feathers, ceramics with some stones, and worked gold and silver. It filled two wagons.

We started out the next day, somewhat slowed by the procession. I sent the Snakes to make sure all the Tepuzteca were of one mind about joining us. It turned out they were. I also had the Snakes set up a yam system through the Tepuzteca land to the north and the south from their centrally located city, Otatlan. I made sure the line connected with the main Cuitlatec town, Mexcaltepec. I insisted on moving along the coast to set up the yam network over the more open land there, before turning inland to the city that was well up in the highlands. Once the yam system was connected with the north and the governor and garrison were in place, I returned to the coast with the remnant Cuitlatec army in tow. The Cuitlatec towns were fairly large and surrounded with many villages. It was a heavily populated country. We continued along the coast to the east and a wild warlike people called the Yope. The Cuitlateca assured us that the Yope would fiercely resist us and we would do well to bypass them entirely. I decided to have the Snakes finish pacifying the south side of the Mexcala River with the help of Tepuztec auxiliaries, while I went after the Yope with the rest of the force. We crossed a river named for Coyuca, a Cuitlateca town at its mouth, and were soon in what was supposed to be Yope territory.

Actually, it proved to be a strange campaign. The territory was very mountainous and forested. Mostly steep ravines rather than valleys cut the mountains, although there was a major river valley in the middle of their country (the mapper had appropriately named it the Yope River). Only along the coast was the going easy, and even then the heavy rains reduced our speed considerably. The few towns we encountered resisted savagely, but futilely. The one large town, a seaside fishing town called Acapulco, was almost completely destroyed by our attack. I liked its location, however, and set up a strong garrison to protect our line of communications. The coastal area was really no problem to pacify, but the nature of the back-country made it much more difficult to subdue. Still, I had men up to the task. I sent the Pigeons and the Deer inland to stamp out all resistance. Both tumen, more than adept at forest warfare, were easily the match for the Yope. There were casualties, of course, and heavier than I would have liked, but the task was completed by the end of the rainy season, in the fall. The remnants of the Yope submitted and eventually made good Mongols.

They were an odd people. They were far more primitive than any others we had encountered in the south were. They seemed to have little use for clothing, and only dressed after marriage and then just in deerskin or leaves. They did grow some crops, but mostly relied on hunting and stealing their neighbors' food. Even so, they were not without resources. We found gold, silver, and copper as well as some precious stones and many animal pelts. Their main deity was the same miscreant Xipe Totec (they called it Totec Tlatlauhqui) we had encountered since we were among the Huaxteca. It seemed strange to me that a marginally agricultural people would revere a spring god. They clothed their idol and their priests in red (Tlatlauhqui meant "red") and enacted the usual flaying rites in their worship. My hostility toward their cult no doubt stiffened their resistance, and we ended up killing all their priests, but I have no regrets. We were able to send Kuyuk quite a bit of "reparations," and I was alerted to and confirmed the presence of iron ore. I marked it carefully on my map for future reference once the area had been fully pacified long enough that we could consider exploiting its resources.

Once we had passed through the Yope, things were very confusing in the south, along and near the coast. The people were not connected politically with each other, and they spoke a bewildering array of languages all mixed in among each other. Only in the north was there some unity of language, first the Tlapaneca (somehow related to Yope), then the Coixca (not unlike Nahual), if not purpose. It did not slow us down much, since there was only spotty resistance in this area. The people were far more agricultural than the Yope and had more to lose by resisting us. Those that did resist, did so vigorously, but most yielded even before we invested them. The land was less broken and wooded here, but it was so by design, for the people had cleared and leveled their fields, constantly expanding the area under cultivation. By early spring, we had pacified the whole area south of the Mexcala River and had encountered elements of Juchi's forces both in the east and in the north.

I learned that Juchi was well to the east of me. Having laboriously fought his way through the Mixteca or Tya Nuu (Men of the Earth), he was now dealing with the Zapoteca or Ben Zah (Cloud People). Again, a stranger from Anahuac had stirred both up to desperate resistance, but the stranger had gone on to the east. Four more Tumen, the Kestrels, Wolves, Bears, and Panthers had joined Juchi for the Ben Zah campaign. He had sent the Hawks and Turtles back home, left the Falcons among the Tya Nuu, and sent the Pheasants to replace the Antelopes in Huexotzinco.

I decided to leave the Pigeons to watch the area south of the Mexcala while I took the others and the auxiliaries and cleared the area north of the river that had not yet been pacified. This time we moved west down the river valley. First, we dealt with the rest of the Coixca, and then I finally made the acquaintance of the Chontal, who had resisted the Snakes and the Pigeons on their march to meet me. These were a mixed lot. Some of their towns were distinct and organized, while others were scattered among ravines, and still others seemed to consist of caves and huts on hillsides. They cultivated extensively, getting good crops out of what looked like marginal land. Their language was very guttural, and I never did learn it. Fortunately, they did not resist us, since our treatment of Alahuitzlan had exposed the lie of Tezozomoc's reports about us.

By late spring, I had dismissed the auxiliaries, and leaving a small group of the Snakes behind to organize and train the Chontal and the Coixca, I went to visit Cuauhnahuac as I had promised almost three years earlier.

The valley of the Tlalhuica was, indeed, very pleasant, and Cuauhnahuac was its nicest spot. Nestled among ravines, it abounded in flowers, fruit, grain, and cotton. The climate was comfortable when I was there, and they assured me it was always so. I sent the Deer back home and sent the Snakes to replace the Beavers and the Wildcats in Anahuac. I ordered the latter home also. Meanwhile, my staff and I spent a most enjoyable few weeks in Cuauhnahuac. The leader of the town again tried to offer me one of his daughters, but I insisted that my particular "tribe" only took one wife, and I already had the one. He thought it was very impractical of me, especially since I had so drastically reduced the supply of young men during my campaigns. I told him that many Mongols did take more than one wife, so he needn't worry about the population. One of Juchi's cousins, Timugen, finally did marry one of the man's daughters. He was thrilled with the union.

Kuyuk finally got another message to me. I was thinking that perhaps he had had enough and would order me home, but it was not to be. I was to go immediately to the eastern extreme of the Totonac lands and there meet the Dog, Marten, and Manati Tumen. They should be there by the fall, just as the rainy season ended. Three newly formed tumen, one from the Huaxteca (the Lizards), and two from the Totonaca (the Monkeys and the Vultures) would also be in position to join me for the campaign. I was to proceed to the east and take the large peninsula of the Maya as well as the land between. Juchi would be continuing along the southern coast, so we should meet up beyond the peninsula, where the land narrowed considerably. There would be guides waiting for me among the Totonaca.

It would be a long journey to the Totonac lands, and I felt I should look in on as many governors and allies as possible along the way to make sure none of those people I had left behind were in any danger. I reluctantly left Cuauhnahuac and went north into

Anahuac to look in on the people there. Tenochtitlan was most central location, so I had the governors and local leaders meet me there. Acamapichtli was my host, and he showed me around the two islands wrested from the lake to form a thriving twin city. Many of the houses were made of dressed stone, and many of the people were well dressed and ornamented as befitted those who chose the winning side in a war. There was a network of canals across the islands greatly facilitating transportation. The society was stratified, but apparently only recently so. It seemed that Acamapichtli was the first official leader the Tenocha had, and he had spread himself liberally among the daughters of the clan leaders resulting in an upper-class of parasites claiming relationship to him and thus exalted status (he was widely believed to be of Toltec lineage, although his mother was a Mexica). It seemed absurd, but was none of my business. The city was thriving, and their only complaint was the need to get drinking water from a spring near the hill called Chapultepec, where we had routed the Tepaneca ambush. I suggested that they build an aqueduct, and they just happened to have plans for one at hand. I had a feeling these people would have to be carefully watched.

There were modest ceremonial centers on both islands. That on Tenochtitlan consisted of a large square facing a modest-sized pyramid at its eastern end topped with twin temples to their main gods, Tlaloc (the rain god) and Huitzilopochtli (the war god). Oddly, the war god's name meant "Southern Huitzilin." It was the Nahual name for a small iridescent bird with fast-beating wings that made a humming sound like a bee—not exactly a bird one would associate with war, although it was rather aggressive. On the pyramid platform front of Tlaloc's temple was the painted statue of a man lying on his back with his knees flexed and his upper torso lifted off the ground. There was a type of receptacle (for the hearts of sacrificial victims) at his waist, and he faced outward from the temple. We had seen such figures before, and I was told that they were of Tolteca origin and were widely used, even in the Maya lands. In front of Huitzilopochtli's temple was a slab of black volcanic rock about two feet high and a foot and a half wide set into the floor. It seemed that sacrificial victims were stretched back over the rock in order to facilitate relieving them of their hearts. I was gratified to note that the area was clean of blood. The actual temples were of carved and painted stone and wood, each decorated with symbols and figures associated with the gods they housed. Inside were idols representing each. Huitzilopochtli was represented as a warrior with a huitzilin helmet, eagle feather shield, and holding a blue spear thrower shaped like a snake. Tlaloc was represented as a sort of water monster, part man and part fish, with goggling eyes and fangs for teeth and holding a bag of seeds and a digging stick.

On the western side of the square across from this pyramid, there was another one under construction. Acamapichtli informed me that it was for a temple to honor Tengri, the Mongol god. I tried to explain that Tengri was an abstract god that was honored but not offered sacrifices and never represented. He said that they would simply put a temple without a roof and without an idol on the pyramid. He assured me that the temple would be painted blue, like the sky. He was really quite pleased with the idea and wondered if perhaps we would send some of our priests to make sure they were properly honoring Tengri. Again, I explained that there were no priests of Tengri, and there was no cult or ritual connected with his worship. He was honored with incense and asked for wisdom and health and nothing more. Of course, I had no intention of telling him about the ongons and the rest of the Mongol pantheon. Cult among the Mongols had always been up to the individual, and I rather liked the system. I emphasized to him that priests had no place among the Mongols, since they were mere parasites who did nothing and demanded much. If he wished to keep his priests employed, he could, but we had none of our own to send him. He seemed genuinely bewildered at this and said he would have to talk to his council about it.

Tlatelolco also had a main temple to Huitzilopochtli, but more significantly, they also had a huge market. This was the size of a small town all contained within a broad open space in front of the temple. Stalls and stands were arranged in rows with areas between them like streets so that the customers could stroll by. The whole was very tidy and organized. Like goods could be found in one area.

Guards patrolled the "streets" to ensure no disturbance occurred and three judges at one end of the market settled any disputes immediately. Payment was in the form of barter, the chocolatl beans or little copper pieces shaped like celts. And the variety of goods available was astounding. One could buy any sort of textile as cloth or cut into any imaginable style of clothing and dyed a startling selection of colors. One could choose from a staggering array of pottery and ceramics. There were raw materials if one wished to make one's own cloth or ceramics. Meat, fish, and eggs were available not only raw and dressed, but also cooked and even still alive, especially birds. There were hides of every animal found anywhere within a few months' travel; feathers of all conceivable hues and textures, worked into banners or loose. Fruit, vegetables, herbs, flowers, and grain were also available, again either cooked or raw. Oils, salt, syrups, honey, and juices could be found. Tools, rope, weapons, nets, boats, furniture, planks, beams, sticks, firewood, charcoal, torches, incense, jewelry, gold, silver, stones, paper, inks, and paints were on sale. Even medicines, salves, nawak'osis, and services such as hair cutting and bathing could be secured. Also slaves could be bought and sold. I told Acamapichtli that slavery was not encouraged among the Mongols, since they could never be trusted.

"First you take away our priests and now our slaves?" He shook his head in disbelief. "You will bring the wrath of both the gods and the nobles on me."

"No, I do not take anything away from you. You may keep both if you like. I only recommend that you avoid being dependent on either. Your priests are demanding of too much blood that could be more valuably used elsewhere, and slaves are unreliable and ultimately dangerous."

"We have ended the sacrifices as you demanded, and the dire predictions of the priests have not occurred. There has been no famine, no pestilence, and the sun has not fallen from the sky. But slaves are most reliable and efficient. We have never had any trouble with them. Their children are free unless they sell them. They can own slaves and property and pass them on to their children. They can even buy their own freedom. Some people even sell themselves into slavery to satisfy a debt or to escape poverty. It is not a bad fate and most accept it quite well."

"You certainly have a different form of slavery than we encountered in the old land. Still, I think you would be better off without it. But that is up to you, not an order. If you feel it best to keep the institution, so be it."

From the hostile or despairing faces of those for sale, I was sure I was right, but I really didn't want to make becoming Mongols onerous for the Mexica. In any event, the market was quite diverting, and my staff and I very much enjoyed ourselves. I even bought a few things to send to Paula for herself and the children. I knew she would have really enjoyed the market. George had a wonderful time sampling all the food. It tended to be spicy like some of the Hanjen food my grandfather Peter loved, but it was a different sort of spice. It tended to stay with you longer. I noticed that they had built a causeway between the two islands and remarked on it to Acamapichtli. He said that it had been just recently completed and that they were thinking about building another one to their subject cities on the peninsula to the south. Ixtapalapa would be the logical terminus. I agreed it was a logical move, but thought it would be rather expensive and labor intensive. He reminded me that the Mexica owned slaves for such work. I wished him well on the project, only suggesting that they leave suitable openings for lake traffic. Again, he happened to have the plans ready, and indeed, there were such openings. But he told me the aqueduct was more important.

I met with the governors and rulers in Acamapichtli's palace. It was large but not particularly ornate. The governors reported no problems in their cities, but did wonder if I shouldn't put one of them or someone new in overall command. It seemed that there was no one to make decisions in matters involving more than one city, and there had been some confusion. I asked the governors if any of them wanted such a position, and they all admitted that they did not. Smoking Mirror also did not want the job. I finally got the second in command of the Snakes, Amantacha, a Wendat, to take the job with the title, administrator of Anahuac. Smoking Mirror assured me that the man was the best choice for the task.

He turned out to be a most fortunate pick. He was headquartered in the palace on Tlatelolco originally built for Cuacuauhtzin and currently vacant.

The new ruler of Texcoco, Techotlalatzin, was presented to me. He informed me that Quinatzin had gotten his wish to duel the Khan, but he had lost the fight, so now they owed their allegiance to the Khan as had been agreed. I studied his eyes for traces of sarcasm, but he seemed to believe what he had just told me. I couldn't imagine Kuyuk accepting a duel with a wily old warrior like Quinatzin. He might well have won such a contest, but he would never have taken the chance. I wondered what really happened. Some years later, I learned that the "duel" took place in Kuyuk's yurt. He had his guards hold Quinatzin while he ran him through with his sword. Then he announced how he had just won an epic battle with a most worthy adversary and had him cremated with much honor, and sent back his ashes to Texcoco. The people either believed the tale or wanted to believe it, but there was no protest, and they were now allies.

There were several new tumen in training from among the people of Anahuac—one each from the Mexica, the Alcolhua, the Tepaneca, the Chalca, and the Otomi. More were in the planning stages. The first five would be ready to march by the fall and were to join Juchi's forces. There was much disagreement over what name they would go by, since they all wanted to be the Eagles or Ocelotl. I suggested that they go by their tribal names instead, for now and later pick an animal that wasn't already taken. Of course, one of them could be the Ocelotl, but only one. They all had suggestions for each other, but these were derogatory, like the Mexica should be the Weeds, the Tepaneca the Ducks, the Alcolhua the Worms, and so on. I reminded them that they were all on the same side now, and that if they could not see themselves in that light, we would have to reorganize the tumen, so that all would be represented in each. They never did get around to picking their animals before events rendered it all moot. I soon left for Chalca.

38

THE OLMECA AND THE MAYA, 18-9 K
(EASTERN MEXICO, YUCATAN, 1386-7)

I stopped in Chalca so that I could see if my merchant spies had found out anything about Tezozomoc. They did not disappoint. They found that he had indeed been busily visiting all the surrounding people and stirring them up to fierce resistance against us. He was now in Mayapan, the capital of a sort of kingdom in Uluumil Kutz (Land of Plenty), the northern part of the Maya peninsula. He had stirred up the rulers against us and even managed to convince the people that we were impious, godless barbarians who would bring the wrath of all the gods against ourselves and any who surrendered to us. Even now, the gods were planning a horrible vengeance against us for denying them the blood they needed. In any event, there was a large army gathering around Mayapan, and we could expect resistance every step of the way. On the other hand, the ruler of Mayapan (his title was Halach uinic, "true man") had forbidden Tezozomoc from leaving Mayapan, so we might finally catch up with him there. It looked like I would have to be very careful during the upcoming campaign. Fortunately, we already had extensive maps of the area, and ideas were quickly coming to mind. I went on to Cholula.

Cholula was thriving once again and was already free of an appointed governor. Their army was training in Huexotzinco with elements from the other cities in the plateau. They had together formed a tumen called the Quetzals and would be able to join me on my campaign if the Pheasants felt they were ready. A second tumen was also under development, but would not be ready for a while. I was taken up to the temple so I could see that no blood had been spilled there, but only incense burned as I had instructed. I also had to endure a "religious dance" they had composed to honor the triumphs of Tengri over the "lesser" local gods. There were then a few more entertainments in the form of acrobatics and demonstrations of skill, then some rather annoying music, and finally a large meal. I left early the next morning to avoid any more fanfare and headed for Huexotzinco.

At Huexotzinco, Taska-abi, a Pansfalaya and the commander of the Pheasants, greeted me warmly and assured me that the Quetzals were ready to go with me. I thanked him and remarked on the marvelous performance in my last campaign of his fellow Pansfalaya who made up the bulk of the Pigeon Tumen. He identified several of his relatives among them, and I commented favorably on all of them much to his pleasure. I suggested he invite his relatives up to visit him since they were only a week or so away. Then I asked him about the campaign his Ordu had just finished.

"It was a brutal affair. Resistance among the Tya Nuu was bitter. Many of our scouts never returned; ambushes were frequent in the mountain passes; traps were encountered everywhere. Our losses were quite heavy, about a quarter of my tumen, worse in the others. Even their women and children fought us like cornered wildcats. It would have been easier to conquer all the Southeastern Tribes with one Ordu than these people with five. I'm glad it's over."

"How is morale?"

"Good. We won, killed all our enemies, covered ourselves with glory, and are now enjoying this wonderful peaceful plateau, full of very comely and friendly women, much in need of men. We are enjoying this assignment."

"You earned it. How is Juchi doing?"

"He seemed troubled most of the time, not the happy, carefree carouser I remember from past campaigns. But he led us confidently and well and continues pushing eastward."

I told him I would remember him to Juchi when I met him eventually and authorized him to stay in Huexotzinco as long as he felt either the locals or his men needed it. I gathered up the Quetzals and continued on my way nearly retracing my journey of three years before. There was no trouble anywhere along my path; we had, indeed, brought peace in our wake. I passed quite a few merchant trains, and all of them thanked me as a representative of the Mongols for making their lives much easier. I supposed that was what Tlacuectli had in mind, but I used the occasions to ask about the Olmeca and the Maya. I got a little more information. They all felt that the Olmeca would not resist us very much and perhaps the Putun Maya would even welcome us, since both relied heavily on trade and knew how we had made it much easier and safer. Mayapan was armed to the teeth and lying in wait for us just across their frontier with the Putun. The other Maya would all likely fight since they enjoyed fighting, but it was hard to predict with how much intensity. There would be less resistance in most other areas since Mayapan had hired so many Ah Canul, or mercenaries from their neighbors to the south and southwest. I was beginning to finalize my plan of attack.

By mid fall, I arrived at Chalchicuelan, a Totonac city on the coast about ninety li north of the Olmeca frontier. It would serve as the supply depot and staging area for the campaign. The Manati, Dogs, and Martens were already encamped to the south of the city, while the Lizards, Monkeys and Vultures were even farther south near the frontier. Scouts had already been sent into the Olmeca country, and early reports indicated no organized resistance from them. I called in the Ordu commanders and explained the first leg of the campaign to them.

The Quetzals would cover the right or southern flank along the mountains; the Martens would be on their left (north), followed in order by the Lizards, Manati, Monkeys, Dogs, and Vultures. Each would advance along a broad front of about forty-five li in width, staying in contact with each flank and with a full complement of scouts in advance. They would visit each town and village found by their scouts with a force sufficient to destroy it if needed and either accept their surrender or destroy them. Should they surrender, their army would be impressed into service as auxiliaries, and if the town was large enough, a governor would be appointed and a garrison left with him. In addition, the yam system was to be extended along the coast and up the major rivers, but that would be done in our wake by a group of Totonaca trained for that purpose. I would wander among the tumen and coordinate any action that required more than one. We would continue until we reached the Putun frontier at which point I would have further instructions for them. I sent them all to their step-off points and told them to start the campaign in six days. When they left, Smoking Mirror came over to me.

"The Olmeca will not resist us and neither will the Putun. The Maya, however, are a great people, very learned and skilled and most brave. It is wrong to destroy them."

"I thought you had never visited them. Why are you so taken with them?"

"One of my father's fellow merchants who often traveled with him was from Temax, a town northeast of Mayapan nearer to the coast. He told me marvelous stories about the Maya and their wondrous cities of old. They studied the skies and knew all the movements of the stars. They knew when to plant and when to harvest, when the earth would move and when the storms would hit. They could even see into the future and foretold their own deaths. Still their wisdom is preserved in many books filled with their marvelously expressive picture writing."

"The Hanjen astronomers were always trying to predict the future by looking at the stars and believed one's moment of birth determined his destiny."

"An interesting thought. I have often wondered how much we really control our destiny."

"I happen to believe that our destiny is entirely in our hands and the result of decisions either we or others make. The stars are most helpful for navigation, but nothing else."

"Perhaps or perhaps not, who can say?"

"Anyway, if the Maya are so enlightened, why are they susceptible to Tezozomoc's lies?"

"They are good lies. We have stopped the human sacrifices. The Maya leaders are also the chief priests, and we have greatly reduced the importance of priests. But the Maya have been corrupted by the Itza, who conquered Uluumil Kutz long ago. They are said to be Toltec, but my father always insisted that they were not. In any case, things are much changed under them, and the old arts do not flourish. At least so said Poot, the merchant from Temax."

"Perhaps we will have a positive effect on them. Once we have removed the tyrants, might not the arts again flourish?"

"Is this your latest justification for our unprovoked aggression? We are fighting to free art?"

"I told you before, the Khan does not need me to justify his orders, just to carry them out."

He almost seemed to regard me with pity as he left, but I didn't let it bother me. I had the campaign to consider. The Olmeca did not call themselves by that name; it was merely a Nahual name for "people of the land where there is oli," (oli was the name for the black material produced from the sap of certain trees, out of which they made the balls for their ball game). They called themselves a number of different names like Cupilco and Coatlicamac. As predicted, when the campaign started, there was almost no resistance, and that which occurred was by accident. We rolled through their land in a few weeks. There was a lot of huffing and puffing among the elite, but little else. The merchants were delighted that we had finally come. The peasants were indifferent to us. The towns were much like those of the Totonaca. There was a central plaza with a temple on one side, the residence of the leader on another, and a ball court on a third. Smaller houses surrounded the central plaza. The people were a mixed lot; this seemed to be something of a melting pot of surrounding tribes. The prevailing language was a Mixteca dialect, but so many of the people spoke other languages that there was no need to learn it.

We next swept into the Putun lands. Here there was no pretense of resistance, and everywhere we were warmly received. All of the leaders immediately allied with us. The Putun towns were much like those of their neighbors, although it was clear that the merchant class was the most important. Indeed, their rulers were taken from the merchant class. Their major city, Xicalanco, was the preeminent market town. They actually called their land Acalan, but were not offended at being called Putun Maya. They had been very helpful to our mapmakers when they passed through and had let them join their merchant expeditions and so map all the trade routes. They were quite excited about the maps and had been using them ever since. They helpfully pointed out anything that had changed since the maps had been made. They were not really organized into a kingdom, but were a loose confederation of towns bound together by self-interest. I assured them our governance would be benign, and we would in no way interfere with their commerce. They organized a large group of guides to help us and set up a system to assure us of all the supplies we needed.

I called together the tumen commanders to explain the next leg of the campaign. I ordered the Quetzals and the Martens to move directly to the Maya frontier in the northeast from the coast. They would spend about two weeks pretending to get organized, and then they would begin a painfully slow advance. They should take all the time they needed to make sure they didn't walk into any traps or ambushes. The rest of us would march southeast and secure a wide steamy river valley north of a small range of mountains. Juchi had sent word that he was well into the valley south of the same range, so we needn't worry about that. Once our valley was secure, we would continue east to the sea, then advance north in a broad front to clear the large peninsula of all resistance. Unlike the decoys in the north, we would move as quickly as possible.

I arranged the tumen in a broad front stretching from the foothills of the small range about three hundred li a little north of east. Each Ordu had to cover a front of sixty li. It was no coincidence that the campaign started in the dry season. Of course the term "dry" was only relative. It was still a dank humid jungle, but at least it didn't rain most of the time, and the rivers and streams were fordable. Wagons were of no use at all in such terrain, and all supplies had to be moved by boat and horseback. Our horses were not at all accustomed to such conditions and many sickened and died. Insects were always present, but various local concoctions repelled them adequately. Snakes and ocelotl (the Maya called them balam) were also a problem, although only to our scouts. Fortunately, all animals shied away from large groups of men.

The jungle proved to be our main adversary all along the valley. We encountered only a few scattered small villages at first which offered no resistance at all; then later on, in the south near the main river, we ran into larger villages and endured a few pitched battles. These were messy affairs difficult to control or coordinate, involving mostly our trying to encircle the enemy and them trying not to be encircled. Visibility was limited and range restricted by the vegetation. Still, we generally got the best of these, and eventually the locals agreed to meet with us. We were to meet at a location they considered to be holy, near the main river.

The site was on the south side of the river at the top of a horseshoe bend in the river. It was a hilly place and covered with dense vegetation. As we drew near, we could see that there were stone buildings visible in the vegetation. It turned out to be ceremonial center that was once part of a good-sized city carved out of the jungle. The hills had been terraced to accommodate the temples. From what we could see, the temples were heavily carved with figures and inscriptions in the Maya picture language. The inscriptions either appeared by themselves or with the figures. No one was able to decipher enough of the writing to make sense out of it, but Smoking Mirror and some of our Putun guides knew a few of the pictures. Smoking Mirror said he saw a date that he calculated to have been five hundred years ago.

The locals seemed to be proud of the site as though they had something to do with it. They called themselves Lacandon and looked rather primitive. Their leaders were adorned in feathers and jade, but they were still a rather rude lot. It seemed inconceivable that they had anything to do with the place. Still, they insisted that their forefathers had built the city as well as others in the area, but they had abandoned them in the distant past, and no one remembered what the city was called. I decided not to press the issue, but got down to the matter at hand. I assured them that our governance would be benign, and we would help them and ensure the free flow of trade. I went through the usual pitch at length and could see that they were impressed. Finally they wanted to know if we were the same people who were fighting their way up the valleys of the Ixil and Jacalteca in the south. Assuming they were referring to Juchi's campaign, I told him we were. They then agreed to join us, since they could see there was no choice. I left a small group with them for communications and took most of their army with me to serve as auxiliaries. I would have liked to explore the ruins, but we had to keep moving.

East and north of the Lacandon and with their help, we found the Chol Maya. These people proved to be spread out over a large area in widely scattered villages and towns. Their resistance was spotty, and only a few villages had to be wiped out. I decided to spread the tumen into the positions we would need for our final assault on the north, and only have two tumen clear out the rest of any resistance from the Chol. I sent the Lizards and Vultures, the southernmost Ordu on to the east in a still broader band, since they could break into smaller groups and the Lacandon could guide them to all the Chol villages. The Lizards were to quickly sweep the southernmost line to the sea and then turn north along the coast. The Vultures would sweep a broader area gradually turning their direction from east to north and moving north on the Lizards' left. The Dogs, Manati, and Monkeys then pivoted to the north and began to sweep northward while broadening their front considerably.

I was with the Dogs when they ran into an interesting group around and on a lake. They called themselves the Itza and insisted that they had been driven out of their great capital Chichen some two hundred years before. They lived on five small islands in the lake and in small settlements scattered on the mainland. They were a stratified society with the priests holding a great deal of power. They had heard of us, had been expecting us, and were willing to talk. I went to their main island (called Tayasil) with a small retinue, but instructed the men to watch carefully for any treachery and be ready with boats to send a strong body of men to our rescue. The island was perhaps five hundred paces long and about two hundred wide. The main ceremonial center occupied the central high ground and was surrounded by houses all the way down to the shore. From the looks of the houses, it was clear that only the highest strata lived on this island. The leader's title was Ahau, and the high priest, who bore the title Ah Kin, assisted him. One of the Putun guides acted as interpreter for us.

"The Putun have assured us that you are a boon to trade, but we have some concern about your reported impiety."

"Since we have met only victory since entering this land, it is obvious that the gods do not find us impious."

"Is it true that you do not give the gods their proper nourishment?"

"No, we do give gods the nourishment we feel is proper."

"Human hearts and blood?"

"Incense."

"How long have you been in this land?"

"We have been here eighteen years."

"The gods have been most patient with you. You are fortunate indeed that others have kept them satisfied for you."

"We now control most of the land, and nowhere do we allow human sacrifice."

"There is far more land to the southeast than you think. Do you really plan to conquer all the world to stamp out human sacrifice?"

"I only plan to obey the Khan's instructions, wherever that takes me. His instructions have brought me here. The rest of the world will have to wait for another day."

"You ask us to choose between your Khan and our gods."

"I ask you to choose between life and death."

"Those who defy the gods have no life."

With that he jumped up and lunged at me. I quickly moved out of the line of his charge, and we all drew our weapons. The two leaders and most of their retainers fell quickly to our swords, and we fought our way to the shore. The mainland shore of the lake closest to us exploded in boats as some of our men rushed to our aid. The rest began to sweep the shores of the lake destroying all in their path. Our armor kept us alive until the rest of the men arrived. Some stayed in the boats and poured arrows into the Itza, the rest joined us, and we began to drive them back toward the ceremonial center. The men still in the boats surrounded the island to prevent any escape, and more of our men attacked the other four islands. Boats floated in mass confusion all over the lake with arrows flying and hand-to-hand combat breaking out whenever possible. On the main island, we reached the center and began mopping up. When resistance stopped, a house-to-house search was instituted to catch and kill any survivors. I sent word to the forces on the mainland to spare any of the peasants that did not resist, but wipe out all of the priests.

The battle was bitter, and the losses heavier than usual since so much of the battle was hand-to-hand. Most of my small escort was wounded, and a few were dead. Smoking Mirror had a bad gash on his forearm; I had a smaller one on my cheek and was covered with bruises from all the blows my armor deflected. Fortunately, I had left my son on shore. When the fighting ended, we had killed all of the upper strata of their society and only peasants were left. I enjoined them to go back to their fields in peace.

A smaller town called Topoxte was found on islands on another lake to the east, but the lesson of Tayasil was not lost on them, and they submitted to us immediately. The rest of the area was sparsely populated with small farming villages of Chol Maya, none of which offered any resistance. In fact, Tayasil turned out to be the only resistance any of my Ordu encountered on our northward march to Uluumil Kutz. By midwinter we were in contact with the Quetzals and Martens. They had only advanced a few miles from the Putun frontier, and the forces of Mayapan were massing for an attack thinking them timid. The land was drier and more open in the north making our horses invaluable. The Manati and Monkeys cut the massed forces off from behind, and both forces fell on the surrounded enemy. Few got away, and we quickly resumed our northward march.

Along the eastern coast of the peninsula, there was no resistance at all, since they heavily traded with and depended on the Putun. Inland, there was a little resistance in the east but almost none in the center and the most in the west. The farther north we moved, the more the resistance stiffened all along the line except for the coast. Before long, the entire east coast was cleared, and the Lizards were soon moving along the north coast. Resistance began to falter, and people either fled to the city of Mayapan or surrendered. Inexorably, we tightened the noose around Mayapan, and by mid spring, six tumen were camped around the bloated walled city. I already had the Dog Tumen detailed to occupy the land. They set up headquarters near the site of Chichen since it was most centrally located.

I was not interested in a long siege and brought up the artillery. The wall was about six feet high, but eight to twelve feet thick and followed the rolling terrain. It was pierced by seven large and five small gateways, all of which were currently blocked by whatever they had at hand. The city was rather egg shaped with the point in the northeast. It was almost six li long (east to west) and about four li wide (north to south). The houses seemed rather scattered about from this vantage point, as though the builders had followed the lay of the land. The ceremonial center was just visible in the center of the western half of the city. It was dominated by a pyramid structure.

I decided to use their wall against them. I lined four of the tumen along all but the western walls about two hundred paces away. Then I massed all the cannon all along the western wall with the Manati and the Monkeys at the ready. I did not want another Tayasil on a larger scale, so I waited for a westerly wind. It did not materialize soon enough, but we did get a totally calm day. It would have to do. We began firing at the stone wall. It shuddered and sent showers of slivers at first away but eventually toward the defenders. Before long there were breeches in several places, but we weren't ready yet. At a signal, a shower of fire arrows rained down on the city from all sides quickly firing the thatch roofs of the city's houses. As the defenders rushed to contend with the enemy within the city, we fired a few more rounds into the first layer of houses and then fired a barrage of rockets to further the spreading conflagration. Soon people could be seen jumping over the wall and fleeing the fire only to be cut down by the surrounding tumen. As the fire died down, I sent in the Manati, the Monkeys, and the auxiliaries to finish off any survivors.

The slaughter went on for most of the day, for there was quite a large population in the city. By nightfall, the task was done. We dumped those who had died fleeing the city back into it and camped around it once more. I had a few men look for Tezozomoc, but his body could not be found. We did find the bodies of many of the ruling class. They had taken refuge in a cenote, a type of sinkhole with water in it, which was used as a well. There had been one in the ceremonial center, and they cleverly used it to avoid the fire, but were cut down where they cowered when our men found the opening and looked in.

Everything of value was removed from the smoldering city, and we left the dead littering its streets. We returned to Chichen to await further instructions, and I sent off a large treasure train for Kuyuk. I spent the time looking over the monuments left by the Maya. Chichen was quite impressive. The Dogs had been clearing the vegetation away from the abandoned city, and it was emerging nicely. Just north of the ceremonial center was a very large cenote with the water level quite far down. According to Smoking Mirror, the priests would periodically hurl a victim into the water, and if he or she survived, it was expected he or she would have a message from the rain god. Since the victims were usually weighted down with gifts for the god, it was most unusual for them to return with a message. A very steep pyramid with very narrow tall steps dominated the ceremonial center itself. East of the pyramid was a large temple with the same reclining figure with a receptacle we had seen in Anahuac. There were also a great number of columns carved with figures of warriors, their prisoners, and priests. To the west was a small temple with carvings of ocelotl devouring human hearts, and beyond, a very elaborate ball court. To the south were another smaller cenote and more temples. One was curiously shaped round with a circular stairway inside. Beyond it was a most elaborately carved temple. The whole front had figures and symbols carved into it. Other temples had a plain stone first level with an elaborate upper level. There were splashes of color and bits of plaster still visible in spots, indicating that the buildings had been plastered and painted. I was also shown some elaborate frescoes. The style was very distinct. There were depictions of battle scenes, ceremonies, sacrifices, and even everyday life. We had also amassed quite a collection of their books and were trying to find someone to translate them into something more readable.

I had just set off to look over another set of ruins when a messenger from Kuyuk overtook me. Expecting another campaign, I returned to Chichen before I looked at it. The message was nothing I expected. He wanted me to dismiss four of the tumen and take elements of one of the remaining ones, preferably one of the local tumen, and proceed south to Juchi's headquarters. There I was to arrest him and return him to Kuyuk in chains. He had already ordered Juchi to halt where he was and dismiss all but his staff and wait for me to join him to return home in triumph. His arrest should be very easy for me under the circumstances. My heart sank. I must have stared into space for hours waving off all attempts at communication from my staff. Then I began pacing around the tent debating with myself. Finally I fell into exhausted if fitful sleep. The next morning, I called in George.

39
THE BARBARIAN POX, 19-20 K
SMALLPOX EPIDEMIC, 1387-8)

George came into the tent with a very concerned look wondering, he later admitted, if his mother had died. I motioned him to sit.

"I have an important mission for you. You are to translate this message from Kuyuk into the old language and take it to Juchi where you will translate it back again for him. You must go right after I send back Kuyuk's messenger with my reply. Once you reach, Juchi you will have to stay with him no matter what happens. Can you do this?"

"Yes, of course, Father."

"Good. Here is the message and some paper. Translate it here and now, and I'll look it over when you are done."

His eyes grew wider when he read the message, but he quietly went to work and did a very good job of translating the message. I admonished him not to tell anyone about the message or his mission but be ready to leave on my notice. I then told him to send in Smoking Mirror. While I waited for the latter to arrive, I composed my reply to Kuyuk. I had just finished it when he came in.

"Who do we attack next?"

"Read for yourself." I handed him Kuyuk's message.

"What will you do?" he returned the note.

"This is my reply: 'It is impossible for me to fully comply with your latest order. Therefore, after doing what I can, I am placing myself under arrest and turning myself in to you at once. I should be there by early summer. I am dismissing my staff and the tumen.'"

"You will not obey the Khan?"

"I can't. He is wrong to move against Juchi, and I cannot be part of it. What I would like to do before I go is to make you governor of Uluumil Kutz and give you my staff. I suspect it will be safer for you and the staff if you remain here out of sight, rather than follow me to my doom. I should think it would be best if your wife and family could join you. I can probably get word to you if he tries to move against you. But I suspect the worst he would do is order you to arrest Juchi. If he does, you could go ahead and make a vague attempt to do so."

"What would you have done if Kuyuk had ordered you to arrest me?"

"Arranged a hunting 'accident' and sent you off to Cuba by boat, while reporting your 'fate' to Kuyuk. However, he would not have ordered your arrest (that is reserved for the Khan's family); he would have ordered your execution. The same awaits me when I reach him, or, perhaps on the way."

"Then why go? Why not have your own 'accident' and disappear to Cuba?"

"Because then my family would be executed in my stead. No, I decided long ago to throw in my lot with the Mongols, and I will not now run from my fate."

"What about George?"

"He will be leaving on a mission shortly, but you know nothing about it."

"I see. I am willing to do what you ask. As it happens, my wife is on her way here now. I was going to ask you to let me stay here for a while anyway since I have grown weary of war. Still, I have thrown my lot in with you and would gladly join you on this journey if you would have me."

"Thank you, my friend. I would indeed enjoy your company, but I value you too much to risk your life. If you return as my companion, you would suffer my fate. I would be a poor friend to ask that."

"And I would be a poor friend not to offer."

"You can do more here. If Juchi survives to become the next Khan, the Khanate will be a better place, and you must help him, for the sake of our children."

"I will do as you ask. It may sound strange, but I am relieved to discover that you would disobey orders for the sake of a friend. There were times when I felt you were too mindless in carrying out orders. Still, I do not feel this is your last journey. I am sure we will meet again."

When he had left, I sat down and wrote a long letter to Paula and a shorter one to Padraig both in the old language. I told Paula about what had happened and urged her not to worry about me but to do what she could to protect the children. I assured her of my love for her and dared to hope that we would meet again. I asked her to translate the letter for Padraig (he never learned the old language). In it, I asked him to send Paula and the children to a safe place and not be able to find it should he be called upon to do so by Kuyuk. I thanked him for his friendship and many kindnesses to my family. I called in a messenger and ordered him to take the messages to the Antelope Ordu by the quickest route and tell no one of his destination or his origin. He saluted and left. Once he was well under way, I called in Kuyuk's messenger and gave him my sealed reply. I told him to take it back to Kuyuk at once. He saluted and left immediately. I then called in my staff and told them that I was returning to the Eagle Ordu at once. I would not need them, just a small escort would do. They would now serve Smoking Mirror, the new governor of Uluumil Kutz. As they left, I nodded to my son and watched from the entrance of my tent as he mounted and headed east toward the coast on his way to Juchi. Then I called in the tumen commanders and gave them their marching home orders. It was perhaps a bit risky to have only one tumen here, but with the help of the Putun Maya, I was certain we would know about any revolt long before it materialized. In any case, the Dogs would set about training a native tumen as soon as possible.

My work done, I walked about the camp and drank in all the sights, sounds, and smells. It had been quite an adventure, my life had been good, and I had no complaints. That night I slept very well. The next morning, I selected a small contingent from the Huaxteca and started on my way back. I went at a good pace but certainly not a messenger's pace. It wouldn't do to arrive in Kuyuk's presence shortly after my message. Once I had passed through

Huaxteca country, I dismissed my escort to visit their families and continued on alone.

It was a strange journey. With no mission on my mind, I was truly able to just enjoy the trip. I didn't carefully notice landmarks or dutifully make maps, but rather reveled in the natural beauty, noticing the subtle changes in vegetation and animal life as I moved north along the coast. I found myself disinclined to hunt, but just ate my dry rations at a yam or more often spent the night at one of the many villages where I was no stranger. I told no one about my likely fate, but instead very much enjoyed their company, trading tales, completely at ease for the first time since I was a child. I felt utterly at peace.

When I pulled into an Ishak village one evening, I was greeted warmly, as usual, and told that there was another visitor there also. This turned out to be Mazatl, Smoking Mirror's wife. She was happy to see me, and I told her that Smoking Mirror was now governor of Uluumil Kutz and regaled her and her two children with tales of the campaign and Smoking Mirror's significant contribution. The children were still a little young to fully understand, but puffed up appropriately. They both had the odd Nahual-type name, the boy was Seven Ocelotl (Chico Ocelotl) and the girl was Three House (Yeyi Calli). I assured them they would love Uluumil Kutz and urged them to learn the language and explore all the ruins. The next morning as we made our farewells, Mazatl took me aside for a private word.

"I know what you think awaits you at the Eagle Ordu, but you are wrong, you still have much to do."

"How can you know? Did Smoking Mirror write you?"

"No. My mother had a vision."

"Your mother? I don't remember meeting her."

"She didn't choose to meet you when you visited our town. She told me that morning that my future husband was among those coming in from the west riding strange beasts. Needless to say, she has the piercing sight."

"What was her vision?"

"She saw you as an old man writing in a book. I showed her the

Mongol writing I had learned, but she said it was another writing, and you were writing your own story and all you had seen."

"But how do you know about my current journey?"

"She told me I would meet you on my way, and I should tell you that you would not die at the Eagle Ordu."

"She didn't elaborate?"

"No. Sometimes she feels one should only be told what one needs to know. She didn't tell me who in your party that day would be my husband, but said I would know at the right time."

I thanked her and continued on my way, turning north away from the coast. I didn't know what to make of her mother's message. I had heard about some people foreseeing the future, but I couldn't imagine what would stay Kuyuk's wrath. No Khan could lightly dismiss disobedience, but it gave me something to think about as I turned the possible scenarios over in my mind for most of that day. That evening, however, I reached another village, put the whole business out of my mind, and went back to enjoying the trip.

The rest of the journey was most pleasant and uneventful. I fully expected to be intercepted at any moment by a group of guards and put in chains for the rest of the trip, but it didn't happen. Everyone greeted me like an old friend, and no one seemed to have an inkling that I was headed for any difficulty. I began to wonder if the messenger had failed to reach Kuyuk. Occasionally, there would be an accident, and a message wouldn't get through. However, there was nothing to do now but continue on my way. It was full summer when I reached the Owl Ordu. There again, I was greeted warmly and had to recount the part of the campaign after their departure for the commander, Tsakaka-sakis, and his staff. I noticed that they were all wearing new raw silk shirts, but didn't comment on it.

The next morning, I moved north on the last leg of the journey. It only took a few days to reach the Eagle Ordu, and still no one came to arrest me, and in the yams along the way no mention was made of any evil fate awaiting me. Even as the Ordu came into view, nothing seemed amiss. The sentry waved me through without comment. I continued into the Ordu and pulled up at Kuyuk's yurt. I asked one of the guards to announce me, but he told me to go rest up from the journey, Kuyuk was aware that I was here and would see me later. Puzzled, I went to visit Okuh-hatuh. He wasn't in, but was at a great meeting of shamans in the west. He was due back that night. I went to the yurt I had left five years before and was greeted enthusiastically by all my neighbors. I chatted with them a bit, then went in and cleaned up. Then I sat and waited for Kuyuk's summons. It came at night. I had just dozed off while reading an old book when one of his guards announced himself outside my yurt. He urged me to come at once. No chains, no arrest. I was waved in quickly by the guards and found myself standing alone in front of Kuyuk who was sitting gloomily in the candlelight. He eyed me coldly for a while, and I remained silent, as was the custom.

"I suppose you wonder why you are still alive?"

"Yes, frankly, I do."

"Don't let it give you any hope. Your life is still, of course, forfeit. However, you still may have a service to perform for me. A service that, most regrettably, no one else can perform."

"A service?"

"I never liked you. I was certain you could not be trusted and one day would betray us. But Kaidu always insisted you were the most faithful of all his men, and he trusted you above the rest of us. Kaidu has proved the fool. What you are is lucky. It is criminal how lucky you are. Had you betrayed me sooner, I would have enjoyed purging our ranks of you and your Ferengi brethren. You are a cowardly, vile, conniving, and untrustworthy race, and I only regret that Khan Ogedai's untimely death prevented the total destruction of your spawning ground. It would have been better had we overrun your puny race instead of the Hanjen. We would still rule in our world instead of having to come into another world as vagabonds and start all over again. And if we did, we wouldn't have our present problem, and you could die, as you richly deserve. On the other hand, perhaps you are not the hope my son thinks you are."

"Juchi is here?" I ignored his diatribe.

"I have no son named Juchi," he screamed at me. "I refer to Ogedai. He seems to think you alone can help."

"How?"

"Are you familiar with the so-called barbarian pox?"

"Yes, I am."

"Is there a cure?"

"No, but there is a marginally effective treatment and a very effective prevention."

"A prevention?"

"Yes, I read a treatise on it in Khanbalikh and asked about it. I was shown how it was done and even did it on Paula and myself."

"And it really works?"

"The treatise insisted that it was always effective, although not always pleasant."

"What do you mean?"

"Well, it involves giving someone a mild case of the disease to prevent the more virulent form. Depending on the relative mildness of the given disease, it can be pleasant or not. Mine was quite mild."

"And you and your wife cannot now get the pox?"

"No, we are immune just like anyone else who has survived the disease. Surely there are some among the Mongols who survived the disease, for it was always breaking out in the old Khanate."

"The ones with the scarred faces, like Batu?"

"Yes."

"And you can perform this prevention technique?"

"With the right ingredients, I can."

"What would you need?"

"I would need to go to the infected people, find one who survives the disease and is the least discomfited by it, gather the scabs from his sores, and use them to give the disease to those who show no symptoms. They in turn would likely have an even milder version of the pox, and their scabs would be used to further spread the immunity. The more often it is done, the milder the disease."

"The Hanjen always have the most disgusting cures for diseases." He grimaced. "How do you impart the disease with the scabs?"

"They are ground into a powder and blown into a nostril."

"How can you say such a thing without retching?" He choked. "And you have had this done to yourself?"

"Yes, it was not particularly unpleasant."

"As I said, you are lucky. Only the most incredible luck would have made you read and remember the one thing that can save your worthless hide now. You will go to the Salmon Ordu at once and stop the epidemic before it reaches us here. Then all of us will undergo your treatment of prevention."

"The pox has stricken the Salmon Ordu? Usually it kills most of those infected."

"And so it has. And it has not stopped there. It is quickly killing all the people thereabouts as well. You must stop it first from moving east, then from moving south. How much help do you need?"

"I can only take those who have survived the disease to help me. It would be monstrous to take anyone else."

"That would only be a handful."

"As more are treated, more can help."

"So be it. If you can stop the disease, you and your family will be exiled instead of killed. Go quickly. I'll send your help after you."

I returned to my yurt and gathered all I would need, some supplies and the hollow metal tube I had kept all these years. I was most concerned about when it had started, for it tended to spread very quickly. Winter would often stop it, and sparse population, but not much else. I jotted down a note to Okuh-hatuh telling him of the Hanjen treatment (boiled mallows mixed with garlic and rice), but cautioned him that it was only marginally effective. Mallows were found locally, and we had brought garlic and rice with us, but only the former was widely used, the latter had given way to other grains over the years. I had some rice in storage and got it and what mallows and garlic I could find among my neighbors to takewith me. I slept until first light, then set out full speed along the yam system toward the Salmon Ordu. When I reached the Hawk Ordu, I showed my brother the metal tube and urged him to make me as many as he could and send them to me as soon as possible along with more of the ingredients of the Hanjen treatment. While there, a few of my helpers showed up. All were much older than I was and quite vigorous for their age. All also bore the mark of their disease and a grimness about their mission.

I had almost reached the Antelope Ordu before it occurred to me that I couldn't trust Kuyuk to keep his word about exiling me. If Smoking Mirror was right about my blind loyalty, perhaps at last I was beginning to see. At least I would be in a position to help my family. The Antelope Ordu was buzzing about the epidemic. Padraig had decided that it would be best if everyone left the Ordu and scattered in all directions except west before the epidemic hit. He held everyone up when he heard that I was coming. It turned out that about the time my notes to him and Paula arrived, he had received an urgent note from Ogedai about the outbreak of the epidemic in the Salmon Ordu. Ogedai was alarmed at the virulence and fast spread of the disease and wisely made special arrangements for the transmission of messages to prevent the disease from spreading that way. Even so, it had been moving eastward inexorably and was already reported among the Nimipu. Padraig had mentioned the disease to Paula before sending her off to safety, and she had told him about the procedure I had done to prevent her from contracting the disease. He, in turn, had sent a note to Ogedai about it in hopes that word would reach Kuyuk, and I might be spared. I thanked him for his efforts but mentioned my doubt that Kuyuk would keep his word. He agreed that I was likely right.

Still, I had my work cut out for me. If the epidemic broke out that long ago, I would have to move as soon as possible. I told Padraig to keep his Ordu intact for now. I would start the process in the yams among the Nimipu and work my way back to the Antelopes. I would have to send people in all directions as soon as I had sufficient scabs from a mild-enough version of the disease. I told him that when I got back again, I would find Paula and treat the children. Until then, he should leave them where they were.

We moved out immediately along the yam network, and after several days, reached a station near the Nimipu frontier where the attendants were down with the disease. I sent one of the men on to the Salmon Ordu to get some of those who may have survived the disease to join me. Meanwhile, we tried to make the attendants as comfortable as possible. Two families of Nimipu attended the yam, and all but one old woman was down with the disease. The children were the worse off at the moment, although their mothers had already died by the time we got there. The younger men were also in very bad shape. The mildest case seemed to be a man about my age, a Mongol who had been on his way to the Salmon Ordu to visit his brother. I got his scabs as soon as they were fully formed. He was pleased that he could be of some help. One by one the others died. We did manage to nurse back one of the older men of the yam, but all the others did not recover. We buried the dead and prevailed upon the recovered traveler and attendant to stay and keep the station open for now.

We moved back to the previous yam, and I explained the situation to them. I suggested that only the middle-aged and older men take the treatment at this time, the rest should move on to the east until I had a safe enough batch for them. The young left, and I treated those left behind. All quickly came down with the disease, and we nursed them as best we could with the Hanjen treatment.

All but one of these eventually recovered, but only one had a fairly mild version of the disease, so again I only gathered his scabs. I was a little surprised that the disease was still so virulent. We continued on to the next yam and went through the same procedure. This time all of the cases were of the milder sort and all survived. At the next yam, I felt confident enough to treat all of the attendants and all of their families. Again the cases were fairly mild, but we had some trouble with the children and only brought them through with great difficulty. At the next yam, I sent the children away, and only treated the adults. This worked quite well, and I had a good "harvest" from them. Still, until I could safely treat the children, I wouldn't feel it was ready for general use. Before we left the yam, a group of volunteers from the Salmon Ordu arrived. They were all marked with the telltale scars and all looked haunted by what they had seen. They told me that the disease had broken out shortly after one of the Koryo ships had put into the Ordu. First those unloading the ship fell ill, and then it spread. The Salmon Ordu was now reduced to a skeleton. Only a few of the older men had not contracted the disease, and only a few dozen of those who had contracted it survived. Ogedai was not among the survivors. He was spared at first and tirelessly worked to help the sick. Then his wife and children got the disease and quickly succumbed. Before long, he, too, came down with it. He was one of the last in the Ordu to die of it. The situation in the villages was worse. Whole villages were dead; with no one to nurse the sick, all had died. The rest of the survivors were busy burning the dead in the surrounding villages. The epidemic was now raging among the Nimipu and even the Nomo and Salst, although it seemed to be skipping around and some villages had been spared so far.

We went on to the next yam and again treated all, even the children. This time all had a much milder form, and I had trouble getting very much of a "harvest" from them. While there, a shipment of the metal tubes arrived from my brother along with a good supply of rice, mallows, and garlic. By now, my helpers were well enough trained, and the material was suitable, so I sent them in all directions to find and treat as many of the still healthy people as they could find. I continued toward the Antelope Ordu yam by yam. Soon I was able to move more quickly since the disease was so mild that it barely slowed any but the children down, and I didn't have to tarry while nursing them all back to health. I made provision for "harvesting" before I went on, however, and urged them to send it on to me as soon as it was available. By the time I reached the Antelope Ordu, I had an excellent supply and was able to treat the entire Ordu and still have enough left to treat my children. Once there were enough sufficiently recovered to take care of the rest, I urged them to also start treating the yam attendants to the east and then went to find Paula.

She and the children were in the high plateau above the Yellow Canyon, and I found them near one of the hot springs. They were gathering in supplies for winter and already had a good deal of dried meat. They were a beautiful sight. I had left Uluumil Kutz thinking I would never see them again, and here they all were. My heart leapt—it was wonderful. I explained to the children of what the treatment consisted and how they would all come down with a very mild form of the disease, but would then never have to fear it again as long as they lived. They all bravely came forward for the treatment, although Ignace was concerned that they wouldn't be able to hunt for winter while they were recovering. I assured him that I would hunt while they were incapacitated and wouldn't leave until all were well again. And, indeed, I hunted while Paula nursed them, and we had a sweet interval as a family for a change.

I felt I had to go back and continue the work to make sure the treatment reached as many people as possible, but asked Paula to keep the children here so that if Kuyuk changed his mind, at least I could be sure they were safe. She reluctantly agreed, but warned me that she would not have much of a life without me. I promised to do nothing foolish and return to her as soon as decently possible. I also decided to send some trusted men from the Antelopes to protect them since raging epidemics tend to affect people in strange ways, turning some into marauding savages and, also, wild animals would be emboldened after encountering such feeble resistance among the sick and might attack the healthy.

When I got back to the Antelope Ordu, Padraig readily assigned a small contingent to guard my family. They considered it an honor since I had saved them from the epidemic. I trained and sent out groups from among the Antelopes, especially to go to the local villages of which they personally knew. I was particularly concerned about the Nomo and the Newe since they were so isolated. I then led another group of them to the Ox Ordu. Since it was mid fall, half of the Oxen went hunting for a few weeks while the other half were treated. When the hunters returned, they would also be treated. I trained another large group to treat the Siksika and the Kensistenoug and suggested that they could continue north and east in the spring. I moved on to the Hawk Ordu. Once the Hawks were recovering, I had the most able go and replace all the yam attendants between them and the Eagles. I treated the attendants as a group at the Hawk Ordu.

When I arrived at the Eagle Ordu, I found Kuyuk far more bitter than grateful. It was as if he held me personally responsible for Ogedai's death. I let him rant and rave as long as he wished. Then I reported on the progress so far and urged that I continue the program in the south in case it broke through from the west coast. I was sure it would not spread north in the winter, but it would really wreak havoc in the heavily populated south. He waved me on with seeming disinterest, and I left. I went to see Okuh-hatuh.

"You have saved us all, Raven," he greeted me.

"No, some nameless Hanjen physician saved us. I merely remembered his treatise."

"Your note helped me understand the nature of the disease. If mallows and garlic were thought to help, then it weakens the heart and is accompanied by a high fever. The rice could easily be exchanged with another grain, since it serves to keep up the patient's strength. I wished I could have studied with these Hanjen of yours. They are quite clever in their use of herbs."

"Yes, they have always been noted for that. I will show you the technique for preventing the illness, and you can be in charge of treating the Eagle Ordu. I think it best I move on to the Owls as soon as possible."

"I would be honored, but why the haste? I have heard that the disease has been stopped."

"I'm afraid it may have spread south along the west coast and could hit the heavily populated areas in the south, where I spent the last five years conquering."

"I have noticed a coldness in Kuyuk when he talks of you. Is there something between you I could try to smooth over?"

"No, it would be best if you didn't mention me to him. He very much wants to execute me and instead had to turn to me for help. He would be likely to strike out at anyone who spoke favorably of me."

"How did this evil happen?"

"He ordered me to arrest Juchi, and I refused."

"Arrest Juchi! Why?"

"He claimed Juchi was plotting against him. It is more likely that he wanted Ogedai to succeed him, but had already named Juchi as his successor. Now I don't know what he'll do. He has no other son and doesn't get along with his brothers. Hopefully he will either reconcile himself to Juchi or die before he has officially repudiated him."

"What will Juchi do?"

"Bide his time and watch his back. I don't think he'll move against his father no matter what happens. He knows it would tear apart everything that Kaidu worked to build. And that he would never do."

"I will do what I can for Kuyuk. He is a most unhappy man since Ogedai died. Perhaps you hadn't heard, but Ogedai's family was with him at the Salmon Ordu, and none survived."

I showed him what to do and moved on south. Once the Owls were treated, I sent elements of them eastward to continue the work in the southeast this winter, then move north in the spring. I continued on south to the Horse Ordu. Here there was no sign of disease, and no one had yet heard of it. I went on to the Coyotl Ordu that had been set up along the middle course of the Thanuge River the previous year. Some word had filtered in to them about the epidemic. Elements of the A'-a' tam had passed on whispers of a great death among the people of the coast. Trade had ended, and all were afraid to cross the Western Desert. Many of the people were moving east in fear, and quite a few of these were camped around the Horse Ordu. Once the efficacy of the treatment was explained, all were eager for it, and again I trained some Ordu members from each of the western tribes to return to their people with the treatment.

It was only when I reached the Lizard Ordu that I encountered resistance to the treatment. I had to demonstrate it on myself first, even though I explained that it would not make me ill at all because I had already undergone the treatment. Once it was clear no harm would come to me, some of those who had served with me stepped forward and accepted treatment; then the rest also went along. There was also resistance among some in the Totonaca Ordu. The Olmeca and the Maya were the most resistant. I had written a letter explaining the situation to Smoking Mirror, and he had come to Coatzacoalcos to meet me and help with the program. The resistance did not surprise him. He told me that although the Maya accepted him and the new "regime," they resisted any change in their way of life. There had been reports of occasional human sacrifice and the underground survival of priests and cult. As long as it was not open, he tolerated it. The Maya were a most kind, generous, and friendly people, but their stubbornness was unsurpassed by any he had met in his travels. He tried a demonstration before a large group of Maya, in which he treated his wife and children and a few volunteers. It did get a few to go along, but rumors ran in all directions about the sinister "true" purpose for the treatment, and it was impossible to gauge how effective the program was. I was able to send a crew to Juchi to treat him and his staff, including George. Kuyuk had made no further move against him, so he was still in the area called Tamoan Chan (Land of the Mists) by the Maya, and was acting as governor. He was in a town called Mixco in the southern highlands. These Maya also greatly resisted the program.

In the western high country, there was much less trouble, and the treatment was accepted almost universally. From Anahuac, I sent men to treat all those in the west and south who would accept the treatment. By the next fall, I felt my work was done, and I began to make my way back home. Some word of the results of the epidemic had finally reached me. It was necessary to send people to the west coast to start up populations again. The peoples around the Salmon Ordu had all but ceased to exist. The Ordu itself was no longer a viable organization, but it was being rebuilt. Kuyuk had ordered Padraig to go and do the task. He was also to rekindle our trading with the Koryo as soon as possible. The epidemic had worked its way south along the coast for a great distance, and the loss of life had been staggering. In the north, the disease skipped around more, and whole villages had been spared long enough to be treated and saved. The Nimipu had lost about half of their western villages, as had the Salst, but the rest only suffered a few spotty losses. The Nomo and Newe had only a few villages stricken, and those were virtually wiped out. None of the people farther east had any losses, and all who were willing were now treated. Provision had also been made to treat every newborn child who had lived a full year. Only the Southeastern tribes had not been treated. I felt that was unwise and found out later on that some of the Ani' Yun'-wiya had surreptitiously offered the treatment to their neighbors and many had accepted. I regretted that I hadn't thought to encourage more such sedition.

40

ASSASSINS, 20-1 K

(TX, LA, MS. TN, KY, IL, MN, ND, MT, 1388-9)

Since it was early winter when I arrived back at the Pelican Ordu, I thought it best to wait until late winter to start back to my family. I wrote a report of my efforts in the south and sent it on to Kuyuk. I explained that I would be checking up on the treatment program in the south and east this winter, but I should be at the Antelope Ordu in the spring, and he could send me a message there regarding my exile destination. Then I went east. I stopped at any village or town that I saw and made sure that all had received the treatment. Occasionally, I would find someone who had missed it and prevail on him to accept it now. A description of the course of the disease was usually enough to turn the trick. I eventually reached the Taunika and treated a few of them. They told me that the Natchez had been offered the treatment but had refused. I thought that imprudent of them and went to visit them. Since they were well aware that we surrounded them and far outnumbered them, they readily, if not enthusiastically acquiesced to my visit. I went to the "Great Sun" himself and asked him why they had refused the treatment we had generously offered to share with them.

"The generosity of one's enemies is always suspect."

"I didn't think we were enemies, but merely neighbors."

"Our gods warned us that your 'treatment' would make us impious, like you, and they would be forced to withhold their favor."

"All the treatment does is keep you from contracting a horrible disease that either disfigures or kills. Other than that it in no way changes you."

"There is no such disease, unless you brought it with you from whatever evil place that spawned you."

"I merely offer you life. I will not force it on you. Wherever the disease came from, it is here and has killed and disfigured many in the west. If it strikes here also, you will almost all die, and I would regret the disappearance of your people."

"You would? Why?"

"Who knows what wisdom you have or what lessons you can teach about the land, the river, the stars, whatever. We have learned much from each of those who have joined us. We have also taught them much. It is always regrettable to waste knowledge."

"How can the impious love the land? You confuse me."

"Perhaps I am not really impious."

"I will send you a group of people to treat. If they suffer no untoward consequences, the rest of us will also submit."

"A wise precaution. I agree to your conditions."

I treated about fifty of them, explained what would happen, and sent them on their way. I went on to visit the Pigeon Ordu and the Pansfalaya. I explained about the Natchez trial of our treatment and told them to treat the rest of the tribe should they agree to be treated. The Pigeons had returned from their occupation duties and wanted to hear about the rest of my campaign. We traded stories for a few days, and then I moved on to Nanih Waiya. I didn't really know why I went there, and I really didn't set out to go there, but I seemed inexorably drawn to the place. It was deserted when I arrived, and I climbed up the mound and sat at its summit. I neither felt nor heard anything special, but it was a peaceful place. I went back down the mound and camped for the night near its base. That night I had no dreams that I could remember. When I awakened, I found an incredibly old, wrinkled dark-skinned man sitting watching me. I rose and greeted him, stirring up the fire against the morning chill. He didn't speak, but fixed me with his dark luminous eyes. Then it occurred to me that he was Kiliahote, the same shaman who had spoken for all the Pansfalaya shaman when they agreed to join us many years before.

"It is remarkable that you have lived to such an old age," I said to him.

"No, not remarkable. Interesting, perhaps, but not remarkable."

"Do you come here to dream dreams?"

"No, do you?"

"I don't usually remember my dreams. I don't know why I came here, but I was drawn here."

"It is a good place. Perhaps it wants to tell you something."

"I heard nothing, but I did find it most peaceful."

"Then perhaps it is peace you need. It is coming, you know. The great death is coming."

"But we have stopped the epidemic. It was indeed a great death in the west, but not here."

"You did stop that death, but it was not the great death. The great death follows, and you will not be able to stop it. But never fear, it will not hurt you, and you were not meant to stop it."

"When will it come?"

"Soon. And when it arrives, it will solve many of your problems."

"Solve problems. How?"

"You will see."

"Will you also live to see it?"

"No."

He said no more, but closed his eyes, and began a sort of low chant. I walked a short distance away to get some water, and when I returned, he was gone. I looked around for him thinking to share some breakfast with him, but he was nowhere to be seen. I thought about what he had said, wondering what other disease would follow us here. There were many of them in the old land, far more than in this one. Not all of them were serious, but there was the epidemic that was reported along the southern coast of the old Khanate. It had seemed to be endemic in a few of the port cities, but it hadn't spread far inland. I couldn't remember the name of it, but it caused painful swelling in the lymph glands and usually resulted in death. I tried to recall what I had read so long ago about diseases, but couldn't think of any other serious one that spread like the barbarian pox. It was also the only one that could be prevented. Whatever the disease would be, I still wished that I could mitigate it. I knew I would try.

I decided to turn north and visit Murenbalikh. On the way, I visited some more villages, not only of the Pansfalaya, but also the Tsoyaha, the Chikasha and the displaced Iyehyeh elites. I noticed that almost all of the locals had changed a little. While the head deformation was still common, fewer of the youngest children showed it. Tattooing was also lessening, as were face painting and bizarre hairstyles. Still, feathers and jewelry were quite prominent, and land cultivation had increased to feed the horses. I also noticed that the people looked healthier, since they had adequate food in their diet. All had experienced a crop failure over the last several years from flooding, late frost, local draught, or whatever, and had received all the grain they needed from their neighbors through the nearby Ordu. Also, the horse enabled them to get meat, especially that of the plains oxen, far more easily. The advantages of being with us were not lost on them. Even the recent war in the south had helped morale, since it was a matter of pride among them to have fought successfully in battles. All this had done much to dispel any lingering hostility among the Chikasha and the exiles. I recognized several of them from the campaign, and they greeted me like an old friend. Only the oldest among them were still a bit distant.

I crossed the Wazhazhe River below the falls and passed the site of the town we had destroyed during the Hotcangara wars. It was hard to detect except for the obvious second growth, mostly evergreens, along the river where their fields had been. The town was hard to find without close inspection. We had not left any of it standing, and the burned wood had long since been reduced into the soil. Still, it was easy to distinguish the site on the bluff overlooking the river, and I thought back on that campaign, when I was younger and life was simpler. I just caught the motion in the trees out of the corner of my eye and dropped to the ground in time to miss the arrow aimed at me. I rolled over into a slight depression and readied an arrow of my own as I scanned the woods carefully. Again a motion alerted me in time to avoid another arrow. I could see the slightest movement in the brush as my assailant moved surreptitiously to the right to get closer to me. I followed the movement for a moment, then let fly an arrow at where I was sure he would be crouching. I heard a cry of pain and rushed forward with my sword drawn.

Doubled up in pain with my arrow deep in his side was an old Hotcangara warrior. He wore the old face paint even though he was dressed for winter hunting. I could see he was mortally wounded, for there was the blank look of death in his eyes beneath the pain and the hate. Even so he wielded a knife at me, although every movement further darkened the light snow on the ground with his blood. I approached him and kicked the knife from his hand with a sudden move. He looked at me for a moment, then put both his hands on my arrow and pulled it out with a strong jerk. Blood shot out of the wound, and he tried to stop it long enough to spit his defiance at me.

"So long you keep your hate, what a waste of your life." I shook my head. "You could have done so much more with yourself."

"Had I killed you," he gasped, "my entire life would have been vindicated. The gods put you in my power and I failed. I curse my fate, and welcome my death."

"Who are you?"

"Theenjaaykay-ea, Tayhah nea's brother," he almost whispered. "I knew you would be here today alone, and I had to try and avenge my people. I curse you with my last breath."

Blood followed his last breath out of his mouth, and soon he was still. I followed his footprints in the snow to see if he was accompanied, but they led to a small campsite. He didn't seem to have a horse, but had come on foot alone. Tayhah nea had been the old Hotcangara war chief we had defeated and killed long ago when we took Murenbalikh. I had assumed his family would have fought alongside and died with him a rash assumption. I wondered why he had focused his hatred on me and how he had known I would be coming by here alone today. I hadn't mentioned it to anyone, but he had been camping overnight waiting for me. I decided to follow his tracks back to his village to see if there was another hotbed of revolt in the area. I tied his body on one of my horses and brought it along with me.

His trail led me north for most of the day passing up the nearby villages. It was crossed by other hunters' trails, but his gait was distinct, enough to easily follow. He must have had a kind of a limp. Near dusk, his trail veered to the west and led me to a small encampment. It consisted of a single winter hut and a sweathouse. The remnants of a summer hut could be seen to one side, collapsed under some snow. There was a small stream meandering through the site. A little patch of smoke drifted out of the hut's smoke hole, so I knew someone was there. I kept watch for a while, and finally, just before the light failed, an old woman came out of the hut and looked up the trail in my direction. I rose up and approached her. She looked searchingly at me focusing her old eyes. Finally seeing who I was she slumped to her knees and began keening a sort of chant. I approached within a few feet of her, alert for any movement from the hut, and waited for her to finish.

"Are you Theenjaaykay -ea's woman?" I asked.

"I am Doecheeinggah, wife of Theenjaaykay-ea. Are you his killer?"

"I am. Will you also attack me?"

"No. I will not die with the foreign metal in me. I will die this night from the cold sleep. I bid you leave me in peace, for I would die alone in the company of my ancestors."

"Is this a burial ground?"

"It is."

"I have his body with me. Would you wish to bury it here?"

"You did not leave him for the beasts?"

"No. I will bring it up for you."

When I got back with the body, she was standing quietly. She took the body off the horse, eschewing any help from me, and, indeed, not needing any. She took him into the hut, then came back out and looked at me for a moment. Her face changed from that of a tired old woman to that of strong vigorous warrior. She fixed her dark eyes on mine.

"For this kindness, I remove his curse on you. You will die of age like me instead of violence like him. When you leave here, go west to the river, then north to the city. Do not come again alone to this land. There are many here who wish you ill. Go now, and do not camp near here."

I knew better than to talk to people when they had that look about them, so I mounted up and rode out of the encampment to the west. There was a full moon giving its eerie light to the leafless forest, so I didn't stop until it dropped below the treetops in front of me. It was well after dawn when I awoke. The weather was still clear and the bright sunlight belied the cold morning air. I continued on to Murenbalikh without further incident, only occasionally meeting lone hunters along my way. They were surprised to see me, but showed no hostility. I reached the city after a few days and found it a bevy of activity. Since all the harvesting and hunting were done, the people were busily engaged in contests of skill and strength or various crafts. I was greeted in a modestly friendly manner as I went through the city to the governor's residence. Tatanka Ska Koda had died a few years before, and the current governor of the city was Patheske, a Hotcangara who had worked his way up through the ranks. I told him about the incident with Theenjaaykay-ea.

"I greatly regret the attack," he said. "I have heard of him, but we thought he had died since he disappeared long ago after his brother was killed. He must have been living alone in the woods all this time, just biding his time. He was something of a shaman in his day and perhaps saw you coming in a vision, but his excitement blurred the vision and he didn't see what would happen to him."

"Do you think that's how he knew I was coming that day, a vision?"

"Yes. It is quite common among our shaman. I can ask one of them to look into your future for you if you wish."

"No, thank you. I prefer to leave the future in the future."

"As you wish. But the good ones can save you a lot of trouble."

"But Theenjaaykay-ea's woman said there were many here who wished me ill. Can that be true? Are many of your people still full of hate?"

"Love and hate are strong emotions. They are not easily given nor are they easily withdrawn. Your people killed many of mine, far more than seemed necessary, and you left many people hating you for it. I would say more of us do not hate you anymore. But those that still do, still do."

"The woman gave me the impression the hostility was directed at me in particular."

"One of our shaman insisted that you, because of your strange looks, were the evil influence that made the Mongols so ruthless. For a while, that view was quite popular, and it was thought if you were to be killed, the Mongols would be more kind to us."

"My position and authority were never that strong. I merely obeyed orders."

"Yes, but the Mongols do not appear that different to us while you do. Of course, I never believed that. Years ago I met a man from an eastern tribe. He said that he had seen men like you almost every year. They fished in large boats and occasionally came ashore for water. His people did not bother them, and they, in turn, seemed to pose no threat."

"You say people that look like me fish off the eastern coast?"

"That is what the man said."

I stayed a few days visiting various acquaintances and trying to find out more about my fishing "relatives." No one knew any more about them, and I toyed with the idea of looking for them, but I wanted to get back to my family before Kuyuk moved against us. I crossed the river to visit the Falcon Ordu. Borgurchi was still the commander, and he welcomed me warmly. We talked about the southern campaign, especially the Tya Nuu portion in which they had taken part. I mentioned my visit with the Pheasants in Huexotzinco and asked about his stint as occupying governor of the Tya Nuu. He said it was an unpleasant business. The people had resigned themselves, and there was no armed resistance, but they were not cooperative. He and the rest of the Ordu had been quite pleased when they were replaced by the Quetzals last year and could finally return. Then, to my surprise, he freely expressed his displeasure with Kuyuk. He had been one of Kaidu's minghan commanders in the original Ordu, and while he revered Kaidu, he felt his son was worse than worthless. He assured me that the only good thing Kuyuk had ever done was to father Juchi. I asked if such opinions were widely held, and he insisted that they were. None of the original Ordu had any respect for Kuyuk, and I should be careful of him since he would likely turn on me one day. I didn't tell him that that day had already come, but rather assured him that I would be careful.

I took the yam system north along the river eventually crossing over to visit my old Ordu, the Wolves. Temur was still in command of them, and he also greeted me warmly. We talked about the southern campaign and especially his part in the campaign against the Ben Zah. It had also been a hard struggle, and they were glad they didn't have to remain on occupation duty. Although he assured me that the Ben Zah women were the most beautiful in the south. I had never seen any of them that I was aware, although I had been fairly close to their land when I was in Tlapan. He told me he could take care of that loss right away and called over an attendant. The man ran out and returned with a woman. She was fairly tall and slim with light skin for a Southerner, like burnished copper, almost translucent. She had large bright eyes, a straight nose and full lips. I had to admit that she was a beauty, perhaps second only to Paula. She fixed a rather puzzled look on me.

"Do you speak the Nahual language?" I asked.

"Yes," she answered in a halting, musical version of that language. "But you cannot be a Mexica."

"No, I am a Mongol."

"The strangest I have yet seen. Are there more like you?"

"Yes, a few. How did you come to be here?"

"I was a slave of the Tya Nuu. I was freed by your forces and tried to return home. When I arrived, my family and my village were all dead also at the hand of your forces. Teghur, the son of Temur, looked on me with favor and brought me back with him. Since I had nowhere else to go, it was a kindness."

"You do not hate those who killed your family?"

"It will not restore them to me, and I cannot help them by joining them in death. Teghur has been a good husband to me, and I have been well received by his family. This is my new home."

"I congratulate you on your wisdom and Teghur on his good fortune in finding you."

"I thank you." She bowed and left.

Since Temur did not speak Nahual very well, I repeated the gist of our conversation for him. He listened intently and smiled.

"My son has chosen quite well for himself. She speaks Mongol quite well now, but it was interesting hearing that strange tongue and trying to catch the words. You should hear their language. They call it Loochi, and it is a very strange, musical language. They convey more meaning with how they speak than which words they use."

"You were right about their beauty, or is she an exception?"

"No, I would say she would be average. They are quite a beautiful people. However, it is no surprise, they allow any deformed infants to die, and their elderly kill themselves rather than grow ugly or senile with age. It is, I suppose, pragmatic, but ruthless."

One could wonder why the Ben Zah did such things. Of course, the Hanjen would often leave baby daughters to die, and the more primitive tribes that lived in harsh land would do the same as the Ben Zah. Still, it was an odd practice for such a settled civilized people. I didn't stay long among the Wolves, but continued on my way north using the yam system. I was within a day's ride of the old training site near Lake Ocheti, when a blizzard kept me trapped in a yam for almost a week. I didn't mind, since the Ocheti shakowin family that ran the yam was wonderful company, and we swapped stories much like I had in that first trip over to the new land.

When the wind finally died down, the snow was a few feet deep and very powdery. I regretted not having my dogsled with me, but the horses were well rested, and I would not have trouble finding the next yam. I set out early and soon found the going quite difficult. We had to high step through the snow, which slowed down both the horses and me and tired us out. I kept changing horses, but we had not gone far when I could see they were all exhausted. I looked about for shelter, but this was a rather flat land; there were few hills and no caves. Quite by chance, I saw an old hut. It was in a screen of pines and was almost invisible, but I had lost my footing and happened to look in its direction as I got up. The hut was not in the best repair, but it was made of wood, and its roof seemed fairly intact. There was enough room in it for the horses, and the door was just high enough to admit them, so I brought them in first and fed and watered them for the night. Since they were in the hut, I could not have a fire, so I ate my dry meal and wrapped myself up for the night.

I woke early the next morning, and after eating got started back on the way to Lake Ocheti. It was again a day of very slow progress. But I did just make it to the yam at dusk. The attendant took my horses from me and shooed me into his yurt. I warmed myself at his fire and was quickly served a bowl of hot broth and some of the mondamin grain. An Anishinabe family attended this yam. They had seen me many years before during my travels here and were glad to see me again. They suggested that I wait a few days until the messenger with the dogsled came back this way. He would then be returning to the Hawk Ordu. He had been headed to one of the Anishinabe villages on Lake Gichigami and should be on his way back soon. Since I wanted to go to the Hawk Ordu, it seemed like a good idea. Actually my own dogsled and team were at the Hawk Ordu with my brother and his family.

Two days later, the messenger came in the late afternoon. He turned out to be my old friend Nitsiza. I had not seen him for some years. It happened that he had been running a yam station north of the Hawk Ordu and had missed the campaign in the south. He had returned to the Ordu as a messenger this winter since their messenger had been killed in an accident. He would return to his station and his family in the spring, however. He did not regret missing the southern campaign, he told me, since he thought it would be too warm there for him, and he didn't want to be so far away from his family. He was delighted to have me along with him. We started out the next day. He gradually brushed me up on my sledding skills during the runs, and we caught up on our past few years each evening at the yams. The passage took two weeks including a day's layover during a freak blizzard.

When we reached the Hawk Ordu, Nitsiza took me right to Henry's yurt. He was glad to see me. I spent a few days with him, and he showed me all that had been going on among his metal workers. More and more of the men seemed to be engaged in making ornaments. Still, enough were making the arrowheads, helmets, swords, and knives. Migizi was still working on making smaller cannon. He had made one with a two-inch muzzle, and it had worked fairly well, except that it was hard to control. He was sure he could make them even smaller, like the one I had given him years before. He had made some just like it, but they had exploded when fired, so he thought he'd work down to that size. He was experimenting with different alloys now. I wished him luck and told him he could keep my small cannon. Henry gave me two raw-silk shirts like those we used to all have when we first came into this land. They were now available again because of the Koryo trade, and he wanted me to have some. I remembered how one had saved me from more serious damage during the Iyehyeh campaign and gratefully put one on before I left. I looked over my sled and made a few minor repairs on it. I rounded up most of the dogs, wrestled them into their harnesses and took a few days turning them back into a cohesive team. I set off again once the team was ready enough.

The first days went smoothly. Since the river was still frozen hard, I had decided to use it with the dogsled so the way would be a lot easier than the constant climbing in and out of ravines up on the plateau. I made quite good time, enabling me to have more time to find the yams in the afternoons, since they were not readily apparent from the river. On the fourth day, I noticed the junction with the Absaroke River and turned into the latter. It was late winter by now, and there was some melting during the day that would refreeze at night. I had to be careful not to set the sled on any wet spot overnight, or I would have to chip it out in the morning. On the sixth day, not long after I left a yam and got back on the river, I was moving along at a good pace when suddenly I felt an impact on my back. At first I felt only surprise, but it was followed by pain. I crouched down and urged the dogs onward as fast as was safe. Another arrow whizzed by my head. A bend in the river came up just in time to save me from another, which shot by just as I turned. I stopped the sled a little farther along and turned it over on its side. Using some of my spare clothes, I made it look like I was dead under the sled. Then I pulled the arrow out of my back and placed it in the dummy. Finally, I took cover nearby under the riverbank overhang behind some rocks. I first readied my bow and some arrows, then felt the wound. The cold did much to minimize the bleeding, and it wasn't a deep wound thanks to all the clothing I was wearing. My raw silk shirt neatly sheathed the arrow in my flesh keeping it from catching when I pulled it out. I stuffed some clean cotton into the wound and crouched down to catch my assailant. I did not have long to wait.

Since he was on horseback, it took him awhile to reach me. He was up on the bluff opposite my position, and seeing my sled, he jumped off and climbed down to the river surface. He approached the sled with his sword drawn, circling behind to avoid the snarling dogs. As soon as he was in range, I shot an arrow into him. I was a little above and to his right, and since he was intent on my decoy, he was taken by surprise. The arrow went deep into his chest, for my range was only about fifty feet. He staggered back from the wound, dropped his sword, and fell down. I rose up, drew my sword, and approached him. It was one of Kuyuk's guards, Macoegee, a Hotcangara. He was mortally wounded and merely looked at me as I drew near.

"Did Kuyuk send you?"

"Perhaps. Perhaps not. Who can tell?"

"You wouldn't be here without Kuyuk's permission. Why do you shield him now? You must know you will die."

"So will you."

With an amazing move for one with such a wound, he lunged at me with a knife. My reflexes did not fail me, and I jumped back in time to miss his thrust. There would be no more from him, however. He landed on his chest and likely forced the arrow deeper, for when I kicked him over with my foot, his lifeless eyes stared ahead. I checked him for any dispatches, but he had none. I went up to his horses. They also bore no dispatch, only food and clothing. I had to think there would be others and that this was done at Kuyuk's bidding, but I had to wonder why. He could easily order me back to the Eagle Ordu and have me slain or order one of the Ordu commanders along the way to arrest me and either kill me on the spot or return me to him. It didn't make sense. I brought the horses down on the river.

I dragged Macoegee into the hiding place I had used and made some hoof coverings for the horses from his clothes. I brought them along with me to the next yam. I asked the attendant about them, claiming to have found them wandering along the river. He said that they were not from his yam, but perhaps from the next one down. I turned them over to him and stayed the night. I was very much on my guard now, so I stayed with the dogs, claiming one of them didn't look well. Nothing happened that night, and I started off early the next morning. That evening, I reached the Antelope Ordu. I went in to see the commander as soon as I arrived. I was surprised to see Padraig. He was obviously troubled, but at the same time most relieved to see me.

"You can't imagine what a relief it is to see you."

"Why are you back here? Have you heard from Kuyuk?"

"I have. I was ordered to return here this winter. If you had not arrived before the spring thaw, I was to kill Paula and the children. If I failed to do so, my whole family would be killed instead. I was sure you would make it, but it is still quite a relief. Why does he hate you so?"

"I don't really know, except that he blames me for the loss of his son. I think it's quite obvious now who sent that assassin to ambush me. Kuyuk wanted me not to reach here so you would have to pick between my family and yours. He hoped you would not be able to kill my family then he could freely move against both of us. He seems to have fixated his hatred on Ferengi."

"He would have won, then. I could not have harmed your family."

"Does he tell you to where I am to be exiled?"

"You won't believe it." He shook his head in disgust. "He has ordered me to take you to the Salmon Order. There you and your family will be placed on the first Koryo ship that comes to trade and returned to the old land."

41

EXILE, 21 K

(MT, WY, ID, WA, OR, 1389)

I had to admit I did not expect Kuyuk to send me back to the old land. I had to sort out what to do next. I told Padraig that I would go get my family from the high plateau and meet him at the Salmon Ordu as soon as weather permitted. He agreed and urged me to be careful and give his best to Paula and the children. I thanked him again and set off up the river early the next morning. The yam system took me much of the way up the Absaroke River, so I "camped" warmly for the first several days. Finally I had to turn south into the Yellow Canyon itself and away from the yams. The snow cover helped me climb up the western ridge of the canyon. It would have been easier to run up the frozen river, but I would never have been able to climb the walls of the canyon near the falls with the sled. The going was slow and rough. I had to spend a few nights under the stars. Howls from wolves made me cast about for a cave the second night. I finally found one and piled up a load of wood for the night. I got the dogs settled inside the cave and the fire going just before nightfall. All night long, the haunting cries of the wolves drew nearer. I kept the fire going until dawn, only sleeping fitfully. I had seen the cold yellow eyes glistening in the night or in my dreams, but there was no sign of them in the morning.

The sky was leaden, and there was moisture in the air that morning, so I fed the dogs quickly and got going. We had just reached the plateau late that morning when the snow began to fall. The flakes were large and wet, limiting visibility, but not impeding the sled. The going was also easier on the flatter terrain of the plateau. Remembering the lay of the land, I bore a little to the southwest to reach the area of the hot springs, west of the lake where I had last found my family. The lake came vaguely into view at last, and

I could just see the steam from the hot springs challenging the cold air and the still-falling snow. I aimed toward the steam and soon found myself in a strange land that was a patchwork of steam, ice, and snow. I halted the sled near one of the hot springs and set up camp. It was still early, but with poor visibility I would never find my family, so I decided I might as well wait for the weather to clear in a comfortable spot. I was really looking forward to a good soak in the warm waters a little way downstream from the hot spring. I settled down the dogs and fed them, then stripped and stepped into the water. The warmth was penetrating and revitalizing. I probed my wound a bit and found it was healing nicely. After a good long soak, I reluctantly got out, gave myself a good rubdown and dressed in fresh clothes. I found it best not to camp too close to the steam, since it would alternately bathe you in damp heat and freeze you as the wind shifted.

The next day was clear and a little warmer. It was spring in most of the land but still winter up here. I began looking around for my family. I looked all around the lake, but saw no sign of them. I was returning to my campsite that evening when I saw a small company of Panai'ti, a tribe related to and much like the Newe. I stopped and hailed them. They greeted me heartily and invited me to join them in their nearby camp for the night. They had been hunting the large reindeer and had found my campsite. They wondered who it was that was up here alone in the winter. I was surprised that they would hunt here in the snow, but they said it was often easier to catch game in the snow, although not with horses. They had a fair-sized campsite laid out near the western edge of the plateau. They had already had some success hunting, although from the taste of the meat, it must have been an ancient and skinny animal. I asked about the pox, and they said that their village had been spared. They had submitted to the treatment, although there were a few villages that had refused it. Most of the villages that had been wiped out by it were in the west near the Nimipu and the Nomo. The latter had also been hit by the pox, but they assured me that the worst damage was beyond the western mountains. They had heard that whole tribes had been annihilated. I suspected that overstated it a bit, but I asked why some of their villages had rejected the treatment.

"Our shaman are split on the treatment. Some say that since the disease followed you from the other land, you would know how to cure it. Others say that we should just stay away from you since the disease followed you and would hit those who came in contact with you, but spare those it could not find."

"I don't know how disease works, or what it is, but this particular disease strikes only large groups of people. It disappears for years, and then comes back again. Only those who survived the disease once or received the treatment remain immune to it. It was also reported to not affect some people, especially those of advanced years, but to be especially merciless on the young."

"All of our diseases come from evil spirits. Perhaps this disease's evil spirit hates the young and thriving."

"Perhaps." I had no intention of debating that point. "But whatever disease comes from the old land to ravage your people, I hope you realize that we never wished it so and will do all we can to stop it."

"We know that you are good people. You have brought peace and plenty into the land. We can walk the land with no fear of our neighbors. If our crops fail, you send us all we need. You have given us a wondrous animal that gives wings to our feet so we never want for meat. It would be folly to expect there would be no price to pay in return. That is not the way life is. Fortune and misfortune are brothers. One can only hope that the latter merely comes to visit not to abide. What say you, Raven?"

"Such wisdom can only come from a chief," I complimented him.

The hunting party had just arrived that morning so they had not seen anyone else on the plateau. I decided to try the southern extension of the plateau the next day. I rose early, ate, bid my hosts farewell, and good hunting and set off for the south. The southern lake was smaller, and there were fewer hot springs, but it was an even better place to hide in the winter, with all its narrow ravines on the western side of the lake. As I approached the entrance to one of the ravines, I saw a man standing with an arrow drawn. I slowed down since it was obviously not a sneak attack. As I got close enough, I stopped the sled and approached him. He lowered the bow and bellowed.

"It is the Raven! He has finally come."

With that I could see a group of men rising up from hiding places and coming toward me. I got close enough to recognize the man who had called out to the others as Itskinaks, a Siksika who was now a jagun commander in the Antelope Ordu. He clapped me on the back in welcome and soon more of the Antelopes surrounded me and welcomed me heartily. Soon a path was made, and Paula came running toward me with the children behind her. I ran toward her, and we held on to each other as if our lives depended on it. It was as though all the anxiety of the past two years could be squeezed out of existence if we only clung hard enough. Reluctantly we let go, and I gave each of the children a big hug. We had a little celebration that night. I talked to Paula and the children alone that night explaining what Kuyuk had ordered.

"I am not sure how, but I do know that we will not return to the old land. We will go to the Salmon Ordu so that Kuyuk cannot strike easily at Padraig. But once there, I will think of a way to stay."

They were all in agreement with me and most anxious to avoid going back to the old land. Mathilde was a young lady now seventeen years old and, while Ignace had been too busy looking after the family to form any attachments and the others were still a little too young, she had fallen in love with a young man from the Antelope Ordu. They wished to marry, and the young man presented himself to me for my approval. He proved to be a Siksika named, oddly enough, Seagull. His actual name was Suyi Piksi, which meant Water Bird, but when he described the bird, it was obviously a seagull, so he had changed his name to Seagull in Mongol. When I explained to him that we were to be exiled, and if he wanted to marry Mathilde, he would have to join us in that exile, he was fully prepared to do so. He said that his vision quest had taken him to a large lake where he had seen a seagull in flight. That led to his name and his conviction that one day he would live near the sea. I asked him where he had been posted since joining the Ordu. He said that he had at first joined the Salmon Ordu, but had only been there a year when he was called home because of his parents' bad health. As it happened, while he was away, the pox had struck, and by the time he was ready to return, the Salmon Ordu had become a shell. He had decided to stay with the Antelopes until a decision had been made about the Salmon Ordu. His jagun had been sent to protect my family. The most wonderful assignment he ever had. Since I was not familiar with the coast, I asked him about the area.

"It is a pleasant place, the winters are mild, there is a lot of rain, but it isn't a soaking rain. There are huge cedar forests, much game, and more fish than one could imagine. The locals are strange looking since they deform their heads, but some of them are very friendly, and all of them are good warriors. There are a lot of languages, however, some not unlike that of the Salst and some like that of the Nimipu, but others very strange indeed. There are even some bands of people with a language like that of the Tinneh that live north of my people. These live in the wild mountain forests, but we were in touch with them, and they had allied with us. Only some of the more northern tribes had refused to ally with us."

"What about in the south? How far south had recruitment reached?"

"I was told that the original recruitment had only reached the people immediately south of the Salst River, but later an expedition was sent south along the coast as far as a large bay, and then it returned through a huge valley between two ranges of mountains. There was some resistance, but eventually all joined or died. South of the bay, there was some recruitment, but it had been sporadic, one band at a time."

"I know the mappers made it all the way down the coast. Why didn't Ogedai follow? Did he ever set up an Ordu in the south?"

"I don't know why he didn't go south, but all our attention was on trade and facilitating the movement of goods along the yam system east to the Eagle Ordu. We had a few outposts along the coast north and south of the Salmon Ordu, but he never established another Ordu, and we spent very little time training recruits. They were mostly used to move goods. I was posted to one of the outposts for a while. It was in the north on a cape across a strait from a large island."

"What was that like?"

"It was wonderful. The local tribe was a kind, peaceful people who called themselves Kwenetchechat; it meant 'cape people' in their language. They showed me how to handle their large boats."

"You learned to use their boats?" Seagull had given me an idea.

"Yes. It isn't too complicated. I could show you once we get to the coast if you like."

"That would be most enlightening."

The next morning, I sent the contingent of Antelopes back home to their Ordu after detaching Seagull. I told Seagull and Mathilde that I fully approved of their marriage, but suggested that they wait until our disposition was more settled, since it was not easy traveling when one was pregnant. They agreed, although reluctantly. There was still quite a bit of snow on the ground, but it was getting soft, and it was clear that we could soon travel on horseback. I had already sent the dogs back with the Antelopes. A few days later, we started west, crossing the mountains by the same high pass I had used years before to enter the plateau. Soon we were making our way through the upper Kimooenim River Valley and the most hospitable villages of the Nomo. Spring was fully in progress in the valley, and only the mountains were still draped in snow. Flowers bloomed everywhere, and Paula and I were reminded of our journey across the prairie in spring many years before, although the vegetation was not nearly as lush in this high valley. We found a few deserted villages on the western fringe of the valley and a few more as we entered Nimipu land. It was eerie spending a night in a totally deserted village, especially since you knew it wasn't abandoned, but wiped out. We finally ran into some Nimipu, and they were most gracious to us. It seemed I was given all the credit for stopping the pox, and they had even named the treatment "the raven's breath."

We passed over the mountains and followed the Salst River to the Salmon Ordu. This was the worst part of the journey. The terrain was no problem, but the sights were. Little more than wild, snarling dogs and skeletons populated a few of the villages. Some of the villages still had people in them, but they looked shattered and haunted, many bore the scars of the pox. The yams were back in operation, and they had a surplus of horses, since so many people had died and left them behind. Some had escaped and were running wild now. The dogs were becoming a threat to the young and the weak, and wolves were also getting quite bold. Until the population rebounded, it would only get worse. Attempts to get people to move west and replace the lost were only somewhat successful. We found several villages of Nimipu, Salst, and Siksika north of the Salst River and some Nomo villages south of it, but only a handful of the people among them came from the more eastern tribes. There was much concern that the pox would hit again. I tried to explain that as long as they had been treated, they had nothing to fear.

We finally reached the Salmon Ordu. Padraig showed me around. The Ordu was on the north side of the mouth of the Salst. The river was very broad at its mouth, nearly twelve li wide. There was a huge snow-capped mountain standing as a sentinel on the southern side, some distance upstream. It had been visible for much of the later days of our journey, and the locals said it was a volcano, although not an active one. Its presence had been the reason the Salmon Ordu was established on the north side of the river. Frankly, since there were two smaller volcanoes on the north side of the river, that weren't as far upstream, I thought they should have put the Ordu on the other side of the river. Seagull had been right about the rain, it wasn't continuous, but there was a lot of it. The cedar forests were amazing. The trees were huge, and the undergrowth was dense.

Apparently only a few hundred of the original Salmon Ordu survived the epidemic, and whole tribes had been wiped out. I asked Padraig how far north and south the pox had spread. He said that to the north it had only affected the coastal tribes and even there had seemed to skip some of the villages completely and had only gotten perhaps fifteen hundred li north when the treatment halted the spread. Most of the tribes south of that point had been greatly reduced and had been forced to consolidate their villages. Inland, the more isolated settlements, especially those in the mountains, had been spared long enough to receive the treatment. The valleys and the heavily populated areas had been devastated. The local Tsinuks had been reduced to a mere fragment, as had the Kalapoewah who lived in the large valley that ran south of the Salst River not far upstream. Along the coast, the tribes had also been greatly reduced to the south, but again in the mountains they fared much better. The disease had been stopped among the Shastika and the Lalacas in the southern interior and the Shagero on the coast. It would have been much worse had there not been some already sparsely populated areas to slow down the spread. Still, much of the coast for about nine hundred li south was currently deserted.

The Koryo had not yet arrived. In fact, there had been no sign of them since that ill-fated ship that brought the pox. Padraig wondered if perhaps they realized what they had unleashed here and were afraid to return. I was sure they would be back, since there was no limit to a merchant's greed. I used the time to learn how to use one of the local boats. The Tsinuks had left a great number of their boats, and these had been piled up for eventual use as firewood. With Seagull's help, my sons and I selected the one in best shape and learned the finer points of operating it. Seagull then painted it in the gaudy style of Xa'ida, an island people far to the north. The bow and stern were painted red with imaginative sea animal designs in black. The center was painted black as was the upper rim on the inside. I finalized my plan. I had the boys get as many water skins as they could find without inviting questions and put them in the boat after filling them. I also bought a good supply of dried ox meat, ostensibly for trading once I arrived in Koryo and put it with my belongings.

It was only a dozen days after our arrival that a sail was sighted, and the merchant fleet came into view. As they approached, I wondered if they carried Kiliahote's "great death" with them. The merchantmen dropped anchor near the shore, and the leader put out to shore with a small escort. Padraig and I waited for them on the shore. The leader bowed formally when he reached the shore, looked us over perhaps expecting to see Ogedai or some other familiar face, and then introduced himself as Yi Mongju, a merchant

from Songjin. I recalled that Songjin was on the northeast coast of
the Koryo peninsula. We introduced ourselves and invited him to
join us for a meal. Over the meal, he apologized for taking so long
to return. It seemed that there had been some turmoil over succession to the throne. The real power was in the hands of Yi Songgye, a
general who was leader of the anti-Yuan faction. He had driven out
the Yuan sympathizers and seized all their lands. The current king
was merely his puppet. Yi Songgye was trying to befriend the rulers
of the Middle Kingdom, the so-called Ming Dynasty. Already, the
Ming pretender had insisted that the name of Koryo be changed
to Chosin, to mark the dynastic change. He then asked if Ogedai's
absence was perhaps due to some sort of upheaval in this land.

"Indeed," I replied. "On your last visit you left behind the so-
called 'barbarian pox.' It killed him and his whole family along with
most of the people in this area. We were able to stop it by using an
old Hanjen method."

"But the pox usually does not spread far or do such damage.
Surely there was some other cause for such destruction."

"The pox was unknown here. Perhaps that made it stronger. In
any case, we hope you will never again put in here with disease as
part of your cargo. If you do, it will not again be forgiven."

"Understandably so," he stammered. "Be assured, never again
will I bring disease with me."

"Good. Now, from what I understand, you exchange silk for
gold. Is that correct?"

"Yes. That seems to be all you want from us and all you have
to trade."

"Perhaps there is more here than you might think. Do you have
any need for copper?"

"Yes, I could take copper. I didn't know you had any to spare.
Silver would also be welcome. Could we interest you in ceramics or
cotton? I see you wear cotton, but perhaps there is a shortage?"

"We have plenty of cotton. In fact, it is superior to yours. The
fibers are longer and produce a sturdier fabric. Your ceramics are
quite fine and delicately wrought, but such things are of no use when
there isn't an elite class. However, if you could persuade a learned

doctor to relocate here, it could be most helpful. Perhaps one who was on the wrong side of the recent unpleasantness?"

"I think I might be able to do that." He brightened. "I might perhaps make up for my last, inadvertent cargo."

"It might. Tell me, if your current rulers are anti-Yuan, how do they allow you to trade with Mongols?"

"One does not always volunteer information that might not be well received. Songjin is far from Kaesong, the capital, and I don't tell the local authorities where I'm going. Besides, as far as is known, the Yuan are all on the Mongolian Plain, and one cannot reach there by boat from Koryo."

"Where do they think you are trading?"

"Yapon-uls, of course. I sail east and the only thing east of Koryo is Yapon-uls. Actually I sail northeast to avoid the Waegu."

"The Waegu?" Padraig had never heard of the Koryo name for the Yapon-khun pirates. The Hanjen called them Wo-koo, and they called themselves Wako.

"They are pirates that live mostly on the west coast of Yapon-uls and on the islands between there and Koryo. Their predations were devastating until General Yi Songgye sent a punitive expedition to wipe out their hiding places. They are far less of a problem now. In fact, they struck our port right after I returned from my last trip here and took all I had. It took two years to build up again."

"Do you not sail along the coast to reach here?" I asked.

"No, the winds and currents take us north of the island of the Ainu, then east across the sea to this place. We return along the coast to the north, then follow the chain of islands west."

"The offshore current here flows north?"

"The current closest to shore flows north, but a little farther out it flows south. Have you an interest in sailing?"

"Only a little. The Khan has exiled me to Koryo and wants you to return there with me."

"But that is impossible. How can I return from Japan with a Mongol Ferengi? You couldn't even pass for an Ainu."

"I'm sure we can reach an understanding. Perhaps if we discussed this alone?" I nodded to Padraig, and he shrugged and left the room leaving the merchant and me alone. "Don't worry, I don't want to return to Koryo with you. I only must leave here with you. Once we are out of sight of land, I will leave your company. This is what we'll do. You will express interest in obtaining one of the local boats. They are quite colorful and finely carved, so your interest will appear plausible. I will show you a fine specimen and offer it to you as a gift. You will accept it and have it placed on your ship just as it is. Once your trading is done, you will take my family and me with you. Once we are out of sight of land, my family and I will 'steal' the boat and escape. You will have no idea what happened to us."

"I will do as you ask. It seems like the best way around an unpleasant situation. Now perhaps after a good night's sleep we can get on with some trade."

I had him shown to his quarters and sat down again with Padraig. "I got him to agree to take me with him. You should write a note to Kuyuk after I go telling him that you saw me get aboard the ships and sail away with them. Also mention that the merchant is willing to trade copper and silver for silk. I don't want us to keep sending all our gold back to the old land. And it may help focus Kuyuk's attention elsewhere."

"I can't believe he's sending you back." Padraig shook his head.

"Don't worry about it. I know we'll see each other again."

The next day, the trading of silk for gold was concluded, and the merchant absently admired one of the local boats. I suggested that he have a look at the boat we had been using while waiting for him. He expressed great admiration for it, and I told him he could have it since I would have no further use for it. He had it taken out to and pulled aboard his ship along with the gold and fresh supplies of food and water. He also took along a sample of our cotton to see if he could find any interest in it. Finally, my family and I said our farewells to Padraig and his family and our other friends. We, along with Seagull, then took our belongings and boarded one of the boats to be ferried out to the ships. We boarded the strange ship, climbing up a rope thrown over the side to us. The merchant welcomed me aboard the ship and asked me to make sure his new boat was properly secure. I looked over the boat carefully and suggested that it be lashed to the outside of the ship so that it could be used quickly in case of emergency. The merchant agreed, and the boat was secured to the side of the ship. As we began to get under way, Seagull and I surreptitiously stowed our things on the boat. I could see that one of the ship's crew had seen us, and I went over to him.

"You look like a bright young man," I said in Hanjen, handing him a small lump of gold. "Perhaps you can do me a service?"

"Oh yes." He smiled broadly. He spoke Hanjen quite well.

"When you return to Koryo, should you encounter anyone knowledgeable about the silk cultivation who might want to leave Koryo, perhaps you might suggest to them an eastward voyage?"

"Would people of Koryo be welcome here?" He seemed surprised.

"If the Mongols were welcomed here, why wouldn't the Koryo be?"

"But silk requires mulberry trees. I have not seen any here."

"There is a type of mulberry in the southeastern part of the land. Are you familiar with silk?" I thought perhaps I had inadvertently found the right man.

"My family cultivates it. It is greatly encouraged now. Would my whole family be welcome here?"

"With such a skill, most certainly."

"I will ask them. I take it you will not be with us for long?"

"Who can tell?" I smiled at him.

He went back to work, and my party kept together near the boat watching the shore recede as we put out to sea. Once we could no longer make out details on the shore, Ignace, Seagull, and I placed arrows in our bows and made a big show of stealing the boat. The ship's crew looked more puzzled than surprised and willingly lowered the boat with us on board into the sea. We stowed our bows and started paddling westward with the oars. Before nightfall we could feel a current pulling us southward and turned into it. As the stars came out, I was able to see that we were still just north of the Salmon Ordu, but well out to sea. By midnight, we were south of the Ordu, but the current was not very swift. I wanted to be sure we were well south of it before turning in toward shore, but I had to allow for the north-running current along the shore. I also had to bear in mind that weather could suddenly turn ugly, and the sea was no place to be when that happened.

We had plenty of food and water, so we had nothing to do but all take turns rowing the boat to help along the sluggish current. I wanted to be at least six hundred li south of the Ordu before turning in to shore. I wanted to reach the mouth of a river called Caiyukla on the map. It was about five hundred li south of the Ordu. A tribe of the same name had populated it, but it was one of the tribes virtually wiped out by the pox. The survivors had concentrated northward with some related tribes around a river called Alsi' (again for the local tribe). I thought it might take six days to get far enough south at the rate we were going. Almost every morning, we were beset by a dense fog that would only slowly lift. Fortunately, the current kept us on course. The sea was full of animals. There was a large relative of the otters we had long enjoyed watching sport on the riverbanks and innumerable seals. On a rare clear day, we even saw a small pod of whales a comfortable distance away. On the third day, the wind began to pick up a little from the north. I was concerned that it might be heralding a storm, but it did increase our speed even though we did not have a sail. By nightfall, when I made another star sighting, I could see that we would only have to continue another day if the wind held up. By dawn, the seas had become a bit rough and the sky was leaden. The wind had not only held all night but had picked up. I decided it was best to make for shore rather than try to ride out what had to be an approaching storm on the sea in a small boat.

We all paddled furiously eastward, while the wind continued to pick up speed and the waves grew higher. Soon we had to dedicate the younger children to bailing the boat as the higher waves began to crash over the boat. Then the rain began to fall. It was a wind-driven rain squall so it actually did not last long, but it nearly swamped the boat, and we all had to bale furiously. Fortunately, Seagull had had the foresight to outfit the boat with wooden bowls for baling. Once the squall passed, the seas began to settle a little, and we continued to paddle eastward with determination. Finally near midday, the land came into view, but it was the mountaintops of the coastal range rather than the shore. By evening, the shore itself was in sight, but it was a jagged rocky shore with many small rock islands full of birds. By now, although the wind drove us shoreward, the current was flowing north, and we had to struggle against it while propelling ourselves toward the shore and avoiding the rocks. Somewhere in the dark, the moon dancing in and out from behind the clouds revealed a sandy beach before us. Summoning what strength we had left, we propelled ourselves toward it and with the help of a good-sized breaker found ourselves at rest on the shore. We got out, wearily pushed our boat farther ashore and then lay down in it for an exhausted sleep. Before allowing myself to sleep, I took a reading on the stars and forced my numb brain to calculate our position before collapsing myself.

It was well past dawn when we began stirring. I was the last to wake, and when I finally did rouse myself, it was to the smell of roasting fish. Seagull had caught them, the children had gathered wood, and Paula had prepared them. I was embarrassed that I had slept so long, but assumed that my age was catching up with me. We very much enjoyed the fish. My calculations of the night before indicated that we were within several li of the Caiyukla River, but I wanted to take another sighting with a clearer head that night and suggested that we camp here for the day and rest up from our voyage. There was no objection, and Ignace went hunting, and Seagull went fishing while I checked over our things for damage. The maps were in waterproof sealskin pouches, so they were in good shape. We still had plenty of dried meat, and it also had remained in good condition. We still had some water, but I sent Mathilde and the younger ones to look for a stream. Paula helped me with our things. After all was accounted for, I took the map of the area up a nearby hill and tried to figure out where we were from it.

This seemed to be a rather heavily wooded area, mostly fir trees. There had been some cutting of trees in the area in the last few years, indicating that there had been a settlement nearby. To the north of my hill was a small row of hills, to the east was a good-sized hill, and to the south there appeared to be a level area leading to what had to be a small river. It was too small to be the Caiyukla, but it might be the unnamed one just north of it. That night was clear, and I took another sighting determining that I was indeed north of the target river. The small unnamed river to the south was shown on the map to drain a lake and might prove quite adequate to our needs. The map also noted a settlement on the lake, and indeed, Ignace's hunting expedition had taken him to the lake, and he had found the now-deserted settlement. He had also found a deer, and we ate well that night.

42
"KORYO," 21-9 K
(SW OR, 1389-97)

The next morning, we dragged our boat well above the beach into the trees. We then took all our belongings and made the trek overland toward the settlement on the lake that Ignace had found. We seemed to be heading southeast and within a few hours were within sight of the lake and the abandoned village. The lake was perhaps six li from east to west and about one and a half li from north to south (it had something of a crescent shape with a finger extending north from the middle). There was a river emptying into its eastern end from the north, and the river draining it was at its western end. The village was nearer the western end, on the northern shore, west of the "finger." It was not very large, only six houses, but the houses were quite large, about fifteen feet wide and thirty to forty feet long. They were made of wooden planks, much like those of the Tsinuks. Each had a large central fire pit with a raised plank floor and plank benches. There was a long pole for smoking meat and skins over the fire pit. There was a small patch of garden where the locals had cultivated a little nawak'osis. We cleaned out two of the houses, the largest and the smallest, and then patched them up with pieces cannibalized from the other houses. We then built a sweat bath, which Seagull felt was essential, and I had finally grown to enjoy.

The next day, Seagull began his "preparations" for his marriage. He was determined to do everything correctly. He set out alone on an expedition to find a worthy bride gift for Paula and me, even though we assured him it wasn't necessary. Mathilde took over fixing up the smaller house to her satisfaction with the enthusiastic help of Ludmilla. Ignace and Theodore went hunting, and I helped Paula fix up our house. It was strange living in a house after all these years in a tent or yurt, and this was a strange house. But we had both lived in houses in Khanbalikh, and starting over like this made us feel young again.

Seagull was gone for quite a while, and Mathilde was beside herself worrying about him, but I assured her, it was not unusual that he was searching long and hard for a worthwhile gift, since he greatly valued her, and our opinion. Meanwhile, the houses were looking quite habitable, and the boys had found considerable game in the surrounding hills. As summer waned, flocks of waterfowl landed in "our" lake, and we added a few of them to our larder. The lake also abounded in fish, and even with my limited skills, we were able to catch quite a few of them as well. We also were able to gather berries. Even though it was late spring, we cleared a patch of ground and planted a small garden with the vegetable seeds Paula had thought to bring along, and it was coming along nicely. There was no shortage of rain, and we were frequently blanketed in fog, but the climate was quite mild.

Finally, in early fall Seagull returned. The boys and I were at the stream that emptied into the lake trying to figure out a way to catch some of the huge salmon that were just beginning to make their run upstream, when we heard horses. Thinking it might be trouble, we put arrows in our bows, hid, and waited to see who it was. Suddenly, out of the woods Seagull emerged riding one horse and leading a dozen more. We jumped up and greeted him. He proudly leaped off his horse, embraced me, and handed me the reins. This was his bride gift to me, horses. It seems he was of a mind to find horses for us all along and remembering how many were running wild to the north, he reasoned that there might also be some to the east. He crossed over the mountains into the large valley between them and another taller range farther east. There he found the remnants of the Kalapoewah at the upper limits of the valley, but farther downriver there were only deserted villages and many horses running wild and free. He quickly rounded up this small herd and got them used to being ridden again. It wasn't too hard, but it did take time. He then brought them back. He had prudently avoided any contact with the locals, just in case he might be recognized. Needless to say I was delighted with the gift. It is very hard to be a Mongol without a horse.

We went back to the houses on horseback with more than a little rowdiness from the boys. Theodore was put in charge of feeding and watering the herd. Mathilde was most relieved to have her intended back in one piece, and Paula was also delighted to have horses again. Seagull showed us how the Tsinuk caught salmon by blocking the stream with nets. He insisted that we first catch one, place it on a stone facing upstream, thank the salmon spirits for letting us catch it, roast it, each eat some of it, then throw the bones back in the river. If we did this each year, we would never want for salmon. It was not the first time things had been delayed by the local beliefs, but it was hard to criticize them, since they merely evinced reverence for the animals on which they depended for sustenance. In a way, I found it both touching and wise.

I asked Seagull if he had some elaborate ritual in mind for marrying Mathilde, but much to my relief he didn't. He would merely purify himself for three days, and then be ready. He did not expect Mathilde to do anything she wasn't accustomed to do. At the end of the third day, he would present himself to us for any ritual we had in mind, and then take his bride. His purification rites were not easy. He rose early in the morning, stoked up the sweat bath, steamed himself, rubbed down with fir boughs, plunged into the lake, and spent the day alone in quiet meditation. He took no food, only drank a little water, and smoked a little nawak'osis during this time. Mathilde spent the time fussing over her wedding outfit and her hair, assisted by her mother and sister. The boys and I caught and smoked salmon. We had cleaned up another of the houses for use as a smoke house (since none of us were very fond of choking) and put it to good use. On the third day, I thought I should ask Mathilde what sort of ceremony she had in mind. That gave her something else to think about for a while, but she finally came back and said she wanted the same ceremony Paula and I had had. Fortunately Paula had a better memory than I had for such things and remembered her uncle's exact words on that day long ago on the banks of the Sungari. I wrote them down and was ready that evening when at last Seagull presented himself.

He had a final surprise for us. He presented us with a huge sturgeon he had caught in our lake. It was already cleaned and roasted. He had dressed in his finest Ordu "uniform" and carried himself with remarkable dignity and strength for a man who must have been starving. Mathilde made a beautiful bride, reminding me very much of her mother. The ritual was mercifully brief, and we had quite a feast to celebrate. Not only was there the sturgeon, but also salmon, venison, duck, the mondamin grain, and other vegetables, followed by bowls of fresh and dried berries. After the feast, Seagull and Mathilde set up housekeeping in the small house.

The fall and winter were not harsh. Although there were some remarkable rainstorms, there was very little snow. We retrieved our boat after the first such storm and found it still seaworthy, although its paint was badly worn. We dragged it back with the help of the horses. The mild weather inspired me to look around a bit at our surroundings. I found the Caiyukla River to the south. It was bounded by tall sand dunes on both sides along the coast. They extended for some distance to the south, but not as far as our river to the north. I decided to call our river the Koryo River, since that was where we were supposed to be. I also named our lake Seagull Lake, for no one could get larger fish out of it with less trouble than he could. There was a smaller lake closer to the coast, and I named it for Mathilde. This caused a little jealousy among the other children, but I promised them a worthwhile landmark when it presented itself.

Another project for the winter was building a forge for Ignace. He wanted to continue honing his skills, and we might need some metalwork before long. He had some iron scraps with him, but there was no coal or iron ore in the surrounding mountains, although there was lime. We did find some scraps of steel around the village, mostly arrowheads and a few copper bangles. I made him one of the double bellows of the Hanjen, which got him temperatures from burning wood just hot enough to do some work.

In the spring, Mathilde, now quite heavy with child, began looking around for certain herbs and other medicinal plants to build up her considerable inventory. Ludmilla had shown some interest and was helping her. Ignace kept us in fresh meat and worked his forge. Theodore had become adept at fishing with Seagull's coaching and added this to his groomsman duties. Paula and I started another garden. Once it was planted, Seagull and I did some reconnoitering. I thought it best that we find out just where around us there were occupied villages. As the population began to rebound from the plague, there would be inevitable expansion, and eventually we might be found.

To the north, we found the remnants of the four tribes that had lived along this part of the coast still clustered in a few villages along the Alsi River about seventy-five li north of our river. There were signs that they were rebounding, however, and they seemed to be close to outgrowing their villages. To the east, the nearest villages were in the upper part of the Kalapoewah Valley, where Seagull had found them last fall, about ninety li away from us. Southeast of us, we had to go to the upper reaches of the Etnemitane River to find the remnants of its namesake tribe. They were beginning to range some distance on their hunting expeditions, but not in our direction. Their nearest village was about one hundred twenty li southeast from us. About the same distance due south of us were the Kusa. They had not been as reduced as some of the others around us. They had villages around an excellent natural harbor as well as along the river that was named for them. The sand dunes north of them tended to channel their expansion inland rather than toward us. It looked like our northern neighbor would be the most likely to come upon us. I decided we would have to check them out every few months, and everyone in the spring.

On our way back from the Kusa, we stopped at any deserted village we found to see if we could find anything of use to us. We found a few scraps of metal, mostly copper, for Ignace, and some decent arrows, but little else. Most of these villages had belonged to the Etnemitane, a somewhat primitive tribe related in language to the faraway Tinneh. We had almost reached the limits of their former territory, when we were astonished to see a bit of smoke coming from one of the houses in a village. We came closer for a look and were surprised to see a young woman, seemingly alone working in front of one of the houses. She was busily preparing a rabbit for a meal. We waited to see if anyone would join her, but as we watched, she roasted the rabbit and cleaned and stretched the skin. Then she ate the small meal with great deliberation, savoring as if she had not eaten in a while. She was definitely alone. We agreed it wasn't safe for her, and I sent Seagull in to see if she would want to go join her people upstream. If she did, he could guide her there, and I would wait for him. I thought it best if I not show my face, since I did stand out in a crowd.

Before long, Seagull was back. The woman was willing to join our "band," but she would not go upriver to her relatives. It turned out that she was not an Etnemitane, but had been married to one. He and her young son had gone to visit the Salmon Ordu shortly after the plague broke out. They had perished, but she was unaware and had finally gone north to find out what had happened to them. She encountered one of the men I had sent to give the treatment and had taken it, thinking that surely her husband and child had also. When she arrived at the Ordu and learned the truth, she returned to her old home in despair only to find it deserted except for her father-in-law. She had nursed him back to health, but he had died during the past winter. She had no one among the Etnemitane who would welcome her back, and indeed might not know any more of them, since most in her village had died. Her birth tribe was from the south, the Da-a-gelma'n, who lived along the river named for them. They had been greatly reduced by the plague, and she had no reason to return to them either. Seagull felt we should let her join us. I had to agree.

She was somewhat taken aback when she first saw me. She had heard that there were pale people like me, but had never seen one before. I explained, that except for Seagull, the entire band she was joining was pale. She felt it could be no worse than getting used to the Etnemitane, and was much better than living alone. She was an attractive woman in her early twenties, and I had to wonder if Ignace would find her so. I explained to her that we would help her fix up a house of her own if she wished or she could live with us. She could help in any way she felt competent to do so, and no particular demands would be made on her. She was most eager to join us.

We found a few more deserted villages on the way, but no more denizens thereof. We finally reached home and introduced our new guest all around. Her name among the Etnemitane had been "Earth Woman" because her people lived "in the ground." Actually their houses were only partially in the ground like those of the Nimipu. In any case, she wanted a new name to go along with her new status and eventually picked Daldal. It seemed to be some sort of private joke with her, since she always laughed when we called her that. She lived for a while with us, and then decided it would be better if she lived in her own home. We helped her fix it up, and eventually, by the fall, Ignace came to us to ask our approval of his marriage to her. She was a wonderful woman, and we thought he had made a wise choice. Oddly, Ignace chose to go through the same purification ritual that Seagull had. He felt it had brought Seagull good fortune. Daldal also went through some sort of ritual, but it was not for men to know about, so I can't report on it. They also wanted the same marriage ritual as Seagull and Mathilde had, and we had another appropriate feast. Meanwhile, Mathilde had delivered a daughter in the summer and named her Christina.

The next few years were peaceful and quiet for us. Mathilde and Seagull had another daughter, Miriam (after Paula's aunt). Ignace and Daldal had a son, Simon (after Paula's grandfather). We planted, harvested, fished, hunted, and kept an eye on our neighbors. As I expected, those in the north began to move. First they moved east up their river, then north and south along its tributary streams, then south to another small river. Soon it became obvious their next move would be still farther south. I figured we only had another few years. The yam system had been restored, but it was on the other side of the mountains with offshoots leading to the tribe concentrations on this side, well north and south of us.

In spring of the fifth year of our "exile," there were a number of developments. The most shocking was that Paula delivered another son. I had thought surely we would have no more, but it happened that she had been suffering from some sort of ailment and finally, Mathilde had come up with a formula that cured it. We named the boy John. Our children also each had another child, Mathilde a boy, Henry, and Ignace a girl, Ruth. It was amazing having little children running around again. We again made the annual check on all our neighbors. The Kusa had begun moving a little north and now occupied the mouth of the Etnemitane River. The Etnemitane had begun to move back down the river and had reached Daldal's old village. The Kalapoewah were moving north down their valley. The northern group had moved to within thirty li of us, and it would be unlikely that they wouldn't eventually notice us while they were hunting. We had to decide what to do next.

I thought it would be safe for us to stay another summer here, but we should move away in the fall, for that was when the hunters ranged the farthest. I decided to make it my job to find another place for us to live. I had Ignace, Theodore, and Seagull take turns watching the encroaching neighbors and, once the garden was planted, went east toward the mountains. Actually, I already had a site in mind and merely wanted to make sure it would do for at least a few years. The site was about forty-five li due east of our current home. It was on the banks of the Caiyukla River at least sixty li from the mouth just after a large northward bend in the river as it came down through the foothills of the coastal mountains. It was a large level area that had once been settled, but was now grassland giving way to a forest. The village site was overgrown, and the planks rotted away. It even looked like there were other still older sites across the river. The river was about a li wide at this point and was moving a little too swiftly at this time of year for me to try a crossing. I could see a couple of mountains to the south and southeast that might serve as observation posts for those directions, but since the most likely encroachment remained from the north, they would likely be of little use. There was plenty of game in the surrounding forest, and the river teemed with fish. The land would be easily usable for cultivation. On the whole, this site was at least as good as our current home and should serve for a few more years.

I returned home and told the others about the site. The boys had seen it already during various hunting expeditions and were enthusiastic about it; the women needed to see it first. Once they had seen it, they also thought it ideal. I felt it would be best if we allowed our "village" to become a bit rundown, and take the best planks from the unused houses and take them to the other site and begin our new village. We built a wagon and began hauling things to the other site. At Ignace's suggestion, we first built him a house, and he and his family moved there to expedite work on the other houses. Every several days, I would haul another wagonload there and stay a couple of days to work on the houses. They were quickly taking shape, and by midsummer all were ready. We moved Paula and the younger children in the late summer and Seagull and Mathilde followed last. He wanted to get a good supply of salmon before leaving. We dismantled and moved Ignace's forge and the sweathouse, harvested the last of our garden, and left the now partially overgrown site. We tried to make it look as much as possible like it had when we found it. I thought it best if we collapse the houses and fire the site so as to further cover our presence there. I reasoned that a fire would explain why the site wasn't more heavily overgrown. I waited until a nearby thunderstorm preceded by much lightning to fire the site. It didn't burn long before the rain moved in and put it out, but it did burn enough.

The winter was pleasantly mild and passed uneventfully. In the spring, we again reconnoitered our neighbors and found little change except in the north. There was now a settlement on the stream fifteen li north of the Koryo. The villagers were no doubt hunting and fishing around our old Lake Seagull. That summer, there were more children, another son for Ignace and Daldal, Peter (over my protest), and another son for Seagull and Mathilde, Leo (some forgotten relative of Paula's we were running out of names). Paula had no more surprises for me, but John was healthy and growing like a weed. All the children seemed to thrive here.

The following spring, Theodore presented himself and requested permission to go on a vision quest. I detected Seagull's hand in this, but I didn't want to deny the boy's request. Still, it was imperative that we not be found, and I emphasized that to him. He understood and said he would go no farther than the mountain to the southeast. I insisted that he wait until our annual neighbor inventory, and he agreed. We found no real change from the year before. I even climbed the mountain and found it unoccupied with no sign of anyone being nearby. When we got back, I wished Theodore good luck on his quest. He was gone longer than I expected, but returned before I got alarmed. He wanted to discuss his quest with Seagull, Ignace, and me as soon as possible. We got together at a spot a little upstream from our settlement. We sat down in a circle, and Theodore began to speak.

"I went directly to the mountain on foot, so it took most of the morning. As Seagull said, the animals did not disturb me as I went. I climbed the mountain and sat near the top, among the trees. I sat there all night and neither saw or dreamed anything. The next morning, I walked to a spot where a cliff gives a clear view toward the west. I drank a little water and sat down. A fog rolled in and covered all the low ground before me leaving only my mountain and the one to the west above the fog cloud. I felt almost like I was floating above the ground. Then I saw an eagle rise up through the fog carrying a fish. He circled majestically looking for his nest. Suddenly a large shadow passed over the sun, and the startled eagle dropped the fish and plunged back into fog to recover it. Looking eastward for the cause of the shadow I saw an isolated cloud, and under it there was a lone raven flying toward the south. I saw no more of the eagle. The fog lifted at midday, and I saw nothing more that day, and returned to my night spot. I remembered no dreams.

"The next morning, I again took up my position on the cliff. There was no fog this time, and I could see the sea to the northwest. Flocks of seabirds were just visible as specks diving into and hovering over the water. Again I saw an eagle rise from below carrying a fish. He flew directly to his nest and fed the fish to his hatchling, bit by bit. The hatchling would not eat, however, but merely sat impassively ignoring the offered morsels. Finally, it crouched down and moved no more. Its parent kept offering it food for a while, then left the nest and flew toward the sea. Another eagle landed on the nest, prodded the hatchling with his beak, then took the fish and flew toward the north. I saw no more that day, but that night I dreamed that an eagle chased a raven through the sky until it lost it in the setting sun. It returned in triumph only to be shot out of the sky by an arrow. Then the raven flew back out of the setting sun.

"The next morning, I returned to the cliff. The eagle's nest was empty, but I saw another eagle rise up from a different nest a little to the south. Its eaglet had just hatched, and it soon returned with a fish to feed it. Its mate followed, and the hatchling ate everything offered to it. That night, I dreamed that an eagle flew up from the south and landed next to a raven. After a moment, the raven flew to the south, while the eagle watched him. I came back this morning after waking from that dream."

"This is not a personal vision, Theodore." Seagull shook his head. "You have seen a vision of the future. On a vision quest, you must wait for a personal vision, one that will have meaning to you alone and will guide you during the rest of your life. This vision will not serve you in that way."

"What do you mean, 'a vision of the future'?" I asked reluctantly.

"He has seen that Kuyuk will be killed, Juchi will take over, and he will send you south."

"I see." I learned long ago not to argue with mystics.

"Perhaps you should try again in the fall, Theodore," he said.

"I will."

My dreams had always been ridiculous and were more irritating because they seemed perfectly reasonable while I was dreaming them. I suppose that was why I had little faith in dreams. Seagull, on the other hand, had complete faith in them and expressed pity for me that I did not dream more. (I had told him I didn't remember my dreams since I found them so stupid.) Actually, even if Kuyuk did die, we had no way of knowing it as isolated as we were. I was curious about what was going on in the rest of the land, but we really had no way of finding out without compromising our position. In the fall, Theodore again went on a vision quest. This time he returned in a few days with a rather serene air about him. He did not request another gathering to discuss his experience, but simply said that his quest had been successful, and he was quite happy about it.

The following spring, there was no more encroachment, but all the settlements we saw were thriving and would likely be expanding again. I thought it best that we check them all again in the fall. More children were born, both daughters, Sarah (my grandmother) to Mathilde and Seagull, and Paulina to Ignace and Daldal. We had found it necessary to enlarge the houses. All was quite fine until late summer when Seagull came to see me and asked me to join him in a sweat bath. We fired it up and entered it. After waiting a few minutes, he spoke.

"I have seen a vision that I must tell you about. There is a great death raging in the land. It is not just in the west this time, but it has spread across the mountains and even to the far south. I have seen that it will not harm you or the other Mongols from the old land, but it will kill me. I do not fear it or the death it brings, but I would not leave my family alone. Should we go to see our neighbors, we will find it, and it will find us. I would, therefore, prefer to stay here with my family, and I urge you not leave our enclave or, if you must, not to return with the death."

"If another plague had attacked the people, I must go at once and see if I can stop it. I can hardly wait here while it destroys all the people. Did you see any detail about the plague in your vision?"

"No, I only know that it kills and that it causes fever and breathing problems."

"I will go alone this year. If I find any signs of plague, I will not return until and unless I am certain there is no further danger."

"I knew you would, and I would have thought less of you if you hadn't. I hope you can stop this death like you did the last one."

"I can't think of any other disease that responds as surely to prevention as the barbarian pox. But perhaps I will recognize the disease and know of some treatment for it."

We rubbed down and plunged into the river. I got out, dried off and went to tell Paula the news. I called a general meeting of the family and explained the situation to them. Ignace and Theodore immediately volunteered to go anyway, but I insisted that they remain and take care of their mother and the other children. Paula was afraid it would mean another long separation, and she clung tightly to me all that night. The next morning, I bid them all goodbye and rode north to see what I would see.

43
THE ZHEN PLAGUE, 29-30 K
(MEASLES EPIDEMIC, 1397-8)

As I drew near the closest village north of our settlement, I could see that something was wrong. Horses were running free. There was no smoke coming from the houses and, indeed, no sign of any activity at all, except for some barking dogs. I went through the village. It had been fairly small, only about a dozen of the large houses. From the look of it, it had been abandoned in the late spring or early summer. There were a few partial skeletons about, picked clean and scattered by the animals. The dogs had found and finished the abandoned stores of smoked salmon and were looking hungrily at my horses and me. They would soon be a wild pack and would likely find my family before long. I decided I couldn't take that chance and shot as many of them as I could before they began to scatter. I waited a while and got a few more when they came back to feed on their dead. I had a feeling this epidemic was going to get ugly. I spent the night in the village, selecting the strongest house and keeping the horses inside with me. The next morning as I left, I shot a few more of the dogs, leaving only a couple.

I continued north and found similar scenes in each village: no people, a few partial skeletons, horses running wild, and hungry and threatening dogs. I thinned out the last group whenever I could. At last I reached the Alsi River and finally found a few people. It looked as though they had again shrunk down to a few scattered villages. As I rode into the closest village, the haunted survivors gathered and stared at me, first in disbelief, then with tears and wailing. Puzzled, I asked why my coming upset them.

"Because you are too late, Raven," one of them wailed. "We are all but gone, and now you come to save us. You never should have left and allowed this to happen."

"Surely you know I was sent away?"

"Yes, we know you would not have chosen to leave us in our hour of need. But it has passed; we are not worth saving any longer. Almost all of our children are dead; most of our young people are dead; only a few of the older people were not taken ill. Our shaman could do nothing. The neighboring tribes were also affected, and their shaman could do nothing. The Ordu could do nothing. The Great Spirit grows weary of us and wants us all dead."

"You are too great a people to go into oblivion so quietly," I chided them. "There are enough of you left to rebuild your tribe. There is always hope where there is life."

"We were already four tribes reduced to one, by the pox. Now we are become nearly invisible by this new plague. Will there not be another in a few years to finish the work of the first two?"

"Not necessarily. A great shaman in the east predicted that this great death would make all the people of the land stronger and enable them to thwart an even greater evil in the distant future. He saw this as a winnowing of the people, and he welcomed it. You have survived two great plagues you must be strong indeed. Would not your children also be strong?"

"Perhaps." There seemed to be a glimmer of hope in them.

I sat down with them and had them describe the disease to me. They said it seemed to come out of nowhere. No one ill visited the village, but all of a sudden people began to take ill. At first, they felt tired and strangely uncomfortable; then they would begin to have a fever with running noses or coughs, and their eyes would become red and sensitive to light. After two or three days, the fever would get worse and a blotchy rash would appear. The rash would first intensify a bright red color, and then it would fade after a few days. Those that recovered would do so at this point. The others either kept the fever or began to feel pain in their ear, throat, chest, or stomach. The second malady would then kill them. I shuddered when I realized what the disease was.

It was the same plague that had killed off my mother and sister and almost got me when I was a child. It was considered to be a type of pox, related to the barbarian pox. The Hanjen thought it was a milder form of the pox, but the Persian al-Razi thought it was worse. It was generally held to only attack children or adults that had lived isolated lives. It left no marks like the pox did, but like it, one could only get it once. One of my teachers told me that he felt it was growing weaker, since it did less damage each time it attacked. He would be surprised to see how strong it had become again. There was no cure and no prevention, but there was treatment.

"Those of you who survived this plague need have no more fear of it," I said. "It can only strike you once. If any of you did not catch it, you may get it if it comes back again. Any children born now may also get the disease if it returns. It cannot be prevented like the pox, and it cannot be cured, but you can treat it. What you must do is make the victim rest and relieve his discomfort. Keep him in the dark, give him your medicines that reduce fever, soothe itching, and relieve chest discomfort. Make sure that they take plenty of liquids and broths to keep up their strength. If you do these things, few will die. Usually it only kills the weak."

They admitted that they had not done all those things. They had treated the fever and some of the other discomforts, but the victims had tried to keep working through the early stages and many lay in the sun thinking it would help heal them. Few of the sick ate much, and caring for the sick became such a full-time occupation, no one else ate properly, either, and almost all came down with it. They thanked me for my advice and promised to try to rebuild their shattered tribe. I was sure they would succeed.

I continued north through more abandoned villages until I finally came upon the remnants of the Tillamook. They were huddled fearfully in a single village on the banks of their namesake river. I managed to inject some hope in them as in their southern neighbors before I moved on. Next, I eventually came upon a band of Tsinuks. They were gamely getting their weirs ready for the salmon runs. They greeted me cheerily and in general seemed much less defeated than their neighbors to the south, and I asked them about their experience with the plague.

"It came and most of us came down with it, but the Koryo shaman at the Salmon Ordu that you had sent for told us how to treat it, and many of us recovered. Even in your absence you saved us, Raven."

I assumed that my suggestion to the Koryo merchant had been followed after all. I wondered why the treatment information had not been sent farther south. I decided it was time to find out what was going on in the world. I continued on to the Salst River and got a ride across in one of the Tsinuk boats. The man who ferried me was greatly honored to have me in his boat. I remounted on the north bank and rode up to the Salmon Ordu. As I approached the first sentry, he just stared at me in disbelief and said not a word. No one challenged me in any way as I went directly to the commander's yurt. At the yurt, the guard merely took my reins and opened the flap to admit me. As I walked in, Padraig, looking much older, glanced up at me and smiled broadly.

"I knew you'd return this year. What have you heard so far?"

"I only know about the arrival of the plague. This spring, no doubt, and on the merchant's ship?"

"We don't really know." He shrugged. "None of the seamen were ill. It broke out after they left. Cho Yi, the Koryo physician you sent us, thinks it was in the silk. Imagine such a thing, a disease hiding in silk. In any case, it first broke out among those handling the cargo, and then spread everywhere. It spread all along the yam system; almost all of the yam families were stricken. From them, it spread all over the land. The death has been daunting. I recognized it as that children's disease we all got when we were young, so did Cho Yi. Then to my surprise, people began dying from it. Even strong vigorous men were dying. Cho Yi told us how to treat it, and more and more men began to recover. I sent word of the treatment along the yam system, but because they had been so devastated by the disease, it did not move quickly at all. Loss of life in the east was quite heavy. I don't know about the far south, but south of here the losses were devastating. I lost about a quarter of the Ordu. All of my children pulled through it, but many others didn't. How is your family?"

"They were well when I left them, but now I'm afraid to return to them. I must talk to this Cho Yi. But first, what else has happened?"

"By midsummer, the plague was under control around here, and
we were able to restaff the yam system, at least to the east. That's
when we found out that it had spread along the system and raged
all over the east. A Tsinuk who had been transferred to the Eagle
Ordu as a minghan commander apparently got word that his wife
and child, who had remained in his home village, had died of the
disease. He blamed Kuyuk for it, and when he got his chance, fired
an arrow into him. Kuyuk died instantly, for it was a great shot.
The Tsinuk was also cut down immediately. Then, since Kuyuk had
never repudiated his original pronouncement, Juchi was sent for to
succeed him. He arrived in the early fall and immediately sent me
the order to find you and send you back to him."

"Did he mention anything about George in his message?"

"No, but George sent you a note also. Here."

George's note indicated that he had come down with the disease,
but had recovered. He also told me that he had married one of the
Ben Zah women and was anxious to have her meet us. He also had
three children he was anxious for us to meet. They had come down
with the disease, but only one of them had succumbed. It had been
a son he had named after me. He had been sickly much of his young
life, but was dearly loved and would be sorely missed. He regretted
that I would not get to meet him. So did I. That put me back in
mind to talk to the physician.

Cho Yi was still fairly young, perhaps in his thirties. He had a
friendly smile and ready wit, unlike most of the rather gruff almost
rude Koryo with whom I was accustomed. He thanked me profusely
for suggesting that the merchant bring a physician with him. He
was very happy in the new land, and best of all, he was alive. He
had received word from his relatives that he was being sought as a
likely supporter of the old regime. It was true; he had been. After
all, his grandfather had been a Mongol, and, although more recent
hard times had forced him to find a profession, his family had once
prospered under the old regime. He felt right at home in the Ordu
and was sure his children would do well in this land.

I told him about my family and asked what he thought I should do. He said it would be best if they could come immediately to him. He suggested that I have them come quickly along the yam system. They should arrive in about five days hopefully before they get too sick. He could then take care of them. In the long run, it was best to catch the disease and get it over with, rather than try to avoid it. I thanked him and returned to Padraig.

"I really should retrieve my family before going on to Juchi. They are about five days' ride south of here, and if the yam system is in order, I should be able to get them here in that time."

"I can go get them for you and send them on to you in the spring. You should get going east before the mountain passes become too difficult to cross. Juchi urgently needs you with him. You must think of more than your family for this is a very difficult time."

"You are right, but it will be very hard for me to go east before I am sure they are safe."

"I can send my son and a large escort to make certain they are safe. They can leave in the morning. As soon as we get them back here safe and sound, I will send you a message. Don't worry about them, just go on and help Juchi. I'll take care of them as though they were my own."

I finally agreed, but with grave misgivings. I wrote a note for Nial, Padraig's son, to give to Paula. I explained where they were and showed him the exact place on the map. Padraig laughed when I told them that we had been in that area all this time. He said that he knew we were somewhere in the land, but he had guessed north rather than south along the coast. He hadn't thought we would try to beat the coastal current. I explained that we had gone beyond the current until we were south enough to make a try for shore. He was shocked that we would go that far out into the ocean in one of the local boats. I assured them they were quite seaworthy. I told them about our experiences, and they told me more about what had happened in the rest of the land.

There had been much resentment over my exile, and Kuyuk had been unable to find anyone like Juchi or me to continue the conquest of the land. He finally ordered Juchi to attack southeastward along the narrow part of the land and take the rest of the Maya lands. He sent him insufficient men to do the job, perhaps with a view toward getting him killed, but Juchi had been progressing steadily anyway and had gotten beyond the last of the Maya when he was recalled to be Khan. He must have run into the plague on his way back. It was likely raging in the south still. Who knew how far it would go? I told them about my experience with the wild dogs and suggested a concerted pruning of their numbers was called for. Unlike wolves, the dogs were used to and insufficiently afraid of humans and could be quite dangerous. They agreed, and Padraig promised to send a reconnaissance in force southward in a few weeks to see what was going on in that direction.

The next morning, I saw off Nial and, with a heavy heart, started on my way back to the Eagle Ordu. It was a very long trip. Even using the yam system, it took almost two months. It was not a pleasant journey either. Not only was I concerned about my family, but also there was much unhappiness all along the route. Most of the yam attendants had lost family members and relatives to the last plague, and all of them blamed Kuyuk in particular and the Mongols in general. I was hard-pressed to pacify their resentments, but most of them knew and trusted me, and I was able to mollify them somewhat. The old Pansfalaya shaman's prophecy came in very handy as a final argument.

There was a dusting of snow on the ground when I reached the Hawk Ordu. Henry and his family were all well. Only his youngest children and his grandchildren had come down with the disease, and all had recovered. He had recognized it immediately, of course, and knew just what to do. Even so, there had been some death in the Ordu and much unrest. Juchi's accession had come just in time to stave off a revolt and civil war. Henry was pessimistic about the future of the Khanate, but had to admit we had no place to go, so we might as well do whatever we could to save it. He surprised me by saying that he felt better about its chance of survival now that I was back. I never realized he had such confidence in me. I told him about my "exile," and brought him up to date on his newest relatives. He told me that he had seen George and his new family, and I would be quite proud of them. I left the next morning.

The Eagle Ordu was blanketed in snow when I arrived, and in fact it had been steadily snowing all during the last day of my journey, making progress increasingly difficult. The sentry came toward me when I drew into view and turned out to be George. He embraced me with more emotion than I was used to, but he had been clearly worried about me, since they expected me sooner and the snowstorm was beginning to look like a blizzard. He led me right to Juchi's yurt. He wanted desperately to take me to meet his family, but Juchi's need was greater he assured me. I asked if Juchi was well, and he replied that he was in good health, but in poor spirits. I didn't know exactly what to expect.

I was ushered immediately into Juchi's yurt by his guard, who gave me a look as if I had just saved his life. I hurried in and found Juchi pacing madly in front of an untouched meal. He stopped when I entered and threw his arms around me in a most unexpected bear hug. Actually it was more like the grasp of a drowning man.

"Thank Tengri, or whatever torturer mocks me from above, that you have made it here at last! Sit, tell me your family is well, and let me bring you into my misery."

"My family was well when I left them, and I should hear about them soon. Padraig urged me to come here immediately, and it looks like he urged me correctly."

"He must be rewarded for that service. I don't know what to do. The Khanate is falling apart. Some of the Ordu have lost half their men. Whole villages have been reduced to bands. Large bands of bandits are roaming the land killing anyone they find and destroying what they can't carry off. Whole tribes are repudiating our alliance and attacking our envoys. In the south, it is even worse. With the Ordu weakened by disease, there are revolts everywhere. There is even word your old friend Tezozomoc is behind it. Furthermore, my uncle is unhappy that I succeeded my father without his being consulted and is threatening to unseat me. Fortunately, he has not gotten any encouragement, but I must deal with him and his sons, before we have civil war."

"Was not Tului head of the Eagle Ordu?"

"He was, but he transferred a few years ago to the Cranes. I think he expected my father to move against him. You must admit it was a good move. Tului's son, Sartak, commands the Falcon Ordu now, so the two Ordu are close together and just across the river from Murenbalikh, long a hotbed of rebellion. But their concentrated strength of numbers proved to be their weakness. The plague devastated the area. The losses in their Ordu were the worst of all. Murenbalikh was also devastated. Still, the longer their challenge goes unanswered, the stronger it will get."

"It would not be good to have one Ordu move against another. Do you know anyone among the Cranes and the Falcons on whom you can rely?"

"Yes, I do. Borgurchi's son Jebei is one of the minghan commanders in the Falcons. Two of Khassar's sons are still with the Cranes. He is here now as commander of the Eagles and most loyal to me. Borgurchi is commander of the Hawks."

"Minghan commanders always are closer to their men than Ordu commanders. Have them arrest your uncle and his sons and bring them to you. You will then have to either execute or exile them. They have left you no choice. I also suggest you decide as soon as possible which of your sons should succeed you and make it generally known so that we don't have a recurrence of this unpleasantness. Have you given that any thought yet?"

"No, I haven't. They are rather young and unformed yet, but I promise to keep an eye on them and decide as soon as possible."

"Good. Once your uncle and cousins are neutralized, you must order all the Ordu to move immediately against the bandits. Such predators are easy to track down for they make no friends and many enemies. Once they are destroyed, you can move against the tribes that have repudiated our alliance. I suspect once they see we are reestablishing control, there will be a change in leadership and a renewal of alliance. I would strongly suggest that you not show any mercy to the leaders who turned on us, but complete mercy to the tribe. As to the south, you must send someone you can trust completely and let him do what he must to restore order. That will free you to deal with the north. You will find it quite taxing enough."

"I only know one such man, Raven. You."

"Surely there is another? I feel you need my help here."

"I do need your help here, but I need it even more in the south. You are the only man loyal enough, wise enough, and brave enough to deal with the south. You must do this for me."

"But I should start right away if I'm to go there and I must know my family is safe before I go."

"You must go as soon as weather permits. Take my sons with you, and I'll keep George with me. I'll send word of your family to you by the fastest courier as soon as it reaches here. Can I count on you?"

"Of course you can. I will leave tomorrow. Have you any word on Smoking Mirror?"

"I reached him right after the plague did. He was too busy to say much, but I have since heard that he had to withdraw to Xicalanco when the Maya revolted. He is probably safe there, but the sooner you arrive, the better. I am appointing you my regent in the south. All our subjects are to obey you as though they were obeying me. It will greatly simplify your efforts. Of course, it would help if I know what you plan to do, so keep me informed as you go along. We don't have a clear picture of the situation, so you will have to adjust to whatever situation you find."

"I see. Is the Horse Ordu still functioning?"

"Yes, they did not suffer much from the plague. They are a tough lot."

"Can you spare them?"

"Yes, and you could also take the Coyotl Ordu. They suffered some losses, but are largely intact and could use some action."

"Very well. Meanwhile, if you need me back here, don't hesitate to send for me."

"I will, but knowing you're within reach will be enough to give me hope. I will also keep you informed about the north."

"Good. It won't do to save the province while the Khanate is lost."

"It will not be lost. We will talk again before you leave. Go meet your son's family. I have some messages to send."

George had taken up residence in my old yurt. It had needed a little renovation but was quite serviceable still. His wife was named Pinopias. She was a beautiful woman. The three surviving children were also quite attractive, with large luminous eyes. I congratulated him on his choice of wives and on his lovely children. Pinopias drew a bath for me, and afterward, I brought them all up to date on our "exile" and on their new relatives, over a light meal. George was very attentive and continued to be curiously tactile, constantly touching his wife, his children, and me. They also seemed to be possessed of the same propensity, and I found it puzzling and, frankly, irritating. I managed to hide my feelings, or at least I thought I had, until we were alone a moment and George asked me if I did not approve of his wife.

"What is not to like?" I was bewildered. "She is beautiful, gracious, attentive, has given you lovely, healthy children, and is even a good cook. Have I done something to offend you?"

"No, it was just that you seem a little cold and stiffen when I touch you. I thought perhaps you were not pleased with us."

"George, you and I campaigned all through the south together for several years. I doubt if in all that time I ever actually touched you. I know we've been apart for several years, but it is you who have changed, not I. I need time to get used to the new you, but alas, I will not have it."

"Oh, of course, I had forgotten. Pinopias has always been so affectionate with me and the children that I have gotten used to it and, it seems, outdone her. I had better be more aware of it so as not to annoy you and the rest of the family when they arrive."

"No, they won't be annoyed, just puzzled. Let them get used to it, slowly. It is a bit overwhelming at first."

"I will tell Pinopias; she'll be so relieved."

I finally drifted off to sleep, and when I awoke the next morning to get ready for my next trip south, I recalled Seagull's interpretation of Theodore's first vision quest attempt. I found it unsettling that such things could be foreseen so accurately, and then remembered what Seagull had predicted as his fate when he told me about the plague. It was maddening that I had to continue traveling before I knew that they were safe. I urged George to be sure and send me word as quickly as possible once he knew their fate. I embraced him and each of his family as warmly as I could, much to their delight and went tramping through the snow to see Juchi.

Juchi introduced me to his two sons, Mukali, the oldest, and Jelme. Both were fine-looking young men. I had not seen them since they were mere boys. I teased Juchi that they must take after their mother since they were much better looking than he was. He laughed heartily and for a moment looked like the young man with whom I had gone to find a new land so long ago. He admonished his sons to follow my every order without question and learn from me as much as possible. He then told them to get my escort ready to leave. When they had left, he turned back to me.

"Don't be easy on them. Make them show their mettle, and tell me honestly how they fare."

"I will."

"I have already sent orders to have my uncle and cousins arrested. I will let them choose death or exile to Koryo. I will spend the rest of the winter visiting each Ordu, shaking up their leadership if necessary and reasserting central command. The bandits will all be dead before next spring, and by next fall, there will be a united Khanate in the north. Once that is done, I will send you as many tumen as you need for your campaign."

"There are sufficient tumen in the south. I would be surprised if any of them have revolted. I think I know where I will find revolt, and I will be ready for it. I suspect the worst of it will be among those people you conquered, so I will welcome your sons' suggestions in dealing with them."

"They are fierce, but we greatly reduced them during the campaign, and the plague must have further scattered them. But you are wise to be aware of them and take them seriously, especially the Tya Nuu. They were the toughest people we subdued. To a lesser degree, the Maya were also tough. They fight valiantly, but can be easily divided and conquered, for they seem to hate each other as much as they hate us. Of course, they also look right at you, agree with everything you say, then go right on doing things the way they are accustomed. You will not find a more obstinate people completely indifferent to new ideas. But you must know that, since you also dealt with them."

"The ones I encountered were not quite the same. They hated their overlord and his mercenaries more that they hated us. At least that was the situation then. I suppose things have changed."

"Indeed. Smoking Mirror will be quite glad to see you. Will you go there first?"

"Yes, but only to gather him up. It is far more important to secure the central plateau of Anahuac first, and then radiate out from there. From what you tell me, I should probably leave the Maya for last."

"I knew you were the right man for the job. I already consider the south dealt with."

I sincerely hoped his faith in me was not misplaced. I also hoped his sons were half the men he was. I had been surprised that he had felt so overwhelmed by the responsibilities of the Khan, but I realized he just needed a plan to follow, some advice to give him a departure point. It was unfortunate he didn't have a Givevneu or a Donduk like his grandfather had. I certainly learned a lot from them. It was a shame Kaidu had not placed Juchi in his council instead of me, or even better, as well as me. In any case, I had confidence in Juchi and felt sure he would pacify the north by next fall. I suspected my task would take a little longer. I joined my escort, and we rode south. The snow was not as deep as we had feared, and we made good progress through it.

We reached the Owl Ordu and were ferried across the river before nightfall to get a head start on the rest of the trip. We headed straight for the Horse Ordu through Kitikiti'sh country. I was greeted like a returning hero in all the villages we encountered. I could see they had suffered some losses from the plague, but they were full of hope and very supportive of the Khanate now that Juchi was the Khan and I was back at his side. They also made a big fuss over Juchi's sons and not a few of their young women made their interest known. I didn't care if they dallied while I slept as long as they were in the saddle the next morning, and they never let me down. I was more interested in any news from the south, but there was none to be had. It took about a month to reach the Horse Ordu.

The Horse Ordu was in good shape. The men were in fighting trim and were only a little under strength. They were most eager for a campaign. They had already cleared their area of the bandit bands and were not looking forward to a quiet winter. Their commander was none other than Isadowa, the son of the Kitikiti'sh chieftain who had guided me to my first encounter with the Kadohadacho and my meeting with Smoking Mirror and his half brother. He was delighted to see me and brought me up to date on all the news of the neighboring tribes. He had not heard much from the south but was finally able to establish contact with the Lizard Ordu in the Huaxteca lands. It had been severely reduced by the plague and was having trouble restoring order. The Coyotl Ordu was also having trouble chasing down all the bands of bandits and would not be able to help me at this point. I was sorry not to have their help, but they did need to restore order locally before going on campaign. In any case, the Horse Ordu consisted of splendid, hardened warriors. I had enough. We set out southward within a few days.

44
RETURN TO ANAHUAC, 30-1 K
(MEXICO, 1398-9)

When we reached the Lizard Ordu, the commander, Juchi's cousin Timugen (Mangku's son), threw his arms around me in greeting. I could see his command was in bad shape. He told me that he had lost about two-thirds of his men to the plague. While he recognized the disease, he had no idea how to treat it. His wife and children had come down with it, and two of the latter succumbed. Finally, word got through on treatment, but the crisis had already passed. Still, they were able to spread the word to the more remote villages and save some lives. Then the revolts started. The Huaxteca had always been a contentious lot, and one of their priests claimed that the plague was Xipe Totec's punishment for not giving him his sacrifices. Fortunately, the revolts were piecemeal and uncoordinated, and he had been able to put them down in detail. The worst was in the south, but he had been able to put that down with the help of the Vultures. There had been very little unrest among the Totonaca, and all of that had been in the form of banditry. The Olmeca and the Putun Maya had also been fairly quiet, although there was considerable banditry among the former. Smoking Mirror had moved to Coatzacoalcos to help put it down. The local Ordu, the Xiuhtototl (the name of a local blue bird), had been hard-pressed. The Putun Maya Ordu, the Flying Fish, had been busy hunting down bandit bands from the Maya. There had been no word from the interior since the plague started, except for the Ralamari, who were still loyal and were trying to recover from the plague.

I commended Timugen on his excellent handling of the situation and thanked him for his information. I told him to send Juchi a complete report on his efforts and try to rebuild his Ordu and the yam system as soon as possible. I would not be able to stay with him, but would have to continue south. Still, I would make sure the yams were intact on my way and stay in touch with him should he need any help. He thanked me for coming and assured me he could handle his area and get the yams north going again. I would find the yams to the south fully functional. I sent Smoking Mirror a note to meet me at the Monkey Ordu if he could safely leave the Olmeca lands, then continued on my way south.

When I reached the Vulture Ordu, I found it under strength, but otherwise well rested and in good shape. The commander, Toolhulhulsote, a Nimipu, assured me the Totonaca were still very much a part of the Khanate and offered his Ordu's services on our campaign. I gladly accepted and sent his Vultures along with most of the Horse Tumen to secure the mountain pass that would take us to the high valleys. I went on to the Monkey Ordu with an escort of a few hundred men. On the way, I could see that the Totonaca had been badly mauled by the plague, but as I had heard, they did not seem to blame us for it and were quite loyal to us. As we approached the Monkey Ordu, a lone, most familiar rider came toward us.

"Mazatl was right about you, Raven," Smoking Mirror called out as I drew near him.

"You mean her mother was right." I laughed. "Is your family well?"

"Yes, quite well, thanks to Mazatl. She has proven quite the herbalist and pulled us through that plague. Are there any more like that we need anticipate?"

"No, I don't think so. That and the pox were the two worst."

"Good. We really couldn't absorb another one like that. How is your family?"

"I really don't know. I had to leave them to rush east to help Juchi."

"When he came through on his way to become Khan he told me he was sure you had never left the land, and he would send for you immediately. Did you ever leave?"

"No. We embarked with the Koryo fleet, but left it once we were out to sea and settled several hundred li south of the Salmon Ordu. But more to the point, what has been happening here?"

Smoking Mirror then brought me up to date. After I left him several years before, all was fine for some time. The Maya seemed indifferent but still cooperated. He had reestablished schools for the more willing among them to learn reading and writing in the Uighur script as well as in the Maya picture writing. He had also established artisan schools to promote their considerable artistic talents. Yet, while they went along with everything he did, they showed no enthusiasm, and he always felt like an outsider. When the plague hit, all the blame was placed on him, and the revolt was general. He had not felt confident enough to send back the Dog Ordu, but had eventually replaced them with the Quetzal Ordu. Their losses to the plague had been bad, but nothing compared to the losses suffered in the retreat to Xicalanco. All along the way, they were set upon by rabid bands of Maya. The Putun Maya had remained loyal and had rallied to his aid clearing their lands of the bandit bands. He felt he would have to leave their Ordu, the Flying Fish, there to ensure continued safety for the Putun. The Olmeca in the cities had also remained loyal, but banditry was rife in the countryside, and he had only just stamped the last of it out. Again, he felt he had to leave the Xiuhtototl there to deal with any further outbreaks. He had brought the remnants of the Quetzal Tumen with him.

Remnants were right there were perhaps a thousand of them. At least they were well rested and anxious to return to their home base. We spent the night with the Monkeys. I told the commander, Sensondacat, a Ka-i-gwu, to send half his force north to replace the Lizard Ordu. I caught Smoking Mirror up on my activities of the last few years that night. He envied me the peace I enjoyed in "exile" and asked if I had heard anything about the Kadohadacho and the Ani' Yun'-wiya. I had only heard that both had remained loyal to us in spite of heavy losses to the plague, but there was so much confusion in the east that I was not sure of my information. Juchi had promised that he would keep me informed. Before I turned in, I wrote Juchi a dispatch detailing what I had learned and telling him of my planned move west.

The next morning, we set out northwestward to the pass near the snow-capped Citlaltepetl. It was late winter, and the pass along the merchant trail would be clear of any snow. As before, we found no resistance along most of the route, but only the same shallow promises of eternal loyalty we had heard before. This time I made each town responsible for a nearby yam station promising them total destruction should any harm come to the station. They were not pleased, but they were not about to argue. It worked also, for just as we were approaching the cliff-top town of Ixtacamaxtitlan, a dispatch arrived from Juchi. I sent a team to find out the disposition of the town while I read Juchi's dispatch.

On top of his dispatch was one from Padraig. I read it first. Nial had reached my family's encampment within five days of setting out and arrived just in time to beat off a bandit attack. The bandits had fired all the houses and were about to make their final rush when Nial arrived. They scattered quickly, but he had managed to kill most of them. Of my family, Ignace, Daldal, and Seagull were badly wounded. Theodore, Ludmilla, and Paula were lightly wounded. The others were unscathed. All but Paula had the early signs of the plague. It was too dangerous to move them north, so Nial kept them where they were to nurse them through their wounds and the plague. Ignace died first, then Daldal, then Seagull, and then Ludmilla. The rest recovered and were returned to the Salmon Ordu. Padraig then sent a large force to the south to stamp out any other bandits. I was devastated. I turned away and leaned heavily against a tree. Smoking Mirror took the note from me, read it, and put a comforting hand on my shoulder. Then he turned and took over for me. I sat down and wrote a long letter to Paula and the children, expressing my deep regret at leaving them behind once too often and taking so long to offer any poor comfort over our devastating loss. I begged them to come to me as soon as they could do so safely, for I could never again leave them alone. I sealed the letter and sent the messenger back with it. Only then did I look at Juchi's letter.

He expressed his regret over my loss. His uncle and cousins had chosen death over exile and were accommodated. The revolts were among elements of the Hotcangara, Iliniwek, Twanhtwanh, Wendat, Great Bay tribes, Menominiwok ininiwok, Amani yukhan, Iyehyeh, and even isolated Northeastern Bands. Once he had reasserted his command, most of the revolts dissipated, but a few were serious, especially among the Wendat and Great Bay tribes. The Southeastern Tribes meanwhile had become involved in a sort of death cult and were causing no end of trouble for the Pigeon and Manati Ordu. Once the revolts were dealt with, he would have to mount a large-scale campaign against them. The Taino and Lucayo had suffered high losses, but also remained loyal except for one of the caciques on Boriquen. The local Ordu, the Agouti, had crushed him.

I turned to find Smoking Mirror and found him demanding the surrender of the leaders of Ixtacamaxtitlan. These were duly handed over, and he ordered their execution. He appointed a new governor and garrison and ordered the town's army to join us immediately. I thanked him for stepping in like that and gave him Juchi's dispatch to read. He breathed a sigh of relief that his and his wife's people had not joined the revolt and then told me what had happened here. The town had revolted against the garrison and driven them out of the town with heavy losses. Under the circumstances, they regretted their rash decision and threw themselves on our mercy. I concurred with his decisions, and we continued west.

As we drew near the eastern plateau, a small party approached us. It turned out to be a delegation from Michikinikwa, the governor I had appointed to Texcalla. He was still in the city even though he had turned governance back to the local leaders some years before. He wanted to assure me that the city was still loyal to the Khanate and would happily welcome me. I thought it odd that he had re-mained and that all members of his delegation were Texcalla. One would think he would send at least one of his original staff, unless none of them had stayed behind with him, which would also be odd. I asked the delegation about the situation on their plateau. They said only Cholula had revolted, the rest were loyal. I asked about Anahuac, and they said that Tezozomoc had returned and turned most of the Tepaneca, Otomi, and Alcolhua against us. They were even now attacking Chalca and the Mexica islands. I thanked them and sent them back with word that we would follow. Then I turned to Smoking Mirror.

"What do you make of it? A trap?"

"It does sound suspicious. I wouldn't expect Cholula to revolt, or Texcalla to remain loyal. I also doubt if the Tepaneca and Alcolhua are united about anything."

"Exactly. What do you suppose they are trying to do? There can't be enough of them left to attack us. We left them in sorry shape, and the plague can't have helped them. What sort of treachery could they be planning?"

"I don't know, but at least we are forewarned."

I sent out the scouts to check the surrounding area for traps, and we moved forward. We reached the edge of the plateau without incident, and the scouts reported no suspicious activity. We continued on to Texcalla and again found nothing threatening. The leader of Texcalla came out to greet me, and I recognized the same one who had surrendered to us many years before. He invited us to enter the city and share his house as long as we wished. I declined and asked him where Michikinikwa was. He said that he had fallen ill and was in bed, but we could visit him if we wished. I again declined and told him to give him our regards. He then said that at least I could join him for a sacrifice to our god Tengri; it would only take a moment. I replied that we did not sacrifice to Tengri, only the Khan could do that. He kept coming up with more reasons for me to go into the city, and I kept turning them away. He began to get desperate and begged me to enter the city for he feared his people would turn against him if they thought I didn't favor them. I still refused telling him to send out some of the leaders of the people, and I would assure them I was not displeased. He eagerly thanked me and said he would do so. As he left, Smoking Mirror and I exchanged a glance. I ordered the men to discreetly surround the city, had the cannon massed nearby and loaded, and sent the scouts out again to look for any possible reinforcements.

I kept a large group of men with me, and as the contingent from the town approached, I had them discreetly ready their arrows. All of the men coming toward us were young, too young to be leaders, and all wore cloaks under which all could conceal their weapons. I bid them stop when they were about fifty feet away, but they kept on coming as if they hadn't heard me. I quickly mounted and rode to the back keeping them fifty feet away. They halted, and the eldest among them asked if they did not have permission to talk with me. I replied that they did, and they could do so from right where they were. He asked if it was true that we still considered them to be our allies. I replied that we did. Could we not share a meal together then to cement our alliance? We could not.

Suddenly, with a shout their swords came out from under their cloaks, and they rushed toward me. My men's arrows quickly cut them down. Even so, one hurled a knife at me that just missed my head. Then a surge of men ran out of the city right into the massed cannon loaded with shrapnel shot. The survivors retreated to the city. Since there was no wall, we shelled the first layer of houses, quickly reducing them to rubble. More sorties came out of the town but were quickly driven back. More and more of the town was reduced to rubble. Finally, when not one building was still standing, we rushed in and finished off the survivors. No sign was found of Michikinikwa. I doubted that he had decided to stay, so I wasn't surprised. I figured that they had come to think that if they could kill me, the men would all go back. I wondered what the real situation was around here. Smoking Mirror was certain there were Tepaneca among the Texcalla dead. We rested a day and moved on toward Huexotzinco.

As we approached the city, a large unarmed (and uncloaked) contingent came toward us. Their spokesman drew near alone and identified himself as the current chief of the city. He assured me of the city's loyalty and had already mobilized his army to join me on my campaign. He was quite willing to step aside if I wished to appoint a governor and station a garrison here. I asked him about the situation in this plateau and in Anahuac. He said that Tezozomoc had returned and had rallied many of his Tepaneca to his cause. He had also gotten support from elements of the Otomi, Matlatzinca, and Mazahuaca. Also some of the Mexica from Tlatelolco had gone over to him. The Alcolhua, Chalca, Tlalhuica, and the rest of the Mexica were against him. He controlled only ruined cities at this time but had a huge band of raiders that had terrorized the whole valley. The five tumen in the valley were badly reduced by the plague and had been unable to stop him. He tried to get this plateau on his side, but Huexotzinco and Cholula would have none of him. He convinced Texcalla that if they killed Smoking Mirror and me, the gods would abandon us, and all the Mongols would be destroyed. He knew nothing about the fate of the missing Michikinikwa. This sounded more like it.

We camped in front of the town for the night, and I sent a messenger to Cholula. He returned early the next morning with a contingent from that city. Their Ordu, the Rabbits, would be formed and ready to join us when we reached the city. The commander of the Rabbits, Sakaceweskam, a Kensistenoug, led the contingent. He assured me that his Ordu was still serviceable even though much reduced. I thanked him and dismissed the Quetzal Ordu to visit their families and then reform at Huexotzinco and stand by if needed. We continued on to Cholula, picked up the Rabbits (there were about four thousand of them), and moved west up the pass toward Anahuac. I sent scouts out ahead of us as usual. I fully expected to find the pass defended, but it was not, and the scouts reported no sign of the enemy on the slopes or beyond. We reached Amecameca without incident. The city was abandoned and had been burned. There were signs of a recent struggle, perhaps within a few weeks. From the looks of it, the people had beaten off an attack with great difficulty, considered their position untenable, and fled toward Chalco. The attackers had then returned and vented their anger on the city. We set up sentries and camped outside the city.

The scouts again reported finding no concentrations of men just small groups of people widely scattered and engaged in peasant activity between Chalco and us. It was hard to believe that the army that destroyed Amecameca so recently had completely left the area. One would expect them to exploit their advantage. I had to think something was going on. Still, it was possible that they didn't think they could challenge a force the size of ours and were waiting for us to break up so they could attack us piecemeal. As Kaidu would have said, one must never count on one's enemies to make the same mistake more than once. Tlalmanalco had also been abandoned and burned, after Amecameca from the signs, and again the fugitives went toward Chalco. We reached Chalco without incident.

Chalco was still inhabited, and there was much rejoicing upon our arrival. The city was in bad shape. Much of their wall was little more than rubble. It seemed the enemy had some cannon, but little ammunition and even less skill at using them. While they had done some damage with them, their limited skill prevented them from causing serious harm. The city was full of refugees from all of the towns and cities in southeastern Anahuac. The head of the city and the acting commander of the Chalca Ordu presented themselves to me. The former was named Mixtzin, a man about my age; the latter was Itzcoatl, one of Acamapichtli's sons. They told me that all the cities had suffered great losses from the plague, and all the priests blamed the Mongols and the abandonment of the sacrifices for the plague. All five Ordu had also suffered greatly from the plague and were now mere shells, barely able to defend their central cities.

Tezozomoc had arrived in the early winter, and all the priests rallied to his side. Most of the Tepaneca and many of the Otomi joined them, even some from the Tepaneca and Otomi tumen deserted to him. The Mazahuaca and Matlatzinca then rallied to him, as did some of the Tlatelolco. There had been fighting ever since. When Tezozomoc first arrived in Anahuac, the Ordu were too busy trying to restore order and remove and burn all the dead to hunt him down. By the time they were able to turn their attention to him, he was too strong to defeat. He now controlled the entire western shore of the lake and much of the northern shore. His armies had overrun and destroyed all of the smaller southern towns. Only Chalca, Xochimilco, and the island towns, Xico and Cuitlahuac, were holding out. Huitzilihuitl, the current Tlatoani of the Mexica, had defeated the Tlatelolca traitors and was in control of both Mexica islands, but their aqueduct had been cut off, and much of their water must be brought in from Ixtapalapa across the causeway. The Alcolhua were also still loyal to the Khanate, although it was likely as much from hostility toward the Tepaneca as fondness for us. Their Ordu had been engaged in defending their northern border and the few Otomi towns that had remained loyal. The remnant of the Otomi Ordu was defending Tizayuca and that of the Tepaneca Ordu was defending Huitzilin, both Otomi towns near the Alcolhua border.

Tezozomoc had learned much during his exile. The Ordu scouts would report no sign of the enemy for days; then suddenly they would find their town surrounded and attacked on all sides. When the Ordu would sortie out of a town, they would find the enemy behind ditches filled with sharpened wooden spikes, preventing them from using their horses. Then they would be showered with darts propelled by atlatl. They had found it necessary to fight defensively from inside the cities. This had only been partially successful, since when repulsed, the enemy would melt away at night and soon appear somewhere else. One by one the towns were becoming indefensible and had to be abandoned. Each victory would bring more of the peasants to Tezozomoc's side. Soon only the Alcolhua would stand in his way.

It wasn't hard to see the problem. Most of the peasants in the valley were Otomi, with little but forced allegiance to the cities and their foreign rulers. Although Tezozomoc was also a foreign ruler, he seemed to be winning, and the winning side was always the best. From what they were telling me, it looked like the wily Tezozomoc had mastered camouflage, infiltration, and mobility. I guessed he was using the horses only for transportation since his people were hardly the match of ours on horseback. The camouflage was also simple: his forces would dress and act like the ubiquitous Otomi peasant. That way they could be anywhere and seem to belong especially with the bulk of the peasantry either uncommitted or on his side. The infiltration was an easily learned skill. He was a stimulating foe.

Smoking Mirror had gone to check on his relatives after we finished talking to the leaders. While he was gone, I had the men start to repair the city walls and set up defensive positions around the town. I sat down to think over the situation. I had on hand the equivalent of one and a half tumen splintered into several separate commands. I decided to keep the Horses intact, but send the other Ordu pieces to replace the Otomi Ordu and elements of the Alcolhua Ordu. It was unfair, perhaps, but I didn't really trust the Tepaneca Ordu. The Mexica Ordu was best kept protecting the lake, and I sent them a message to that effect. When Smoking Mirror returned, he reported that his relatives had suffered heavily from the plague, but the survivors were now in good spirits since our advent. I told him what I had in mind to do.

"The only way to defeat Tezozomoc with the forces at hand is by turning his strategy against him. I want the loyal Otomi to infiltrate his forces and tell me when, where, and how he plans to attack. With enough notice, I can spring a surprise on him and begin to roll back his gains. As we are more successful, the peasants will desert him."

"It is a good plan, if the Otomi will cooperate. Are you sure they will?"

"No, but it makes sense for them to do so, if there is any ambition among them. They have been mostly treated like chattel in this valley. If I promise them the Tepaneca lands, or much of them, they will be highly motivated."

"They are the only ones who could do it for you. Any of the others would be spotted and killed."

"I know."

It seemed prudent to assume there were spies everywhere, so I sent Smoking Mirror to intercept the Otomi Ordu en route through Alcolhua lands while I made a big show of sending out patrols and scouts to look for the enemy. So the effort was not a total waste, I told the scouts to count the number of peasant men they saw while on patrol. Word began to filter in that there had been an attack on one of the smaller Tlalhuica towns, then on one of the loyal Otomi towns, then on one of the northern Alcolhua towns. I didn't move, but kept on sending out patrols and scouts and tallying up the scouts' peasant numbers. Smoking Mirror returned from his mission and told me that the Ordu had agreed to help, and about two hundred of the men were "deserting" to Tezozomoc's army. More and more hit-and-run attacks were reported in the north, obviously suggesting that I should take the Horse Tumen and head north to stop them.

At last, the scouts reported a dramatic rise in peasant numbers in the area, so I decided to take the bait. I led the Horses north about a day's ride, and then we filtered back part of the way at night hiding in a forest. We remained hidden the next day lighting no fires and making almost no noise. Toward evening, a lone peasant was seen on the path through our forest. He was captured and proved to be one of our Otomi spies. He informed me that by dawn, about twenty thousand warriors would surround Chalco. Since we had left, they would dig the ditch only north of the town this time. At dawn, they would fire rockets into the town and then attack on all sides. Another of our spies had gone into the town and warned Smoking Mirror. I got the men up, and we rode in a big circle around to the east remaining in the forest. Before dawn, we left the forest and moved first south, then east, at full speed, changing horses frequently.

Before long, we could hear the rockets and soon found ourselves cutting our way through a surprised rear guard that was holding the enemy's horses. We rounded up the horses and stampeded them ahead of us toward the city. The forces were struggling on the walls, and cannon was occasionally heard firing into the assaulting forces. I had the men split and fan out around the city, trampling and firing arrows into the attackers. As we pressed our advantage, the men in the city counterattacked, and soon the enemy were fleeing desperately to the rear or to the lake. When we reached the lake, we turned back and chased down and killed as many as we could find. When we finished, late in the morning, it took the rest of the day to pile up their dead. There were a few Tepaneca elites among them, but Tezozomoc was not among them. The wounded were dispatched except for a few obviously Otomi warriors. These were patched up and sent home with a warning that if we found them again among our enemies, they would die. They gratefully told us that Tezozomoc was in the ruins of Azcapotzalco preparing a trap for the Horse Tumen, which he thought would be in the north. They also assured me that we had destroyed about half of his whole army.

I was fairly sure the Chalco area was secure, so I mounted up the Horses and moved west along the lakeshore. I moved slowly so that word of the defeat would have time to spread and sink in. By the time we reached Xochimilco, my spies reported that most of the Otomi had deserted Tezozomoc. He had planned an ambush in the north, but most of the men he sent to spring it had instead gone home. Only his own Tepaneca and the few remaining Tlatelolca were still with him. The Matlatzinca and Mazahuaca had withdrawn to their valley in the west and would likely be approaching soon to cut a deal. Meanwhile, many of the Otomi deserters were forming bands to attack Tezozomoc's forces.

I picked up my pace, and soon we were moving through the deserted Tepaneca cities again much like we had so many years before. My scouts reported a concentration of Tepaneca in the same Chapultepec area again apparently lying in ambush. They couldn't get a good fix on the numbers, but it seemed like a large group. Somehow, I doubted that Tezozomoc would stand and fight. I sent a message to the Mexica to have an arc of boats full of warriors in position around the lakeshore of Azcapotzalco by dawn. We drew near to Chapultepec, and I set up a skeleton camp with many fires and a lot of noise. Meanwhile, I led the Horses on a wide arc around the forces on the hill and directly to Azcapotzalco. By dawn, we were in position around the ruined city and had already apprehended several of their messengers. Once the sun was up, we showed ourselves to the besieged. We began to fire the cannon at what few targets remained. Defenders organized and tried to rush us, but there were too few of them. A few boats tried to escape but were cut off by the Mexica. Attempts were made to surrender, but I would have none of it. Finally resistance ended, and I sent the men in to finish off any survivors. Finally Tezozomoc had been brought to ground. He was among the dead. One of our shells had caused the house in which he was hiding to collapse, and his body was dragged out of the rubble. I made quite sure he was dead this time, by having his head removed before burning. I still wondered how he ever escaped us at Mayapan. I had the city demolished completely and forbade it ever being rebuilt. In a way, I was sorry I never got to meet the man, but then I might have shown him mercy and that would have been a big mistake.

The rest of the Tepaneca were rounded up with little trouble and presented to me. I had the elites separated from the rest and executed. I gave the remainder the city of Tlacopan to rebuild and organize under an appointed governor, Ixtlilxochitl, one of the Mexica leader Huitzilihuitl's sons. I gave him a strong Otomi garrison and charged him to rule well. I gave the Mexica control of Chapultepec and the area around it. I gave the Alcolhua control over the two Tepaneca cities nearest to them across the lake, Ecatepec and Tulpetlac, as well as the surrounding towns and land. I gave the Xochimilca Tlapan and the rest of the Tepaneca land, except for Tlacopan, of course, which I turned over to the Otomi. I then called a meeting of all leaders in the valley.

We met in Tlatelolco at the palace of the administrator of Anahuac. The first task was to replace the administrator, Amantacha, who had died during the plague and, since communications had been cut off, was never replaced. Looking things over, I could see that there was no one with enough stature who could be spared from more pressing tasks to take over this one. I appointed instead a council of leaders to settle matters between them, and should a consensus not be reached, they could appeal to me or to whomever I appointed once I left the area, for a final decision. They agreed and promised to cooperate. I then charged them to concentrate all their energy in rebuilding their people.

45
KHAN OF ANAHUAC, 31-45 K
(MEXICO, 1399-1413)

I remained in Tlatelolco for the rest of the spring accepting
sheepish delegations from the surrounding area and opening up
communications with our "allies" by reestablishing the yam system
in all directions. To the north, there was not far to go, only the larger
Otomi cities and the Ralamari beyond. The east was also in good
shape. The south was still mostly loyal. The Tlalhuica had remained
steadfast and had struggled with Tezozomoc and his allies. Beyond
them, the losses from the plague had been devastating, and there
was no organized resistance anywhere as far as the coast. Even the
Yope had remained loyal.

To the west, the Matlatzinca and the Mazahuaca had already
thrown themselves on our mercy assuring us that they had been
told the Mongol Khanate had fallen apart, and bandits were invad-
ing from the east. I took a few towns away from them and sent
their pitiful armies east to assist the Flying Fish Ordu against the
Maya. Few of them would ever return. Farther west, the Otomi, the
Purepecha, and the various others had also been too devastated by
the plague to revolt, but there was much lawlessness and banditry
with which we would have to deal. It was a miserable, nasty job, and
I sent the Horse Ordu to take care of it. I thought it would be good
experience for Juchi's sons, so I sent them along. Isadowa spent the
next three years chasing down and wiping out bandits. The people
were most grateful and assisted the effort greatly. The yam system
was fully restored by the end of the first year.

To the southeast, things were uncertain. It seemed that the Ben
Zah had not revolted or turned to banditry, but the Tya Nuu had
done both and had attacked the Ben Zah, their old enemies. By
midsummer, I led a group of understrength tumen that just about

equaled one on a punitive expedition against the Tya Nuu. To my relief, the Coyotl Tumen was able to join me in mid campaign, and the Tya Nuu were subdued by late fall. It was a brutal campaign, and they were not much of a people when it was over. The Ben Zah were very glad we came and offered much assistance. I reorganized them into an ally granting them local autonomy much like the loyal tribes in the north. This made us even more popular with them, and they assisted our continuing campaign with a moderate force of warriors. By the late fall, I was south of the Olmeca lands chasing down more bandits when a pile of dispatches from Juchi finally reached me.

He had crushed all the revolts, wiped out all the bandits, and was now leading a campaign against the Southeastern Cities. Padraig had swept the entire western coast and found the once populous area devastated. He was organizing and training an Ordu near the large bay he had named Raven Bay. They would be called the Ravens. My family had moved east and was on its way to Tlatelolco. I should turn over my campaign to Smoking Mirror and return there myself since I was now the Khan of Anahuac! I was stunned. He went on to explain that he would now be the Khakhan of the Blue Sky, and I would still report to him, but to no one else. My Khanate would include all of the area he and I had conquered for his father. He thought this arrangement would be the most practical since the original Khanate had become too large to govern properly. He hoped I would accept the position because I was the only one he could trust. I showed the dispatches to Smoking Mirror. I watched him read them and could tell when he got to the last one. His mouth hung open, and he looked up at me in disbelief.

"It is beyond belief, Raven," he finally said, his eyes shining. "For many of the last several years I wondered if I had done wrong in throwing my lot in with the Mongols. With this act, Juchi has restored all my original faith. You must accept. It will let all know that competence and intelligence is rewarded in the Khanate. I can't tell you how many people have wished you were Khan and longed for your wise guidance during the dark years of Kuyuk. Do not let some misguided modesty deprive these desperate people of the good leadership that can bring them back from the abyss."

I was stunned again. I had no idea Smoking Mirror held me in such esteem. It took a while for it all to sink in. I thought of my family. As Khan, I would only rarely have to travel, and when I did it would be with a large retinue and all my family. It would not be an easy job, but I would draw much comfort from their constant presence, especially Paula. To be able to sleep each night with her in my arms for the rest of my life was worth all the problems running a Khanate would bring. I wondered if I could do it. Well, I watched the incomparable Kaidu in action, I suffered under the incompetent Kuyuk, and I managed my little family on my own for several years. As long as I remembered who I was and where I had been, I should be able to do a satisfactory job. Was it a good idea to split the Khanate? That was a tough call. When Chingis' Khanate was split up among his descendants, they eventually went to war with each other, encroaching on each other's territory. But then, they never had agreed to Kubilai being the Khakhan, nor could they agree to any of the others deserving that title. As of now, there would be no problem, here. Juchi was my friend as well as ruler and my loyalty to him was so complete that should another dispatch arrive in a few days changing everything, I would obey it. But what would happen after he and I were gone? What if there was another Kuyuk among either Juchi's sons or mine? Was the division good for the people? I shared these last thoughts with Smoking Mirror, who had been sitting quietly watching me turn all this over in my mind.

"A most worthy concern, Raven, further proof that you would be a most unusual ruler, perhaps the best ever known in these lands. The very fact that the good of the people enters your mind, frees me of all concern for it. It will be most interesting to see you make all of the decisions that affect your people while keeping in mind their welfare. It is also most heartening that Juchi seems to share your concern for the people he governs. It bodes well for the land that you and he rule most of it in these difficult times. I doubt if your children would be so different from you. The acorn does not fall far from the oak. Of course, there is no need to have your children succeed you; you could appoint another."

"I have often wondered about that, but it occurs to me that as much intrigue as is involved when the choice of succession must be made within one family, it could become intolerable if it was thrown open to the whole realm. Still, if none of the sons are competent, a good ruler should look elsewhere."

"I don't think you will have that problem, but your son might."

"Who can say? In any case, the Khakhan must approve anyone I suggest as my successor, and could easily overrule me."

"So it has always been. Perhaps one day it will be different. I really like the way the Ani' Yun'-wiya run things."

"But they endlessly talk about everything. One's entire life would be spent in meetings trying to find a consensus. And, as difficult as it is in the one tribe, imagine what it would be like for a very disparate group of tribes. It simply wouldn't work."

"Maybe not, but I wish it could be tried."

I didn't want to say it, but if such were the government of the Khanate, I would not even consider leading it. I would surely go mad within a few weeks. I could never understand why he liked that system. While it did remove any rationale for dissent, it did not end it. Smoking Mirror had too much faith in human goodness. Perhaps that was good for him. I wrote Juchi a note thanking him for his confidence in me and agreeing to take over Anahuac for him. I also reiterated my loyalty to him and acknowledged his authority over me. Meanwhile, I had a decision to make about the current campaign. We needed to restore order, but I wasn't sure we had enough men to take on the Maya. Already, the tumen with me were in need of a rest. I ordered the Coyotl to remain and hunt down bandits until I could relieve them. I put Smoking Mirror in charge of the entire eastern frontier ordering him to first restore order, then take back the Maya lands when we could send him enough forces to do the job. I suggested that he set up his headquarters in Xicalanco.

We moved north over the mountains, escorted by all the Ordu remnants from Anahuac and traveled together as far as Coatzacoalcos. There Smoking Mirror was reunited with his family. Mazatl congratulated me on becoming Khan and urged me to take along

Chico Ocelotl, now called Tepeyolotl (Heart of the Hill), to serve me and learn. The boy was about eighteen and a fine-looking lad, tall like his father but less gaunt and with a smaller nose. I readily agreed and thanked her again for her mother's predictions. She smiled and told me not to worry about the future. I didn't press her for any further predictions. Smoking Mirror moved east to Xicalanco, and I went north to the Monkey Ordu.

The Monkeys were in fairly good shape and up to about six thousand men. I ordered them to go south and replace the Coyotl Ordu and report directly to Smoking Mirror in Xicalanco. I sent him a note telling him of the replacement and another note to the now returned Lizards to send half of their men south to replace the Monkeys. I then went on to the pass leading up to Anahuac. When we neared Ahuilizapan, I noticed a large force camped just outside the city. They proved to be a contingent from the Eagle Ordu. They were escorting my family! I thanked them for their protection and sent them back to help Juchi on his campaign. They gave me a shield-beating salute as the new Khan of Anahuac. With them, I sent a note to Juchi thanking him for the escort of my family and telling him of my disposition of the eastern frontier and urging him to send me any Ordu he could spare when his campaign was over so we could again assert our authority over the Maya. The official work done, I went into my family's tent, and we held on to each other and wept over our losses.

I noticed that Mathilde was not among them and asked after her. It seemed that she had become very withdrawn over her loss and had declined to come east with the others. She even turned her children over to Paula and withdrew into the forest alone. No one could talk any sense into her or get her to think of her children. Padraig sent a party to find her, and when they did, she was at our old encampment and had recently died. There were no signs of violence; they found her in her tent with a peaceful smile on her face. She was buried next to Seagull. I looked at her children and wanted to be mad at her, but couldn't. It was unusual for a woman to love her husband more than her children, but I could understand it. The truth was that even though I was devastated at the loss of half my children, I would have been destroyed had Paula died and not even the Khanate or the children could have brought me back. But I would miss Mathilde, Ignace, Ludmilla, Seagull, and Daldal. They were wonderful people whom I genuinely loved. We had all become quite close during our "exile," and the losses were hard.

Paula had acquired a couple of unattached women to help with all the children, for there were ten of them, and the oldest, Christina, was only eight years old. One of the women was an older widow, an aunt of Seagull named Nahtahki. The other was a young niece of the shaman Okuh-hatuh named Natomah. I was pleased that we would bring a bit of the north with us since I always felt it was more wholesome than the south. Although unquestionably the southerners were more sophisticated and cultured, the northerners were more spiritual and in tune with the land. It was a good influence, and I made a note to be sure the children all spent a few of their formative years in the north.

The ascent to Anahuac was slow and pleasant with much time taken to visit the towns along the way. We were especially well received in Cholula and Chalco along the way. But still, nothing compared to the reception in Tenochtitlan. We went around the lake from Chalco to Ixtapalapa, and as we cleared the top of the hill, before us we could see the city gleaming across the causeway with feather banners of every color floating lightly in the gentle breeze. All along the causeway were people holding reeds. Our path along the causeway was strewn with flower petals. The leaders of all the cities met us and led us in procession across to Tenochtitlan. We were led directly to the Temple of Tengri, a plain flat stone altar painted blue atop a very high pyramid. On the altar was readied a censor full of a kind of incense. I was asked to light it. I did, and it signaled the beginning of general feast, with much music, acrobatics, singing, dancing, food beyond belief, and the heady scent of innumerable flower petals raining down on us.

Late that night, we were led in triumph to the palace in Tlatelolco, but the next day we had to visit Texcoco, then Xochimilco, and so on until we had been feted at each major city of Anahuac. Then came invitations from the neighboring valleys. I put off all of these except Cuauhnahuac since I wanted to show it to Paula. She immediately fell in love with it, and I asked the ruler to allot me a plot on which to build a summer residence. He was thrilled, and it took some trouble to persuade him that my needs were modest I wouldn't need three mountains and a forest, just a small piece of land. He insisted on building it for me, and again it took some doing to convince him we didn't want a huge palace, just a modestly large house, big enough for the whole family. We worked out the plans, chose the site and I left it in his hands to complete. It was done by early summer and served me every summer while I was Khan.

Word came from Juchi that the campaign against the Southeastern Cities had concluded. All of them were now subject to us. The strange death cult was probably due to the staggering losses they suffered from the plague. Whole cities were wiped out, and the survivors began to worship Death as a god. Their cult was bloody, and he felt it necessary to wipe it out. The remnants of the people were rebuilding their tribes. He was sure that the population of the area was only about a quarter of what it had been. None of the tumen were up to full strength yet, but he would begin sending them one at a time every few months to wear down the Maya resistance. Once I had rebuilt a few of my tumen, I could finish them off. It was thoughtful of him to want to give me the credit for retaking the Maya lands, but I felt I was finished being a warrior. Unless there was no alternative, I would not lead in battle again.

About the time the Horses returned from the west, I had many of my tumen up to strength, and I sent five of them to Smoking Mirror to retake the last of the Maya lands. The campaign lasted almost a year, but in the end, he was again governor of the Maya. My son Theodore and Juchi's two sons served in the campaign with distinction. I sent Tepeyolotl to help organize a new Ordu in the west. There was a small outbreak of bandit activity there, and there was finally enough population to support an Ordu. So it went for those first years, there were a few small outbreaks of banditry, and we stamped them out quickly. The weather was good, the crops plentiful, and the population grew. There were isolated outbreaks of the plague, but with fewer deaths. Theodore took a wife from among the

Ben Zah as had his brother George. The younger children grew like weeds, and I made sure they spent some years in the north, among the Siksika for Mathilde and Seagull's children, and among Hawk Ordu for Ignace and Daldal's children. On a whim, I sent John to visit Smoking Mirror, and when he returned, he wanted to visit the Ani' Yun'-wiya. I let him visit Mazatl's family for a few years, and he came back a very thoughtful, introspective young boy.

Henry managed to come down for a visit the year before he died. He looked over and approved of the iron works we had set up in Tenanco in the old Yope territory. It supplied all the iron for the Khanate for a long time. As usual, each Ordu and most of the larger cities also had their own ironworkers. More widespread was work in gold, silver, and copper. There was a great demand for bangles. I was always being presented with something or other made of gold, but unless it was artistically executed, I just stored it in the treasury. The more artistic pieces were displayed about the palace. Feathers were also in great demand for ornamentation and decoration, and I was often presented with some beautifully wrought capes and mantles and even headpieces. Again I displayed some and gave out some as gifts as necessary.

The people were much given to festivals and pageantry, and I encouraged the leaders to continue with their customs as before as long as there was no bloodshed. In general, I tried to interfere as little as possible with the cities, but made sure the borders were secure, bandits were hunted down, commerce was safe, and any natural disasters were ameliorated. Of the latter, there were occasional earthquakes, floods, hurakan, droughts, and volcanoes. Some of these were more disastrous than others were, but we were able to deal with everyone's needs. This went a long way toward dispelling the influence of the priests. They seized on every disaster as a sign of their particular god's punishment, but when an Ordu quickly arrived with food, clothing, and shelter, no one listened to the priests. Before long, most of them rethought their situation and came around to support the Khanate. A few, however, continued to cause trouble and eventually had to be eliminated. Not surprisingly, this caused little trouble among the people. It is difficult to miss a parasite.

Most of the people continued to have slaves, but whenever any were given to me, I would free them and pay them a wage to work for me if they wished or let them go their way. It would be nice to report that my practice spread among the people, but it didn't. They thought me rather eccentric. I was also considered eccentric because I wouldn't marry the daughters the various leaders offered me and so build up a proper harem. I had to go to some lengths not to hurt anyone's feelings, but I so rewarded them for offering that it would have been difficult for them to take offence. I did encourage my staff to marry out of their tribe and so to strengthen our unity. I made sure that taxes were not onerous. Ordu had to be supported wherever they were stationed, and a small levy was used to support my staff, but no one suffered from taxation, and it was always suspended in case of any disaster. Mine was a most benign rule.

Still, this was not a people given to living in peace, and warriors had to have their wars. The obvious target was the southeast beyond the Maya. Actually keeping the restive Maya in check was the real reason I decided on another campaign. It began some eight years after I became khan. Juchi had come down for a visit and mentioned that many of the young men were getting bored with Ordu duty and wanted to see some action. He was toying with the idea of wiping out the hostile cannibals on the island chain east of the Taino islands. Already the local Ordu had driven them out of some of the islands, but they still remained on the outermost island and the islands south of it. I suggested that such a campaign would not really solve his problem since a single Island Ordu could handle them if he ordered it. I suggested that instead we could penetrate the southeast with four Ordu at a time, two in the north and two in the south until all the Ordu had had a chance to participate. It would give me a chance to wear down the flower of the Maya youth before it turned on us again, and it would give the northern Ordu a difficult and challenging campaign. However, I felt that we should always offer alliance to the people we meet, not just conquer like he and I had been forced to do. He was pleased with the idea and suggested that George and Mukali be the leaders of the two wings. I suggested that Jelme should be George's second in command and

Tepeyolotl Mukali's. He agreed and further suggested that both campaigns should report to Smoking Mirror and he should be consulted for any difficulties rather than us since he was much closer to the area. He could send us reports on their progress. I enthusiastically concurred, and we called in George and Mukali.

The two were excited about leading a campaign, even if it might prove to be largely peaceful, and were pleased with their seconds and the short line of communication. George decided on the southern part, and Mukali was quite satisfied with the northern part. I suggested that they each take a northern and a southern tumen, to further cement unity between the two khanates. They thought that was a good idea. Juchi suggested that they be ready to begin their campaign at the start of the dry season in the late fall. They went off to organize their staffs. Juchi then told me that, of course, all of the new territory would be in my khanate. It was logical for it to be so, but I thanked him anyway.

"Have you given any thought to succession?" I asked him.

"Much thought, actually. While Mukali is the better soldier, I think Jelme would be the better Khan. What do you think?"

"I agree, but will Mukali accept your decision in peace?"

"I hope so. I have already told the council my decision, so there is nothing he can do about it in any case. This campaign is his last chance to convince me he is more than just a good warrior. We must instruct Tepeyolotl to take over and send him back in chains if he does not obey his orders. Can he be counted on to do so?"

"I'm sure he can. He has his father's loyalty and good sense. If we instruct him to do so, he will."

"Good. Now, what about you? Will it be George, Theodore, or John?"

"My decision is easy. Only George would want the job. Theodore is too introspective to be khan, but would be an invaluable advisor for George. John seems to be more interested in medicine. Neither will begrudge George the Khanate, and George will be loyal to you and your successors."

"The truth is, if you had not survived my father's plots, there was no one else that I could have given half my Khanate and trusted to remain loyal to me. As for George, I know him best of all your sons and would trust him with my life, just as you trusted me with his."

The campaign began that fall, and the people first encountered proved to be as intractable as the Maya and in fact were likely related to them. George had the easier way, since the southern part was generally more open and dry, while the northern part was jungle. Resistance was stiffer in the north, and Mukali performed bravely and irreproachably throughout the campaign. He imprudently marched back along his path of victory at the end of the campaign and died of a snakebite. He always camped out in the open with his men instead of in a tent, and during the night he was bitten. He was found dead the next morning. It removed the potential succession problem, but was a terrible waste. George and Jelme were unscathed during the campaign, but Tepeyolotl was wounded severely near the end of the campaign and was evacuated by boat. The sea and our faithful allies the Putun Maya kept the northern campaign supplied. The Ben Zah kept the southern campaign supplied by caravan. The steady supplies and the endless line of fresh troops were too much for the locals and gradually resistance lessened. Then it was renewed vigorously along the last part of the isthmus when they encountered a people called Cuna. While they were rather primitive, they were formidable warriors well able and willing to defend their land from any intrusion. In the end, we could afford the losses better than they could, and they had to submit. By the time we reached the end of their lands, all the Ordu had been bloodied in campaign, and we could call a halt and absorb the new lands.

Three Ordu were left behind to keep the peace, but there was no trouble as it became clear we were more of a boon than a curse. The several chiefdoms that joined us freely prospered with the improved trade and the safety net the Khanate provided them. Within a year, one of the occupying Ordu was replaced with a local levy. Within three years, all the Ordu were local. The campaign accomplished all we wanted. The Maya hotheads were thinned out considerably, and all the tumen got a chance to see some action. Smoking Mirror's authority was extended over the conquered lands of the isthmus, and his son was assigned to be his assistant.

Since he was to be my successor, I assigned George to be the head of my council. It was fairly large, but was only advisory. The heads of the Mexica, Alcolhua, and Chalca were on it, and there was a representative from each of the allied peoples. I would also rotate two seats among the conquered people, except those that had revolted like the Maya, the Tepaneca, and the Tya Nuu. Any leader was allowed to see me, and anybody was allowed to see the leader of the local Ordu to redress any grievance. Eventually we set up a cadre of judges to handle civil and criminal problems to relieve the Ordu commanders of that onerous chore. This was based on a system already in use locally when we took over.

In my sixty-second year, I put George in charge of the Khanate and with the rest of my family went north to visit Juchi. We left in the fall and spent the whole winter leisurely moving northward visiting anyone we knew or thought we knew along the way. Smoking Mirror and his family came out to meet us along the way and go along with us. We were warmly received in every town along the way. Each Ordu we visited turned out in full array to great me with the shield-beating salute. Smoking Mirror and I exchanged glances frequently when we came upon a familiar sight, but found we didn't need to say much to each other. We arrived at the Eagle Ordu in the late spring. The plains were dressed in their most beautiful flowers, and Juchi, himself, came out to meet me and lead me into the Ordu. We were met with a shield-beating salute that shook the earth. We spent the rest of spring and most of the summer getting reacquainted, hunting, visiting the other Ordu, and discussing everything and anything. Padraig and his family arrived in early summer and stayed with us several weeks. Both his and Mathilde's hair were completely white, all his children were grown and had children of their own except for a late daughter they'd had. She was named Paula and was about John's age, fifteen. Unfortunately John was not with us for this trip since he was still with Mazatl's family among the Ani' Yun'-wiya, but he planned to join us before we left, since he wanted to study with Okuh-hatuh in the Eagle Ordu.

Much had happened in the north in my absence. The Koryo

trade had continued and had expanded to include cotton, ginseng root, and other raw materials for medicines from us and porcelains, finished medicines, and rice from them. A fledgling silk industry had been established (by the family of the young sailor I had spoken to so long ago) in the land of the Pansfalaya where there were plentiful mulberry trees to feed the silkworms. More Koryo immigrants had arrived at the Salmon Ordu and were bringing their valuable skills to serve the Khanate. More of the northern Tinneh had joined the Khanate, as had many isolated bands of the Kutchin people in the northwest. The Inuit, however, still preferred to live in peace independently. Also in the north, a shipful of people as pale as me were seen cutting wood and sailing east with it. This occurred in a large bay east of the larger Inuit Bay. The local Inuit reported that the ships came irregularly—often at intervals of several years. These people lived in the east on a large island with no trees where there are also many Inuit. Juchi had decided not to bother them since they caused no trouble.

Another incursion by pale people had resulted in some conflict. The people that I had heard about earlier who fished along the coast and sometimes put into shore for varying lengths of time ran afoul of a patrol from the Panther Ordu. They assumed an attack rather than a mere inquiry and fled to their ships leaving behind much of their dried fish. The patrol took the fish. A watch had been posted for them so that contact might be made with them. Meanwhile, Padraig's youngest son Pierre was sent the Panther Ordu with the thought that perhaps they wouldn't run off if they saw someone like them. So far their ships had been seen, but they had not put into shore since the incident a few years ago. None of the locals interviewed had any contact with them or knew from where they come.

The Natchez people had begun to unravel after the second plague (the Zhen plague). The Great Sun and most of his family had died of it, and since they could offer no help to those suffering from it, the people began to drift away to the Taunika and Pansfalaya. They no longer existed as an independent people. Smoking Mirror was not sorry to hear of their passing, but I was sorry they could not adjust and add to the Khanate instead of being brushed aside by it. The Southeastern cities were also greatly reduced and were only now returning to prosperity and starting to grow again.

The small islands south and east of the Taino islands had been conquered, and the cannibal people absorbed into the Taino. The leader of the expedition, the head of the Dog Ordu, Chekika (my long-ago Calusa observer), was convinced that they were the same people, only less civilized. At the end of the southern chain of islands was a fairly large landmass. Most of the people in the immediate area near the last island seemed to be related to the cannibals and Taino, at least in language and practices. Mapping of the land had begun and already a few mappers had been attacked, so a punitive expedition was being organized. The land could possibly be connected to our isthmus. We had just begun mapping the area beyond our border, since it had taken so long to properly map the difficult terrain of the isthmus itself. That bordering area was also a very dense jungle and was not lending itself to easy mapping. So far we were not having any trouble with the locals. Padraig thought it would be better to first map the coastline from the sea and then later fill the blanks in between. I agreed that that would be useful, except that since the mappers would have to put into shore every night, they would be at the mercy of whatever tribe was there, and it would be hard to support them or know where they were to rescue them. We had been sending mappers with all major trading expeditions into the landmass, but their efforts had not yet been properly collated. I could report that there was a massive mountain range not far inland from the coast, but that was all I had noticed on the map fragments. I promised to send detailed maps as soon as they were available.

Juchi thought we would likely have to mount another expedition in a few years to keep the warriors happy and suggested we take the coastal area between the isthmus and the end of the island chain, assuming the area was connected and not just some large islands. We should know that before we started the campaign. Meanwhile, he was experimenting with larger boats, built by Koryo immigrants along the lines of their merchant ships. The work was being done on the southern coast near the Pansfalaya lands. The first ship should be ready for launching soon and would begin taking soundings off the coast, mapping channels and reefs, and getting a feel for the prevailing winds offshore. It would also serve to train men for shipboard service, and as the fleet grew, elements would be sent south to serve my khanate as well. It would greatly facilitate movement of troops and supplies during the upcoming campaign. A similar program was just getting under way at the Salmon Ordu and would greatly facilitate the movement of goods along the west coast. There was no plan to eventually compete with the Koryo merchants with our new fleet. It was only intended for use off our own shores. I was greatly impressed with Juchi's foresight in this matter and promised to have soundings taken off as much of our coast as possible, as far out as possible.

Padraig left a few weeks before I did. About a week before we left, John arrived from the southeast, and Migizi and my nephew Henry arrived from the Hawk Ordu. John was turned over to Okuh-hatuh who was delighted to have a new apprentice. Henry and Migizi had a surprise for me. After many years of experimentation, Migizi had finally developed a small cannon that could be held and shot by one man. It was not yet as accurate as an arrow, nor could it be fired at the same rate, but it delivered a devastating wound from a small solid shot. They demonstrated it for me. It looked a little like the model I had given Migizi so long ago, except that it had a much longer muzzle and a longer stock. It was loaded just like a cannon and fired just like a cannon. It was rather heavy and best aimed from a laying position, with the weight of the weapon supported by the ground. It also had a fairly strong recoil. Still, it wasn't impossible to use, and a line of them could deliver a crushing blow to an attacking mass. I suggested that a portion of a tumen should be armed with them and trained to use them. If they proved useful, we could expand their use. Juchi agreed and ordered the Hawk Ordu to develop such a cadre. Migizi promised to refine his weapon. Henry told me that both of Migizi's sons were working with him, as was one of his own sons. He was certain we were on to something.

When I took leave of Juchi, we both pledged to meet again in five years. Little did we know that would not be possible.

46

THE SOUTHERN CAMPAIGN AND RETIREMENT,
48-77 K
(MEXICO CITY & CUERNAVACA, 1416-45)

Three years after our meeting, we began the new campaign. Our fleet was now plying our eastern coasts and was readied to deliver an Ordu from the northern khanate to the mainland across from the terminus of the island chain. The southern Ordu would travel overland through the isthmus. George would command my forces, and Jelme would lead the northern forces. The coast had been mapped between the terminus of the island chain and the isthmus, and, indeed, it was connected. We also had determined that there were mainly moderately sized chiefdoms in the western part of the area and smaller ones in the eastern part. There was a very large bay almost midway between the jump-off points that could serve as a rendezvous for the two wings. The coastal terrain varied from jungle at both jump-off points to cultivated lands and arid scrublands in between. The interior was still something of a mystery, except for the areas mapped by our merchants. These were mostly confined to the western area. There were at least three lines of mountains with valleys in between them. The western valley was more narrow and shallow, the eastern very broad and deep with a mighty river (the Yuma) in its midst. The easternmost mountain line extended almost to the sea, but the other two stopped well short, leaving a large heavily cultivated alluvial plain along the coast. We knew that the people on this coastal plain were divided into two major people, the Sinu in the center and west and the Tairona in the east. Both were moderately developed chiefdoms engaged in agriculture and quite skilled in gold working. Neither people were united under a single chief, but were rather split into chiefdoms of varying size and strength. To the south of the isthmus along the coastal jungle were a more primitive people called the Choco who were much like the Cuna, although not as fierce. They had been much impressed by our defeat of the Cuna and had been joining us one band at a time over the years and aiding our mapping of their area. We also knew of a people called the Quimbaya that lived in the middle part of the western valley. They were also heavily engaged in agriculture and quite skilled at gold working. There were also a people called the Muisca that lived on high plateaus in the eastern line of mountains. They also cultivated crops, but were less skilled in gold working. They were known to mine salt and the beautiful clear dark green stone (emerald) that was highly prized as an ornamental. I had seen a few of them in Tenochtitlan (where they were called quetzalitzli) and often wondered where they were from. These last two peoples were not in the target area of our campaign, however.

As usual, the Maya Ordu would be the first to go. I decided to use five tumen initially. Each would cover an area about sixty li wide and would march eastward along the coast until they reached the large bay. Juchi was also sending five tumen and had already stock-piled supplies in the last island of the chain guarded by the first of the tumen. They would begin sailing to the mainland as soon as the next tumen arrived on the fleet. It would take a while before all five tumen were in place, but the first ones would begin moving inland and approaching the locals. They would move down to the mouth of a large river called the Warao, after the people living in its large delta. After securing that area, they would wait for the arrival of the other tumen before moving west along a similar three hundred li wide path from the coast. My tumen would arrive in twos and begin contacting the locals immediately east of the Choco and moving well inland into the first line of mountains before pivoting north along the shore. Both wings would receive fresh tumen during the campaign to either replace or supplement the original five as needed.

Our part of the campaign went quite smoothly at first. The small groups in the foothills and northern end of the first mountain line needed little persuasion to join us. Isolated bands attacked us and were wiped out. The Sinu tried to talk us to death, but in the end most of their chiefs submitted with only token reluctance. The

Tairona refused to have anything to do with us, however. None of the chiefs would join, and in fact, they joined forces to resist us and even had the temerity to attack us first. Their attack was beaten off when the artillery opened up on them. Shaken, they retreated to their larger cities, but would not surrender. George then cut them off landward and began gradually enveloping them toward the sea by besieging and reducing their southern and eastern cities first and holding lines to the sea. There was an isolated mountain group close to the sea. Most of their major cities were on the northern and western foothills of this group. George manned the line with three tumen and sent the other two east. One went around the mountain group and attacked from the northeast, and the other went through the mountains and attacked from the southeast. The resistance was fierce, and at the critical moment, two fresh tumen arrived from the isthmus to roll over their last strongholds. George was loath to wipe the Tairona out as was our custom because he was quite impressed by their large cities, canals, and roads. These last were their undoing since we utilized them to our great benefit during the campaign. Instead, he executed the chiefs and most of the ruling class and organized the people along the lines of the Putun Maya as a craft and mercantile people. He sent for some the Putun Maya to settle among them and expedite the transition. He sent me a long report on his decisions and asked for my approval. I was quite impressed by his actions and praised him lavishly. The Tairona eventually proved invaluable. Over the years, they began to use the Putun Maya boats and ply the coasts of the land in all directions greatly increasing the flow of goods and were essential in the further mapping of what proved to be a huge landmass. East of the Tairona, the land was more arid and the people were loosely organized seminomadic tribes hunting, fishing, or gathering. They generally were happy to join us. We reached the large bay first and swept a large area around it.

The northern group arrived shortly after our Ordu had finished rounding the bay. They had met varied resistance, but had taken a long time to get into position because of the long distances they had to travel. The campaigns were becoming a logistical nightmare for the northern Ordu, and some other arrangement would have to be made. While George and Jelme were discussing the problem, word reached them that Juchi had died. Theodore was placed in command of mopping up and consolidating the new lands, and they returned north. Word also reached me, and with a heavy heart, I also made my way north with Paula. I arrived first, not surprisingly, and offered my condolences to Juchi's wife and daughters. Juchi had already been buried according to custom so I could only bid him farewell in my mind. When Jelme and George arrived, Jelme was immediately proclaimed Khakhan, and George and I pledged our continued allegiance.

Jelme had always been a thoughtful young man, and he had matured into a decisive, insightful man, a credit to his father. He immediately called a council meeting and graciously invited George and I to attend. He retained his father's council although he added a few new members. He confirmed my position as Khan of Anahuac and asked if I were ready to name a successor among my sons. I immediately named George, and Jelme confirmed him before the council, making the succession official. I thanked him for his confidence in my family and me. He thanked me for my long and unswerving loyalty. He then told me that if I ever grew weary of ruling, I could abdicate, I didn't have to die to leave the position. That gave me something to think about on the way back, and indeed, some three years later, when I was sure all was well in every part of my Khanate, I turned it over to George and retired to Cuauhnahuac.

On the way back from the Eagle Ordu, George told me what Jelme had decided to do about the southern landmass. Since we were each in possession of a portion of it, he would rotate tumen to the eastern part while we would rotate them to the western part to keep the peace. The next time we decided on a campaign, we should organize a volunteer grouping of tumen made up from the standing Ordu. These would be sent to the frontier as they were organized and would only travel with their personal weapons. The occupying Ordu would also guard a supply depot complete with cannon and horses enough for several tumen. This would take a while to set up, but then it would take a while to pacify the new areas also. This organization would prevent all the disruptive movement of tumen over ever-increasing distances, especially over the ocean. We would be free to extend our portion whenever we chose; there would be no further need of acting in concert. He also felt we should place someone in charge of our portion of the area. I decided to leave Theodore in charge and sent his family to join him. Jelme placed Kaidu, Mukali's oldest son, in command of his part. Kaidu had been a member of his staff during the campaign and had served with distinction.

When I retired, I only pressed George to keep me up on the latest map additions; otherwise, I would in no way annoy him. He could seek my advice if he wished, but I knew he didn't need it. I must admit, George followed my instructions to the letter. He sent me copies of all the latest map fragments and otherwise did not bother me. There are those who would have been offended by this, but I was relieved. Paula and I took long rides in the beautiful hills around our home and occasionally undertook a long journey to visit Smoking Mirror. If the summer was particularly hot, George would stay with us for a while, but he never talked over affairs of the Khanate; we only discussed the family. John eventually came back to join us with his wife, Wurteh, an Ani' Yun'-wiya related to Mazatl. She had insisted on taking a new name on being married and had settled on Moonlight, since there had been a full moon on the night they had met. This was rendered Metztlaconac or "Glowing Moon" in Nahual. John had become much interested in healing the sick, but did not use the rituals he had learned to perform, only the medicines and treatments he had mastered. He felt the ritual was only for show and did nothing to help. He was very gentle and patient with the ill and did what he could to help them. He grew to be quite revered by his patients, but he was never satisfied and went on long journeys to learn new techniques and find new medicines.

Theodore would occasionally send me a summary report of what was happening on the frontier. He had been sending merchant trains farther and farther into the landmass. The coastal mapping had been hampered in the west by a north-flowing coastal current, but they had eventually discovered a south-flowing current farther out to sea that eventually turned and met the coastal current, thus describing a circular flow. They took advantage of this and finally mapped the northern part of the coast as well as the currents. The mapping ships would run into primitive rafts and small boats with fishermen occasionally, but these would flee landward, and we did not bother them. On land, we were slowly moving along the coast, which was a dense jungle for at least as far down the coast from the isthmus as we had penetrated. The people on the coast remained primitive, like the Choco, but they had heard rumors of a great kingdom to the south ruled by a god. The people of this kingdom were called the Chimu and their capital was called Chan Chan. As with most such rumors, there was likely some truth to it, but only some. I suspected it would turn out to be another stratified society like the Natchez, who had also been ruled by a "god," the Great Sun.

Word would also come from the other frontier, although indirectly through George. While the western coast of the landmass seemed to extend generally southward, with only a few capes and bays to break it up, the eastern coast continued to extend eastward, seemingly endlessly, although it was also tending a little south. It, too, was mostly jungle and primitive people. Kaidu had also been expanding along the coast, but the people were only slightly cooperative and even then, inconsistently. They seemed to want nothing from us or anyone else, except for wives (for whom they raided each other). They were also quite adept at fading into the jungle and making themselves invisible. More than one punitive expedition returned empty-handed. Jelme was becoming impatient with the frustration, and Kaidu had begun turning one tribe against another to thin them out. I thought this was wrong, but it was not my place to chide him about it. Later, the Zhen epidemic broke out among the locals and greatly weakened them. As it happened, this epidemic struck just as a large-scale punitive expedition was getting under way, and before long they had swept a long stretch of the coast free of any hostile tribes.

I was sorry to hear that the plague had struck there for I was worried about how far it would spread. Indeed, it came right around the coast and eventually was raging in our areas of the southern land-mass. It eventually spread throughout both Khanates also, but this time did its damage only to the young. In the south, however, it was devastating to all ages. It took many years to rebuild the populations under our control. We had little information how much damage occurred beyond our control, but suspected it was considerable. The plague did have the effect of the Quimbaya sending emissaries to us for help and soon joining us as allies to secure that help. The Muisca did not seem to be affected at first, but eventually they, too, were devastated. They did not ask for any help, however, nor did they join us. External trade ended for a few years while supplies were brought in to help rebuild the people. A few more of the coastal peoples also joined us, as did the people south of the Quimbaya. These were small chieftaincies with organized societies based on agriculture and fishing, but they were so devastated they could not function independently and were heartened by our acceptance of the Quimbaya.

Over the years, our mappers kept working the coast, and when the trade resumed, the interior was also partially sketched in. The western coast bulged westward not far south of the Choco area. It was a gradual bulge that seemed to end in a large bay with several islands, but it continued to bulge south of the bay for about six hundred li before finally tending back eastward. The Chimu people proved to be in this area but contact was limited. Somewhere along the Chimu coast, the south-flowing coastal current, which we had discovered south of the circular current, was overwhelmed by the north-flowing offshore current, and mapping became quite slow. The current extended too far out to sea for our boats, although there was some talk of trying to cross it, get as far south as possible, then rejoin and ride it and the prevailing winds back north along the coast. This expedition was still being planned. In the east, the wind blew toward shore, and the currents flowed west. Still, they had mapped the coast at least as far as a mighty river with an enormous mouth filled with islands. They were still mapping the islands but had ascertained that the coast continued generally eastward beyond the river. We were much farther south along our coast than they were, but not much farther in terms of coastline. No information on the people encountered was coming from the eastern mappers.

Smoking Mirror died not long after the Zhen plague outbreak. Mazatl only lived about a year longer. The same year, Padraig and Mathilde died within a few days of each other. One by one, all the people I knew were dying, not by the plague, just by advancing years. I was amazed that I continued to enjoy good health, and although it seemed to take me longer to get up in the morning, I was still able to do so. I suspect I was kept young because there were always children about. John's family lived with us, of course, and he had three children. Also one or more of our grandchildren and their families were usually visiting us at all times. John had gone to help with the plague and was gone for almost four years. He was even more quiet and introspective when he returned, but he didn't seem to want to discuss his experiences. A few months after his return, Metztlaconac died of a mysterious ailment. John had tried all he knew to try, but was unable to diagnose the ailment or cure it. He was able to alleviate the great pain she was suffering. After she died, he went on another journey, back to the Eagle Ordu to confer with Okuh-hatuh, then on to the Salmon Ordu to talk to Cho Yi. While he was gone, George died suddenly and was succeeded by his eldest son, John. Paula and I went to Tlatelolco for the funeral and the installation of the new Khan. We had decided on cremation rather than the Mongol hidden burial. A large pyre was erected at the foot of the temple to Tengri and John set the flame. The ashes were gathered and thrown into the lake, near its middle. It was strange burying another one of our children. The installation ceremony was just like the one for George. All the local Ordu filled the square in full regalia and, when John was proclaimed Khan, beat their shields with their swords.

When my son John returned home some years later, he had a new wife, Paula, Padraig and Mathilde's youngest child. She had been married to Skolaskin, a Salst minghan commander in the Salmon Ordu, but he had died in a hunting accident. She also had three children from her first marriage and brought them with her. Their timing couldn't have been better, because my Paula died the day after their arrival. She died peacefully in her sleep. She had seemed just fine that day and had not mentioned any pain. I was crushed by her loss, but with all the activity around me, I was unable to give myself over to grief, except at night when I would feel truly alone. Then every morning the children would come into my room and get me up to tell them stories. I began thinking often of the past and the full life I had lived. I was ready to die, but didn't and couldn't understand why. Then John told me his Paula was with child. I had thought she was a little too old for that, but John, himself, had been something of a late child also. In due time a son was born. They insisted on naming him Karl. So it was I came to write this journal. Now, perhaps this journal was the last thing I had to do before I die, and finally I can join my Paula.

Since beginning this book, I have been dreaming frequently and remembering the dreams. Instead of the ridiculous dreams I had when I was younger, these are wonderful dreams of my journeys with Paula. We are both young and happy. The last thing I see before I awaken is her smiling face. The dreams are so vivid that I can feel the cool and wet and hot and dry. I can smell the tundra, the plain, the flowers, the forest, and the sea. Last night I dreamed of Grandfather George, Givevneu, and Kaidu. They were standing together at the mouth of a cave or tunnel. They turned toward me and extended their arms to welcome me. Perhaps it is finally my time. I hope so.

47
CUAUHNAHUAC, 77 K
CUERNAVACA, MX, 1445)

My father died in his sleep the night after he finished writing. I found the last page on his table when the children who found him the next morning came to get me. He had a wonderful smile on his face, but then, (at least in my memory) he had always been a happy man, able to see his way clearly no matter what happened. I could never understand him. I didn't know he was writing what seems to be a journal or more accurately a memoir. He never mentioned it to me or anyone else, but I've got the whole of it and will read it. His remains were taken to Tlatelolco and cremated with full honors as befits a Khan. My nephew John, the current Khan, lit the pyre and carried the ashes to the center of the lake with great ceremony. Rather than grieved, the crowd seemed almost reverent. There was barely a sound from them. Few of them knew him, of course, and not that many more remembered his reign, but all knew of him, and he was always spoken of with reverence, at least, in my hearing. I always found that puzzling. He unquestionably deserved respect, and he had mine, but reverence seems a bit much. Perhaps his memoir will shed some light on this for me.

Having read his memoirs, I am amazed at how little I knew of, or indeed, thought of our coming to this land. It was a remarkable trek. The founding and growth of the Khanate was also remarkable, spawned as it was by little more than one man's vision. And to think that my father was uniquely involved almost from the beginning and was instrumental in carrying out that vision. All of my life the only danger I faced, of which I was aware, was from the elements. I have never been involved in any military campaign except indirectly treating the wounded. Neither have I done any exploring or mapping or trading. I have, however, wandered over much of the land and visited places my father never saw, and everywhere I went I never sensed any danger from any man. That is the legacy of the Mongols. My father played a large part in that legacy, but also, he had his own legacy, that of the good ruler. He was scrupulously fair, completely honest, and utterly devoid of arrogance. The only inaccuracies in his memoirs, which I can detect, are those which people he trusted told him. I am surprised he didn't see through them, but who would expect his oldest friends and his sons to lie to him. I think perhaps now I should set the record straight.

The first deception was regarding the Southeast Campaign that added the isthmus to the Khanate. My father never seemed to know that Juchi ordered George and Mukali to add the territory without regard to the wishes of the locals; they were only given the chance to join before they were attacked. Otherwise, there would have been very little land added to the Khanate. I guess he never realized that George was more loyal to Juchi than to him. Then there was the matter of Mukali's "accident" on his return trip. He was ordered to return by land "to make sure the land was pacified," and a man loyal to Jelme and familiar with snakes made sure Mukali had his accident. Since Juchi ordered him to return by land, I have always felt he had a part in his son's demise, but I could never get any confirmation. Smoking Mirror was shocked when he learned about it, but he had no love for Mukali, since he held him responsible for his son's near-fatal wounding. I was surprised that he never told my father the real story. I suspect, my father never asked about it, and knowing Smoking Mirror, he would never have volunteered such information.

The first campaign in the southern landmass was also conducted in the same manner. George did break precedence by not wiping out the Tairona, and there was some grumbling about it, but no one was prepared to question him openly. The real reason he spared them was because he was much taken with their goldsmithing and was sure it would prove a valuable asset. His wife also greatly treasured gold bangles and received quite a load of them from him. I should also mention that George was most unfair to the Maya Tumen. In each campaign their losses were alarming. They were never supported with artillery and were always employed in any frontal assault on a difficult position. They are a fearless people and fierce warriors and were led to believe they were being honored rather than deliberately being killed off. To be fair, it was a prudent policy, for they are a difficult people. In all the time I spent among them, I never felt truly accepted nor did I have a clue what they were thinking about me or about what I told them. I was, however, always treated respectfully by them, and they were always kind to and generous with me. I will always have the greatest respect for them. I do suspect that Smoking Mirror would have lived longer if he ruled over a more pliable people. He was smart to maintain his capital among the far more cooperative Putun Maya.

There was some talk about Juchi's death in the Eagle Ordu, but Jelme was far away at the time, and Juchi was hardly a young man by then. I am puzzled that my father maintained a high opinion of Jelme. The latter was always quite clever, but he never impressed me as being thoughtful. Perhaps my father was blinded by loyalty to Juchi, or perhaps subsequent events forever soured me on the man. This brings me to the final error. I found out from Theodore that the outbreak of the Zhen plague in the southern landmass was no accident. It seems that there occurred a minor outbreak of the disease in one of the more isolated Northeast Bands not long after they incongruously received a gift of silk cloth from Jelme. This outbreak was reported to Jelme in a dispatch from the nearby Ordu, which had already sent help. Not nearly long enough afterward, a small party arrived to replace the "diseased" silk for the band. They gathered up the silk and passed out new cloth. Then they departed to "destroy" the contaminated silk. They next time they were seen, they had embarked to join the new campaign in the south and were carrying curious bundles along with their personal weapons. When they arrived in the south, they sent gifts of silk to several of the more truculent tribes as "a peace offering." Not long after the gifts arrived, the plague broke out. While it was unquestionably a very effective move, the plague spread far beyond the target tribes and moved back to strike our people. The results were devastating, and I labored mightily for four years to end it, four years that I would have preferred spending with my family and especially my wife who died shortly after my return.

Other than these few things, the book is quite accurate as far as I know. I will make sure the rest of the family reads the book, but I do not intend to write any more. Perhaps one of the children will pick up the narrative later on.

APPENDIX 1
DRAMATIS PERSONAE
BOOK 1

Acamapichtli—first "ruler" of the city of Tenochtitlan (Mexico), an historical figure (r. 1372–91) who served the Tepaneca faithfully. In the book, his fate is quite different.

Adihanin—Kadohadacho (Caddo)—Smoking Mirror's Kadohadacho name.

Al-Razi—Persian physician working in Baghdad who clinically described and distinguished measles and smallpox in AD 910.

Amantacha—Wendat (Huron), second in command of the Snake Ordu and later named administrator of Anahuac.

Atabeyra—Taino fertility goddess.

Bela IV, King of Hungary, 1206–1270. His army was crushed at Mohi by the Mongol invasion of Europe in 1241.

Bimiibatod Omasus—Anishinabe (Chippewa), second in command of the Wildcat Ordu, who becomes the governor of the Purepecha (Tarascans).

Carpini , John of—a Franciscan friar sent in 1245 as an envoy by Pope Innocent IV to find out about the Mongols, to protest their invasion of 1241, and to enlist them in a war against the Muslims. He returned in 1247.

Chekika—Calusa observer, younger brother of the main chief. He rises through the ranks to become a tumen commander.

Chico Ocelotl—Smoking Mirror's son's birth name, he later becomes Tepeyolotl.

Chingis Khan—(1167–1227) founder of the Mongol Empire, conquered Northern China, Iran, Afghanistan, Turkistan and much of Southern Russia.

Cho Yi—Koryo (Korean) physician who immigrates to the Salmon Ordu. He helps ameliorate the measles epidemic.

Christina—daughter of a Nestorian priest and Karl's mother.

Christina—eldest daughter of Karl's brother Henry (1365–1403).

Christina—eldest daughter of Mathilde and Seagull, (1391–1455).

Cuacuauhtzin—son of Tezozomoc and first ruler of Tlatilulco, an historical figure who closely tied his city to his Tepaneca. In the book, he dies in battle.

Cuchiyaga—Calusa principle chief.

Curicaueri—principle god of the Purepecha (Tarascans). He seems to have been a fire or volcano god.

Daldal—Da-a-gelma'n (Takelma) widow, marries Ignace, Karl's second son. Daldal is the name of a mythical hero of her tribe.

Donduk—second in command of the Ordu under Kaidu, organizes the forest Ordu, and leads them in the forest theatre of the second Hotcangara (Chiwere Sioux) Campaign and in the Mingue Campaign. He also serves as governor of the Mingue lands, trains the Pigeon Ordu and finally the Alligator Ordu, serving as the first commander of both. He dies in 1381.

Doqus—wife of Henry, Karl's brother.

Gagewin—Anishinabe (Chippewa) chief who shows Karl an alternate iron ore deposit (the Mesabi Range in Minnesota).

George Waldmann—(d. 1368) grandfather of Karl, works as an ironmonger in Khanbalikh and sees to Karl's education.

George Waldmann—Karl's first son (1371–1432), succeeds him as Khan of Anahuac.

Givevneu—shaman of Kaidu's tumen. He is originally from the An'kalym (Chuckchi), a people from northeastern Siberia. His original name is Blocknot. He dies in 1381.

Henry Waldman—Karl's father, works as a swordsmith; moves to the northeast frontier of the Khanate with Kaidu, commander of the tumen stationed there.

Henry Waldman—Karl's brother (1340–1405), works as a swordsmith.

Henry—Henry's eldest son (1360–1411), also a swordsmith.

Henry—first son of Mathilde and Seagull (1395–1446).

Huitzilopochtli—"Southern Hummingbird," the principle god of the Mexica (Aztecs). He was a war god.

Ibrahim—a Muslim chemist, one of Karl's teachers in Khanbalikh.

Ignace—Karl's second son (1375–98).

Inoli—Ani' Yun'-wiya (Cherokee) member of Karl's staff during the Huaxteca campaign who is made governor of the first town that surrenders.

Isadowa—Kitikiti'sh (Wichita) guide, son of Howitscahde, led Karl to the Kadohadacho (Caddo). He is commander of the Horse Ordu during Karl's second Southern Campaign.

Jelme—Juchi's second son and successor (r. 1415–45).

John—Henry's second son (1363–1422), also a swordsmith.

John—Karl's youngest son, (1395–65), a physician and father of Karl, the Crow.

Juchi—grandson of Kaidu, son of Kuyuk, explorer and frequent companion of Karl. He goes on to become the 3rd Khan of the Blue Sky (r. 1398–15).

Kaidu—Mongol officer appointed commander of the tumen stationed on the northeast frontier of the Khanate. He pares down his tumen and leads them to America. He becomes the first Khan of the Khanate of the Blue Sky. He dies in 1382.

Ushesees—Ani' Yun'-wiya (Cherokee) chief of the town Kituhwa, where Karl meets with the assembled tribal representatives several times while they consider joining the Mongols.

Karl Waldmann—(The Raven) narrator of Book One, born in Khanbalikh (modern Beijing) in 1350, in the final decades of the Yuan or Mongol Dynasty. Son of Henry and Christina. He becomes the first Khan of Anahuac.

Karl Waldmann—(The Crow) narrator of Book Two, youngest son of Karl (The Raven's) youngest son, John. Born in Cuauhnahuac (Cuernavaca) has a most varied career.

Katalsta—Ani' Yun'-wiya (Cherokee) original name of Smoking Mirror's wife, Mazatl.

Katan—brother of Yesui, early teacher of Karl.

Kiliahote—Pansfalaya (Choctaw) shaman who advises the tribe to join the Mongols. He makes some disturbing predictions.

Kuang Tung—a Chinese engineer and one of Karl's teachers in Khanbalikh.

Kubilai Khan—5th Supreme Khan (r. 1260–94), conquered the rest of China, founded the Yuan Dynasty. He was the Khan visited by Marco Polo.

Kuyuk Khan—3rd Supreme Khan (r. 1246–8), visited by John of Carpini.

Kuyuk—oldest son of Kaidu, becomes head of the Owl Ordu and later succeeds Kaidu as 2nd Khan of the Blue Sky (r. 1382–98).

Kwesh—a distinguished chief of the Titskan watitch (Tonkawa) who joins the Mongols with his band and helps bring in the rest of the tribe also.

Leo—second son of Mathilde and Seagull (1396–1461).

Ludmilla—Karl's second daughter (1381–98).

Mangku—Kaidu's second son, becomes leader of the Hawk Ordu. He dies in 1381.

Mathilde—wife of Padraig, a descendant of Breton adventurers, related to Pierre Boucher.

Mathilde Waldman—first daughter of Karl (1373–99).

Mato Anahtaka—Ocheti shakowin (Dakota Sioux) leader who is the second commander of the Pigeon Ordu.

Mazatl—Ani' Yun'-wiya (Cherokee) daughter of Ostenako and wife of Smoking Mirror. Her original name is Katalsta.

Menawa—Kofitachiki (Cofitachiqui—an independent city-state of the Muskhogean people who were known as the Creeks in historic times) high chief.

Metztlaconac—Ani' Yun'-wiya (Cherokee) first wife of John, Karl's youngest son. Her original name is Wurteh.

Michikinikwa—Twanhtwanh (Miami) member of Karl's staff who is appointed governor of Texcalla (Tlaxcalla).

Migizi—Anishinabe (Chippewa) metalworker who works on muskets.

Miriam—second daughter of Mathilde and Seagull (1393–1413).

Mixcoatl—principle god of Texcalla (Tlaxcalla), a hunting god.

Motsoyouf—Dzitsiista (Cheyenne) recruit who urges his tribe to join the Mongols, later becomes a mapper.

Mukali—Juchi's eldest son, who leads and dies during the Isthmus (Central American) campaign.

Munche Canche—Peace Chief of the Hotcangara (Chiwere Sioux) who surrenders their main city (Cahokia—is the current name; what they called it is unknown) to the Mongols.

Nahtahki—Siksika (Blackfoot) aunt of Seagull who helps Karl and Paula with the children after her nephew's death.

Naukum—Givevneu's brother, head of his native An'kalym village.

Nial—one of Padraig's sons.

Nitsiza—Kawchodinne guide who leads the migrating Ordu through Tinneh country (the Mackenzie River Valley), then joins them as their first native recruit. He later runs a yam station north of the Hawk Ordu.

Odinigun—Anishinabe recruit who leads Karl to copper and iron ore and later becomes a metal worker.

Ogedai—younger brother of Juchi, first commander of the Salmon Ordu, he dies during the smallpox epidemic of 1388.

Okuh-hatuh—Dzitsiista (Cheyenne) who studies under and succeeds Givevneu as shaman of the Eagle Ordu.

Ollikut—Nimipu (Nez Perce) chief recruited by Karl, and who favors confederation with the Mongols.

Ootoyuk—Inuit adventurer from Taukujaa's village who goes as far east as the mouth of the Mackenzie River.

Opiyel-Guaobiran—dog deity of the Taino, he apparently guides the dead into the next world.

Ostenako—Ani' Yun'-wiya (Cherokee) chief of the revered town, Itsati.

Padraig O'Byrne—(1348–1425) a soldier (descended from Irish adventurers) who joins Karl and the Ordu of Kaidu after the fall of Khanbalikh.

Patheske—Hotcangara (Chiwere Sioux) who becomes the second governor of Murenbalikh (Cahokia).

Paula—daughter of an itinerant Polish merchant, Karl's wife.

Paulina—second daughter of Ignace and Daldal (1397–1461).

Peter—Karl's maternal grandfather. He is a Persian and a Nestorian Christian priest and helps educate Karl.

Peter—second son of Ignace and Daldal (1395–1442).

Pierre Boucher—goldsmith at the court of Kubilai Khan.

Pinopias—Ben Zah (Zapotec) wife of George, Karl's oldest son.

Quetzalcoatl—the "Feathered Serpent" god of wind, rain, or earth to many of the tribes of Mexico.

Quinatzin—ruler of the Alcolhua, an historical figure who kept Tezozomoc's ambitions in check as long as he lived. In the book, Kuyuk treacherously kills him.

Ruth—first daughter of Ignace and Daldal (1394–1455).

Sakaceweskam—Kensistenoug (Cree) commander of the Rabbit Ordu during Karl's second southern campaign.

Sanukh—distinguished chief of the Titskan watitch (Tonkawa), who joins the Mongols with his band and eventually brings in the rest of his tribe.

Sarah—third daughter of Mathilde and Seagull (1397–1465).

Sartak—son of Tului, cousin of Juchi, head of the Falcon Ordu, conspires with his father against Juchi's accession.

Seagull—Siksika (Blackfoot) soldier, member of the Antelope Ordu, who marries Mathilde, Karl's daughter.

Sensondacat—Ka-i-gwu (Kiowa) commander of the Monkey Ordu during Karl's second southern campaign.

Sharitarish—Chahiksichahiks (Pawnee) chief who sets up a meeting of the tribal confederacy with Karl.

Simon—first son of Ignace and Daldal (1393–1448).

Skolaskin—Salst (Salish) minghan commander in the Salmon Ordu, the first husband of Paula, Padraig and Mathilde's youngest daughter.

Smoking Mirror—"brother" of the chief of the Kadohadacho (Caddo). He is sent to observe the Mongols for a year and eventually joins them and becomes a close friend and frequent companion of Karl. He is appointed governor of Uluumil Kutz (Northern Yucatan). He is later made governor of all the Maya lands (d. 1425).

Steek-cha-komico—Southeastern Tribe (Creek) chief of a group of towns just east of the Pansfalaya (Choctaw) on the East Union River (Black Warrior River).

Talaswaima—Hopitu-shinumu (Hopi) guide, the only member of his tribe to join the Mongols at first. Accompanies Karl on first trip south.

Taska-abi—Pansfalaya (Choctaw), first commander of the Pheasant Ordu.

Tariacuri—legendary founder of the Purepecha (Tarascan) Empire.

Tatanka Ska Koda—Ocheti shakowin chief who joined the Mongols when first recruited and goes on to become governor of Murenbalikh.

Taukujaa—Inuit (or Eskimo) guide, accompanies Karl and Juchi across the Bering Sea to his native village on the Seward Peninsula.

Tayhah nea—Hotcangara (Chiwere Sioux) war chief, leads ambush against the Mongols in the second battle during the first Hotcangara Campaign and dies during the second campaign.

Techotlalatzin—Ruler of Texcoco and the Alcolhua after Quinatzin, an historical figure whose fate in the book is more benign.

Temur—second in command of the Wolf Ordu under Karl during the Mingue Campaign. He commands them during and after the third Hotcangara Campaign.

Tengri—"The Blue Sky" principle god of the Mongols.

Texcatlipoca—"Smoking Mirror," a Toltec god, revered mostly in the Mexican high plateau.

Tezozomoc—ruler of the Tepaneca, an historical figure who eventually conquered most of the Valley of Mexico before the rise of the Aztecs. In the book, his campaign is derailed, but he remains a problem, true to his nature.

Theodore—Karl's third son (1380–1453). He becomes the first Khan of the Clouds (Western South America).

Timugen—cousin of Juchi and member of Karl's staff during the Southern Campaign. He marries one of the daughters of the ruler of Cuauhnahuac (Cuernavaca).

Tlacuectli—Chalca merchant, father of Smoking Mirror.

Tlaloc—rain god revered by most of the natives of Mexico.

Toghon Temur—(r. 1333–70), last Yuan Emperor of China, driven out of China in 1368 by the founder of the Ming Dynasty.

Togun—a cousin of Kaidu and first commander of the Kestrel Ordu.

Toolhulhulsote—Nimipu (Nez Perce) commander of the Vulture Ordu during Karl's second southern campaign.

Tsakaka-sakis—Hewaktokto (Hidatsa), second commander of the Owl Ordu.

Tsu Chi'a—Karl's last teacher in Khanbalikh.

Tului—Kaidu's youngest son, becomes head of the Eagle Ordu. He later moves to the Crane Ordu and conspires against the accession of Juchi.

Tustenuckochee—Southeastern Tribe (Creek [Alabama]) chief of the town of Albayamule and its satellite towns.

Ushesees—Ani' Yun'-wiya (Cherokee) chief of Kituhwa, one of their sacred towns.

Ussu—Mongol Doqus' brother, accompanies Karl on first westward trek. He temporarily commands the Wildcat Ordu.

Wabokieshiek—Hotcangara (Chiwere Sioux) war chief who leads the ill-fated revolt crushed by the Third Hotcangara Campaign.

Wahsakapeequay—Kensistenoug (Cree) wife of Juchi.

Wanbli Sapa—Ocheti shakowin (Dakota Sioux) scout who goes on the reconnoiter of the Hotcangara (Chiwere Sioux). He is the second commander of the Fox Ordu.

Wihio—Dzitsiista (Cheyenne) member of Karl's staff who is made governor of Panuco, the first Huaxteca town to surrender without a fight.

Wurteh—Ani' Yun'-wiya (Cherokee) first wife of Karl's son John. She is related to Mazatl.

Xayacamachan—ruler of Huexotzinco, an historical figure who makes his city the most powerful in the Valley of Puebla. In the book, he dies defending his city.

Xipe Totec—"Flayed One," a spring god of most of the Mexican tribes.

Xolotl—a legendary figure who ruled the entire Valley of Mexico
   in antiquity. Both Quinatzin and Tezozomoc claimed their
   hegemony over the valley because of their decent from him.

Yacateuctli—Toltec merchant god.

Yesui—a Mongol widow, second wife of Henry, stepmother to
   Karl.

Yeyi Calli—Smoking Mirror's daughter.

Yi Mongju—Koryo (Korean) merchant from Songjin on the
   northeast coast of Korea who trades with the Mongols.

Yi Songgye—Koryo (Korean) general, an historical figure who
   deposed the king and took over the government, founding his
   own dynasty.

Yocahu—principle god of the Taino, probably connected with a
   volcano.

Zhu Yuanzhang —(r. 1368–98), founder of the Ming Dynasty,
   reigned under the name Hung-wu.

APPENDIX 2

GLOSSARY
BOOK 1

agouti—(Taino) a rabbitlike animal native to the West Indies.

ahau —(Maya) title of the chief of the "Itza" Maya of Tayasil.

ah canul —(Maya) mercenaries imported from other tribes.

ah kin —(Maya) title of the high priest.

amayxoya —(Caddo) the warrior class of the Caddoan tribes.

arban—(Mongol) military unit of ten.

Atali—(Cherokee) eastern Cherokee dialect.

balam—(Maya) jaguar.

batey—(Taino) the "ball" game as played by the Taino.

cacique—(Taino) major chieftain of the Taino, head of whole areas.
There were five such on Aiti (Hispaniola), and nine on Boriquen
(Puerto Rico).

caddi —(Caddo) the town and village chiefs of the Caddoan
tribes.

canahas —(Caddo) the elders of the Caddoan tribes.

cazabi—(Taino) bread made from the manioc root.

cazonci—(Tarascan) the principle ruler of the Tarascans.

chaya—(Caddo) the "pages" of the Caddoan tribes.

chinampa—(Nahual) "islands" in Lake Texcoco made of contained
dredged lakebed used for cultivation of crops and flowers.

chocolatl—(Nahual) chocolate.

conna—(Caddo) the Caddoan shaman.

coyotl—(Nahual) coyote.

Elati —(Cherokee) western Cherokee dialect.

Ferengi—(Mongol) derived from the word Frank, it was the generic
term for all European people.

halach uinic—(Maya) "true man" the ruler of a Maya town.

hamaca—(Taino) a hammock made of cotton mesh.

Hanjen—(Mongol) northern (Chin or Han) Chinese.

hurakan—(Taino) hurricane.

jagun—(Mongol) military unit of one hundred.

kashim—(Mongol) the name of the elite guard assigned to protect the Khan.

ke'let—(Chukchi) the "evil" spirits responsible for all disease and misfortune. The shaman would struggle with them in the spirit world during trance to force them to leave.

kumis—(Mongol) fermented mare's milk.

Loochi—Zapoteca name for their language.

li—(Chinese) distance measurement about 1/3 mile.

maguey—(Nahual) multipurpose plant native to Mexico.

manidoo—(Algonquin) impersonal supernatural power that can be controlled or manipulated under certain circumstances.

manoomin—(Chippewa) wild rice.

matapi—(Taino) a long tubular basketlike container used to squeeze the juice out of the grated manioc tubers.

mico—(Muskhogean) a village or town chief.

miigis shell—(Chippewa) a sacred cowry shell that led the Chippewa from the "eastern sea" to Madeline Island in Lake Superior.

minghan—(Mongol)—military unit of one thousand.

mondamin—(Chippewa) corn or maize.

mukamur—(Tungus) intoxicating mushroom of eastern Siberia.

Nahual—(Nahual) language of the Aztecs among others in the Valley of Mexico. Was supposedly the language of the Toltecs.

nawak'osis—(Siksika) tobacco.

ocelotl—(Nahual) jaguar.

oli—(Nahual) rubber.

ongons—(Mongol) familial gods or demigods who would look after the family members, the flocks, etc. They were usually felt cutouts.

Ordu—(Mongol) a camp, semifixed. In the book, it is the organizational name for each tumen.

Semujen—(Mongol) non-Chinese Asians.

Sungjen—(Mongol) southern (Sung) Chinese.

tanmas—(Caddo) Kadohadacho announcer (like a town crier).

tobaco (Taino) cigarlike version of tobacco.

travois—(French) a sledlike device used by natives for hauling loads consisting of two poles attached to a harness tied to a dog or horse on one end and dragged on the ground on the other end.

tumbaga (Taino) the name of a copper-gold alloy highly prized by the Taino for its reddish color.

tumen—(Mongol) a military unit of 10,000 soldiers, organized into groups of 10, 100, and 1000. Historically, they were like a small mobile city, in that they were completely self-sufficient. In the book, each tumen is headquartered in a separate Ordu.

Xinesi—(Caddo) Kadohadacho principle chief and high priest.

yacatas—(Tarascan) odd-shaped temple-tombs of the "kings" of the Tarascans.

yam—(Mongol) stations set up along main travel routes about 25 to 30 miles apart where a traveler or messenger could get food, shelter, and a change of horses as needed. There was often a contingent of soldiers to guard each post.

yoca—(Taino) the yucca or manioc plant.

yurt—(Mongol) a large circular tent made of felt over a wicker frame. The upper part was conical with a small round neck projecting as a chimney. It could be set up or taken down in a half an hour.

ziinzibaakwad—(Chippewa) maple sugar.

APPENDIX 3

TRIBAL NAMES

In the book I have tried to use the names the various Aboriginal American tribes actually called themselves. This is not always possible since some of the names have been lost and many of the tribes referred to themselves by the name of their village or current chief. Most of the names we have grown familiar with are corruptions of the (often unflattering) name used for a tribe by a neighboring tribe. I have taken some liberties with some of the names, but the following list should help clear up any confusion. There is no unanimity of opinion as to where these tribes were in the late 14th century, but I have placed them based on the best information I could glean combined with a bit of speculation based partially on legendary native movements and partially on where they were at first contact. The Aboriginal Americans were not a static people, but migrated to a greater or lesser degree for a variety of reasons. It should also be pointed out that there was a massive die-off in the Southeastern U.S. after the incursions of several Spanish expeditions (Pardo, Narvaez, de Leon, and De Soto) because of the diseases they brought with them. This greatly changed the native people of that area making it rather speculative as to what they were really like at the time of the book. As to the Asian tribes, where possible I have used the names they called themselves, but where that was not available I have used the name we now have for them.

A'-a' tam—the Piman tribes of the Uto-Aztecan language family. This would include the Pima and Papago. I have placed them from the lower Salt and middle Gila rivers in Arizona south to the west coast of the Sea of Cortez north of the Yaqui River. They were an agricultural people that originally lived in Pueblos.

Abenaki —generic name used by the Algonquin-speaking tribes to identify those of their people that lived along the New England coast.

Absaroke (Crows)—a Siouan people who split off from the Hidatsa and were at the confluence of the Yellowstone and Missouri rivers at the time of the book.

Akawai —a Cariban-speaking tribe (Acawai) found inland from the Locono from eastern Venezuela to eastern Guyana.

Acuera—a Timacua tribe, which I place in central Florida between the Oklawaha and St. Johns rivers.

Ahitchita—a Muskhogean tribe (Hitchiti) originally living around a town by the same name on the Chattahoochee River in Western Georgia. The remnant of the tribe became part of the Lower Creeks.

Ainu—a Paleo-Asiatic people that are the original inhabitants of the Japanese island of Hokkaido and also Sakhalin Island to the north. At the time of the book, they were still in power on their islands.

Ais—a Timacua tribe, which I place on the east coast of Florida roughly between Melbourne and Fort Pierce.

Alba ayamule—a Creek town near Montgomery, Alabama, whose survivors are sometimes called the Alabama. In the book, the town controls most of southern Alabama.

Alcolhua—An Oto-Manguean people that lived on the eastern side of Lake Texcoco in the Valley of Mexico and had Texcoco as their capitol. At the time of the book, they were still a power. Historically, they were conquered by the Tepanecas and then joined the Mexica in overthrowing the Tepaneca and forming the Triple Alliance that became the Aztecs.

Algonquin—a language group of tribes found along the east coast from North Carolina to Newfoundland and inland to the Rockies in Canada but only in a narrow band along the U.S. coast, including all of Delaware, New Jersey, and New England and Eastern North Carolina, Virginia, Maryland, Pennsylvania, and New York. In general, they were of hunter-gatherer inclination, although the more southern groups all raised crops and tended to be fairly sedentary. Their tribal organization tended to be loose and their society fairly egalitarian.

Alnanbai —an Algonquin-speaking tribe (Abnaki) that lived in the western Maine valleys of the Kennebec, Androscoggin, and Saco rivers.

Alsi—a Yakonan tribe (Alsea) that lived along the Alsea River on the Oregon Coast.

Altamaha—a town in Central Georgia along the lower Ocmulgee River. It was likely the chief Yamasee town.

Amani yukhan—a Siouan people who ultimately became the Virginia Sioux tribes (Manahoac, Monacan, Moneton, Nahyssan, Occaneechi, Saponi, and Tutelo). At the time of the book, I place them in the upper Ohio Valley from near Cincinnati to near Pittsburgh. This would make them neighbors of the Dhegiba Sioux and would place their migration east later than some authorities maintain.

Anishinabe—an Algonquian tribe (Chippewa) who lived around Lake Superior especially on the northwestern and southern shores in Ontario, Minnesota, and Wisconsin.

Ani' Yun'-wiya—an Iroquoian tribe (Cherokee) whom I place in the Southern Blue Ridge and Smoky Mountains and the surrounding Piedmont from the New to the Hiawassee rivers. This is a little north of their position at first contact.

An'kalym—a part of the Paleo-Asiatic people (Chuckchi) that lived on the Chuckchi Peninsula in Northeastern Siberia. This was the group that lived off the sea rather than by herding reindeer.

A'palachi—a Timacua tribe (Appalachee) whom I place on the lower Apalachicola and Ochlockonee rivers.

A'shiwi—a Pueblo people (Zuni) that I place along a narrow band from the Tomochic River in Western Chihuahua to the area around Flagstaff, Arizona.

Atavillo —a tribe on unknown language that lived in the upper Rimac Valley in southern Peru.

Athabaskan—a language group of tribes that at contact was found mostly on the northwest corner of the North American continent (Alaska and Central West Canada), except for the coast. There were also isolated tribes in Montana, Idaho, Washington, Oregon, and California as well as the Southwestern U.S. and Northern Mexico. At the time of the book, only the last group (Northern Mexico) is not in place, but is on its way.

Atirhagenrat—an Iroquoian tribe (Neutrals) that I place on both shores of the eastern end of Lake Erie. This is somewhat east of their location at contact.

Aymara —language group spoken by twelve related tribes that lived on the high plain around Lake Titicaca in southern Peru and northern Bolivia. In the book, it is the name given to all of these tribes.

Ayrate —the Ani' Yun'-wiya (Cherokee) dialect that predominated in the eastern piedmont area of the southern Appalachians from north central Georgia to north central North Carolina. The dialects were quite different, but just mutually intelligible.

Awenro'ron'non—an Iroquoian tribe (Wenrohronon) that I place along the upper Allegheny River in Northwest Pennsylvania. This is well south of their contact location.

Ayawak'a —Quechua name for the tribe living south of the Calua in northern Peru. It is uncertain what they called themselves. The name means "shrine of the corpse."

Ben Zah—an Oto-Manguean tribe (Zapotecs) that lived in most of the Mexican state of Oaxaca. They are an old civilization that had been invaded by the Mixtecs first and later by the Aztecs. At contact they still controlled the southern half of their land.

Beothuk—the now extinct tribe that lived on Newfoundland. They and their language appear unrelated to their neighbors.

Bi' Ixula —a Wakashan tribe (Bellacoola) living around the area of King Island in western British Columbia.

Borum —a tribe (Botocudo) that lived originally inland in the mountains of southeastern Brazil but moved to the coast to raid. They were very warlike attacking all their neighbors and eventually the Portuguese settlers. In the book, they are along the coast south of Rio de Janeiro.

Caddoan—a language family that lived from the Red River in Louisiana to the Kansas River in Kansas including much of

Arkansas, Louisiana, and Oklahoma and parts of Texas and Kansas. They were a sedentary and agricultural people of varying degrees of social stratification and religious complexity. Many of them engaged in human sacrifice.

Calua —small tribe (Calva) of uncertain language that lived in northern Peru around the modern city of Suyo.

Calusa—the tribe of no certain linguistic affinity that lived in the Everglades of South Florida and in the Keys.

Canari —a tribe that lived in southwest Ecuador on the coast and inland from the Gulf of Guayaquil in the area of Cuenca. Their language was not preserved, and their descendants speak Quechua.

Casca-yunga —tribe that lived south of the Chacha on the upper Maranon River near the Chillao.

Catlo'ltx —a Salishian tribe (Comox) living along the eastern coast of Vancouver Island, British Columbia, between the Puntlatch and Kwakiutl.

Cayapo —a large Ge tribe living in the Mato Grosso area of southeastern Brazil in the southern part of the state of Goias, the western part of the state of Minas Gerais, and the northern part of the state of Sao Paolo.

Chacha —a tribe (Chachapoya) living on the middle Maranon River Valley. There were said to have unusually light skin.

Chahiksichahiks—a Caddoan tribe (Pawnee) whom I place in eastern Nebraska and Kansas along the North Loup, middle Platte, Republican, Smoky Hill, and Kansas rivers.

Chalca—a city state in the Valley of Mexico at the southeastern end of the original lake. It was thought to be ruled by descendants of the Toltecs. At the time of the book, it was allied with Huexotzinco and being attacked by the Tepaneca. At contact, it was ruled by the Aztecs.

Chango —the Atacama people that lived in isolated villages along the Chilean coast from the Atacama Desert to perhaps as far as the Maule River. They spoke a dialect that might be related to Kakan.

Charrua —a Chana-speaking people that lived in all of modern

Uruguay as well as parts of bordering Brazil and Argentina. At some point they were split into five sub tribes: the Yaro, the Guenoa, the Bohane, the Minuan, and the Charrua.

Chavchuvat—a part of the Paleo-Asiatic people (Chuckchi) that lived on the Chuckchi Peninsula in Northeastern Siberia. These were the ones that lived by herding reindeer. The Koryaks that herded reindeer also sometimes called themselves by this name.

Cheroenhaka—an Iroquoian tribe (Nottoway). In the book, I use the name for the Nottoway, Menherrin, and Tuscarora tribes, which I place in Central and Southern Virginia, still united as one tribe. This is northwest of their contact positions. Their dialects are similar enough that it is likely they were still united at the time of the book.

Chichimeca—the various Oto-Manguean tribes living north and west of the Valley of Mexico as unorganized bands. They would periodically spill into the valley and mix with or displace those they found. At first this would be the Otomi who are likely the original inhabitants of the valley, but later other similar groups who had been variously civilized. The Aztecs are the most well known such group.

Chikasha—a Muskhogean tribe (Chickasaw) whom I place in North Central Mississippi. This is a small area within their location at contact. At the time of the book, they had fairly recently split off from their original tribe—most probably the Choctaw.

Chillao —tribe that lived south of the Chacha on the upper Maranon River near the Casca-yunga.

Ch'i-tan —a Mongol-speaking people (Khitans) that conquered part of North China and established the Liao Dynasty (916–1125). They refused to be sinicized and treated the Chinese as inferiors. They were overthrown by the Jurchen.

Chiwaro —a linguistically isolated tribe (Jivaro) living in a large area of southeast Ecuador and north central Peru in the jungles of the eastern foothills of the Andes. They are famous in recent times for shrinking heads and killing missionaries. They resisted conquest into modern times except for their westernmost divisions, the Palta and Malacata, who had moved into the mountains.

Chono —the Chilean tribe just south of the Re Che. Their language and culture were nothing like that of the Re Che. They are likely related to the Alacaluf and the other tribes farther south. Their language has been almost completely lost.

Chontal—a people living in North Central Guerrero whose language is hard to classify. At contact they were subject to the Aztecs.

Chumash —a Hokan-speaking tribe living along the coast, the offshore islands, and the mountains from Moro Bay to just north of Santa Monica in Southern California.

Ciboney—an Arawakan people that along with the Guanahatabey had been displaced from most of the Greater Antilles by the Taino. They still existed at contact in the Western tip of Hispaniola and in the cays of Southern Cuba. They were a primitive people who lived off the sea.

Coixca—a Uto-Aztecan people living in Northern Guerrero on both sides of the upper Balsas River. At contact they were subject to the Aztecs.

Colli —tribe living in the lower and middle Chillon River Valley just north of modern Lima, Peru.

Conchuco —Quechua name for the province and perhaps the tribe living on the west bank of the upper Maranon River in central Peru.

Coosa—an ancient Muskhogean town of a people whose remnants   became members of the Upper Creeks. It was situated along the Coosa River in Northern Alabama.

Cuitlatec—a people of uncertain language that lived in Western Guerrero between the Petatlan and Coyuca rivers from the mountains to the shore. At contact they had been conquered by the Aztecs.

Cusabo—a possibly Muskhogean group of tribes that lived on the coast between Charleston, SC and the Savannah River. This group included the Combahee, Edisto, Etiwaw, Kiawaw, St. Helena, Stono, Wapoo, and Westo tribes. In the book, I am intentionally vague about them.

Da-a-gelma'n—a Penutian tribe (Takelma) forming their own language isolate (Takilman). They lived along the middle portion of the Rogue River in Southern Oregon.

Dinne —the name of the Athabaskan tribes that migrated from Canada into the Southwestern U.S. and became known as Apache and Navaho. In the book, they are still scattered between southern Montana and the Four Corners area with a few isolated related groups in Idaho, Oregon, and California.

Dzitsiista—an Algonquian tribe (Cheyenne) whom I place around the Minnesota and Red rivers in western Minnesota and eastern North Dakota.

Eskualdunac—a people of uncertain language classification (Basques) living in north central Spain and southwestern France on both sides of the Pyrenees Mountains. There is ample evidence that they were fishing for cod off the coast of New England long before Columbus.

Etchareottine—an Athabaskan tribe (Slaveys) that live west and south of Great Slave Lake in Canada's Northwest Territories.

Etnemitane—an Athabaskan tribe (Umpqua) that lived along the upper Umpqua River in Southern Oregon. They lived off the river and were not as developed as their neighbors.

Even—a Tungus people that live along the northern shore of the Okhotsk Sea in Eastern Siberia and well inland along the Omolon River. They appear to be a combination of a people very like the Evenks and the original people of the area, the Yukaghir. At the time of the book, this process was well under way, but not yet complete.

Evenks—a Tungus people that live along the western shore of the Sea of Okhotsk and far inland into Siberia.

Genakin —a tribe (Puelche) that lived in the northern Pampas of Argentina from the Rio de la Plata to the Rio Negro and west to the Andean foothills. Historically, as in the book, they fought desperately for their freedom. Their language does not seem related to that of their immediate neighbors except the tribal fragments called the Pampas, Serrano, and Querandi, who do not appear in the book and were all likely originally part of the Genakin.

Great Bay Tribes—a term used in the book for the Algonquian

tribes living around the Chesapeake Bay. This would include the Nanticoke, Conoy, and Powhatan.

Great Sound Tribes—a term used in the book for the Algonquian tribes living along the mainland opposite the Outer Banks of North Carolina. This would include the Pamlico, Weapemeoc, Moratok, Machapunga, Hatteras, and Chowanoc tribes.

Guanahatabey —an Arawakan people living in western Cuba where they were pushed by the Taino. They were quite primitive, living off the sea.

Guarani —a large language family extending from southern Brazil to the Parana Delta. In the book, the name designates the small isolate in the Parana Delta.

Guayana —a Ge-speaking tribe (Caingang) that lived in the area of Sao Paolo in southeastern Brazil.

Hais—a Caddoan-speaking tribe (Eyeish) with a dialect rather distinct from other Caddoan tribes. They lived in the area eastern Texas to northwest Louisiana at the time of the book.

Halkome'lem —a Salishian tribe (Stalo) that lived on the lower Frazier River in southwestern British Columbia. In the book, they are combined as one tribe with the Cowichan who lived on the southeastern coast of Vancouver Island.

Hamakhava—the California Shoshonean name for the Tzinama-a.

Han—the dominant Chinese ethnic group. From an amalgam of the tribes subject to the Han Dynasty in the 3rd and 4th century AD, and not jealous of their separate identity, they have gone on absorbing neighboring people so that they make up about 94 percent of the Chinese population today. Even so, there are some fifty minorities still identifiable in China. The Han state was between the Yangtze and Yellow rivers and spread south to Hainan Island, west to part of modern Sinkiang Province, north into Manchuria and Korea and east to the China Sea.

Hasinai—a Caddoan confederacy of related tribes that centered on the Hainai tribe. They were in the Northeast Texas area, from Dallas to the Red River.

Haush —a tribe living on the southeastern tip of Tierra del Fuego (off the southern tip of Chile). They are related to the Shelknam and likely migrated from Patagonia before them. They speak a dialect of the Tshon family, which is just intelligible to the Shelknam.

Hewaktokto—a Siouan tribe (Hidatsa) which I place on the Missouri River between the Little Missouri and the Knife rivers.

Hobe—a Timacua tribe historically located in the Palm Beach area of the Southeastern Florida Coast.

Hopitu-shinumu—a Uto-Aztecan tribe (Hopi) living in the 14th century along the Colorado and the Little Colorado rivers in north central Arizona.

Hotcangara—a Siouan people that in the book represents the Winnebago and Chiwere Sioux (Oto, Iowa, and Missouri) tribes. Most evidence suggests that the people that occupied the great city now called Cahokia, near East St. Louis, Illinois, were a Siouan tribe. A process of elimination tends to make this group of Sioux the likeliest candidates. The languages of these tribes are mutually comprehensible, so their separation was fairly recent and perhaps incomplete at the time of the book. The name "Hotcangara" means "people of the parent speech" and was used, in contact times, to refer to the Winnebago.

Hsiung-nu —Altaic-speaking nomads from Inner Mongolia that coalesced into a powerful tribe dominating Mongolia and Chinese Turkistan. They raided the northern frontier of the Han Dynasty for centuries, finally conquering and displacing them as the Chao Dynasty (AD 304–52). They ruled over most of North China but were under constant pressure from all sides and fragmented in small states until they were unified under the Chinese Sui Dynasty (AD 581–618).

Huacrachucu —Quechua name for a province and possibly a tribe on the east bank of the upper Maranon River in central Peru.

Huamachucu —Quechua name for the people living just south of the Q'asa-marka, to whom they were related. They too were allied to the Chimu.

Huancavilca —a tribe living on the Santa Elena Peninsula in southwestern Ecuador, around and west of Guayaquil. Their language was lost but thought to be distinct from that of their neighbors.

Huaxteca—a Mayan people (Huastecs) who lived in Northeastern Mexico between the Vinazco and the Soto la Marina rivers encompassing the southern parts of Tamaulipas and Nuevo Leon, Northern Vera Cruz, Hidalgo, and Queretaro and most of San Luis Potosi. In contact times, they had been driven a little east and had lost some cities to the Aztecs.

Huexotzinco—a city-state in the Valley of Puebla, Central Mexico. At the time of the book, it was the ascendant city in the valley, dominating its neighboring cities and intruding itself westward into the Valley of Mexico. By contact times, it belonged to Texcalla.

Iliniwek—an Algonquian tribe (Illinois) which I place at the southern end of Lake Michigan from Grand River in Michigan to the Illinois-Wisconsin border, including much of Northwestern Indiana and Southwestern Michigan.

Inka —the dominant tribe (Inca) of Peru at contact. Its empire stretched from southern Colombia to northwest Argentina and northern Chile at the time of the conquest. In the book, their expansion was just beginning.

Inuit—the Eskimo people that live along the shore of Northern and Western Alaska and Northern Canada.

Inuna-ina—an Algonquian tribe (Arapaho) which I place on the Assiniboin River in southern Manitoba, Canada.

Ipai —a Yuman-speaking people (Digueno) that lived in modern San Diego County, California.

Iroquoian—a language family of tribes ranging from the Saint Lawrence River south through New York, Pennsylvania and along the Blue Ridge Mountains to North Carolina. They were sedentary and agricultural, but often warlike.

Ishak—(Atakapa) a separate linguistic group (sometimes they are considered a Macro-Algonquian language isolate). I place them in a narrow band along the Gulf Coast from Vermilion Bay, Louisiana, to the Brazos River, Texas.

Itza—a Maya people allegedly connected to the Toltecs. They set up a Toltec-like city in Northern Yucatan (Chichen Itza) which was eventually overthrown and its survivors fled south to Lake Tayasil where they still were at the time of contact.

Iyehyeh—name used in the book for the various Siouan tribes that lived in the Carolinas (Catawba, Cheraw, Sugaree, Waxhaw, Congaree, Santee, Winyaw, Etiwaw, Sewee, Waccamaw, Wateree, Cape Fear, Keyauwee, Sissipahaw, Adshusher, Shakori, Pedee, Wocoon, Saponi, and Eno).

Jurchen —a Tungus-speaking tribe (Jurchids) that originated in the forests and mountains of Eastern Manchuria. They went on to become horsemen and soon were threatening both the Ch'i-tans and the Koreans. In 1115, their ruler declared himself emperor of the Chin Dynasty (1115–1234) and began to overrun the Ch-i-tan lands. By 1125, the Ch'i-tans were scattered, and the Jurchids began spreading south and eventually ruled most of the Yellow River Valley. They were, in turn, brushed aside by the Mongols under Chingis and Kubilai (1212–34).

Kadohadacho—a Caddoan tribe, the leading or most distinguished tribe of the Hasinai Confederacy of Caddoan tribes. I place the Kadohadacho along the lower Canadian and Cimarron rivers, and the Arkansas River from the Nebraska border to the Neosho River in eastern Oklahoma.

Ka-i-gwu—a tribe (Kiowa) and linguistic family probably related to Uto-Aztecan that lived at the headwaters of the Missouri River.

Kaina—a division (Bloods) of the Siksika (Blackfoot). At the time of the book, this division was probably just developing.

Kakan —the name of the language of the Diaguita tribe of northern Chile and northwestern Argentina. The tribe apparently expanded into Chile at some point. The language is an isolate, probably related to Argentinean language groups.

Kalapoewah—a Penutian tribe (Kalapooian) that lived in the watershed of the Willamette and Umpqua rivers and in the Willamette Valley above the falls, Oregon. They hunted and dug up roots.

Kanale—a possible Zaparoan-speaking tribe (Canelo) that lived in the jungles of the eastern foothills of the Andes in east central

Ecuador north of the Chiwaro.

Kanastoge—an Iroquoian tribe (Conestoga or Susquehanna) that lived on the Susquehanna River in Pennsylvania and Maryland.

Kaniengehaga—an Iroquoian tribe (Mohawk), the easternmost of that language group that lived along the middle Mohawk River in Central New York. They were one of the Five Nations of historic times.

Kasihta—a town on the banks of the Chattahoochee River a few miles below Kawita, Georgia. The inhabitants later became Lower Creeks.

Kawchodinne—an Athabaskan tribe (Hares) who lived between the Mackenzie River and Great Bear Lake in Canada's Northwest Territories.

Kawesqar—a tribe (Alacaluf) living along the coast and on the islands of southern Chile, south of the Chono. They were much like the Chono in culture and likely spoke a similar language.

Kensistenoug—an Algonquian tribe (Cree) who were found in Canada in a broad band from central Saskatchewan to Hudson Bay, including most of central Manitoba and much of Ontario.

K'eres—a linguistic family of Pueblo Indians (Keresan) living west of the upper Rio Grande in West Central New Mexico around Acoma.

Khitans—a Tungus people that consolidated into a federation of tribes in Eastern Inner Mongolia in AD 905. In 926, their Khan (Yeh-lu A-pao-chi) declared himself emperor and adopted the dynastic name, Liao. By 937, they controlled the Beijing area and continued to rule the northeastern tip of China as the Liao Dynasty until 1125 when the Jurchen overthrew them. Some of them fled west among the Uighurs and formed the state called Kara Khitai, which was later conquered by the Mongols.

Kicho—a Chibchan-speaking tribe (Quijo) living in north central Ecuador. They are likely related to the Chibchan-speaking tribes to their west in the mountains (the Panzaleo), with whom they were friendly and shared many traits.

Kigzh—a Uto-Aztecan-speaking tribe (Gabrielinos) that lived in what is now Los Angeles County, California.

Kitikiti'sh—a Caddoan tribe (Wichita) which I place along the middle Arkansas River, the Neosho River, and Osage River in southeastern Kansas and southwestern Missouri.

Kituhwa—the Ani' Yun'-wiya (Cherokee) dialect spoken along the Tuckasegee River in western North Carolina around the principle city by the same name. This may have been the original language, since Kituhwa was considered by many of the Cherokee to be their first town, but it is uncertain.

Kiwigapawa—an Algonquian tribe (Kickapoo) whom I place in eastern Michigan from Saginaw Bay to Lake Erie and in the tip of Ontario between Lake Huron and Lake Erie.

Koasati—a town probably on Pine Island in the Tennessee River whose remnants became Upper Creeks. In the book, they are among the few future Creeks that join the Mongols.

Kofan—a tribe (Cofan) of uncertain language that lived in south central Colombia and northeast Ecuador in the jungles of the eastern foothills of the Andes just east and northeast of the Kicho.

Kofitachiki—a Muskhogean tribe (Cofitachiqui) whose survivors became part of the Lower Creeks. It was a large chiefdom located along much of the Savannah River to the Wateree River except for the coast.

Kusa—a Penutian tribe (Kusan) that lived along the Coos River and Bay as well as the lower Coquille River in southeastern Oregon. They were sedentary and agricultural.

Kutchakutchin—an Athabaskan tribe (Kutchin) that lived on both banks of the Yukon River between Birch Creek and the Porcupine rivers in Northeastern Alaska.

Kutonaqa—a tribe (Kutenai) and a distinct language family possibly related to Algonquian that lived in the Rockies from Southeastern British Columbia to Northern Idaho and the northwestern tip of Montana.

Kuweveka paiya—a Yuman tribe (Yavapai) that lived in the northwest quadrant of Arizona perhaps as far east as the Rio Verde and the

Salt River, but east and south of the Colorado River.

Kwakiutl—Wakashan tribe (actually an amalgam of small related bands) that lived on both shores of Queen Charlotte Sound and northern Vancouver Island in southwestern British Columbia, Canada.

Kwawia—a Uto-Aztecan-speaking tribe (Cahuilla) that lived in the desert area south of the San Bernardino Mountains and north of the Santa Rosa Mountains in southwestern San Bernardino County California, south of the Takhtam (Serrano).

Kwenetchechat—a Wakashan tribe (Makah) that lived on Cape Flattery in Northwest Washington. They exploited the sea much like their relatives farther north.

Kwenio'gwen—an Iroquois tribe (Cayuga) one of those that became the Five Nations. At the time of the book, they are still not united to the other tribes and were found around Lake Cayuga in West Central New York.

Kwichana—a Hokan tribe (Yuma) that lived along the lower Colorado River around its junction with the Gila River.

Lacandon—a Mayan tribe that lived along the Usumacinta and Pasion rivers in Chiapas Mexico and Guatemala. They have remained rather primitive, unlike their relatives.

Lalacas—a Latuami tribe (Modoc) that lived in northeastern California and south central Oregon.

Lampa—tribe living in the upper Chillon and Chancay valleys in southern Peru near the Ocro, with whom they were usually fighting.

Latacunga—tribe living in north central Ecuador around Quito. Also called the Panzaleo or Kito.

Leni lenape—Algonquian tribe (Delaware) that lived in eastern Pennsylvania, New Jersey, and southeastern New York.

'Lingit—an Athabaskan tribe (Tlingit) located along the Alaskan panhandle from Prince William Sound to Dixon Entrance.

Locono—general name the Arawakan tribes along the north coast of South America from eastern Venezuela to western French Guiana used for themselves.

Lucayo—the Taino bands living on the Bahamas, Turks and Caicos

Islands north of the Greater Antilles.

Lygitann'ytan—the Koryak name for the Chuckchi.

Macuni—a Mashacali-speaking tribe that lived in the mountains in the eastern part of the state of Minas Gerais in southeastern Brazil.

Mahican—an Algonquian tribe that lived in the upper Hudson River Valley extending a little into Massachusetts and Vermont.

Mashacali—a separate linguistic family that lived along the Mucuri River in southeastern Brazil.

Matlatzinca—an Oto-Manguean people that lived in the Valley of Toluca west of the Valley of Mexico. At contact they were subject to the Aztecs.

Maya—a people with a long history of development. They began in the highlands of Guatemala, then gradually moved north into the Yucatan peninsula. They left behind ruins of many great ceremonial centers. They wrote many books in their picture language but only a few survived the conquest. They fought against themselves frequently and were unable to form any sort of empire. They spread north as far as Tamaulipas, Mexico, (the Huastecs) but otherwise dominated the Yucatan peninsula of Mexico along with most of the states of Tabasco and Chiapas and also Belize, Guatemala, and part of Honduras and El Salvador.

Mayapan—a Maya state centered on the city of Mayapan that controlled much of Northern Yucatan at the time of the book. At contact it was just another Maya city.

Mazahuaca—an Oto-Manguean people that lived just north of the Matlatzinca in the Valley of Toluca and the hills north of it. At contact they were subject to the Aztecs.

Menominiwok ininiwok—Algonquian tribe (Menominee) living along both shores of Upper Lake Michigan from Green Bay and the Leelanau Peninsula to just before Mackinaw Island and including most of the habitable islands in that region of the lake.

Meritong—a subdivision of the Coroado tribe, a Puri-Coroado-speaking people that lived inland north and west of Rio de

Janeiro, Brazil. At the time of the book, the Puri and Coroado were still one tribe.

Merkits—a Tungus tribe living near Lake Baikal. They were often at odds with the Mongols but united with them under Chingis and remained an integral part of them.

Mexica—the probably Oto-Manguean people that took up Nahual, a Uto-Aztecan language at some point before contact. At the time of the book, they were subjects of the Tepanecs living on two islands near the western shores of Lake Texcoco, Tenochtitlan, and Tlatelolco. Historically, they joined in a revolt that overthrew the Tepanecs and formed part of the Triple Alliance that became the Aztecs.

Mingue—one of the Algonquian terms for the Northern Iroquois.

Minuan—a subtribe of the Charrua that lived in northeastern Argentina between the Uruguay and Parana rivers.

Mocozo—a Timacuan tribe that I place in an extended area around Lake Kissimmee in South Central Florida.

Mongols—a Tungus people originally from the forests and mountains south of Lake Baikal. They migrated south to the Onon River around AD 900 and there formed a number of tribes most of whom were herdsmen. These continued in obscurity used as pawns by the Chinese, Khitans, and Jurchens until they consolidated under Chingis in 1203. He was named Khan in 1206 and began to form one of the largest empires in history. His grandson Kubilai conquered the rest of China and founded the Yuan Dynasty (1264–1368). The Mongols were eventually driven back to Mongolia by a popular Chinese revolt that led to the Ming Dynasty (1368–644).

Moyopampa—Quechua name for the tribe living in a low extension of the Andes northeast of the Chacha. The name means "round valley."

Muskhogean—a language family (sometimes classified as Macro-Algonquian) found mostly in the Southeastern U.S. from the Mississippi River to the Georgia Coast, from Southern Tennessee and South Carolina to the Gulf, and including most of Florida.

They tended to be a sedentary people living in towns and villages and cultivating extensively.

Nahani—Athabaskan tribe that lived in the Rockies from northern British Columbia to the Yukon Territory, Canada.

Na-I-shan-dina—an Athabaskan-speaking tribe (Kiowa Apache) that attatched itself to the Kiowa. I place them along the Yellowstone River in south central Montana and the upper Belle Fourche River in western South Dakota.

Nanai—a Tungus people of apparently mixed background living on the middle Amur River in northeast China and southeast Siberia.

Narragansett—Algonquin-speaking tribe that lived in Rhode Island from Providence River to Pawcatuck River. In historic times, they first grew large with refugees from other tribes, then were destroyed during King Philip's War.

Natchez—a Muskhogean tribe that lived along the east bank of the Mississippi River in the area of Natchez, Mississippi.

Nausets—an Algonquin speaking people living on Cape Cod, Massachusetts, east of Bass River. They were either part of or subject to the Wampanoag. In historic times, they were peaceful and helped the Pilgrim Colony.

Ne-e-noilno—an Algonquin-speaking people (Montagnais) that were found in southeastern Quebec, Canada, north of the St. Lawrence River and east of St. Maurice River. In the book, they would be one of the Northeastern Bands.

Newe—a Uto-Aztecan-speaking people (southern Shoshone) who were around and to the south of the Great Salt Lake in Utah at the time of the book.

Niantic—an Algonquin-speaking tribe occupying the coast of eastern Connecticut and western Rhode Island from Narragansett Bay to the Connecticut River. In historic times, they were divided into two by the Pequot tribe. They were generally allied with the Narragansett tribe.

Nicarao—a Nahual-speaking people that migrated in the 11th century to the area between Lake Nicaragua and the Pacific Ocean.

Nimipu—a Sahaptian tribe (Nez Perce) who lived along the Salmon, lower Snake and upper Columbia rivers in Idaho, Washington, and Oregon. In the book, I include most of the Sahaptian tribes under this name.

Nivkh—a Paleo-Asiatic people living on the lower Amur River in Southeastern Siberia.

Nomo—a Uto-Aztecan-speaking people (northern Shoshone) which I place in southern Idaho, especially along the Snake River and from northern Utah to northwestern Wyoming. This would be the northern end of their location at contact.

Nonoalco—a possibly mythical people of great artistic talent whom the legends credit for building all the great cities in the Valley of Anahuac and the surrounding areas.

Northeastern Bands—the name used in the book for the Algonquin tribes living largely as scattered bands in New England and Eastern Canada. This would include the Nipissing, Temiscaming, Abittibi, Algonkin, Nascapee, Montagnais, Mistassin, Bersiamite, Papinachois, Micmac, Malecite, Passamaquoddy, Arosaguntacook, Sokoki, Penobscot, Norridgewock, Pennacook, Massachuset, Wampanoag, Narraganset, Nipmuc, Montauk, and Wapinger.

Nukfila—the "Creek" name for either the Utina or all the Timacua-speaking tribes.

Numakiki—a Siouan tribe (Mandan) that lived along the middle Missouri River, from the Knife to the Cheyenne rivers in central North and South Dakota. An isolated group lived near the confluence of the Belle Fourche and Cheyenne rivers in south western South Dakota.

Numu—a Uto-Aztecan-speaking tribe (Northern Paiute—Mono) living in the mountains of central eastern California and western Nevada.

Nuwu—a Uto-Aztecan-speaking tribe (Southern Paiute—Chemehuevi) that lived in the deserts and mountains of central and eastern San Bernardino County, California. At some point after the time of the book, they moved east to the Colorado River displacing the Yuman-speaking people there.

Nymil"u—a Paleo-Asiatic people (Koryaks) living north of and on the northern neck of the Kamchatka Peninsula in Eastern Siberia.

Ocale—a Timacua tribe that lived in Central Florida between the Withlacoochee and Oklawaha rivers.

Ocheti shakowin—a Siouan tribal group (Dakota), which went on to separate into Santee, Yankton, and Teton Sioux. In the book, they are still united and live a sedentary life in a large part of Minnesota from the Mississippi River to the Duluth area.

Ocro—tribe living in the upper Chillon and Chancay valleys in southern Peru near the Lampa with whom they often fought.

Ojibwa—the Cree name for the Anishinabe (Chippewa).

Okimulgis—an old Muskhogean town (Okmulgee) located on the east bank of the Okmulgee River south of Macon. Its people were probably Hitchiti.

Olmeca—a largely Zoquean-speaking people that were a mixture of the various tribes in the area. They were not the same Olmecs who flourished in the area long before. They were called Olmeca because "oli," or rubber, could be found in the area and gave their name to the earlier civilization.

Oneniute'ron'non—an Iroquoian tribe (Seneca) that lived between Seneca Lake and the Geneva River in West New York. Historically, they were one of the Five Nations.

Ononta'ge—an Iroquoian tribe (Onondaga) that lived along Onondaga Creek and Lake and north to Lake Ontario. They were one of the Five Nations.

Otomi—an Oto-Manguean people that lived in and north and east of the Valley of Mexico. They were probably the original inhabitants of the valley. At the time of the book, they dominated the northern shore of Lake Texcoco as well as most of the states of Hidalgo and Queretaro, along with parts of Tlaxcalla, Puebla, and Vera Cruz. At contact they were mostly under the Aztecs.

Ottare—Ani' Yun'-wiya (Cherokee) dialect spoken by those living in the Smoky Mountains (southern Appalachian) from northwest Georgia to southwest Virginia, except for the area of the Tuckasegee River in North Carolina. It was different but just mutually intelligible to the others.

Ozita—a Timacua tribe that lived along the southern shore of Tampa Bay in Western Florida.

Pache—a Chibchan-speaking tribe (also Panche) that lived along the upper reaches of the Magdalena River in south central Colombia.

Palta—a division of the Chiwaro that moved into the mountains from the jungles to the east. They lived in southern Ecuador around Loja southward into northeast Peru near Jaen.

Panai'ti—a Shoshonean people (Bannock) that lived in the eastern parts of Shoshonean lands. It is not clear if they were separate at the time of the book, and I make their distinctness vague.

Pansfalaya—a Muskhogean tribe (Choctaw) that held sway over all but the northern tip and the northwest edge and the coast of Mississippi.

Pantch—a possibly Muskhogean tribe (Chitimacha) that was located along the Mississippi Delta in Southern Louisiana.

Pashohan—the Caddoan name for the "Hotcangara" Sioux.

Patasho—a possibly language isolate, they were found inland from the coast of Brazil around the 17° S parallel.

Paya—a possibly Chibchan-speaking tribe that lived along the northeast coast of Honduras.

Pensacola—a Timacuan tribe that lived along the lower Escambia and Yellow rivers and around Pensacola Bay.

Pesmokanti—Algonquin-speaking tribe (Passamaquoddy) part of the Abenaki Confederacy. They were found along the St. Croix River between Maine and New Brunswick. In the book, they are one of the Northeastern Bands.

Piegan—a division of the Siksika (Blackfoot). At the time of the book, this division was probably just beginning.

Pinco—a tribe living at the headwaters of the Maranon River in south central Peru.

Pioje—a Tucanoan-speaking tribe, the eastern division of the Encabellado tribe living in north central Ecuador in the jungles of the eastern foothills of the Andes.

Potano—a Timacua tribe that lived in northern Florida from the

Santa Fe River to Orange Lake and west to the Suwannee River (the Gainesville area).

Potawatamink—an Algonquian tribe (Potawatomi) that I place from Sault Ste. Marie and Manitoulin Island in Lake Huron to the headwaters of the Mattagami River.

Purepecha—a people (Tarascans) whose language forms an isolate. They lived in most of the state of Michoacan, Mexico, and were still an independent entity at contact. At the time of the book, they were just becoming an "empire" and only dominated a small area around Lake Patzcuaro. It is unclear where they came from.

Puruha—the tribe occupying central Ecuador around Riobamba and Guano.

Putun Maya—a group of Maya that lived along the coast just east of the Yucatan peninsula in the Mexican states of Tabasco, Campeche, and Chiapas. They were formidable traders ranging all along the Atlantic coasts of Mexico and Central America and probably to many of the westernmost Caribbean islands (Cuba, the Caymans, and Jamaica).

Q'asa-marka—the Quechua name for a powerful state (Caxamarca) allied to the Chimu Empire. They lived around the city of Cajamarca in northern Peru. It is not known what their original name was. The name means "town in a ravine."

Qin—a Chinese-speaking northwestern Chinese tribe and state (Chin) that overthrew and replaced the Zhou Dynasty in 221 BC. It greatly expanded and consolidated China, but only lasted until the death of the first emperor in 210 BC, after which civil wars broke out again. The Western name for the Middle Kingdom (China) comes from the name of this state.

Ralamari—a Uto-Aztecan tribe (Tarahumare) that lived in the mountains of north central Mexico in most of the states of Zacatecas and Coahuilla and in parts of Jalisco, Guanajuato, and San Luis Potosi. They were still independent at contact.

Re Che—the tribe that lived in middle Chile. They used to be called Araucan but more recently are called Mapuche, the name of one of their divisions. The other divisions are Picunche, Wiyiche, and Chilote. Long after contact, a group crossed the Andes into Argentina. In the book, they are all still west of the Andes between the Limari River and Chiloe Island. Their language is an apparent isolate.

Saktchi Huma—a Muskhogean tribe (Chakchiuma) that was closely related to the Choctaw and Chickasaw. In the book, they are a small tribe in Northwestern Mississippi, near the Yazoo River.

Salishian—a language family of tribes found in the Northwest. It includes the Flatheads, Spokan, Kalispel, Cour d' Alene, Pisquow, Sinkiuse, Methow, Okinagan, Shuswap, Ntlakyapamuk, Lillooet, Bellacoola, Comox, Cowichan, Squamish, Songish, Nisqualli, Twana, Chehalis, and Tillamook.

Salst—a Salishian tribe (Flathead) that lived in northeastern Washington, Northern Idaho, and just into Montana. In the book, all the Salishian tribes are called Salst.

Saturiwa—a Timacuan tribe that lived along the lower St. Johns River in Northeastern Florida.

Sekani—Athabaskan tribe living along the Rockies from west central Alberta to east and central British Columbia, Canada.

Shagero—an Algonquian tribe (Yurok) that lived along the mouth of the Klamath River in Northern California.

Shahi'yena—Sioux name for the Dzitsiistas (Cheyenne).

Shang—a Chinese-speaking north China dynasty (and possibly the name of their tribe) that ruled over part of northern China (most of the Yellow River Valley) from 1500 BC to 1122 BC. It was overthrown by the Zhou Dynasty.

Shastika—a Hokan tribe (Shasta) living in Northern California.

Shawunogi—an Algonquian tribe (Shawnee) that I place in Central Indiana. This is west of their contact location (Central Ohio).

Shelknam—a tribe living on most of Tierra del Fuego (southern tip of Chile). Their language belongs to the Tshon family, and they most likely migrated from Patagonia in two waves at some point after their relatives the Haush. The northern and southern Shelknam have different dialects and culture and were often at odds. They and the Haush were called Ona by the Yamana and some books refer to them by that name.

Siksika—an Algonquian tribe (Blackfoot) whom I place roaming the prairies of Southern Alberta and Saskatchewan along the Saskatchewan River. At the time of the book, the Bloods and Piegans were still united with the Blackfoot.

Siouan Tribes—an agricultural people of decreasing sophistication from south to north. They were at the time of the book in a broad band from Minnesota to Missouri, into the Central Plains along the Missouri River, and east along the Ohio River as far as the Pennsylvania border. They also had an isolated group in much of the Carolinas. At the time of contact, the northern groups had moved into the plains (Dakota and Chiwere) or up the Missouri (Dhegiba) or down the Mississippi (Quapaw and Biloxi), and the Virginia Sioux were in place in much of Central Virginia.

Southeastern Cities—a term used in the book to refer to the cities of the Muskhogean people that refuse to join the Mongols. After contact, the remnants of these people who were greatly reduced by plagues became the Creeks.

Surreche—a Timacuan tribe that lived between Cape Canaveral and the upper St. Johns River on the central east coast of Florida.

Taino—an Arawakan people that lived mostly in the Greater Antilles (Cuba, Hispaniola, Puerto Rico, and Jamaica), but also in the Western Lesser Antilles. They migrated up from Venezuela and gradually displaced the Ciboney, an earlier migratory group from the same area. They, in turn, were displaced from the Southern Lesser Antilles by the Caribs, yet another group from the same place. They were very agricultural and traded extensively.

Takhtam—a Uto-Aztecan-speaking people (Serrano) living in the southwestern part of San Bernardino County, California.

Tamien—a Penutian-speaking people who belonged to subgroup called Costanoan and lived in modern Santa Clara County, California.

Tamoyo—a Tupian-speaking tribe that lived in the area around modern Rio de Janeiro, Brazil. Like all Tupian tribes, they migrated from the interior displacing the original tribe, the Tapuya.

Tanish—a Caddoan tribe (Arikira) which at the time of the book was divided into two groups along the mid Missouri River. One was near the White River in central South Dakota and the other was between the Niobrara and the Big Nemaha rivers in eastern Nebraska.

Tarama—Quechua name for a tribe living along the Montoro River south of Lake Junin in central Peru. At the time of the book, they were subject to the Inka.

Tatars—a Tungus tribe that split off from the Mongols at the Onon River. They were heavily embroiled as mercenaries and ill-used the Mongols frequently. Once the latter got the upper hand under Chingis, the Tatars ceased to exist as a separate tribe. Chingis killed all their men and incorporated the women and children into the Mongols.

Tatsanottine—an Athabaskan tribe (Yellowknives) that lived northeast of Great Slave Lake in Canada's Northwest Territories.

Taunika—a Muskhogean tribe (Tunica) that lived along the West Bank of the Mississippi River from the Red River to the Arkansas River and on the East Bank over to the Yazoo River.

Tekesta—a Timacua tribe that lived in the Miami area of Southeastern Florida.

Tepaneca—an Oto-Manguean-speaking people that lived on the western shore of Lake Texcoco. At the time of the book, they were beginning to dominate the valley. Historically, they conquered most of it before falling to the Triple Alliance that became the Aztecs. They were still under the Aztecs at contact.

Tepuztec—a people in the northern part the Mexican state of Guerrero between the Balsas River and the mountains to the south. Historically, they were conquered by the Aztecs and remained under them at contact.

Texcalla—an Oto-Manguean-speaking city-state (Tlaxcalla) in the Puebla Valley that at the time of the book was dominated by Huexotzinco. Historically, they came to dominate the Puebla Valley and remained independent of the Aztecs. At contact they first fought, then joined Cortez.

T'han-u-ge—a group of Pueblo tribes (Tano) that form their own language group with the Tewa, Jemez, Tigua, and Piro tribes (Tanoan). I place them on the upper Rio Grande around Santa Fe, New Mexico.

Thilanottine—an Athabaskan tribe (Chipewya) that lived in Northern Manitoba and Saskatchewan and Southeastern Northwest Territories of Canada.

Tiionen'iote'—an Iroquoian tribe (Oneida) that lived in the area south of Lake Oneida in Central New York. They were one of the Five Nations.

Timacua—a language family whose members lived in most of Florida. Some authorities refer to the Utina tribe as the Timacua proper while still using the name for all the Florida tribes. They were all agriculturally active, often planting two crops a year. The individual tribal names used in the book are at best suspect. There is very little reliable information on their language or what the various city-states called themselves.

Tinneh—an Athabaskan family consisting of the Hares, Yellowknives, Beavers, Slaveys, Dogribs, and Chipewya tribes of Northwestern Canada.

Titskan Wa'titch—a difficult-to-classify group (Tonkawa) that forms its own language group (sometimes they are considered Macro-Algonquian). They occupied much of central Texas and lived a mean hunter-gatherer life.

Ti'wan—a group of Pueblo tribes (Tigua) of the Tanoan language group. I place them along the Upper Rio Grande from Taos to Socorro.

Tlalhuica—a Uto-Aztecan people that lived south of the Valley of Mexico, in the states of Morelos and Mexico. At contact they were under the Aztecs.

Tlapaneca—a Hokan people that lived in Eastern Guerrero, western Oaxaca and Southern Puebla in southern Mexico. At contact they were under control of the Aztecs.

Tocobaga—a Timacua tribe that lived along the Gulf Coast of Florida between Tampa Bay and the Withlacoochee River.

T'o-pa—a Turkic speaking people from Mongolia that conquered part of North China forming the Northern Wei Dynasty (AD

386–534). They adopted Buddhism and became Sinicized and absorbed by the Sui Dynasty.

Totonaca—a Penutian-speaking people (Totonacs) that lived on Mexico's Gulf Coast between the Cazones and Papaloapan rivers in the states of Vera Cruz and Puebla. At contact they were tributaries of the Aztecs. Cortez landed in their territory.

Tremembe—a tribe living on the northeastern Brazilian coast from the Tury River to the Baia de Marajo. Their language is unknown, but it was not Tupi-Guarani.

Tsalagi—the Muskhogean (Creek) name for the Ani' Yun'-wiya (Cherokee).

Tsattine—an Athabaskan tribe (Beavers) found in northern and central Alberta, Canada. The Sarci were a splinter group in southern Alberta, north and east of the Siksika (Blackfoot).

Tsimshian—a Salishian tribe living along the lower Skeena River and the adjoining coastal area in western British Columbia, Canada.

Tsinuk—a Penutian people (Chinooks) that lived on the lower Columbia River along the Washington and Oregon border.

Tsoyaha—the name used in the book for the Yuchi, a difficult-to-classify tribe (usually considered Macro-Siouan) that I place in Central Tennessee along and between the Cumberland and Tennessee rivers, a little west of where they were found at first contact.

Tungus—the Altaic-speaking people of eastern subarctic Siberia. The term is sometimes used for all the Altaic people living in bands in Siberia.

Tupinamba—a Tupi-Guarani-speaking tribe that lived along the coast of Brazil from the Amazon River to Sao Paolo with some interruptions from other tribes. They had migrated from the interior in waves displacing first the original inhabitants and then each other.

Twanhtwanh—an Algonquian tribe (Miami) that I place in the northwest quarter of Ohio at the time of the book. This is east of their contact position.

Tya Nuu—a Mixe-Zoquean people (Mixtecs) that lived in the

mountainous areas of Southern Puebla and Northern Oaxaca. They are an old civilization that may be the descendants of the builders of Teotihuacán. They began conquering the Zapotecan lands only to be attacked themselves by the Aztecs and largely absorbed except for the state of Teotitlan, which was considered an ally. That was the situation at contact.

Tzinama-a—a Yuman-speaking tribe (Mohave) living along both sides of the lower Colorado River between Needles and Black Canyon, on the border of Arizona and California.

Ukwunu—a Muskhogean tribe (Oconee) that lived along the Oconee River in East Central Georgia. They were probably related to the Hitchiti and followed them to become the Lower Creeks.

Urriparacushi—a Timacuan tribe that lived in Central Florida in the area between Winter Garden and the Withlacoochee River.

Ute—a Uto-Aztecan tribe that I place roaming the Great Basin including Southeast Oregon, Nevada, most of Utah, and part of Wyoming, Colorado, Arizona, and California. They were hunter-gatherers who eked out a precarious existence in a hostile environment. At contact they had split into the Paiutes and Utes and shared much of their area with the Shoshone.

Utina—a Timacuan tribe that lived in North Central Florida between the St. Johns and upper Santa Fe rivers.

Wacata—a Timacuan tribe that lived along the Southeast Coast of Florida in the Fort Pierce area.

Wahili—a Muskhogean people (Guale) whose remnants probably became part of the Lower Creeks. They lived at the mouth of the Altamaha River in Georgia.

Wako—14th and 15th century Japanese pirates that plundered merchant shipping in the East China Sea, Yellow Sea, and Sea of Japan. They would also attack port cities and sack them. The disorganized Japanese authorities winked at their privations, while the Chinese and Koreans struggled to suppress them with varying success. Once trade became important enough to the Japanese, they were stopped.

Wampo—Quechua name for the tribe (Huambo) that lived south

of the Wanka-pampa in northern Peru. It is uncertain if this is the name of the tribe since the word means "boat." The Inka province was also called Cutervos, which might be the actual name of the tribe or perhaps there were two tribes in the province. In the book, I call the people in this area Wampo.

Wanka—Quechua name for the tribe (Huanca) that lived between the cities of Huancayo and Jauja in southern Peru. The name means "field guardian." At the time of the book, they were already subject to the Inka.

Wanka-pampa—Quechua name for the tribe (Huncapampa) occupying the area around the modern city of Huancabamba in northern Peru. It is not known what they called themselves. The name means "valley of the field guardian."

Wappinger—an Algonquian-speaking tribe related to the Mahicans and the Delaware and living in southeastern New York (around Poughkeepsie) and western Connecticut. In historic times, they formed a confederacy with related tribes from the east bank of the Hudson River (from Poughkeepsie to Manhattan) to the Connecticut River.

Waylya—Quechua name for a tribe (Huayla) that lived along the Huaylas River in west central Peru. The name means "meadow."

Wazhazhe—a Siouan people that eventually became the Dhegiba Sioux (Ponca, Omaha, Osage, Kansa, and Quapaw). In the book, they are found still united in the middle Ohio Valley from the Wabash to a little beyond Cincinnati. The traditions of these tribes put them in this general area at the time of the book.

Welel—a Hokan-speaking tribe (Esselen) living in the rough coastal country south of Monterrey Bay, California.

Wendat—an Iroquois tribe (Huron) living along the St. Lawrence River from Lake Erie to Montreal.

Xa'ida—a Skittagetan-speaking tribe (possibly Athabaskan) (Haida) living on the Queen Charlotte Islands off the coast of British Columbia.

Yamana—a tribe (also called Yahgan) living on the islands along the southern coast of Tierra del Fuego (southernmost Chile). Their language is an isolate. It appears they may have either displaced or replaced the Alacaluf in their territory.

Yamasi—a Muskhogean tribe (Yamasee) living along Coastal Georgia at the time of the book. Historically, they disappeared into the Seminoles after much warfare.

Yanktonai—a Siouan tribe (Yankton), a division of the Lakota. In the book, the term is used for the Assiniboin that are thought to have broken off from the Yankton and moved to southeastern Manitoba, where they emulated the Cree.

Yatasi—Caddoan tribe found in northwest Arkansas, southwest Missouri and eastern Oklahoma at the time of the book.

Ychma—a tribe living along the lower and middle portions of the Rimac and Lurin valleys in southwestern Peru around and south of Lima.

Yenresh—an Iroquois tribe (Erie) whom I place in a thin band along the southern shore of Lake Erie from the middle of Ohio to the New York border. This is a little west of their contact location.

Yokut—a Penutian-speaking people living all along the San Joachin Valley of Southern California.

Yope—a people that lived along the Papagallo River and its tributaries in Southern Guerrero, Mexico, and spoke a difficult language to classify. At contact they were still independent, although almost surrounded by the Aztecs.

Yuit—the name the Inuit (Eskimos) of Siberia call themselves.

Yukaghur—a Paleo-Asiatic people that lived in the area north of the Sea of Okhost. They were generally absorbed by the Evens, a Tungus people that moved into their area from the west.

Yupigyt—the name the Chuckchi called the Eskimos.

Yustaga—a Timacua tribe living between the Aucilla and the Suwannee rivers on the Gulf Coast of Florida.

Zhou—a Chinese-speaking northwestern Chinese tribe and dynasty (Chou) that overthrew the Shang Dynasty in 1122 and greatly expanded their territory over all of North China and even into the Yangtze River Valley in the south. Around 500 BC, their authority began to wane, and it was finally overthrown by another northwestern state, the Qin.

APPENDIX 4

GEOGRAPHICAL NAMES

It was only logical that the Mongols would not name geographical features the same as generations of European explorers. Like the latter, some of their names would reflect their ancestral homeland and heroes. Also like the latter, some of the names would be those used by the local inhabitants, or the name of a nearby tribe or village. Where possible, the local names were used. Below are the names used in the book coupled with the names found on modern maps.

Absaroke River—Yellowstone River, NW Wyoming to NW North Dakota.

Ahatam River—Gila River, SW New Mexico to SW Arizona.

Aiti—Hispaniola Island, West Indies (Haiti and Dominican Republic).

Albayamule River—Tallapoosa and Alabama rivers, EC to SW Alabama.

Alnanbai River—Kennebec River, WC to SE Maine.

Alsi River—Alsea River, W Oregon.

Amgun River—Amgun River, SE Siberia.

Amona Island—Mona Island, between Puerto Rico and Hispaniola.

Anahuac—"the One World" the Nahual term for the Valley of Mexico.

Andahualya —also called Chanca, Inka province west of Cuzco in SC Peru.

Andahuaylas —capital of Andahualya province. It is still so named and is in SC Peru.

Angara —Inka province south of Wanka on lower Montero River in SC Peru.

Apurimac River—major river in C Peru.

Aralbalikh —port near site of Port au Prince, Haiti.

Ashiwi River—Salt River, SC Arizona.

Atacames —principle city of the tribe now called Esmeraldas just east of the town of Esmeraldas in NW Ecuador.

Bayern —the German word for Bavaria a state in S Germany.

Bear River—James River, E North Dakota to E South Dakota.

Beaver River—Silver Creek, W Montana.

Bio Bio River —large river in C Chile.

Bira River —Bira River, SE Siberia.

Boriquen—Puerto Rico, West Indies.

Black Hill River—Cheyenne River, W South Dakota.

Bright Burning River—Blackfoot River, W Montana.

Caiyukla River—Siuslaw River, W Oregon.

Capawake —Wampanoag name for Martha's Vineyard, SE Massachusetts.

Cara —Trinidad, West Indies. The name means "Land of Hummingbirds."

Cathay —Medieval European name for China.

Cautin River —river in S. Chile, flows into the Imperial River.

Cayambe —town NE of Quito, Ecuador. It was the principle town of the Cara tribe.

Champa —ancient kingdom in southern Viet Nam.

Chan Chan—capital of the Chimu Empire, near Trujillo, NW Peru.

Chesapeake—Great Bay Tribe (Powhatan) town in south Norfolk, Virginia.

Chicama River—NW Peru.

Chingis River—Delaware River, E Pennsylvania.

Choapa River—C Chile.

Chosin—name of Korea under the Yi Dynasty (1392–1910).

Chot —(or Chotuna) Chimu city near modern Chiclayo, NW Peru.

Chuncumayo—Almodena River —larger river south of Inka Cuzco into which the Huatanay and Tullumayo rivers flow. It is a tributary of the Urubamba River.

Churning White Water River—Clearwater River, N Idaho.

Cincay Qoca —Inka province just south of Huanuco around Lake

Junin in C Peru.

Cincay Qoca Lake—Lake Junin in C Peru. The name means "Lynx Lake."

Cipango —Medieval European name for Japan.

Coal River—Powder River, NE Wyoming to SE Montana.

Coaxomulco —Coajomulco—town on road from Mexico City and Cuernavaca, Mexico.

Column Tower River—Belle Fourche River, NE Wyoming.

Coosa River—Coosa River, NW Georgia to C Alabama.

Cozumel—large island off the NE coast of the Yucatan Peninsula in SE Mexico.

Cuauhnahuac—Cuernavaca, Morelos, Mexico.

Cuautla —town about 25 miles ESE of Cuernavaca, Mexico.

Cuba—Cuba, West Indies.

Cusabo River—Chattooga, Tugalu and Savannah rivers, Georgia – So. Carolina Border.

Cuttatawomen River —Rappahannock River, N Virginia. Cuzco— the Inka capital, still so named in S Peru.

Da-a-gelma'n River—Rogue River, SW Oregon.

Dark Boiling Creek—Donaker Creek, W Montana.

Deep Cut River —Hay River, NW Alberta, Canada.

Dehcho River—Mackenzie River, W Northwest Territories, Canada.

Donostia —Basque name for San Sebastian in NC Spain.

Dsidsila'letc —Salst (Duwamish—Salishian) village on site of modern Seattle, WA.

Duwamish River—flows through Seattle, WA.

Dzilam —Dzilam Gonzalez—small town near NC coast of the Yucatan Peninsula in SE Mexico.

East Chesapeake River —East Branch Elizabeth River, SE Virginia.

East Tsoyaha River—Cumberland River, SE Kentucky, N Tennessee to NW Kentucky.

East Union River—Black Warrior River, W. Alabama.

Estatoe—Ani' Yun'-wiya (Cherokee) town below junction of Chattooga and Tallulah rivers in NW South Carolina.

Etiwaw River—Wando River, SE South Carolina.

Etnemitane River—Umpqua River, SW Oregon.

Feather River—Rosebud Creek, S Montana.

Fujian Province—province in SE China across the Taiwan Straight from Taiwan.

Fuzhou—port near Charleston, South Carolina.

Gaztela—Basque name for the province of Castile, C Spain.

Georgbalikh—port on site of Lima, Peru.

Gichigami Lake—Lake Superior.

Gipuzkoa—Basque name for the province of Guipuzcoa, NC Spain.

Great Bay—Chesapeake Bay, Virginia and Maryland.

Great Falls River—Sun River, W Montana.

Great Open Place Among the Mountains River—Big Hole R., W Mont.

Great Sea—the Asiatic term for the Pacific Ocean.

Great Sound—Currituck, Albemarle and Pamlico Sounds, No. Carolina.

Guanahani—Lucayo name for "San Salvador" Columbus' first landfall.

Guaura River—Huaura River, WC Peru.

Haton Xauxa—capital of the Inka province of Wanka, modern Jauja in SC Peru.

Hehlashishe River—Wabash River, W Indiana.

Henribalikh—port on site of Valparaiso, Chile.

Hewaktokto River—Little Missouri River, SW North Dakota.

Higuey—province in SE Aiti (SE Dominican Republic).

Hokomawanank River—Roanoke River, S Virginia to NE North Carolina.

Hopitu River—Colorado River, Colorado to Baja California, Mexico.

Hormuz—Arab city on the north shore of the Straight of Hormuz SW Iran.

Horn River—Tongue River, NC Wyoming to SE Montana.

Huanuco—northernmost Inka province at the time of the book, 1460. It was centered around the city of the same name in C

Peru.

Huatanay—western of two rivers that framed Inka Cuzco.

Huaxteca River—Tamesi River, Tamaulipas, Mexico.

Huaxtepec—(Oaxtepec) town 21 miles E of Cuernavaca, Mexico.

Huaylas River—the Santa River in WC Peru.

Huichahue River—S Chile, flows into the Tolten River.

Ignacebalikh—port on site of Puerto Montt, S. Chile.

Imaklik—Big Diomede Island, Bering Strait.

Inaklik—Little Diomede Island, Bering Strait.

Inuit Bay—Hudson Bay, NC Canada.

Inuna-ina River—Assiniboin River, S Manitoba, Canada.

Ipai Bay—San Diego Bay, SW California.

Isadowa River—Canadian River, NE New Mexico, NW Texas to C Oklahoma.

Ishak River—Sabine River, NE Texas to SW Louisiana.

Itsati—a Cherokee town (Echota) located on the south side of the Little Tennessee River below Citico Creek in Tennessee (Monroe Co.). Several other Cherokee towns shared the name but this one was the first and most important in the time frame of the book.

Itsati River—Little Tennessee River, SW North Carolina to E Tennessee.

Kaachxana-aakw—Tlingit village—modern Wrangel, AK.

Kadohadacho River—Arkansas River, SE Colorado to SE Arkansas.

Kaidubalikh—port on site of Rio de Janeiro, Brazil.

Kalinta River—Salinas River, WC California.

Kalinta-ruk—village near mouth of the Salinas River, WC California.

Karakorum—the old Mongol capitol, in NC Mongolia.

Karamuren River—the Mongol name for the Amur River, SE Siberia.

Kasihta River—Chattahoochee and Apalachicola rivers, W Georgia to NW Florida.

Kayung—Haida village on Graham Island, BC, Canada.

Kensistenoug River—Sheyenne River, E North Dakota.

Keowee—Ani' Yun'-wiya (Cherokee) town near Port George, South Carolina.

Keowee River—Keowee and Seneca rivers, NW South Carolina.

Keres River—San Jose River, WC New Mexico.

Khanate River—Athabasca River, WC to NE Alberta, Canada.

Khanbalikh—the Mongol name for Tatu (later Beijing), the Yuan Dynasty Capital of China. In the book it is also the name of the capital of the Khakhanate of the Blue Sky, in the area of Sioux City, Iowa.

Khartsgaibalikh—(Hawk City)—town that evolved from the old Hawk Ordu, near Riverdale, ND.

Khereekhot—(Mongol for Crow Town) Baie St. Paul, Quebec, Canada.

Khilbalikh—(Mongol for Boundary City) settlement on site of modern Brownsville, TX.

Khon Kheree—(Mongol for Raven) port on site of San Francisco, California.

Kimooenim River—Snake River, NW Wyoming to SE Washington.

Kitikitish River—Neosho River, E Kansas to NE Oklahoma.

Kituhwa—the principal city of the Cherokee. It was on the Tuckasegee River near Bryson City, North Carolina. Although the individual Cherokee towns were independent, this one held a sort of primacy of dignity if not authority. It was held to be their first town in the area after they migrated from the north.

Kitwilksheba—Tsimshian village at mouth of Skeena River in WC BC, Canada.

Koryo—old name for Korea.

Koryo River—Sutton Creek, W Oregon.

Kubilai River—Susquehanna River, C Pennsylvania.

Kujujuk—port near Houston, Texas.

Kuli—now Calicut, a Medieval kingdom on the SW coast of India.

Kuriltai Balikh—(Kuriltai City)—village that was founded on the site of the proclamation of the Khanate of the Blue Sky about 9 miles NNW of Blue Ridge, AB, Canada.

Kusa River—Coos River, SW Oregon.

Kutcha River—Porcupine River, NE Alaska, N Yukon Territory, Canada.

Kwakwakas—Kwakiutl village on west coast of Guilford Island, SW BC, Canada.

Kwesh River—Brazos River, C Texas.

Kytmin—Inuit name for a mountain on Cape Dezneva, NE Siberia.

Laha River—Laja River, C Chile. It flows into the Bio Bio.

Lambayeque River—the Chancay River, NW Peru.

Lanka—Sinhalese name for Ceylon, modern Sri Lanka.

Lapurdi—Basque name for province of Labourd, SW France.

Leni Lenape River—Hudson River, E New York.

Liamuiga—St. Kitts, West Indies. The name means "The Fertile Island."

Liao River—Liao River, S Manchuria.

Limari River—N Chile.

Little Sungari River—Milk River, NE Montana.

Lollelhue River—S Chile.

Longjiang—port and shipbuilding center in north Norfolk, Virginia.

Madinina—Martinique, West Indies. The name means "Island of Flowers."

Mahican River—Mohawk River, C New York.

Malacca—Medieval kingdom on site of modern Melaka, Malaysia.

Malindi—Medieval kingdom on site of modern Malindi, Kenya.

Manta—principle town of the tribe called Manta on NW coast of Ecuador.

Maricao River—W Puerto Rico.

Mataquito River—C Chile.

Mathilde Lake—Sutton Lake, W. Oregon.

Maule River—C Chile.

Maullin River—S Chile.

Merkit River—Madison River, W Montana.

Mexcala River—Balsas River, Southern Mexico.

Michigamaw Lake—Lake Michigan.

Mingue Lake—Lake Ontario.

Missi Sipi River—Mississippi River, NC Minnesota to SE Louisiana.

Mixquic—town 7 miles SW of Chalco now on the SE edge of Mexico City, Mexico.

Moche River—NW Peru.

Mongol River—Missouri River, SW Montana to EC Missouri.

Montauk Island—Long Island, New York.

Murenbalikh—"Cahokia" near East St. Louis, Illinois.

Nanih Waiya—sacred place of the Choctaw, now an historical site in EC Mississippi.

Naishandina River—Bighorn River, N Wyoming to S Montana.

Nanjing—port and shipbuilding city near Everet, Washington.

Nansamund River—Nansemund River, SE Virginia.

Naparoa—Basque name for the province of Navarre, NC Spain.

Nashanekammuck—small Wampanoag village on Capawake (Martha's Vineyard), in SW part of island.

Nauset Peninsula—Cape Cod, E Massachusetts.

Nikwasi –Cherokee town on site of Franklin, North Carolina.

Nimipu River—Salmon River, N Idaho.

Nitsiza River—Liard River, SW Northwest Territories, Canada.

Nomo River—Boise River, C Idaho.

North Aniyunwiya River—Shenandoah River, WC Virginia to NE West Virginia.

North Branch River—Henry's Fork, S Idaho.

North Chahicks River—North Platte River, SW Wyoming to E Nebraska.

North Chesapeake River—Lafayette River, SE Virginia.

North Dzitsiista River—Red River, W Minnesota to S Manitoba, Canada.

North Numakiki River—Knife River, C North Dakota.

Ocheti Lake—Mille Lacs, E Minnesota.

Onawmanient River—Chickahominy River, C Virginia.

Onon River—NE Mongolia to SE Siberia.

Ottawa Lake—Lake Huron.

Otumba—town 8 miles east of Teotihuacán, Mexico.

Owl River—Republican and Kansas rivers—E Colorado, S Nebraska to NC Kansas.

Pachachaca River—a tributary of the Apurimac River in SC Peru. It formed the eastern border of Inka Andahualya Province.

Pah-Chu-Laka Falls—Shoshone Falls, SC Idaho.

Palta River—the Huancapampa River between the Chotano River and the Maranon rivers in NC Peru.

Pacatnamu—Chimu city near mouth of the Jepetepec River, modern Pascamayo, NW Peru.

Pachacoto River—small river emptying into the upper reaches of the Santa River in WC Peru.

Pansfalaya River—Pearl River, CS Mississippi.

Panuco River—Panuco River, San Luis Potosi to Vera Cruz, Mexico.

Paula River—Judith River, C Montana.

Paulpa—Digueno village on site of San Diego, California.

Peaku River—Pecos River, E New Mexico to W Texas.

Pensacola River—Conecuh and Escambia rivers, S Alabama to NW Florida.

Pioje River—Napo River, NC Ecuador to NE Peru.

Pissasec River—South Anna—Pamunkey River, C Virginia.

Plains Oxen River—Elkhorn River, NC to E Nebraska.

Posol-mi—village at south end of San Francisco Bay, WC California.

Potomac River—Potomac River, N Virginia.

Powhatan River—James River, S Virginia.

Pyeyek—Inuit name for Cape Prince of Wales, W Alaska.

Red River—Red River, N Texas to E Louisiana.

Ruin River—San Juan River, WC New Mexico to EC Arizona.

Sabino—Abnaki village on west bank of the Kennebec River near its mouth. Home village of Aspenquid, brother-in-law of Karl (the Crow) in Book 2 .

Saint Jean de Luz—coastal town in SW France.

Salmon Sound—(Tsagaalzh in Mongol)—Puget Sound, NW Washington.

Salst River—Flathead, Clark Fork, Pend Oreille and Columbia rivers, W Montana to W Oregon and Washington.

Salt River—Saline River, S Arkansas.

Saturiwa River—St. Johns River, NE Florida.

Seagull Lake—Mercer Lake, W Oregon.

Secotan River—Pamlico River, E North Carolina.

Seet Kah—Tlingit settlement at modern Petersburg, AK.

Setacoo—Cherokee town near Decatur, Tennessee.

Sewee River—Santee River, Congaree—Santee River, C South Carolina.

Sharbalikh—(Ox City)—town that evolved from the old Plains Oxen (Bison) Ordu, near Culbertson MT.

Sharitarish River—Smoky Hill River, W to C Kansas.

Sharp Bitterroot River—Bitterroot River, W Montana.

Shining River—South Fork and Sun rivers, W Montana.

Siksika River—South Saskatchewan River, S Alberta to C Saskatchewan, Canada.

Sitka—Tlingit village on Baranoff Island, SE AK.

Small River—St. Regis River, W Montana.

South Aniyunwiya River—Hiawassee River, N Georgia to SE Tennessee.

South Chahicks River—South Platte River, SW Wyoming to E Nebraska.

South Chesapeake River—South Branch Elizabeth River, SE Virginia.

South Dzitsiista River—Minnesota River, SW Minnesota.

South Fork River—Clark Fork to Flathead River, W Montana.

South Numakiki River—Cheyenne River, W South Dakota.

South Salst River—Coeur d'Alene—Spokane rivers, N Idaho, E Washington.

Sparkling Cold Seeking River—South Fork, Flathead River, NW Montana.

Stampede River—Muddy Creek, SC Nebraska.

Stikine River—(Great River in Tlingit) from NW BC, Canada to SE AK.

Stono River—Cooper River, E South Carolina.

Sungari River—Sungari River NC Manchuria.

Tacatacuru Island—Cumberland Island, SE Georgia.

Tamalameque—capital of Khanate of the Clouds, between modern towns of Mata de Cana and Regidor on east bank of the Magdalena River in NC Colombia.

Tamoan Chan—Southern Yucatan Peninsula, Mexico.

Tatar River—Gallatin River, W Montana.

Tauxenent River—Bull Run Creek—Occoquan River, N Virginia.

Tegulunbalikh—port on site of Buenos Aires, Argentina.

Tenayuca—town at the end of causeway leading NW from Tlatelolco. It is now part of Mexico City, Mexico.

Tenochtitlan—the southern of two island cities in the WC part of Lake Texcoco, settled by the Mexica, leading tribe of what became the Aztecs. It is now part of the center of Mexico City, Mexico.

Teotihuacán—ruins of a large ancient city about 32 miles NE of Tenochtitlan, with well preserved pyramids and other structures. The name means "City of the Gods" and the site was revered in precontact Mexico.

Tepeapulco—town 26 miles ENE of the site of Teotihuacán, NE of Mexico City, Mexico.

Tepexpan—town 24 miles NW of Tenochtitlan (center of Mexico City, Mexico). It was near the NW shore of Lake Texcoco.

Tepeyac—town on mainland connected to Tlatelolco by a causeway leading NE of the city. Now it is part of Mexico City.

Tepozteco—mountain just north of Tepoztlan, Mexico.

Tepoztlan—town NE of Cuernavaca, Mexico. It is the legendary birthplace of Quetzalcoatl.

Tezontepec—Villa Tezontepec, a town about 50 miles NE of Tenochtitlan (center of Mexico City, Mexico.

Thanuge River—Rio Grande NC New Mexico to SE Texas.

Theodorbalikh—port on site of Talcahuano (near Concepcion), Chile.

Titskan River—Atascosa River, S Texas.

Tlacotenco—town about 25 miles SSE of Tenochtitlan (center of

Mexico City, Mexico) just north of the Tlaloc Volcano and just west of its extensive lava beds. It is now part of Mexico City.

Tlahuac—town on southern shore of the peninsula jutting into Lake Texcoco from the east. It is now part of Mexico City.

Tlatelolco—northern of two island cities in the WC part of Lake Texcoco, settled by the Mexica, leading tribe of what become the Aztecs. It is now part of the center of Mexico City, Mexico.

Tlayacapan—town about 20 miles ENE of Cuernavaca, Mexico.

Tolcayuca—town about 50 miles NNE of Tenochtitlan (center of Mexico City, Mexico).

Tolten River—S Chile.

Tonggye—Town on western side of Mobile Bay, south of Mobile, Alabama. It was named for a province on the NE coast of Korea from which most of the Korean immigrants in the book came.

Tonggye Bay—Mobile Bay, SW Alabama.

Tsimshian River—Skeena River WC BC, Canada.

Tugaloo—Cherokee town now under Lake Hartwell in NE Georgia.

Tullumayo River—Rodadero River—eastern of two rivers that framed Inka Cuzco.

Tulancingo—town about 70 miles NE of Tenochtitlan (center of Mexico City, Mexico).

Tultepec—town 15 miles north of Tenochtitlan (center of Mexico City), Mexico. It is now part of Mexico City, Mexico.

Tulyehualco—town on southern shore of Lake Texcoco at the southern terminus of the causeway to Iztapalapa.

Tunessee—Cherokee town north of the junction of the Tennessee and Little Tennessee rivers.

Tungus River—Marias River NC Montana.

Tutalosi—Kofitachiki town near Augusta, Georgia.

Tuxla—Putun Maya settlement at site of Santa Marta, Colombia.

Twanh Lake—Lake Erie.

Ukwunu River—Oconee River, C Georgia.

Uluumil Kutz—Northern Yucatan Peninsula, Mexico.

Union River—Tombigbee River, W Alabama.

Urubamba River –a major river in C Peru.

Ussuri River—Ussuri River, SE Siberia.

Vilcas—Inka province SE of Angara around modern city of Ayacucho in SC Peru.

Viru River—WC Peru.

Wahili River—Altamaha River, E Georgia.

Wampo River—Chotano River in NC Peru.

Wan-ka-pampa River—Huancabamba River, NC Peru.

Warao River—Orinoco River, S to NE Venezuela.

Wazhazhe River—Ohio River, SW Pennsylvania to S Illinois—W Kentucky.

Wendat River—St. Lawrence River, E Ontario and Quebec, Canada.

West Tsoyaha River—Tennessee River, NE Tennessee to W Kentucky.

White Mountain Top River—North Fork, Salmon River, C Idaho.

Winnipeg Lake—Lake Winnipeg, Manitoba, Canada.

Winyaw River—Yadkin and Pee Dee rivers, NC North Carolina to NE South Carolina.

Wooded Lake—Lake of the Woods, Minnesota, Ontario and Manitoba.

Xaymaca—Jamaica, West Indies.

Xequetepeque River—Jequetepec River, NW Peru.

Yagueca—town and province in W Boriquen (Puerto Rico).

Yaguez River—W Puerto Rico.

Yangzi—port on site of Boston, Massachusetts.

Yauhtepec—town about 15 miles ESE of Cuernavaca, Mexico.

Yecapixtla—town about 17 miles E of Yauhtepec, Mexico.

Yukanah River—Yukon River, Central Alaska, Yukon Territory, Canada.

Yumabalikh—port on site of Baranquilla, Colombia.

Yuma River—Magdalena River, SW to NW Colombia.

Zheng He—Port at site of S Manhattan Island, (New York City) New York.